# The Writings of Lactantius

# The Writings of Lactantius

# The Writings of Lactantius

© Lighthouse Publishing 2025

Written by: Lanctantius (250-325)
Translated: Rev. Alexander Roberts D.D. (1826-1901)
Translated by: Rev. William Fletcher in June, 1886
Updated into Modern U.S English: A.M. Overett (b.1960)

All rights reserved. Without limiting the rights under copyright reserved above, no part of this publication may be reproduced, stored in a retrieval system, or transmitted, in any form or by any means (electronic, mechanical, photocopying, recording or otherwise), without the prior written permission of the copyright owner of this book.

Published by
Lighthouse Publishing
SAN 257-4330
228 Freedom Parkway
Hoschton, GA 30548
United States of America

www.lighthousechristianpublishing.com

# INTRODUCTORY NOTICE
*To*
# LACTANTIUS.

[a.d. 260—330.] Reaching, at last, the epoch of Constantine, perhaps the reader will share my own feelings, as those of—

"One who long, in thickets and in brakes
Entangled, winds now this way, and now that,
His devious course uncertain, seeking home,
But finds at last a greensward smooth and large,
Courageous, and refreshed for future toil."

How strange it seems, after three centuries since John the Baptist suffered, to gain a moment when kings are not actually persecuting Christ in His servants!

How marvelous the change must have been in the experience of the primitive faithful; the Roman Emperor not ashamed of Jesus, and setting up the cross on the standards of his legions! Tertullian, *De Fuga,* and the troubles of Cyprian about *The Lapsed,* are matters of the past. As in a moment, God has changed the world for His people, and their perils become as suddenly reversed. The world's favor begins to be the trial of faith, as its hatred before. The mild contemplative attitude of the Church at this period is something surprising. It accepts with little exultation this miracle of the Master; but so long has it been habituated to persecution, that it finds much of its discipline, and not less of its prevailing spirit, neutralized by its very triumph. No more the martyr's heroic testimony and his crown beyond this life; no such call for the celibate as had been enforced before in tomes of the Christian literature; and what need now of Antony's invitation to the desert and the cell? But, on the other hand, these ascetic forms of heroic faith were all that were now left to minister to the martyr-spirit, and to perpetuate the habits enforced upon the early believers. The hermitage and the monastery assumed a new attractiveness, and became dear to sentiment, as to principle before. We must not be surprised, then, at the tendencies of the age now rapidly developed; but let us rejoice for a moment in the times of refreshing from the Lord now at last vouchsafed to that "little flock" to which He had promised the kingdom. The "conversion of Constantine," as it is called, introduced the most marvelous revolution in human empire, in practical thought, and in the laws and manners of mankind, ever known in the history of the world. It is amazing how little the men of the epoch itself glorified their own introduction to "marvelous light," and how very little the Church has left us, to tell the story of its emotions when first it found itself at rest from fiery persecutions, or when came forth from the Emperor the Edict of Milan for the legal observance of "the Day of the Sun."1 What a day that Easter was, when, emerging from the catacombs and other dens and caves of the earth, the Church herself seemed as one risen from the dead!

We may be sure there were tears of joy and warm embraces among kindred long torn asunder by their common exposures to fire and sword. We cannot imagine, indeed, all, that was in the hearts of those Christian families that now kept holyday together in the face of the world, and sang fearlessly in holy places their anthem, "Christ is risen from the dead." But a moment's thought we ought to give, as we pass into a stage of history entirely fresh and new, to the power of God thus manifested. The miracle thus wrought by the ascended Christ needs no aid from the supposed "vision of Constantine" to make it a supernatural exhibition of His glory who is "King of kings and Lord of lords."

Arnobius wrote to the minds of perplexed Pilates asking "What is truth" in a new spirit, and not indisposed to wash their own hands of the blood of Jesus, though not prepared to believe and be baptized. His pupil finds a better sort of Pilate in the Emperor and in his period. Constantine is a pagan still at heart, but he is convinced of the truth that Christ has a kingdom "not of this world;" and he must have this credit, above the Antonines, that he recognized in the Christians not only his best and most loyal subjects, but men of a character altogether superior to that of the heathen, who had so long been the councilors of the empire. He was one, also, who accepted "the logic of events," and who came to terms with the inevitable in time to turn it to his own advantage.

I think Constantine had read the *Apologies* addressed to the Antonines by Justin Martyr, and was at first disposed only to accept the plea for Christians so far forth as Justin had urged it. Going so far, he was led beyond his positive convictions to measures of policy which identified him with the Church. That the Church was distrustful of him, and doubted how long the Imperial favor might be relied upon, is also apparent. This doubt accounts, in some degree, for the great moderation of the Church in accepting benefits from him, and in withholding notes of triumph. She instinctively foresaw Julians in the way, and expected reactionary periods. She forbore to baptize the Emperor, and encouraged his disposition to postpone. It was as when "the wolf of Benjamin" was introduced to the disciples: "they were afraid of him, and believed not that he was a disciple."

Lactantius, moved, perhaps, by Hosius or Eusebius, undertakes the instruction of the Emperor, while seeming only to copy the example of Justin writing to Antoninus Pius. The *Institutes,* it is true, had been begun at an earlier date; but he economizes, for a new purpose, the material, in which, perhaps, he had only purposed to follow up the work of his teacher, in language better fitted to the polite, for refuting heathenism. I cannot doubt that he aimed, in pure Latinity, to win the Emperor and his court to a deeper and purer conviction of divine truth: to more than a feeble and possibly superstitious idea that it was useless to contend with it, and that the gods of the empire were impotent to protect themselves against Christian progress and its masterly exposures of their shame and nothingness.

In language which has given him the title of the Christian Cicero, Lactantius employs Cicero himself as a defender of the truth; correcting him, indeed, and overruling his mistakes, rebuking his pusillanimity, and justly censuring him, (1) in philosophy, for declaring it no rule of action, however ennobling its precepts; and (2) in religion, for not venturing to profess conclusions to which his reasoning necessarily tend. All this is admirably adapted to carry on the work of Christian Fathers and Apologists under the change of times. He and Arnobius furnish but a supplement to the real teachers of the Church, and are not to be always depended on in statements of doctrine. They write like earnest converts, but not like theologians; yet, although their loose expressions are often inconsistent one with another, it is manifest that their design is to support orthodoxy as it had been defined by abler expounders. I think the large respect which Lactantius pays to the testimony of the Sibyls was addressed to the class with which he had to deal. Constantine was greatly influenced by such testimonies, if we may judge from his own liberal quotations4 and his comments on the *Pollio* of Virgil, to which, as a Christian oracle, our author may have introduced him. In short, the day had come in which it could no longer be said with strict propriety of phrase, "Not many mighty, not many noble, are called;" and Lactantius accepted, as his mission, the enforcement, before such a class, of despised truths which the great had persecuted in vain for centuries. He drew them thus to the conclusion that God had indeed "chosen the foolish things of the world to confound the wise, and the weak things of the world to confound the things which are mighty; and base things of the world, and things which are despised, hath God chosen, yea, and things which are not, to bring to naught things that are." Such was the prophecy of St. Paul, and the *Labarum* uplifted by Cæsar's legions proclaimed the fulfillment.

    I have little doubt that Lactantius was of heathen parentage, and was converted late in life. To his eternal honor he was not a "fair-weather Christian," but boldly confessed the faith amid the fires of the last and most terrible of the great persecutions. Its probable date suggests that his treatise on the persecutors may have been a far-reaching effort to dissuade the Cæsars of a later age from trying to restore "the gods to Latium."

I confess my own partiality to our author, and the interest with which his writings continue to impress me, even now. In youth (*Consule Planco*) I brought to his pages an enthusiastic appreciation of the genius which had adorned the very dawn of Christian civilization by works of literary merit not inferior to those of the Augustan age. The crabbed Latinity of Tertullian has charms, indeed, of its own sort: it was the shaggy raiment of the ascetic and the confessor, "always bearing about in his own body the dying of the Lord Jesus." It befitted the age and the man, and those awful realities with which Christians had then to deal. Not words, but things, were their one concern. It is pleasant to find, however, that Christianity is not incapable of meeting all sorts and conditions of men; and Lactantius' was doubtless the instrument of Providence in bearing the testimony of Jesus, "even before kings," in language which promised to Roman letters the new and commanding development imparted to its language by Christianity, which has made it imperishable, and more truly "eternal" than Rome itself.

The following is the Introductory Notice of the reverend translator:—

Lactantius has always held a very high place among the Christian Fathers, not only on account of the subject-matter of his writings, but also on account of the varied erudition, the sweetness of expression, and the grace and elegance of style, by which they are characterized. It appears, therefore, more remarkable that so little is known with certainty respecting his personal history. We are unable to fix with precision either the place or time of his birth, and even his name has been the subject of much discussion. It is known that he was a pupil of Arnobius, who gave lectures in rhetoric at Sicca in Africa. Hence it has been supposed that Lactantius was a native of Africa, while others have maintained that he was born in Italy, and that his birthplace probably was Firmium, on the Adriatic. He was probably born about the middle of the third century, since he is spoken of as far advanced in life about a.d. 315. He is usually denominated "Lucius Cælius Firmianus Lactantius;" but the name Cæcilius is sometimes substituted for Cælius, and it is uncertain whether Firmianus is a family name or a local designation. Some have even supposed that be received the name of *Lactantius* from the milky softness of his style.

He attained to great eminence as a teacher of rhetoric, and his fame far outstripped the reputation of his master Arnobius. Such, indeed, was his celebrity, that he was invited by the Emperor Diocletian to settle at Nicomedia, and there practice his art. He appears, however to have met with so little success in that city, as to have been reduced to extreme indigence. Abandoning his profession as a pleader, he devoted himself to literary composition. It was probably at this period that he embraced the Christian faith, and we may perhaps be justified in supposing some connection between his poverty and his change of religion. He was afterwards called to settle in Gaul, probably about a.d. 315, and the Emperor Constantine entrusted to him the education of his son Crispus. He is believed to have died at Trèves about a.d. 325.

His principal work is *The Christian Institutions,* or an *Introduction to True Religion,* in seven books, designed to supersede the less complete treatises of Minucius Felix, Tertullian, and Cyprian. In these books, each of which has a distinct title, and constitutes a separate essay, he demonstrates the falsehood of the pagan religion, shows the vanity of the heathen philosophy, and undertakes the defense of the Christian religion against its adversaries. He also sets forth the nature of righteousness, gives instructions concerning the true worship of God, and treats of the punishment of the wicked, and the reward of the righteous in everlasting happiness.

To the *Institutions* is appended an epitome dedicated to Pentadius. The authorship of this abridgment has been questioned in modem times; but it is expressly assigned to Lactantius by Hieronymus. The greater part of the work was wanting in the earlier editions, and it was not until the beginning of the eighteenth century that it was discovered nearly entire.

In the treatise on *The Anger of God* is directed mainly against the tenets of the Epicureans and Stoics, who maintained that the deeds of men could produce no emotions of pleasure or anger in the Deity. Lactantius holds that the love of the good necessarily implies the hatred of evil; and that the tenets of these philosophers, as tending to overthrow the doctrine of future rewards and punishments, are subversive of the principles of true religion.

In the treatise on *The Workmanship of God,* or *The Formation of Man,* the author dwells upon the wonderful construction of the human frame, and the adaptation of means to ends therein displayed, as proofs of the wisdom and goodness of God. The latter part of the book contains speculations concerning the nature and origin of the soul.

In the treatise on the *Deaths of Persecutors,* an argument for the truth of the Christian religion is derived from the fact, that those emperors who had been most distinguished as persecutors of the Christians, were special objects of divine vengeance.

To these treatises are usually appended some poetical works which have been attributed to Lactantius, but it is very questionable whether any of them were really written by him.

The poem on the *Phoenix* appears to be of a comparatively modern date.

That on *Easter* is believed to have been composed by Venantius Honorianus Clementianus Fortunatus in the sixth century.

The poem on the *Passion of the Lord,* though much admired both in its language and style of thought, bears the impress of a later age.

There is also a collection of *A Hundred Enigmas,* which has been attributed to Lactantius; but there is good reason to suppose that they are not the production of his pen. Heumann endeavored to prove that *Symposium* is the title of the work, and that no such person as Symposius ever existed. But this opinion is untenable. It is true that Hieronymus speaks of Lactantius as the author of a Symposium, but there are no grounds for supposing that the work was of a light and trifling character: it was probably a serious dialogue.

The style of Lactantius has been deservedly praised for the dignity, elegance, and clearness of expression by which it is characterized, and which have gained for him the appellation of the Christian Cicero. His writings everywhere give evidence of his varied and extensive erudition, and contain much valuable information respecting the systems of the ancient philosophers. But his claims as a theologian are open to question; for he holds peculiar opinions on many points, and he appears more successful as an opponent of error than as a maintainer of the truth. Lactantius has been charged with a leaning to Manicheism, but the charge appears to be unfounded.

The translation has been made from Migne's edition, from which most of the notes have been taken. The quotations from Virgil have been given in the words of Conington's translation, and those from Lucretius in the words of Munro.

# The Divine Institutes

## Book I

### Of the false worship of the gods.

**Preface.—of what great value the knowledge of the truth is and always has been.**

Men of great and distinguished talent, when they had entirely devoted themselves to learning, holding in contempt all actions both private and public, applied to the pursuit of investigating the truth whatever labor could be bestowed upon it; thinking it much more excellent to investigate and know the method of human and divine things, than to be entirely occupied with the heaping up of riches or the accumulation of honors. For no one can be made better or more just by these things, since they are frail and earthly, and pertain to the adorning of the body only. Those men were indeed most deserving of the knowledge of the truth, which they so greatly desired to know, that they even preferred it to all things. For it is plain that some gave up their property, and altogether abandoned the pursuit of pleasures, that, being disengaged and without impediment, they might follow the simple truth, and it alone. And so greatly did the name and authority of the truth prevail with them, that they proclaimed that the reward of the greatest good was contained in it. But they did not obtain the object of their wish, and at the same time lost their labor and industry; because the truth, that is the secret of the Most High God, who created all things, cannot be attained by our own ability and perceptions. Otherwise there would be no difference between God and man, if human thought could reach to the counsels and arrangements of that eternal majesty. And because it was impossible that the divine method of procedure should become known to man by his own efforts, God did not suffer man any longer to err in search of the light of wisdom, and to wander through inextricable darkness without any result of his labor, but at length opened his eyes, and made the investigation of the truth His own gift, so that He might show the nothingness of human wisdom, and point out to man wandering in error the way of obtaining immortality.

But since few make use of this heavenly benefit and gift, because the truth lies hidden veiled in obscurity; and it is either an object of contempt to the learned because it has not suitable defenders, or is hated by the unlearned on account of its natural severity, which the nature of men inclined to vices cannot endure: for because there is a bitterness mingled with virtues, while vices are seasoned with pleasure, offended by the former and soothed by the latter, they are borne headlong, and deceived by the appearance of good things, they embrace evils for goods,—I have believed that these errors should be encountered, that both the learned may be directed to true wisdom, and the unlearned to true religion. And this profession is to be thought much better, more useful and glorious, than that of oratory, in which being long engaged, we trained young men not to virtue, but altogether to cunning wickedness. Certainly we shall now much more rightly discuss respecting the heavenly precepts, by which we may be able to instruct the minds of men to the worship of the true majesty. Nor does he deserve so well respecting the affairs of men, who imparts the knowledge of speaking well, as he who teaches men to live in piety and innocence; on which account the philosophers were in greater glory among the Greeks than the orators. For they, *the philosophers*, were considered teachers of right living, which is far more excellent, since to speak well belongs only to a few, but to live well belongs to all. Yet that practice in fictitious suits has been of great advantage to us, so that we are now able to plead the cause of truth with greater copiousness and ability of speaking; for although the truth may be defended without eloquence, as it often has been defended by many, yet it needs to be explained, and in a measure discussed, with distinctness and elegance of speech, in order that it may flow with greater power into the minds of men, being both provided with its own force, and adorned with the brilliancy of speech.

**Chap. I. — Of religion and wisdom.**

We undertake, therefore, to discuss religion and divine things. For if some of the greatest orators, veterans as it were of their profession, having completed the works of their pleadings, at last gave themselves up to philosophy, and regarded that as a most just rest from their labors, if they tortured their minds in the investigation of those things which could not be found out, so that they appear to have sought for themselves not so much leisure as occupation, and that indeed with much greater trouble than in their former pursuit; how much more justly shall I betake myself as to a most safe harbor, to that pious, true, and divine wisdom, in which all things are ready for utterance, pleasant to the hearing, easy to be understood, honorable to be undertaken! And if some skillful men and arbiters of justice composed and published Institutions of civil law, by which they might lull the strife and contentions of discordant citizens, how much better and more rightly shall we follow up in writing the divine Institutions, in which we shall not speak about rain-droppings, or the turning of waters, or the preferring of claims, but we shall speak of hope, of life, of salvation, of immortality, and of God, that we may put an end to deadly superstitions and most disgraceful errors.

And we now commence this work under the auspices of your name, O mighty Emperor Constantine, who were the first of the Roman princes to repudiate errors, and to acknowledge and honor the majesty of the one and only true God. For when that most happy day had shone upon the world, in which the Most High God raised you to the prosperous height of power, you entered upon a dominion which was salutary and desirable for all, with an excellent beginning, when, restoring justice which had been overthrown and taken away, you expiated the most shameful deed of others. In return for which action God will grant to you happiness, virtue, and length of days, that even when old you may govern the state with the same justice with which you began in youth, and may hand down to your children the guardianship of the Roman name, as you yourself received it from your father. For to the wicked, who still rage against the righteous in other parts of the world, the Omnipotent will also repay the reward of their wickedness with a severity proportioned to its tardiness; for as He is a most indulgent Father towards the godly, so is He a most upright Judge against the ungodly. And in my desire to defend His religion and divine worship, to whom can I rather appeal, whom can I address, but him by whom justice and wisdom have been restored to the affairs of men?

Therefore, leaving the authors of this earthly philosophy, who bring forward nothing certain, let us approach the right path; for if I considered these to be sufficiently suitable guides to a good life, I would both follow them myself, and exhort others to follow them. But since they disagree among one another with great contention, and are for the most part at variance with themselves, it is evident that their path is by no means straightforward; since they have severally marked out distinct ways for themselves according to their own will, and have left great confusion to those who are seeking for the truth. But since the truth is revealed from heaven to us who have received the mystery of true religion, and since we follow God, the teacher of wisdom and the guide to truth, we call together all, without any distinction either of sex or of age, to heavenly pasture. For there is no more pleasant food for the soul than the knowledge of truth, to the maintaining and explaining of which we have destined seven books, although the subject is one of almost boundless and immeasurable labor; so that if anyone should wish to dilate upon and follow up these things to their full extent, he would have such an exuberant supply of subjects, that neither books would find any limit, nor speech any end. But on this account we will put together all things briefly, because those things which we are about to bring forward are so plain and lucid, that it seems to be more wonderful that the truth appears so obscure to men, and to those especially who are commonly esteemed wise, or because men will only need to be trained by us,—that is, to be recalled from the error in which they are entangled to a better course of life.

And if, as I hope, we shall attain to this, we will send them to the very fountain of learning, which is most rich and abundant, by copious draughts of which they may appease the thirst conceived within, and quench their ardor. And all things will be easy, ready of accomplishment, and clear to them, if only they are not annoyed at applying patience in reading or hearing to the perception of the discipline of wisdom. For many, pertinaciously adhering to vain superstitions, harden themselves against the manifest truth, not so much deserving well of their religions, which they wrongly maintain, as they deserve ill of themselves; who, when they have a straight path, seek devious windings; who leave the level ground that they may glide over a precipice; who leave the light, that, blind and enfeebled, they may lie in darkness. We must provide for these, that they may not fight against themselves, and that they may be willing at length to be freed from inveterate errors. And this they will assuredly do if they shall at any time see for what purpose they were born; for this is the cause of their perverseness,—namely, ignorance of themselves: and if any one, having gained the knowledge of the truth, shall have shaken off this ignorance, he will know to what object his life is to be directed, and how it is to be spent. And I thus briefly define the sum of this knowledge, that neither is any religion to be undertaken without wisdom, nor any wisdom to be approved of without religion.

### Chap. II.—That there is a providence in the affairs of men.

Having therefore undertaken the office of explaining the truth, I did not think it so necessary to take my commencement from that inquiry which naturally seems the first, whether there is a providence which consults for all things, or all things were either made or are governed by chance; which sentiment was introduced by Democritus, and confirmed by Epicurus. But before them, what did Protagoras effect, who raised doubts respecting the gods; or Diagoras afterwards, who excluded them; and some others, who did not hold the existence of gods, except that there was supposed to be no providence? These, however, were most vigorously opposed by the other philosophers, and especially by the Stoics, who taught that the universe could neither have been made without divine intelligence, nor continue to exist unless it were governed by the highest intelligence. But even Marcus Tullius, although he was a defender of the Academic system, discussed at length and on many occasions respecting the providence which governs affairs, confirming the arguments of the Stoics, and himself adducing many new ones; and this he does both in all the books of his own philosophy, and especially in those which treat of the nature of the gods.

And it was no difficult task, indeed, to refute the falsehoods of a few men who entertained perverse sentiments by the testimony of communities and tribes, who on this one point had no disagreement. For there is no one so uncivilized, and of such an uncultivated disposition, who, when he raises his eyes to heaven, although he knows not by the providence of what God all this visible universe is governed, does not understand from the very magnitude of the objects, from their motion, arrangement, constancy, usefulness, beauty, and temperament, that there is some providence, and that that which exists with wonderful method must have been prepared by some greater intelligence. And for us, assuredly, it is very easy to follow up this part as copiously as it may please us. But because the subject has been much agitated among philosophers, and they who take away providence appear to have been sufficiently answered by men of sagacity and eloquence, and because it is necessary to speak, in different places throughout this work which we have undertaken, respecting the skill of the divine providence, let us for the present omit this inquiry, which is so closely connected with the other questions, that it seems possible for us to discuss no subject, without at the same time discussing the subject of providence.

## Chap. III.—Whether the universe is governed by the power of one god or of many.

Let the commencement of our work therefore be that inquiry which closely follows and is connected with the first: Whether the universe is governed by the power of one God or of many. There is no one, who possesses intelligence and uses reflection, who does not understand that it is one Being who both created all things and governs them with the same energy by which He created them. For what need is there of many to sustain the government of the universe? Unless we should happen to think that, if there were more than one, each would possess less might and strength. And they who hold that there are many gods, do indeed effect this; for those gods must of necessity be weak, since individually, without the aid of the others, they would be unable to sustain the government of so vast a mass. But God, who is the Eternal Mind, is undoubtedly of excellence, complete and perfect in every part. And if this is true, He must of necessity be one. For power or excellence, which is complete, retains its own peculiar stability. But that is to be regarded as solid from which nothing can be taken away, that as perfect to which nothing can be added.

Who can doubt that he would be a most powerful king who should have the government of the whole world? And not without reason, since all things which everywhere exist would belong to him, since all resources from all quarters would be centered in him alone. But if more than one divide the government of the world, undoubtedly each will have less power and strength, since everyone must confine himself within his prescribed portion. In the same manner also, if there are more gods than one, they will be of less weight, others having in themselves the same power. But the nature of excellence admits of greater perfection in him in whom the whole is, than in him in whom there is only a small part of the whole. But God, if He is perfect, as He ought to be, cannot but be one, because He is perfect, so that all things may be in Him. Therefore the excellences and powers of the gods must necessarily be weaker, because so much will be wanting to each as shall be in the others; and so the more there are, so much the less powerful will they be. Why should I mention that this highest power and divine energy is altogether incapable of division? For whatever is capable of division must of necessity be liable to destruction also. But if destruction is far removed from God, because He is incorruptible and eternal, it follows that the divine power is incapable of division. Therefore God is one, if that which admits of so great power can be nothing else: and yet those who deem that there are many gods, say that they have divided their functions among themselves; but we will discuss all these matters at their proper places. In the meantime, I affirm this, which belongs to the present subject. If they have divided their functions among themselves, the matter comes back to the same point, that any one of them is unable to supply the place of all. He cannot, then, be perfect who is unable to govern all things while the others are unemployed. And so is comes to pass, that for the government of the universe there is more need of the perfect excellence of one than of the imperfect powers of many. But he who imagines that so great a magnitude as this cannot be governed by one Being, is deceived. For he does not comprehend how great are the might and power of the divine majesty, if he thinks that the one God, who had power to create the universe, is also unable to govern that which He has created. But if he conceives in his mind how great is the immensity of that divine work, when before it was nothing, yet that by the power and wisdom of God it was made out of nothing—a work which could only be commenced and accomplished by one—he will now understand that that which has been established by one is much more easily governed by one.

Someone may perhaps say that so immense a work as that of the universe could not even have been fabricated except by many. But however many and however great he may consider them,—whatever magnitude, power, excellence, and majesty he may attribute to the many,—the whole of that I assign to one, and say that it exists in one: so that there is in Him such an amount of these properties as can neither be conceived nor expressed. And since we fail in this subject, both in perception and in words—for neither does the human breast admit the light of so great understanding, nor is the mortal tongue capable of explaining such great subjects—it is right that we should understand and say this very same thing. I see, again, what can be alleged on the other hand, that those many gods are such as we hold the one God to be. But this cannot possibly be so, because the power of these gods individually will not be able to proceed further, the power of the others meeting and hindering them. For either each must be unable to pass beyond his own limits, or, if he shall have passed beyond them, he must drive another from his boundaries. They who believe that there are many gods, do not see that it may happen that some may be opposed to others in their wishes, from which circumstance disputing and contention would arise among them; as Homer represented the gods at war among themselves, since some desired that Troy should be taken, others opposed it. The universe, therefore, must be ruled by the will of one. For unless the power over the separate parts be referred to one and the same providence, the whole itself will not be able to exist; since each takes care of nothing beyond that which belongs peculiarly to him, just as warfare could not be carried on without one general and commander. But if there were in one army as many generals as there are legions, cohorts, divisions, and squadrons, first of all it would not be possible for the army to be drawn out in battle array, since each would refuse the peril; nor could it easily be governed or controlled, because all would use their own peculiar counsels, by the diversity of which they would inflict more injury than they would confer advantage. So, in this government of the affairs of nature, unless there shall be one to whom the care of the whole is referred, all things will be dissolved and fall to decay.

But to say that the universe is governed by the will of many, is equivalent to a declaration that there are many minds in one body, since there are many and various offices of the members, so that separate minds may be supposed to govern separate senses; and also the many affections, by which we are accustomed to be moved either to anger, or to desire, or to joy, or to fear, or to pity, so that in all these affections as many minds may be supposed to operate; and if anyone should say this, he would appear to be destitute even of that very mind, which is one. But if in one body one mind possesses the government of so many things, and is at the same time occupied with the whole, why should anyone suppose that the universe cannot be governed by one, but that it can be governed by more than one? And because those maintainers of many gods are aware of this, they say that they so preside over separate offices and parts, that there is still one chief ruler. The others, therefore, on this principle, will not be gods, but attendants and ministers, whom that one most mighty and omnipotent appointed to these offices, and they themselves will be subservient to his authority and command. If, therefore, all are not equal to one another, all are not gods; for that which serves and that which rules cannot be the same. For if God is a title of the highest power, He must be incorruptible, perfect, incapable of suffering, and subject to no *other* being; therefore they are not gods whom necessity compels to obey the one greatest God. But because they who hold this opinion are not deceived without cause, we will presently lay open the cause of this error. Now, let us prove by testimonies the unity of the divine power.

**Chap. IV.—That the one god was foretold even by the prophets.**

The prophets, who were very many, proclaim and declare the one God; for, being filled with the inspiration of the one God, they predicted things to come, with agreeing and harmonious voice. But those who are ignorant of the truth do not think that these prophets are to be believed; for they say that those voices are not divine, but human. Forsooth, because they proclaim one

God, they were either madmen or deceivers. But truly we see that their predictions have been fulfilled, and are in course of fulfilment daily; and their foresight, agreeing as it does to one opinion, teaches that they were not under the impulse of madness. For who possessed of a frenzied mind would be able, I do not say to predict the future, but even to speak coherently? Were they, therefore, who spoke such things deceitful? What was so utterly foreign to their nature as a system of deceit, when they themselves restrained others from all fraud? For to this end were they sent by God, that they should both be heralds of His majesty, and correctors of the wickedness of man.

Moreover, the inclination to feign and speak falsely belongs to those who covet riches, and eagerly desire gains,—a disposition which was far removed from those holy men. For they so discharged the office entrusted to them, that, disregarding all things necessary for the maintenance of life, they were so far from laying up store for the future, that they did not even labor for the day, content with the unstored food which God had supplied; and these not only had no gains, but even endured torments and death. For the precepts of righteousness are distasteful to the wicked, and to those who lead an unholy life. Wherefore they, whose sins were brought to light and forbidden, most cruelly tortured and slew them. They, therefore, who had no desire for gain, had neither the inclination nor the motive for deceit. Why should I say that some of them were princes, or even kings, upon whom the suspicion of covetousness and fraud could not possibly fall, and yet they proclaimed the one God with the same prophetic foresight as the others?

### Chap. V.—Of the testimonies of poets and philosophers.

But let us leave the testimony of prophets, lest a proof derived from those who are universally disbelieved should appear insufficient. Let us come to authors, and for the demonstration of the truth let us cite as witnesses those very persons whom they are accustomed to make use of against us,—I mean poets and philosophers. From these we cannot fail in proving the unity of God; not that they had ascertained the truth, but that the force of the truth itself is so great, that no one can be so blind as not to see the divine brightness presenting itself to his eyes. The poets, therefore, however much they adorned the gods in their poems, and amplified their exploits with the highest praises, yet very frequently confess that all things are held together and governed by one spirit or mind. Orpheus, who is the most ancient of the poets, and coeval with the gods themselves,—since it is reported that he sailed among the Argonauts together with the sons of Tyndarus and Hercules,—speaks of the true and great God as the first-born, because nothing was produced before Him, but all things sprung from Him. He also calls Him Phanes because when as yet there was nothing He first appeared and came forth from the infinite. And since he was unable to conceive in his mind the origin and nature of this Being, he said that He was born from the boundless air: "The first-born, Phaethon, son of the extended air;" for he had nothing more to say. He affirms that this Being is the Parent of all the gods, on whose account He framed the heaven, and provided for His children that they might have a habitation and place of abode in common: "He built for immortals an imperishable home." Thus, under the guidance of nature and reason, he understood that there was a power of surpassing greatness which framed heaven and earth. For he could not say that Jupiter was the author of all things, since he was born from Saturn; nor could he say that Saturn himself was their author, since it was reported that he was produced from the heaven; but he did not venture to set up the heaven as the primeval god, because he saw that it was an element of the universe, and must itself have had an author. This consideration led him to that first-born god, to whom he assigns and gives the first place.

Homer was able to give us no information relating to the truth, for he wrote of human rather than divine things. Hesiod was able, for he comprised in the work of one book the generation of the gods; but yet he gave us no information, for he took his commencement not from God the Creator, but from chaos, which is a confused mass of rude and unarranged matter; whereas he ought first to have explained from what source, at what time, and in what manner, chaos itself had begun to exist or to have consistency. Without doubt, as all things were placed in order, arranged, and made by some artificer, so matter itself must of necessity have been formed by some being. Who, then, made it except God, to whose power all things are subject? But he shrinks from admitting this, while he dreads the unknown truth. For, as he wished it to appear, it was by the inspiration of the Muses that he poured forth that song on Helicon; but he had come after previous meditation and preparation.

Maro was the first of our poets to approach the truth, who thus speaks respecting the highest God, whom he calls Mind and Spirit:—

> "Know first, the heaven, the earth, the main,
> The moon's pale orb, the starry train,
> Are nourished by a Soul,
> A Spirit, whose celestial flame
> Glows in each member of the frame,
> And stirs the mighty whole."

And lest anyone should happen to be ignorant what that Spirit was which had so much power, he has declared it in another place, saying: "For the Deity pervades all lands, the tracts of sea and depth of heaven; the flocks, the herds, and men, and all the race of beasts, each at its birth, derive their slender lives from Him."

Ovid also, in the beginning of his remarkable work, without any disguising of the name, admits that the universe was arranged by God, whom he calls the Framer of the world, the Artificer of all things. But if either Orpheus or these poets of our country had always maintained what they perceived under the guidance of nature, they would have comprehended the truth, and gained the same learning which we follow.

But thus far of the poets. Let us come to the philosophers, whose authority is of greater weight, and their judgment more to be relied on, because they are believed to have paid attention, not to matters of fiction, but to the investigation of the truth. Thales of Miletus, who was one of the number of the seven wise men, and who is said to have been the first of all to inquire respecting natural causes, said that water was the element from which all things were produced, and that God was the mind which formed all things from water. Thus he placed the material of all things in moisture; he fixed the beginning and cause of their production in God. Pythagoras thus defined the being of God, "as a soul passing to and fro, and diffused through all parts of the universe, and through all nature, from which all living creatures which are produced derive their life." Anaxagoras said that God was an infinite mind, which moves by its own power. Antisthenes maintained that the gods of the people were many, but that the God of nature was one only; that is, the Fabricator of the whole universe. Cleanthes and Anaximenes assert that the air is the chief deity; and to this opinion our poet has assented: "Then almighty father Æther descends in fertile showers into the bosom of his joyous spouse; and great himself, mingling with her great body, nourishes all her offspring." Chrysippus speaks of God as a natural power endowed with divine reason, and sometimes as a divine necessity. Zeno also speaks of Him as a divine and natural law. The opinion of all these, however uncertain it is, has reference to one point,—to their agreement in the existence of one providence. For whether it be nature, or æther, or reason, or mind, or a fatal necessity, or a divine law, or if you term it anything else, it is the same which is called by us God. Nor does the diversity of titles prove an obstacle, since by their very signification they all refer to one object. Aristotle, although he is at variance with himself, and both utters and holds sentiments opposed to one another, yet upon the whole bears witness that one Mind presides over the universe. Plato, who is judged the wisest of all, plainly and openly maintains the rule of one God; nor does he name Him Æther, or Reason, or Nature, but, as He truly is, God, and that this universe, so perfect and wonderful, was fabricated by Him. And Cicero, following and imitating him in many instances, frequently acknowledges God, and calls Him supreme, in those books which he wrote on the subject of laws; and he adduces proof that the universe is governed by Him, when he argues respecting the nature of the gods in this way: "Nothing is superior to God: the world must therefore be governed by Him. Therefore God is obedient or subject to no nature; consequently He Himself governs all nature." But what God Himself is he defines in his *Consolation*: "Nor can God Himself, as He is comprehended by us, be comprehended in any other way than as a mind free and unrestrained, far removed from all mortal materiality, perceiving and moving all things."

How often, also, does Annæus Seneca, who was the keenest Stoic of the Romans, follow up with deserved praise the supreme Deity! For when he was discussing the subject of premature death, he said "You do not understand the authority and majesty of your Judge, the Ruler of the world, and the God of heaven and of all gods, on whom those deities which we separately worship and honor are dependent." Also in his *Exhortations*: "This Being, when He was laying the first foundations of the most beautiful fabric, and was commencing this work, than which nature has known nothing greater or better, that all things might serve their own rulers, although He had spread Himself out through the whole body, yet He produced gods as ministers of His kingdom." And how many other things like to our own writers did he speak on the subject of God! But these things I put off for the present, because they are more suited to other parts of the subject. At present it is enough to demonstrate that men of the highest genius touched upon the truth, and almost grasped it, had not custom, infatuated by false opinions, carried them back; by which custom they both deemed that there were other gods, and believed that those things which

God made for the use of man, as though they were endowed with perception, were to be held and worshipped as gods.

**Chap. VI.—Of divine testimonies, and of the sibyls and their predictions.**

Now let us pass to divine testimonies; but I will previously bring forward one which resembles a divine testimony, both on account of its very great antiquity, and because he whom I shall name was taken from men and placed among the gods. According to Cicero, Caius Cotta the pontiff, while disputing against the Stoics concerning superstitions, and the variety of opinions which prevail respecting the gods, in order that he might, after the custom of the Academics, make everything uncertain, says that there were five Mercuries; and having enumerated four in order, says that the fifth was he by whom Argus was slain, and that on this account he fled into Egypt, and gave laws and letters to the Egyptians. The Egyptians call him Thoth; and from him the first month of their year, that is, September, received its name among them. He also built a town, which is even now called in Greek Hermopolis (the town of Mercury), and the inhabitants of Phenæ honor him with religious worship. And although he was a man, yet he was of great antiquity, and most fully imbued with every kind of learning, so that the knowledge of many subjects and arts acquired for him the name of Trismegistus. He wrote books, and those in great numbers, relating to the knowledge of divine things, in which he asserts the majesty of the supreme and only God, and makes mention of Him by the same names which we use—God and Father. And that no one might inquire His name, he said that He was without name, and that on account of His very unity He does not require the peculiarity of a name. These are his own words: "God is one, but He who is one only does not need a name; for He who is self-existent is without a name." God, therefore, has no name, because He is alone; nor is there any need of a proper name, except in cases where a multitude of persons requires a distinguishing mark, so that you may designate each person by his own mark and appellation. But God, because He is always one, has no peculiar name.

It remains for me to bring forward testimonies respecting the sacred responses and predictions, which are much more to be relied upon. For perhaps they against whom we are arguing may think that no credence is to be given to poets, as though they invented fictions, nor to philosophers, inasmuch as they were liable to err, being themselves but men. Marcus Varro, than whom no man of greater learning ever lived, even among the Greeks, much less among the Latins, in those books respecting divine subjects which he addressed to Caius Cæsar the chief pontiff, when he was speaking of the Quindecemviri, says that the Sibylline books were not the production of one Sibyl only, but that they were called by one name Sibylline, because all prophetesses were called by the ancients Sibyls, either from the name of one, the Delphian priestess, or from their proclaiming the counsels of the gods. For in the Æolic dialect they used to call the gods by the word Sioi, not Theoi; and for counsel they used the word bule, not boule;—and so the Sibyl received her name as though Siobule. But he says that the Sibyls were ten in number, and he enumerated them all under the writers, who wrote an account of each: that the *first* was from the Persians, and of her Nicanor made mention, who wrote the exploits of Alexander of Macedon;—the *second* of Libya, and of her Euripides makes mention in the prologue of the Lamia;—the *third* of Delphi, concerning whom Chrysippus speaks in that book which he composed concerning divination;—the *fourth* a Cimmerian in Italy, whom Nævius mentions in his books of the Punic war, and Piso in his annals;—the *fifth* of Erythræa, whom Apollodorus of Erythræa affirms to have been his own countrywoman, and that she foretold to the Greeks when they were setting out for Ilium, both that Troy was doomed to destruction, and that Homer would write falsehoods;—the *sixth* of Samos, respecting whom Eratosthenes writes that he had found a written notice in the ancient annals of the Samians. The *seventh* was of Cumæ, by name Amalthæa, who is termed by some Herophile, or Demophile, and *they say* that she brought nine books to the king Tarquinius Priscus, and asked for them three hundred philippics, and that the king refused so great a price, and derided the madness of the woman; that she, in the sight of the king, burnt three of the books, and demanded the same price for those which were left; that Tarquinias much more considered the woman to be mad; and that when she again, having burnt three other books, persisted in asking the same price, the king was moved, and bought the remaining books for the three hundred pieces of gold: and the number of these books was afterwards increased, after the rebuilding of the Capitol; because they were collected from all cities of Italy and Greece, and especially from those of Erythræa, and were brought to Rome, under the name of whatever Sibyl they were. *Further*, that the *eighth* was from the Hellespont, born in the Trojan territory, in the village of Marpessus, about the town of Gergithus; and Heraclides of Pontus writes that she lived in the times of Solon and Cyrus;—the *ninth* of Phrygia, who gave oracles at Ancyra;—the *tenth* of Tibur, by name Albunea, who is worshipped at Tibur as a goddess, near the banks of the river Anio, in the depths of which her statue is said to have been found, holding in her hand a book. The senate transferred her oracles into the Capitol.

  The predictions of all these Sibyls are both brought forward and esteemed as such, except those of the Cumæan Sibyl, whose books are concealed by the Romans; nor do they consider it lawful for them to be inspected by anyone but the Quindecemviri. And there are separate books the production of each, but because these are inscribed with the name of the Sibyl they are believed to be the work of one; and they are confused, nor can the productions of each be distinguished and assigned to their own authors, except in the case of the Erythræan Sibyl, for she both inserted her own true name in her verse, and predicted that she would be called Erythræan, though she was born at Babylon. But we also shall speak of the Sibyl without any distinction, wherever we shall have occasion to use their testimonies. All these Sibyls, then, proclaim one God, and especially the Erythræan, who is regarded among the others as more celebrated and noble; since Fenestella, a most diligent writer, speaking of the Quindecemviri, says that, after the rebuilding of the Capitol, Caius Curio the consul proposed to the senate that ambassadors should be sent to Erythræ to search out and bring to Rome the writings of the Sibyl; and that, accordingly, Publius Gabinius, Marcus Otacilius, and Lucius Valerius were sent, who conveyed to Rome about a thousand verses written out by private persons. We have shown before that Varro made the same statement. Now in these verses which the ambassadors brought to Rome, are these testimonies respecting the one God:—

1. "One God, who is alone, most mighty, uncreated."

This is the only supreme God, who made the heaven, and decked it with lights.

2. "But there is one only God of pre-eminent power, who made the heaven, and sun, and stars, and moon, and fruitful earth, and waves of the water of the sea."

And since He alone is the framer of the universe, and the artificer of all things of which it consists or which are contained in it, it testifies that He alone ought to be worshipped:—

3. "Worship Him who is alone the ruler of the world, who alone was and is from age to age."
Also another Sibyl, whoever she is, when she said that she conveyed the voice of God to men, thus spoke:—

4. "I am the one only God, and there is no other God."

I would now follow up the testimonies of the others, were it not that these are sufficient, and that I reserve others for more befitting opportunities. But since we are defending the cause of truth before those who err from the truth and serve false religions, what kind of proof ought we to bring forward against them, rather than to refute them by the testimonies of their own gods?

### Chap. VII.—Concerning the testimonies of Apollo and the gods.

Apollo, indeed, whom they think divine above all others, and especially prophetic, giving responses at Colophon,—I suppose because, induced by the pleasantness of Asia, he had removed from Delphi,—to someone who asked who He was, or what God was at all, replied in twenty-one verses, of which this is the beginning:—

"Self-produced, untaught, without a mother, unshaken, a name not even to be comprised in word, dwelling in fire, this is God; and we His messengers are a slight portion of God."

Can any one suspect that this is spoken of Jupiter, who had both a mother and a name? Why should I say that Mercury, that thrice greatest, of whom I have made mention above, not only speaks of God as "without a mother," as Apollo does, but also as "without a father," because He has no origin from any other source but Himself? For He cannot be produced from any one, who Himself produced all things. I have, as I think, sufficiently taught by arguments, and confirmed by witnesses, that which is sufficiently plain by itself, that there is one only King of the universe, one Father, one God.

But perchance someone may ask of us the same question which Hortensius asks in Cicero: If God is one only, what solitude can be happy? As though we, in asserting that He is one, say that He is desolate and solitary. Undoubtedly He has ministers, whom we call messengers. And that is true, which I have before related, that Seneca said in his *Exhortations* that God produced ministers of His kingdom. But these are neither gods, nor do they wish to be called gods or to be worshipped, inasmuch as they do nothing but execute the command and will of God. Nor, however, are they gods who are worshipped in common, whose number is small and fixed. But if the worshippers of the gods think that they worship those beings whom we call the ministers of the Supreme God, there is no reason why they should envy us who say that there is one God, and deny that there are many. If a multitude *of gods* delights them, we do not speak of twelve, or three hundred and sixty-five as Orpheus did; but we convict them of innumerable errors on the other side, in thinking that they are so few. Let them know, however, by what name they ought to be called, lest they do injury to the true God, whose name they set forth, while they assign it to more than one. Let them believe their own Apollo, who in that same response took away from the other gods their name, as he took away the dominion from Jupiter. For the third verse shows that the ministers of God ought not to be called gods, but angels. He spoke falsely respecting himself, indeed; for though he was of the number of demons, he reckoned himself among the angels of God, and then in other responses he confessed himself a demon. For when he was asked how he wished to be supplicated, he thus answered:—

"O all-wise, all-learned, versed in many pursuits, hear, O demon."

And so, again, when at the entreaty of someone he uttered an imprecation against the Sminthian Apollo, he began with this verse:—

"O harmony of the world, bearing light, all-wise demon."

What therefore remains, except that by his own confession he is subject to the scourge of the true God and to everlasting punishment? For in another response he also said:—

"The demons who go about the earth and about the sea
Without weariness, are subdued beneath the scourge of God."

We speak on the subject of both in the second book. In the meantime it is enough for us that while he wishes to honor and place himself in heaven, he has confessed, as the nature of the matter is, in what manner they are to be named who always stand beside God.

Therefore let men withdraw themselves from errors; and laying aside corrupt superstitions, let them acknowledge their Father and Lord, whose excellence cannot be estimated, nor His greatness perceived, nor His beginning comprehended. When the earnest attention of the human mind and its acute sagacity and memory has reached Him, all ways being, as it were, summed up and exhausted, it stops, it is at a loss, it fails; nor is there anything beyond to which it can proceed. But because that which exists must of necessity have had a beginning, it follows that since there was nothing before Him, He was produced from Himself before all things. Therefore He is called by Apollo "self-produced," by the Sibyl "self-created," "uncreated," and "unmade." And Seneca, an acute man, saw and expressed this in his *Exhortations*. "We," he said, "are dependent upon another." Therefore we look to someone to whom we owe that which is most excellent in us. Another brought us into being, another formed us; but God of His own power made Himself.

**Chap. viii.—that god is without a body, nor does he need difference of sex for procreation.**

It is proved, therefore, by these witnesses, so numerous and of such authority, that the universe is governed by the power and providence of one God, whose energy and majesty Plato in the *Timæus* asserts to be so great, that no one can either conceive it in his mind, or give utterance to it in words, on account of His surpassing and incalculable power. And then can anyone doubt whether anything can be difficult or impossible for God, who by His providence designed, by His energy established, and by His judgment completed those works so great and wonderful, and even now sustains them by His spirit, and governs them by His power, being incomprehensible and unspeakable, and fully known to no other than Himself? Wherefore, as I often reflect on the subject of such great majesty, they who worship the gods sometimes appear so blind, so incapable of reflection, so senseless, so little removed from the mute animals, as to believe that those who are born from the natural intercourse of the sexes could have had anything of majesty and divine influence; since the Erythræan Sibyl says: "It is impossible for a God to be fashioned from the loins of a man and the womb *of a woman.*" And if this is true, as it really is, it is evident that Hercules, Apollo, Bacchus, Mercury, and Jupiter, with the rest, were but men, since they were born from the two sexes. But what is so far removed from the nature of God as that operation which He Himself assigned to mortals for the propagation of their race, and which cannot be affected without corporeal substance?

Therefore, if the gods are immortal and eternal, what need is there of the other sex, when they themselves do not require succession, since they are always about to exist? For assuredly in the case of mankind and the other animals, there is no other reason for difference of sex and procreation and bringing forth, except that all classes of living creatures, inasmuch as they are doomed to death by the condition of their mortality, may be preserved by mutual succession. But God, who is immortal, has no need of difference of sex, nor of succession. Someone will say *that this arrangement is necessary,* in order that He may have some to minister to Him, or over whom He may bear rule. What need is there of the female sex, since God, who is almighty, is able to produce sons without the agency of the female? For if He has granted to certain minute creatures that they

"Should gather offspring for themselves with their mouth from leaves and sweet herbs," why should anyone think it impossible for God Himself to have offspring except by union with the other sex? No one, therefore, is so thoughtless as not to understand that those were mere mortals, whom the ignorant and foolish regard and worship as gods. Why, then, someone will say, were they believed to be gods? Doubtless because they were very great and powerful kings; and since, on account of the merits of their virtues, or offices, or the arts which they discovered, they were beloved by those over whom they had ruled, they were consecrated to *lasting* memory. And if any one doubts this, let him consider their exploits and deeds, the whole of which both ancient poets and historians have handed down.

## Chap. IX.—Of Hercules and his life and death.

Did not Hercules, who is most renowned for his valor, and who is regarded as an Africanus among the gods, by his debaucheries, lusts, and adulteries, pollute the world, which he is related to have traversed and purified? And no wonder, since he was born from an adulterous intercourse with Alcmena.

What divinity could there have been in him, who, enslaved to his own vices, against all laws, treated with infamy, disgrace, and outrage, both males and females? Nor, indeed, are those great and wonderful actions which he performed to be judged such as to be thought worthy of being attributed to divine excellence. For what! Is it so magnificent if he overcame a lion and a boar; if he shot down birds with arrows; if he cleansed a royal stable; if he conquered a virago, and deprived her of her belt; if he slew savage horses together with their master? These are the deeds of a brave and heroic man, but still a man; for those things which he overcame were frail and mortal. For there is no power so great, as the orator says, which cannot be weakened and broken by iron and strength. But to conquer the mind, and to restrain anger, is the part of the bravest man; and these things he never did or could do: for one who does these things I do not compare with excellent men, but I judge him to be most like to a god.

I could wish that he had added *something* on the subject of lust, luxury, desire, and arrogance, so as to complete the excellence of him whom he judged to be like to a god. For he is not to be thought braver who overcomes a lion, than he who overcomes the violent wild beast shut up within himself, viz. anger; or he who has brought down most rapacious birds, than he who restrains most covetous desires; or he who subdues a warlike Amazon, than he who subdues lust, the vanquisher of modesty and fame; or he who cleanses a stable from dung, than he who cleanses his heart from vices, which are more destructive evils because they are peculiarly his own, than those which might have been avoided and guarded against. From this it comes to pass, that he alone ought to be judged a brave man who is temperate, moderate, and just. But if any one considers what the works of God are, he will at once judge all these things, which most trifling men admire, to be ridiculous. For they measure them not by the divine power of which they are ignorant, but by the weakness of their own strength. For no one will deny this, that Hercules was not only a servant to Eurystheus, a king, which to a certain extent may appear honorable, but also to an unchaste woman, Omphale, who used to order him to sit at her feet, clothed with her garments, and executing an appointed task. Detestable baseness! But such was the price at which pleasure was valued. What! Someone will say, do you think that the poets are to be believed? Why should I not think so? For it is not Lucilius who relates these things, or Lucian, who spared not men nor gods, but these especially who sing the praises of the gods.

Whom, then, shall we believe, if we do not credit those who praise them? Let him who thinks that these speak falsely produce other authors on whom we may rely, who may teach us who these gods are, in what manner and from what source they had their origin, what is their strength, what their number, what their power, what there is in them which is admirable and worthy of adoration—what mystery, in short, more to be relied on, and more true. He will produce no such authorities. Let us, then, give credence to those who did not speak for the purpose of censure, but to proclaim their praise. He sailed, then, with the Argonauts, and sacked Troy, being enraged with Laomedon on account of the reward refused to him, by Laomedon, for the preservation of his daughter, from which circumstance it is evident at what time he lived. He also, excited by rage and madness, slew his wife, together with his children. Is this he whom men consider a god? But his heir Philoctetes did not so regard him, who applied a torch to him when about to be burnt, who witnessed the burning and wasting of his limbs and sinews, who buried his bones and ashes on Mount OEta, in return for which office he received his arrows.

**Chap. X.—Of the life and actions of Æsculapius, Apollo, Neptune, Mars, Castor and Pollux, mercury and Bacchus.**

What other action worthy of divine honors, except the healing of Hippolytus, did Æsculapius perform, whose birth also was not without disgrace to Apollo? His death was certainly more renowned, because he earned the distinction of being struck with lightning by a god. Tarquitius, in a dissertation concerning illustrious men, says that he was born of uncertain parents, exposed, and found by some hunters; that he was nourished by a dog, and that, being delivered to Chiron, he learned the art of medicine. He says, moreover, that he was a Messenian, but that he spent some time at Epidaurus. Tully also says that he was buried at Cynosuræ. What was the conduct of Apollo, his father? Did he not, on account of his impassioned love, most disgracefully tend the flock of another, and build walls for Laomedon, having been hired together with Neptune for a reward, which could with impunity be withheld from him? And from him first the perfidious king learned to refuse *to carry out* whatever contract he had made with gods. And he also, while in love with a beautiful boy, offered violence to him, and while engaged in play, slew him.

Mars, when guilty of homicide, and set free from the charge of murder by the Athenians through favor, lest he should appear to be too fierce and savage, committed adultery with Venus. Castor and Pollux, while they are engaged in carrying off the wives of others, ceased to be twin-brothers. For Idas, being excited with jealousy on account of the injury, transfixed one *of the brothers* with his sword. And the poets relate that they live and die alternately: so that they are now the most wretched not only of the gods, but also of all mortals, inasmuch as they are not permitted to die once only. And yet Homer, differing from the other poets, simply records that they both died. For when he represented Helen as sitting by the side of Priam on the walls of Troy, and recognizing all the chieftains of Greece, but as looking in vain for her brothers only, he added to his speech a verse of this kind:—

"Thus she; unconscious that in Sparta they,
Their native land, beneath the sod were laid."

What did Mercury, a thief and spendthrift, leave to contribute to his fame, except the memory of his frauds? Doubtless he was deserving of heaven, because he taught the exercises of the palæstra, and was the first who invented the lyre. It is necessary that Father Liber should be of chief authority, and of the first rank in the senate of the gods, because he was the only one of them all, except Jupiter, who triumphed, led an army, and subdued the Indians. But that very great and unconquered Indian commander was most shamefully overpowered by love and lust. For, being conveyed to Crete with his effeminate retinue, he met with an unchaste woman on the shore; and in the confidence inspired by his Indian victory, he wished to give proof of his manliness, lest he should appear too effeminate. And so he took to himself in marriage that woman, the betrayer of her father, and the murderer of her brother, after that she had been deserted and repudiated by another husband; and he made her Libera, and with her ascended into heaven.

What was the conduct of Jupiter, the father of all these, who in the customary prayer is styled Most Excellent and Great? Is he not, from his earliest childhood, proved to be impious, and almost a parricide, since he expelled his father from his kingdom, and banished him, and did not await his death though he was aged and worn out, such was his eagerness for rule? And when he had taken his father's throne by violence and arms, he was attacked with war by the Titans, which was the beginning of evils to the human race; and when these had been overcome and lasting peace procured, he spent the rest of his life in debaucheries and adulteries. I forbear to mention the virgins whom he dishonored. For that is wont to be judged endurable. I cannot pass by the cases of Amphitryon and Tyndarus, whose houses he filled to overflowing with disgrace and infamy. But he reached the height of impiety and guilt in carrying off the royal boy. For it did not appear enough to cover himself with infamy in offering violence to women, unless he also outraged his own sex. This is true adultery, which is done against nature. Whether he who committed these crimes can be called Greatest is a matter of question, undoubtedly he is not the Best; to which name corrupters, adulterers, and incestuous persons have no claim; unless it happens that we men are mistaken in terming those who do such things wicked and abandoned, and in judging them most deserving of every kind of punishment. But Marcus Tullius was foolish in upbraiding Caius Verres with adulteries, for Jupiter, whom he worshipped, committed the same; and in upbraiding Publius Clodius with incest with his sister, for he who was Best and Greatest had the same person both as sister and wife.

**Chap. xi.—of the origin, life, reign, name and death of Jupiter, and of Saturn and Uranus.**

Who, then, is so senseless as to imagine that he reigns in heaven who ought not even to have reigned on earth? It was not without humor that a certain poet wrote of the triumph of Cupid: in which book he not only represented Cupid as the most powerful of the gods, but also as their conqueror. For having enumerated the loves of each, by which they had come into the power and dominion of Cupid, he sets in array a procession, in which Jupiter, with the other gods, is led in chains before the chariot of him, celebrating a triumph. This is elegantly pictured by the poet, but it is not far removed from the truth. For he who is without virtue, who is overpowered by desire and wicked lusts, is not, *as the poet feigned*, in subjection to Cupid, but to everlasting death. But let us cease to speak concerning morals; let us examine the matter, in order that men may understand in what errors they are miserably engaged. The common people imagine that Jupiter reigns in heaven; both learned and unlearned are alike persuaded of this. For both religion itself, and prayers, and hymns, and shrines, and images demonstrate this. And yet they admit that he was also descended from Saturn and Rhea. How can he appear a god, or be believed, as the poet says, to be the author of men and all things, when innumerable thousands of men existed before his birth—those, for instance, who lived during the reign of Saturn, and enjoyed the light sooner than Jupiter? I see that one god was king in the earliest times, and another in the times that followed. It is therefore possible that there may be another hereafter. For if the former kingdom was changed, why should we not expect that the latter may possibly be changed, unless by chance it was possible for Saturn to produce one more powerful than himself, but impossible for Jupiter so to do? And yet the divine government is always unchangeable; or if it is changeable, which is an impossibility, it is undoubtedly changeable at all times.

Is it possible, then, for Jupiter to lose his kingdom as his father lost it? It is so undoubtedly. For when that deity had spared neither virgins nor married women, he abstained from Thetis only in consequence of an oracle which foretold that whatever son should be born from her would be greater than his father. And first of all there was in him a want of foreknowledge not befitting a god; for had not Themis related to him future events, he would not have known them of his own accord. But if he is not divine, he is not indeed a god; for the name of divinity is derived from god, as humanity is from man. Then there was a consciousness of weakness; but he who has feared, must plainly have feared one greater than himself. But he who does this assuredly knows that he is not the greatest, since something greater can exist. He also swears most solemnly by the Stygian marsh: "Which is set forth the sole object of religious dread to the gods above." What is this object of religious dread? Or by whom is it set forth? Is there, then, some mighty power which may punish the gods who commit perjury? What is this great dread of the infernal marsh, if they are immortal? Why should they fear that which none are about to see, except those who are bound by the necessity of death? Why, then, do men raise their eyes to the heaven? Why do they swear by the gods above, when the gods above themselves have recourse to the infernal gods, and find among them an object of veneration and worship? But what is the meaning of that saying, that there are fates whom all the gods and Jupiter himself obey? If the power of the Parcæ is so great, that they are of more avail than all the heavenly gods, and their ruler and lord himself, why should not they be rather said to reign, since necessity compels all the gods to obey their laws and ordinances? Now, who can entertain a doubt that he who is subservient to anything cannot be greatest? For if he were so, he would not receive fates, but would appoint them. Now I return to another subject which I had omitted. In the case of one goddess only he exercised self-restraint, though he was deeply enamored of her; but this was not from any virtue, but through fear of a successor. But this fear plainly denotes one who is both mortal and feeble, and of no weight: for at the very hour of his birth he might have been put to death, as his elder brother had been put to death; and if it had been possible for him to have lived, he would never have given up the supreme power to a younger brother. But Jupiter himself having been preserved by stealth, and stealthily nourished, was called Zeus, or Zen, not, as they imagine, from the fervor of heavenly fire, or because he is the giver of life, or because he breathes life into living creatures, which power belongs to God alone; for how can he impart the breath of life who has himself received it from another source? But he was so called because he was the first who lived of the male children of Saturn. Men, therefore, might have had another god as their ruler, if Saturn had not been deceived by his wife. But it will be said the poets feigned these things. Whoever entertains this opinion is in error. For they spoke respecting men; but in order that they might embellish those whose memory they used to celebrate with praises, they said that they were gods. Those things, therefore, which they spoke concerning them as gods were feigned, and not those which they spoke concerning them as men; and this will be manifest from an instance which we will bring forward. When about to offer violence to Danae, he poured into her lap a great quantity of golden coins. This was the price which he paid for her dishonor. But the poets who spoke about him as a god, that they might not weaken the authority of his supposed majesty, feigned that he himself descended in a shower of gold, making use of the same figure with which they speak of showers of iron when they describe a multitude of darts and arrows. He is said to have carried away Ganymede by an eagle; it is a picture of the poets. But he either carried him off by a legion, which has an eagle for its standard; or the ship on board of which he was placed had its tutelary deity in the shape of an eagle, just as it had the effigy of a bull when he seized Europa and conveyed her across the sea. In the same manner, it is related that he changed Io, the daughter of Inachus, into a heifer. And in order that she might escape the anger of Juno, just as she was, now covered with bristly hair, and in the shape of a heifer, she is said to have swam over the sea, and to have come into Egypt; and there, having recovered her former appearance, she became the goddess who is now called Isis. By what argument, then, can it be proved that Europa did not sit on the bull, and that Io was not changed into a heifer? Because there is a fixed day in the annals on which the voyage of Isis is celebrated; from which fact we learn that she did not swim across the sea, but sailed over. Therefore they who appear to themselves to be wise because they understand that there cannot be a living and earthly body in heaven, reject the whole story of Ganymede as false, and perceive that the occurrence took place on earth, inasmuch as the matter and the lust itself is earthly. The poets did not therefore invent these transactions, for if they were to do so they would be most worthless; but they added a certain color to the transactions. For it was not for the purpose of detraction that they said these things, but from a desire to embellish them. Hence men are deceived; especially because, while they think that all these things are feigned by the poets, they worship that of which they are ignorant. For they do not know what is the limit of poetic license, how far it is allowable to proceed in fiction, since it is the business of the poet with some gracefulness to change and transfer actual occurrences into other representations by oblique transformations. But to feign the whole of that which you relate, that is to be foolish and deceitful rather than to be a poet.

But grant that they feigned those things which are believed to be fabulous, did they also feign those things which are related about the female deities and the marriages of the gods? Why, then, are they so represented, and so worshipped? Unless by chance not the poets only, but painters also, and statuaries, speak falsehoods. For if this is the Jupiter who is called by you a god, if it is not he who was born from Saturn and Ops, no other image but his alone ought to have been placed in all the temples. What meaning have the effigies of women? What the doubtful sex? In which, if this Jupiter is represented, the very stones will confess that he is a man. They say that the poets have spoken falsely, and yet they believe them: yes, truly they prove by the fact itself that the poets did not speak falsely; for they so frame the images of the gods, that, from the very diversity of sex, it appears that these things which the poets say are true. For what other conclusion does the image of Ganymede and the effigy of the eagle admit of, when they are placed before the feet of Jupiter in the temples, and are worshipped equally with himself, except that the memory of impious guilt and debauchery remains forever? Nothing, therefore, is wholly invented by the poets: something perhaps is transferred and obscured by oblique fashioning, under which the truth was enwrapped and concealed; as that which was related about the dividing of the kingdoms by lot. For they say that the heaven fell to the share of Jupiter, the sea to Neptune, and the infernal regions to Pluto. Why was not the earth rather taken as the third portion, except that the transaction took place on the earth? Therefore it is true that they so divided and portioned out the government of the world, that the empire of the east fell to Jupiter, a part of the west was allotted to Pluto, who had the surname of Agesilaus; because the region of the east, from which light is given to mortals, seems to be higher, but the region of the west lower. Thus they so veiled the truth under a fiction, that the truth itself detracted nothing from the public persuasion. It is manifest concerning the share of Neptune; for we say that his kingdom resembled that unlimited authority possessed by Mark Antony, to whom the senate had decreed the power of the maritime coast, that he might punish the pirates, and tranquillize the whole sea. Thus all the maritime coasts, together with the islands, fell to the lot of Neptune. How can this be proved? Undoubtedly ancient stories attest it. Euhemerus, an ancient author, who was of the city of Messene, collected the actions of Jupiter and of the others, who are esteemed gods, and composed a history from the titles and sacred inscriptions which were in the most ancient temples, and especially in the sanctuary of the Triphylian Jupiter, where an inscription indicated that a golden column had been placed by Jupiter himself, on which column he wrote an account of his exploits, that posterity might have a memorial of his actions. This history was translated and followed by Ennius, whose words are these: "Where Jupiter gives to Neptune the government of the sea, that he might reign in all the islands and places bordering on the sea."

The accounts of the poets, therefore, are true, but veiled with an outward covering and show. It is possible that Mount Olympus may have supplied the poets with the hint for saying that Jupiter obtained the kingdom of heaven, because Olympus is the common name both of the mountain and of heaven. But the same history informs us that Jupiter dwelt on Mount Olympus, when it says: "At that time Jupiter spent the greatest part of his life on Mount Olympus; and they used to resort to him thither for *the administration of* justice, if any matters were disputed. Moreover, if anyone had found out any new invention which might be useful for human life, he used to come thither and display it to Jupiter." The poets transfer many things after this manner, not for the sake of speaking falsely against the objects of their worship, but that they may by variously colored figures add beauty and grace to their poems. But they who do not understand the manner, or the cause, or the nature of that which is represented by figure, attack the poets as false and sacrilegious. Even the philosophers were deceived by this error; for because these things which are related about Jupiter appeared unsuited to the character of a god, they introduced two Jupiters, one natural, the other fabulous. They saw, on the one hand, that which was true, that he, forsooth, concerning whom the poets speak, was man; but in the case of that natural Jupiter, led by the common practice of superstition, they committed an error, inasmuch as they transferred the name of a man to God, who, as we have already said, because He is one only, has no need of a name. But it is undeniable that he is Jupiter who was born from Ops and Saturn. It is therefore an empty persuasion on the part of those who give the name of Jupiter to the Supreme God. For some are in the habit of defending their errors by this excuse; for, when convinced of the unity of God, since they cannot deny this, they affirm that they worship Him, but that it is their pleasure that He should be called Jupiter. But what can be more absurd than this? For Jupiter is not accustomed to be worshipped without the accompanying worship of his wife and daughter. From which his real nature is evident; nor is it lawful for that name to be transferred thither, where there is neither any Minerva nor Juno. Why should I say that the peculiar meaning of this name does not express a divine, but human power? For Cicero explains the names Jupiter and Juno as being derived from giving help; and Jupiter is so called as if he were a helping father,—a name which is ill adapted to God: for to help is the part of a man conferring some aid upon one who is a stranger, and in a case where the benefit is small. No one implores God to help him, but to preserve him, to give him life and safety, which is a much greater and more important matter than to help.

And since we are speaking of a father, no father is said to help his sons when he begets or brings them up. For that expression is too insignificant to denote the magnitude of the benefit derived from a father. How much more unsuitable is it to God, who is our true Father, by whom we exist, and whose we are altogether, by whom we are formed, endued with life, and enlightened, who bestows upon us life, gives us safety, and supplies us with various kinds of food! He has no apprehension of the divine benefits who thinks that he is only aided by God. Therefore he is not only ignorant, but impious, who disparages the excellency of the supreme power under the name of Jupiter. Wherefore, if both from his actions and character we have proved that Jupiter was a man, and reigned on earth, it only remains that we should also investigate his death. Ennius, in his sacred history, having described all the actions which he performed in his life, at the close thus speaks: Then Jupiter, when he had five times made a circuit of the earth, and bestowed governments upon all his friends and relatives, and left laws to men, provided them with a settled mode of life and corn, and given them many other benefits, and having been honored with immortal glory and remembrance, left lasting memorials to his friends, and when his age was almost spent, he changed his life in Crete, and departed to the gods. And the Curetes, his sons, took charge of him, and honored him; and his tomb is in Crete, in the town of Cnossus, and Vesta is said to have founded this city; and on his tomb is an inscription in ancient Greek characters, "Zan Kronou," which is in Latin, "Jupiter the son of Saturn." This undoubtedly is not handed down by poets, but by writers of ancient events; and these things are so true, that they are confirmed by some verses of the Sibyls, to this effect:—

> "Inanimate demons, images of the dead,
> Whose tombs the ill-fated Crete possesses as a boast."

Cicero, in his treatise concerning the Nature of the Gods, having said that three Jupiters were enumerated by theologians, adds that the third was of Crete, the son of Saturn, and that his tomb is shown in that island. How, therefore, can a god be alive in one place, and dead in another; in one place have a temple, and in another a tomb? Let the Romans then know that their Capitol, that is the chief head of their objects of public veneration, is nothing but an empty monument.

Let us now come to his father who reigned before him, and who perhaps had more power in himself, because he is said to be born from the meeting of such great elements. Let us see what there was in him worthy of a god, especially that he is related to have had the golden age, because in his reign there was justice in the earth. I find something in him which was not in his son. For what is so befitting the character of a god, as a just government and an age of piety? But when, on the same principle, I reflect that he is a son, I cannot consider him as the Supreme God; for I see that there is something more ancient than himself,— namely, the heaven and the earth. But I am in search of a God beyond whom nothing has any existence, who is the source and origin of all things. He must of necessity exist who framed the heaven itself, and laid the foundations of the earth. But if Saturn was born from these, as it is supposed, how can he be the chief God, since he owes his origin to another? Or who presided over the universe before the birth of Saturn? But this, as I recently said, is a fiction of the poets. For it was impossible that the senseless elements, which are separated by so long an interval, should meet together and give birth to a son, or that he who was born should not at all resemble his parents, but should have a form which his parents did not possess.

Let us therefore inquire what degree of truth lies hid under this figure. Minucius Felix, in his treatise which has the title of *Octavius*, alleged these proofs: "That Saturn, when he had been banished by his son, and had come into Italy, was called the son of Coelus (heaven), because we are accustomed to say that those whose virtue we admire, or those who have unexpectedly arrived, have fallen from heaven; and that he was called the son of earth, because we name those who are born from unknown parents sons of earth." These things, indeed, have some resemblance to the truth, but are not true, because it is evident that even during his reign he was so esteemed. He might have argued thus: That Saturn, being a very powerful king, in order that the memory of his parents might be preserved, gave their names to the heaven and earth, whereas these were before called by other names, for which reason we know that names were applied both to mountains and rivers. For when the poets speak of the offspring of Atlas, or of the river Inachus, they do not absolutely say that men could possibly be born from inanimate objects; but they undoubtedly indicate those who were born from those men, who either during their lives or after their death gave their names to mountains or rivers. For that was a common practice among the ancients, and especially among the Greeks. Thus we have heard that seas received the names of those who had fallen into them, as the Ægean, the Icarian, and the Hellespont. In Latium, also, Aventinus gave his name to the mountain on which he was buried; and Tiberinus, or Tiber, gave his name to the river in which he was drowned. No wonder, then, if the names of those who had given birth to most powerful kings were attributed to the heaven and earth. Therefore it appears that Saturn was not born from heaven, which is impossible, but from that man who bore the name of Uranus. And Trismegistus attests the truth of this; for when he said that very few had existed in whom there was perfect learning, he mentioned by name among these his relatives, Uranus, Saturn, and Mercury. And because he was ignorant of these things, he gave another account of the matter; how he might have argued, I have shown. Now I will say in what manner, at what time, and by whom this was done; for it was not Saturn who did this, but Jupiter. Ennius thus relates in his sacred history: "Then Pan leads him to the mountain, which is called the pillar of heaven. Having ascended thither, he surveyed the lands far and wide, and there on that mountain he builds an altar to Coelus; and Jupiter was the first who offered sacrifice on that altar. In that place he looked up to heaven, by which name we now call it, and that which was above the world which was called the firmament, and he gave to the heaven its name from the name of his grandfather; and Jupiter in prayer first gave the name of heaven to that which was called firmament, and he burnt entire the victim which he there offered in sacrifice." Nor is it here only that Jupiter is found to have offered sacrifice. Cæsar also, in Aratus, relates that Aglaosthenes says that when he was setting out from the island of Naxos against the Titans, and was offering sacrifice on the shore, an eagle flew to Jupiter as an omen, and that the victor received it as a good token, and placed it under his own protection. But the sacred history testifies that even beforehand an eagle had sat upon his head, and portended to him the kingdom. To whom, then, could Jupiter have offered sacrifice, except to his grandfather Coelus, who, according to the saying of Euhemerus, died in Oceania, and was buried in the town of Aulatia?

**Chap. xii.—that the stoics transfer the figments of the poets to a philosophical system.**

Since we have brought to light the mysteries of the poets, and have found out the parents of Saturn, let us return to his virtues and actions. He was, *they say*, just in his rule. First, from this very circumstance he is not now a god, inasmuch as he has ceased to be. In the next place, he was not even just, but impious not only towards his sons, whom he devoured, but also towards his father, whom he is said to have mutilated. And this may perhaps have happened in truth. But men, having regard to the element which is called the heaven, reject the whole fable as most foolishly invented; though the Stoics, (according to their custom) endeavor to transfer it to a physical system, whose opinion Cicero has laid down in his treatise concerning the Nature of the Gods. They held, he says, that the highest and ethereal nature of heaven, that is, of fire, which by itself produced all things, was without that part of the body which contained the productive organs. Now this theory might have been suitable to Vesta, if she were called a male. For it is on this account that they esteem Vesta to be a virgin, inasmuch as fire is an incorruptible element; and nothing can be born from it, since it consumes all things, whatever it has seized upon. Ovid in the *Fasti* says: "Nor do you esteem Vesta to be anything else than a living flame; and you see no bodies produced from flame. Therefore she is truly a virgin, for she sends forth no seed, nor receives it, and loves the attendants of virginity."

This also might have been ascribed to Vulcan, who indeed is supposed to be fire, and yet the poets did not mutilate him. It might also have been ascribed to the sun, in whom is the nature and cause of the productive powers. For without the fiery heat of the sun nothing could be born, or have increase; so that no other element has greater need of productive organs than heat, by the nourishment of which all things are conceived, produced, and supported. Lastly, even if the case were as they would have it, why should we suppose that Coelus was mutilated, rather than that he was born without productive organs? For if he produces by himself, it is plain that he had no need of productive organs, since he gave birth to Saturn himself; but if he had them, and suffered mutilation from his son, the origin of all things and all nature would have perished. Why should I say that they deprive Saturn himself not only of divine, but also of human intelligence, when they affirm that Saturn is he who comprises the course and change of the spaces and seasons, and that he has that very name in Greek? For he is called Cronos, which is the same as Chronos, that is, a space of time. But he is called Saturn, because he is satiated with years. These are the words of Cicero, setting forth the opinion of the Stoics: "The worthlessness of these things any one may readily understand. For if Saturn is the son of Coelus, how could Time have been born from Coelus, or Coelus have been mutilated by Time, or afterwards could Time have been despoiled of his sovereignty by his son Jupiter? Or how was Jupiter born from Time? Or with what years could eternity be satiated, since it has no limit?"

## Chap. xiii.—how vain and trifling are the interpretations of the stoics respecting the gods, and in them concerning the origin of Jupiter, concerning Saturn and Ops.

If therefore these speculations of the philosophers are trifling, what remains, except that we believe it to be a matter of fact that, being a man, he suffered mutilation from a man? Unless by chance any one esteems him as a god who feared a co-heir; whereas, if he had possessed any divine knowledge, he ought not to have mutilated his father, but himself, to prevent the birth of Jupiter, who deprived him of the possession of his kingdom. And he also, when he had married his sister Rhea, whom in Latin we call Ops, is said to have been warned by an oracle not to bring up his male children, because it would come to pass that he should be driven into banishment by a son. And being in fear of this, it is plain that he did not devour his sons, as the fables report, but put them to death; although it is written in sacred history that Saturn and Ops, and other men, were at that time accustomed to eat human flesh, but that Jupiter, who gave to men laws and civilization, was the first who by an edict prohibited the use of that food. Now if this is true, what justice can there possibly have been in him? But let us suppose it to be a fictitious story that Saturn devoured his sons, only true after a certain fashion; must we then suppose, with the vulgar, that he has eaten his sons, who has carried them out to burial? But when Ops had brought forth Jupiter, she stole away the infant, and secretly sent him into Crete to be nourished. Again, I cannot but blame his want of foresight. For why did he receive an oracle from another, *and not from himself?* Being placed in heaven, why did he not see the things which were taking place on earth? Why did the Corybantes with their cymbals escape his notice? Lastly, why did there exist any greater force which might overcome his power? Doubtless, being aged, he was easily overcome by one who was young, and despoiled of his sovereignty. He was therefore banished and went into exile; and after long wanderings came into Italy in a ship, as Ovid relates in his *Fasti*:—

"The cause of the ship remains to be explained. The scythe-bearing god came to the Tuscan river in a ship, having first traversed the world."

Janus received him wandering and destitute; and the ancient coins are a proof of this, on which there is a representation of Janus with a double face, and on the other side a ship; as the same poet adds:—

"But pious posterity represented a ship on the coin, bearing testimony to the arrival of the stranger god."

Not only therefore all the poets, but the writers also of ancient histories and events, agree that he was a man, inasmuch as they handed down to memory his actions in Italy: of Greek writers, Diodorus and Thallus; of Latin writers, Nepos, Cassius, and Varro. For since men lived in Italy after a rustic fashion,—

"He brought the race to union first,
Erewhile on mountain tops dispersed,
And gave them statutes to obey,
And willed the land wherein he lay
Should Latium's title bear."

Does any one imagine him to be a god, who was driven into banishment, who fled, who lay hid? No one is so senseless. For he who flees, or lies hid, must fear both violence and death.

Orpheus, who lived in more recent times than his, openly relates that Saturn reigned on earth and among men:—

"First Cronus ruled o'er men on earth,
And then from Cronus sprung the mighty king,
The widely sounding Zeus."

And also our own Maro says:

"This life the golden Saturn led on earth;"

and in another place:—

"That was the storied age of gold,
So peacefully, serenely rolled
The years beneath his reign."

The poet did not say in the former passage that he led this life in heaven, nor in the latter passage that he reigned over the gods above. From which it appears that he was a king on earth; and this he declares more plainly in another place:—

"Restorer of the age of gold,
In lands where Saturn ruled of old."

Ennius, indeed, in his *translation of* Euhemerus says that Saturn was not the first who reigned, but his father Uranus. In the beginning, he says, Coelus first had the supreme power on the earth. He instituted and prepared that kingdom in conjunction with his brothers. There is no great dispute, if there is doubt, on the part of the greatest authorities respecting the son and the father. But it is possible that each may have happened: that Uranus first began to be pre-eminent in power among the rest, and to have the chief place, but not the kingdom; and that afterwards Saturn acquired greater resources, and took the title of king.

## Chap. xiv.—what the sacred history of euhemerus and ennius teaches concerning the gods.

Now, since the sacred history differs in some degree from those things which we have related, let us open those things which are contained in the true writings that we may not, in accusing superstitions, appear to follow and approve of the follies of the poets. These are the words of Ennius: "Afterwards Saturn married Ops. Titan, who was older *than Saturn*, demands the kingdom for himself. Upon this their mother Vesta, and their sisters Ceres and Ops, advise Saturn not to give up the kingdom to his brother. Then Titan, who was inferior in person to Saturn, on that account, and because he saw that his mother and sisters were using their endeavors that Saturn might reign, yielded the kingdom to him. He therefore made an agreement with Saturn, that if any male children should be born to him, he would not bring them up. He did so for this purpose, that the kingdom might return to his own sons. Then, when a son was first born to Saturn, they slew him. Afterwards twins were born, Jupiter and Juno. Upon this they present Juno to the sight of Saturn, and secretly hide Jupiter, and give him to Vesta to be brought up, concealing him from Saturn. Ops also brings forth Neptune without the knowledge of Saturn, and secretly hides him. In the same manner Ops brings forth twins by a third birth, Pluto and Glauca. Pluto in Latin is Dispater; others call him Orcus. Upon this they show to Saturn the daughter Glauca, and conceal and hide the son Pluto. Then Glauca dies while yet young." This is the lineage of Jupiter and his brothers, *as these things are written*, and the relationship is handed down to us after this manner from the sacred narrative. Also shortly afterwards he introduces these things: "Then Titan, when he learned that sons were born to Saturn, and secretly brought up, secretly takes with him his sons, who are called Titans, and seizes his brother Saturn and Ops, and encloses them within a wall, and places over them a guard."

The truth of this history is taught by the Erythræan Sibyl, who speaks almost the same things, with a few discrepancies, which do not affect the subject-matter itself. Therefore Jupiter is freed from the charge of the greatest wickedness, according to which he is reported to have bound his father with fetters; for this was the deed of his uncle Titan, because he, contrary to his promise and oath, had brought up male children. The rest of the history is thus put together. *It is said* that Jupiter, when grown up, having heard that his father and mother had been surrounded with a guard and imprisoned, came with a great multitude of Cretans, and conquered Titan and his sons in an engagement, and rescued his parents from imprisonment, restored the kingdom to his father, and thus returned into Crete. Then, after these things, *they say* that an oracle was given to Saturn, bidding him to take heed lest his son should expel him from the kingdom; that he, for the sake of weakening the oracle and avoiding the danger, laid an ambush for Jupiter to kill him; that Jupiter, having learned the plot, claimed the kingdom for himself afresh, and banished Saturn; and that he, when he had been tossed over all lands, followed by armed men whom Jupiter had sent to seize or put him to death, scarcely found a place of concealment in Italy.

### Chap. xv.—how they who were men obtained the name of gods.

Now, since it is evident from these things that they were men, it is not difficult to see in what manner they began to be called gods. For if there were no kings before Saturn or Uranus, on account of the small number of men who lived a rustic life without any ruler, there is no doubt but in those times men began to exalt the king himself, and his whole family, with the highest praises and with new honors, so that they even called them gods; whether on account of their wonderful excellence, men as yet rude and simple really entertained this opinion, or, as is commonly the case, in flattery of present power, or on account of the benefits by which they were set in order and reduced to a civilized state. Afterwards the kings themselves, since they were beloved by those whose life they had civilized, after their death left regret of themselves. Therefore men formed images of them, that they might derive some consolation from the contemplation of their likenesses; and proceeding further through love of their worth, they began to reverence the memory of the deceased, that they might appear to be grateful for their services, and might attract their successors to a desire of ruling well. And this Cicero teaches in his treatise on the Nature of the Gods, saying "But the life of men and common intercourse led to the exalting to heaven by fame and goodwill men who were distinguished by their benefits. On this account Hercules, on this Castor and Pollux, Æsculapius and Liber" were ranked with the gods. And in another passage: "And in most states it may be understood, that for the sake of exciting valor, or that the men most distinguished for bravery might more readily encounter danger on account of the state, their memory was consecrated with the honor paid to the immortal gods." It was doubtless on this account that the Romans consecrated their Cæsars, and the Moors their kings. Thus by degrees religious honors began to be paid to them; while those who had known them, first instructed their own children and grandchildren, and afterwards all their posterity, in the practice of this rite. And yet these great kings, on account of the celebrity of their name, were honored in all provinces.

But separate people privately honored the founders of their nation or city with the highest veneration, whether they were men distinguished for bravery, or women admirable for chastity; as the Egyptians honored Isis, the Moors Juba, the Macedonians Cabirus, the Carthaginians Uranus, the Latins Faunus, the Sabines Sancus, the Romans Quirinus. In the same manner truly Athens worshipped Minerva, Samos Juno, Paphos Venus, Lemnos Vulcan, Naxos Liber, and Delos Apollo. And thus various sacred rites have been undertaken among different peoples and countries, inasmuch as men desire to show gratitude to their princes, and cannot find out other honors which they may confer upon the dead. Moreover, the piety of their successors contributed in a great degree to the error; for, in order that they might appear to be born from a divine origin, they paid divine honors to their parents, and ordered that they should be paid by others. Can anyone doubt in what way the honors paid to the gods were instituted, when he reads in Virgil the words of Æneas giving commands to his friends:—

> "Now with full cups libation pour
> To mighty Jove, whom all adore,
> Invoke Anchises' blessed soul."

And he attributes to him not only immortality, but also power over the winds:—

> "Invoke the winds to speed our flight,
> And pray that he we hold so dear
> May take our offerings year by year,
> Soon as our promised town we raise,
> In temples sacred to his praise."

In truth, Liber and Pan, and Mercury and Apollo, acted in the same way respecting Jupiter, and afterwards their successors did the same respecting them. The poets also added their influence, and by means of poems composed to give pleasure, raised them to the heaven; as is the case with those who flatter kings, even though wicked, with false panegyrics. And this evil originated with the Greeks, whose levity being furnished with the ability and copiousness of speech, excited in an incredible degree mists of falsehoods. And thus from admiration of them they first undertook their sacred rites, and handed them down to all nations. On account of this vanity the Sibyl thus rebukes them:—

> "Why trustest thou, O Greece, to princely men?
> Why to the dead dost offer empty gifts?
> Thou offerest to idols; this error who suggested,

That thou shouldst leave the presence of the mighty God, and make these offerings?"

Marcus Tullius, who was not only an accomplished orator, but also a philosopher, since he alone was an imitator of Plato, in that treatise in which he consoled himself concerning the death of his daughter, did not hesitate to say that those gods who were publicly worshipped were men. And this testimony of his ought to be esteemed the weightier, because he held the priesthood of the augurs, and testifies that he worships and venerates the same gods. And thus within the compass of a few verses he has presented us with two facts. For while he declared his intention of consecrating the image of his daughter in the same manner in which they were consecrated by the ancients, he both taught that they were dead, and showed the origin of a vain superstition. "Since, in truth," he says, "we see many men and women among the number of the gods, and venerate their shrines, held in the greatest honor in cities and in the country, let us assent to the wisdom of those to whose talents and inventions we owe it that life is altogether adorned with laws and institutions, and established on a firm basis. And if any living being was worthy of being consecrated, assuredly it was this. If the offspring of Cadmus, or Amphitryon, or Tyndarus, was worthy of being extolled by fame to the heaven, the same honor ought undoubtedly to be appropriated to her. And this indeed I will do; and with the approbation of the gods, I will place you the best and most learned of all women in their assembly, and will consecrate you to the estimation of all men." Someone may perhaps say that Cicero raved through excessive grief. But, in truth, the whole of that speech, which was perfect both in learning and in its examples, and in the very style of expression, gave no indications of a distempered mind, but of constancy and judgment; and this very sentence exhibits no sign of grief. For I do not think that he could have written with such variety, and copiousness, and ornament, had not his grief been mitigated by reason itself, and the consolation of his friends and length of time. Why should I mention what he says in his books concerning the Republic, and also concerning glory? For in his treatise on the Laws, in which work, following the example of Plato, he wished to set forth those laws which he thought that a just and wise state would employ, he thus decreed concerning religion: "Let them reverence the gods, both those who have always been regarded as gods of heaven, and those whose services *to men* have placed them in heaven: Hercules, Liber, Æsculapius, Castor, Pollux, and Quirinus." Also in his Tusculan Disputations, when he said that heaven was almost entirely filled with the human race, he said: "If, indeed, I should attempt to investigate ancient accounts, and to extract from them those things which the writers of Greece have handed down, even those who are held in the highest rank as gods will be found to have gone from us into heaven. Inquire whose sepulchers are pointed out in Greece: remember, since you are initiated, what things are handed down in the mysteries; and then at length you will understand how widely this *persuasion* is spread." He appealed, as it is plain, to the conscience of Atticus, that it might be understood from the very mysteries that all those who are worshipped were men; and when he acknowledged this without hesitation in the case of Hercules, Liber, Æsculapius, Castor and Pollux, he was afraid openly to make the same admission respecting Apollo and Jupiter their fathers, and likewise respecting Neptune, Vulcan, Mars, and Mercury, whom he termed the greater gods; and therefore he says that this opinion is widely spread, that we may understand the same concerning Jupiter and the other more ancient gods: for if the ancients consecrated their memory in the same manner in which he says that he will consecrate the image and the name of his daughter, those who mourn may be pardoned, but those who believe it cannot be pardoned. For who is so infatuated as to believe that heaven is opened to the dead at the consent and pleasure of a senseless multitude? Or that any one is able to give to another that which he himself does not possess? Among the Romans, Julius was made a god, because it pleased a guilty man, Antony; Quirinus was made a god, because it seemed good to the shepherds, though one of them was the murderer of his twin brother, the other the destroyer of his country. But if Antony had not been consul, in return for his services towards the state Caius Cæsar would have been without the honor even of a dead man, and that, too, by the advice of his father-in-law Piso, and of his relative Lucius Cæsar, who opposed the celebration of the funeral, and by the advice of Dolabella the consul, who overthrew the column in the forum, that is, his monuments, and purified the forum. For Ennius declares that Romulus was regretted by his people, since he represents the people as thus speaking, through grief for their lost king: "O Romulus, Romulus, say what a guardian of your country the gods produced you? You brought us forth within the regions of light. O father, O sire, O race, descended from the gods." On account of this regret they more readily believed Julius Proculus uttering falsehoods, who was suborned by the fathers to announce to the populace that he had seen the king in a form more majestic than that of a man; and that he had given command to the people that a temple should be built to his honor, that he was a god, and was called by the name of Quirinus. By which deed he at once persuaded the people that Romulus had gone to the gods, and freed the senate from the suspicion of having slain the king.

**Chap. xvi. — By what argument it is proved that those who are distinguished by a difference of sex cannot be gods.**

I might be content with those things which I have related, but there still remain many things which are necessary for the work which I have undertaken. For although, by destroying the principal part of superstitions, I have taken away the whole, yet it pleases me to follow up the remaining parts, and more fully to refute so inveterate a persuasion, that men may at length be ashamed and repent of their errors. This is a great undertaking, and worthy of a man. "I proceed to release the minds of men from the ties of superstitions," as Lucretius says; and he indeed was unable to effect this, because he brought forward nothing true. This is our duty, who both assert the existence of the true God and refute false deities. They, therefore, who entertain the opinion that the poets have invented fables about the gods, and yet believe in the existence of female deities, and worship them, are unconsciously brought back to that which they had denied—that they have sexual intercourse, and bring forth. For it is impossible that the two sexes can have been instituted except for the sake of generation. But a difference of sex being admitted, they do not perceive that conception follows as a consequence. And this cannot be the case with a God. But let the matter be as they imagine; for they say that there are sons of Jupiter and of the other gods. Therefore new gods are born, and that indeed daily, for gods are not surpassed in fruitfulness by men. It follows that all things are full of gods without number, since forsooth none of them dies. For since the multitude of men is incredible, and their number not to be estimated—though, as they are born, they must of necessity die—what must we suppose to be the case with the gods who have been born through so many ages, and have remained immortal? How is it, then, that so few are worshipped? Unless we think by any means that there are two sexes of the gods, not for the sake of generation, but for mere gratification, and that the gods practice those things which men are ashamed to do, and to submit to. But when any are said to be born from any, it follows that they always continue to be born, if they are born at any time; or if they ceased at any time to be born, it is befitting that we should know why or at what time they so ceased. Seneca, in his books of moral philosophy, not without some pleasantry, asks, "What is the reason why Jupiter, who is represented by the poets as most addicted to lust, ceased to beget children? Was it that he was become a sexagenarian, and was restrained by the Papian law? Or did he obtain the privileges conferred by having three children? Or did the sentiment at length occur to him, 'What you have done to another, you may expect from another;' and does he fear lest anyone should act towards him as he himself did to Saturn?" But let those who maintain that they are gods, see in what manner they can answer this argument which I shall bring forward. If there are two sexes of the gods, conjugal intercourse follows; and if this takes place, they must have houses, for they are not without virtue and a sense of shame, so as to do this openly and promiscuously, as we see that the brute animals do. If they have houses, it follows that they also have cities; and for this we have the authority of Ovid, who says, "The multitude of gods occupy separate places; in this front the powerful and illustrious inhabitants of heaven have placed their dwellings." If they have cities, they will also have fields. Now who cannot see the consequence,—namely, that they plough and cultivate their lands? And this is done for the sake of food. Therefore they are mortal. And this argument is of the same weight when reversed. For if they have no lands, they have no cities; and if they have no cities, they are also without houses. And if they have no houses, they have no conjugal intercourse; and if they are without this, they have no female sex. But we see that there are females among the gods also. Therefore there are not gods. If anyone is able, let him do away with this argument. For one thing so follows the other, that it is impossible not to admit these last things. But no one will refute even the former argument. Of the two sexes the one is stronger, the other weaker. For the males are more robust, the females more feeble. But a god is not liable to feebleness; therefore there is no female sex. To this is added that last conclusion of the former argument, that there are no gods, since there are females also among the gods.

**Chap. xvii.—concerning the same opinion of the stoics, and concerning the hardships and disgraceful conduct of the gods.**

On these accounts the Stoics form a different conception of the gods; and because they do not perceive what the truth is, they attempt to join them with the system of natural things. And Cicero, following them, brought forward this opinion respecting the gods and their religions. Do you see then, he says, how an argument has been drawn from physical subjects which have been well and usefully found out, to the existence of false and fictitious gods? And this circumstance gave rise to false opinions and turbulent errors, and almost old-womanly superstitions. For both the forms of the gods, and their ages, and clothing and ornaments, are known to us; and moreover their races, and marriages, and all their relationships, and all things reduced to the similitude of human infirmity. What can be said more plain, more true? The chief of the Roman philosophy, and invested with the most honorable priesthood, refutes the false and fictitious gods, and testifies that their worship consists of almost old-womanly superstitions: he complains that men are entangled in false opinions and turbulent errors. For the whole of his third book respecting the Nature of the Gods altogether overthrows and destroys all religion. What more, therefore, is expected from us? Can we surpass Cicero in eloquence? By no means; but confidence was wanting to him, being ignorant of the truth, as he himself simply acknowledges in the same work. For he says that he can more easily say what is not, than what is; that is, that he is aware that *the received system* is false, but is ignorant of the truth. It is plain, therefore, that those who are supposed to be gods were but men, and that their memory was consecrated after their death. And on this account also different ages and established representations of form are assigned to each, because their images were fashioned in that dress and *of that* age at which death arrested each.

Let us consider, if you please, the hardships of the unfortunate gods. Isis lost her son; Ceres her daughter; Latona, expelled and driven about over the earth, with difficulty found a small island where she might bring forth. The mother of the gods both loved a beautiful youth, and also mutilated him when found in company with a harlot; and on this account her sacred rites are now celebrated by the Galli as priests. Juno violently persecuted harlots, because she was not able to conceive by her brother. Varro writes, that the island Samos was before called Parthenia, because Juno there grew up, and there also was married to Jupiter. Accordingly there is a most noble and ancient temple of hers at Samos, and an image fashioned in the dress of a bride; and her annual sacred rites are celebrated after the manner of a marriage. If, therefore, she grew up, if she was at first a virgin and afterwards a woman, he who does not understand that she was a human being confesses himself a brute. Why should I speak of the lewdness of Venus, who ministered to the lusts of all, not only gods, but also men? For from her infamous debauchery with Mars she brought forth Harmonia; from Mercury she brought forth Hermaphroditus, who was born of both sexes; from Jupiter Cupid; from Anchises Æneas; from Butes Eryx; from Adonis she could bring forth no offspring, because he was struck by a boar, and slain, while yet a boy. And she first instituted the art of courtesanship, as is contained in the sacred history; and taught women in Cyprus to seek gain by prostitution, which she commanded for this purpose, that she alone might not appear unchaste and a courter of men beyond other females. Has she, too, any claim to religious worship, on whose part more adulteries are recorded than births? But not even were those virgins who are celebrated able to preserve their chastity inviolate. For from what source can we suppose that Erichthonius was born? Was it from the earth, as the poets would have it appear? But the circumstance itself cries out. For when Vulcan had made arms for the gods, and Jupiter had given him the option of asking for whatever reward he might wish, and had sworn, according to his custom, by the infernal lake, that he would refuse him nothing which he might ask, then the lame artificer demanded Minerva in marriage. Upon this the excellent and mighty Jupiter, being bound by so great an oath, was not able to refuse; he, however, advised Minerva to oppose and defend her chastity. Then in that struggle they say that Vulcan shed his seed upon the earth, from which source Erichthonius was born: and that this name was given to him from ἔριδος and χθονός, that is, from the contest and the ground. Why, then, did she, a virgin, entrust that boy shut up with a dragon and sealed to three virgins born from Cecrops? An evident case of incest, as I think, which can by no means be glossed over. Another, when she had almost lost her lover, who was torn to pieces by his madened horses, called in the most excellent physician Æsculapius for the treatment of the youth; and when he was healed,

> "Trivia kind her favourite hides,
> And to Egeria's care confides,
> To live in woods obscure and lone,
> And lose in Virbius' name his own."

What is the meaning of this so diligent and anxious care? Why this secret abode? Why this banishment, either to so great a distance, or to a woman, or into solitude? Why, in the next place, the change of name? Lastly, why such a determined hatred of horses? What do all these things imply, but the consciousness of dishonor, and a love by no means consistent with a virgin? There was evidently a reason why she undertook so great a labor for a youth so faithful, who had refused compliance with the love of his stepmother.

**Chap. xviii.—on the consecration of gods, on account of the benefits which they conferred upon men.**

In this place also they are to be refuted, who not only admit that gods have been made from men, but even boast of it as a subject of praise, either on account of their valor, as Hercules, or of their gifts, as Ceres and Liber, or of the arts which they discovered, as Æsculapius or Minerva. But how foolish these things are, and how unworthy of being the causes why men should contaminate themselves with inexpiable guilt, and become enemies to God, in contempt of whom they undertake offerings to the dead, I will show from particular instances. They say that it is virtue which exalts man to heaven,—not, however, that concerning which philosophers discuss, which consists in goods of the soul, but this connected with the body, which is called fortitude; and since this was pre-eminent in Hercules, it is believed to have deserved immortality. Who is so foolishly senseless as to judge strength of body to be a divine or even a human good, when it has been assigned in greater measure to cattle, and it is often impaired by one disease, or is lessened by old age itself, and altogether fails? And so Hercules, when he perceived that his muscles were disfigured by ulcers, neither wished to be healed nor to grow old, that he might not at any time appear to have less strength or comeliness than he once had. They supposed that he ascended into heaven from the funeral pile on which he had burnt himself alive; and those very qualities which they most foolishly admired, they expressed by statues and images, and consecrated, so that they might forever remain as memorials of the folly of those who had believed that gods owed their origin to the slaughter of beasts. But this, perchance, may be the fault of the Greeks, who always esteemed most trifling things as of the greatest consequence. What is the case of our own countrymen? Are they more wise? For they despise valor in an athlete, because it produces no injury; but in the case of a king, because it occasions widely-spread disasters, they so admire it as to imagine that brave and warlike generals are admitted to the assembly of the gods, and that there is no other way to immortality than to lead armies, to lay waste the territory of others, to destroy cities, to overthrow towns, to put to death or enslave free peoples. Truly the greater number of men they have cast down, plundered, and slain, so much the more noble and distinguished do they think themselves; and ensnared by the show of empty glory, they give to their crimes the name of virtue. I would rather that they should make to themselves gods from the slaughter of wild beasts, than approve of an immortality so stained with blood. If anyone has slain a single man, he is regarded as contaminated and wicked, nor do they think it lawful for him to be admitted to this earthly abode of the gods. But he who has slaughtered countless thousands of men, has inundated plains with blood, and infected rivers, is not only admitted into the temple, but even into heaven. In Ennius Africanus thus speaks: "If it is permitted anyone to ascend to the regions of the gods above, the greatest gate of heaven is open to me alone."

Because, in truth, he extinguished and destroyed a great part of the human race. Oh how great the darkness in which you were involved, O Africanus, or rather O poet, in that you imagined the ascent to heaven to be open to men through slaughters and bloodshed! And Cicero also assented to this delusion. It is so in truth, he said, O Africanus, for the same gate was open to Hercules; as though he himself had been doorkeeper in heaven at the time when this took place. I indeed cannot determine whether I should think it a subject of grief or of ridicule, when I see grave and learned, and, as they appear to themselves, wise men, involved in such miserable waves of errors. If this is the virtue which renders us immortal, I for my part should prefer to die, rather than to be the cause of destruction to as many as possible. If immortality can be obtained in no other way than by bloodshed, what will be the result if all shall agree to *live in harmony*? And this may undoubtedly be realized, if men would cast aside their pernicious and impious madness, and live in innocence and justice. Shall no one, then, be worthy of heaven? Shall virtue perish, because it will not be permitted men to rage against their fellowmen? But they who reckon the overthrow of cities and people as the greatest glory will not endure public tranquility: they will plunder and rage; and by the infliction of outrageous injuries will disturb the compact of human society, that they may have an enemy whom they may destroy with greater wickedness than that with which they attacked.

    Now let us proceed to the remaining subjects. The conferring of benefits gave the name of gods to Ceres and Liber. I am able to prove from the sacred writings that wine and corn were used by men before the offspring of Coelus and Saturnus. But let us suppose that they were introduced by these. Can it appear to be a greater thing to have collected corn, and having bruised it, to have taught men to make bread; or to have pressed grapes gathered from the vine, and to have made wine, than to have produced and brought forth from the earth corn itself, or the vine? God, indeed, may have left these things to be drawn out by the ingenuity of man; yet all things must belong to Him, who gave to man both wisdom to discover, and those very things which might be discovered. The arts also are said to have gained immortality for their inventors, as medicine for Æsculapius, the craft of the smith for Vulcan. Therefore let us worship those also who taught the art of the fuller and of the shoemaker. But why is not honor paid to the discoverer of the potter's art? Is it that those rich men despise Samian vessels? There are also other arts, the inventors of which greatly profited the life of man. Why have not temples been assigned to them also? But doubtless it is Minerva who discovered all, and therefore workmen offer prayers to her. Such, then, was the low condition from which Minerva ascended to heaven. Is there truly any reason why anyone should leave the worship of Him who created the earth with its living creatures, and the heaven with its stars, for the adoration of her who taught men to set up the woof? What place does he hold who taught the healing of wounds in the body? Can he be more excellent than Him who formed the body itself, and the power of sensibility and of life? Finally, did he contrive and bring to light the herbs themselves, and the other things in which the healing art consists?

**Chap. xix.—that it is impossible for anyone to worship the true god together with false deities.**

But someone will say that this Supreme Being, who made all things, and those also who conferred on men particular benefits, are entitled to their respective worship. First of all, it has never happened that the worshipper of these has also been a worshipper of God. Nor can this possibly happen. For if the honor paid to Him is shared by others, He altogether ceases to be worshipped, since His religion requires us to believe that He is the one and only God. The excellent poet exclaims, that all those who refined life by the invention of arts are in the lower regions, and that even the discoverer himself of such a medicine and art was thrust down by lightning to the Stygian waves, that we may understand how great is the power of the Almighty Father, who can extinguish even gods by His lightnings. But ingenious men perchance thus reasoned with themselves: Because God cannot be struck with lightning, it is manifest that the occurrence never took place; nay, rather, because it did take place, it is manifest that the person in question was a man, and not a god. For the falsehood of the poets does not consist in the deed, but in the name. For they feared evil, if, in opposition to the general persuasion, they should acknowledge that which was true. But if this is agreed upon among themselves, that gods were made from men, why then do they not believe the poets, if at any time they describe their banishments and wounds, their deaths, and wars, and adulteries? From which things it may be understood that they could not possibly become gods, since they were not even good men, and during their life they performed those actions which bring forth everlasting death.

**Chap. xx.—of the gods peculiar to the Romans, and their sacred rites.**

I now come to the superstitions peculiar to the Romans, since I have spoken of those which are common. The wolf, the nurse of Romulus, was invested with divine honors. And I could endure this, if it had been the animal itself whose figure she bears. Livy relates that there was an image of Larentina, and indeed not of her body, but of her mind and character. For she was the wife of Faustulus, and on account of her prostitution she was called among the shepherds wolf, that is, harlot, from which also the brothel derives its name. The Romans doubtless followed the example of the Athenians in representing her figure. For when a harlot, by name Leæna, had put to death a tyrant among them, because it was unlawful for the image of a harlot to be placed in the temple, they erected the effigy of the animal whose name she bore. Therefore, as the Athenians erected a monument from the name, so did the Romans from the profession *of the person thus honored*. A festival was also dedicated to her name, and the Larentinalia were instituted. Nor is she the only harlot whom the Romans worship, but also Faula, who was, as Verrius writes, the paramour of Hercules. Now how great must that immortality be thought which is attained even by harlots! Flora, having obtained great wealth by this practice, made the people her heir, and left a fixed sum of money, from the annual proceeds of which her birthday might be celebrated by public games, which they called Floralia. And because this appeared disgraceful to the senate, in order that a kind of dignity might be given to a shameful matter, they resolved that an argument should be taken from the name itself. They pretended that she was the goddess who presides over flowers, and that she must be appeased, that the crops, together with the trees or vines, might produce a good and abundant blossom. The poet followed up this idea in his *Fasti*, and related that there was a nymph, by no means obscure, who was called Chloris, and that, on her marriage with Zephyrus, she received from her husband as a wedding gift the control over all flowers. These things are spoken with propriety, but to believe them is unbecoming and shameful. And *when the truth is in question*, ought disguises of this kind to deceive us? Those games, therefore, are celebrated with all wantonness, as is suitable to the memory of a harlot. For besides licentiousness of words, in which all lewdness is poured forth, women are also stripped of their garments at the demand of the people, and then perform the office of mime players, and are detained in the sight of the people with indecent gestures, even to the satiating of unchaste eyes.

    Tatius consecrated an image of Cloacina, which had been found in the great sewer; and because he did not know whose likeness it was, he gave it a name from the place. Tullus Hostilius fashioned and worshipped Fear and Pallor. What shall I say respecting him, but that he was worthy of having his gods always at hand, as men commonly wish? The conduct of Marcus Marcellus concerning the consecration of Honor and Valor differs from this in goodness of the names, but agrees with it in reality. The senate acted with the same vanity in placing Mind among the gods; for if they had possessed any intelligence, they would never have undertaken sacred rites of this kind. Cicero says that Greece undertook a great and bold design in consecrating the images of Cupids and Loves in the gymnasia: it is plain that he flattered Atticus, and jested with his friend. For that ought not to have been called a great design, or a design at all, but the abandoned and deplorable wickedness of unchaste men, who exposed their children, whom it was their duty to train to an honorable course, to the lust of youth, and wished them to worship gods of profligacy, in those places especially where their naked bodies were exposed to the gaze of their corruptors, and at that age which, through its simplicity and incautiousness, can be enticed and ensnared before it can be on its guard. What wonder, if all kinds of profligacy flowed from this nation, among whom vices themselves have the sanction of religion, and are so far from being avoided, that they are even worshipped? And therefore, as though he surpassed the Greeks in prudence, he subjoined to this sentence as follows: "Vices ought not to be consecrated, but virtues." But if you admit this, O Marcus Tullius, you do not see that it will come to pass that vices will break in together with virtues, because evil things adhere to those which are good, and have greater influence on the minds of men; and if you forbid these to be consecrated, the same Greece will answer you that it worships some gods that it may receive benefits, and others that it may escape injuries.

For this is always the excuse of those who regard their evils as gods, as the Romans esteem Blight and Fever. If, therefore, vices are not to be consecrated, in which I agree with you, neither indeed are virtues. For they have no intelligence or perception of themselves; nor are they to be placed within walls or shrines made of clay, but within the breast; and they are to be enclosed within, lest they should be false if placed without man. Therefore I laugh at that illustrious law of yours which you set forth in these words: "But those things on account of which it is given to man to ascend into heaven—*I speak of* mind, virtue, piety, faith—let there be temples for their praises." But these things cannot be separated from man. For if they are to be honored, they must necessarily be in man himself. But if they are without man, what need is there to honor those things which you do not possess? For it is virtue, which is to be honored, and not the image of virtue; and it is to be honored not by any sacrifice, or incense, or solemn prayer, but only by the will and purpose. For what else is it to honor virtue, but to comprehend it with the mind, and to hold it fast? And as soon as anyone begins to wish for this, he attains it. This is the only honor of virtue; for no other religion and worship is to be held but that of the one God. To what purport is it, then, O wisest man, to occupy with superfluous buildings places which may turn out to the service of men? To what purport is it to establish priests for the worship of vain and senseless objects? To what purport to immolate victims? To what purport to bestow such great expenditure on the forming or worshipping of images? The human breast is a stronger and more uncorrupted temple: let this rather be adorned, let this be filled with the true deities. For they who thus worship the virtues—that is, who pursue the shadows and images of virtues—cannot hold the very things which are true. Therefore there is no virtue in any one when vices bear rule; there is no faith when each individual carries off all things for himself; there is no piety when avarice spares neither relatives nor parents, and passion rushes to poison and the sword: no peace, no concord, when wars rage in public, and in private enmities prevail even to bloodshed; no chastity when unbridled lusts contaminate each sex, and the whole body in every part. Nor, however, do they cease to worship those things which they flee from and hate. For they worship with incense and the tips of their fingers those things which they ought to have shrunk from with their inmost feelings; and this error is altogether derived from their ignorance of the principal and chief good.

When their city was occupied by the Gauls, and the Romans, who were besieged in the Capitol, had made military engines from the hair of the women, they dedicated a temple to the Bald Venus. They do not therefore understand how vain are their religions, even from this very fact, that they jeer at them by these follies. They had perhaps learned from the Lacedæmonians to invent for themselves gods from events. For when they were besieging the Messenians, and they (the Messenians) had gone out secretly, escaping the notice of the besiegers, and had hastened to plunder Lacedæmon, they were routed and put to flight by the Spartan women. But the Lacedæmonians, having learned the stratagem of the enemy, followed. The women in arms went out to a distance to meet them; and when they saw that their husbands were preparing themselves for battle, supposing them to be Messenians, they laid bare their persons. But the men, recognizing their wives, and excited to passion by the sight, rushed to promiscuous intercourse, for there was not time for discrimination. In like manner, the youths who had on a former occasion been sent by the same people, having intercourse with the virgins, from whom the Partheniæ were born, in memory of this deed erected a temple and statue to armed Venus. And although this originated in a shameful cause, yet it seems better to have consecrated Venus as armed than bald. At the same time an altar was erected also to Jupiter Pistor (the baker), because he had admonished them in a dream to make all the corn which they had into bread, and throw it into the camp of the enemy; and when this was done, the siege was ended, since the Gauls despaired of being able to reduce the Romans by want.

    What a derision of religious rites is this! I were a defender of these, what could I complain of so greatly as that the name of gods had come into such contempt as to be mocked by the most disgraceful names? Who would not laugh at the goddess Fornax, or rather that learned men should be occupied with celebrating the Fornacalia? Who can refrain from laughter on hearing of the goddess Muta? They say that she is the goddess from whom the Lares were born, and they call her Lara, or Larunda. What advantage can she, who is unable to speak, afford to a worshipper? Caca also is worshipped, who informed Hercules of the theft of his oxen, having obtained immortality through the betrayal of her brother; and Cunina, who protects infants in the cradle, and keeps off witchcraft; and Stercutus, who first introduced the method of manuring the land; and Tutinus, before whom brides sit, as an introduction to the marriage rites; and a thousand other fictions, so that they who regarded these as objects of worship may be said to be more foolish than the Egyptians, who worship certain monstrous and ridiculous images. These however, have some delineation of form. What shall I say of those who worship a rude and shapeless stone under the name of Terminus? This is he whom Saturnus is said to have swallowed in the place of Jupiter; nor is the honor paid to him undeservedly. For when Tarquinius wished to build the Capitol, and there were the chapels of many gods on that spot, he consulted them by augury whether they would give way to Jupiter; and when the rest gave way, Terminus alone remained. From which circumstance the poet speaks of the immoveable stone of the Capitol. Now from this very fact how great is Jupiter found to be, to whom a stone did not give way, with this confidence, perhaps, because it had rescued him from the jaws of his father! Therefore, when the Capitol was built, an aperture was left in the roof above Terminus himself, that, since he had not given way, he might enjoy the free heaven; but they did not themselves enjoy this, who imagined that a stone enjoyed it. And therefore they make public supplications to him, as to the god who is the guardian of boundaries; and he is not only a stone, but sometimes also a stock. What shall I say of those who worship such objects, unless—that they above all others are stones and stocks?

**Chap. xxi.—of certain deities peculiar to barbarians, and their sacred rites; and in like manner concerning the romans.**

We have spoken of the gods themselves who are worshipped; we must now speak a few words respecting their sacrifices and mysteries. Among the people of Cyprus, Teucer sacrificed a human victim to Jupiter, and handed down to posterity that sacrifice which was lately abolished by Hadrian when he was emperor. There was a law among the people of

Tauris, a fierce and inhuman nation, *by which it was ordered* that strangers should be sacrificed to Diana; and this sacrifice was practiced through many ages. The Gauls used to appease Hesus and Teutas with human blood. Nor, indeed, were the Latins free from this cruelty, since Jupiter Latialis is even now worshipped with the offering of human blood. What benefit do they who offer such sacrifices implore from the gods? Or what are such deities able to bestow on the men by whose punishments they are propitiated? But this is not so much a matter of surprise with respect to barbarians, whose religion agrees with their character. But are not our countrymen, who have always claimed for themselves the glory of gentleness and civilization, found to be more inhuman by these sacrilegious rites? For these ought rather to be esteemed impious, who, though they are embellished with the pursuits of liberal training, turn aside from such refinement, than those who, being ignorant and inexperienced, glide into evil practices from their ignorance of those which are good. And yet it is plain that this rite of immolating human victims is ancient, since Saturn was honored in Latium with the same kind of sacrifice; not indeed that a man was slain at the altar, but that he was thrown from the Milvian bridge into the Tiber. And Varro relates that this was done in accordance with an oracle; of which oracle the last verse is to this effect: "And offer heads to Ades, and to the father a man." And because this appears ambiguous, both a torch and a man are accustomed to be thrown to him. But it is said that sacrifices of this kind were put an end to by Hercules when he returned from Spain; the custom still continuing, that instead of real men, images made from rushes were cast forth, as Ovid informs us in his *Fasti*: "Until the Tirynthian came into these lands, gloomy sacrifices were annually offered in the Leucadian manner: he threw into the water Romans made of straw; do you, after the example of Hercules, cast in the images of human bodies."

The Vestal virgins make these sacred offerings, as the same poet says: "Then also a virgin is accustomed to cast from the wooden bridge the images of ancient men made from rushes."

For I cannot find language to speak of the infants who were immolated to the same Saturn, on account of his hatred of Jupiter. To think that men were so barbarous, so savage, that they gave the name of sacrifice to the slaughter of their own children, that is, to a deed foul, and to be held in detestation by the human race; since, without any regard to parental affection, they destroyed tender and innocent lives, at an age which is especially pleasing to parents, and surpassed in brutality the savageness of all beasts, which—savage as they are—still love their offspring! O incurable madness! What more could those gods do to them, if they were most angry, than they now do when propitious, when they defile their worshippers with parricide, visit them with bereavements, and deprive them of the sensibilities of men? What can be sacred to these men? Or what will they do in profane places, who commit the greatest crimes amidst the altars of the gods? Pescennius Festus relates in the books of his History by a Satire, that the Carthaginians were accustomed to immolate human victims to Saturn; and when they were conquered by Agathocles, the king of the Sicilians, they imagined that the god was angry with them; and therefore, that they might more diligently offer an expiation, they immolated two hundred sons of their nobles: "So great the ills to which religion could prompt, which has oft times produced wicked and impious deeds." What advantage, then, did the men propose by that sacrifice, when they put to death so large a part of the state, as not even Agathocles had slain when victorious?

From this kind of sacrifices those public rites are to be judged *signs* of no less madness; some of which are in honor of the mother of the gods, in which men mutilate themselves; others are in honor of Virtus, whom they also call Bellona, in which the priests make offspring not with the blood of another victim, but with their own. For, cutting their shoulders, and thrusting forth drawn swords in each hand, they run, they are beside themselves, they are frantic. Quintilian therefore says excellently in his *Fanatic*: "If a god compels this, he does it in anger." Are even these things sacred? Is it not better to live like cattle, than to worship deities so impious, profane, and sanguinary? But we will discuss at the proper time the source from which these errors and deeds of such great disgrace originated. In the meantime, let us look also to other matters which are without guilt, that we may not seem to select the worse parts through the desire of finding fault. In Egypt there are sacred rites in honor of Isis, since she either lost or found her little son. For at first her priests, having made their bodies smooth, beat their breasts, and lament, as the goddess herself had done when her child was lost. Afterwards the boy is brought forward, as if found, and that mourning is changed into joy. Therefore Lucan says, "And Osiris never sufficiently sought for." For they always lose, and they always find him. Therefore in the sacred rites there is a representation of a circumstance which really occurred; and which assuredly declares, if we have any intelligence, that she was a mortal woman, and almost desolate, had she not found one person. And this did not escape the notice of the poet himself; for he represents Pompey when a youth as thus speaking, on hearing the death of his father: "I will now draw forth the deity Isis from the tomb, *and send her* through the nations; and I will scatter through the people Osiris covered with wood." This Osiris is the same whom the people call Serapis. For it is customary for the names of the dead who are deified to be changed, that no one, as I believe, may imagine them to be men. For Romulus after his death became Quirinus, and Leda became Nemesis, and Circe Marica; and Ino, when she had leapt into the sea, was called Leucothea; and the mother Matuta; and her son Melicerta was called Palæmon and Portumnus. And the sacred rites of the Eleusinian Ceres are not unlike these. For as in those *which have been mentioned* the boy Osiris is sought with the wailing of his mother, so in these Proserpine is carried away to contract an incestuous marriage with her uncle; and because Ceres is said to have sought for her in Sicily with torches lighted from the top of Etna, on this account her sacred rites are celebrated with the throwing of torches.

At Lampsacus the victim to he offered to Priapus is an ass, and the cause of the sacrifice of this animal is thus set forth in the *Fasti*:—When all the deities had assembled at the festival of the Great Mother, and when, satiated with feasting, they were spending the night in sport, they say that Vesta had laid herself on the ground for rest, and had fallen asleep, and that Priapus upon this formed a design against her honor as she slept; but that she was aroused by the unseasonable braying of the ass on which Silenus used to ride, and that the design of the insidious plotter was frustrated. On this account they say that the people of Lampsacus were accustomed to sacrifice an ass to Priapus, as though it were in revenge; but among the Romans the same animal was crowned at the Vestalia (festival of Vesta) with loaves, in honor of the preservation of her chastity. What is baser, what more disgraceful, than if Vesta is indebted to an ass for the preservation of her purity? But the poet invented a fable. But was that more true which is related by those who wrote "Phenomena," when they speak concerning the two stars of Cancer, which the Greeks call asses? That they were asses which carried across father Liber when he was unable to cross a river, and that he rewarded one of them with the power of speaking with human voice; and that a contest arose between him and Priapus; and Priapus, being worsted *in the contest*, was enraged, and slew the victor. This truly is much more absurd. But poets have the license of saying what they will. I do not meddle with a mystery so odious; nor do I strip Priapus of his disguise, lest something deserving of ridicule should be brought to light. It is true the poets invented these fictions, but they must have been invented for the purpose of concealing some greater depravity. Let us inquire what this is. But in fact it is evident. For as the bull is sacrificed to Luna, because he also has horns as she has; and as "Persia propitiates with a horse Hyperion surrounded with rays, that a slow victim may not be offered to the swift god;" so in this case no more suitable victim could be found than that which resembled him to whom it is offered.

At Lindus, which is a town of Rhodes, there are sacred rites in honor of Hercules, the observance of which differs widely from all other rites; for they are not celebrated with words of good omen (as the Greeks term it), but with reviling and cursing. And they consider it a violation of the sacred rites, if at any time during the celebration of the solemnities a good word shall have escaped from any one even inadvertently. And this is the reason assigned for this practice, if indeed there can be any reason in things utterly senseless. When Hercules had arrived at the place, and was suffering hunger, he saw a ploughman at work, and began to ask him to sell one of his oxen. But the ploughman replied that this was impossible, because his hope of cultivating the land depended altogether upon those two bullocks. Hercules, with his usual violence, because he was not able to receive one of them, killed both. But the unhappy man, when he saw that his oxen were slain, avenged the injury with reviling,—a circumstance which afforded gratification to the man of elegance and refinement. For while he prepares a feast for his companions, and while he devours the oxen of another man, he receives with ridicule and loud laughter the bitter reproaches with which the other assails him. But when it had been determined that divine honors should be paid to Hercules in admiration of his excellence, an altar was erected in his honor by the citizens, which he named, from the circumstance, the yoke of oxen; and at this altar two yoked oxen were sacrificed, like those which he had taken from the ploughman. And he appointed the same man to be his priest, and directed him always to use the same reviling in offering sacrifice, because he said that he had never feasted more pleasantly. Now these things are not sacred, but sacrilegious, in which that is said to be enjoined, which, if it is done in other things, is punished with the greatest severity. What, moreover, do the rites of the Cretan Jupiter himself show, except the manner in which he was withdrawn from his father, or brought up? There is a goat belonging to the nymph Amalthea, which gave suck to the infant; and of this goat Germanicus Cæsar thus speaks, in his poem translated from Aratus:—

"She is supposed to be the nurse of Jupiter; if in truth the infant Jupiter pressed the faithful teats of the Cretan goat, which attests the gratitude of her lord by a bright constellation."

Musæus relates that Jupiter, when fighting against the Titans, used the hide of this goat as a shield, from which circumstance he is called by the poets shield-bearer. Thus, whatever was done in concealing the boy, that also is done by way of representation in the sacred rites. Moreover, the mystery of his mother also contains the same *story* which Ovid sets forth in the *Fasti*:—

"Now the lofty Ida resounds with tinklings, that the boy may cry in safety with infant mouth. Some strike their shields with stakes, some beat their empty helmets. This is the employment of the Curetes, this of the Corybantes. The matter was concealed, and imitations of the ancient deed remain; the attendant goddesses shake instruments of brass, and hoarse hides. Instead of helmets they strike cymbals, and drums instead of shields; the flute gives Phrygian strains, as it gave before."

Sallust rejected this opinion altogether, as though invented by the poets, and wished to give an ingenious explanation of the reasons for which the Curetes are said to have nourished Jupiter; and he speaks to this purport: Because they were the first to understand the worship of the deity, that therefore antiquity, which exaggerates all things, made them known as the nourishers of Jupiter. How much this learned man was mistaken, the matter itself at once declares. For if Jupiter holds the first place, both among the gods and in religious rites, if no gods were worshipped by the people before him, because they who are worshipped were not yet born; it appears that the Curetes, on the contrary, were the first who did not understand the worship of the deity, since all error was introduced by them, and the memory of the true God was taken away. They ought therefore to have understood from the mysteries and ceremonies themselves, that they were offering prayers to dead men. I do not then require that anyone should believe the fictions of the poets. If any one imagines that these speak falsely, let him consider the writings of the pontiffs themselves, and weigh whatever there is of literature pertaining to sacred rites: he will perhaps find more things than we bring forward, from which he may understand that all things which are esteemed sacred are empty, vain, and fictitious. But if anyone, having discovered wisdom, shall lay aside his error, he will assuredly laugh at the follies of men who are almost without understanding: I mean those who either dance with unbecoming gestures, or run naked, anointed, and crowned with chaplets, either wearing a mask or besmeared with mud. What shall I say about shields now putrid with age? When they carry these, they think that they are carrying gods themselves on their shoulders. For Furius Bibaculus is regarded among the chief examples of piety, who, though he was prætor, nevertheless carried the sacred shield, preceded by the lictors, though his office *as proetor* gave him an exemption from this duty. He was therefore not Furius, but altogether mad, who thought that he graced his prætorship by this service. Deservedly then, since these things are done by men not unskillful and ignorant, does Lucretius exclaim:—

"O foolish minds of men! O blinded breasts! In what darkness of life and in how great dangers is passed this term of life, whatever be its duration!"

Who that is possessed of any sense would not laugh at these mockeries, when he sees that men, as though bereft of intelligence, do those things seriously, which if anyone should do in sport, he would appear too full of sport and folly?

**Chap. xxii.—who was the author of the vanities before described in Italy among the Romans, and who among other nations.**

The author and establisher of these vanities among the Romans was that Sabine king who especially engaged the rude and ignorant minds of men with new superstitions: and that he might do this with some authority, he pretended that he had meetings by night with the goddess Egeria. There was a very dark cavern in the grove of Aricia, from which flowed a stream with a never failing spring. Hither he was accustomed to withdraw himself without any witnesses, that he might be able to pretend that, by the admonition of the goddess his wife, he delivered to the people those sacred rites which were most acceptable to the gods. It is evident that he wished to imitate the craftiness of Minos, who concealed himself in the cave of Jupiter, and, after a long delay there, brought forward laws, as though delivered to him by Jupiter, that he might bind men to obedience not only by the authority of his government, but also by the sanction of religion. Nor was it difficult to persuade shepherds. Therefore he instituted pontiffs, priests, Salii, and augurs; he arranged the gods in families; and by these means he softened the fierce spirits of the new people and called them away from warlike affairs to the pursuit of peace. But though he deceived others, he did not deceive himself. For after many years, in the consulship of Cornelius and Bebius, in a field belonging to the scribe Petilius, under the Janiculum, two stone chests were found by men who were digging, in one of which was the body of Numa, in the other seven books in Latin respecting the law of the pontiffs, and the same number written in Greek respecting systems of philosophy, in which he not only annulled the religious rites which he himself had instituted, but all others also. When this was referred to the senate, it was decreed that these books should be destroyed. Therefore Quintus Petilius, the prætor who had jurisdiction in the city, burnt them in an assembly of the people. This was a senseless proceeding; for of what advantage was it that the books were burnt, when the cause on account of which they were burnt—that they took away the authority due to religion—was itself handed down to memory? Everyone then in the senate was most foolish; for the books might have been burnt, and yet the matter itself have been unknown. Thus, while they wish to prove even to posterity with what piety they defended religious institutions, they lessened the authority of the institutions themselves by their testimony.

But as Pompilius was the institutor of foolish superstitions among the Romans, so also, before Pompilius, Faunus was in Latium, who both established impious rites to his grandfather Saturnus, and honored his father Picus with a place among the gods, and consecrated his sister Fatua Fauna, who was also his wife; who, as Gabius Bassus relates, was called Fatua because she had been in the habit of foretelling their fates to women, as Faunus did to men. And Varro writes that she was a woman of such great modesty, that, as long as she lived, no male except her husband saw her or heard her name. On this account women sacrifice to her in secret, and call her the Good Goddess. And Sextus Claudius, in that book which he wrote in Greek, relates that it was the wife of Faunus who, because, contrary to the practice and honor of kings, she had drunk a jar of wine, and had become intoxicated, was beaten to death by her husband with myrtle rods. But afterwards, when he was sorry for what he had done, and was unable to endure his regret for her, he paid her divine honors. For this reason they say that a covered jar of wine is placed at her sacred rites. Therefore Faunus also left to posterity no slight error, which all that are intelligent see through. For Lucilius in these verses derides the folly of those who imagine that images are gods: "The terrestrial Lamiæ, which Faunus and Numa Pompilius and others instituted; at and these he trembles, he places everything in this. As infant boys believe that every statue of bronze is a living man, so these imagine that all things feigned are true: they believe that statues of bronze contain a heart. It is a painter's gallery; there is nothing true; all things are fictitious." The poet, indeed, compares foolish men to infants. But I say that they are much more senseless than infants. For they (infants) suppose that images are men, whereas these take them for gods: the one through their age, the others through folly, imagine that which is not true: at any rate, the one soon ceased to be deceived; the foolishness of the others is permanent, and always increases. Orpheus was the first who introduced the rites of father Liber into Greece; and he first celebrated them on a mountain of Boeotia, very near to Thebes, where Liber was born; and because this mountain continually resounded with the strains of the lyre, it was called Cithæron. Those sacred rites are even now called Orphic, in which he himself was lacerated and torn in pieces; and he lived about the same time with Faunus. But which of them was prior in age admits of doubt, since Latinus and Priam reigned during the same years, as did also their fathers Faunus and Laomedon, in whose reign Orpheus came with the Argonauts to the coast of the Trojans.

Let us therefore advance further, and inquire who was really the first author of the worship of the gods. Didymus, in the books of his commentary on Pindar, says that Melisseus, king of the Cretans, was the first who sacrificed to the gods, and introduced new rites and parades of sacrifices. He had two daughters, Amalthæa and Melissa, who nourished the youthful Jupiter with goats' milk and honey. Hence that poetic fable derived its origin, that bees flew to the child, and filled his mouth with honey. Moreover, he says that Melissa was appointed by her father the first priestess of the Great Mother; from which circumstance the priests of the same Mother are still called Melissæ. But the sacred history testifies that Jupiter himself, when he had gained possession of power, arrived at such insolence that he built temples in honor of himself in many places. For when he went about to different lands, on his arrival in each region, he united to himself the kings or princes of the people in hospitality and friendship; and when he was departing from each, he ordered that a shrine should be dedicated to himself in the name of his host, as though the remembrance of their friendship and league could thus be preserved. Thus temples were founded in honor of Jupiter Atabyrius and Jupiter Labrandius; for Atabyrius and Labrandius were his entertainers and assistants in war. Temples were also built to Jupiter Laprius, to Jupiter

Molion, to Jupiter Casius, and others, after the same manner. This was a very crafty device on his part, that he might both acquire divine honor for himself, and a perpetual name for his entertainers in conjunction with religious observances. Accordingly they were glad, and cheerfully submitted to his command, and observed annual rites and festivals for the sake of *handing down* their own name. Æneas did something like this in Sicily, when he gave the name of his host Acestes to a city which he had built, that Acestes might afterwards joyfully and willingly love, increase, and adorn it. In this manner Jupiter spread abroad through the world the observance of his worship, and gave an example for the imitation of others. Whether, then, the practice of worshipping the gods proceeded from Melisseus, as Didymus related, or from Jupiter also himself, as Euhemerus says, the time is still agreed upon when the gods began to be worshipped. Melisseus, indeed, was much prior in time, inasmuch as he brought up Jupiter his grandson. It is therefore possible that either before, or while Jupiter was yet a boy, he taught the worship of the gods, namely, the mother of his foster-child, and his grandmother Tellus, who was the wife of Uranus, and his father Saturnus; and he himself, by this example and institution, may have exalted Jupiter to such pride, that he afterwards ventured to assume divine honors to himself.

**Chap. xxiii.—of the ages of vain superstitions, and the times at which they commenced.**

Now, since we have ascertained the origin of vain superstitions, it remains that we should also collect the times during which they whose memory is honored lived. Theophilus, in his book written to Autolycus respecting the times, says that Thallus relates in his history, that Belus, who is worshipped by the Babylonians and Assyrians, is found to have lived 322 years before the Trojan war; that Belus, moreover, was contemporary with Saturnus, and that they both grew up at one time;—which is so true, that it may be inferred by reason itself. For Agamemnon, who carried on the Trojan war, was the fourth in descent from Jupiter; and Achilles and Ajax were of the third descent from him; and Ulysses was related in the same degree. Priam, indeed, was distant by a long series of descents. But according to some authorities, Dardanus and Iasius were sons of Coritus, not of Jupiter. For if it had been so, Jupiter could not have formed that unchaste connection with Ganymede, his own descendant. Therefore, if you divide the years which are in agreement, the number will be found in harmony with the parents of those whom I have named above. Now, from the destruction of the Trojan city fourteen hundred and seventy years are made up. From this calculation of times, it is manifest that Saturnus has not been born more than eighteen hundred years, and he also was the father of all the gods. Let them not glory, then, in the antiquity of their sacred rites, since both their origin and system and times have been ascertained. There still remain some things which may be of great weight for the disproving of false religions; but I have determined now to bring this book to an end, that it may not exceed moderate limits. For those things must be followed up more fully, that, having refuted all things which seem to oppose the truth, we may be able to instruct in true religion men who, through ignorance of good things, wander in uncertainty. But the first step towards wisdom is to understand what is false; the second, to ascertain what is true. Therefore he who shall have profited by this first discussion of mine, in which we have exposed false things, will be excited to the knowledge of the truth, than which no pleasure is more gratifying to man; and he will now be worthy of the wisdom of heavenly training, who shall approach with willingness and preparation to the knowledge of the other subjects.

# The divine institutes.

## Book II.

## Of the Origin of Error.

**Chap. i.—that forgetfulness of reason makes men ignorant of the true god, whom they worship in adversity and despise in prosperity.**

Although I have shown in the first book that the religious ceremonies of the gods are false, because those in whose honor the general consent of men throughout the world by a foolish persuasion undertook various and dissimilar rites were mortals, and when they had completed their *term of* life, yielded to a divinely appointed necessity and died, yet, lest any doubt should be left, this second book shall lay open the very fountain of errors, and shall explain all the causes by which men were deceived, so that at first they believed that they were gods, and afterwards with an inveterate persuasion persevered in the religious observances which they had most perversely undertaken. For I desire, O Emperor Constantine, now that I have proved the emptiness of these things, and brought to light the impious vanity of men, to assert the majesty of the one God, undertaking the more useful and greater duty of recalling men from crooked paths, and of bringing them back into favor with themselves, that they may not, as some philosophers do, so greatly despise themselves, nor think that they are weak and useless, and of no account, and altogether born in vain. For this notion drives many to vicious pursuits. For while they imagine that we are a care to no God, or that we are about to have no existence after death, they altogether give themselves to the indulgence of their passions; and while they think that it is allowed them, they eagerly apply themselves to the enjoyment of pleasures, by which they unconsciously run into the snares of death; for they are ignorant as to what is reasonable conduct on the part of man: for if they wished to understand this, in the first place they would acknowledge their Lord, and would follow after virtue and justice; they would not subject their souls to the influence of earth-born fictions, nor would they seek the deadly fascinations of their lusts; in short, they would value themselves highly, and would understand that there is more in man than appears; and that they cannot retain their power and standing unless men lay aside depravity, and undertake the worship of their true Parent. I indeed, as I ought, often reflecting on the sum of affairs, am accustomed to wonder that the majesty of the one God, which keeps together and rules all things, has come to be so forgotten, that the only befitting object of worship is, above all others, the one which is especially neglected; and that men have sunk to such blindness, that they prefer the dead to the true and living God, and those who are of the earth, and buried in the earth, to Him who was the Creator of the earth itself.

And yet this impiety of men might meet with some indulgence if the error entirely arose from ignorance of the divine name. But since we often see that the worshippers of other gods themselves confess and acknowledge the Supreme God, what pardon can they hope for their impiety, who do not acknowledge the worship of Him whom man cannot altogether be ignorant of? For both in swearing, and in expressing a wish, and in giving thanks, they do not name Jupiter, or a number of gods, but God; so entirely does the truth of its own accord break forth by the force of nature even from unwilling breasts. And this, indeed, is not the case with men in their prosperity. For then most of all does God escape the memory of men, when in the enjoyment of His benefits they ought to honor His divine beneficence. But if any weighty necessity shall press them, then they remember God. If the terror of war shall have resounded, if the pestilential force of diseases shall have overhung them, if long-continued drought shall have denied nourishment to the crops, if a violent tempest or hail shall have assailed them, they betake themselves to God, aid is implored from God, God is entreated to succor them. If anyone is tossed about on the sea, the wind being furious, it is this *God* whom he invokes. If anyone is harassed by any violence, he implores His aid. If anyone, reduced to the last extremity of poverty, begs for food, he appeals to God alone, and by His divine and matchless name alone he seeks to gain the compassion of men. Thus they never remember God, unless it be while they are in trouble. When fear has left them, and the dangers have withdrawn, then in truth they quickly hasten to the temples of the gods: they pour libations to them, they sacrifice to them, and they crown them with garlands. But to God, whom they called upon in their necessity itself, they do not give thanks even in word. Thus from prosperity arises luxury; and from luxury, together with all other vices, there arises impiety towards God.

From what cause can we suppose this to arise? Unless we imagine that there is some perverse power which is always hostile to the truth, which rejoices in the errors of men, whose one and only task it is perpetually to scatter darkness, and to blind the minds of men, lest they should see the light,—lest, in short, they should look to heaven, and observe the nature of their own body, the origin of which we shall relate at the proper place; but now let us refute fallacies. For since other animals look down to the ground, with bodies bending forward, because they have not received reason and wisdom, whereas an upright position and an elevated countenance have been given to us by the Creator God, it is evident that these ceremonies paid to the gods are not in accordance with the reason of man, because they bend down the heaven-sprung being to the worship of earthly objects. For that one and only Parent of ours, when He created man,—that is, an animal intelligent and capable of exercising reason,—raised him from the ground, and elevated him to the contemplation of his Creator. As an ingenious poet has well represented it:—

"And when other animals bend forward and look to the earth, He gave to man an elevated countenance, and commanded him to look up to the heaven, and to raise his countenance erect to stars."

From this circumstance the Greeks plainly derived the name ἄνθρωπος, because he looks upward. They therefore deny themselves, and renounce the name of man, who do not look up, but downward: unless they think that the fact of our being upright is assigned to man without any cause. God willed that we should look up to heaven, and undoubtedly not without reason. For both the birds and almost all of the dumb creation see the heaven, but it is given to us in a peculiar manner to behold the heaven as we stand erect, that we may seek religion there; that since we cannot see God with our eyes, we may with our mind contemplate Him, whose throne is there: and this cannot assuredly be done by him who worships brass and stone, which are earthly things. But it is most incorrect that the nature of the body, which is temporary, should be upright, but that the soul itself, which is eternal, should be abject; whereas the figure and position have no other signification, except that the mind of man ought to look in the same direction as his countenance, and that his soul ought to be as upright as his body, so that it may imitate that which it ought to rule. But men, forgetful both of their name and nature, cast down their eyes from the heaven, and fix them upon the ground, and fear the works of their own hands, as though anything could be greater than its own artificer.

**Chap. ii.—what was the first cause of making images; of the true likeness of god, and the true worship of him.**

What madness is it, then, either to form those objects which they themselves may afterwards fear, or to fear the things which they have formed? But, they say, we do not fear the images themselves, but those beings after whose likeness they were formed, and to whose names they are dedicated. You fear them doubtless on this account, because you think that they are in heaven; for if they are gods, the case cannot be otherwise. Why, then, do you not raise your eyes to heaven, and, invoking their names, offer sacrifices in the open air? Why do you look to walls, and wood, and stone, rather than to the place where you believe them to be? What is the meaning of temples and altars? What, in short, of the images themselves, which are memorials either of the dead or absent? For the plan of making likenesses was invented by men for this reason, that it might be possible to retain the memory of those who had either been removed by death or separated by absence. In which of these classes, then, shall we reckon the gods? If among the dead, who is so foolish as to worship them? If among the absent, then they are not to be worshipped, if they neither see our actions nor hear our prayers. But if the gods cannot be absent,—for, since they are divine, they see and hear all things, in whatever part of the universe they are,—it follows that images are superfluous, since the gods are present everywhere, and it is sufficient to invoke with prayer the names of those who hear us. But if they are present, they cannot fail to be at hand at their own images. It is entirely so, as the people imagine, that the spirits of the dead wander about the tombs and relics of their bodies. But after that the deity has begun to be near, there is no longer need of his statue.

For I ask, if anyone should often contemplate the likeness of a man who has settled in a foreign land, that he may thus solace himself for him who is absent, would he also appear to be of sound mind, if, when the other had returned and was present, he should persevere in contemplating the likeness, and should prefer the enjoyment of it, rather than the sight of the man himself? Assuredly not. For the likeness of a man appears to be necessary at that time when he is far away; and it will become superfluous when he is at hand. But in the case of God, whose spirit and influence are diffused everywhere, and can never be absent, it is plain that an image is always superfluous. But they fear lest their religion should be altogether vain and empty if they should see nothing present which they may adore, and therefore they set up images; and since these are representations of the dead, they resemble the dead, for they are entirely destitute of perception. But the image of the ever-living God ought to be living and endued with perception. But if it received this name from resemblance, how can it be supposed that these images resemble God, which have neither perception nor motion? Therefore the image of God is not that which is fashioned by the fingers of men out of stone, or bronze, or other material, but man himself, since he has both perception and motion, and performs many and great actions. Nor do the foolish men understand, that if images could exercise perception and motion, they would of their own accord adore men, by whom they have been adorned and embellished, since they would be either rough and unpolished stone, or rude and unshapen wood, had they not been fashioned by man.

Man, therefore, is to be regarded as the parent of these images; for they were produced by his instrumentality, and through him they first had shape, figure, and beauty. Therefore he who made them is superior to the objects which were made. And yet no one looks up to the Maker Himself, or reverences Him: he fears the things which he has made, as though there could be more power in the work than in the workman. Seneca, therefore, rightly says in his moral treatises: They worship the images of the gods, they supplicate them with bended knee, they adore them, they sit or stand beside them through the whole day, they offer to them contributions, they slay victims; and while they value these *images* so highly, they despise the artificers who made them. What is so inconsistent, as to despise the statuary and to adore the statue; and not even to admit to your society him who makes your gods? What force, what power can they have, when he who made them has none? But he was unable to give to these even those powers which he had, the power of sight, of hearing, of speech, and of motion. Is anyone so foolish as to suppose that there is anything in the image of a god, in which there is nothing even of a man except the mere resemblance? But no one considers these things; for men are imbued with this persuasion, and their minds have thoroughly imbibed the deception of folly. And thus beings endowed with sense adore objects which are senseless, rational beings adore irrational objects, those who are alive adore inanimate objects, those sprung from heaven adore earthly

objects. It delights me, therefore, as though standing on a lofty watch-tower, from which all may hear, to proclaim aloud that saying of
Persius:—

"O souls bent down to the earth, and destitute of heavenly things?"

Rather look to the heaven, to the sight of which God your Creator raised you. He gave to you an elevated countenance; you bend it down to the earth; you depress to things below those lofty minds, which are raised together with their bodies to their parent, as though it repented you that you were not born quadrupeds. It is not befitting that the heavenly being should make himself equal to things which are earthly, and incline to the earth. Why do you deprive yourselves of heavenly benefits, and of your own accord fall prostrate upon the ground? For you do wretchedly roll yourselves on the ground, when you seek here below that which you ought to have sought above. For as to those vain and fragile productions, the work of man's hands, from whatever kind of material they are formed, what are they but earth, out of which they were produced? Why, then, do you subject yourselves to lower objects? Why do you place the earth above your heads? For when you lower yourselves to the earth, and humiliate yourselves, you sink of your own accord to hell, and condemn yourselves to death; for nothing is lower and more humble than the earth, except death and hell. And if you wished to escape these, you would despise the earth lying beneath your feet, preserving the position of your body, which you received upright, in order that you might be able to direct your eyes and your mind to Him who made it. But to despise and trample upon the earth is nothing else than to refrain from adoring images, because they are made of earth; also not to desire riches, and to despise the pleasures of the body, because wealth, and the body itself, which we make use of as a lodging, is but earth. Worship a living being, that you may live; for he must necessarily die who has subjected himself and his soul to the dead.

### Chap. iii.—that Cicero and other men of learning erred in not turning away the people from error.

But what does it avail thus to address the vulgar and ignorant, when we see that learned and prudent men, though they understand the vanity of these ceremonies, nevertheless through some perverseness persist in the worship of those very objects which they condemn? Cicero was well aware that the deities which men worshipped were false. For when he had spoken many things which tended to the overthrow of religious ceremonies, he said nevertheless that these matters ought not to be discussed by the vulgar, lest such discussion should extinguish the system of religion which was publicly received. What can you do respecting him, who, when he perceives himself to be in error, of his own accord dashes himself against the stones, that all the people may stumble? Or tears out his own eyes, that all may be blind? who neither deserves well of others, whom he suffers to be in error, nor of himself, since he inclines to the errors of others, and makes no use of the benefit of his own wisdom, so as to carry out in action the conception of his own mind, but knowingly and consciously thrusts his foot into the snare, that he also may be taken with the rest, whom he ought, as the more prudent, to have extricated? Nay rather, if you have any virtue, Cicero, endeavor to make the people wise: that is a befitting subject, on which you may expend all the powers of your eloquence. For there is no fear lest speech should fail you in so good a cause, when you have often defended even bad ones with copiousness and spirit. But truly you fear the prison of Socrates, and on that account you do not venture to undertake the advocacy of truth. But, as a wise man, you ought to have despised death. And, indeed, it would have been much more glorious to die on account of good words than on account of reviling. Nor would the renown of your Philippics have been more advantageous to you than the dispersion of the errors of mankind, and the recalling of the minds of men to a healthy state by your disputation.

But let us make allowance for timidity, which ought not to exist in a wise man. Why, then, are you yourself engaged in the same error? I see that you worship things of earth made by the hand: you understand that they are vain, and yet you do the same things which they do, whom you confess to be most foolish. What, therefore, did it profit you that you saw the truth, which you were neither about to defend nor to follow? If even they who perceive themselves to be in error err willingly, how much more so do the unlearned vulgar, who delight in empty processions, and gaze at all things with boyish minds! They are delighted with trifling things, and are captivated with the form of images; and they are unable to weigh every object in their own minds, so as to understand that nothing which is beheld by the eyes of mortals ought to be worshipped, because it must necessarily be mortal. Nor is it matter of surprise if they do not see God, when they themselves do not even see man, whom they believe that they see. For this, which falls under the notice of the eyes, is not man, but the receptacle of man, the quality and figure of which are not seen from the lineaments of the vessel which contains them, but from the actions and character. They, therefore, who worship images are *mere* bodies without men, because they have given themselves to corporeal things, and do not see anything with the mind more than with the body; whereas it is the office of the soul to perceive those things more clearly which the eye of the body cannot behold. And that philosopher and poet severely accuses those men as humble and abject, who, in opposition to the design of their nature, prostrate themselves to the worship of earthly things; for he says:—

"And they abase their souls with fear of the gods, and weigh and press them down to earth."

When he said these things, indeed, his meaning was different—that nothing was to be worshipped, because the gods do not regard the affairs of men.

In another place, at length, he acknowledges that the ceremonies and worship of the gods is an unavailing office:—

"Nor is it any piety to be often seen with veiled head to turn to a stone, and approach every altar, and fall prostrate on the ground, and spread the hands before the shrines of the gods, and sprinkle the altars with much blood of beasts, and to offer vow after vow."

And assuredly if these things are useless, it is not right that sublime and lofty souls should be called away and depressed to the earth, but that they should think only of heavenly things.

False religious systems, therefore, have been attacked by more sagacious men, because they perceived their falsehood; but the true *religion* was not introduced, because they knew not what and where it was. They therefore so regarded it as though it had no existence, because they were unable to find it in its truth. And in this manner they fell into a much greater error than they who held a religion which was false. For those worshippers of fragile images, however foolish they may be, inasmuch as they place heavenly things in things which are earthly and corruptible, yet retain something of wisdom, and may be pardoned, because they hold the chief duty of man, if not in reality, yet still in their purpose; since, if not the only, yet certainly the greatest difference between men and the beasts consists in religion. But this latter class, in proportion to their superior wisdom, in that they understood the error of false religion, rendered themselves so much the more foolish, because they did not imagine that some religion was true. And thus, because it is easier to judge of the affairs of others than of their own, while they see the downfall of others, they have not observed what was before their own feet. On either side is found the greatest folly, and a certain trace of wisdom; so that you may doubt which are rather to be called more foolish—those who embrace a false religion, or those who embrace none. But (as I have said) pardon may be granted to those who are ignorant and do not own themselves to be wise; but it cannot be extended to those who, while they profess wisdom, rather exhibit folly. I am not, indeed, so unjust as to imagine that they could divine, so that they might find out the truth by themselves; for I acknowledge that this is impossible. But I require from them that which they were able to perform by reason itself. For they would act more prudently, if they both understood that some *form of* religion is true, and if, while they attacked false *religions*, they openly proclaimed that men were not in possession of that which is true.

But this consideration may perhaps have influenced them, that if there were any true religion, it would exert itself and assert its authority, and not permit the existence of anything opposed to it. For they were unable to see at all, on what account, or by whom, and in what manner true religion was depressed, which partakes of a divine mystery and a heavenly secret. And no man can know this by any means, unless he is taught. The sum of the matter is this: The unlearned and the foolish esteem false religions as true, because they neither know the true nor understand the false. But the more sagacious, because they are ignorant of the true, either persist in those religions which they know to be false, that they may appear to possess something; or worship nothing at all, that they may not fall into error, whereas this very thing partakes largely of error, under the figure of a man to imitate the life of cattle. To understand that which is false is truly the part of wisdom, but of human wisdom. Beyond this step man cannot proceed, and thus many of the philosophers have taken away religious institutions, as I have pointed out; but to know the truth is the part of divine wisdom. But man by himself cannot attain to this knowledge, unless he is taught by God. Thus philosophers have reached the height of human wisdom, so as to understand that which is not; but they have failed in attaining the power of saying that which really is. It is a well-known saying of

Cicero: "I wish that I could as easily find out the truth as I can refute false things." And because this is beyond the power of man's condition, the capability of this office is assigned to us, to whom God has delivered the knowledge of the truth; to the explaining of which the four last books shall be devoted. Now, in the meantime, let us bring to light false things, as we have begun to do.

**Chap. iv.—of images, and the ornaments of temples, and the contempt in which they are held even by the heathens themselves.**

What majesty, then, can images have, which were altogether in the power of puny man, either that they should be formed into something else, or that they should not be made at all? On which account Priapus thus speaks in Horace:

"Formerly I was the trunk of a fig-tree, a useless log, when the carpenter, at a loss whether he should make a bench or a Priapus, decided that it should be a god. Accordingly I am a god, a very great terror to thieves and birds."

Who would not be at ease with such a guardian as this? For thieves are so foolish as to fear the figure of Priapus; though the very birds, which they imagine to be driven away by fear of his scythe, settle upon the images which are skillfully made, that is, which altogether resemble men, build their nests there, and defile them. But Flaccus, as a writer of satire, ridiculed the folly of men. But they who make the images fancy that they are performing a serious business. In short, that very great poet, a man of sagacity in other things, in this alone displayed folly, not like a poet, but after the manner of an old woman, when even in those most highly-finished books he orders this to be done:—

"And let the guardianship of Priapus of the Hellespont, who drives away thieves and birds with his willow scythe, preserve them."

Therefore they adore mortal things, as made by mortals. For they may be broken, or burnt, or be destroyed. For they are often apt to be broken to pieces, when houses fall through age, and when, consumed by conflagration, they waste away to ashes; and in many instances, unless aided by their own magnitude, or protected by diligent watchfulness, they become the prey of thieves. What madness is it, then, to fear those objects for which either the downfall of a building, or fires, or thefts, may be feared! What folly, to hope for protection from those things which are unable to protect themselves! What perversity, to have recourse to the guardianship of those which, when injured, are themselves unavenged, unless vengeance is exacted by their worshippers! Where, then, is truth? Where no violence can be applied to religion; where there appears to be nothing which can be injured; where no sacrilege can be committed.

But whatever is subjected to the eyes and to the hands, that, in truth, because it is perishable, is inconsistent with the whole subject of immortality. It is in vain, therefore, that men set off and adorn their gods with gold, ivory, and jewels, as though they were capable of deriving any pleasure from these things. What is the use of precious gifts to insensible objects? Is it the same which the dead have? For as they embalm the bodies of the dead, wrap them in spices and precious garments, and bury them in the earth, so they honor the gods, who when they were made did not perceive it, and when they are worshipped have no knowledge of it; for they did not receive sensibility on their consecration. Persius was displeased that golden vessels should be carried into the temples, since he thought it superfluous that that should be reckoned among religious offerings which was not an instrument of sanctity, but of avarice. For these are the things which it is better to offer as a gift to the god whom you would rightly worship:—

"Written law and the divine law of the conscience, and the sacred recesses of the mind, and the breast imbued with nobleness."

A noble and wise sentiment. But he ridiculously added this: that there is this gold in the temples, as there are dolls presented to Venus by the virgin; which perhaps he may have despised on account of their smallness. For he did not see that the very images and statues of the gods, wrought in gold and ivory by the hand of Polycletus, Euphranor, and Phidias, were nothing more than large dolls, not dedicated by virgins, to whose sports some indulgence may be granted, but by bearded men. Therefore Seneca deservedly laughs at the folly even of old men. We are not (he says) boys twice, as is commonly said, but are always so. But there is this difference, that *when men* we have greater subjects of sport. Therefore men offer to these dolls, which are of large size, and adorned as though for the stage, both perfumes, and incense, and odors: they sacrifice to these costly and fattened victims, which have a mouth, but one that is not suitable for eating; to these they bring robes and costly garments, though they have no need of clothing; to these they dedicate gold and silver, of which they who receive them are as destitute as they who have given them.

And not without reason did Dionysius, the despot of Sicily, when after a victory he had become master of Greece, despise, and plunder and jeer at such gods, for he followed up his sacrilegious acts by jesting words. For when he had taken off a golden robe from the statue of the Olympian Jupiter, he ordered that a woolen garment should be placed upon him, saying that a golden robe was heavy in summer and cold in winter, but that a woolen one was adapted to each season. He also took off the golden beard from Æsculapius, saying that it was unbecoming and unjust, that while his father Apollo was yet smooth and beardless, the son should be seen to wear a beard before his father. He also took away the bowls, and spoils, and some little images which were held in the extended hands of the statues, and said that he did not take them away, but received them: for that it would be very foolish and ungrateful to refuse to receive good things, when offered voluntarily by those from whom men were accustomed to implore them. He did these things with impunity, because he was a king and victorious. Moreover, his usual good fortune also followed him; for he lived even to old age, and handed down the kingdom in succession to his son. In his case, therefore, because men could not punish his sacrilegious deeds, it was befitting that the gods should be their own avengers. But if any humble person shall have committed any such crime, there are at hand for his punishment the scourge, fire, the rack, the cross, and whatever torture men can invent in their anger and rage. But when they punish those who have been detected in the act of sacrilege, they themselves distrust the power of their gods. For why should they not leave to them especially the opportunity of avenging themselves, if they think that they are able to do so? Moreover, they also imagine that it happened through the will of the deities that the sacrilegious robbers were discovered and arrested; and their cruelty is instigated not so much by anger as by fear, lest they themselves should be visited with punishment if they failed to avenge the injury done to the gods. And, in truth, they display incredible shallowness in imagining that the gods will injure them on account of the guilt of others, who by themselves were unable to injure those very persons by whom they were profaned and plundered. But, in fact, they have often themselves also inflicted punishment on the sacrilegious: that may have occurred even by chance, which has sometimes happened, but not always. But I will show presently how that occurred. Now in the meantime I will ask, why did they not punish so many and such great acts of sacrilege in Dionysius, who insulted the gods openly, and not in secret? Why did they not repel this sacrilegious man, possessed of such power, from their temples, their ceremonies, and their images? Why, even when he had carried off their sacred things, had he a prosperous voyage—as he himself, according to his custom, testified in joke? Do you see, he said to his companions who feared shipwreck, how prosperous a voyage the immortal gods themselves give to the sacrilegious? But perhaps he had learnt from Plato that the gods have no power.

What of Caius Verres? Whom his accuser Tully compares to this same Dionysius, and to Phalaris, and to all tyrants. Did he not pillage the whole of Sicily, carrying away the images of the gods, and the ornaments of the temples? It is idle to follow up each particular instance: I would fain make mention of one, in which the accuser, with all the force of eloquence—in short, with every effort of voice and of body—lamented about Ceres of Catina, or of Henna: the one of whom was of such great sanctity, that it was unlawful for men to enter the secret recesses of her temple; the other was of such great antiquity, that all accounts relate that the goddess herself first discovered grain in the soil of Henna, and that her virgin daughter was carried away from the same place. Lastly, in the times of the Gracchi, when the state was disturbed both by seditions and by portents, on its being discovered in the Sibylline predictions that the most ancient Ceres ought to be appeased, ambassadors were sent to Henna. This Ceres, then, either the most holy one, whom it was unlawful for men to behold even for the sake of adoration, or the most ancient one, whom the senate and people of Rome had appeased with sacrifices and gifts, was carried away with impunity by Caius Verres from her secret and ancient recesses, his robber slaves having been sent in. The same *orator*, in truth, when he affirmed that he had been entreated by the Sicilians to undertake the cause of the province, made use of these words: "That they had now not even any gods in their cities to whom they might betake themselves, since Verres had taken away the most sacred images from their most venerable shrines." As though, in truth, if Verres had taken them away from the cities and shrines, he had also taken them from heaven. From which it appears that those gods have nothing in them more than the material of which they are made. And not without reason did the Sicilians have recourse to you, O Marcus Tullius, that is, to a man; since they had for three years experienced that those gods had no power. For they would have been most foolish if they had fled for protection against the injuries of men, to those who were unable to be angry with Caius Verres on their own behalf. But, *it will be urged*, Verres was condemned on account of these deeds. Therefore he was not punished by the gods, but by the energy of Cicero, by which he either crushed his defenders or withstood his influence. Why should I say that, in the case of Verres himself, that was not so much a condemnation as a respite from labor? So that, as the immortal gods had given a prosperous voyage to Dionysius when he was carrying off the spoils of gods, so also they appear to have bestowed on Verres quiet repose, in which he might with tranquility enjoy the fruits of his sacrilege. For when civil wars afterwards raged, being removed from all danger and apprehension, under the cloak of condemnation he heard of the disastrous misfortunes and miserable deaths of others; and he who appeared to have fallen while all retained their position, he alone, in truth, retained his position while all fell; until the proscription of the triumvirs,—that very proscription, indeed, which carried off Tully, the avenger of the violated majesty of the gods,—carried him off, satiated at once with the enjoyment of the wealth which he had gained by sacrilege, and with life, and worn out by old age. Moreover, he was fortunate in this very circumstance, that before his own death he heard of the cruelest end of his accuser; the gods doubtless providing that this sacrilegious man and spoiler of their worship should not die before he had received consolation from revenge.

**Chap. v.—that god only, the creator of all things, is to be worshipped, and not the elements or heavenly bodies; and the opinion of the stoics is refuted, who think that the stars and planets are gods.**

How much better, therefore, is it, leaving vain and insensible objects, to turn our eyes in that direction where is the seat and dwelling-place of the true God; who suspended the earth on a firm foundation, who bespangled the heaven with shining stars; who lighted up the sun, the most bright and matchless light for the affairs of men, in proof of His own single majesty; who girded the earth with seas, and ordered the rivers to flow with perpetual course!

"He also commanded the plains to extend themselves, the valleys to sink down, the woods to be covered with foliage, the stony mountains to rise."

All these things truly were not the work of Jupiter, who was born seventeen hundred years ago; but of the same, "that framer of all things, the origin of a better world," who is called God, whose beginning cannot be comprehended, and ought not to be made the subject of inquiry. It is sufficient for man, to his full and perfect wisdom, if he understands the existence of God: the force and sum of which understanding is this, that he look up to and honor the common Parent of the human race, and the Maker of wonderful things. Whence some persons of dull and obtuse mind adore as gods the elements, which are both created objects and are void of sensibility; who, when they admired the works of God, that is, the heaven with its various lights, the earth with its plains and mountains, the seas with their rivers and lakes and fountains, struck with admiration of these things, and forgetting the Maker Himself, whom they were unable to see, began to adore and worship His works. Nor were they able at all to understand how much greater and more wonderful He is, who made these things out of nothing. And when they see that these things, in obedience to divine laws, by a perpetual necessity are subservient to the uses and interests of men, they nevertheless regard them as gods, being ungrateful towards the divine bounty, so that they preferred their own works to their most indulgent God and Father. But what wonder is it if uncivilized or ignorant men err, since even philosophers of the Stoic sect are of the same opinion, so as to judge that all the heavenly bodies which have motion are to be reckoned in the number of gods; inasmuch as the Stoic Lucilius thus speaks in Cicero: "This regularity, therefore, in the stars, this great agreement of the times in such various courses during all eternity, are unintelligible to me without the exercise of mind, reason, and design; and when we see these things in the constellations, we cannot but place these very objects in the number of the gods." And he thus speaks a little before: "It remains," he says, "that the motion of the stars is voluntary; and he who sees these things, would act not only unlearnedly, but also impiously, if he should deny it." We in truth firmly deny it; and we prove that you, O philosophers, are not only unlearned and impious, but also blind, foolish, and senseless, who have surpassed in shallowness the ignorance of the uneducated. For they regard as gods *only* the sun and moon, but you the stars also.

    Make known to us, therefore, the mysteries of the stars, that we may erect altars and temples to each; that we may know with what rites and on what day to worship each, with what names and with what prayers we should call on them; unless perhaps we ought to worship gods so innumerable without any discrimination, and gods so minute in a mass. Why should I mention that the argument by which they infer that all the heavenly bodies are gods, tends to the opposite conclusion? For if they imagine that they are gods on this account, because they have their courses fixed and in accordance with reason, they are in error. For it is evident from this that they are not gods, because it is not permitted them to deviate from their prescribed orbits. But if they were gods, they would be borne hither and thither in all directions without any necessity, as living creatures on the earth, who wander hither and thither as they please, because their wills are unrestrained, and each is borne wherever inclination may have led it. Therefore the motion of the stars is not voluntary, but of necessity, because they obey the laws appointed for them. But when he was arguing about the courses of the stars, while he understood from the very harmony of things and times that they were not by chance, he judged that they were voluntary; as though they could not be moved with such order and arrangement, unless they contained within them an understanding acquainted with its own duty. Oh, how difficult is truth to those who are ignorant of it! How easy to those who know it! If, he says, the motions of the stars are not by chance, nothing else remains but that they are voluntary; nay, in truth, as it is plain that they are not by chance, so is it clear that they are not voluntary. Why, then, in completing their courses, do they preserve their regularity? Undoubtedly God, the framer of the universe, so arranged and contrived them, that they might run through their courses in the heaven with a divine and wonderful order, to accomplish the variations of the successive seasons. Was Archimedes of Sicily able to contrive a likeness and representation of the universe in hollow brass, in which he so arranged the sun and moon, that they effected, as it were every day, motions unequal and resembling the revolutions of the heavens, and that sphere, while it revolved, exhibited not only the approaches and withdrawing of the sun, or the increase and waning of the moon, but also the unequal courses of the stars, whether fixed or wandering? Was it then impossible for God to plan and create the originals, when the skill of man was able to represent them by imitation? Would the Stoic, therefore, if he should have seen the figures of the stars painted and fashioned in that brass, say that they moved by their own design, and not by the genius of the artificer? There is therefore in the stars design, adapted to the accomplishment of their courses; but it is the design of God, who both made and governs all things, not of the stars themselves, which are thus moved. For if it had been His will that the sun should remain fixed, it is plain that there would be perpetual day. Also if the stars had no motions, who doubts that there would have been eternal night? But that there might be vicissitudes of day and night, it was His will that the stars should move, and move with such variety that there might not only be mutual interchanges of light and darkness, by which alternate courses of labor and rest might be established, but also *interchanges* of cold and heat, that the power and influence of the different seasons might be adapted either to the production or the ripening of the crops. And because philosophers did not see this skill of the divine power in contriving the movements of the stars, they supposed them to be living, as though they moved with feet and of their own accord, and not by the divine intelligence. But who does not understand why God contrived them? Doubtless lest, as the light of the sun was withdrawn, a night of excessive darkness should become too oppressive with its foul and dreadful gloom, and should be injurious to the living. And so He both bespangled the heaven with wondrous variety, and tempered the darkness itself with many and minute lights. How much more wisely therefore does Naso judge, than they who think that they are devoting themselves to the pursuit of wisdom, in thinking that those lights were appointed by God to remove the gloom of darkness! He concludes the book, in which he briefly comprises the phenomena *of nature*, with these three verses:—

"These images, so many in number, and of such a figure, God placed in the heaven; and having scattered them through the gloomy darkness, He ordered them to give a bright light to the frosty night." But if it is impossible that the stars should be gods, it follows that the sun and moon cannot be gods, since they differ from the light of the stars in magnitude only, and not in their design. And if these are not gods, the same is true of the heaven, which contains them all.

**Chap. vI.—that neither the whole universe nor the elements are god, nor are they possessed of life.**

In like manner, if the land on which we tread, and which we subdue and cultivate for food, is not a god, then the plains and mountains will not be gods; and if these are not so, it follows that the whole of the earth cannot appear to be God. In like manner, if the water, which is adapted to the wants of living creatures for the purpose of drinking and bathing, is not a god, neither are the fountains *gods* from which the water flows. And if the fountains are not gods, neither are the rivers, which are collected from the fountains. And if the rivers also are not gods, it follows that the sea, which is made up of rivers, cannot be considered as God. But if neither the heaven, nor the earth, nor the sea, which are the parts of the world, can be gods, it follows that the world altogether is not God; whereas the same Stoics contend that it is both living and wise, and therefore God. But in this they are so inconsistent, that nothing is said by them which they do not also overthrow. For they argue thus: It is impossible that that which produces from itself sensible objects should itself be insensible. But the world produces man, who is endowed with sensibility; therefore it must also itself be sensible. Also they argue: that cannot be without sensibility, a part of which is sensible; therefore, because man is sensible, the world, of which man is a part, also possesses sensibility. The propositions themselves are true, that that which produces a being endowed with sense is itself sensible; and that that possesses sense, a part of which is endowed with sense. But the assumptions by which they draw their conclusions are false; for the world does not produce man, nor is man a part of the world. For the same God who created the world, also created man from the beginning: and man is not a part of the world, in the same manner in which a limb is a part of the body; for it is possible for the world to be without man, as it is for a city or house. Now, as a house is the dwelling-place of one man, and a city of one people, so also the world is the abode of the whole human race; and that which is inhabited is one thing, that which inhabits another. But these persons, in their eagerness to prove that which they had falsely assumed, that the world is possessed of sensibility, and is God, did not perceive the consequences of their own arguments. For if man is a part of the world, and if the world is endowed with sensibility because man is sensible, therefore it follows that, because man is mortal, the world must also of necessity be mortal, and not only mortal, but also liable to all kinds of disease and suffering. And, on the contrary, if the world is God, its parts also are plainly immortal: therefore man also is God, because he is, as you say, a part of the world. And if man, then also both beasts of burden and cattle, and the other kinds of beasts and of birds, and fishes, since these also in the same manner are possessed of sensibility, and are parts of the world. But this is endurable; for the Egyptians worship even these. But the matter comes to this: that even frogs, and gnats, and ants appear to be gods, because these also have sensibility, and are parts of the world. Thus arguments drawn from a false *source* always lead to foolish and absurd conclusions. Why should I mention that the same *philosophers* assert that the world was constructed for the sake of gods and men as a common dwelling? Therefore the world is neither god, nor living, if it has been made: for a living creature is not made, but born; and if it has been built, it has been built as a house or ship *is built*. Therefore there is a builder of the world, *even* God; and the world which has been made is distinct from Him who made it. Now, how inconsistent and absurd it is, that when they affirm that the heavenly fires and the other elements of the world are gods, they also say that the world itself is God! How is it possible that out of a great heap of gods one God can be made up? If the stars are gods, it follows that the world is not God, but the dwelling-place of gods. But if the world is God, it follows that all the things which are in it are not gods, but members of God, which clearly cannot by themselves take the name of God. For no one can rightly say that the members of one man are many men; but, however, there is no similar comparison between a living being and the world. For because a living being is endowed with sensibility, its members also have sensibility; nor do they become senseless unless they are separated from the body. But what resemblance does the world present to this? Truly they themselves tell us, since they do not deny that it was made, that it might be, as it were, a common abode for gods and men. If, therefore, it has been constructed as an abode, it is neither itself God, nor are the elements which are its parts; because a house cannot bear rule over itself, nor can the parts of which a house consists. Therefore they are refuted not only by the truth, but even by their own words. For as a house, made for the purpose of being inhabited, has no sensibility by itself, and is subject to the master who built or inhabits it; so the world, having no sensibility of itself, is subject to God its Maker, who made it for His own use.

### Chap. vii.—of god, and the religious rites of the foolish; of avarice, and the authority of ancestors.

The foolish, therefore, err in a twofold manner: first, in preferring the elements, that is, the works of God, to God *Himself*; secondly, in worshipping the figures of the elements themselves under human form. For they form the images of the sun and moon after the fashion of men; also those of fire, and earth, and sea, which they call Vulcan, Vesta, and Neptune. Nor do they openly sacrifice to the elements themselves. Men are possessed with so great a fondness for representations, that those things which are true are now esteemed of less value: they are delighted, in fact, with gold, and jewels, and ivory. The beauty and brilliancy of these things dazzle their eyes, and they think that there is no religion where these do not shine. And thus, under pretense of *worshipping* the gods, avarice and desire are worshipped. For they believe that the gods love whatever they themselves desire, whatever it is, on account of which thefts and robberies and murders daily rage, on account of which wars overthrow nations and cities throughout the whole world. Therefore they consecrate their spoils and plunder to the gods, who must undoubtedly be weak, and destitute of the highest excellence, if they are subject to desires. For why should we think them celestial if they long for anything from the earth, or happy if they are in want of anything, or uncorrupted if they take pleasure in those things in the pursuit of which the desire of men is not unreservedly condemned? They approach the gods, therefore not so much on account of religion, which can have no place in badly acquired and corruptible things, as that they may gaze upon the gold, and view the brilliancy of polished marble or ivory, that they may survey with unwearied contemplation garments adorned with precious stones and colors, or cups studded with glittering jewels. And the more ornamented are the temples, and the more beautiful the images, so much the greater majesty are they believed to have: so entirely is their religion confined to that which the desire of men admires.

    These are the religious institutions handed down to them by their ancestors, which they persist in maintaining and defending with the greatest obstinacy. Nor do they consider of what character they are; but they feel assured of their excellence and truth on this account, because the ancients have handed them down; and so great is the authority of antiquity, that it is said to be a crime to inquire into it. And thus it is everywhere believed as ascertained truth. In short, in Cicero, Cotta thus speaks to Lucilius: "You know, Balbus, what is the opinion of Cotta, what the opinion of the pontiff. Now let me understand what your sentiments are: for since you are a philosopher, I ought to receive from you a reason for your religion; but in the case of our ancestors it is reasonable to believe them, though no reason is alleged by them." If you believe, why then do you require a reason, which may have the effect of causing you not to believe? But if you require a reason, and think that the subject demands inquiry, then you do not believe; for you make inquiry with this view, that you may follow it when you have ascertained it. Behold, reason teaches you that the religious institutions of the gods are not true: what will you do? Will you prefer to follow antiquity or reason? And this, indeed, was not imparted to you by another, but was found out and chosen by yourself, since you have entirely uprooted all religious systems. If you prefer reason, you must abandon the institutions and authority of our ancestors, since nothing is right but that which reason prescribes. But if piety advises you to follow your ancestors, then admit that they were foolish, who complied with religious institutions invented contrary to reason; and that you are senseless, since you worship that which you have proved to be false. But since the name of ancestors is so greatly objected to us, let us see, I pray, who those ancestors were from whose authority it is said to be impious to depart.

Romulus, when he was about to found the city, called together the shepherds among whom he had grown up; and since their number appeared inadequate to the founding of the city, he established an asylum. To this all the most abandoned men flocked together indiscriminately from the neighboring places, without any distinction of condition. Thus he brought together the people from all these; and he chose into the senate those who were oldest, and called them Fathers, by whose advice he might direct all things. And concerning this senate, Propertius the elegiac poet thus speaks:—

"The trumpet used to call the ancient Quirites to an assembly; those hundred in the field often formed the senate. The senate-house, which now is raised aloft and shines with the well-robed senate, received the Fathers clothed in skins, rustic spirits."

These are the Fathers whose decrees learned and sagacious men obey with the greatest devotion; and all posterity must judge that to be true and unchangeable which an hundred old men clothed in skins established at their will; who, however, as has been mentioned in the first book, were enticed by Pompilius to believe the truth of those sacred rites which he himself delivered. Is there any reason why their authority should be so highly esteemed by posterity, since during their life no one either high or low judged them worthy of affinity?

**Chap. viii.—of the use of reason in religion; and of dreams, auguries, oracles, and similar portents.**

It is therefore right, especially in a matter on which the whole plan of life turns, that everyone should place confidence in himself, and use his own judgment and individual capacity for the investigation and weighing of the truth, rather than through confidence in others to be deceived by their errors, as though he himself were without understanding. God has given wisdom to all alike, that they might be able both to investigate things which they have not heard, and to weigh things which they have heard. Nor, because they preceded us in time, did they also outstrip us in wisdom; for if this is given equally to all, we cannot be anticipated in it by those who precede us. It is incapable of diminution, as the light and brilliancy of the sun; because, as the sun is the light of the eyes, so is wisdom the light of man's heart. Wherefore, since wisdom—that is, the inquiry after truth—is natural to all, they deprive themselves of wisdom, who without any judgment approve of the discoveries of their ancestors, and like sheep are led by others. But this escapes their notice, that the name of ancestors being introduced, they think it impossible that they themselves should have more knowledge because they are called descendants, or that the others should be unwise because they are called ancestors. What, therefore, prevents us from taking a precedent from them, that as they handed down to posterity their false inventions, so we who have discovered the truth may hand down better things to our posterity? There remains therefore a great subject of inquiry, the discussion of which does not come from talent, but from knowledge: and this must be explained at greater length, that nothing at all may be left in doubt. For perhaps someone may have recourse to those things which are handed down by many and undoubted authorities; that those very persons, whom we have shown to be no gods, have often displayed their majesty both by prodigies, and dreams, and auguries, and oracles. And, indeed, many wonderful things may be enumerated, and especially this, that Accius Navius, a consummate augur, when he was warning Tarquinius Priscus to undertake the commencement of nothing new without the previous sanction of auguries, and the king, detracting from the credit due to his art, told him to consult the birds, and then to announce to him whether it was possible for that which he himself had conceived in his mind to be accomplished, and Navius affirmed that it was possible; then take this whetstone, he said, and divide it with a razor. But the other without any hesitation took and cut it.

In the next place is the fact of Castor and Pollux having been seen in the Latin war at the lake of Juturna washing off the sweat of their horses, when their temple which adjoins the fountain had been open of its own accord. In the Macedonian war the same *deities*, mounted on white horses, are said to have presented themselves to Publius Vatienus as he went to Rome at night, announcing that King Perseus had been vanquished and taken captive on that day, the truth of which was proved by letters received from Paulus a few days afterwards. That also is wonderful, that the statue of Fortune, in the form188 of a woman, is reported to have spoken more than once; also that the statue of Juno Moneta, when, on the capture of Veii, one of the soldiers, being sent to remove it, sportively and in jest asked whether she wished to remove to Rome, answered that she wished it. Claudia also is set forth as an example of a miracle. For when, in accordance with the Sibylline books, the Idæan mother was sent for, and the ship in which she was conveyed had grounded on a shoal of the river Tiber, and could not be moved by any force, they report that Claudia, who had been always regarded as unchaste on account of her excess in personal adornment, with bended knees entreated the goddess, if she judged her to be chaste, to follow her girdle; and thus the ship, which could not be moved by all the strong men, was moved by a single woman. It is equally wonderful, that during the prevalence of a pestilence, Æsculapius, being called from Epidaurus, is said to have released the city of Rome from the long-continued plague.

Sacrilegious persons can also be mentioned, by the immediate punishment of whom the gods are believed to have avenged the injury done to them. Appius Claudius the censor having, against the advice of the oracle, transferred the sacred rites of Hercules to the public slaves, was deprived of his eyesight; and the Potitian *gens*, which abandoned its privilege, within the space of one year became extinct. Likewise the censor Fulvius, when he had taken away the marble tiles from the temple of the Lacinian Juno, to cover the temple of the equestrian Fortuna, which he had built at Rome, was deprived of his senses, and having lost his two sons who were serving in Illyricum, was consumed with the greatest grief of mind. Turullius also, the lieutenant of Mark Antony, when he had cut down a grove of Æsculapius in Cos, and built a fleet, was afterwards slain at the same place by the soldiers of Cæsar. To these examples is added Pyrrhus, who, having taken away money from the treasure of the Locrian Proserpine, was shipwrecked, and dashed against the shores near to the temple of the goddess, so that nothing was found uninjured except that money. Ceres of Miletus also gained for herself great veneration among men. For when the city had been taken by Alexander, and the soldiers had rushed in to plunder her temple, a flame of fire suddenly thrown upon them blinded them all.

There are also found dreams which seem to show the power of the gods. For it is said that Jupiter presented himself to Tiberius Atinius, a plebeian, in his sleep, and enjoined him to announce to the consuls and senate, that in the last Circensian games a public dancer had displeased him, because a certain Antonius Maximus had severely scourged a slave under the *furca* in the middle of the circus, and had led him to punishment, and that on this account the games ought to be repeated. And when he had neglected this command, he is said on the same day to have lost his son, and to have been himself seized by a severe disease; and that when he again perceived the same image asking whether he had suffered sufficient punishment for the neglect of his command, he was carried on a litter to the consuls; and having explained the whole matter in the senate, he regained strength of body, and returned to his house on foot. And that dream also was not less wonderful, to which it is said that Augustus Cæsar owed his preservation. For when in the civil war with Brutus he was afflicted with a severe disease, and had determined to abstain from battle, the image of Minerva presented itself to his physician Artorius, advising him that Cæsar should not confine himself to the camp on account of his bodily infirmity. He was therefore carried on a litter to the army, and on the same day the camp was taken by Brutus. Many other examples of a similar nature may be brought forward; but I fear that, if I shall delay too long in the setting forth of contrary subjects, I may either appear to have forgotten my purpose, or may incur the charge of loquacity.

**Chap. ix.—of the devil, the world, god, providence, man, and his wisdom.**

I will therefore set forth the method of all these things, that difficult and obscure subjects may be more easily understood; and I will bring to light all these deceptions of the pretended deity, led by which men have departed very far from the way of truth. But I will retrace the matter far back from its source; that if any, unacquainted with the truth and ignorant, shall apply himself to the reading *of this book*, he may be instructed, and may understand what can in truth be "the source and origin of these evils;" and having received light, may perceive his own errors and those of the whole human race.

Since God was possessed of the greatest foresight for planning, and of the greatest skill for carrying out in action, before He commenced this business of the world,—inasmuch as there was in Him, and always is, the fountain of full and most complete goodness,—in order that goodness might spring as a stream from Him, and might flow forth afar, He produced a Spirit like to Himself, who might be endowed with the perfections of God the Father. But how He willed that, I will endeavor to show in the fourth book. Then He made another being, in whom the disposition of the divine origin did not remain. Therefore he was infected with his own envy as with poison, and passed from good to evil; and at his own will, which had been given to him by God unfettered, he acquired for himself a contrary name. From which it appears that the source of all evils is envy. For he envied his predecessor, who through his steadfastness is acceptable and dear to God the Father. This being, who from good became evil by his own act, is called by the Greeks diabolus: we call him accuser, because he reports to God the faults to which he himself entices us. God, therefore, when He began the fabric of the world, set over the whole work that first and greatest Son, and used Him at the same time as a counsellor and artificer, in planning, arranging, and accomplishing, since He is complete both in knowledge, and judgment, and power; concerning whom I now speak more sparingly, because in another place both His excellence, and His name, and His nature must be related by us. Let no one inquire of what materials God made these works so great and wonderful: for He made all things out of nothing.

Nor are the poets to be listened to, who say that in the beginning was a chaos, that is, a confusion of matter and the elements; but that God afterwards divided all that mass, and having separated each object from the confused heap, and arranged them in order, He constructed and adorned the world. Now it is easy to reply to these persons, who do not understand the power of God: for they believe that He can produce nothing, except out of materials already existing and prepared; in which error philosophers also were involved. For Cicero, while discussing the nature of the gods, thus speaks: "First of all, therefore, it is not probable that the matter from which all things arose was made by divine providence, but that it has, and has had, a force and nature of its own. As therefore the builder, when he is about to erect any building, does not himself make the materials, but uses those which are already prepared, and the statuary also *uses* the wax; so that divine providence ought to have had materials at hand, not of its own production, but already prepared for use. But if matter was not made by God, then neither was the earth, and water, and air, and fire, made by God." Oh, how many faults there are in these ten lines! First, that he who in almost all his other disputations and books was a maintainer of the divine providence, and who used very acute arguments in assailing those who denied the existence of a providence, now himself, as a traitor or deserter, endeavored to take away providence; in whose case, if you wish to oppose him, neither consideration nor labor is required: it is only necessary to remind him of his own words. For it will be impossible for Cicero to be more strongly refuted by anyone than by Cicero himself. But let us make this concession to the custom and practice of the Academics, that men are permitted to speak with great freedom, and to entertain what sentiments they may wish. Let us examine the sentiments themselves. It is not probable, he says, that matter was made by God. By what arguments do you prove this? For you gave no reason for its being improbable. Therefore, on the contrary, it appears to me exceedingly probable; nor does it appear so without reason, when I reflect that there is something more in God, whom you verily reduce to the weakness of man, to whom you allow nothing else but the mere workmanship. In what respect, then, will that divine power differ from man, if God also, as man does, stands in need of the assistance of another? But He does stand in need of it, if He can construct nothing unless He is furnished with materials by another. But if this is the case, it is plain that His power is imperfect, and he who prepared the material must be judged more powerful. By what name, therefore, shall he be called who excels God in power?—since it is greater to make that which is one's own, than to arrange those things which are another's. But if it is impossible that anything should be more powerful than God, who must necessarily be of perfect strength, power, and intelligence, it follows that He who made the things which are composed of matter, made matter also. For it was neither possible nor befitting that anything should exist without the exercise of God's power, or against His will. But it is probable, he says, that matter has, and always has had, a force and nature of its own. What force could it have, without anyone to give it? What nature, without anyone to produce it? If it had force, it took that force from someone. But from whom could it take it, unless it were from God? Moreover, if it had a nature, which plainly is so called from being produced, it must have been produced. But from whom could it have derived its existence, except God? For nature, from which you say that all things had their origin, if it has no understanding, can make nothing. But if it has the power of producing and making, then it has understanding, and must be God. For that force can be called by no other name, in which there is both the foresight to plan, and the skill and power to carry into effect. Therefore Seneca, the most intelligent of all the Stoics, says better, who saw "that nature was nothing else but God." Therefore he says, "Shall we not praise God, who possesses natural excellence?" For He did not learn it from anyone. Yes, truly, we will praise Him; for although it is natural to Him, He gave it to Himself, since God Himself is nature. When, therefore, you assign the origin of all things to nature, and take it from God, you are in the same difficulty:—

"You pay your debt by borrowing, Geta."

For while simply changing the name, you clearly admit that it was made by the same person by whom you deny that it was made.

There follows a most senseless comparison. "As the builder," he says, "when he is about to erect any building, does not himself make the materials, but uses those which are already prepared, and the statuary also the wax; so that divine providence ought to have had materials at hand, not of its own production, but already prepared for use." Nay rather it ought not; for God will have less power if He makes from materials already provided, which is the part of man. The builder will erect nothing without wood, for he cannot make the wood itself; and not to be able to do this is the part of human weakness. But God Himself makes the materials for Himself, because He has the power. For to have the power is the property of God; for if He is not able, He is not God. Man produces *his works* out of that which already exists, because through his mortality he is weak, and through his weakness his power is limited and moderate; but God produces His works out of that which has no existence, because through His eternity He is strong, and through His strength His power is immense, which has no end or limit, like the life of the Maker Himself. What wonder, then, if God, when He was about to make the world, first prepared the material from which to make it, and prepared it out of that which had no existence? Because it is impossible for God to borrow anything from another source, inasmuch as all things are in Himself and from Himself. For if there is anything before Him, and if anything has been made, *but* not by Him, He will therefore lose both the power and the name of God. But it may be said matter was never made, like God, who out of matter made this world. In that case, it follows that two eternal *principles* are established, and those indeed opposed to one another, which cannot happen without discord and destruction. For those things which have a contrary force and method must of necessity come into collision. In this manner it will be impossible that both should be eternal, if they are opposed to one another, because one must overpower the other. Therefore the nature of that which is eternal cannot be otherwise than simple, so that all things descended from that source as from a fountain. Therefore either God proceeded from matter, or matter from God. Which of these is truer, is easily understood. For of these two, one is endued with sensibility, the other is insensible. The power of making anything cannot exist, except in that which has sensibility, intelligence, reflection, and the power of motion. Nor can anything be begun, or made, or completed, unless it shall have been foreseen by reason how it shall be made before it exists, and how it shall endure after it has been made. In short, he *only* makes anything who has the will to make it, and hands to complete that which he has willed. But that which is insensible always lies inactive and torpid; nothing can originate in that source where there is no voluntary motion. For if every animal is possessed of reason, it is certain that it cannot be produced from that which is destitute of reason, nor can that which is not present in the original source be received from any other quarter. Nor, however, let it disturb any one, that certain animals appear to be born from the earth. For the earth does not give birth to these of itself, but the Spirit of God, without which nothing is produced. Therefore God did not arise from matter, because a being endued with sensibility can never spring from one that is insensible, a wise one from one that is irrational, one that is incapable of suffering from one that can suffer, an incorporeal being from a corporeal one; but matter is rather from God. For whatever consists of a body solid, and capable of being handled, admits of an external force. That which admits of force is capable of dissolution; that which is dissolved perishes; that which perishes must necessarily have had an origin; that which had an origin had a source from which it originated, that is, some maker, who is intelligent, foreseeing, and skilled in making. There is one assuredly, and that no other than God. And since He is possessed of sensibility, intelligence, providence, power, and vigor, He is able to create and make both animated and inanimate objects, because He has the means of making everything. But matter cannot always have existed, for if it had existed it would be incapable of change. For that which always was, does not cease always to be; and that which had no beginning must of necessity be without an end. Moreover, it is easier for that which had a beginning to be without an end, than for that which had no beginning, to have an end. Therefore if matter was not made, nothing can be made from it. But if nothing can be made from it, then matter itself can have no existence. For matter is that out of which something is made. But everything out of which anything is made, inasmuch as it has received the hand of the artificer, is destroyed, and begins to be some other thing. Therefore, since matter had an end, at the time when the world was made out of it, it also had a beginning. For that which is destroyed was *previously* built up; that which is loosened was *previously* bound up; that which is brought to an end was begun. If, then, it is inferred from its change and end, that matter had a beginning, from whom could that beginning have been, except from God? God, therefore, is the only being who was not made; and therefore He can destroy other things, but He Himself cannot be destroyed. That which was in Him will always be permanent, because He has not been produced or sprung from any other source; nor does His birth depend on any other object, which being changed may cause His dissolution. He is of Himself, as we said in the first book; and therefore He is such as He willed that He should be, incapable of suffering, unchangeable, incorruptible, blessed, and eternal.

But now the conclusion, with which Tully finished the sentiment, is much more absurd. "But if matter," he says, "was not made by God, the earth indeed, and water, and air, and fire, were not made by God." How skillfully he avoided the danger! For he stated the former point as though it required no proof, whereas it was much more uncertain than that on account of which the statement was made. If matter, he says, was not made by God, the world was not made by God. He preferred to draw a false inference from that which is false, than a true one from that which is true. And though uncertain things ought to be proved from those which are certain, he drew a proof from an uncertainty, to overthrow that which was certain. For, that the world was made by divine providence (not to mention Trismegistus, who proclaims this; not to mention the verses of the Sibyls, who make the same announcement; not to mention the prophets, who with one impulse and with harmonious voice bear witness that the world was made, and that it was the workmanship of God), even the philosophers almost universally agree; for this is the opinion of the Pythagoreans, the Stoics, and the Peripatetics, who are the chief of every sect. In short, from those first seven wise men, even to Socrates and Plato, it was held as an acknowledged and undoubted fact; until many ages afterwards the crazy Epicurus lived, who alone ventured to deny that which is most evident, doubtless through the desire of discovering novelties, that he might found a sect in his own name. And because he could find out nothing new, that he might still appear to disagree with the others, he wished to overthrow old opinions. But in this all the philosophers who snarled around him, refuted him. It is more certain, therefore, that the world was arranged by providence, than that matter was collected by providence. Wherefore he ought not to have supposed that the world was not made by divine providence, because its matter was not made by divine providence; but because the world was made by divine providence, *he ought to have concluded* that matter also was made by the Deity. For it is more credible that matter was made by God, because He is all-powerful, than that the world was not made by God, because nothing can be made without mind, intelligence, and design. But this is not the fault of Cicero, but of the sect. For when he had undertaken a disputation, by which he might take away the nature of the gods, respecting which philosophers prated, in his ignorance of the truth he imagined that the Deity must altogether be taken away. He was able therefore to take away the gods, for they had no existence. But when he attempted to overthrow the divine providence, which is in the one God, because he had begun to strive against the truth, his arguments failed, and he necessarily fell into this pitfall, from which he was unable to withdraw himself. Here, then, I hold him firmly fixed; I hold him fastened to the spot, since Lucilius, who disputed on the other side, was silent. Here, then, is the turning-point; on this everything depends. Let Cotta disentangle himself, if he can, from this difficulty; let him bring forward arguments by which he may prove that matter has always existed, which no providence made. Let him show how anything ponderous and heavy either could exist without an author or could be changed, and how that which always was ceased to be, so that that which never was might begin to be. And if he shall prove these things, then, and not till then, will I admit that the world itself was not established by divine providence, and yet in making this admission I shall hold him fast by another snare. For he will turn round again to the same point, to which he will be unwilling *to return*, so as to say that both the matter of which the world consists, and the world which consists of matter, existed by nature; though I contend that nature itself is God. For no one can make wonderful things, that is, things existing with the greatest order, except one who has intelligence, foresight, and power. And thus it will come to be seen that God made all things, and that nothing at all can exist which did not derive its origin from God.

But the same, as often as he follows the Epicureans, and does not admit that the world was made by God, is wont to inquire by what hands, by what machines, by what levers, by what contrivance, He made this work of such magnitude. He might see, if he could have lived at that time in which *God* made it. But, that man might not look into the works of God, He was unwilling to bring him into this world until all things were completed. But he could not be brought in: for how could he exist while the heaven above was being built, and the foundations of the earth beneath were being laid; when humid things, perchance, either benumbed with excessive stiffness were becoming congealed, or seethed with fiery heat and rendered solid were growing hard? Or how could he live when the sun was not yet established, and neither corn nor animals were produced? Therefore it was necessary that man should be last made, when the finishing hand had now been applied to the world and to all other things. Finally, the sacred writings teach that man was the last work of God, and that he was brought into this world as into a house prepared and made ready; for all things were made on his account. The poets also acknowledge the same. Ovid, having described the completion of the world, and the formation of the other animals, added:—

"An animal more sacred than these, and more capacious of a lofty mind, was yet wanting, and which might exercise dominion over the rest. Man was produced."

So impious must we think it to search into those things which God wished to be kept secret! But his inquiries were not made through a desire of hearing or learning, but of refuting; for he was confident that no one could assert that. As though, in truth, it were to be supposed that these things were not made by God, because it cannot be plainly seen in what manner they were created! If you had been brought up in a well-built and ornamented house, and had never seen a workshop, would you have supposed that that house was not built by man, because you did not know how it was built? You would assuredly ask the same question about the house which you now ask about the world—by what hands, with what implements, man had contrived such great works; and especially if you should see large stones, immense blocks, vast columns, the whole work lofty and elevated, would not these things appear to you to exceed the measure of human strength, because you would not know that these things were made not so much by strength as by skill and ingenuity?

But if man, in whom nothing is perfect, nevertheless effects more by skill than his feeble strength would permit, what reason is there why it should appear to you incredible, when it is alleged that the world was made by God, in whom, since He is perfect, wisdom can have no limit, and strength no measure? His works are seen by the eyes; but how He made them is not seen even by the mind, because, as Hermes says, the mortal cannot draw nigh to (that is, approach nearer, and follow up with the understanding) the immortal, the temporal to the eternal, the corruptible to the incorruptible. And on this account the earthly animal is as yet incapable of perceiving heavenly things, because it is shut in and held as it were in custody by the body, so that it cannot discern all things with free and unrestrained perception. Let him know, therefore, how foolishly he acts, who inquires into things which are indescribable. For this is to pass the limits of one's own condition, and not to understand how far it is permitted man to approach. In short, when God revealed the truth to man, He wished us only to know those things which it concerned man to know for the attainment of life; but as to the things which related to a profane and eager curiosity He was silent, that they might be secret. Why, then, do you inquire into things which you cannot know, and if you knew them you would not be happier. It is perfect wisdom in man, if he knows that there is but one God, and that all things were made by Him.

**Chap. X.—Of the World, and Its Parts, the Elements and Seasons.**

Now, having refuted those who entertain false sentiments respecting the world and God its Maker, let us return to the divine workmanship of the world, concerning which we are informed in the sacred writings of our holy religion. Therefore, first of all, God made the heaven, and suspended it on high, that it might be the seat of God Himself, the Creator. Then He founded the earth, and placed it under the heaven, as a dwelling-place for man, with the other races of animals. He willed that it should be surrounded and held together by water. But He adorned and filled His own dwelling-place with bright lights; He decked it with the sun, and the shining orb of the moon, and with the glittering signs of the twinkling stars; but He placed on the earth the darkness, which is contrary to these. For of itself the earth contains no light, unless it receives it from the heaven, in which He placed perpetual light, and the gods above, and eternal life; and, on the contrary, He placed on the earth darkness, and the inhabitants of the lower regions, and death. For these things are as far removed from the former ones, as evil things are from good, and vices from virtues. He also established two parts of the earth itself opposite to one another, and of a different character,—namely, the east and the west; and of these the east is assigned to God, because He Himself is the fountain of light, and the enlightener of all things, and because He makes us rise to eternal life. But the west is ascribed to that disturbed and depraved mind, because it conceals the light, because it always brings on darkness, and because it makes men die and perish in their sins. For as light belongs to the east, and the whole course of life depends upon the light, so darkness belongs to the west: but death and destruction are contained in darkness. Then He measured out in the same way the other parts,—namely, the south and the north, which parts are closely united with the two former. For that which is more glowing with the warmth of the sun, is nearest to and closely united with the east; but that which is torpid with colds and perpetual ice belongs to the same division as the extreme west. For as darkness is opposed to light, so is cold to heat. As, therefore, heat is nearest to light, so is the south to the east; and as cold is nearest to darkness, so is the northern region to the west. And He assigned to each of these parts its own time,—

namely, the spring to the east, the summer to the southern region, the autumn belongs to the west, and the winter to the north. In these two parts also, the southern and the northern, is contained a figure of life and death, because life consists in heat, death in cold. And as heat arises from fire, so does cold from water. And according to the division of these parts He also made day and night, to complete by alternate succession with each other the courses and perpetual revolutions of time, which we call years. The day, which the first east supplies, must belong to God, as all things do, which are of a better character. But the night, which the extreme west brings on, belongs, indeed, to him whom we have said to be the rival of God.

And even in the making of these God had regard to the future; for He made them so, that a representation of true religion and of false superstitions might be shown from these. For as the sun, which rises daily, although it is but one,—from which Cicero would have it appear that it was called Sol, because the stars are obscured, and it alone is seen,—yet, since it is a true light, and of perfect fullness, and of most powerful heat, and enlightens all things with the brightest splendor; so God, although He is one only, is possessed of perfect majesty, and might, and splendor. But night, which we say is assigned to that depraved adversary of God, shows by a resemblance the many and various superstitions which belong to him. For although innumerable stars appear to glitter and shine, yet, because they are not full and solid lights, and send forth no heat, nor overpower the darkness by their multitude, therefore these two things are found to be of chief importance, which have power differing from and opposed to one another—heat and moisture, which God wonderfully designed for the support and production of all things. For since the power of God consists in heat and fire, if He had not tempered its ardor and force by mingling matter of moisture and cold, nothing could have been born or have existed, but whatever had begun to exist must immediately have been destroyed by conflagration. From which also some philosophers and poets said that the world was made up of a discordant concord; but they did not thoroughly understand the matter. Heraclitus said that all things were produced from fire; Thales of Miletus from water. Each saw something *of the truth*, and yet each was in error: for if one *element* only had existed, water could not have been produced from fire, nor, on the other hand, could fire from water; but it is more true that all things were produced from a mingling of the two. Fire, indeed, cannot be mixed with water, because they are opposed to each other; and if they came into collision, the one which proved superior must destroy the other. But their substances may be mingled. The substance of fire is heat; of water, moisture. Rightly therefore does Ovid say:

"For when moisture and heat have become mingled, they conceive, and all things arise from these two. And though fire is at variance with water, moist vapor produces all things, and discordant concord is adapted to production."

For the one element is, as it were, masculine; the other, as it were, feminine: the one active, the other passive. And on this account it was appointed by the ancients that marriage contracts should be ratified by the solemnity of fire and water, because the young of animals are furnished with a body by heat and moisture, and are thus animated to life.

For, since every animal consists of soul and body, the material of the body is contained in moisture, that of the soul in heat: which we may know from the offspring of birds; for though these are full of thick moisture, unless they are cherished by creative heat, the moisture cannot become a body, nor can the body be animated with life. Exiles also were accustomed to be forbidden the use of fire and water: for as yet it seemed unlawful to inflict capital punishment on any, however guilty, inasmuch as they were men. When, therefore, the use of those things in which the life of men consists was forbidden, it was deemed to be equivalent to the actual infliction of death on him who had been thus sentenced. Of such importance were these two elements considered, that they believed them to be essential for the production of man, and for the sustaining of his life. One of these is common to us with the other animals, the other has been assigned to man alone. For we, being a heavenly and immortal race, make use of fire, which is given to us as a proof of immortality, since fire is from heaven; and its nature, inasmuch as it is moveable and rises upward, contains the principle of life. But the other animals, inasmuch as they are altogether mortal, make use of water only, which is a corporeal and earthly element. And the nature of this, because it is moveable, and has a downward inclination, shows a figure of death. Therefore the cattle do not look up to heaven, nor do they entertain religious sentiments, since the use of fire is removed from them. But from what source or in what manner God lighted up or caused to flow these two principal elements, fire and water, He who made them alone can know.

**Chap. XI.—Of Living Creatures, of Man; Prometheus, Deucalion, the ParcÆ.**

Therefore, having finished the world, He commanded that animals of various kinds and of dissimilar forms should be created, both great and smaller. And they were made in pairs, that is, one of each sex; from the offspring of which both the air and the earth and the seas were filled. And God gave nourishment to all these by their kinds from the earth, that they might be of service to men: some, for instance, were for food, others for clothing; but those which are of great strength He gave, that they might assist in cultivating the earth, whence they were called beasts of burthen. And thus, when all things had been settled with a wonderful arrangement, He determined to prepare for Himself an eternal kingdom, and to create innumerable souls, on whom He might bestow immortality. Then He made for Himself a figure endowed with perception and intelligence, that is, after the likeness of His own image, than which nothing can be more perfect: He formed man out of the dust of the ground, from which he was called man, because He was made from the earth. Finally,

Plato says that the human form was godlike; as does the Sibyl, who says,—

"Thou art my image, O man, possessed of right reason."

The poets also have not given a different account respecting this formation of man, however they may have corrupted it; for they said that man was made by Prometheus from clay. They were not mistaken in the matter itself, but in the name of the artificer. For they had never come into contact with a line of the truth; but the things which were handed down by the oracles of the prophets, and contained in the sacred book of God; those things collected from fables and obscure opinion, and distorted, as the truth is wont to be corrupted by the multitude when spread abroad by various conversations, everyone adding something to that which he had heard,— those things they comprised in their poems; and in this, indeed, *they acted* foolishly, in that they attributed so wonderful and divine a work to man. For what need was there that man should be formed of clay, when he might be generated in the same way in which Prometheus himself was born from Iapetus? For if he was a man, he was able to beget a man, but not to make one. But his punishment on Mount Caucasus declares that he was not of the gods. But no one reckoned his father Iapetus or his uncle Titan as gods, because the high dignity of the kingdom was in possession of Saturn only, by which he obtained divine honors, together with all his descendants. This invention of the poets admits of refutation by many arguments. It is agreed by all that the deluge took place for the destruction of wickedness, and for its removal from the earth. Now, both philosophers and poets, and writers of ancient history, assert the same, and in this they especially agree with the language of the prophets. If, therefore, the flood took place for the purpose of destroying wickedness, which had increased through the excessive multitude of men, how was Prometheus the maker of man, when his son Deucalion is said by the same writers to have been the only one who was preserved on account of his righteousness? How could a single descent and a single generation have so quickly filled the world with men? But it is plain that they have corrupted this also, as they did the former account; since they were ignorant both at what time the flood happened on the earth, and who it was that deserved on account of his righteousness to be saved when the human race perished, and how and with whom he was saved: all of which are taught by the inspired writings. It is plain, therefore, that the account which they give respecting the work of Prometheus is false.

But because I had said that the poets are not accustomed to speak that which is altogether untrue, but to wrap up in figures and thus to obscure their accounts, I do not say that they spoke falsely in this, but that first of all Prometheus made the image of a man of rich and soft clay, and that he first originated the art of making statues and images; inasmuch as he lived in the times of Jupiter, during which temples began to be built, and new modes of worshipping the gods introduced. And thus the truth was corrupted by falsehood; and that which was said to have been made by God began also to be ascribed to man, who imitated the divine work. But the making of the true and living man from clay is the work of God. And this also is related by Hermes, who not only says that man was made by God, after the image of God, but he even tried to explain in how skillful a manner He formed each limb in the human body, since there is none of them which is not as available for the necessity of use as for beauty. But even the Stoics, when they discuss the subject of providence, attempt to do this; and Tully followed them in many places. But, however, he briefly treats of a subject so copious and fruitful, which I now pass over on this account, because I have lately written a particular book on this subject to my disciple Demetrianus. But I cannot here omit that which some erring philosophers say, that men and the other animals arose from the earth without any author; whence that expression of Virgil:—

"And the earth-born race of men raised its head from the hard fields."

And this opinion is especially entertained by those who deny the existence of a *divine* providence. For the Stoics attribute the formation of animals to divine skill. But Aristotle freed himself from labor and trouble, by saying that the world always existed, and therefore that the human race, and the other things which are in it, had no beginning, but always had been, and always would be. But when we see that each animal separately, which had no previous existence, begins to exist, and ceases to exist, it is necessary that the whole race must at some time have begun to exist, and must cease at some time because it had a beginning.

For all things must necessarily be comprised in three periods of time—the past, the present, and the future. The commencement belongs to the past, existence to the present, dissolution to the future. And all these things are seen in the case of men individually: for we begin when we are born; and we exist while we live; and we cease when we die. On which account they would have it that there are three Parcæ: one who warps the web of life for men; the second, who weaves it; the third, who cuts and finishes it. But in the whole race of men, because the present time only is seen, yet from it the past also, that is, the commencement, and the future, that is, the dissolution, are inferred. For since it exists, it is evident that at some time it began to exist, for nothing can exist without a beginning; and because it had a beginning, it is evident that it will at some time have an end. For that cannot, as a whole, be immortal, which consists of mortals. For as we all die individually, it is possible that, by some calamity, all may perish simultaneously: either through the unproductiveness of the earth, which sometimes happens in particular cases; or through the general spread of pestilence, which often desolates separate cities and countries; or by the conflagration of the world, as is said to have happened in the case of Phaethon; or by a deluge, as is reported in the time of

Deucalion, when the whole race was destroyed with the exception of one man. And if this deluge happened by chance, it might assuredly have happened that he who was the only survivor should perish. But if he was reserved by the will of divine providence, as it cannot be denied, to recruit mankind, it is evident that the life and the destruction of the human race are in the power of God. And if it is possible for it to die altogether, because it dies in parts, it is evident that it had an origin at some time; and as the liability to decay bespeaks a beginning, so also it gives proof of an end. And if these things are true, Aristotle will be unable to maintain that the world also itself had no beginning. But if Plato and Epicurus extort this from Aristotle, yet Plato and Aristotle, who thought that the world would be everlasting, will, notwithstanding their eloquence, be deprived of this also by Epicurus, because it follows, that, *as it had a beginning*, it must also have an end. But we will speak of these things at greater length in the last book. Now let us revert to the origin of man.

**Chap. XII.—That Animals Were Not Produced Spontaneously, but by a Divine Arrangement, of Which God Would Have Given Us the Knowledge, If It Were Advantageous for Us to Know It.**

They say that at certain changes of the heaven, and motions of the stars, there existed a kind of maturity for the production of animals; and thus that the new earth, retaining the productive seed, brought forth of itself certain vessels after the likeness of wombs, respecting which Lucretius says,—

"Wombs grew attached to the earth by roots;"

and that these, when they had become mature, being rent by the compulsion of nature, produced tender animals; afterwards, that the earth itself abounded with a kind of moisture which resembled milk, and that animals were supported by this nourishment. How, then, were they able to endure or avoid the force of the cold or of heat, or to be born at all, since the sun would scorch them or the cold contract them? But, they say, at the beginning of the world there was no winter nor summer, but a perpetual spring of an equable temperature. Why, then, do we see that none of these things now happens? Because, they say, it was necessary that it should once happen, that animals might be born; but after they began to exist, and the power of generation was given to them, the earth ceased to bring forth, and the condition of time was changed. Oh, how easy it is to refute falsehoods! In the first place, nothing can exist in this world which does not continue permanent, as it began. For neither were the sun and moon and stars then uncreated; nor, having been created, were they without their motions; nor did that divine government, which manages and rules their courses, fail to begin *its exercise* together with them. In the next place, if it is as they say, there must of necessity be a providence, and they fall into that very condition which they especially avoid. For while the animals were yet unborn, it is plain that someone provided that they should be born, that the world might not appear gloomy with waste and desolation. But, that they might be produced from the earth without the office of parents, provision must have been made with great judgment; and in the next place, that the moisture condensed from the earth might be formed into the various figures of bodies; and also that, having received from the vessels with which they were covered the power of life and sensation, they might be poured forth, as it were, from the womb of mothers, is a wonderful and indescribable provision. But let us suppose that this also happened by chance; the circumstances which follow assuredly cannot be by chance,—that the earth should at once flow with milk, and that the temperature of the atmosphere should be equable. And if these things plainly happened, that the newly born animals might have nourishment, or be free from danger, it must be that someone provided these things by some divine counsel.

But who is able to make this provision except God? Let us, however, see whether the circumstance itself which they assert could have taken place, that men should be born from the earth. If any one considers during how long a time and in what manner an infant is reared, he will assuredly understand that those earth-born children could not possibly have been reared without someone to bring them up. For they must have lain for many months cast forth, until their sinews were strengthened, so that they had power to move themselves and to change their place, which can scarcely happen within the space of one year. Now see whether an infant could have lain through many months in the same manner and in the same place where it was cast forth, without dying, overwhelmed and corrupted by that moisture of the earth which it supplied for the sake of nourishment, and by the excrements of its own body mixed together. Therefore it is impossible but that it was reared by someone; unless, indeed, all animals are born not in a tender condition, but grown up: and it never came into their mind to say this. Therefore the whole of that method is impossible and vain; if that can be called method by which it is attempted that there shall be no method. For he who says that all things are produced of their own accord, and attributes nothing to divine providence, he assuredly does not assert, but overthrows method. But if nothing can be done or produced without design, it is plain that there is a divine providence, to which that which is called design peculiarly belongs. Therefore God, the Contriver of all things, made man. And even Cicero, though ignorant of the sacred writings, saw this, who in his treatise on the Laws, in the first book, handed down the same thing as the prophets; and I add his words: "This animal, foreseeing, sagacious, various, acute, gifted with memory, full of method and design, which we call man, was produced by the supreme Deity under remarkable circumstances; for this alone of so many kinds and natures of animals, partakes of judgment and reflection, when all other animals are destitute of them." Do you see that the man, although far removed from the knowledge of the truth, yet, inasmuch as he held the image of wisdom, understood that man could not be produced except by God? But, however, there is need of divine testimony, lest that of man should be insufficient. The Sibyl testifies that man is the work of God:—

"He who is the only God being the invincible Creator, He Himself fixed the figure of the form of men, He Himself mixed the nature of all belonging to the generation of life."

The sacred writings contain statements to the same effect. Therefore God discharged the office of a true father. He Himself formed the body; He Himself infused the soul with which we breathe. Whatever we are, it is altogether His work. In what manner He effected this He would have taught us, if it were right for us to know; as He taught us other things, which have conveyed to us the knowledge both of ancient error and of true light.

**Chap. XIII.—Why Man is of Two Sexes; what is His First Death, and What the Second and of the Fault and Punishment of Our First Parents.**

When, therefore, He had first formed the male after His own likeness, then He also fashioned woman after the image of the man himself, that the two by their union might be able to perpetuate their race, and to fill the whole earth with a multitude. But in the making of man himself He concluded and completed the nature of those two materials which we have spoken of as contrary to each other, fire and water. For having made the body, He breathed into it a soul from the vital source of His own Spirit, which is everlasting, that it might bear the similitude of the world itself, which is composed of opposing elements. For he consists of soul and body, that is, as it were, of heaven and earth: since the soul by which we live, has its origin, as it were, out of heaven from God, the body out of the earth, of the dust of which we have said that it was formed. Empedocles—whom you cannot tell whether to reckon among poets or philosophers, for he wrote in verse respecting the nature of things, as did Lucretius and Varro among the Romans—determined that there were four elements, that is, fire, air, water, and earth; perhaps following Trismegistus, who said that our bodies were composed of these four elements by God, for *he said* that they contained in themselves something of fire, something of air, something of water, and something of earth, and *yet* that they were neither fire, nor air, nor water, nor earth. And these things indeed are not false; for the nature of earth is contained in the flesh, that of moisture in the blood, that of air in the breath, that of fire in the vital heat. But neither can the blood be separated from the body, as moisture is from the earth; nor the vital heat from the breath, as fire from the air: so that of all things only two elements are found, the whole nature of which is included in the formation of our body. Man, therefore, was made from different and opposite substances, as the world itself was made from light and darkness, from life and death; and he has admonished us that these two things contend against each other in man: so that if the soul, which has its origin from God, gains the mastery, it is immortal, and lives in perpetual light; if, on the other hand, the body shall overpower the soul, and subject it to its dominion, it is in everlasting darkness and death. And the force of this is not that it altogether annihilates the souls of the unrighteous, but subjects them to everlasting punishment.

We term that punishment the second death, which is itself also perpetual, as also is immortality. We thus define the first death: Death is the dissolution of the nature of living beings; or thus: Death is the separation of body and soul. But we thus define the second death: Death is the suffering of eternal pain; or thus: Death is the condemnation of souls for their deserts to eternal punishments. This does not extend to the dumb cattle, whose spirits, not being composed of God, but of the common air, are dissolved by death. Therefore in this union of heaven and earth, the image of which is developed in man, those things which belong to God occupy the higher part, namely the soul, which has dominion over the body; but those which belong to the devil occupy the lower part, manifestly the body: for this, being earthly, ought to be subject to the soul, as the earth is to heaven. For it is, as it were, a vessel which this heavenly spirit may employ as a temporary dwelling. The duties of both are—for the latter, which is from heaven and from God, to command; but for the former, which is from the earth and the devil, to obey. And this, indeed, did not escape the notice of a dissolute man, Sallust, who says: "But all our power consists in the soul and body; we use the soul to command, the body rather to obey." It had been well if he had lived in accordance with his words; for he was a slave to the most degrading pleasures, and he destroyed the efficacy of his sentiment by the depravity of his life. But if the soul is fire, as we have shown, it ought to mount up to heaven as fire, that it may not be extinguished; that is, *it ought to rise* to the immortality which is in heaven. And as fire cannot burn and be kept alive unless it be nourished by some rich fuel in which it may have sustenance, so the fuel and food of the soul is righteousness alone, by which it is nourished unto life. After these things, God, having made man in the manner in which I have pointed out, placed him in paradise, that is, in a most fruitful and pleasant garden, which He planted in the regions of the East with every kind of wood and tree, that he might be nourished by their various fruits; and being free from all labors, might devote himself entirely to the service of God his Father.

Then He gave to him fixed commands, by the observance of which he might continue immortal; or if he transgressed them, be punished with death. It was enjoined that he should not taste of one tree only which was in the midst of the garden, in which He had placed the knowledge of good and evil. Then the accuser, envying the works of God, applied all his deceits and artifices to beguile the man, that he might deprive him of immortality. And first he enticed the woman by fraud to take the forbidden fruit, and through her instrumentality he also persuaded the man himself to transgress the law of God. Therefore, having obtained the knowledge of good and evil, he began to be ashamed of his nakedness, and hid himself from the face of God, which he was not before accustomed to do. Then God drove out the man from the garden, having passed sentence upon the sinner, that he might seek support for himself by labor. And He surrounded the garden itself with fire, to prevent the approach of the man until He execute the last judgment on earth; and having removed death, recall righteous men, His worshippers, to the same place; as the sacred writers teach, and the Erythræan Sibyl, when she says: "But they who honor the true God inherit everlasting life, themselves inhabiting together paradise, the beautiful garden, forever." But since these are the last things, we will treat of them in the last part of this work. Now let us explain those which are first. Death therefore followed man, according to the sentence of God, which even the Sibyl teaches in her verse, saying: "Man made by the very hands of God, whom the serpent treacherously beguiled that he might come to the fate of death, and receive the knowledge of good and evil." Thus the life of man became limited in duration; but still, however, long, inasmuch as it was extended to a thousand years. And when Varro was not ignorant of this, handed down as it is in the sacred writings, and spread abroad by the knowledge of all, he endeavored to give reasons why the ancients were supposed to have lived a thousand years. For he says that among the Egyptians months are accounted as years: so that the circuit of the sun through the twelve signs *of the zodiac* does not make a year, but the moon, which traverses that sign-bearing circle in the space of thirty days; which argument is manifestly false. For no one then exceeded the thousandth year. But now they who attain to the hundredth year, which frequently happens, undoubtedly live a thousand and two hundred months. And competent authorities report that men are accustomed to reach one hundred and twenty years. But because Varro did not know why or when the life of man was shortened, he himself shortened it, since he knew that it was possible for man to live a thousand and four hundred months.

**Chap. XIV.—Of Noah the Inventor of Wine, Who First Had Knowledge of the Stars, and of the Origin of False Religions.**

But afterwards God, when He saw the earth filled with wickedness and crimes, determined to destroy mankind with a deluge; but, however, for renewing the multitude, He chose one man, who, when all were corrupted, stood forth pre-eminent, as a remarkable example of righteousness. He, when six hundred years old, built an ark, as God had commanded him, in which he himself was saved, together with his wife and three sons, and as many daughters-in-law, when the water had covered all the loftiest mountains. Then when the earth was dry, God, execrating the wickedness of the former age, that the length of life might not again be a cause of meditating evils, gradually diminished the age of man by each successive generation, and placed a limit at a hundred and twenty years, which it might not be permitted to exceed. But he, when he went forth from the ark, as the sacred writings inform us, diligently cultivated the earth, and planted a vineyard with his own hand. From which circumstance they are refuted who regard Bacchus as the author of wine. For he not only preceded Bacchus, but also Saturn and Uranus, by many generations. And when he had first taken the fruit from the vineyard, having become merry, he drank even to intoxication, and lay naked. And when one of his sons, whose name was Cham, had seen this, he did not cover his father's nakedness, but went out and told the circumstance to his brothers also. But they, having taken a garment, entered with their faces turned backwards, and covered their father. And when their father became aware of what had been done he disowned and sent away his son. But he went into exile, and settled in a part of that land which is now called Arabia; and that land was called from him Chanaan, and his posterity Chanaanites. This was the first nation which was ignorant of God, since its prince and founder did not receive from his father the worship of God, being cursed by him; and thus he left to his descendants ignorance of the divine nature.

From this nation all the nearest people flowed as the multitude increased. But the descendants of his father were called Hebrews, among whom the religion of the true God was established. But from these also in after times, when their number was multiplied exceedingly, since the small extent of their settlements could not contain them, then young men, either sent by their parents or of their own accord, by the compulsion of poverty, leaving their own lands to seek for themselves new settlements, were scattered in all directions, and filled all the islands and the whole earth; and thus being torn away from the stem of their sacred root, they established for themselves at their own discretion new customs and institutions. But they who occupied Egypt were the first of all who began to look up to and adore the heavenly bodies. And because they did not shelter themselves in houses on account of the quality of the atmosphere, and the heaven is not overspread with any clouds in that country, they observed the courses of the stars, and their obscurations, while in their frequent adorations they more carefully and freely beheld them. Then afterwards, induced by certain prodigies, they invented monstrous figures of animals, that they might worship them; the authors of which we will presently disclose. But the others, who were scattered over the earth, admiring the elements of the world, began to worship the heaven, the sun, the earth, the sea, without any images and temples, and offered sacrifices to them in the open air, until in process of time they erected temples and statues to the most powerful kings, and originated the practice of honoring them with victims and odors; and thus wandering from the knowledge of God, they began to be heathens. They err, therefore, who contend that the worship of the gods was from the beginning of the world, and that heathenism was prior to the religion of God: for they think that this was discovered afterwards, because they are ignorant of the source and origin of the truth. Now let us return to the beginning of the world.

**Chap. XV.—Of the Corruption of Angels, and the Two Kinds of Demons.**

When, therefore, the number of men had begun to increase, God in His forethought, lest the devil, to whom from the beginning He had given power over the earth, should by his subtlety either corrupt or destroy men, as he had done at first, sent angels for the protection and improvement of the human race; and inasmuch as He had given these a free will, He enjoined them above all things not to defile themselves with contamination from the earth, and thus lose the dignity of their heavenly nature. He plainly prohibited them from doing that which He knew that they would do, that they might entertain no hope of pardon. Therefore, while they abode among men, that most deceitful ruler of the earth, by his very association, gradually enticed them to vices, and polluted them by intercourse with women. Then, not being admitted into heaven on account of the sins into which they had plunged themselves, they fell to the earth. Thus from angels the devil makes them to become his satellites and attendants. But they who were born from these, because they were neither angels nor men, but bearing a kind of mixed nature, were not admitted into hell, as their fathers were not into heaven. Thus there came to be two kinds of demons; one of heaven, the other of the earth. The latter are the wicked spirits, the authors of all the evils which are done, and the same devil is their prince. Whence Trismegistus calls him the ruler of the demons. But grammarians say that they are called demons, as though *doemones*, that is, skilled and acquainted with matters: for they think that these are gods. They are acquainted, indeed, with many future events, but not all, since it is not permitted them entirely to know the counsel of God; and therefore they are accustomed to accommodate their answers to ambiguous results. The poets both know them to be demons, and so describe them. Hesiod thus speaks:—

"These are the demons according to the will of Zeus, Good, living on the earth, the guardians of mortal men."

And this is said for this purpose, because God had sent them as guardians to the human race; but they themselves also, though they are the destroyers of men, yet wish themselves to appear as their guardians, that they themselves may be worshipped, and God may not be worshipped. The philosophers also discuss the subject of these beings. For Plato attempted even to explain their natures in his "Banquet;" and Socrates said that there was a demon continually about him, who had become attached to him when a boy, by whose will and direction his life was guided. The art also and power of the Magi altogether consists in the influences of these; invoked by whom they deceive the sight of men with deceptive illusions, so that they do not see those things which exist, and think that they see those things which do not exist. These contaminated and abandoned spirits, as I say, wander over the whole earth, and contrive a solace for their own perdition by the destruction of men. Therefore they fill every place with snares, deceits, frauds, and errors; for they cling to individuals, and occupy whole houses from door to door, and assume to themselves the name of genii; for by this word they translate demons in the Latin language. They consecrate these in their houses, to these they daily pour out libations of wine, and worship the wise demons as gods of the earth, and as averters of those evils which they themselves cause and impose. And these, since spirits are without substance and not to be grasped, insinuate themselves into the bodies of men; and secretly working in their inward parts, they corrupt the health, hasten diseases, terrify their souls with dreams, harass their minds with phrenzies, that by these evils they may compel men to have recourse to their aid.

**Chap. XVI.—That Demons Have No Power Over Those Who are Established in the Faith.**

And the nature of all these deceits is obscure to those who are without the truth. For they think that those demons profit them when they cease to injure, whereas they have no power except to injure. Someone may perchance say that they are therefore to be worshipped, that they may not injure, since they have the power to injure. They do indeed injure, but those only by whom they are feared, whom the powerful and lofty hand of God does not protect, who are uninitiated in the mystery of truth. But they fear the righteous, that is, the worshippers of God, adjured by whose name they depart from the bodies *of the possessed*: for, being lashed by their words as though by scourges, they not only confess themselves to be demons, but even utter their own names—those which are adored in the temples—which they generally do in the presence of their own worshippers; not, it is plain, to the disgrace of religion, but *to the disgrace* of their own honor, because they cannot speak falsely to God, by whom they are adjured, nor to the righteous, by whose voice they are tortured. Therefore oft times having uttered the greatest howling, they cry out that they are beaten, and are on fire, and that they are just on the point of coming forth: so much power has the knowledge of God, and righteousness! Whom, therefore, can they injure, except those whom they have in their own power? In short, Hermes affirms that those who have known God are not only safe from the attacks of demons, but that they are not even bound by fate. "The only protection," he says, "is piety, for over a pious man neither evil demon nor fate has any power: for God rescues the pious man from all evil; for the one and only good thing among men is piety." And what piety is, he testifies in another place, in these words: "For piety is the knowledge of God." Asclepius also, his disciple, more fully expressed the same sentiment in that finished discourse which he wrote to the king. Each of them, in truth, affirms that the demons are the enemies and harassers of men, and on this account Trismegistus calls them wicked angels; so far was he from being ignorant that from heavenly beings they were corrupted, and began to be earthly.

### Chap. XVII.—That Astrology, Soothsaying, and Similar Arts are the Invention of Demons.

These were the inventors of astrology, and soothsaying, and divination, and those productions which are called oracles, and necromancy, and the art of magic, and whatever evil practices besides these men exercise, either openly or in secret. Now all these things are false of themselves, as the Erythræan Sibyl testifies:—

> "Since all these things are erroneous,
> Which foolish men search after day by day."

But these same authorities by their countenance cause it to be believed that they are true. Thus they delude the credulity of men by lying divination, because it is not expedient for them to lay open the truth. These are they who taught men to make images and statues; who, in order that they might turn away the minds of men from the worship of the true God, cause the countenances of dead kings, fashioned and adorned with exquisite beauty, to be erected and consecrated, and assumed to themselves their names, as though *they were assuming* some characters. But the magicians, and those whom the people truly call enchanters, when they practice their detestable arts, call upon them by their true names, those heavenly names which are read in the sacred writings. Moreover, these impure and wandering spirits, that they may throw all things into confusion, and overspread the minds of men with errors, interweave and mingle false things with true. For they themselves feigned that there are many heavenly beings, and one king of all, Jupiter; because there are many spirits of angels in heaven, and one Parent and Lord of all, God. But they have concealed the truth under false names, and withdrawn it from sight.

For God, as I have shown in the beginning, does not need a name, since He is alone; nor do the angels, inasmuch as they are immortal, either suffer or wish themselves to be called gods: for their one and only duty is to submit to the will of God, and not to do anything at all except at His command. For we say that the world is so governed by God, as a province is by its ruler; and no one would say that his attendants are his sharers in the administration of the province, although business is carried on by their service. And yet these can effect something contrary to the commands of the ruler, through his ignorance; which is the result of man's condition. But that guardian of the world and ruler of the universe, who knows all things, from whose divine eyes nothing is concealed, has alone with His Son the power over all things; nor is there anything in the angels except the necessity of obedience. Therefore they wish no honor to be paid to them, since all their honor is in God. But they who have revolted from the service of God, because they are enemies of the truth, and betrayers of God attempt to claim for themselves the name and worship of gods; not that they desire any honor (for what honor is there to the lost?), nor that they may injure God, who cannot be injured, but that they may injure men, whom they strive to turn away from the worship and knowledge of the true Majesty, that they may not be able to obtain immortality, which they themselves have lost through their wickedness. Therefore they draw on darkness, and overspread the truth with obscurity, that men may not know their Lord and Father. And that they may easily entice them, they conceal themselves in the temples, and are close at hand at all sacrifices; and they often give prodigies, that men, astonished by them, may attach to images a belief in their divine power and influence. Hence it is that the stone was cut by the augur with a razor; that Juno of Veii answered that she wished to remove to Rome; that Fortuna Muliebris announced the threatening danger; that the ship followed the hand of Claudia; that Juno when plundered, and the Locrian Proserpine, and the Milesian Ceres, punished the sacrilegious; that Hercules exacted vengeance from Appius, and Jupiter from Atinius, and Minerva from Cæsar. Hence it was that the serpent sent for from Epidaurus freed the city of Rome from pestilence. For the chief of the demons was himself carried thither in his own form, without any dissembling; if indeed the ambassadors who were sent for that purpose brought with them a serpent of immense size.

But they especially deceive in the case of oracles, the juggleries of which the profane cannot distinguish from the truth;

and therefore they imagine that commands, and victories, and wealth, and prosperous issues of affairs, are bestowed by them,— in short, that the state has often been freed from imminent dangers by their interposition; which dangers they have both announced, and when appeased with sacrifices, have averted. But all these things are deceits. For since they have a presentiment of the arrangements of God, inasmuch as they have been His ministers, they interpose themselves in these matters, that whatever things have been accomplished or are in the course of accomplishment by God, they themselves may especially appear to be doing or to have done; and as often as any advantage is hanging over any people or city, according to the purpose of God, either by prodigies, or dreams, or oracles, they promise that they will bring it to pass, if temples, honors, and sacrifices are given to them. And on the offering of these, when the necessary result comes to pass, they acquire for themselves the greatest veneration. Hence temples are vowed, and new images consecrated; herds of victims are slain; and when all these things are done, yet the life and safety of those who have performed them are not the less sacrificed. But as often as dangers threaten, they profess that they are angry on account of some light and trifling cause; as Juno was with Varro, because he had placed a beautiful boy on the carriage of Jupiter to guard the dress, and on this account the Roman name was almost destroyed at Cannæ. But if Juno feared a second Ganymede, why did the Roman youth suffer punishment? Or if the gods regard the leaders only, and neglect the rest of the multitude, why did Varro alone escape who acted thus, and why was Paulus, who was innocent, slain? Assuredly nothing then happened to the Romans by "the fates of the hostile Juno," when Hannibal by craft and valor dispatched two armies of the Roman people. For Juno did not venture either to defend Carthage, where were her arms and chariot, or to injure the Romans; for

> "She had heard that sons of Troy
> Were born her Carthage to destroy."

But these are the delusions of those who, concealing themselves under the names of the dead, lay snares for the living. Therefore, whether the impending danger can be avoided, they wish it to appear that they averted it, having been appeased; or if it cannot be avoided, they contrive that it may appear to have happened through disregard of them. Thus they acquire to themselves authority and fear from men, who are ignorant of them. By this subtlety and by these arts they have caused the knowledge of the true and only God to fail among all nations. For, being destroyed by their own vices, they rage and use violence that they may destroy others. Therefore these enemies of the human race even devised human victims, to devour as many lives as possible.

**Chap. XVIII.—Of the Patience and Vengeance of God, the Worship of Demons, and False Religions.**

Someone will say, Why then does God permit these things to be done, and not apply a remedy to such disastrous errors? That evils may be at variance with good; that vices may be opposed to virtues; that He may have some whom He may punish, and others whom He may honor. For He has determined at the last times to pass judgment on the living and the dead, concerning which judgment I shall speak in the last book. He delays, therefore, until the end of the times shall come, when He may pour out His wrath with heavenly power and might, as

> "Prophecies of pious seers
> Ring terror in the 'wildered ears."

But now He suffers men to err, and to be impious even towards Himself, just, and mild, and patient as He is. For it is impossible that He in whom is perfect excellence should not also be of perfect patience. Whence some imagine, that God is altogether free from anger, because He is not subject to affections, which are perturbations of the mind; for every animal which is liable to affections and emotions is frail. But this persuasion altogether takes away truth and religion. But let this subject of discussing the anger of God be laid aside for the present; because the matter is very copious, and to be more widely treated in a work devoted to the subject. Whoever shall have worshipped and followed these most wicked spirits, will neither enjoy heaven nor the light, which are God's; but will fall into those things which we have spoken of as being assigned in the distribution of things to the prince of the evil ones himself,— namely, into darkness, and hell, and everlasting punishment.

I have shown that the religious rites of the gods are vain in a threefold manner: In the first place, because those images which are worshipped are representations of men who are dead; and that is a wrong and inconsistent thing, that the image of a man should be worshipped by the image of God, for that which worships is lower and weaker *than that which is worshipped:* then that it is an inexpiable crime to desert the living in order that you may serve memorials of the dead, who can neither give life nor light to anyone, for they are themselves without it: and that there is no other God but one, to whose judgment and power every soul is subject. In the second place, that the sacred images themselves, to which most senseless men do service, are destitute of all perception, since they are earth. But who cannot understand that it is unlawful for an upright animal to bend itself that it may adore the earth? which is placed beneath our feet for this purpose, that it may be trodden upon, and not adored by us, who have been raised from it, and have received an elevated position beyond the other living creatures, that we may not turn ourselves again downward, nor cast this heavenly countenance to the earth, but may direct our eyes to that quarter to which the condition of their nature has directed, and that we may adore and worship nothing except the single deity of our only Creator and Father, who made man of an erect figure, that we may know that we are called forth to high and heavenly things. In the third place, because the spirits which preside over the religious rites themselves, being condemned and cast off by God, wallow over the earth, who not only are unable to afford any advantage to their worshippers, since the power of all things is in the hands of one alone, but even destroy them with deadly attractions and errors; since this is their daily business, to involve men in darkness, that the true God may not be sought by them. Therefore they are not to be worshipped, because they lie under the sentence of God. For it is a very great crime to devote one's self to the power of those whom, if you follow righteousness, you are able to excel in power, and to drive out and put to flight by adjuration of the divine name. But if it appears that these religious rites are vain in so many ways as I have shown, it is manifest that those who either make prayers to the dead, or venerate the earth, or make over their souls to unclean spirits, do not act as becomes men, and that they will suffer punishment for their impiety and guilt, who, rebelling against God, the Father of the human race, have undertaken inexpiable rites, and violated every sacred law.

### Chap. XIX.—Of the Worship of Images and Earthly Objects.

Whoever, therefore, is anxious to observe the obligations to which man is liable, and to maintain a regard for his nature, let him raise himself from the ground, and, with mind lifted up, let him direct his eyes to heaven: let him not seek God under his feet, nor dig up from his footprints an object of veneration, for whatever lies beneath man must necessarily be inferior to man; but let him seek it aloft, let him seek it in the highest place: for nothing can be greater than man, except that which is above man. But God is greater than man: therefore He is above, and not below; nor is He to be sought in the lowest, but rather in the highest region. Wherefore it is undoubted that there is no religion wherever there is an image. For if religion consists of divine things, and there is nothing divine except in heavenly things; it follows that images are without religion, because there can be nothing heavenly in that which is made from the earth. And this, indeed, may be plain to a wise man from the very name. For whatever is an imitation, that must of necessity be false; nor can anything receive the name of a true object which counterfeits the truth by deception and imitation. But if all imitation is not particularly a serious matter, but as it were a sport and jest, then there is no religion in images, but a mimicry of religion. That which is true is therefore to be preferred to all things which are false; earthly things are to be trampled upon, that we may obtain heavenly things. For this is the state of the case, that whosoever shall prostrate his soul, which has its origin from heaven, to the shades beneath, and the lowest things, must fall to that place to which he has cast himself. Therefore he ought to be mindful of his nature and condition, and always to strive and aim at things above. And whoever shall do this, he will be judged altogether wise, he just, he a man: he, in short, will be judged worthy of heaven whom his Parent will recognize not as abject, nor cast down to the earth after the manner of the beasts, but rather standing and upright as He made him.

**Chap. XX.—Of Philosophy and the Truth.**

A great and difficult portion of the work which I have undertaken, unless I am deceived, has been completed; and the majesty of heaven supplying the power of speaking, we have driven away inveterate errors. But now a greater and more difficult contest with philosophers is proposed to us, the height of whose learning and eloquence, as some massive structure, is opposed to me. For as in the former case we were oppressed by a multitude, and almost by the universal agreement of all nations, so in this subject we are oppressed by the authority of men excelling in every kind of praise. But who can be ignorant that there is more weight in a smaller number of learned men than in a greater number of ignorant persons? But we must not despair that, under the guidance of God and the truth, these also may be turned aside from their opinion; nor do I think that they will be so obstinate as to deny that they behold with sound and open eyes the sun as he shines in his brilliancy. Only let that be true which they themselves are accustomed to profess, that they are possessed with the desire of investigation, and I shall assuredly succeed in causing them to believe that the truth which they have long sought for has been at length found, and to confess that it could not have been found by the abilities of man.

# The divine institutes

## Book III.

## Of the False Wisdom of Philosophers.

### Chap. I.—A Comparison of the Truth with Eloquence: Why the Philosophers Did Not Attain to It. Of the Simple Style of the Scriptures.

Since it is supposed that the truth still lies hidden in obscurity—either through the error and ignorance of the common people, who are the slaves of various and foolish superstitions, or through the philosophers, who by the perverseness of their minds confuse rather than throw light upon it—I could wish that the power of eloquence had fallen to my lot, though not such as it was in Marcus Tullius, for that was extraordinary and admirable, but in some degree approaching it; that, being supported as much by the strength of talent as it has weight by its own force, the truth might at length come forth, and having dispelled and refuted public errors, and the errors of those who are considered wise, might introduce among the human race a brilliant light. And I could wish that this were so, for two reasons: either that men might more readily believe the truth when adorned with embellishments, since they even believe falsehood, being captivated by the adornment of speech and the enticement of words; or, at all events, that the philosophers themselves might be overpowered by us, most of all by their own arms, in which they are accustomed to pride themselves and to place confidence.

But since God has willed this to be the nature of the case, that simple and undisguised truth should be more clear, because it has sufficient ornament of itself, and on this account it is corrupted when embellished with adorning from without, but that falsehood should please by means of a splendor not its own, because being corrupt of itself it vanishes and melts away, unless it is set off and polished with decoration sought from another source; I bear it with equanimity that a moderate degree of talent has been granted to me. But it is not in reliance upon eloquence, but upon the truth, that I have undertaken this work,—a work, perhaps, too great to be sustained by my strength; which, however, even if I should fail, the truth itself will complete, with the assistance of God, whose office this is. For when I know that the greatest orators have often been overcome by pleaders of moderate ability, because the power of truth is so great that it defends itself even in small things by its own clearness: why should I imagine that it will be overwhelmed in a cause of the greatest importance by men who are ingenious and eloquent, as I admit, but who speak false things; and not that it should appear bright and illustrious, if not by our speech, which is very feeble, and flows from a slight fountain, but by its own light? Nor, if there have been philosophers worthy of admiration on account of their literary erudition, should I also yield to them the knowledge and learning of the truth, which no one can attain to by reflection or disputation. Nor do I now disparage the pursuit of those who wished to know the truth, because God has made the nature of man most desirous of arriving at the truth; but I assert and maintain this against them, that the effect did not follow their honest and well-directed will, because they neither knew what was true in itself, nor how, nor where, nor with what mind it is to be sought. And thus, while they desire to remedy the errors of men, they have become entangled in snares and the greatest errors. I have therefore been led to this task of refuting philosophy by the very order of the subject which I have undertaken.

For since all error arises either from false religion or from wisdom, in refuting error it is necessary to overthrow both. For inasmuch as it has been handed down to us in the sacred writings that the thoughts of philosophers are foolish, this very thing is to be proved by fact and by arguments, that no one, induced by the honorable name of wisdom, or deceived by the splendor of empty eloquence, may prefer to give credence to human rather than to divine things. Which things, indeed, are related in a concise and simple manner. For it was not befitting that, when God was speaking to man, He should confirm His words by arguments, as though He would not otherwise be regarded with confidence: but, as it was right, He spoke as the mighty Judge of all things, to whom it belongs not to argue, but to pronounce sentence. He Himself, as God, is truth. But we, since we have divine testimony for everything, will assuredly show by how much surer arguments truth may be defended, when even false things are so defended that they are accustomed to appear true. Wherefore there is no reason why we should give so much honor to philosophers as to fear their eloquence. For they might speak well as men of learning; but they could not speak truly, because they had not learned the truth from Him in whose power it was. Nor, indeed, shall we effect anything great in convicting them of ignorance, which they themselves very often confess. Since they are not believed in that one point alone in which alone they ought to have been believed, I will endeavor to show that they never spoke so truly as when they uttered their opinion respecting their own ignorance.

### Chap. II.—Of Philosophy, and How Vain Was Its Occupation in Setting Forth the Truth.

Now, since the falsehood of superstitions has been shown in the two former books, and the origin itself of the whole error has been set forth, it is the business of this book to show the emptiness and falsehood of philosophy also, that, all error being removed, the truth may be brought to light and become manifest. Let us begin, therefore, from the common name of philosophy, that when the head itself is destroyed, an easier approach may be open to us for demolishing the whole body; if indeed that can be called a body, the parts and members of which are at variance with one another, and are not united together by any connecting link, but, as it were, dispersed and scattered, appear to palpitate rather than to live. Philosophy is (as the name indicates, and they themselves define it) the love of wisdom. By what argument, then, can I prove that philosophy is not wisdom, rather than by that derived from the meaning of the name itself? For he who devotes himself to wisdom is manifestly not yet wise, but devotes himself to the subject that he may be wise. In the other arts it appears what this devotedness effects, and to what it tends: for when any one by learning has attained to these, he is now called, not a devoted follower of the profession, but an artificer. But it is said it was on account of modesty that they called themselves devoted to wisdom, and not wise. Nay, in truth, Pythagoras, who first invented this name, since he had a little more wisdom than those of early times, who regarded themselves as wise, understood that it was impossible by any human study to attain to wisdom, and therefore that a perfect name ought not to be applied to an incomprehensible and imperfect subject. And, therefore, when he was asked what was his profession, he answered that he was a philosopher, that is, a searcher after wisdom. If, therefore, philosophy searches after wisdom, it is not wisdom itself, because it must of necessity be one thing which searches, and another which is searched for; nor is the searching itself correct, because it can find nothing.

But I am not prepared to concede even that philosophers are devoted to the pursuit of wisdom, because by that pursuit there is no attaining to wisdom. For if the power of finding the truth were connected with this pursuit, and if this pursuit were a kind of road to wisdom, it would at length be found. But since so much time and talent have been wasted in the search for it, and it has not yet been gained, it is plain that there is no wisdom there. Therefore they who apply themselves to philosophy do not devote themselves to the pursuit of wisdom; but they themselves imagine that they do so, because they know not where that is which they are searching for, or of what character it is. Whether, therefore, they devote themselves to the pursuit of wisdom or not, they are not wise, because that can never be discovered which is either sought in an improper manner, or not sought at all. Let us look to this very thing, whether it is possible for anything to be discovered by this kind of pursuit, or nothing.

**Chap. III.—Of What Subjects Philosophy Consists, and Who Was the Chief Founder of the Academic Sect.**

Philosophy appears to consist of two subjects, knowledge and conjecture, and of nothing more. Knowledge cannot come from the understanding, nor be apprehended by thought; because to have knowledge in oneself as a peculiar property does not belong to man, but to God. But the nature of mortals does not receive knowledge, except that which comes from without. For on this account the divine intelligence has opened the eyes and ears and other senses in the body that by these entrances knowledge might flow through to the mind. For to investigate or wish to know the causes of natural things,—whether the sun is as great as it appears to be, or is many times greater than the whole of this earth; also whether the moon be spherical or concave; and whether the stars are fixed to the heaven, or are borne with free course through the air; of what magnitude the heaven itself is, of what material it is composed; whether it is at rest and immoveable, or is turned round with incredible swiftness; how great is the thickness of the earth, or on what foundations it is poised and suspended,—to wish to comprehend these things, I say, by disputation and conjectures, is as though we should wish to discuss what we may supposed to be the character of a city in some very remote country, which we have never seen, and of which we have heard nothing more than the name. If we should claim to ourselves knowledge in a matter of this kind, which cannot be known, should we not appear to be mad, in venturing to affirm that in which we may be refuted? How much more are they to be judged mad and senseless, who imagine that they know natural things, which cannot be known by man! Rightly therefore did Socrates, and the Academics who followed him, take away knowledge, which is not the part of a disputant, but of a diviner. It remains that there is in philosophy conjecture only; for that from which knowledge is absent, is entirely occupied by conjecture. For every one conjectures that of which he is ignorant. But they who discuss natural subjects, conjecture that they are as they discuss them. Therefore they do not know the truth, because knowledge is concerned with that which is certain, conjecture with the uncertain.

Let us return to the example before mentioned. Come, let us conjecture about the state and character of that city which is unknown to us in all respects except in name. It is probable that it is situated on a plain, with walls of stone, lofty buildings, many streets, magnificent and highly adorned temples. Let us describe, if you please, the customs and deportment of the citizens. But when we shall have described these, another will make opposite statements; and when he also shall have concluded, a third will arise, and others after him; and they will make very different conjectures to those of ours. Which therefore of all is truer? Perhaps none of them. But all things have been mentioned which the nature of the circumstances admits, so that some one of them must necessarily be true. But it will not be known who has spoken the truth. It may possibly be that all have in some degree erred *in their description*, and that all have in some degree attained to the truth. Therefore we are foolish if we seek this by disputation; for someone may present himself who may deride our conjectures, and esteem us as mad, since we wish to conjecture the character of that which we do not know. But it is unnecessary to go in quest of remote cases, from which perhaps no one may come to refute us. Come, let us conjecture what is now going on in the forum, what in the senate house. That also is too distant. Let us say what is taking place with the interposition of a single wall; no one can know this but he who has heard or seen it. No one therefore ventures to say this, because he will immediately be refuted not by words, but by the presence of the fact itself. But this is the very thing which philosophers do, who discuss what is taking place in heaven, but think that they do that with impunity, because there is no one to refute their errors. But if they were to think that someone was about to descend who would prove them to be mad and false, they would never discuss those subjects at all which they cannot possibly know. Nor, however, is their shamelessness and audacity to be regarded as more successful because they are not refuted; for God refutes them to whom alone the truth is known, although He may seem to connive at their conduct, and He reckons such wisdom of men as the greatest folly.

### Chap. IV.—That Knowledge is Taken Away by Socrates, and Conjecture by Zeno.

Zeno and the Stoics, then, were right in repudiating conjecture. For to conjecture that you know that which you do not know, is not the part of a wise, but rather of a rash and foolish man. Therefore if nothing can be known, as Socrates taught, or ought to be conjectured, as Zeno taught, philosophy is entirely removed. Why should I say that it is not only overthrown by these two, who were the chiefs of philosophy, but by all, so that it now appears to have been long ago destroyed by its own arms? Philosophy has been divided into many sects; and they all entertain various sentiments. In which do we place the truth? It certainly cannot be in all. Let us point out someone; it follows that all the others will be without wisdom. Let us pass through them separately; in the same manner, whatever we shall give to one we shall take away from the others. For each particular sect overturns all others, to confirm itself and its own *doctrines:* nor does it allow wisdom to any other, lest it should confess that it is itself foolish; but as it takes away others, so is it taken away itself by all others. For they are nevertheless philosophers who accuse it of folly. Whatever sect you shall praise and pronounce true, that is censured by philosophers as false. Shall we therefore believe one which praises itself and its doctrine, or the many which blame the ignorance of each other? That must of necessity be better which is held by great numbers, than that which is held by one only. For no one can rightly judge concerning himself, as the renowned poet testifies; for the nature of men is so arranged, that they see and distinguish the affairs of others better than their own. Since, therefore, all things are uncertain, we must either believe all or none: if we are to believe no one, then the wise have no existence, because while they separately affirm different things they think themselves wise; if all, it is equally true that there are no wise men, because all deny the wisdom of each individually. Therefore all are in this manner destroyed; and as those fabled sparti of the poets, so these men mutually slay one another, so that no one remains of all; which happens on this account, because they have a sword, but have no shield. If, therefore, the sects individually are convicted of folly by the judgment of many sects, it follows that all are found to be vain and empty; and thus philosophy consumes and destroys itself. And since Arcesilas the founder of the Academy understood this, he collected together the mutual censures of all, and the confession of ignorance made by distinguished philosophers, and armed himself against all. Thus he established a new philosophy of not philosophizing. From this founder, therefore, there began to be two kinds of philosophy: one the old one, which claims to itself knowledge; the other a new one, opposed to the former, and which detracts from it. Between these two kinds of philosophy I see that there is disagreement, and as it were civil war. On which side shall we place wisdom, which cannot be torn asunder? If the nature of things can be known, this troop of recruits will perish; if it cannot, the veterans will be destroyed: if they shall be equal, nevertheless philosophy, the guide of all, will still perish, because it is divided; for nothing can be opposed to itself without its own destruction. But if, as I have shown, there can be no inner and peculiar knowledge in man on account of the frailty of the human condition, the party of Arcesilas prevails. But not even will this stand firm, because it cannot be the case that nothing at all is known.

### Chap. V.—That the Knowledge of Many Things is Necessary.

For there are many things which nature itself, and frequent use, and the necessity of life, compel us to know.

Accordingly you must perish, unless you know what things are useful for life, in order that you may seek them; and what are dangerous, that you may shun and avoid them. Moreover, there are many things which experience finds out. For the various courses of the sun and moon, and the motions of the stars, and the computation of times, have been discovered, and the nature of bodies, and the strength of herbs by students of medicine, and by the cultivators of the land the nature of soils, and signs of future rains and tempests have been collected. In short, there is no art which is not dependent on knowledge. Therefore Arcesilas ought, if he had any wisdom, to have distinguished the things which were capable of being known, and those which were incapable. But if he had done this, he would have reduced himself to the common herd. For the common people have sometimes more wisdom, because they are only so far wise as is necessary. And if you inquire of them whether they know anything or nothing, they will say that they know the things which they know, and will confess that they are ignorant of what they are ignorant. He was right, therefore, in taking away the systems of others, but he was not right in laying the foundations of his own. For ignorance of all things cannot be wisdom, the peculiar property of which is knowledge. And thus, when he overcame the philosophers, and taught that they knew nothing, he himself also lost the name of philosopher, because his system is to know nothing. For he who blames others because they are ignorant, ought himself to have knowledge; but when he knows nothing, what perverseness or what insolence it is, to constitute himself a philosopher on account of that very thing for which he takes away the others! For it is in their power to answer thus: If you convict us of knowing nothing, and therefore of being unwise because we know nothing, does it follow that you are not wise, because you confess that you know nothing? What progress, therefore, did Arcesilas make, except that, having dispatched all the philosophers, he pierced himself also with the same sword?

## Chap. VI.—Of Wisdom, and the Academics, and Natural Philosophy.

Does wisdom therefore nowhere exist? Yes, indeed, it was amongst them, but no one saw it. Some thought that all things could be known: these were manifestly not wise. Others thought that nothing could be known; nor indeed were these wise: the former, because they attributed too much to man; the latter, because they attributed too little. A limit was wanting to each on either side. Where, then, is wisdom? It consists in thinking neither that you know all things, which is the property of God; nor that you are ignorant of all things, which is the part of a beast. For it is something of a middle character which belongs to man, that is, knowledge united and combined with ignorance. Knowledge in us is from the soul, which has its origin from heaven; ignorance from the body, which is from the earth: whence we have something in common with God, and with the animal creation. Thus, since we are composed of these two elements, the one of which is endowed with light, the other with darkness, a part of knowledge is given to us, and a part of ignorance. Over this bridge, so to speak, we may pass without any danger of falling; for all those who have inclined to either side, either towards the left hand or the right, have fallen. But I will say how each part has erred. The Academics argued from obscure subjects, against the natural philosophers, that there was no knowledge; and satisfied with the examples of a few incomprehensible subjects, they embraced ignorance as though they had taken away the whole of knowledge, because they had taken it away in part. But natural philosophers, on the other hand, derived their argument from those things which are open, *and inferred* that all things could be known, and, satisfied with things which were manifest, retained knowledge; as if they had defended it altogether, because they had defended it in part. And thus neither the one saw what was clear, nor the others what was obscure; but each party, while they contended with the greatest ardor either to retain or to take away knowledge only, did not see that there would be placed in the middle that which might guide them to wisdom.

But Arcesilas, who teaches that there is no knowledge, when he was detracting from Zeno, the chief of the Stoics, that he might altogether overthrow philosophy on the authority of Socrates, undertook this opinion to affirm that nothing could be known. And thus he disproved the judgment of the philosophers, who had thought that the truth was drawn forth, and found out by their talents,—namely, because that wisdom was mortal, and, having been instituted a few ages before, had now attained to its greatest increase, so that it was now necessarily growing old and perishing, the Academy suddenly arose, the old age, as it were, of philosophy, which might dispatch it now withering. And Arcesilas rightly saw that they are arrogant, or rather foolish, who imagine that the knowledge of the truth can be arrived at by conjecture. But no one can refute one speaking falsely, unless he who shall have previously known what is true; but Arcesilas, endeavoring to do this without a knowledge of the truth, introduced a kind of philosophy which we may call unstable or inconstant. For, that nothing may be known, it is necessary that something be known. For if you know nothing at all, the very knowledge that nothing can be known will be taken away. Therefore he who pronounces as a sentiment that nothing is known, professes, as it were, some conclusion already arrived at and known: therefore it is possible for something to be known.

Of a similar character to this is that which is accustomed to be proposed in the schools as an example of the kind of fallacy called asystaton; that someone had dreamt that he should not believe dreams. For if he did believe them, then it follows that he ought not to believe them. But if he did not believe them, then it follows that he ought to believe them. Thus, if nothing can be known, it is necessary that this fact must be known, that nothing is known. But if it is known that nothing can be known, the statement that nothing can be known must as a consequence be false. Thus there is introduced a tenet opposed to itself, and destructive of itself. But the evasive man wished to take away learning from the other philosophers, that he might conceal it at his home. For truly he is not for taking it from himself who affirms anything that he may take it from others: but he does not succeed; for it shows itself, and betrays its plunderer. How much more wisely and truly he would act, if he should make an exception, and say that the causes and systems of heavenly things only, or natural things, because they are hidden, cannot be known, for there is no one to teach them; and ought not to be inquired into, for they cannot be found out by inquiry! For if he had brought forward this exception, he would both have admonished the natural philosophers not to search into those things which exceeded the limit of human reflection; and would have freed himself from the ill-will arising from calumny, and would certainly have left us something to follow. But now, since he has drawn us back from following others, that we may not wish to know more than we are capable of knowing, he has no less drawn us back from himself also. For who would wish to labor lest he should know anything? Or to undertake learning of this kind that he may even lose ordinary knowledge? For if this learning exists, it must necessarily consist of knowledge; if it does not exist, who is so foolish as to think that that is worthy of being learned, in which either nothing is learned, or something is even unlearned? Wherefore, if all things cannot be known, as the natural philosophers thought, nor nothing, as the Academics taught, philosophy is altogether extinguished.

### Chap. VII.—Of Moral Philosophy, and the Chief Good.

Let us now pass to the other part of philosophy, which they themselves call moral, in which is contained the method of the whole of philosophy, since in natural philosophy there is only delight, in this there is utility also. And since it is more dangerous to commit a fault in arranging the condition of life and in forming the character, greater diligence must be used, that we may know how we ought to live. For in the former subject some indulgence may be granted: for whether they say anything, they bestow no advantage; or if they foolishly rave, they do no injury. But in this subject there is no room for difference of opinion, none for error. All must entertain the same sentiments, and philosophy itself must give instructions as it were with one mouth; because if any error shall be committed, life is altogether overthrown. In that former part, as there is less danger, so there is more difficulty; because the obscurity of the subject compels us to entertain different and various opinions. But in this, as there is more danger, so there is less difficulty; because the very use of the subjects and daily experiments are able to teach what is truer and better. Let us see, therefore, whether they agree, or what *assistance* they give us for the better guidance of life. It is not necessary to enlarge on every point; let us select one, and especially that which is the chief and principal thing, in which the whole of wisdom centers and depends. Epicurus deems that the chief good consists in pleasure of mind, Aristippus in pleasure of the body. Callipho and Dinomachus united virtue with pleasure, Diodorus with the privation of pain, Hieronymus placed the chief good in the absence of pain; the Peripatetics, again, in the goods of the mind, the body, and fortune. The chief good of Herillus is knowledge; that of Zeno, to live agreeably to nature; that of certain Stoics, to follow virtue. Aristotle placed the chief good in integrity and virtue. These are the sentiments of nearly all. In such a difference of opinions, whom do we follow? Whom do we believe? All are of equal authority. If we are able to select that which is better, it follows that philosophy is not necessary for us; because we are already wise, inasmuch as we judge respecting the opinions of the wise. But since we come for the sake of learning wisdom, how can we judge, who have not yet begun to be wise? Especially when the Academic is close at hand, to draw us back by the cloak, and forbid us to believe anyone, without bringing forward that which we may follow.

**Chap. VIII.—Of the Chief Good, and the Pleasures of the Soul and Body, and of Virtue.**

What then remains, but that we leave raving and obstinate wranglers, and come to the judge, who is in truth the giver of simple and calm wisdom? Which is able not only to mold us, and lead us into the way, but also to pass an opinion on the controversies of those men. This teaches us what is the true and highest good of man; but before I begin to speak on this subject, all those opinions must be refuted, that it may appear that no one of those *philosophers* was wise. Since the inquiry is respecting the duty of man, the chief good of the chief animal ought to be placed in that which it cannot have in common with the other animals. But as teeth are the peculiar property of wild beasts, horns of cattle, and wings of birds, so something peculiar to himself ought to be attributed to man, without which he would lose the fixed order of his condition. For that which is given to all for the purpose of life or generation, is indeed a natural good; but still it is not the greatest, unless it be peculiar to each class. Therefore he was not a wise man who believed that pleasure of the mind is the chief good, since that, whether it be freedom from anxiety or joy, is common to all. I do not consider Aristippus even worthy of an answer; for since he is always rushing into pleasures of the body, and is only the slave of sensual indulgences, no one can regard him as a man: for he lived in such a manner that there was no difference between him and a brute, except this only, that he had the faculty of speech. But if the power of speaking were given to the ass, or the dog, or swine, and you were to inquire from these why they so furiously pursue the females, that they can scarcely be separated from them, and even neglect their food and I drink; why they either drive away other males, or do not abstain from the pursuit even when vanquished, but often, when bruised by stronger animals, they are more determined in their pursuit; why they dread neither rain nor cold; why they undertake labor, and do not shrink from danger;— what other answer will they give, but that the chief good is bodily pleasure?—that they eagerly seek it, in order that they may be affected with the most agreeable sensations; and that these are of so much importance, that, for the sake of attaining them, they imagine that no labor, nor wounds, nor death itself, ought to be refused by them? Shall we then seek precepts of living from these men, who have no other feelings than those of the irrational creatures?

The Cyrenaics say that virtue itself is to be praised on this account, because it is productive of pleasure. True, says the filthy dog, or the swine wallowing in the mire. For it is on this account that I contend with my adversary with the utmost exertion of strength, that my valor may procure for me pleasure; of which I must necessarily be deprived if I shall come off vanquished. Shall we therefore learn wisdom from these men, who differ from cattle and the brutes, not in feeling, but in language? To regard the absence of pain as the chief good, is not indeed the part of Peripatetic and Stoic, but of clinical philosophers. For who would not imagine that the discussion was carried on by those who were ill, and under the influence of some pain? What is so ridiculous, as to esteem that the chief good which the physician is able to give? We must therefore feel pain in order that we may enjoy good; and that, too, severely and frequently, that afterwards the absence of pain may be attended with greater pleasure. He is therefore most wretched who has never felt pain, because he is without that which is good; whereas we used to regard him as most happy, because he was without evil. He was not far distant from this folly, who said that the entire absence of pain was the chief good. For, besides the fact that every animal avoids pain, who can bestow upon himself that good, towards the obtaining of which we can do no more than wish? But the chief good cannot make any one happy, unless it shall be always in his power; and it is not virtue, nor learning, nor labor, which affords this to man, but nature herself bestows it upon all living creatures. They who joined pleasure with virtuous principle, wished to avoid this common blending together of all, but they made a contradictory kind of good; since he who is abandoned to pleasure must of necessity be destitute of virtuous principle, and he who aims at principle must be destitute of pleasure.

The *chief* good of the Peripatetics may possibly appear excessive, various, and—excepting those goods which belong to the mind, and what they are is a great subject of dispute—common to man with the beasts. For goods belonging to the body—that is, safety, freedom from pain, health—are no less necessary for dumb creatures than for man; and I know not if they are not more necessary for them, because man can be relieved by remedies and services, the dumb animals cannot. The same is true of those which they call the goods of fortune; for as man has need of resources for the support of life, so have they need of prey and pasture. Thus, by introducing a good which is not within the power of man, they made man altogether subject to the power of another. Let us also hear Zeno, for he at times dreams of virtue. The chief good, he says, is to live in accordance with nature. Therefore we must live after the manner of the brutes. For in these are found all the things which ought to be absent from man: they are eager for pleasures, they fear, they deceive, they lie in wait, they kill; and that which is especially to the point, they have no knowledge of God. Why, therefore, does he teach me to live according to nature, which is of itself prone to a worse course, and under the influence of some more soothing blandishments plunges headlong into vices? Or if he says that the nature of brutes is different from the nature of man, because man is born to virtue, he says something to the purpose; but, however, it will not be a definition of the chief good, because there is no animal which does not live in accordance with its nature.

He who made knowledge the chief good, gave something peculiar to man; but men desire knowledge for the sake of something else, and not for its own sake. For who is contented with knowing, without seeking some advantage from his knowledge? The arts are learned for the purpose of being put into exercise; but they are exercised either for the support of life, or pleasure, or for glory. That, therefore, is not the chief good which is not sought for on its own account. What difference, therefore, does it make, whether we consider knowledge to be the chief good, or those very things which knowledge produces from itself, that is, means of subsistence, glory, pleasure? And these things are not peculiar to man, and therefore they are not the chief goods; for the desire of pleasure and of food does not exist in man alone, but also in the brutes. How is it with regard to the desire of glory? Is it not discovered in horses, since they exult in victory, and are grieved when vanquished? "So great is their love of praises, so great is their eagerness for victory." Nor without reason does that most excellent poet say that we must try "what grief they feel when overcome, and how they rejoice in victory." But if those things which knowledge produces are common to man with other animals, it follows that knowledge is not the chief good. Moreover, it is no slight fault of this definition that bare knowledge is set forth. For all will begin to appear happy who shall have the knowledge of any art, even those who shall know mischievous subjects; so that he who shall have learned to mix poisons, is as happy as he who has learned to apply remedies. I ask, therefore, to what subject knowledge is to be referred. If to the causes of natural things, what happiness will be proposed to me, if I shall know the sources of the Nile, or the vain dreams of the natural philosophers respecting the heaven? Why should I mention that on these subjects there is no knowledge, but mere conjecture, which varies according to the abilities of men? It only remains that the knowledge of good and evil things is the chief good. Why, then, did he call knowledge the chief good more than wisdom, when both words have the same signification and meaning? But no one has yet said that the chief good is wisdom, though this might more properly have been said. For knowledge is insufficient for the undertaking of that which is good and avoiding that which is evil, unless virtue also is added. For many of the philosophers, though they discussed the nature of good and evil things, yet from the compulsion of nature lived in a manner different from their discourse, because they were without virtue. But virtue united with knowledge is wisdom.

It remains that we refute those also who judged virtue itself to be the chief good, and Marcus Tullius was also of this opinion; and in this they were very inconsiderate. For virtue itself is not the chief good, but it is the contriver and mother of the chief good; for this cannot be attained without virtue. Each point is easily understood. For I ask whether they imagine that it is easy to arrive at that distinguished good, or that it is reached only with difficulty and labor? Let them apply their ingenuity, and defend error. If it is easily attained to, and without labor, it cannot be the chief good. For why should we torment ourselves, why wear ourselves out with striving day and night, seeing that the object of our pursuit is so close at hand, that anyone who wishes may grasp it without any effort of the mind? But if we do not attain even to a common and moderate good except by labor, since good things are by their nature arduous and difficult, whereas evil things have a downward tendency, it follows that the greatest labor is necessary for the attainment of the greatest good. And if this is most true, then there is need of another virtue, that we may arrive at that virtue which is called the chief good; but this is incongruous and absurd, that virtue should arrive at itself by means of itself. If no good can be reached unless by labor, it is evident that it is virtue by which it is reached, since the force and office of virtue consist in the undertaking and carrying through of labors. Therefore the chief good cannot be that by which it is necessary to arrive at another. But they, since they were ignorant of the effects and tendency of virtue, and could discover nothing more honorable, stopped at the very name of virtue, and said that it ought to be sought, though no advantage was proposed from it; and thus they fixed for themselves a good which itself stood in need of a good. From these Aristotle was not far removed, who thought that virtue together with honor was the chief good; as though it were possible for any virtue to exist unless it were honorable, and as though it would not cease to be virtue if it had any measure of disgrace. But he saw that it might happen that a bad opinion is entertained respecting virtue by a depraved judgment, and therefore he thought that deference should be paid to what in the estimation of men constitutes a departure from what is right and good, because it is not in our power that virtue should be honored simply for its own deserts.

For what is honorable character, except perpetual honor, conferred on any one by the favorable report of the people? What, then, will happen, if through the error and perverseness of men a bad reputation should ensue? Shall we cast aside virtue because it is judged to be base and disgraceful by the foolish? And since it is capable of being oppressed and harassed, in order that it may be of itself a peculiar and lasting good, it ought to stand in need of no outward assistance, so as not to depend by itself upon its own strength, and to remain steadfast. And thus no good is to be hoped by it from man, nor is any evil to be refused.

### Chap. IX.—Of the Chief Good, and the Worship of the True God, and a Refutation of Anaxagoras.

I now come to the chief good of true wisdom, the nature of which is to be determined in this manner: first, it must be the property of man alone, and not belong to any other animal; secondly, it must belong to the soul only, and not be shared with the body; lastly, it cannot fall to the lot of anyone without knowledge and virtue. Now this limitation excludes and does away with all the opinions of those *whom I have mentioned;* for their sayings contain nothing of this kind. I will now say what this is, that I may show, as I designed, that all philosophers were blind and foolish, who could neither see, nor understand, nor surmise at any time what was fixed as the chief good for man. Anaxagoras, when asked for what purpose he was born, replied that he might look upon the heaven and the sun. This expression is admired by all, and judged worthy of a philosopher. But I think that he, being unprepared with an answer, uttered this at random, that he might not be silent. But if he had been wise, he ought to have considered and reflected with himself; for if anyone is ignorant of his own condition, he cannot even he a man. But let us imagine that the saying was not uttered on the spur of the moment. Let us see how many and what great errors he committed in three words. First, he erred in placing the whole duty of man in the eyes alone, referring nothing to the mind, but everything to the body. But if he had been blind, would he lose the duty of a man, which cannot happen without the ruin of the soul? What of the other parts of the body? Will they be destitute, each of its own duty? Why should I say that more depends upon the ears than upon the eye, since learning and wisdom can be gained by the ears only, but not by the eyes only? Were you born for the sake of seeing the heaven and the sun? Who introduced you to this sight? Or what does your vision contribute to the heaven and the nature of things? Doubtless that you may praise this immense and wonderful work. Therefore confess that God is the Creator of all things, who introduced you into this world, as a witness and praiser of His great work. You believe that it is a great thing to behold the heaven and the sun: why, therefore, do you not give thanks to Him who is the author of this benefit? Why do you not measure with your mind the excellence, the providence, and the power of Him whose works you admire? For it must be, that He who created objects worthy of admiration, is Himself much more to be admired. If anyone had invited you to dinner, and you had been well entertained, should you appear in your senses, if you esteemed the mere pleasure more highly than the author of the pleasure? So entirely do philosophers refer all things to the body, and nothing at all to the mind, nor do they see beyond that which fails under their eyes. But all the offices of the body being put aside, the business of man is to be placed in the mind alone. Therefore we are not born for this purpose, that we may see those things which are created, but that we may contemplate, that is, behold with our mind, the Creator of all things Himself. Wherefore, if anyone should ask a man who is truly wise for what purpose he was born, he will answer without fear or hesitation, that he was born for the purpose of worshipping God, who brought us into being for his cause, that we may serve Him. But to serve God is nothing else than to maintain and preserve justice by good works. But he, as a man ignorant of divine things, reduced a matter of the greatest magnitude to the least, by selecting two things only, which he said were to be beheld by him. But if he had said that he was born to behold the world, although he would comprise all things in this, and would use an expression of greater sound, yet he would not have completed the duty of man; for as much as the soul excels the body, so much does God excel the world, for God made and governs the world. Therefore it is not the world which is to be contemplated by the eye, for each is a body; but it is God who is to be contemplated by the soul: for God, being Himself immortal, willed that the soul also should be everlasting. But the contemplation of God is the reverence and worship of the common Parent of mankind. And if the philosophers were destitute of this, and in their ignorance of divine things prostrated themselves to the earth, we must suppose that Anaxagoras neither beheld the heaven nor the sun, though he said that he was born that he might behold them. The object proposed to man is therefore plain and easy, if he is wise; and to it especially belongs humanity. For what is humanity itself, but justice? What is justice, but piety? And piety is nothing else than the recognition of God as a parent.

**Chap. X.—It is the Peculiar Property of Man to Know and Worship God.**

Therefore the chief good of man is in religion only; for the other things, even those which are supposed to be peculiar to man, are found in the other animals also. For when they discern and distinguish their own voices by peculiar marks among themselves, they seem to converse: they also appear to have a kind of smile, when with soothed ears, and contracted mouth, and with eyes relaxed to sportiveness, they fawn upon man, or upon their own mates and young. Do they not give a greeting which bears some resemblance to mutual love and indulgence? Again, those creatures which look forward to the future and lay up for themselves food, plainly have foresight. Indications of reason are also found in many of them. For since they desire things useful to themselves, guard against evils, avoid dangers, prepare for themselves lurking-places standing open in different places with various outlets, assuredly they have some understanding. Can anyone deny that they are possessed of reason, since they often deceive man himself? For those which have the office of producing honey, when they inhabit the place assigned to them, fortify a camp, construct dwellings with unspeakable skill, and obey their king; I know not if there is not in them perfect prudence. It is therefore uncertain whether those things which are given to man are common to him with other living creatures: they are certainly without religion. I indeed thus judge, that reason is given to all animals, but to the dumb creatures only for the protection of life, to man also for its prolongation. And because reason itself is perfect in man, it is named wisdom, which renders man distinguished in this respect, that to him alone it is given to comprehend divine things. And concerning this the opinion of Cicero is true: "Of so many kinds of animals," he says, "there is none except man which has any knowledge of God; and among men themselves, there is no nation either so uncivilized or so savage, which, even if it is ignorant of due conceptions of the Deity, does not know that some conception of Him ought to be entertained." From which it is effected, that he acknowledges God, who, as it were, calls to mind the source from which he is sprung. Those philosophers, therefore, who wish to free the mind from all fear, take away even religion, and thus deprive man of his peculiar and surpassing good, which is distinct from living uprightly, and from everything connected with man, because God, who made all living creatures subject to man, also made man subject to Himself. What reason is there why they should also maintain that the mind is to be turned in the same direction to which the countenance is raised? For if we must look to the heaven, it is undoubtedly for no other reason than on account of religion; if religion is taken away, we have nothing to do with the heaven. Therefore we must either look in that direction or bend down to the earth. We are not able to bend down to the earth, even if we should wish, since our posture is upright. We must therefore look up to the heaven, to which the nature of the body calls us. And if it is admitted that this must be done, it must either be done with this view, that we may devote ourselves to religion, or that we may know the nature of the heavenly objects. But we cannot by any means know the nature of the heavenly objects, because nothing of that kind can be found out by reflection, as I have before shown. We must therefore devote ourselves to religion, and he who does not undertake this prostrates himself to the ground, and, imitating the life of the brutes, abdicates the office of man. Therefore the ignorant are wiser; for although they err in choosing religion, yet they remember their own nature and condition.

### Chap. XI.—Of Religion, Wisdom, and the Chief Good.

It is agreed upon, therefore, by the general consent of all mankind, that religion ought to be undertaken; but we have to explain what errors are committed on this subject. God willed this to be the nature of man, that he should be desirous and eager for two things, religion and wisdom. But men are mistaken in this, that they either undertake religion and pay no attention to wisdom, or they devote themselves to wisdom alone, and pay no attention to religion, though the one cannot be true without the other. The consequence is, that they fall into a multiplicity of religions, but false ones, because they have left wisdom, which could have taught them that there cannot be many gods; or they devote themselves to wisdom, but a false wisdom, because they have paid no attention to the religion of the Supreme God, who might have instructed them to the knowledge of the truth. Thus men who undertake either of these courses follow a devious path, and one full of the greatest errors, inasmuch as the duty of man, and all truth, are included in these two things which are inseparably connected. I wonder, therefore, that there was none at all of the philosophers who discovered the abode and dwelling-place of the chief good. For they might have sought it in this manner. Whatever the greatest good is, it must be an object proposed to all men. There is pleasure, which is desired by all; but this is common also to man with the beasts, and has not the force of the honorable, and brings a feeling of satiety, and when it is in excess is injurious, and it is lessened by advance of age, and does not fall to the lot of many: for they who are without resources, who constitute the greater part of men, must also be without pleasure. Therefore pleasure is not the chief good; but it is not even a good. What shall we say of riches? This is much truer of them. For they fall to the lot of fewer men, and that generally by chance; and they often fall to the indolent, and sometimes by guilt, and they are desired by those who already possess them. What shall we say of sovereignty itself? That does not constitute the chief good: for all cannot reign, but it is necessary that all should be capable of attaining the chief good.

Let us therefore seek something which is held forth to all. Is it virtue? It cannot be denied that virtue is a good, and undoubtedly a good for all men. But if it cannot be happy because its power and nature consist in the endurance of evil, it assuredly is not the chief good. Let us seek something else. But nothing can be found more beautiful than virtue, nothing more worthy of a wise man. For if vices are to be avoided on account of their deformity, virtue is therefore to be desired on account of its beauty. What then? Can it be that that which is admitted to be good and honorable should be requited with no reward, and be so unproductive as to procure no advantage from itself? That great labor and difficulty and struggling against evils with which this life is filled, must of necessity produce some great good. But what shall we say that it is? Pleasure? But nothing that is base can arise from that which is honorable. Shall we say that it is riches? Or commands? But these things are frail and uncertain. Is it glory? Or honor? Or a lasting name? But all these things are not contained in virtue itself, but depend upon the opinion and judgment of others. For virtue is often hated and visited with evil. But the good which arises from it ought to be so closely united with it as to be incapable of being separated or disunited from it; and it cannot appear to be the chief good in any other way than if it belongs peculiarly to virtue, and is such that nothing can be added to it or taken from it. Why should I say that the duties of virtue consist in the despising of all these things? For not to long for, or desire, or love pleasures, riches, dominions, and honors, and all those things which are esteemed as goods, as others do overpowered by desire, that assuredly is virtue. Therefore it effects something else more sublime and excellent; nor does anything struggle against these present goods but that which longs for greater and truer things. Let us not despair of being able to find it, if we turn our thoughts in all directions; for no slight or trifling rewards are sought.

**Chap. XII.—Of the Twofold Conflict of Body and Soul; And of Desiring Virtue on Account of Eternal Life.**

But our inquiry is as to the object for which we are born: and thus we are able to trace out what is the effect of virtue. There are two parts of which man is made up, soul and body. There are many things peculiar to the soul, many peculiar to the body, many common to both, as is virtue itself; and as often as this is referred to the body, it is called fortitude for the sake of distinction. Since, therefore, fortitude is connected with each, a contest is proposed to each, and victory held forth to each from the contest: the body, because it is solid, and capable of being grasped, must contend with objects which are solid and can be grasped; but the soul, on the other hand, because it is slight and subtle, and invisible, contends with those enemies who cannot be seen and touched. But what are the enemies of the soul, but lusts, vices, and sins? And if virtue shall have overcome and put to flight these, the soul will be pure and free from stain. Whence, then, are we able to collect what are the effects of fortitude of soul? Doubtless from that which is closely connected with it, and resembles it, that is, from fortitude of the body; for when this has come to any encounter and contest, what else does it seek from victory but life? For whether you contend with a man or beast, the contest is for safety. Therefore, as the body obtains by victory its preservation from destruction, so the soul obtains a continuation of its existence; and as the body, when overcome by its enemies, suffers death, so the soul, when overpowered by vices, must die. What difference, therefore, will there be between the contest carried on by the soul and that carried on by the body, except that the body seeks for temporal, but the soul eternal life? If, therefore, virtue is not happy by itself, since its whole force consists, as I have said, in the enduring of evils; if it neglects all things which are desired as goods; if in its highest condition it is exposed to death, inasmuch as it often refuses life, which is desired by others, and bravely undergoes death, which others fear; if it must necessarily produce some great good from itself, because labors, endured and overcome even until death, cannot fail of obtaining a reward; if no reward, such as it deserves, is found on earth, inasmuch as it despises all things which are frail and transitory, what else remains but that it may effect some heavenly reward, since it treats with contempt all earthly things, and may aim at higher things, since it despises things that are humble? And this *reward* can be nothing else but immortality.

With good reason, therefore, did Euclid, no obscure philosopher, who was the founder of the system of the Megareans, differing from the others, say that that was the chief good which was unvarying and always the same. He certainly understood what is the nature of the chief good, although he did not explain in what it consisted; but it consists of immortality, nor anything else at all, inasmuch as it alone is incapable of diminution, or increase, or change. Seneca also unconsciously happened to confess that there is no other reward of virtue than immortality. For in praising virtue in the treatise which he wrote on the subject of premature death, he says: "Virtue is the only thing which can confer upon us immortality, and make us equal to the gods." But the Stoics also, whom he followed, say that no one can be made happy without virtue. Therefore, the reward of virtue is a happy life, if virtue, as it is rightly said, makes a happy life. Virtue, therefore, is not, as they say, to be sought on its own account, but on account of a happy life, which necessarily follows virtue. And this argument might have taught them in what the chief good consisted. But this present and corporeal life cannot be happy, because it is subjected to evils through the body. Epicurus calls God happy and incorruptible, because He is everlasting. For a state of happiness ought to be perfect, so that there may be nothing which can harass, or lessen, or change it. Nor can anything be judged happy in other respects, unless it be incorruptible. But nothing is incorruptible but that which is immortal. Immortality therefore is alone happy, because it can neither be corrupted nor destroyed. But if virtue falls within the power of man, which no one can deny, happiness also belongs to him. For it is impossible for a man to be wretched who is endued with virtue. If happiness falls within his power, then immortality, which is possessed of the attribute of happiness, also belongs to him.

The chief good, therefore, is found to be immortality alone, which pertains to no other animal or body; nor can it happen to anyone without the virtue of knowledge, that is, without the knowledge of God and justice. And how true and right is the seeking for this, the very desire of this life shows: for although it be but temporary, and most full of labor, yet it is sought and desired by all; for both old men and boys, kings and those of the lowest station, in fine, wise as well as foolish, desire this. Of such value, as it seemed to Anaxagoras, is the contemplation of the heaven and the light itself, that men willingly undergo any miseries on this account. Since, therefore, this short and laborious life, by the general consent not only of men, but also of other animals, is considered a great good, it is manifest that it becomes also a very great and perfect good if it is without an end and free from all evil. In short, there never would have been anyone who would despise this life, however short it is, or undergo death, unless through the hope of a longer life. For those who voluntarily offered themselves to death for the safety of their countrymen, as Menoeceus did at Thebes, Codrus at Athens, Curtius and the two Mures at Rome, would never have preferred death to the advantages of life, unless they had thought that they should attain to immortality through the estimation of their countrymen; and although they were ignorant of the life of immortality, yet the reality itself did not escape their notice. For if virtue despises opulence and riches because they are frail, and pleasures because they are of brief continuance, it therefore despises a life which is frail and brief, that it may obtain one which is substantial and lasting. Therefore reflection itself, advancing by regular order, and weighing everything, leads us to that excellent and surpassing good, on account of which we are born. And if philosophers had thus acted, if they had not preferred obstinately to maintain that which they had once apprehended, they would undoubtedly have arrived at this truth, as I have lately shown. And if this was not the part of those who extinguish the heavenly souls together with the body, yet those who discuss the immortality of the soul ought to have understood that virtue is set before us on this account, that, lusts having been subdued, and the desire of earthly things overcome, our souls, pure and victorious, may return to God, that is, to their original source. For it is on this account that we alone of living creatures are raised to the sight of the heaven, that we may believe that our chief good is in the highest place. Therefore we alone receive religion, that we may know from this source that the spirit of man is not mortal, since it longs for and acknowledges God, who is immortal.

Therefore, of all the philosophers, those who have embraced either knowledge or virtue as the chief good, have kept the way of truth, but have not arrived at perfection. For these are the two things which together make up that which is sought for. Knowledge causes us to know by what means and to what end we must attain; virtue causes us to attain to it. The one without the other is of no avail; for from knowledge arises virtue, and from virtue the chief good is produced. Therefore a happy life, which philosophers have always sought, and still do seek, has no existence either in the worship of the gods or in philosophy; and on this account they were unable to find it, because they did not seek the highest good in the highest place, but in the lowest. For what is the highest but heaven, and God, from whom the soul has its origin? And what is the lowest but the earth, from which the body is made? Therefore, although some philosophers have assigned the chief good, not to the body, but to the soul, yet, inasmuch as they have referred it to this life, which has its ending with the body, they have gone back to the body, to which the whole of this time which is passed on earth has reference. Therefore it was not without reason that they did not attain to the highest good; for whatever looks to the body only, and is without immortality, must necessarily be the lowest. Therefore happiness does not fall to the condition of man in that manner in which philosophers thought; but it so falls to him, not that he should then be happy, when he lives in the body, which must undoubtedly be corrupted in order to its dissolution; but then, when, the soul being freed from intercourse with the body, he lives in the spirit only. In this one thing alone can we be happy in this life, if we appear to be unhappy; if, avoiding the enticements of pleasures, and giving ourselves to the service of virtue only, we live in all labors and miseries, which are the means of exercising and strengthening virtue; if, in short, we keep to that rugged and difficult path which has been opened for us to happiness. The chief good therefore which makes men happy cannot exist, unless it be in that religion and doctrine to which is annexed the hope of immortality.

## Chap. XIII.—Of the Immortality of the Soul, and of Wisdom, Philosophy, and Eloquence.

The subject seems to require in this place, that since we have taught that immortality is the chief good, we should prove this also, that the soul is immortal. On which subject there is great disputation among philosophers; nor have they who held true opinions respecting the soul been able to explain or prove anything: for, being destitute of divine knowledge, they neither brought forward true arguments by which they might overcome, nor evidence by which they might convince. But we shall treat of this question more conveniently in the last book, when we shall have to discuss the subject of a happy life. There remains that third part of philosophy, which they call Logic, in which the whole subject of dialectics and the whole method of speaking are contained. Divine learning does not stand in need of this, because the seat of wisdom is not the tongue, but the heart; and it makes no difference what kind of language you employ, for the question is not about words, but facts. And we are not disputing about the grammarian or the orator, whose knowledge is concerned with the proper manner of speaking, but about the wise man, whose learning is concerned with the right manner of living. But if that system of natural philosophy before mentioned is not necessary, nor this of logic, because they are not able to render a man happy, it remains that the whole force of philosophy is contained in the ethical part alone, to which Socrates is said to have applied himself, laying aside the others. And since I have shown that philosophers erred in this part also, who did not grasp the chief good, for the sake of gaining which we are born; it appears that philosophy is altogether false and empty, since it does not prepare us for the duties of justice, nor strengthen the obligations and settled course of man's life. Let them know, therefore, that they are in error who imagine that philosophy is wisdom; let them not be drawn away by the authority of any one; but rather let them incline to the truth, and approach it. There is no room for rashness here; we must endure the punishment of our folly to all eternity, if we shall be deceived either by an empty character or a false opinion. But man, such as he is, if he trusts in himself, that is, if he trusts in man, is (not to say foolish, in that he does not see his own error) undoubtedly arrogant, in venturing to claim for himself that which the condition of man does not admit of.

And how much that greatest author of the Roman language is deceived, we may see from that sentiment of his; for when, in his "Books on Offices," he had said that philosophy is nothing else than the desire of wisdom, and that wisdom itself is the knowledge of things divine and human, added: "And if anyone censures the desire of this, I do not indeed understand what there is which he imagines praiseworthy. For if enjoyment of the mind and rest from cares is sought, what enjoyment can be compared with the pursuits of those who are always inquiring into something which has reference to and tends to promote a good and happy life? Or if any account is taken of consistency and virtue, either this is the study by which we may attain them, or there is none at all. To say that there is no system in connection with the greatest subjects, when none of the least is without a system, is the part of men speaking inconsiderately, and erring in the greatest subjects. But if there is any discipline of virtue, where shall it be sought when you have departed from that kind of learning?" For my own part, although I endeavored to attain in some degree to the means of acquiring learning, on account of my desire to teach others, yet I have never been eloquent, inasmuch as I never even engaged in public speaking; but the goodness of the cause cannot fail of itself to make me eloquent, and for its clear and copious defense the knowledge of divinity and the truth itself are sufficient. I could wish, therefore, that Cicero might for a short time rise from the dead, that a man of such consummate eloquence might be taught by an insignificant person who is devoid of eloquence, first, what that is which is deemed worthy of praise by him who blames that study which is called philosophy; and in the next place, that it is not that study by which virtue and justice are learned, nor any other, as he thought; and lastly, that since there is a discipline of virtue, he might be taught where it is to be sought, when you have laid aside that kind of learning, which he did not seek for the sake of hearing and learning. For from whom could he hear when no one knew it? But, as his usual practice was in pleading causes, he wished to press *his opponent* by questioning, and thus to lead him to confession, as though he were confident that no answer could be given to show that philosophy was not the instructress of virtue. And in the Tusculan disputations he openly professed this, turning his speech to philosophy, as though he was showing himself off by a declamatory style of speaking. "O philosophy, thou guide of life," he says; "O thou investigator of virtue, and expeller of vices; what could not only we, but the life of men, have effected at all without thee? Thou hast been the inventor of laws, thou the teacher of morals and discipline;"—as though, indeed, she could perceive anything by herself, and he were not rather to be praised who gave her. In the same manner he might have given thanks to food and drink, because without these life could not exist; yet these, while they minister to sense, confer no benefit. But as these things are the nourishment of the body, so wisdom is of the soul.

## Chap. XIV.—That Lucretius and Others Have Erred, and Cicero Himself, in Fixing the Origin of Wisdom.

Lucretius, accordingly, acts more correctly in praising him who was the first discoverer of wisdom; but he acts foolishly in this, that he supposed it to be discovered by a man,—as though that man whom he praises had found it lying somewhere as flutes at the fountain, according to the legends of the poets. But if he praised the inventor of wisdom as a god,—for thus he speaks:—

"No one, I think, who is formed of mortal body. For if we must speak, as the acknowledged majesty of the subject itself demands, he was a god, he was a god, most noble Memmius,"—

yet God ought not to have been praised on this account, because He discovered wisdom, but because He created man, who might be capable of receiving wisdom. For he diminishes the praise who praises a part only of the whole. But he praised Him as a man; whereas He ought to have been esteemed as a God on this very account, because He found out wisdom. For thus he speaks:—

"Will it not be right that this man should be enrolled among the gods?" From this it appears, either that he wished to praise Pythagoras, who was the first, as I have said, to call himself a philosopher; or Thales of Miletus, who is reported to have been the first who discussed the nature of things. Thus, while he seeks to exalt, he has depressed the thing itself. For it is not great if it could have been discovered by man. But he may be pardoned as a poet. But that same accomplished orator, that same consummate philosopher, also censures the Greeks, whose levity he always accuses, and yet imitates. Wisdom itself, which at one time he calls the gift, at another time the invention, of the gods, he fashions after the manner of the poets, and praises on account of its beauty. He also grievously complains that there have been some who disparaged it. "Can anyone," he says, "dare to censure the parent of life, and to defile himself with this guilt of parricide, and to be so impiously ungrateful?"

Are we then parricides, Marcus Tullius, and in your judgment worthy to be sewed up in a bag, who deny that philosophy is the parent of life? Or you, who are so impiously ungrateful towards God (not this god whose image you worship as he sits in the Capitol, but Him who made the world and created man, who bestowed wisdom also among His heavenly benefits), do you call her the teacher of virtue or the parent of life, having learned from whom, one must be in much greater uncertainty than he was before? For of what virtue is she the teacher? For philosophers to the present time do not explain where she is situated. Of what life is she the parent? Since the teachers themselves have been worn out by old age and death before they have determined upon the befitting course of life. Of what truth can you hold her forth as an explorer? Since you often testify that, in so great a multitude of philosophers, not a single wise man has yet existed. What, then, did that mistress of life teach you? Was it to assail with reproaches the most powerful consul, and by your envenomed speeches to render him the enemy of his country? But let us pass by those things, which may be excused under the name of fortune. You applied yourself, in truth, to the study of philosophy, and so, indeed, that no one ever applied himself more diligently; since you were acquainted with all the systems of philosophy, as you yourself are accustomed to boast, and elucidated the subject itself in Latin writings, and displayed yourself as an imitator of Plato. Tell us, therefore, what you have learned, or in what sect you have discovered the truth. Doubtless it was in the Academy which you followed and approved. But this teaches nothing, excepting that you know your own ignorance. Therefore your own books refute you, and show the nothingness of the learning which may be gained from philosophy for life. These are your words: "But to me we appear not only blind to wisdom, but dull and obtuse to those very things which may appear in some degree to be discerned." If, therefore, philosophy is the teacher of life, why did you appear to yourself blind, and dull, and obtuse? Whereas you ought, under her teaching, both to perceive and to be wise, and to be engaged in the clearest light. But how you confessed the truth of philosophy we learn from the letters addressed to your son, in which you advise him that the precepts of philosophy ought to be known, but that we must live as members of a community.

What can be spoken so contradictory? If the precepts of philosophy ought to be known, it is on this account that they ought to be known, in order to our living well and wisely. Or if we must live as members of a community, then philosophy is not wisdom, if it is better to live in accordance with society than with philosophy. For if that which is called philosophy be wisdom, he assuredly lives foolishly who does not live according to philosophy. But if he does not live foolishly who lives in accordance with society, it follows that he who lives according to philosophy lives foolishly. By your own judgment, therefore, philosophy is condemned of folly and emptiness. And you also, in your *Consolation*, that is, not in a work of levity and mirth, introduced this sentiment respecting philosophy: "But I know not what error possesses us, or deplorable ignorance of the truth." Where, then, is the guidance of philosophy? Or what has that parent of life taught you, if you are deplorably ignorant of the truth? But if this confession of error and ignorance has been extorted almost against your will from your innermost breast, why do you not at length acknowledge to yourself the truth, that philosophy which, though it teaches nothing, you extolled with praises to the heavens, cannot be the teacher of virtue?

**Chap. XV.—The Error of Seneca in Philosophy, and How the Speech of Philosophers is at Variance with Their Life.**

Under the influence of the same error (for who could keep the right course when Cicero is in error?), Seneca said: "Philosophy is nothing else than the right method of living, or the science of living honorably, or the art of passing a good life. We shall not err in saying that philosophy is the law of living well and honorably. And he who spoke of it as a rule of life, gave to it that which was its due." He evidently did not refer to the common name of philosophy; for, since this is diffused into many sects and systems, and has nothing certain—nothing, in short, respecting which all agree with one mind and one voice,—what can be so false as that philosophy should be called the rule of life, since the diversity of its precepts hinders the right way and causes confusion? Or the law of living well, when its subjects are widely discordant? Or the science of passing life, in which nothing else is effected by its repeated contradictions than general uncertainty? For I ask whether he thinks that the Academy is philosophy or not? I do not think that he will deny it. And if this is so, none of these things, therefore, is in agreement with philosophy; which renders all things uncertain, abrogates law, esteems art as nothing, subverts method, distorts rule, and entirely takes away knowledge. Therefore all those things are false, because they are inconsistent with a system which is always uncertain, and up to this time explaining nothing. Therefore no system, or science, or law of living well, has been established, except in this the only true and heavenly wisdom, which had been unknown to philosophers. For that earthly wisdom, since it is false, becomes varied and manifold, and altogether opposed to itself. And as there is but one founder and ruler of the world, God, and as truth is one; so wisdom must be one and simple, because, if anything is true and good, it cannot be perfect unless it is the only one of its kind. But if philosophy were able to form the life, no others but philosophers would be good, and all those who had not learned it would be always bad. But since there are, and always have been, innumerable persons who are or have been good without any learning, but of philosophers there has seldom been one who has done anything praiseworthy in his life; who is there, I pray, who does not see that those men are not teachers of virtue, of which they themselves are destitute? For if anyone should diligently inquire into their character, he will find that they are passionate, covetous, lustful, arrogant, wanton, and, concealing their vices under a show of wisdom, doing those things at home which they had censured in the schools.

Perhaps I speak falsely for the sake of bringing an accusation. Does not Tullius both acknowledge and complain of the same thing? "How few," he says, "of philosophers are found of such a character, so constituted in soul and life, as reason demands! How few who think true instruction not a display of knowledge, but a law of life! How few who are obedient to themselves, and submit to their own decrees! We may see some of such levity and ostentation, that it would be better for them not to have learned at all; others eagerly desirous of money, others of glory; many the slaves of lusts, so that their speech wonderfully disagrees with their life." Cornelius Nepos also writes to the same Cicero: "So far am I from thinking that philosophy is the teacher of life and the completer of happiness, that I consider that none have greater need of teachers of living than many who are engaged in the discussion of this subject. For I see that a great part of those who give most elaborate precepts in their school respect-modesty and self-restraint, live at the same time in the unrestrained desires of all lusts." Seneca also, in his *Exhortations*, says: "Many of the philosophers are of this description, eloquent to their own condemnation: for if you should hear them arguing against avarice, against lust and ambition, you would think that they were making a public disclosure of their own character, so entirely do the censures which they utter in public flow back upon themselves; so that it is right to regard them in no other light than as physicians, whose advertisements contain medicines, but their medicine chests poison. Some are not ashamed of their vices; but they invent defenses for their baseness, so that they may appear even to sin with honor." Seneca also says: "The wise man will even do things which he will not approve of, that he may find means of passing to the accomplishment of greater things; nor will he abandon good morals, but will adapt them to the occasion; and those things which others employ for glory or pleasure, he will employ for the sake of action." Then he says shortly afterwards: "All things which the luxurious and the ignorant do, the wise man also will do, but not in the same manner, and with the same purpose. But it makes no difference with what intention you act, when the action itself is vicious; because acts are seen, the intention is not seen."

Aristippus, the master of the Cyrenaics, had a criminal intimacy with Lais, the celebrated courtesan; and that grave teacher of philosophy defended this fault by saying, that there was a great difference between him and the other lovers of Lais, because he himself possessed Lais, whereas others were possessed by Lais. O illustrious wisdom, to be imitated by good men! Would you, in truth, entrust your children to this man for education that they might learn to possess a harlot? He said that there was some difference between himself and the dissolute, that they wasted their property, whereas he lived in indulgence without any cost. And in this the harlot was plainly the wiser, who had the philosopher as her creature, that all the youth, corrupted by the example and authority of the teacher, might flock together to her without any shame. What difference therefore did it make, with what intention the philosopher betook himself to that most notorious harlot, when the people and his rivals saw him more depraved than all the abandoned? Nor was it enough to live in this manner, but he began also to teach lusts; and he transferred his habits from the brothel to the school, contending that bodily pleasure was the chief good. Which pernicious and shameful doctrine has its origin not in the heart of the philosopher, but in the bosom of the harlot.

For why should I speak of the Cynics, who practiced licentiousness in public? What wonder if they derived their name and title from dogs, since they also imitated their life? Therefore there is no instruction of virtue in this sect, since even those who enjoin more honorable things either themselves do not practice what they advise; or if they do (which rarely happens), it is not the system which leads them to that which is right, but nature which often impels even the unlearned to praise.

**Chap. XVI.—That the Philosophers Who Give Good Instructions Live Badly, by the Testimony of Cicero; Therefore We Should Not So Much Devote Ourselves to the Study of Philosophy as to Wisdom.**

But when they give themselves up to perpetual sloth, and undertake no exercise of virtue, and pass their whole life in the practice of speaking, in what light ought they to be regarded rather than as triflers? For wisdom, unless it is engaged on some action on which it may exert its force, is empty and false; and Tullius rightly gives the preference, above teachers of philosophy, to those men employed in civil affairs, who govern the state, who found new cities or maintain with equity those already founded, who preserve the safety and liberty of the citizens either by good laws or wholesome counsels, or by weighty judgments. For it is right to make men good rather than to give precepts about duty to those shut up in corners, which precepts are not observed even by those who speak them; and inasmuch as they have withdrawn themselves from true actions, it is manifest that they invented the system of philosophy itself, for the purpose of exercising the tongue, or for the sake of pleading. But they who merely teach without acting, of themselves detract from the weight of their own precepts; for who would obey, when they who give the precepts themselves teach disobedience? Moreover, it is a good thing to give right and honorable precepts; but unless you also practice them it is a deceit, and it is inconsistent and trifling to have goodness not in the heart, but on the lips.

It is not therefore utility, but enjoyment, which they seek from philosophy. And this Cicero indeed testified. "Truly," he says, "all their disputation, although it contains most abundant fountains of virtue and knowledge, yet, when compared with their actions and accomplishments, I fear lest it should seem not to have brought so much advantage to the business of men as enjoyment to their times of relaxation." He ought not to have feared, since he spoke the truth; but as if he were afraid lest he should be arraigned by the philosophers on a charge of betraying a mystery, he did not venture confidently to pronounce that which was true, that they do not dispute for the purpose of teaching, but for their own enjoyment in their leisure; and since they are the advisers of actions, and do not themselves act at all, they are to be regarded as mere talkers. But assuredly, because they contributed no advantage to life, they neither obeyed their own decrees, nor has any one been found, through so many ages, who lived in accordance with their laws. Therefore philosophy must altogether be laid aside, because we are not to devote ourselves to the pursuit of wisdom, for this has no limit or moderation; but we must be wise, and that indeed quickly. For a second life is not granted to us, so that when we seek wisdom in this life we may be wise in that; each result must be brought about in this life. It ought to be quickly found, in order that it may be quickly taken up, lest any part of life should pass away, the end of which is uncertain. Hortensius in Cicero, contending against philosophy, is pressed by a clever argument; inasmuch as, when he said that men ought not to philosophize, he seemed nevertheless to philosophize, since it is the part of the philosophers to discuss what ought and what ought not to be done in life. We are free and exempt from this calumny, who take away philosophy, because it is the invention of human thought; we defend wisdom, because it is a divine tradition, and we testify that it ought to be taken up by all. He, when he took away philosophy without introducing anything better, was supposed to take away wisdom; and on that account was more easily driven from his opinion, because it is agreed upon that man is not born to folly, but to wisdom.

Moreover, the argument which the same Hortensius employed has great weight also against philosophy,—namely, that it may be understood from this, that philosophy is not wisdom, since its beginning and origin are apparent. When, he says, did philosophers begin to exist? Thales, *as I imagine*, was the first, and his age was recent. Where, then, among the more ancient men did that love of investigating the truth lie hid? Lucretius also says:—

"Then, too, this nature and system of things has been discovered lately, and I the very first of all have only now been found able to transfer it into native words."

And Seneca says: "There are not yet a thousand years since the beginnings of wisdom were undertaken." Therefore mankind for many generations lived without system. In ridicule of which, Persius says:—

"When wisdom came to the city,
Together with pepper and palms;"

as though wisdom had been introduced into the city together with savory merchandise. For if it is in agreement with the nature of man, it must have had its commencement together with man; but if it is not in agreement with it, human nature would be incapable of receiving it. But, inasmuch as it has received it, it follows that wisdom has existed from the beginning: therefore philosophy, inasmuch as it has not existed from the beginning, is not the same true wisdom. But, in truth, the Greeks, because they had not attained to the sacred letters of truth, did not know how wisdom was corrupted. And, therefore, since they thought that human life was destitute of wisdom, they invented philosophy; that is, they wished by discussion to tear up the truth which was lying hid and unknown to them: and this employment, through ignorance of the truth, they thought to be wisdom.

### Chap. XVII.—He Passes from Philosophy to the Philosophers, Beginning with Epicurus; And How He Regarded Leucippus and Democritus as Authors of Error.

I have spoken on the subject of philosophy itself as briefly as I could; now let us come to the philosophers, not that we may contend with these, who cannot maintain their ground, but that we may pursue those who are in flight and driven from our battlefield. The system of Epicurus was much more generally followed than those of the others; not because it brings forward any truth, but because the attractive name of pleasure invites many. For every one is naturally inclined to vices. Moreover, for the purpose of drawing the multitude to himself, he speaks that which is specially adapted to each character separately. He forbids the idle to apply himself to learning; he releases the covetous man from giving largesses to the people; he prohibits the inactive man from undertaking the business of the state, the sluggish from bodily exercise, the timid from military service. The irreligious is told that the gods pay no attention to the conduct of men; the man who is unfeeling and selfish is ordered to give nothing to anyone, for that the wise man does everything on his own account. To a man who avoids the crowd, solitude is praised. One who is too sparing, learns that life can be sustained on water and meal. If a man hates his wife, the blessings of celibacy are enumerated to him; to one who has bad children, the happiness of those who are without children is proclaimed; against unnatural parents it is said that there is no bond of nature. To the man who is delicate and incapable of endurance, it is said that pain is the greatest of all evils; to the man of fortitude, it is said that the wise man is happy even under tortures. The man who devotes himself to the pursuit of influence and distinction is enjoined to pay court to kings; he who cannot endure annoyance is enjoined to shun the abode of kings. Thus the crafty man collects an assembly from various and differing characters; and while he lays himself out to please all, he is more at variance with himself than they all are with one another. But we must explain from what source the whole of this system is derived, and what origin it has.

Epicurus saw that the good are always subject to adversities, poverty, labors, exile, and loss of dear friends. On the contrary, he saw that the wicked were happy; that they were exalted with influence, and loaded with honors; he saw that innocence was unprotected, that crimes were committed with impunity: he saw that death raged without any regard to character, without any arrangement or discrimination of age; but that some arrived at old age, while others were carried off in their infancy; that some died when they were now robust and vigorous, that others were cut off by an untimely death in the first flower of youth; that in wars the better men were especially overcome and slain. But that which especially moved him, was the fact that religious men were especially visited with weightier evils, whereas he saw that less evils or none at all fell upon those who altogether neglected the gods, or worshipped them in an impious manner; and that even the very temples themselves were often set on fire by lightning. And of this Lucretius complains, when he says respecting the god:—

"Then he may hurl lightnings, and often throw down his temples, and withdrawing into the deserts, there spend his rage in practicing his bolt, which often passes the guilty by, and strikes dead the innocent and unoffending."

But if he had been able to collect even a small particle of truth, he would never say that the god throws down his own temples, when he throws them down on this account, because they are not his. The Capitol, which is the chief seat of the Roman city and religion, was struck with lightning and set on fire not once only, but frequently. But what was the opinion of clever men respecting this is evident from the saying of Cicero, who says that the flame came from heaven, not to destroy that earthly dwelling-place of Jupiter, but to demand a loftier and more magnificent abode. Concerning which transaction, in the books respecting his consulship, he speaks to the same purport as Lucretius:—

"For the father thundering on high, throned in the lofty Olympus, himself assailed his own citadels and famed temples, and cast fires upon his abode in the Capitol.

In the obstinacy of their folly, therefore, they not only did not understand the power and majesty of the true God, but they even increased the impiety of their error, in endeavoring against all divine law to restore a temple so often condemned by the judgment of Heaven.

Therefore, when Epicurus reflected on these things, induced as it were by the injustice of these matters (for thus it appeared to him in his ignorance of the cause and subject), he thought that there was no providence. And having persuaded himself of this, he undertook also to defend it, and thus he entangled himself in inextricable errors. For if there is no providence, how is it that the world was made with such order and arrangement? He says: There is no arrangement, for many things are made in a different manner from that in which they ought to have been made. And the divine man found subjects of censure. Now, if I had leisure to refute these things separately, I could easily show that this man was neither wise nor of sound mind. Also, if there is no providence, how is it that the bodies of animals are arranged with such foresight, that the various members, being disposed in a wonderful manner, discharge their own offices individually? The system of providence, he says, contrived nothing in the production of animals; for neither were the eyes made for seeing, nor the ears for hearing, nor the tongue for speaking, nor the feet for walking; inasmuch as these were produced before it was possible to speak, to hear, to see, and to walk. Therefore these were not produced for use; but use was produced from them. If there is no providence, why do rains fall, fruits spring up, and trees put forth leaves? These things, he says, are not always done for the sake of living creatures, inasmuch as they are of no benefit to providence; but all things must be produced of their own accord. From what source, therefore, do they arise, or how are all things which are carried on brought about? There is no need, he says, of supposing a providence; for there are seeds floating through the empty void, and from these, collected together without order, all things are produced and take their form. Why, then, do we not perceive or distinguish them? Because, he says, they have neither any color, nor warmth, nor smell; they are also without flavor and moisture; and they are so minute, that they cannot be cut and divided.

Thus, because he had taken up a false principle at the commencement, the necessity of the subjects which followed led him to absurdities. For where or from whence are these atoms? Why did no one dream of them besides Leucippus only? From whom Democritus, having received instructions, left to Epicurus the inheritance of his folly. And if these are minute bodies, and indeed solid, as they say, they certainly are able to fall under the notice of the eyes. If the nature of all things is the same, how is it that they compose various objects? They meet together, he says, in varied order and position as the letters which, though few in number, by variety of arrangement make up innumerable words. But it is urged the letters have a variety of forms. And so, he says, have these first principles; for they are rough, they are furnished with hooks, they are smooth. Therefore they can be cut and divided, if there is in them any part which projects. But if they are smooth and without hooks, they cannot cohere. They ought therefore to he hooked, that they may be linked together one with another. But since they are said to be so minute that they cannot be cut asunder by the edge of any weapon, how is it that they have hooks or angles? For it must be possible for these to be torn asunder, since they project. In the next place, by what mutual

## The Writings of Lactatius

compact, by what discernment, do they meet together, so that anything may be constructed out of them? If they are without intelligence, they cannot come together in such order and arrangement; for nothing but reason can bring to accomplishment anything in accordance with reason. With how many arguments can this trifling be refuted! But I must proceed with my subject. This is he

"Who surpassed in intellect the race of man, and quenched the light of all, as the ethereal sun arisen quenches the stars."

Which verses I am never able to read without laughter. For this was not said respecting Socrates or Plato, who are esteemed as kings of philosophers, but concerning a man who, though of sound mind and vigorous health, raved more senselessly than anyone diseased. And thus the most vain poet, I do not say adorned, but overwhelmed and crushed, the mouse with the praises of the lion. But the same man also releases us from the fear of death, respecting which these are his own exact words:—

"When we are in existence, death does not exist; when death exists, we have no existence: therefore death is nothing to us."

How cleverly he has deceived us! As though it were death now completed which is an object of fear, by which sensation has been already taken away, and not the very act of dying, by which sensation is being taken from us. For there is a time in which we ourselves even yet exist, and death does not yet exist; and that very time appears to be miserable, because death is beginning to exist, and we are ceasing to exist.

Nor is it said without reason that death is not miserable. The approach of death is miserable; that is, to waste away by disease, to endure the thrust, to receive the weapon in the body, to be burnt with fire, to be torn by the teeth of beasts. These are the things which are feared, not because they bring death, but because they bring great pain. But rather make out that pain is not an evil. He says it is the greatest of all evils. How therefore can I fail to fear, if that which precedes or brings about death is an evil? Why should I say that the argument is false, inasmuch as souls do not perish? But, he says, souls do perish; for that which is born with the body must perish with the body. I have already stated that I prefer to put off the discussion of this subject, and to reserve it for the last part of my work, that I may refute this persuasion of Epicurus, whether it was that of Democritus or Dicæarchus, both by arguments and divine testimonies. But perhaps he promised himself impunity in the indulgence of his vices; for he was an advocate of most disgraceful pleasure, and said that man was born for its enjoyment. Who, when he hears this affirmed, would abstain from the practice of vice and wickedness? For; if the soul is doomed to perish, let us eagerly pursue riches, that we may be able to enjoy all kinds of indulgence; and if these are wanting to us, let us take them away from those who have them by stealth, by stratagem, or by force, especially if there is no God who regards the actions of men: as long as the hope of impunity shall favor us, let us plunder and put to death. For it is the part of the wise man to do evil, if it is advantageous to him, and safe; since, if there is a God in heaven, He is not angry with anyone. It is also equally the part of the foolish man to do good; because, as he is not excited with anger, so he is not influenced by favor. Therefore let us live in the indulgence of pleasures in every possible way; for in a short time we shall not exist at all. Therefore let us suffer no day, in short, no moment of time, to pass away from us without pleasure; lest, since we ourselves are doomed to perish, the life which we have already spent should itself also perish.

Although he does not say this in word, yet he teaches it in fact. For when he maintains that the wise man does everything for his own sake, he refers all things which he does to his own advantage. And thus he who hears these disgraceful things, will neither think that any good thing ought to be done, since the conferring of benefits has reference to the advantage of another; nor that he ought to abstain from guilt, because the doing of evil is attended with gain. If any chieftain of pirates or leader of robbers were exhorting his men to acts of violence, what other language could he employ than to say the same things which Epicurus says: that the gods take no notice; that they are not affected with anger nor kind feeling; that the punishment of a future state is not to be dreaded, because souls die after death, and that there is no future state of punishment at all; that pleasure is the greatest good; that there is no society among men; that everyone consults for his own interest; that there is no one who loves another, unless it be for his own sake; that death is not to be feared by a brave man, nor any pain; for that he, even if he should be tortured or burnt, should say that he does not regard it. There is evidently sufficient cause why anyone should regard this as the expression of a wise man, since it can most fittingly be applied to robbers!

### Chap. XVIII.—The Pythagoreans and Stoics, While They Hold the Immortality of the Soul, Foolishly Persuade a Voluntary Death.

Others, again, discuss things contrary to these, namely, that the soul survives after death; and these are chiefly the Pythagoreans and Stoics. And although they are to be treated with indulgence because they perceive the truth, yet I cannot but blame them, because they fell upon the truth not by their opinion, but by accident. And thus they erred in some degree even in that very matter which they rightly perceived. For, since they feared the argument by which it is inferred that the soul must necessarily die with the body, because it is born with the body, they asserted that the soul is not born with the body, but rather introduced into it, and that it migrates from one body to another. They did not consider that it was possible for the soul to survive the body, unless it should appear to have existed previously to the body. There is therefore an equal and almost similar error on each side.

But the one side are deceived with respect to the past, the other with respect to the future. For no one saw that which is most true, that the soul is both created and does not die, because they were ignorant why that came to pass, or what was the nature of man. Many therefore of them, because they suspected that the soul is immortal, laid violent hands upon themselves, as though they were about to depart to heaven. Thus it was with Cleanthes and Chrysippus, with Zeno, and Empedocles, who in the dead of night cast himself into a cavity of the burning Ætna, that when he had suddenly disappeared it might be believed that he had departed to the gods; and thus also of the Romans Cato died, who through the whole of his life was an imitator of Socratic ostentation. For Democritus was of another persuasion. But, however,

"By his own spontaneous act he offered up his head to death; "

and nothing can be more wicked than this. For if a homicide is guilty because he is a destroyer of man, he who puts himself to death is under the same guilt, because he puts to death a man. Yea, that crime may be considered to be greater, the punishment of which belongs to God alone. For as we did not come into this life of our own accord; so, on the other hand, we can only withdraw from this habitation of the body which has been appointed for us to keep, by the command of Him who placed us in this body that we may inhabit it, until He orders us to depart from it; and if any violence is offered to us, we must endure it with equanimity, since the death of an innocent person cannot be unavenged, and since we have a great Judge who alone always has the power of taking vengeance in His hands.

All these philosophers, therefore, were homicides; and Cato himself, the chief of Roman wisdom, who, before he put himself to death, is said to have read through the treatise of Plato which he wrote on the immortality of the soul, and was led by the authority of the philosopher to the commission of this great crime; yet he, however, appears to have had some cause for death in his hatred of slavery. Why should I speak of the Ambraciot, who, having read the same treatise, threw himself into the sea, for no other cause than that he believed Plato?—a doctrine altogether detestable and to be avoided, if it drives men from life. But if Plato had known and taught by whom, and how, and to whom, and on account of what actions, and at what time, immortality is given, he would neither have driven Cleombrotus nor Cato to a voluntary death, but he would have trained them to live with justice. For it appears to me that Cato sought a cause for death, not so much that he might escape from Caesar, as that he might obey the decrees of the Stoics, whom he followed, and might make his name distinguished by some great action; and I do not see what evil could have happened to him if he had lived. For Caius Caesar, such was his clemency, had no other object, even in the very heat of civil war, than to appear to deserve well of the state, by preserving two excellent citizens, Cicero and Cato. But let us return to those who praise death as a benefit. You complain of life as though you had lived, or had ever settled with yourself why you were born at all. May not therefore the true and common Father of all justly find fault with that saying of Terence:—

"First, learn in what life consists; then, if you shall be dissatisfied with life, have recourse to death."

You are indignant that you are exposed to evils; as though you deserved anything good, who are ignorant of your Father, Lord, and King; who, although you behold with your eyes the bright light, are nevertheless blind in mind, and lie in the depths of the darkness of ignorance. And this ignorance has caused that some have not been ashamed to say, that we are born for this cause, that we may suffer the punishment of our crimes; but I do not see what can be more senseless than this. For where or what crimes could we have committed when we did not even exist? Unless we shall happen to believe that foolish old man, who falsely said *that he had lived before, and* that in his former life he had been Euphorbus. He, I believe, because he was born of an ignoble race, chose for himself a family from the poems of Homer. O wonderful and remarkable memory of Pythagoras! O miserable forgetfulness on the part of us all, since we know not who we were in our former life! But perhaps it was caused by some error, or favor, that he alone did not touch the abyss of Lethe, or taste the water of oblivion; doubtless the trifling old man (as is wont to be the case with old women who are free from occupation) invented fables as it were for credulous infants. But if he had thought well of those to whom he spoke these things; if he had considered them to be men, he would never have claimed to himself the liberty of uttering such perverse falsehoods. But the folly of this most trifling man is deserving of ridicule. What shall we do in the case of Cicero, who, having said in the beginning of his *Consolation* that men were born for the sake of atoning for their crimes, afterwards repeated the assertion, as though rebuking him who does not imagine that life is a punishment? He was right, therefore, in saying beforehand that he was held by error and wretched ignorance of the truth.

**Chap. XIX.—Cicero and Others of the Wisest Men Teach the Immortality of the Soul, But in an Unbelieving Manner; And that a Good or an Evil Death Must Be Weighed from the Previous Life.**

But those who assert the advantage of death, because they know nothing of the truth, thus reason: If there is nothing after death, death is not an evil; for it takes away the perception of evil. But if the soul survives, death is even an advantage; because immortality follows. And this sentiment is thus set forth by Cicero concerning the Laws: "We may congratulate ourselves, since death is about to bring either a better state than that which exists in life, or at any rate not a worse. For if the soul is in a state of vigor without the body, it is a divine life; and if it is without perception, assuredly there is no evil." Cleverly argued, as it appeared to himself, as though there could be no other state. But each conclusion is false. For the sacred writings teach that the soul is not annihilated; but that it is either rewarded according to its righteousness, or eternally punished according to its crimes. For neither is it right, that he who has lived a life of wickedness in prosperity should escape the punishment which he deserves; nor that he who has been wretched on account of his righteousness, should be deprived of his reward. And this is so true, that Tully also, in his *Consolation*, declared that the righteous and the wicked do not inhabit the same abodes. For those same wise men, he says, did not judge that the same course was open for all into the heaven; for they taught that those who were contaminated by vices and crimes were thrust down into darkness, and lay in the mire; but that, on the other hand, souls that were chaste, pure, upright, and uncontaminated, being also refined by the study and practice of virtue, by a light and easy course take their flight to the gods, that is, to a nature resembling their own. But this sentiment is opposed to the former argument. For that is based on the assumption that every man at his birth is presented with immortality. What distinction, therefore, will there be between virtue and guilt, if it makes no difference whether a man be Aristides or Phalaris, whether he be Cato or Catiline? But a man does not perceive this opposition between sentiments and actions, unless he is in possession of the truth. If anyone, therefore, should ask me whether death is a good or an evil, I shall reply that its character depends upon the course of the life. For as life itself is a good if it is passed virtuously, but an evil if it is spent viciously, so also death is to be weighed in accordance with the past actions of life. And so it comes to pass, that if life has been passed in the service of God, death is not an evil, for it is a translation to immortality. But if not so, death must necessarily be an evil, since it transfers men, as I have said, to everlasting punishment.

What, then, shall we say, but that they are in error who either desire death as a good, or flee from life as an evil? Unless they are most unjust, who do not weigh the fewer evils against the greater number of blessings. For when they pass all their lives in a variety of the choicest gratifications, if any bitterness has chanced to succeed to these, they desire to die; and they so regard it as to appear never to have fared well, if at any time they happen to fare ill. Therefore they condemn the whole of life, and consider it as nothing else than filled with evils. Hence arose that foolish sentiment, that this state which we imagine to be life is death, and that that which we fear as death is life; and so that the first good is not to be born, that the second is an early death. And that this sentiment may be of greater weight, it is attributed to Silenus. Cicero in his *Consolation* says: "Not to be born is by far the best thing, and not to fall upon these rocks of life. But the next thing is, if you have been born, to die as soon as possible, and to flee from the violence of fortune as from a conflagration." That he believed this most foolish expression appears from this, that he added something of his own for its embellishment. I ask, therefore, for whom he thinks it best not to be born, when there is no one at all who has any perception; for it is the perception which causes anything to be good or bad. In the next place, why did he regard the whole of life as nothing else than rocks, and a conflagration; as though it were either in our power not to be born, or life were given to us by fortune, and not by God, or as though the course of life appeared to bear any resemblance to a conflagration?

The saying of Plato is not dissimilar, that he gave thanks to nature, first that he was born a human being rather than a dumb animal; in the next place, that he was a man rather than a woman; that he was a Greek rather than a barbarian; lastly, that he was an Athenian, and that he was born in the time of Socrates. It is impossible to say what great blindness and errors are produced by ignorance of the truth would altogether contend that nothing in the affairs of men was ever spoken more foolishly. As though, if he had been born a barbarian, or a woman, or, in fine, an ass, he would be the same Plato, and not that very being which had been produced. But he evidently believed Pythagoras, who, in order that he might prevent men from feeding on animals, said that souls passed from the bodies of men to the bodies of other animals; which is both foolish and impossible. It is foolish, because it was unnecessary to introduce souls that have long existed into new bodies, when the same Artificer who at one time had made the first, was always able to make fresh ones; it is impossible, because the soul endued with right reason can no more change the nature of its condition, than fire can rush downwards, or, like a river, pour its flame obliquely. The wise man therefore imagined, that it might come to pass that the soul which was then in Plato might be shut up in some other animal, and might be endued with the sensibility of a man, so as to understand and grieve that it was burthened with an incongruous body. How much more rationally would he have acted, if he had said that he gave thanks because he was born with a good capacity, and capable of receiving instruction, and that he was possessed of those resources which enabled him to receive a liberal education! For what benefit was it that he was born at Athens? Have not many men of distinguished talent and learning lived in other cities, who were better individually than all the Athenians? How many thousands must we believe that there were, who, though born at Athens, and in the times of Socrates, were nevertheless unlearned and foolish? For it is not the walls or the place in which any one was born that can invest a man with wisdom. Of what avail was it to congratulate himself that he was born in the times of Socrates? Was Socrates able to supply talent to learners? It did not occur to Plato that Alcibiades also, and Critias, were constant hearers of the same Socrates, the one of whom was the most active enemy of his country, the other the cruelest of all tyrants.

**Chap. XX.—Socrates Had More Knowledge in Philosophy than Other Men, Although in Many Things He Acted Foolishly.**

Let us now see what there was so great in Socrates himself, that a wise man deservedly gave thanks that he was born in his times. I do not deny that he was a little more sagacious than the others who thought that the nature of things could be comprehended by the mind. And in this I judge that they were not only senseless, but also impious; because they wished to send their inquisitive eyes into the secrets of that heavenly providence. We know that there are at Rome, and in many cities, certain sacred things which it is considered impious for men to look upon. Therefore they who are not permitted to pollute those objects abstain from looking upon them; and if by error or some accident a man has happened to see them, his guilt is expiated first by his punishment, and afterwards by a repetition of sacrifice. What can you do in the case of those who wish to pry into unpermitted things? Truly they are much more wicked who seek to profane the secrets of the world and this heavenly temple with impious disputations, than those who entered the temple of Vesta, or the Good Goddess, or Ceres. And these shrines, though it is not lawful for men to approach them, were yet constructed by men. But these men not only escape the charge of impiety, but, that which is much more unbecoming, they gain the fame of eloquence and the glory of talent. What if they were able to investigate anything? For they are as foolish in asserting as they are wicked in searching out; since they are neither able to find out anything, nor, even if they had found out anything, to defend it. For if even by chance they have seen the truth—a thing which often happens—they so act that it is refuted by others as false. For no one descends from heaven to pass sentence on the opinions of individuals; wherefore no one can doubt that those who seek after these things are foolish, senseless, and insane.

Socrates therefore had something of human wisdom, who, when he understood that these things could not possibly be ascertained, removed himself from questions of this kind; but I fear that he so acted in this alone. For many of his actions are not only undeserving of praise, but also most deserving of censure, in which things he most resembled those of his own class. Out of these I will select one which may be judged of by all. Socrates used this well-known proverb: "That which is above us is nothing to us." Let us therefore fall down upon the earth, and use as feet those hands which have been given us for the production of excellent works. The heaven is nothing to us, to the contemplation of which we have been raised; in fine, the light itself can have no reference to us; undoubtedly the cause of our sustenance is from heaven. But if he perceived this, that we ought not to discuss the nature of heavenly things, he was unable even to comprehend the nature of those things which he had beneath his feet. What then? Did he err in his words? It is not probable; but he undoubtedly meant that which he said, that we are not to devote ourselves to religion; but if he were openly to say this, no one would suffer it.

For who cannot perceive that this world, completed with such wonderful method, is governed by some providence, since there is nothing which can exist without someone to direct it? Thus, a house deserted by its inhabitant fails to decay; a ship without a pilot goes to the bottom; and a body abandoned by the soul wastes away. Much less can we suppose that so great a fabric could either have been constructed without an Artificer, or have existed so long without a Ruler. But if he wished to overthrow those public superstitions, I do not disapprove of this; yea, I shall rather praise it, if he shall have found anything better *to take their place*. But the same man swore by a dog and a goose. Oh buffoon (as Zeno the Epicurean says), senseless, abandoned, desperate man, if he wished to scoff at religion; madman, if he did this seriously, so as to esteem a most base animal as God! For who can dare to find fault with the superstitions of the Egyptians, when Socrates confirmed them at Athens by his authority? But was it not a mark of consummate vanity, that before his death he asked his friends to sacrifice for him a cock which he had vowed to Æsculapius? He evidently feared lest he should be put upon his trial before Rhadamanthus, the judge, by Æsculapius on account of the vow. I should consider him most mad if he had died under the influence of disease. But since he did this in his sound mind, he who thinks that he was wise is himself of unsound mind. Behold one in whose times the wise man congratulates himself as having been born!

### Chap. XXI.—Of the System of Plato, Which Would Lead to the Overthrow of States.

Let us, however, see what it was that he learned from Socrates, who, having entirely rejected natural philosophy, betook himself to inquiries about virtue and duty. And thus I do not doubt that he instructed his hearers in the precepts of justice. Therefore, under the teaching of Socrates, it did not escape the notice of Plato, that the force of justice consists in equality, since all are born in an equal condition. Therefore (he says) they must have nothing private or their own; but that they may be equal, as the method of justice requires, they must possess all things in common. This is capable of being endured, as long as it appears to be spoken of money. But how impossible and how unjust this is, I could show by many things. Let us, however, admit its possibility. For grant that all are wise, and despise money. To what, then, did that community lead him? Marriages also, he says, ought to be in common; so that many men may flock together like dogs to the same woman, and he who shall be superior in strength may succeed in obtaining her; or if they are patient as philosophers, they may await their turns, as in a brothel. Oh the wonderful equality of Plato! Where, then, is the virtue of chastity? Where conjugal fidelity? And if you take away these, all justice is taken away. But he also says that states would be prosperous, if either philosophers were their kings, or their kings were philosophers. But if you were to give the sovereignty to this man of such justice and equity, who had deprived some of their own property, and given to some the property of others, he would prostitute the modesty of women; a thing which was never done, I do not say by a king, but not even by a tyrant.

But what motive did he advance for this most degrading advice? The state will be in harmony, and bound together with the bonds of mutual love, if all shall be the husbands, and fathers, and wives, and children of all. What a confusion of the human race is this? How is it possible for affection to be preserved where there is nothing certain to be loved? What man will love a woman, or what woman a man, unless they shall always have lived together,—unless devotedness of mind, and faith mutually preserved, shall have made their love indivisible? But this virtue has no place in that promiscuous pleasure. Moreover, if all are the children of all, who will be able to love children as his own, when he is either ignorant or in doubt whether they are his own? Who will bestow honor upon any one as a father, when he does not know from whom he was born? From which it comes to pass, that he not only esteems a stranger as a father, but also a father as a stranger. Why should I say that it is possible for a wife to be common, but impossible for a son, who cannot be conceived except from one? The community, therefore, is lost to him alone, nature herself crying out against it. It remains that it is only for the sake of concord that he would have a community of wives. But there is no more vehement cause of discords, than the desire of one woman by many men. And in this Plato might have been admonished, if not by reason, yet certainly by example, both of the dumb animals, which fight most vehemently on this account, and of men, who have always carried on most severe wars with one another on account of this matter.

**Chap. XXII.—Of the Precepts of Plato, and Censures of the Same.**

It remains that the community of which we have spoken admits of nothing else but adulteries and lusts, for the utter extinction of which virtue is especially necessary. Therefore he did not find the concord which he sought, because he did not see whence it arises. For justice has no weight in outward circumstances, not even in the body, but it is altogether employed on the mind of man. He, therefore, who wishes to place men on an equality, ought not to take away marriage and wealth, but arrogance, pride, and haughtiness, that those who are powerful and lifted up on high may know that they are on a level even with the most needy. For insolence and injustice being taken from the rich, it will make no difference whether some are rich and others poor, since they will be equal in spirit, and nothing but reverence towards God can produce this result. He thought, therefore, that he had found justice, whereas he had altogether removed it, because it ought not to be a community of perishable things, but of minds. For if justice is the mother of all virtues, when they are severally taken away, it is also itself overthrown. But Plato took away above all things frugality, which has no existence when there is no property of one's own which can be possessed; he took away abstinence, since there will be nothing belonging to another from which one can abstain; he took away temperance and chastity, which are the greatest virtues in each sex; he took away self-respect, shame, and modesty, if those things which are accustomed to be judged base and disgraceful begin to be accounted honorable and lawful. Thus, while he wishes to confer virtue upon all, he takes it away from all. For the ownership of property contains the material both of vices and of virtues, but a community of goods contains nothing else than the licentiousness of vices. For men who have many mistresses can be called nothing else than luxurious and prodigal. And likewise women who are in the possession of many men, must of necessity be not adulteresses, because they have no fixed marriage, but prostitutes and harlots. Therefore he reduced human life, I do not say to the likeness of dumb animals, but of the herds and brutes. For almost all the birds contract marriages, and are united in pairs, and defend their nests, as though their marriage-beds, with harmonious mind, and cherish their own young, because they are well known to them; and if you put others in their way, they repel them. But this wise man, contrary to the custom of men, and contrary to nature, chose more foolish objects of imitation; and since he saw that the duties of males and females were not separated in the case of other animals, he thought that women also ought to engage in warfare, and take a share in the public counsels, and undertake magistracies, and assume commands.

And therefore he assigned to them horses and arms: it follows that he should have assigned to men wool and the loom, and the carrying of infants. Nor did he see the impossibility of what he said, from the fact that no nation has existed in the world so foolish or so vain as to live in this manner.

### Chap. XXIII.—Of the Errors of Certain Philosophers, and of the Sun and Moon.

Since, therefore, the leading men among the philosophers are themselves discovered to be of such emptiness, what shall we think of those lesser ones, who are accustomed never to appear to themselves so wise, as when they boast of their contempt of money? Brave spirit! But I wait to see their conduct, and what are the results of that contempt. They avoid as an evil, and abandon the property handed down to them from their parents. And lest they should suffer shipwreck in a storm, they plunge headlong of their own accord in a calm, being resolute not by virtue, but by perverse fear; as those who, through fear of being slain by the enemy, slay themselves, that by death they may avoid death. So these men, without honor and without influence, throw away the means by which they might have acquired the glory of liberality. Democritus is praised because he abandoned his fields, and suffered them to become public pastures. I should approve of it, if he had given them. But nothing is done wisely which is useless and evil if it is done by all. But this negligence is tolerable. What shall I say of him who changed his possessions into money, which he threw into the sea? I doubt whether he was in his senses, or deranged. Away, he says, ye evil desires, into the deep. I will cast you away, lest I myself should be cast away by you. If you have so great a contempt for money, employ it in acts of kindness and humanity, bestow it upon the poor; this, which you are about to throw away, may be a succor to many, so that they may not die through famine, or thirst, or nakedness. Imitate at least the madness and fury of Tuditanus; scatter abroad your property to be seized by the people. You have it in your power both to escape the possession of money, and yet to lay it out to advantage; for whatever has been profitable to many is securely laid out.

But who approves of the equality of faults as laid down by Zeno? But let us omit that which is always received with derision by all. This is sufficient to prove the error of this madman, that he places pity among vices and diseases. He deprives us of an affection, which involves almost the whole course of human life. For since the nature of man is more feeble than that of the other animals, which divine providence has armed with natural means of protection, either to endure the severity of the seasons or to ward off attacks from their bodies, because none of these things has been given to man, he has received in the place of all these things the affection of pity, which is truly called humanity, by which we might mutually protect each other. For if a man were rendered savage by the sight of another man, which we see happen in the case of those animals which are of a solitary nature, there would be no society among men, no care or system in the building of cities; and thus life would not even be safe, since the weakness of men would both be exposed to the attacks of the other animals, and they would rage among themselves after the manner of wild beasts. Nor is his madness less in other things.

For what can be said respecting him who asserted that snow was black? How naturally it followed, that he should also assert that pitch was white! This is he who said that he was born for this purpose, that he might behold the heaven and the sun, who beheld nothing on the earth when the sun was shining. Xenophanes most foolishly believed mathematicians who said that the orb of the moon was eighteen times larger than the earth; and, as was consistent with this folly, he said that within the concave surface of the moon there was another earth, and that there another race of men live in a similar manner to that in which we live on this earth. Therefore these lunatics have another moon, to hold forth to them a light by night, as this does to us. And perhaps this globe of ours may be a moon to another earth below this. Seneca says that there was one among the Stoics who used to deliberate whether he should assign to the sun also its own inhabitants; he acted foolishly in doubting. For what injury would he have inflicted if he had assigned them? But I believe the heat deterred him, so as not to imperil so great a multitude; lest, if they should perish through excessive heat, so great a calamity should be said to have happened by his fault.

**Chap. XXIV.—Of the Antipodes, the Heaven, and the Stars.**

How is it with those who imagine that there are antipodes opposite to our footsteps? Do they say anything to the purpose? Or is there any one so senseless as to believe that there are men whose footsteps are higher than their heads? Or that the things which with us are in a recumbent position, with them hang in an inverted direction? That the crops and trees grow downwards? That the rains, and snow, and hail fall upwards to the earth? And does anyone wonder that hanging gardens are mentioned among the Seven Wonders of the World, when philosophers make hanging fields, and seas, and cities, and mountains? The origin of this error must also be set forth by us. For they are always deceived in the same manner. For when they have assumed anything false in the commencement of their investigations, led by the resemblance of the truth, they necessarily fall into those things which are its consequences. Thus they fall into many ridiculous things; because those things which are in agreement with false things, must themselves be false. But since they placed confidence in the first, they do not consider the character of those things which follow, but defend them in every way; whereas they ought to judge from those which follow, whether the first are true or false.

What course of argument, therefore, led them to the idea of the antipodes? They saw the courses of the stars travelling towards the west; they saw that the sun and the moon always set towards the same quarter, and rise from the same. But since they did not perceive what contrivance regulated their courses, nor how they returned from the west to the east, but supposed that the heaven itself sloped downwards in every direction, which appearance it must present on account of its immense breadth, they thought that the world is round like a ball, and they fancied that the heaven revolves in accordance with the motion of the heavenly bodies; and thus that the stars and sun, when they have set, by the very rapidity of the motion of the world are borne back to the east. Therefore they both constructed brazen orbs, as though after the figure of the world, and engraved upon them certain monstrous images, which they said were constellations. It followed, therefore, from this rotundity of the heaven, that the earth was enclosed in the midst of its curved surface. But if this were so, the earth also it must be like a globe; for that could not possibly be anything but round, which was held enclosed by that which was round. But if the earth also were round, it must necessarily happen that it should present the same appearance to all parts of the heaven; that is, that it should raise aloft mountains, extend plains, and have level seas. And if this were so, that last consequence also followed, that there would be no part of the earth uninhabited by men and the other animals. Thus the rotundity of the earth leads, in addition, to the invention of those suspended antipodes.

But if you inquire from those who defend these marvelous fictions, why all things do not fall into that lower part of the heaven, they reply that such is the nature of things, that heavy bodies are borne to the middle, and that they are all joined together towards the middle, as we see spokes in a wheel; but that the bodies which are light, as mist, smoke, and fire, are borne away from the middle, so as to seek the heaven. I am at a loss what to say respecting those who, when they have once erred, consistently persevere in their folly, and defend one vain thing by another; but that I sometimes imagine that they either discuss philosophy for the sake of a jest, or purposely and knowingly undertake to defend falsehoods, as if to exercise or display their talents on false subjects. But I should be able to prove by many arguments that it is impossible for the heaven to be lower than the earth, were is not that this book must now be concluded, and that some things still remain, which are more necessary for the present work. And since it is not the work of a single book to run over the errors of each individually, let it be sufficient to have enumerated a few, from which the nature of the others may be understood.

## Chap. XXV.—Of Learning Philosophy, and What Great Qualifications are Necessary for Its Pursuit.

We must now speak a few things concerning philosophy in general, that having strengthened our cause we may conclude. That greatest imitator of Plato among our writers thought that philosophy was not for the multitude, because none but learned men could attain to it. "Philosophy," says Cicero, "is contented with a few judges, of its own accord designedly avoiding the multitude." It is not therefore wisdom, if it avoids the concourse of men; since, if wisdom is given to man, it is given to all without any distinction, so that there is no one at all who cannot acquire it. But they so embrace virtue, which is given to the human race, that they alone of all appear to wish to enjoy that which is a public good; being as envious as if they should wish to bind or tear out the eyes of others that they may not see the sun. For what else is it to deny wisdom to men, than to take away from their minds the true and divine light? But if the nature of man is capable of wisdom, it was befitting that both workmen, and country people, and women, and all, in short, who bear the human form, should be taught to be wise; and that the people should be brought together from every language, and condition, and sex, and age. Therefore it is a very strong argument that philosophy neither tends to wisdom, nor is of itself wisdom, that its mystery is only made known by the beard and cloak of the philosophers. The Stoics, moreover, perceived this, who said that philosophy was to be studied both by slaves and women; Epicurus also, who invites those who are altogether unacquainted with letters to philosophy; and Plato also, who wished to compose a state of wise men.

They attempted, indeed, to do that which truth required; but they were unable to proceed beyond words. First, because instruction in many arts is necessary for an application to philosophy. Common learning must be acquired on account of practice in reading, because in so great a variety of subjects it is impossible that all things should be learned by hearing, or retained in the memory. No little attention also must be given to the grammarians, in order that you may know the right method of speaking. That must occupy many years. Nor must there be ignorance of rhetoric, that you may be able to utter and express the things which you have learned. Geometry also, and music, and astronomy, are necessary, because these arts have some connection with philosophy; and the whole of these subjects cannot be learned by women, who must learn within the years of their maturity the duties which are hereafter about to be of service to them for domestic uses; nor by servants, who must live in service during those years especially in which they are able to learn; nor by the poor, or laborers, or rustics, who have to gain their daily support by labor. And on this account Tully says that philosophy is averse from the multitude. But yet Epicurus will receive the ignorant. How, then, will they understand those things which are said respecting the first principles of things, the perplexities and intricacies of which are scarcely attained to by men of cultivated minds?

Therefore, in subjects which are involved in obscurity, and confused by a variety of intellects, and set off by the studied language of eloquent men, what place is there for the unskillful and ignorant? Lastly, they never taught any women to study philosophy, except Themiste only, within the whole memory of man; nor slaves, except Phædo only, who is said, when living in oppressive slavery, to have been ransomed and taught by Cebes. They also enumerate Plato and Diogenes: these, however, were not slaves, though they had fallen into servitude, for they had been taken captive. A certain Aniceris is said to have ransomed

Plato for eight sesterces. And on this account Seneca severely rebuked the ransomer himself, because he set so small value upon Plato. He was a madman, as it seems to me, who was angry with a man because he did not throw away much money; doubtless he ought to have weighed gold as though to ransom the corpse of Hector, or to have insisted upon the payment of more money than the seller demanded. Moreover, they taught none of the barbarians, with the single exception of Anacharsis the Scythian, who never would have dreamed of philosophy had he not previously learned both language and literature.

## Chap. XXVI.—It is Divine Instruction Only Which Bestows Wisdom; And of What Efficacy the Law of God is.

That, therefore, which they perceived to be justly required by the demands of nature, but which they were themselves unable to perform, and saw that the philosophers could not effect, is accomplished only by divine instruction; for that only is wisdom. Doubtless they were able to persuade anyone who do not even persuade themselves of anything; or they will crush the desires, moderate the anger, and restrain the lusts of any one, when they themselves both yield to vices, and acknowledge that they are overpowered by nature. But what influence is exerted on the souls of men by the precepts of God, because of their simplicity and truth, is shown by daily proofs. Give me a man who is passionate, scurrilous, and unrestrained; with a very few words of God,

"I will render him as gentle as a sheep."

Give me one who is grasping, covetous, and tenacious; I will presently restore him to you liberal, and freely bestowing his money with full hands. Give me a man who is afraid of pain and death; he shall presently despise crosses, and fires, and the bull of Phalaris. Give me one who is lustful, an adulterer, a glutton; you shall presently see him sober, chaste, and temperate. Give me one who is cruel and bloodthirsty: that fury shall presently be changed into true clemency. Give me a man who is unjust, foolish, an evil-doer; forthwith he shall be just, and wise, and innocent: for by one laver all his wickedness shall be taken away. So great is the power of divine wisdom, that, when infused into the breast of man, by one impulse it once for all expels folly, which is the mother of faults, for the effecting of which there is no need of payment, or books, or nightly studies. These results are accomplished gratuitously, easily, and quickly, if only the ears are open and the breast thirsts for wisdom. Let no one fear: we do not sell water, nor offer the sun for a reward. The fountain of God, most abundant and most full, is open to all; and this heavenly light rises for all, as many as have eyes. Did any of the philosophers effect these things, or is he able to effect them if he wishes? For though they spend their lives in the study of philosophy, they are neither able to improve any other person nor themselves (if nature has presented any obstacle). Therefore their wisdom, doing its utmost, does not eradicate, but hide vices. But a few precepts of God so entirely change the whole man, and having put off the old man, render him new, that you would not recognize him as the same.

**Chap. XXVII.—How Little the Precepts of Philosophers Contribute to True Wisdom, Which You Will Find in Religion Only.**

What, then? Do they enjoin nothing similar? Yes, indeed, many things; and they frequently approach the truth. But those precepts have no weight, because they are human, and are without a greater, that is, that divine authority. No one therefore believes them, because the hearer imagines himself to be a man, just as he is, who enjoins them. Moreover, there is no certainty with them, nothing which proceeds from knowledge. But since all things are done by conjecture, and many differing and various things are brought forward, it is the part of a most foolish man to be willing to obey their precepts, since it is doubted whether they are true or false; and therefore no one obeys them, because no one wishes to labor for an uncertainty. The Stoics say that it is virtue which can alone produce a happy life. Nothing can be said with greater truth. But what if he shall be tormented, or afflicted with pain? Will it be possible for anyone to be happy in the hands of the executioners? But truly pain inflicted upon the body is the material of virtue; therefore he is not wretched even in tortures. Epicurus speaks much more strongly. The wise man, he says, is always happy; and even when shut up in the bull of Phalaris he will utter this speech: "It is pleasant, and I do not care for it." Who would not laugh at him? Especially, because a man who is devoted to pleasure took upon himself the character of a man of fortitude, and that to an immoderate degree; for it is impossible that anyone should esteem tortures of the body as pleasures, since it is sufficient for discharging the office of virtue that one sustains and endures them. What do you, Stoics, say? What do you, Epicurus? The wise man is happy even when he is tortured. If it is on account of the glory of his endurance, he will not enjoy it, for perchance he will die under the tortures. If it is on account of the recollection of the deed, either he will not perceive it if souls shall perish, or, if he shall perceive it, he will gain nothing from it.

What other advantage is there then in virtue? What happiness of life? Is it that a man may die with equanimity? You present to me the advantage of a single hour, or perhaps moment, for the sake of which it may not be expedient to be worn out by miseries and labors throughout the whole of life. But how much time does death occupy? On the arrival of which it now makes no difference whether you shall have undergone it with equanimity or not. Thus it happens that nothing is sought from virtue but glory. But this is either superfluous and short-lived, or it will not follow from the depraved judgments of men. Therefore there is no fruit from virtue where virtue is subject to death and decay. Therefore they who said these things saw a certain shadow of virtue; they did not see virtue itself. For they had their eyes fixed on the earth, nor did they raise their countenances on high that they might behold her

"Who showed herself from the quarters of heaven."

This is the reason why no one obeys their precepts; inasmuch as they either train men to vices, if they defend pleasure; or if they uphold virtue, they neither threaten sin with any punishment, except that of disgrace only, nor do they promise any reward to virtue, except that of honor and praise only, since they say that virtue is to be sought for its own sake, and not on account of any other object. The wise man therefore is happy under tortures; but when he suffers torture on account of his faith, on account of justice, or on account of God, that endurance of pain will render him most happy. For it is God alone who can honor virtue, the reward of which is immortality alone. And they who do not seek this, nor possess religion, with which eternal life is connected, assuredly do not know the power of virtue, the reward of which they are ignorant; nor look towards heaven, as they themselves imagine that they do, when they inquire into subjects which do not admit of investigation, since there is no other cause for looking towards heaven, unless it be either to undertake religion, or to believe that one's soul is immortal. For if any one understands that God is to be worshipped, or has the hope of immortality set before him, his mind is in heaven; and although he may not behold it with his eyes, yet he does behold it with the eye of his soul. But they who do not take up religion are of the earth, for religion is from heaven; and they who think that the soul perishes together with the body, equally look down towards the earth: for beyond the body, which is earth, they see nothing further, which is immortal. It is therefore of no profit that man is so made, that with upright body he looks towards heaven, unless with mind raised aloft he discerns God, and his thoughts are altogether engaged upon the hope of everlasting life.

## Chap. XXVIII.—Of True Religion and of Nature. Whether Fortune is a Goddess, and of Philosophy.

Wherefore there is nothing else in life on which our plan and condition can depend but the knowledge of God who created us, and the religious and pious worship of Him; and since the philosophers have wandered from this, it is plain that they were not wise. They sought wisdom, indeed; but because they did not seek it in a right manner, they sunk down to a greater distance, and fell into such great errors, that they did not even possess common wisdom. For they were not only unwilling to maintain religion, but they even took it away; while, led on by the appearance of false virtue, they endeavor to free the mind from all fear: and this overturning of religion gains the name of nature. For they, either being ignorant by whom the world was made, or wishing to persuade men that nothing was completed by divine intelligence, said that nature was the mother of all things, as though they should say that all things were produced of their own accord: by which word they altogether confess their own ignorance. For nature, apart from divine providence and power, is absolutely nothing. But if they call God nature, what perverseness is it, to use the name of nature rather than of God! But if nature is the plan, or necessity, or condition of birth, it is not by itself capable of sensation; but there must necessarily be a divine mind, which by its foresight furnishes the beginning of their existence to all things. Or if nature is heaven and earth, and everything which is created, nature is not God, but the work of God.

By a similar error they believe in the existence of fortune, as a goddess mocking the affairs of then with various casualties, because they know not from what source things good and evil happen to them. They think that they are brought together to do battle with her; nor do they assign any reason by whom and on what account they are thus matched; but they only boast that they are every moment carrying on a contest for life and death with fortune. Now, as many as have consoled any persons on account of the death and removal of friends, have censured the name of fortune with the most severe accusations; nor is there any disputation of theirs on the subject of virtue, in which fortune is not harassed. M. Tullius, in his *Consolation*, says that he has always fought against fortune, and that she was always overpowered by him when he had valiantly beaten back the attacks of his enemies; that he was not subdued by her even then, when he was driven from his home and deprived of his country; but then, when he lost his dearest daughter, he shamefully confesses that he is overcome by fortune. I yield, he says, and raise my hand. What is more wretched than this man, who thus lies prostrate? He acts foolishly, he says; but it is one who professes that he is wise. What, then, does the assumption of the name imply? What that contempt of things which is laid claim to with magnificent words? What that dress, so different from others? Or why do you give precepts of wisdom at all, if no one has yet been found who is wise? And does anyone bear ill-will to us because we deny that philosophers are wise, when they themselves confess that they neither have knowledge nor wisdom? For if at any time they have so failed that they are not even able to feign anything, as their practice is in other cases, then in truth they are reminded of their ignorance; and, as though in madness, they spring up and exclaim that they are blind and foolish. Anaxagoras pronounces that all things are overspread with darkness. Empedocles complains that the paths of the senses are narrow, as though for his reflections he had need of a chariot and four horses. Democritus says that the truth lies sunk in a well so deep that it has no bottom; foolishly, indeed, as he says other things. For the truth is not, as it were, sunk in a well to which it was permitted him to descend, or even to fall, but, as it were, placed on the highest top of a lofty mountain, or in heaven, which is most true. For what reason is there why he should say that it is sunk below rather than that it is raised aloft? Unless by chance he preferred to place the mind also in the feet, or in the bottom of the heels, rather than in the breast or in the head.

So widely removed were they from the truth itself, that even the posture of their own body did not admonish them, that the truth must be sought for by them in the highest place. From this despair arose that confession of Socrates, in which he said that he knew nothing but this one thing alone, that he knew nothing. From this flowed the system of the Academy, if that is to be called a system in which ignorance is both learnt and taught. But not even those who claimed for themselves knowledge were able consistently to defend that very thing which they thought that they knew. For since they were not in agreement with one another, through their ignorance of divine things they were so inconsistent and uncertain, and often asserting things contrary to one another, that you are unable to determine and decide what their meaning was. Why therefore should you fight against those men who perish by their own sword? Why should you labor to refute those whom their own speech refutes and presses? Aristotle, says Cicero, accusing the ancient philosophers, declares that they are either most foolish or most vainglorious, since they thought that philosophy was perfected by their talents; but that he saw, because a great addition had been made in a few years, that philosophy would be complete in a short time. What, then, was that time? In what manner, when, or by whom, was philosophy completed? For that which he said, that they were most foolish in supposing that philosophy was made perfect by their talents, is true; but he did not even himself speak with sufficient discretion, who thought that it had either been begun by the ancients, or increased by those who were more recent, or that it would shortly be brought to perfection by those of later times. For that can never be investigated which is not sought by its own way.

### Chap. XXIX.—Of Fortune Again, and Virtue.

But let us return to the subject which we laid aside. Fortune, therefore, by itself, is nothing; nor must we so regard it as though it had any perception, since fortune is the sudden and unexpected occurrence of accidents. But philosophers, that they may not sometimes fail to err, wish to be wise in a foolish matter; and say that she is not a goddess, as is generally believed, but a god. Sometimes, however, they call this god nature, sometimes fortune, "because he brings about," says the same Cicero, "many things unexpected by us, on account of our want of intelligence and our ignorance of causes." Since, therefore, they are ignorant of the causes on account of which anything is done, they must also be ignorant of him who does them. The same writer, in a work of great seriousness, in which he was giving to his son precepts of life drawn from philosophy, says, "Who can be ignorant that the power of fortune is great on either side? For both when we meet with a prosperous breeze from her we gain the issues which we desire, and when she has breathed contrary to us we are dashed on the rocks." First of all, he who says that nothing can be known, spoke this as though he himself and all men had knowledge. Then he who endeavors to render doubtful even the things which are plain, thought that this was plain, which ought to have been to him especially doubtful; for to a wise man it is altogether false. Who, he says, knows not? I indeed know not. Let him teach me, if he can, what that power is, what that breeze, and what the contrary breath.

It is disgraceful, therefore, for a man of talent to say that, which if you were to deny it, he would be unable to prove. Lastly, he who says that the assent must be withheld because it is the part of a foolish man rashly to assent to things which are unknown to him, he, I say, altogether believed the opinions of the vulgar and uninstructed, who think that it is fortune which gives to men good and evil things. For they represent her image with the horn of plenty and with a rudder, as though she both gave wealth and had the government of human affairs. And to this opinion Virgil assented, who calls fortune omnipotent; and the historian who says, But assuredly fortune bears sway in everything. What place, then, remains for the other gods? Why is she not said to reign by herself, if she has more power than others; or why is she not alone worshipped, if she has power in all things? Or if she inflicts evils only, let them bring forward some cause why, if she is a goddess, she envies men, and desires their destruction, though she is religiously worshipped by them; why she is more favorable to the wicked and more unfavorable to the good; why she plots, afflicts, deceives, exterminates; who appointed her as the perpetual harasser of the race of men; why, in short, she has obtained so mischievous a power, that she renders all things illustrious or obscure according to her caprice rather than in accordance with the truth. Philosophers, I say, ought rather to have inquired into these things, than rashly to have accused fortune, who is innocent: for although she has some existence, yet no reason can be brought forward by them why she should be as hostile to men as she is supposed to be. Therefore all those speeches in which they rail at the injustice of fortune, and in opposition to fortune arrogantly boast of their own virtues, are nothing else but the ravings of thoughtless levity.

Wherefore let them not envy us, to whom God has revealed the truth: who, as we know that fortune is nothing, so also know that there is a wicked and crafty spirit who is unfriendly to the good, and the enemy of righteousness, who acts in opposition to God; the cause of whose enmity we have explained in the second book. He therefore lays plots against all; but those who are ignorant of God he hinders by error, he overwhelms with folly, he overspreads with darkness, that no one may be able to attain to the knowledge of the divine name, in which alone are contained both wisdom and everlasting life. Those, on the other hand, who know God, he assails with wiles and craft, that he may ensnare them with desire and lust, and when they are corrupted by the blandishments of sin, may impel them to death; or, if he shall have not succeeded by stratagem, he attempts to cast them down by force and violence. For on this account he was not at once thrust down by God to punishment at the original transgression, that by his malice he may exercise man to virtue: for unless this is in constant agitation, unless it is strengthened by continual harassing, it cannot be perfect, inasmuch as virtue is dauntless and unconquered patience in enduring evils. From which it comes to pass that there is no virtue if an adversary is wanting. When, therefore, they perceived the force of this perverse power opposed to virtue, and were ignorant of its name, they invented for themselves the senseless name of fortune; and how far this is removed from wisdom, Juvenal declares in these verses:—

"No divine power is absent if there is prudence; but we make you a goddess, O Fortune, and place you in heaven."

It was folly, therefore, and error, and blindness, and, as Cicero says, ignorance of facts and causes, which introduced the names of Nature and Fortune. But as they are ignorant of their adversary, so also they do not indeed know virtue the knowledge of which is derived from the idea of an adversary. And if this is joined with wisdom, or, as they say, is itself also wisdom, they must be ignorant in what subjects it is contained. For no one can possibly be furnished with true arms if he is ignorant of the enemy against whom he must be armed; nor can he overcome his adversary, who in fighting does not attack his real enemy, but a shadow. For he will be overthrown, who, having his attention fixed on another object, shall not previously have foreseen or guarded against the blow aimed at his vitals.

**Chap. XXX.—The Conclusion of the Things Before Spoken; And by What Means We Must Pass from the Vanity of the Philosophers to True Wisdom, and the Knowledge of the True God, in Which Alone are Virtue and Happiness.**

I have taught, as far as my humble talents permitted, that the philosophers held a course widely deviating from the truth. I perceive, however, how many things I have omitted, because it was not my province to enter into a disputation against philosophers. But it was necessary for me to make a digression to this subject, that I might show that so many and great intellects have expended themselves in vain on false subjects, lest anyone by chance being shut out by corrupt superstitions, should wish to betake himself to them as though about to find some certainty. Therefore the only hope, the only safety for man, is placed in this doctrine, which we defend. All the wisdom of man consists in this alone, the knowledge and worship of God: this is our tenet, this our opinion. Therefore with all the power of my voice I testify, I proclaim, I declare: Here, here is that which all philosophers have sought throughout their whole life; and yet, they have not been able to investigate, to grasp, and to attain to it, because they either retained a religion which was corrupt, or took it away altogether. Let them therefore all depart, who do not instruct human life, but throw it into confusion. For what do they teach? Or whom do they instruct, who have not yet instructed themselves? Whom are the sick able to heal, whom can the blind guide? Let us all, therefore, who have any regard for wisdom, betake ourselves to this subject. Or shall we wait until Socrates knows something? Or Anaxagoras finds light in the darkness? Or until Democritus draws forth truth from the well? Or Empedocles extends the paths of his soul? Or until Arcesilas and Carneades see, and feel, and perceive?

Lo, a voice from heaven teaching the truth, and displaying to us a light brighter than the sun itself. Why are we unjust to ourselves, and delay to take up wisdom, which learned men, though they wasted their lives in its pursuit, were never able to discover. Let him who wishes to be wise and happy hear the voice of God, learn righteousness, understand the mystery of his birth, despise human affairs, embrace divine things, that he may gain that chief good to which he was born. Having overthrown all false religions, and having refuted all the arguments, as many as it was customary or possible to bring forward in their defense; then, having proved the systems of philosophy to be false, we must now come to true religion and wisdom, since, as I shall teach, they are both connected together; that we may maintain it either by arguments, or by examples, or by competent witnesses, and may show that the folly with which those worshippers of gods do not cease to upbraid us, has no existence with us, but lies altogether with them. And although, in the former books, when I was contending against false religions, and in this, when I was overthrowing false wisdom, I showed where the truth is, yet the next book will more plainly indicate what is true religion and what true wisdom.

# The divine institutes

## Book IV.

## Of True Wisdom and Religion.

### Chap. I.—Of the Former Religion of Men, and How Error Was Spread Over Every Age, and of the Seven Wise Men of Greece.

When I reflect, O Emperor Constantine, and often revolve in my mind the original condition of men, it is accustomed to appear alike wonderful and unworthy that, by the folly of one age embracing various superstitions, and believing in the existence of many gods, they suddenly arrived at such ignorance of themselves, that the truth being taken away from their eyes, the religion of the true God was not observed, nor the condition of human nature, since men did not seek the chief good in heaven, but on earth. And on this account assuredly the happiness of the ancient ages was changed. For, having left God, the parent and founder of all things, men began to worship the senseless works of their own hands. And what were the effects of this corruption, or what evils it introduced, the subject itself sufficiently declares. For, turning away from the chief good, which is blessed and everlasting on this account, because it cannot be seen, or touched, or comprehended, and from the virtues which are in agreement with that good, and which are equally immortal, gliding down to these corrupt and frail gods, and devoting themselves to those things by which the body only is adorned, and nourished, and delighted, they sought eternal death for themselves, together with their gods and goods relating to the body, because all bodies are subject to death. Superstitions of this kind, therefore, were followed by injustice and impiety, as must necessarily be the case. For men ceased to raise their countenances to the heaven; but, their minds being depressed downwards, clung to goods of the earth, as they did to earth-born superstitions. There followed the disagreement of mankind, and fraud, and all wickedness; because, despising eternal and incorruptible goods, which alone ought to be desired by man, they rather chose temporal and short-lived things, and greater trust was placed by men in evil, inasmuch as they preferred vice to virtue, because it had presented itself as nearer at hand.

Thus human life, which in former ages had been occupied with the clearest light, was overspread with gloom and darkness; and in conformity with this depravity, when wisdom was taken away, then at length men began to claim for themselves the name of wise. For at the time when all were wise, no one was called by that name. And would that this name, once common to all the class, though reduced to a few, still retained its power! For those few might perhaps be able, either by talent, or by authority, or by continual exhortations, to free the people from vices and errors. But so entirely had wisdom died out, that it is evident, from the very arrogance of the name, that no one of those who were so called was really wise. And yet, before the discovery of this philosophy, as it is termed, there are said to have been seven, who, because they ventured to inquire into and discuss natural subjects, deserved to be esteemed and called wise men.

O wretched and calamitous age, in which through the whole world there were only seven who were called by the name of men, for no one can justly be called a man unless he is wise! But if all the others besides themselves were foolish, even they themselves were not wise, because no one can be truly wise in the judgment of the foolish. So far were they removed from wisdom, that not even afterwards, when learning increased, and many and great intellects were always intent upon this very subject, could the truth be perceived and ascertained. For, after the renown of those seven wise men, it is incredible with how great a desire of inquiring into the truth all Greece was inflamed. And first of all, they thought the very name of wisdom arrogant, and did not call themselves wise men, but desirous of wisdom. By which deed they both condemned those who had rashly arrogated to themselves the name of wise men, of error and folly, and themselves also of ignorance, which indeed they did not deny. For wherever the nature of the subject had, as it were, laid its hands upon their minds, so that they were unable to give any account, they were accustomed to testify that, they knew nothing, and discerned nothing. Wherefore they are found to be much wiser, who in some degree saw themselves, than those who had believed that they were wise.

## Chap. II.—Where Wisdom is to Be Found; Why Pythagoras and Plato Did Not Approach the Jews.

Wherefore, if they were not wise who were so called, nor those of later times, who did not hesitate to confess their want of wisdom, what remains but that wisdom is to be sought elsewhere, since it has not been found where it was sought. But what can we supposed to have been the reason why it was not found, though sought with the greatest earnestness and labor by so many intellects, and during so many ages, unless it be that philosophers sought for it out of their own limits? And since they traversed and explored all parts, but nowhere found any wisdom, and it must of necessity be somewhere, it is evident that it ought especially to be sought there where the title of folly appears; under the covering of which God hides the treasury of wisdom and truth, lest the secret of His divine work should be exposed to view. Whence I am accustomed to wonder that, when Pythagoras, and after him Plato, inflamed with the love of searching out the truth, had penetrated as far as to the Egyptians, and Magi, and Persians, that they might become acquainted with their religious rites and institutions (for they suspected that wisdom was concerned with religion), they did not approach the Jews only, in whose possession alone it then was, and to whom they might have gone more easily. But I think that they were turned away from them by divine providence, that they might not know the truth, because it was not yet permitted for the religion of the true God and righteousness to become known to men of other nations. For God had determined, as the last time drew near, to send from heaven a great leader, who should reveal to foreign nations that which was taken away from a perfidious and ungrateful people. And I will endeavor to discuss the subject in this book, if I shall first have shown that wisdom is so closely united with religion, that the one cannot be separated from the other.

## Chap. III.—Wisdom and Religion Cannot Be Separated: the Lord of Nature Must Necessarily Be the Father of Every One.

The worship of the gods, as I have taught in the former book, does not imply wisdom; not only because it gives up man, who is a divine animal, to earthly and frail things, but because nothing is fixed in it which may avail for the cultivation of the character and the framing of the life; nor does it contain any investigation of the truth, but only the rite of worship, which does not consist in the service of the mind, but in the employment of the body. And therefore that is not to be deemed true religion, because it instructs and improves men by no precepts of righteousness and virtue. Thus philosophy, inasmuch as it does not possess true religion, that is, the highest piety, is not true wisdom. For if the divinity which governs this world supports mankind with incredible beneficence, and cherishes it as with paternal indulgence, wishes truly that gratitude should be paid, and honor given to itself, man cannot preserve his piety if he shall prove ungrateful for the heavenly benefits; and this is certainly not the part of a wise man. Since, therefore, as I have said, philosophy and the religious system of the gods are separated, and far removed from each other; seeing that some are professors of wisdom, through whom it is manifest that there is no approach to the gods, and that others are priests of religion, through whom wisdom is not learned; it is manifest that the one is not true wisdom, and that the other is not true religion. Therefore philosophy was not able to conceive the truth, nor was the religious system of the gods able to give an account of itself, since it is without it. But where wisdom is joined by an inseparable connection with religion, both must necessarily be true; because in our worship we ought to be wise, that is, to know the proper object and mode of worship, and in our wisdom to worship, that is, to complete our knowledge by deed and action.

Where, then, is wisdom joined with religion? There, indeed, where the one God is worshipped, where life and every action is referred to one source, and to one supreme authority: in short, the teachers of wisdom are the same, who are also the priests of God. Nor, however, let it affect any one, because it often has happened, and may happen, that some philosopher may undertake a priesthood of the gods; and when this happens, philosophy is not, however, joined with religion; but philosophy will both be unemployed amidst sacred rites, and religion will be unemployed when philosophy shall be treated of. For that system of religious rites is dumb, not only because it relates to gods who are dumb, but also because its observance is by the hand and the fingers, not by the heart and tongue, as is the case with ours, which is true. Therefore religion is contained in wisdom, and wisdom in religion. The one, then, cannot be separated from the other; because wisdom is nothing else but the worship of the true God with just and pious adoration. But that the worship of many gods is not in accordance with nature, may be inferred and conceived even by this argument: that every god who is worshipped by man must, amidst the solemn rites and prayers, be invoked as father, not only for the sake of honor, but also of reason; because he is both more ancient than man, and because he affords life, safety, and sustenance, as a father does. Therefore Jupiter is called father by those who pray to him, as is Saturnus, and Janus, and Liber, and the rest in order; which Lucilius laughs at in the council of the gods: "So that there is none of us who is not called excellent father of the gods; so that father Neptunus, Liber, father Saturnus, Mars, Janus, father Quirinus, are called after one name." But if nature does not permit that one man should have many fathers (for he is produced from one only), therefore the worship of many gods is contrary to nature, and contrary to piety.

One only, therefore, is to be worshipped, who can truly be called Father. He also must of necessity be Lord, because as He has power to indulge, so also has He power to restrain. He is to be called Father on this account, because He bestows upon us many and great things; and Lord on this account, because He has the greatest power of chastising and punishing. But that He who is Father is also Lord, is shown even by reference to civil law. For who will be able to bring up sons, unless he has the power of a lord over them? Nor without reason is he called father of a household, although he only has sons: for it is plain that the name of father embraces also slaves, because "household" follows; and the name of "household" comprises also sons, because the name of "father" precedes: from which it is evident, that the same person is both father of his slaves and lord of his sons. Lastly, the son is set at liberty as if he were a slave; and the liberated slave receives the name of his patron, as if he were a son. But if a man is named father of a household, that it may appear that he is possessed of a double power, because as a father he ought to indulge, and as a lord to restrain, it follows that he who is a son is also a slave, and that he who is a father is also a lord. As, therefore, by the necessity of nature, there cannot be more than one father, so there can only be one lord. For what will the slave do if many lords shall give commands at variance with each other? Therefore the worship of many gods is contrary to reason and to nature, since there cannot be many fathers or lords; but it is necessary to consider the gods both as fathers and lords.

Therefore the truth cannot be held where the same man is subject to many fathers and lords, where the mind, drawn in different directions to many objects, wanders to and fro, hither and thither. Nor can religion have any firmness, when it is without a fixed and settled dwelling-place. Therefore there can be no true worship of many gods; just as that cannot be called matrimony, in which one woman has many husbands, but she will either be called a harlot or an adulteress. For when a woman is destitute of modesty, chastity, and fidelity, she must of necessity be without virtue. Thus also the religious system of the gods is unchaste and unholy, because it is destitute of faith, for that unsettled and uncertain honor has no source or origin.

## Chapter IV.—Of Wisdom Likewise, and Religion, and of the Right of Father and Lord.

By these things it is evident how closely connected are wisdom and religion. Wisdom relates to sons, and this relation requires love; religion to servants, and this relation requires fear. For as the former are bound to love and honor their father, so are the latter bound to respect and venerate their lord. But with respect to God, who is one only, inasmuch as He sustains the twofold character both of Father and Lord, we are bound both to love Him, inasmuch as we are sons, and to fear Him, inasmuch as we are servants. Religion, therefore, cannot be divided from wisdom, nor can wisdom be separated from religion; because it is the same God, who ought to be understood, which is the part of wisdom, and to be honored, which is the part of religion. But wisdom precedes, religion follows; for the knowledge of God comes first, His worship is the result of knowledge. Thus in the two names there is but one meaning, though it seems to be different in each case. For the one is concerned with the understanding, the other with action. But, however, they resemble two streams flowing from one fountain. But the fountain of wisdom and religion is God; and if these two streams shall turn aside from Him, they must be dried up: for they who are ignorant of Him cannot be wise or religious.

Thus it comes to pass that philosophers, and those who worship *many* gods, either resemble disinherited sons or runaway slaves, because the one do not seek their father, nor the other their master. And as they who are disinherited do not attain to the inheritance of their father, nor runaway slaves impunity, so neither will philosophers receive immortality, which is the inheritance of the heavenly kingdom, that is, the chief good, which they especially seek; nor will the worshippers of gods escape the penalty of everlasting death, which is the punishment of the true Master against those who are deserters of His majesty and name. But that God is Father and also Lord was unknown to both, to the worshippers of the gods as well as to the professors of wisdom themselves: inasmuch as they either thought that nothing at all was to be worshipped; or they approved of false religions; or, although they understood the strength and power of the Supreme God (as Plato, who says that there is one God, Creator of the world, and Marcus Tullius, who acknowledges that man has been produced by the Supreme God in an excellent condition), nevertheless they did not render the worship due to Him as to the supreme Father, which was their befitting and necessary duty. But that the gods cannot be fathers or lords, is declared not only by their multitude, as I have shown above, but also by reason: because it is not reported that man was made by gods, nor is it found that the gods themselves preceded the origin of man, since it appears that there were men on the earth before the birth of Vulcan, and Liber, and Apollo, and Jupiter himself. But the creation of man is not accustomed to be assigned to Saturnus, nor to his father Coelus.

But if none of those who are worshipped is said to have originally formed and created man, it follows that none of these can be called the father of man, and so none of them can be God. Therefore it is not lawful to worship those by whom man was not produced, for he could not be produced by many. Therefore the one and only God ought to be worshipped, who was before Jupiter, and Saturnus, and Coelus himself, and the earth. For He must have fashioned man, who, before the creation of man, finished the heaven and the earth. He alone is to be called Father who created us; He alone is to be considered Lord who rules, who has the true and perpetual power of life and death. And he who does not adore Him is a foolish servant, who flees from or does not know his Master; and an undutiful son, who either hates or is ignorant of his true Father.

### Chap. V.—The Oracles of the Prophets Must Be Looked Into; And of Their Times, and the Times of the Judges and Kings.

Now, since I have shown that wisdom and religion cannot be separated, it remains that we speak of religion itself, and wisdom. I am aware, indeed, how difficult it is to discuss heavenly subjects; but still the attempt must be ventured, that the truth may be made clear and brought to light, and that many may be freed from error and death, who despise and refuse the truth, while it is concealed under a covering of folly. But before I begin to speak of God and His works, I must first speak a few things concerning the prophets, whose testimony I must now use, which I have refrained from doing in the former books. Above all things, he who desires to comprehend the truth ought not only to apply his mind to understand the utterances of the prophets, but also most diligently to inquire into the times during which each one of them existed, that he may know what future events they predicted, and after how many years their predictions were fulfilled. Nor is there any difficulty in making these computations; for they testified under what king each of them received the inspiration of the Divine Spirit. And many have written and published books respecting the times, making their commencement from the prophet Moses, who lived about seven hundred years before the Trojan War. But he, when he had governed the people for forty years, was succeeded by Joshua, who held the chief place twenty-seven years.

After this they were under the government of judges during *three hundred and seventy* years. Then their condition was changed, and they began to have kings; and when they had ruled during *four hundred and fifty years*, until the reign of Zedekiah, the Jews having been besieged by the king of Babylon, and carried into captivity, endured a long servitude, until, in the seventieth year afterwards, the captive Jews were restored to their own lands and settlements by Cyrus the elder, who attained the supreme power over the Persians, at the time when Tarquinius Superbus reigned at Rome. Wherefore, since the whole series of times may be collected both from the Jewish histories and from those of the Greeks and Romans, the times of the prophets individually may also be collected; the last of whom was Zechariah, and it is agreed on that he prophesied in the time of King Darius, in the second year of his reign, and in the eighth month. Of so much greater antiquity are the prophets found to be than the Greek writers. And I bring forward all these things that they may perceive their error who endeavor to refute Holy Scripture, as though it were new and recently composed, being ignorant from what fountain the origin of our holy religion flowed. But if anyone, having put together and examined the times, shall duly lay the foundation of learning, and fully ascertain the truth, he will also lay aside his error when he has gained the knowledge of the truth.

**Chap. VI.—Almighty God Begat His Son; And the Testimonies of the Sibyls and of Trismegistus Concerning Him.**

God, therefore, the contriver and founder of all things, as we have said in the second book, before He commenced this excellent work of the world, begat a pure and incorruptible Spirit, whom He called His Son. And although He had afterwards created by Himself innumerable other beings, whom we call angels, this first-begotten, however, was the only one whom He considered worthy of being called by the divine name, as being powerful in His Father's excellence and majesty. But that there is a Son of the Most High God, who is possessed of the greatest power, is shown not only by the unanimous utterances of the prophets, but also by the declaration of Trismegistus and the predictions of the Sibyls. Hermes, in the book which is entitled *The Perfect Word*, made use of these words: "The Lord and Creator of all things, whom we have thought right to call God, since He made the second God visible and sensible. But I use the term sensible, not because He Himself perceives (for the question is not whether He Himself perceives), but because He leads to perception and to intelligence. Since, therefore, He made Him first, and alone, and one only, He appeared to Him beautiful, and most full of all good things; and He hallowed Him, and altogether loved Him as His own Son." The Erythræan Sibyl, in the beginning of her poem, which she commenced with the Supreme God, proclaims the Son of God as the leader and commander of all, in these verses:—

"The nourisher and creator of all things, who placed the sweet breath in all, and made God the leader of all."

And again, at the end of the same poem:—

"But whom God gave for faithful men to honor."

And another Sibyl enjoins that He ought to be known:—

"Know Him as your God, who is the Son of God."

Assuredly He is the very Son of God, who by that most wise King Solomon, full of divine inspiration, spoke these things which we have added: "God founded me in the beginning of His ways, in His work before the ages. He set me up in the beginning, before He made the earth, and before He established the depths, before the fountains of waters came forth: the Lord begat me before all the hills; He made the regions, and the uninhabitable boundaries under the heaven. When He prepared the heaven, I was by Him: and when He separated His own seat, when He made the strong clouds above the winds, and when He strengthened the mountains, and placed them under heaven; when He laid the strong foundations of the earth, I was with Him arranging all things. I was He in whom He delighted: I was daily delighted, when He rejoiced, the world being completed." But on this account Trismegistus spoke of Him as "the artificer of God," and the Sibyl calls Him "Counsellor," because He is endowed by God the Father with such wisdom and strength, that God employed both His wisdom and hands in the creation of the world.

### Chap. VII.—Of the Name of Son, and Whence He is Called Jesus and Christ.

Someone may perhaps ask who this is who is so powerful, so beloved by God, and what name He has, who was not only begotten at first before the world, but who also arranged it by His wisdom and constructed it by His might. First of all, it is befitting that we should know that His name is not known even to the angels who dwell in heaven, but to Himself only, and to God the Father; nor will that name be published, as the sacred writings relate, before that the purpose of God shall be fulfilled. In the next place, we must know that this name cannot be uttered by the mouth of man, as Hermes teaches, saying these things: "Now the cause of this cause is the will of the divine good which produced God, whose name cannot be uttered by the mouth of man." And shortly afterwards to His Son: "There is, O Son, a secret word of wisdom, holy respecting the only Lord of all things, and the God first perceived by the mind, to speak of whom is beyond the power of man." But although His name, which the supreme Father gave Him from the beginning, is known to none but Himself, nevertheless He has one name among the angels, and another among men, since He is called Jesus among men: for Christ is not a proper name, but a title of power and dominion; for by this the Jews were accustomed to call their kings. But the meaning of this name must be set forth, on account of the error of the ignorant, who by the change of a letter are accustomed to call Him Chrestus. The Jews had before been directed to compose a sacred oil, with which those who were called to the priesthood or to the kingdom might be anointed. And as now the robe of purple is a sign of the assumption of royal dignity among the Romans, so with them the anointing with the holy oil conferred the title and power of king. But since the ancient Greeks used the word χρίεσθαι to express the art of anointing, which they now express by ἀλείφεσθαι, as the verse of Homer shows,

"But the attendants washed, and anointed them with oil;"

on this account we call Him Christ, that is, the Anointed, who in Hebrew is called the Messias. Hence in some Greek writings, which are badly translated from the Hebrew, the word eleimmenos is found written, from the word aleiphesthai, anointing. But, however, by either name a king is signified: not that He has obtained this earthly kingdom, the time for receiving which has not yet arrived, but that He sways a heavenly and eternal kingdom, concerning which we shall speak in the last book. But now let us speak of His first nativity.

**Chap. VIII.—Of the Birth of Jesus in the Spirit and in the Flesh: of Spirits and the Testimonies of Prophets.**

For we especially testify that He was twice born, first in the spirit, and afterwards in the flesh. Whence it is thus spoken by Jeremiah: "Before I formed Thee in the womb I knew Thee." And likewise by the same: "Who was blessed before He was born;" which was the case with no one else but Christ. For though He was the Son of God from the beginning, He was born again a second time according to the flesh: and this twofold birth of His has introduced great terror into the minds of men, and overspread with darkness even those who retained the mysteries of true religion. But we will show this plainly and clearly, that they who love wisdom may be more easily and diligently instructed. He who hears the Son of God mentioned ought not to conceive in his mind so great impiety as to think that God begat Him by marriage and union with a woman, which none does but an animal possessed of a body, and subject to death. But with whom could God unite Himself, since He is alone? Or since His power was so great, that He accomplished whatever He wished, assuredly He did not require the co-operation of another for procreation. Unless by chance we shall [profanely] imagine, as Orpheus supposed, that God is both male and female, because otherwise He would have been unable to beget, unless He had the power of each sex, as though He could have intercourse with Himself, or without such intercourse be unable to produce.

But Hermes also was of the same opinion, when he says that He was "His own father," and "His own mother." But if this were so, as He is called by the prophets father, so also He would be called mother. In what manner, then, did He beget Him? First of all, divine operations cannot be known or declared by anyone; but nevertheless the sacred writings teach us, in which it is laid down that this Son of God is the speech, or even the reason of God, and also that the other angels are spirits of God. For speech is breath sent forth with a voice signifying something. But, however, since breath and speech are sent forth from different parts, inasmuch as breath proceeds from the nostrils, speech from the mouth, the difference between the Son of God and the other angels is great. For they proceeded from God as silent spirits, because they were not created to teach the knowledge of God, but for His service. But though He is Himself also a spirit, yet He proceeded from the mouth of God with voice and sound, as the Word, on this account indeed, because He was about to make use of His voice to the people; that is, because He was about to be a teacher of the knowledge of God, and of the heavenly mystery to be revealed to man: which word also God Himself first spoke, that through Him He might speak to us, and that He might reveal to us the voice and will of God.

With good reason, therefore, is He called the Speech and the Word of God, because God, by a certain incomprehensible energy and power of His majesty, enclosed the vocal spirit proceeding from His mouth, which he had not conceived in the womb, but in His mind, within a form which has life through its own perception and wisdom, and He also fashioned other spirits of His into angels. Our spirits are liable to dissolution, because we are mortal: but the spirits of God both live, and are lasting, and have perception; because He Himself is immortal, and the Giver both of perception and life. Our expressions, although they are mingled with the air, and fade away, yet generally remain comprised in letters; how much more must we believe that the voice of God both remains forever, and is accompanied with perception and power, which it has derived from God the Father, as a stream from its fountain! But if any one wonders that God could be produced from God by a putting forth of the voice and breath, if he is acquainted with the sacred utterances of the prophets he will cease to wonder. That Solomon and his father David were most powerful kings, and also prophets, may perhaps be known even to those who have not applied themselves to the sacred writings; the one of whom, who reigned subsequently to the other, preceded the destruction of the city of Troy by *one hundred and forty* years. His father, the writer of sacred hymns, thus speaks in the thirty-second Psalm: "By the word of God were the heavens made firm; and all their power by the breath of His mouth." And also again in the forty-fourth Psalm: "My heart hath given utterance to a good word; I speak of my doings towards the king;" testifying, in truth, that the works of God are known to no other than to the Son alone, who is the Word of God, and who must reign forever. Solomon also shows that it is the Word of God, and no other, by whose hands these works of the world were made. "I," He says, "came forth out of the mouth of the Most High before all creatures: I caused the light that failed not to arise in the heavens, and covered the whole earth with a cloud. I have dwelt in the height, and my throne is in the pillar of the cloud." John also thus taught: "In the beginning was the Word, and the Word was with God, and the Word was God. The same was in the beginning with God. All things were made by Him, and without Him was not anything made."

### Chap. IX.—Of the Word of God.

But the Greeks speak of Him as the Logos, more befittingly than we do as the word, or speech: for Logos signifies both speech and reason, inasmuch as He is both the voice and the wisdom of God. And of this divine speech not even the philosophers were ignorant, since Zeno represents the Logos as the arranger of the established order of things, and the framer of the universe: whom also He calls Fate, and the necessity of things, and God, and the soul of Jupiter, in accordance with the custom, indeed, by which they are wont to regard Jupiter as God. But the words are no obstacle, since the sentiment is in agreement with the truth. For it is the spirit of God which he named the soul of Jupiter. For Trismegistus, who by some means or other searched into almost all truth, often described the excellence and majesty of the word, as the instance before mentioned declares, in which he acknowledges that there is an ineffable and sacred speech, the relation of which exceeds the measure of man's ability. I have spoken briefly, as I have been able, concerning the first nativity. Now I must more fully discuss the second, since this is the subject most controverted, that we may hold forth the light of understanding to those who desire to know the truth.

**Chap. X.—Of the Advent of Jesus; Of the Fortunes of the Jews, and Their Government, Until the Passion of the Lord.**

In the first place, then, men ought to know that the arrangements of the Most High God have so advanced from the beginning, that it was necessary, as the end of the world approached, that the Son of God should descend to the earth, that He might build a temple for God, and teach righteousness; but, however, not with the might of an angel or with heavenly power, but in the form of man and in the condition of a mortal, that when He had discharged the office of His ministry, He might be delivered into the hands of wicked men, and might undergo death, that, having subdued this also by His might, He might rise again, and bring to man, whose nature He had put on and represented, the hope of overcoming death, and might admit him to the rewards of immortality. And that no one may be ignorant of this arrangement, we will show that all things were foretold which we see fulfilled in Christ. Let no one believe our assertion unless I shall show that the prophets before a long series of ages published that it should come to pass at length that the Son of God should be born as a man, and perform wonderful deeds, and sow the worship of God throughout the whole earth, and at last be crucified, and on the third day rise again. And when I shall have proved all these things by the writings of those very men who treated with violence their God who had assumed a mortal body, what else will prevent it from being manifest that true wisdom is conversant with this religion only? Now the origin of the whole mystery is to be related.

Our ancestors, who were chiefs of the Hebrews, when they were distressed by famine and want, passed over into Egypt, that they might obtain a supply of corn; and sojourning there a long time, they were oppressed with an intolerable yoke of slavery. Then God pitied them, and led them out, and freed them from the hand of the king of the Egyptians, after *four hundred and thirty* years, under the leadership of Moses, through whom the law was afterwards given to them by God; and in this leading out God displayed the power of His majesty. For He made His people to pass through the midst of the Red Sea, His angel going before and dividing the water, so that the people might walk over the dry land, of whom it might more truly be said (as the poet says), that "the wave, closing over him after the appearance of a mountain, stood around him." And when he heard of this, the tyrant of the Egyptians followed with this great host of his men, and rashly entering the sea which still lay open, was destroyed, together with his whole army, by the waves returning to their place. But the Hebrews, when they had entered into the wilderness, saw many wonderful deeds. For when they suffered thirst, a rock having been struck with a rod, a fountain of water sprung forth and refreshed the people. And again, when they were hungry, a shower of heavenly nourishment descended. Moreover, also, the wind brought quails into their camp, so that they were not only satisfied with heavenly bread, but also with more choice banquets. And yet, in return for these divine benefits, they did not pay honor to God; but when slavery had been now removed from them, and their thirst and hunger laid aside, they fell away into luxury, and transferred their minds to the profane rites of the Egyptians. For when Moses, their leader, had ascended into the mountain, and there tarried forty days, they made the head of an ox in gold, which they call Apis, that it might go before them as a standard. With which sin and crime God was offended, and justly visited the impious and ungrateful people with severe punishments, and made them subject to the law which He had given by Moses.

But afterwards, when they had settled in a desert part of Syria, the Hebrews lost their ancient name; and since the leader of their host was Judas, they were called Jews, and the land which they inhabited Judæa. And at first, indeed, they were not subject to the dominion of Kings, but civil Judges presided over the people and the law: they were not, however, appointed only for a year, as the Roman consuls, but supported by a perpetual jurisdiction. Then, the name of Judges being taken away, the kingly power was introduced. But during the government of the Judges the people had often undertaken corrupt religious rites; and God, offended by them, as often brought them into bondage to strangers, until again, softened by the repentance of the people, He freed them from bondage. Likewise under the Kings, being oppressed by wars with their neighbors on account of their iniquities, and at last taken captive and led to Babylon, they suffered punishment for their impiety by oppressive slavery, until Cyrus came to the kingdom, who immediately restored the Jews by an edict. Afterwards they had tetrarchs until the time of Herod, who was in the reign of Tiberius Cæsar; in whose fifteenth year, in the consulship of the two Gemini, on the 23d of March, the Jews crucified Christ. This series of events, this order, is contained in the secrets of the sacred writings. But I will first show for what reason Christ came to the earth, that the foundation and the system of divine religion may be manifest.

## Chap. XI.—Of the Cause of the Incarnation of Christ.

When the Jews often resisted wholesome precepts, and departed from the divine law, going astray to the impious worship of false gods, then God filled just and chosen men with the Holy Spirit, appointing them as prophets in the midst of the people, by whom He might rebuke with threatening words the sins of the ungrateful people, and nevertheless exhort them to repent of their wickedness; for unless they did this, and, laying aside their vanities, return to their God, it would come to pass that He would change His covenant, that is, bestow the inheritance of eternal life upon foreign nations, and collect to Himself a more faithful people out of those who were aliens by birth. But they, when rebuked by the prophets, not only rejected their words; but being offended because they were upbraided for their sins, they slew the prophets themselves with studied tortures: all which things are sealed up and preserved in the sacred writings. For the prophet Jeremiah says: "I sent to you my servants the prophets; I sent them before the morning light; but ye did not hearken, nor incline your ears to hear, when I spoke unto you: let every one of you turn from his evil way, and from your most corrupt affections; and ye shall dwell in the land which I gave to you and to your fathers forever. Walk you not after strange gods, to serve them; and provoke me not to anger with the works of your hands, that I should destroy you." The prophet Ezra also, who was in the times of the same Cyrus by whom the Jews were restored, thus speaks: "They rebelled against Thee, and cast Thy law behind their backs, and slew Thy prophets which testified against them, that they might turn unto Thee."

The prophet Elias also, in the third book of Kings: "I have been very jealous for the Lord God of hosts, because the children of Israel have forsaken Thee, thrown down Thine altars, and slain Thy prophets with the sword; and I only am left, and they seek my life to take it away." On account of these impieties of theirs He cast them off for ever; and so He ceased to send to them prophets. But He commanded His own Son, the first-begotten, the maker of all things, His own counsellor, to descend from heaven, that He might transfer the sacred religion of God to the Gentiles, that is, to those who were ignorant of God, and might teach them righteousness, which the perfidious people had cast aside. And He had long before threatened that He would do this, as the prophet Malachi shows, saying: "I have no pleasure in you, saith the Lord, and I will not accept an offering from your hands; for from the rising of the sun even unto its setting, my name shall be great among the Gentiles." David also in the seventeenth Psalm says: "Thou wilt make me the head of the heathen; a people whom I have not known shall serve me." Isaiah also thus speaks: "I come to gather all nations and tongues; and they shall come and see my glory; and I will send among them a sign, and I will send those that escape of them unto the nations which are afar off, which have not heard my fame; and they shall declare my glory among the Gentiles." Therefore, when God wished to send to the earth one who should measure His temple, He was unwilling to send him with heavenly power and glory, that the people who had been ungrateful towards God might be led into the greatest error, and suffer punishment for their crimes, since they had not received their Lord and God, as the prophets had before foretold that it would thus happen. For Isaiah whom the Jews most cruelly slew, cutting him asunder with a saw, thus speaks: "Hear, O heaven; and give ear, O earth: for the Lord hath spoken, I have begotten sons, and lifted them up on high, and they have rejected me. The ox knoweth his owner, and the ass his master's stall; but Israel hath not known, my people has not understood." Jeremiah also says, in like manner: "The turtle and the swallow hath known her time, and the sparrows of the field have observed the times of their coming: but my people have not known the judgment of the Lord. How do you say, We are wise, and the law of the Lord is with us? The meting out is in vain; the scribes are deceived and confounded: the wise men are dismayed and taken, for they have rejected the word of the Lord."

Therefore (as I had begun to say), when God had determined to send to men a teacher of righteousness, He commanded Him to be born again a second time in the flesh, and to be made in the likeness of man himself, to whom he was about to be a guide, and companion, and teacher. But since God is kind and merciful to His people, He sent Him to those very persons whom He hated, that He might not close the way of salvation against them forever, but might give them a free opportunity of following God, that they might both gain the reward of life if they should follow Him (which many of them do, and have done), and that they might incur the penalty of death by their fault if they should reject their King. He ordered Him therefore to be born again among them, and of their seed, lest, if He should be born of another nation, they might be able to allege a just excuse from the law for their rejection of Him; and at the same time, that there might be no nation at all under heaven to which the hope of immortality should be denied.

**Chap. XII.—Of the Birth of Jesus from the Virgin; Of His Life, Death, and Resurrection, and the Testimonies of the Prophets Respecting These Things.**

Therefore the Holy Spirit of God, descending from heaven, chose the holy Virgin that He might enter into her womb. But she, being filled by the possession of the Divine Spirit, conceived; and without any intercourse with a man, her virgin womb was suddenly impregned. But if it is known to all that certain animals are accustomed to conceive by the wind and the breeze, why should anyone think it wonderful when we say that a virgin was made fruitful by the Spirit of God, to whom whatever He may wish is easy? And this might have appeared incredible, had not the prophets many ages previously foretold its occurrence. Thus Solomon speaks: "The womb of a virgin was strengthened, and conceived; and a virgin was made fruitful, and became a mother in great pity." Likewise the prophet Isaiah, whose words are these: "Therefore God Himself shall give you a sign: Behold, a virgin shall conceive, and bear a son; and ye shall call His name Emmanuel." What can be more manifest than this?

This was read by the Jews, who denied Him. If anyone thinks that these things are invented by us, let him inquire of them, let him take especially from them: the testimony is sufficiently strong to prove the truth, when it is alleged by enemies themselves. But He was never called Emmanuel, but Jesus, who in Latin is called Saving, or Savior, because He comes bringing salvation to all nations. But by this name the prophet declared that God incarnate was about to come to men. For Emmanuel signifies God with us; because when He was born of a virgin, men ought to confess that God was with them, that is, on the earth and in mortal flesh. Whence David says in the eighty-fourth Psalm, "Truth has sprung out of the earth;" because God, in whom is truth, hath taken a body of earth, that He might open a way of salvation to those of the earth. In like manner Isaiah also: "But they disbelieved, and vexed His Holy Spirit; and He was turned to be their enemy. And He Himself fought against them, and He remembered the days of old, who raised up from the earth a shepherd of the sheep." But who this shepherd was about to be, he declared in another place, saying: "Let the heavens rejoice, and let the clouds put on righteousness; let the earth open, and put forth a Savior. For I the Lord have begotten Him." But the Savior is, as we have said before, Jesus. But in another place the same prophet also thus proclaimed: "Behold, unto us a child is born, unto us a Son is given, whose dominion is upon His shoulders, and His name is called Messenger of great counsel." For on this account He was sent by God the Father that He might reveal to all the nations which are under heaven the sacred mystery of the only true God, which was taken away from the perfidious people, who oft times sinned against God. Daniel also foretold similar things: "I saw," he said, "in a vision of the night, and, behold, one like the Son of man coming with the clouds of heaven, and He came even to the Ancient of days. And they who stood by brought Him near before Him. And there was given unto Him a kingdom, and glory, and dominion; and all people, tribes, and languages shall serve Him: and His dominion is everlasting, which shall never pass away, and His kingdom shall not be destroyed." How then do the Jews both confess and expect the Christ of God? Who rejected Him on this account, because He was born of man. For since it is so arranged by God that the same Christ should twice come to the earth, once to announce to the nations the one God, then again to reign, why do they who did not believe in His first advent believe in the second?

But the prophet comprises both His advents in few words. Behold, he says, one like the Son of man coming with the clouds of heaven. He did not say, like the Son of God, but the Son of man, that he might show that He had to be clothed with flesh on the earth, that having assumed the form of a man and the condition of mortality, He might teach men righteousness; and when, having completed the commands of God, He had revealed the truth to the nations, He might also suffer death, that He might overcome and lay open the other world also, and thus at length rising again, He might proceed to His Father borne aloft on a cloud. For the prophet said in addition: And came even to the Ancient of days, and was presented to Him. He called the Most High God the Ancient of days, whose age and origin cannot be comprehended; for He alone was from generations, and He will be always to generations. But that Christ, after His passion and resurrection, was about to ascend to God the Father, David bore witness in these words in the Psalm: "The Lord said unto my Lord, Sit Thou at my right hand, until I make Thine enemies Thy footstool." Whom could this prophet, being himself a king, call his Lord, who sat at the right hand of God, but Christ the Son of God, who is King of kings and Lord of lords? And this is more plainly shown by Isaiah, when he says: "Thus saith the Lord God to my Lord Christ, whose right hand I have holden; I will subdue nations before Him, and will break the strength of kings. I will open before Him gates, and the cities shall not be closed. I will go before Thee, and will make the mountains level; and I will break in pieces the gates of brass, and shatter the bars of iron; and I will give Thee the hidden and invisible treasures, that Thou mayest know that I am the Lord God, which call Thee by Thy name, the God of Israel." Lastly, on account of the goodness and faithfulness which He displayed towards God on earth, there was given to Him a kingdom, and glory, and dominion; and all people, tribes, and languages shall serve Him; and His dominion is everlasting, and that which shall never pass away, and His kingdom shall not be destroyed. And this is understood in two ways: that even now He has an everlasting dominion, when all nations and all languages adore His name, confess His majesty, follow His teaching, and imitate His goodness: He has power and glory, in that all tribes of the earth obey His precepts. And also, when He shall come again with majesty and glory to judge every soul, and to restore the righteous to life, then He shall truly have the government of the whole earth: then, every evil having been removed from the affairs of men, a golden age (as the poets call it), that is, a time of righteousness and peace, will arise. But we will speak of these things more fully in the last book, when we shall speak of His second advent; now let us treat of His first advent, as we began.

### Chap. XIII.—Of Jesus, God and Man; and the Testimonies of the Prophets Concerning Him.

Therefore the Most High God, and Parent of all, when He had purposed to transfer His religion, sent from heaven a teacher of righteousness, that in Him or through Him He might give a new law to new worshippers; not as He had before done, by the instrumentality of man. Nevertheless it was His pleasure that He should be born as a man, that in all things He might be like His supreme Father. For God the Father Himself, who is the origin and source of all things, inasmuch as He is without parents, is most truly named by Trismegistus "fatherless" and "motherless," because He was born from no one. For which reason it was befitting that the Son also should be twice born, that He also might become "fatherless" and "motherless." For in His first nativity, which was spiritual, He was "motherless," because He was begotten by God the Father alone, without the office of a mother. But in His second, which was in the flesh, He was born of a virgin's womb without the office of a father, that, bearing a middle substance between God and man, He might be able, as it were, to take by the hand this frail and weak nature of ours, and raise it to immortality. He became both the Son of God through the Spirit, and the Son of man through the flesh,—that is, both God and man. The power of God was displayed in Him, from the works which He performed; the frailty of the man, from the passion which He endured: on what account He undertook it I will mention a little later. In the meantime, we learn from the predictions of the prophets that He was both God and man—composed of both natures. Isaiah testifies that He was God in these words: "Egypt is wearied, and the merchandise of Ethiopia, and the Sabæans, men of stature, shall come over unto Thee, and shall be Thy servants: and they shall walk behind Thee; in chains they shall fall down unto Thee, and shall make supplication unto Thee, Since God is in Thee, and there is no other God besides Thee. For Thou art God, and we knew Thee not, the God of Israel, the Savior. They shall all be confounded and ashamed who oppose Thee, and shall fall into confusion." In like manner the prophet Jeremiah thus speaks: "This is our God, and there shall none other be compared unto Him. He hath found out all the way of knowledge, and hath given it unto Jacob His servant, and to Israel His beloved. Afterward He was seen upon earth, and dwelt among men."

David also, in the forty-fourth Psalm: "Thy throne, O God, is for ever and ever; a scepter of righteousness is the scepter of Thy kingdom. Thou hast loved righteousness, and hated wickedness; therefore God, Thy God, hath anointed Thee with the oil of gladness." By which word he also shows His name, since (as I have shown above) He was called Christ from His anointing. Then, that He was also man, Jeremiah teaches, saying: "And He is a man, and who hath known Him?" Also Isaiah: "And God shall send to them a man, who shall save them, shall save them by judging." But Moses also, in Numbers, thus speaks: "There shall arise a star out of Jacob, and a man shall spring forth from Israel." On which account the Milesian Apollo, being asked whether He was God or man, replied in this manner: "He was mortal as to His body, being wise with wondrous works; but being taken with arms under Chaldean judges, with nails and the cross He endured a bitter end." In the first verse he spoke the truth, but he skillfully deceived him who asked the question, who was entirely ignorant of the mystery of the truth. For he appears to have denied that He was God. But when he acknowledges that He was mortal as to the flesh, which we also declare, it follows that as to the spirit He was God, which we affirm. For why would it have been necessary to make mention of the flesh, since it was sufficient to say that He was mortal? But being pressed by the truth, he could not deny the real state of the case; as that which he says, that He was wise.

What do you reply to this, Apollo? If he is wise, then his system of instruction is wisdom, and no other; and they are wise who follow it, and no others. Why then are we commonly esteemed as foolish, and visionary, and senseless, who follow a Master who is wise even by the confession of the gods themselves? For in that he said that He wrought wonderful deeds, by which He especially claimed faith is His divinity, he now appears to assent to us, when he says the same things in which we boast. But, however, he recovers himself, and again has recourse to demoniacal frauds. For when he had been compelled to speak the truth, he now appeared to be a betrayer of the gods and of himself, unless he had, by a deceptive falsehood, concealed that which the truth had extorted from him. He says, therefore, that He did indeed perform wonderful works, yet not by divine power, but by magic. What wonder if Apollo thus persuaded men ignorant of the truth, when the Jews also, worshippers (as they seemed to be) of the Most High God, entertained the same opinion, though they had every day before their eyes those miracles which the prophets had foretold to them as about to happen, and yet they could not be induced by the contemplation of such powers to believe that He whom they saw was God? On this account, David, whom they especially read above the other prophets, in the twenty-seventh Psalm thus condemns them:

"Render to them their desert, because they regard not the works of the Lord." Both David himself and other prophets announced that of the house of this very David, Christ should be born according to the flesh. Thus it is written in Isaiah: "And in that day there shall be a root of Jesse, and He who shall arise to rule over the nations, in Him shall the Gentiles trust; and His rest shall be glorious." And in another place: "There shall come forth a rod out of the stem of Jesse, and a blossom shall grow out of his root; and the Spirit of God shall rest upon Him, the spirit of wisdom and understanding, the spirit of counsel and of might, the spirit of knowledge and of piety; and He shall be filled with the spirit of fear of the Lord." Now Jesse was the father of David, from whose root he foretold that a blossom would arise; namely him of whom the Sibyl speaks, "A pure blossom shall spring forth."

Also in the second book of Kings, the prophet Nathan was sent to David, who wished to build a temple for God; and this was the word of the Lord to Nathan, saying: "Go and tell my servant David, Thus saith the Lord Almighty, Thou shall not build me a house for me to dwell in; but when thy days be fulfilled, and thou shalt sleep with thy fathers, I will raise up thy seed after thee, and I will establish His kingdom. He shall build me a house for my name, and I will set up His throne forever; and I will be to Him for a father, and He shall be to me for a son; and His house shall be established, and His kingdom forever." But the reason why the Jews did not understand these things was this, because Solomon the son of David built a temple for God, and the city which he called from his own name, Jerusalem. Therefore they referred the predictions of the prophets to him. Now Solomon received the government of the kingdom from his father himself. But the prophets spoke of Him who was then born after that David had slept with his fathers. Besides, the reign of Solomon was not everlasting; for he reigned forty years. In the next place, Solomon was never called the son of God, but the son of David; and the house which he built was not firmly established, as the Church, which is the true temple of God, which does not consist of walls, but of the heart and faith of the men who believe on Him, and are called faithful. But that temple of Solomon, inasmuch as it was built by the hand, fell by the hand. Lastly, his father, in the Psalm, prophesied in this manner respecting the works of his son: "Except the Lord build the house, they have labored in vain that built it; except the Lord keep the city, the watchman hath waked but in vain."

**Chap. XIV.—Of the Priesthood of Jesus Foretold by the Prophets.**

From which things it is evident that all the prophets declared concerning Christ, that it should come to pass at some time, that being born with a body of the race of David, He should build an eternal temple in honor of God, which is called the Church, and assemble all nations to the true worship of God. This is the faithful house, this is the everlasting temple; and if anyone hath not sacrificed in this, he will not have the reward of immortality. And since Christ was the builder of this great and eternal temple, He must also have an everlasting priesthood in it; and there can be no approach to the shrine of the temple, and to the sight of God, except through Him who built the temple. David in the Psalm teaches the same, saying: "Before the morning-star I begat Thee. The Lord hath sworn, and will not repent; Thou art a priest forever, after the order of Melchisedec." Also in the first book of Kings: "And I will raise me up a faithful Priest, who shall do all things that are in mine heart; and I will build him a sure house; and he shall walk in my sight all his days." But who this was about to be, to whom God promised an everlasting priesthood, Zechariah most plainly teaches, even mentioning His name: "And the Lord God showed me Jesus the great Priest standing before the face of the angel of the Lord, and the adversary was standing at His right hand to resist Him. And the Lord said unto the adversary, The Lord who hath chosen Jerusalem rebuke thee; and lo, a brand plucked out of the fire. And Jesus was clothed with filthy garments, and He was standing before the face of the angel. And He answered and spoke unto those that stood around before His face, saying, Take away the filthy garments from Him, and clothe Him with a flowing garment, and place a fair miter upon His head; and they clothed Him with a garment, and placed a fair miter upon His head. And the angel of the Lord stood, and protested, saying to Jesus: Thus saith the Lord of hosts, If Thou wilt walk in my ways, and keep my precepts, Thou shalt judge my house, and I will give Thee those that may walk with Thee in the midst of these that stand by. Hear, therefore, O Jesus, Thou great Priest."

Who, therefore, would not believe that the Jews were then deprived of understanding, who, when they read and heard these things, laid impious hands upon their God? But from the time in which Zechariah lived, until the fifteenth year of the reign of Tiberius Cæsar, in which Christ was crucified, nearly five hundred years are reckoned; since he flourished in the time of Darius and Alexander, who lived not long after the banishment of Tarquinius Superbus. But they were again misled and deceived in the same manner, in supposing that these things were spoken concerning Jesus the son of Nave, who was the successor of Moses, or concerning Jesus the high priest the son of Josedech; to whom none of those things which the prophet related was suited. For they were never clothed in filthy garments, since one of them was a most powerful prince, and the other high priest; or suffered any adversity, so that they should be regarded as a brand plucked from the fire: not did they ever stand in the presence of God and the angels; nor did the prophet speak of the past so much as of the future. He spoke, therefore, of Jesus the Son of God, to show that He would first come in humility and in the flesh. For this is the filthy garment, that He might prepare a temple for God, and might be scorched as a brand with fire—that is, might endure tortures from men, and at last be extinguished. For a half-burnt brand drawn forth from the hearth and extinguished, is commonly so called. But in what manner and with what commands He was sent by God to the earth, the Spirit of God declared through the prophet, teaching us that when He had faithfully and uniformly fulfilled the will of His supreme Father, He should receive judgment and an everlasting dominion. If, He says, Thou wilt walk in my ways, and keep my precepts, then Thou shalt judge my house. What these ways of God were, and what His precepts, is neither doubtful nor obscure. For God, when He saw that wickedness and the worship of false gods had so prevailed throughout the world, that His name had now also been taken away from the memory of men (since even the Jews, who alone had been entrusted with the secret of God, had deserted the living God, and, ensnared by the deceits of demons, had gone astray, and turned aside to the worship of images, and when rebuked by the prophets did not choose to return to God), He sent His Son as an ambassador to men, that He might turn them from their impious and vain worship to the knowledge and worship of the true God; and also that He might turn their minds from foolishness to wisdom, and from wickedness to deeds of righteousness. These are the ways of God, in which He enjoined Him to walk. These are the precepts which He ordered to be observed. But He exhibited faith towards God. For He taught that there is but one God, and that He alone ought to be worshipped. Nor did He at any time say that He Himself was God; for He would not have maintained His faithfulness, if, when sent to abolish the false gods, and to assert the existence of the one God, He had introduced another besides that one. This would have been not to proclaim one God, nor to do the work of Him who sent Him, but to discharge a peculiar office for Himself, and to separate Himself from Him whom He came to reveal. On which account, because He was so faithful, because He arrogated nothing at all to Himself, that He might fulfil the commands of Him who sent Him, He received the dignity of everlasting Priest, and the honor of supreme King, and the authority of Judge, and the name of God.

**Chap. XV.—Of the Life and Miracles of Jesus, and Testimonies Concerning Them.**

Having spoken of the second nativity, in which, He showed Himself in the flesh to men, let us come to those wonderful works, on account of which, though they were signs of heavenly power, the Jews esteemed Him a magician. When He first began to reach maturity He was baptized by the prophet John in the river Jordan, that He might wash away in the spiritual laver not His own sins, for it is evident that He had none, but those of the flesh, which He bare; that as He saved the Jews by undergoing circumcision, so He might save the Gentiles also by baptism—that is, by the pouring forth of the purifying dew. Then a voice from heaven was heard: "Thou art my Son, to-day have I begotten Thee." Which voice is found to have been foretold by David. And the Spirit of God descended upon Him, formed after the appearance of a white dove. From that time He began to perform the greatest miracles, not by magical tricks, which display nothing true and substantial, but by heavenly strength and power, which were foretold even long ago by the prophets who announced Him; which works are so many, that a single book is not sufficient to comprise them all. I will therefore enumerate them briefly and generally, without any designation of persons and places, that I may be able to come to the setting forth of His passion and cross, to which my discourse has long been hastening. His powers were those which Apollo called wonderful: that wherever He journeyed, by a single word, and in a single moment, He healed the sick and infirm, and those afflicted with every kind of disease: so that those who were deprived of the use of all their limbs, having suddenly received power, were strengthened, and themselves carried their couches, on which they had a little time before been carried. But to the lame, and to those afflicted with some defect of the feet, He not only gave the power of walking, but also of running. Then, also, if any had their eyes blinded in the deepest darkness, He restored them to their former sight. He also loosened the tongues of the dumb, so that they discoursed and spoke eloquently. He also opened the ears of the deaf, and caused them to hear; He cleansed the polluted and the blemished. And He performed all these things not by His hands, or the application of any remedy, but by His word and command, as also the Sibyl had foretold: "Doing all things by His word, and healing every disease."

Nor, indeed, is it wonderful that He did wonderful things by His word, since He Himself was the Word of God, relying upon heavenly strength and power. Nor was it enough that He gave strength to the feeble, soundness of body to the maimed, health to the sick and languishing, unless He also raised the dead, as it were unbound from sleep, and recalled them to life.

And the Jews, then, when they saw these things, contended that they were done by demoniacal power, although it was contained in their secret writings that all things should thus come to pass as they did. They read indeed the words of other prophets, and of Isaiah, saying: "Be strong, ye hands that are relaxed; and ye weak knees, be comforted. Ye who are of a fearful heart, fear not, be not afraid: our Lord shall execute judgment; He Himself shall come and save us. Then shall the eyes of the blind be opened, and the ears of the deaf shall hear: then shall the lame man leap as a deer, and the tongue of the dumb speak plainly: for in the wilderness water hath broken forth, and a stream in the thirsty land." But the Sibyl also foretold the same things in these verses:—

"And there shall be a rising again of the dead; and the course of the lame shall be swift, and the deaf shall hear, and the blind shall see, the dumb shall speak."

On account of these powers and divine works wrought by Him when a great multitude followed Him of the maimed, or sick, or of those who desired to present their sick to be healed, He went up into a desert mountain to pray there. And when He had tarried there three days, and the people were suffering from hunger, He called His disciples, and asked what quantity of food they had with them. But they said that they had five loaves and two fishes in a wallet. Then He commanded that these should be brought forward, and that the multitude, distributed by fifties, should recline *on the ground*. When the disciples did this, He Himself broke the bread in pieces, and divided the flesh of the fishes, and in His hands both of them were increased. And when He had ordered the disciples to set them before the people, five thousand men were satisfied, and moreover twelve baskets were filled from the fragments which remained. What can be more wonderful, either in narration or in action? But the Sibyl had before foretold that it would take place, whose verses are related to this effect:—

"With five loaves at the same time, and with two fishes, He shall satisfy five thousand men in the wilderness; And afterwards taking all the fragments that remain, He shall fill twelve baskets to the hope of many."

I ask, therefore, what the art of magic could have contrived in this case, the skill of which is of avail for nothing else than for deceiving the eyes? He also, when He was about to retire to a mountain, as He was wont, for the sake of prayer, directed His disciples to take a small ship and go before Him. But they, setting out when evening was now coming on, began to be distressed through a contrary wind. And when they were now in the midst of the sea, then, setting His feet on the sea, He came up to them, walking as though on the solid ground, not as the poets fable Orion walking on the sea, who, while a part of his body was sunk in the water,

"With his shoulder rises above the waves."

And again, when He had gone to sleep in the ship, and the wind had begun to rage, even to the extremity of danger, being aroused from sleep, He immediately ordered the wind to be silent; and the waves, which were borne with great violence, were still, and immediately at His word there followed a calm.

But perhaps the sacred writings speak falsely, when they teach that there was such power in Him, that by His command He compelled the winds to obey, the seas to serve Him, diseases to depart, the dead to be submissive. Why should I say that the Sibyls before taught the same things in their verses? One of whom, already mentioned, thus speaks:—

"He shall still the winds by His word, and calm the sea as it rages, treading with feet of peace and in faith."

And again another, which says:—

"He shall walk on the waves, He shall release men from disease. He shall raise the dead, and drive away many pains; and from the bread of one wallet there shall be a satisfying of men."

Some, refuted by these testimonies, are accustomed to have recourse to the assertion that these poems were not by the Sibyls, but made up and composed by our own writers. But he will assuredly not think this who has read Cicero, and Varro, and other ancient writers, who make mention of the Erythræan and the other Sibyls, from whose books we bring forward these examples; and these authors died before the birth of Christ according to the flesh. But I do not doubt that these poems were in former times regarded as ravings, since no one then understood them. For they announced some marvelous wonders, of which neither the manner, nor the time, nor the author was signified. Lastly, the Erythræan Sibyl says that it would come to pass that she would be called mad and deceitful. But assuredly

"They will say that the Sibyl
Is mad, and deceitful: but when all things shall come to pass, then ye will remember me; and no one will any longer Say that I, the prophetess of the great God, am mad."

Therefore they were neglected for many ages; but they received attention after the nativity and passion of Christ had revealed secret things. Thus it was also with the utterances of the prophets, which were read by the people of the Jews for fifteen hundred years and more, but yet were not understood until after Christ had explained them both by His word and by His works. For the prophets spoke of Him; nor could the things which they said have been in any way understood, unless they had been altogether fulfilled.

### Chap. XVI.—Of the Passion of Jesus Christ; That It Was Foretold.

I come now to the passion itself, which is often cast in our teeth as a reproach: that we worship a man, and one who was visited and tormented with remarkable punishment: that I may show that this very passion was undergone by Him in accordance with a great and divine plan, and that goodness and truth and wisdom are contained in it alone. For if He had been most happy on the earth, and had reigned through all His life in the greatest prosperity, no wise man would either have believed Him to be a God, or judged Him worthy of divine honor: which is the case with those who are destitute of true divinity, who not only look up to perishable riches, and frail power, and the advantages arising from the benefit of another, but even consecrate them, and knowingly do service to the memory of the dead, worshipping fortune when it is now extinguished, which the wise never regarded as an object of worship even when alive and present with them. For nothing among earthly things can be venerable and worthy of heaven; but it is virtue alone, and justice alone, which can be judged a true, and heavenly, and perpetual good, because it is neither given to anyone, nor taken away. And since Christ came upon earth, supplied with virtue and righteousness, yea rather, since He Himself is virtue, and Himself righteousness, He descended that He might teach it and mold the character of man. And having performed this office and embassy from God, on account of this very virtue which He at once taught and practiced, He deserved, and was able, to be believed a God by all nations. Therefore, when a great multitude from time to time flocked to Him, either on account of the righteousness which He taught or on account of the miracles which He worked, and heard His precepts, and believed that He was sent by God, and that He was the Son of God, then the rulers and priests of the Jews, excited with anger because they were rebuked by Him as sinners, and perverted by envy, because, while the multitude flocked to Him, they saw themselves despised and deserted, and (that which was the crowning point of their guilt) blinded by folly and error, and unmindful of the instructors sent from heaven, and of the prophets, they caballed against Him, and conceived the impious design of putting Him to death, and torturing Him: of which the prophets had long before written.

For both David, in the beginning of his Psalms, foreseeing in spirit what a crime they were about to commit, says, "Blessed is the man who hath not walked in the way of the ungodly; "and Solomon in the book of Wisdom used these words: "Let us defraud the righteous, for he is unpleasant to us, and upbraided us with our offences against the law. He makes his boast that he has the knowledge of God; and he called himself the Son of God. He is made to reprove our thoughts: it grieves us even to look upon him: for his life is not like the life of others; his ways are of another fashion. We are counted by him as triflers, he withdraweth himself from our ways as from filthiness; he commended greatly the latter end of the just, and boasted that he has God for his Father. Let us see, therefore, if his words be true; let us prove what end he shall have; let us examine him with rebukes and torments that we may know his meekness, and prove his patience; let us condemn him to a shameful death. Such things have they imagined, and have gone astray. For their own folly hath blinded them, and they do not understand the mysteries of God." Does he not describe that impious design entered into by the wicked against God, so that he clearly appears to have been present? But from Solomon, who foretold these things, to the time of their accomplishment, ten hundred and ten years intervened. We feign nothing; we add nothing. They who performed the actions had these accounts; they, against whom these things were spoken, read them. But even now the inheritors of their name and guilt have these accounts, and in their daily readings re-echo their own condemnation as foretold by the voice of the prophets; nor do they ever admit them into their heart, which is also itself a part of their condemnation. The Jews, therefore, being often reproved by Christ, who upbraided them with their sins and iniquities, and being almost deserted by the people, were stirred up to put Him to death.

Now His humility emboldened them to this deed. For when they read with what great power and glory the Son of God was about to descend from heaven, but on the other hand saw Jesus humble, peaceful, of low condition, without comeliness, they did not believe that He was the Son of God, being ignorant that two advents on His part were foretold by the prophets: the first, obscure in humility of the flesh; the other, manifest in the power of His majesty. Of the first David thus speaks in the seventy-first Psalm: "He shall descend as rain upon a fleece; and in His days shall righteousness spring forth, and abundance of peace, as long as the moon is lifted up." For as rain, if it descends upon a fleece, cannot be perceived, because it makes no sound; so he said that Christ would come to the earth without exciting the notice of any, that He might teach righteousness and peace. Isaiah also thus spoke: "Lord, who hath believed our report? And to whom is the arm of the Lord revealed? We made proclamation before Him as children, and as a root in a thirsty land: He has no form nor glory; and we saw Him, and He had no form nor comeliness. But His form was without honor, and defective beyond the rest of men. He is a man acquainted with grief, and knowing how to endure infirmity, because He turned His face away from us; and He was not esteemed. He carries our sins, and He endures pain for us: and we thought that He Himself was in pain, and grief, and vexation. But He was wounded for our transgressions, He was bruised for our offences; the chastisement of our peace was upon Him, by His bruises we are healed. All we like sheep have gone astray, and God hath delivered Him up for our sins." And in the same manner the Sibyl spoke: "Though an object of pity, dishonored, without form, He will give hope to those who are objects of pity." On account of this humility they did not recognize their God, and entered into the detestable design of depriving Him of life, who had come to give them life.

## Chap. XVII.—Of the Superstitions of the Jews, and Their Hatred against Jesus.

But they alleged other causes for their anger and envy, which they bore shut up within in their hearts—namely, that He destroyed the obligation of the law given by Moses; that is, that He did not rest on the Sabbath, but labored for the good of men; that He abolished circumcision; that He took away the necessity of abstaining from the flesh of swine;—in which things the mysteries of the Jewish religion consist. On this account, therefore, the rest of the people, who had not yet withdrawn to Christ, were incited by the priests to regard Him as impious, because He destroyed the obligation of the law of God, though He did this not by His own judgment, but according to the will of God, and after the predictions of the prophets. For Micah announced that He would give a new law, in these terms: "The law shall go forth of Zion, and the word of the Lord from Jerusalem. And He shall judge among many people, and rebuke strong nations." For the former law, which was given by Moses, was not given on Mount Zion, but on Mount Horeb; and the Sibyl shows that it would come to pass that this law would be destroyed by the Son of God:—

"But when all these things which I told you shall be accomplished, then all the law is fulfilled with respect to Him."

But even Moses himself, by whom the law was given which they so tenaciously maintain, though they have fallen away from God, and have not acknowledged God, had foretold that it would come to pass that a very great prophet would be sent by God, who should be above the law, and be a bearer of the will of God to men. In Deuteronomy he thus left it written: "And the Lord said unto me, I will raise them up a Prophet from among their brethren, like unto thee; and I will put my word in His mouth, and He shall speak unto them all that I shall command Him. And whosoever will not hearken to those things which that Prophet shall speak in my name, I will require it of him." The Lord evidently announced by the law-giver himself that He was about to send His own Son—that is, a law alive, and present in person, and destroy that old law given by a mortal, that by Him who was eternal He might ratify afresh a law which was eternal.

In like manner, Isaiah thus prophesied concerning the abolition of circumcision: "Thus saith the Lord to the men of Judah who dwell at Jerusalem, Break up your fallow ground, and sow not among thorns. Circumcise yourselves to the Lord your God, and take away the foreskins of your heart, lest my fury come forth like fire, and burn that none can quench it." Also Moses himself says: "In the last days the Lord shall circumcise thine heart to love the Lord thy God." Also Jesus the son of Nun, his successor, said: "And the Lord said unto Jesus, Make thee knives of flint very sharp, and sit and circumcise the children of Israel the second time." He said that this second circumcision would be not of the flesh, as the first was, which the Jews practice even now, but of the heart and spirit, which was delivered by Christ, who was the true Jesus. For the prophet does not say, "And the Lord said unto me," but "unto Jesus," that he might show that God was not speaking of him, but of Christ, to whom God was then speaking. For that Jesus represented Christ: for when he was at first called Auses, Moses, foreseeing the future, ordered that he should be called Jesus; that since he had been chosen as the leader of the warfare against Amalek, who was the enemy of the children of Israel, he might both subdue the adversary by the emblem of the name, and lead the people into the land of promise. And for this reason he was also successor to

Moses, to show that the new law given by Christ Jesus was about to succeed to the old law which was given by Moses. For that circumcision of the flesh is plainly irrational; since, if God had so willed it, He might so have formed man from the beginning, that he should be without a foreskin. But it was a figure of this second circumcision, signifying that the breast is to be laid bare; that is, that we ought to live with an open and simple heart, since that part of the body which is circumcised has a kind of resemblance to the heart, and is to be treated with reverence. On this account God ordered that it should be laid bare, that by this argument He might admonish us not to have our breast hidden in obscurity; that is, not to veil any shameful deed within the secrets of conscience. This is the circumcision of the heart of which the prophets speak, which God transferred from the mortal flesh to the soul, which alone is about to endure. For being desirous of promoting our life and salvation in accordance with His own goodness, in that circumcision He hath set before us repentance, that if we lay open our hearts,—that is if we confess our sins and make satisfaction to God,—we shall obtain pardon, which is denied to those who are obstinate and conceal their faults, by Him who regards not the outward appearance, as man does, but the innermost secrets of the heart.

The forbidding of the flesh of swine also has the same intention; for when God commanded them to abstain from this, He willed that this should be especially understood, that they should abstain from sins and impurities. For this animal is filthy and unclean, and never looks up to heaven, but prostrates itself to the earth with its whole body and face: it is always the slave of its appetite and food; nor during its life can it afford any other service, as the other animals do, which either afford a vehicle for riding, or aid in the cultivation of the fields, or draw wagons by their neck, or carry burthens on their back, or furnish a covering with their skins, or abound with a supply of milk, or keep watch for guarding our houses. Therefore He forbade them to use the flesh of the pig for food, that is, not to imitate the life of swine, which are nourished only for death; lest, by devoting themselves to their appetite and pleasures, they should be useless for working righteousness, and should be visited with death. Also that they should not immerse themselves in foul lusts, as the sow, which wallows in the mire; of that they do not serve earthly images, and thus defile themselves with mud: for they do bedaub themselves with mud who worship gods, that is, who worship mud and earth. Thus all the precepts of the Jewish law have for their object the setting forth of righteousness, since they are given in a mysterious manner, that under the figure of carnal things those which are spiritual might be known.

**Chap. XVIII.—Of the Lord's Passion, and that It Was Foretold.**

When, therefore, Christ fulfilled these things which God would have done, and which He foretold many ages before by His prophets, incited by these things, and ignorant of the sacred Scriptures, they conspired together to condemn their God. And though He knew that this would come to pass, and repeatedly said that He must suffer and be put to death for the salvation of many, nevertheless He withdrew Himself with His disciples, not that He might avoid that which it was necessary for Him to undergo and endure, but that He might show what ought to take place in every persecution, that no one should appear to have fallen into it through his own fault: and He announced that it would come to pass that He should be betrayed by one of them. And thus Judas, induced by a bribe, delivered up to the Jews the Son of God. But they took and brought Him before Pontius Pilate, who at that time was administering the province of Syria as governor, and demanded that He should be crucified, though they laid nothing else to His charge except that He said that He was the Son of God, the King of the Jews; also His own saying, "Destroy this temple, which was forty-six years in building, and in three days I will raise it up again without hands,"—signifying that His passion would shortly take place, and that He, having been put to death by the Jews, would rise again on the third day.

For He Himself was the true temple of God. They inveighed against these expressions of His, as ill-omened and impious. And when Pilate had heard these things, and He said nothing in His own defense, he gave sentence that there appeared nothing deserving of condemnation in Him. But those most unjust accusers, together with the people whom they had stirred up, began to cry out, and with loud voices to demand His crucifixion.

Then Pontius was overpowered both by their outcries, and by the instigation of Herod the tetrarch, who feared lest he should be deposed from his sovereignty. He did not, however, himself pass sentence, but delivered Him up to the Jews, that they themselves might judge Him according to their law. Therefore they led Him away when He had been scourged with rods, and before they crucified Him they mocked Him; for they put upon Him a scarlet robe, and a crown of thorns, and saluted Him as King, and gave Him gall for food, and mingled for Him vinegar to drink. After these things they spat upon His face, and struck Him with the palms of their hands; and when the executioners themselves contended about His garments, they cast lots among themselves for His tunic and mantle. And while all these things were doing, He uttered no voice from His mouth, as though He were dumb. Then they lifted Him up in the midst between two malefactors, who had been condemned for robbery, and fixed Him to the cross. What can I here deplore in so great a crime? Or in what words can I lament such great wickedness? For we are not relating the crucifixion of Gavius, which Marcus Tullius followed up with all the spirit and strength of his eloquence, pouring forth as it were the fountains of all his genius, proclaiming that it was an unworthy deed that a Roman citizen should be crucified in violation of all laws. And although He was innocent, and undeserving of that punishment, yet He was put to death, and that, too, by an impious man, who was ignorant of justice. What shall I say respecting the indignity of this cross, on which the Son of God was suspended and nailed? Who will be found so eloquent, and supplied with so great an abundance of deeds and words, what speech flowing with such copious exuberance, as to lament in a befitting manner that cross, which the world itself, and all the elements of the world, bewailed?

But that these things were thus about to happen, was announced both by the utterances of the prophets and by the predictions of the Sibyls. In Isaiah it is found thus written: "I am not rebellious, nor do I oppose: I gave my back to the scourge, and my cheeks to the hand: I turned not away my face from the foulness of spitting." In like manner David, in the thirty-fourth Psalm: "The abject were gathered together against me, and they knew me not: they were dispersed, nor did they feel remorse; they tempted me, and greatly derided me; and they gnashed upon me with their teeth." The Sibyl also showed that the same things would happen:—

"He shall afterwards come into the hands of the unjust and the faithless; and they shall inflict on God blows with impure hands, and with polluted mouths they shall send forth poisonous spittle; and He shall then absolutely give His holy back to stripes."

Likewise respecting His silence, which He perseveringly maintained even to His death, Isaiah thus spoke again: "He was led as a sheep to the slaughter; and as a lamb before the shearer is dumb, so He opened not His mouth." And the above-mentioned Sibyl said:—

"And being beaten, He shall be silent, lest anyone should know what the Word is, or whence it came, that it may speak with mortals; and He shall wear the crown of thorns."

But respecting the food and the drink which they offered to Him before they fastened Him to the cross, David thus speaks in the sixty-eighth Psalm: "And they gave me gall for my meat; and in my thirst they gave me vinegar to drink." The Sibyl foretold that this also would happen:—

"They gave me gall for my food, and for my thirst vinegar; this inhospitable table they will show."

And another Sibyl rebukes the land of Judæa in these verses:—

"For you, entertaining hurtful thoughts, did not recognize your God sporting with mortal thoughts; but crowned Him with a crown of thorns, and mingled dreadful gall."

Now, that it would come to pass that the Jews would lay hands upon their God, and put Him to death, these testimonies of the prophets foretold. In Esdras it is thus written: "And Ezra said to the people, This Passover is our Savior and our refuge. Consider and let it come into your heart, that we have to abase Him in a figure; and after these things we will hope in Him, lest this place be deserted forever, saith the Lord God of hosts. If you will not believe Him, nor hear His announcement, ye shall be a derision among the nations." From which it appears that the Jews had no other hope, unless they purified themselves from blood, and put their hopes in that very person whom they denied. Isaiah also points out their deed, and says: "In His humiliation His judgment was taken away. Who shall declare His generation? For His life shall be taken away from the earth; from the transgressions of my people He was led away to death. And I will give Him the wicked for His burial, and the rich for His death, because He did no wickedness, nor spoke guile with His mouth. Wherefore He shall obtain many, and shall divide the spoils of the strong; because He was delivered up to death, and was reckoned among the transgressors; and He bore the sins of many, and was delivered up on account of their transgressions." David also, in the ninety-third Psalm: "They will hunt after the soul of the righteous, and condemn the innocent blood; and the Lord is become my refuge." Also Jeremiah: "Lord, declare it unto me, and I shall know. Then I saw their devices; I was led as an innocent lamb to the sacrifice; they meditated a plan against me, saying, Come, let us send wood into his bread, and let us sweep away his life from the earth, and his name shall no more be remembered." Now the wood signifies the cross, and the bread His body; for He Himself is the food and the life of all who believe in the flesh which He bare, and on the cross upon which He was suspended.

Respecting this, however, Moses himself more plainly spoke to this effect, in Deuteronomy: "And Thy life shall hang before Thine eyes; and Thou shall fear day and night, and shalt have no assurance of Thy life." And the same again in Numbers: "God is not in doubt as a man, nor does He suffer threats as the son of man." Zechariah also thus wrote: "And they shall look on me, whom they pierced." Also David in the twenty-first Psalm: "They pierced my hands and my feet; they numbered all my bones; they themselves looked and stared upon me; they divided my garments among them; and upon my vesture they did cast lots." It is evident that the prophet did not speak these things concerning himself. For he was a king, and never endured these sufferings; but the Spirit of God, who was about to suffer these things, after *ten hundred and fifty* years, spoke by him. For this is the number of years from the reign of David to the crucifixion of Christ. But Solomon also, his son, who built Jerusalem, prophesied that this very city would perish in revenge for the sacred cross: "But if ye turn away from me, saith the Lord, and will not keep my truth, I will drive Israel from the land which I have given them; and this house which I have built for them in my name, I will cast it out from all: and Israel shall be for perdition and a reproach to the people; and this house shall be desolate, and every one that shall pass by it shall be astonished, and shall say, Why hath God done these evils to this land and to this house? And they shall say, Because they forsook the Lord their God, and persecuted their King most beloved by God, and crucified Him with great degradation, therefore hath God brought upon them these evils."

## Chap. XIX.—Of the Death, Burial, and Resurrection of Jesus; And the Predictions of These Events.

What more can now be said respecting the crime of the Jews, than that they were then blinded and seized with incurable madness, who read these things daily, and yet neither understood them, nor were able to be on their guard so as not to do them? Therefore, being lifted up and nailed to the cross, He cried to the Lord with a loud voice, and of His own accord gave up His spirit. And at the same hour there was an earthquake; and the veil of the temple, which separated the two tabernacles, was rent into two parts; and the sun suddenly withdrew its light, and there was darkness from the sixth even to the ninth hour. Of which event the prophet Amos testifies: "And it shall come to pass in that day, saith the Lord, that the sun shall go down at noon, and the daylight shall be darkened; and I will turn your feasts into mourning, and your songs into lamentation." Also Jeremiah: "She who brings forth is affrighted, and vexed in spirit; her sun is gone down while it was yet mid-day; she hath been ashamed and confounded; and the residue of them will I give to the sword in the sight of their enemies." And the Sibyl:—

"And the veil of the temple shall be rent, and at midday there shall be dark vast night for three hours,"

When these things were done, even by the heavenly prodigies, they were not able to understand their crime.

But since He had foretold that on the third day He should rise again from the dead, fearing lest, the body having been stolen by the disciples, and removed, all should believe that He had risen, and there should be a much greater disturbance among the people, they took Him down from the cross, and having shut Him up in a tomb, they securely surrounded it with a guard of soldiers. But on the third day, before light, there was an earthquake, and the sepulcher was suddenly opened; and the guard, who were astonished and stupefied with fear, seeing nothing, He came forth uninjured and alive from the sepulcher, and went into Galilee to seek His disciples: but nothing was found in the sepulcher except the grave-clothes in which they had enclosed and wrapped His body. Now, that He would not remain in hell, but rise again on the third day, had been foretold by the prophets. David says, in the fifteenth Psalm: "Thou wilt not leave my soul in hell; neither wilt Thou suffer Thine holy one to see corruption." Also in the third Psalm: "I laid me down to sleep, and took my rest, and rose again, for the Lord sustained me." Hosea also, the first of the twelve prophets, testified of His resurrection: "This my Son is wise, therefore He will not remain in the anguish of His sons: and I will redeem Him from the power of the grave. Where is thy judgment, O death? Or where is thy sting?" The same also in another place: "After two days, He will revive us in the third day." And therefore the Sibyl said, that after three days' sleep he would put an end to death:—

"And after sleeping three days, He shall put an end to the fate of death; and then, releasing Himself from the dead, He shall come to light, first showing to the called ones the beginning of the resurrection."

For He gained life for us by overcoming death. No hope, therefore, of gaining immortality is given to man, unless he shall believe on Him, and shall take up that cross to be borne and endured.

**Chap. XX.—Of the Departure of Jesus into Galilee after His Resurrection; And of the Two Testaments, the Old and the New.**

Therefore He went into Galilee, for He was unwilling to show Himself to the Jews, lest He should lead them to repentance, and restore them from their impiety to a sound mind. And *there He* opened to His disciples again assembled the writings of Holy Scripture, that is, the secrets of the prophets;

which before His suffering could by no means be understood, for they told of Him and of His passion. Therefore Moses, and the prophets also themselves, call the law which was given to the Jews a testament: for unless the testator shall have died, a testament cannot be confirmed; nor can that which is written in it be known, because it is closed and sealed. And thus, unless Christ had undergone death, the testament could not have been opened; that is, the mystery of God could not have been unveiled and understood.

But all Scripture is divided into two Testaments. That which preceded the advent and passion of Christ—that is, the law and the prophets—is called the Old; but those things which were written after His resurrection are named the New Testament. The Jews make use of the Old, we of the New: but yet they are not discordant, for the New is the fulfilling of the Old, and in both there is the same testator, even Christ, who, having suffered death for us, made us heirs of His everlasting kingdom, the people of the Jews being deprived and disinherited. As the prophet Jeremiah testifies when he speaks such things: "Behold, the days come, saith the Lord, that I will make a new testament to the house of Israel and the house of Judah, not according to the testament which I made to their fathers, in the day that I took them by the hand to bring them out of the land of Egypt; for they continued not in my testament, and I disregarded them, saith the Lord." Also in another place he says in like manner: "I have forsaken my house, I have given up mine heritage into the hand of its enemies. Mine heritage is become unto me as a lion in the forest; it hath cried out against me, therefore have I hated it." Since the inheritance is His heavenly kingdom, it is evident that He does not say that He hates the inheritance itself, but the heirs, who have been ungrateful towards Him, and impious. Mine heritage, he says, is become unto me as a lion; that is, I am become a prey and a devouring to my heirs, who have slain me as the flock. It hath cried out against me; that is, they have pronounced against me the sentence of death and the cross. For that which He said above, that He would make a new testament to the house of Judah, shows that the old testament which was given by Moses was not perfect; but that that which was to be given by Christ would be complete. But it is plain that the house of Judah does not signify the Jews, whom He casts off, but us, who have been called by Him out of the Gentiles, and have by adoption succeeded to their place, and are called sons of the Jews, which the Sibyl declares when she says:—

"The divine race of the blessed, heavenly Jews."

But what that race was about to be, Isaiah teaches, in whose book the Most High Father addresses His Son: "I the Lord God have called Thee in righteousness, and will hold Thine hand, and will keep Thee: and I have given Thee for a covenant of my race, for a light of the Gentiles; to open the eyes of the blind, to bring out the prisoners from the prison, and them that sit in darkness out of the prison-house." When, therefore, we who were in time past as it were blind, and as it were shut up in the prison of folly, were sitting in darkness, ignorant of God and of the truth, we have been enlightened by Him, who adopted us by His testament; and having freed us from cruel chains, and brought us out to the light of wisdom, He admitted us to the inheritance of His heavenly kingdom.

**Chap. XXI.—Of the Ascension of Jesus, and the Foretelling of It; And of the Preaching and Actions of the Disciples.**

But when He had made arrangements with His disciples for the preaching of the Gospel and His name, a cloud suddenly surrounded Him, and carried Him up into heaven, on the fortieth day after His passion, as Daniel had shown that it would be, saying: "And, behold, one like the Son of man came with the clouds of heaven, and came to the Ancient of days." But the disciples, being dispersed through the provinces, everywhere laid the foundations of the Church, themselves also in the name of their divine Master doing many and almost incredible miracles; for at His departure He had endowed them with power and strength, by which the system of their new announcement might be founded and confirmed. But He also opened to them all things which were about to happen, which Peter and Paul preached at Rome; and this preaching being written for the sake of remembrance, became permanent, in which they both declared other wonderful things, and also said that it was about to come to pass, that after a short time God would send against them a king who would subdue the Jews, and level their cities to the ground, and besiege the people themselves, worn out with hunger and thirst. Then it should come to pass that they should feed on the bodies of their own children, and consume one another. Lastly, that they should be taken captive, and come into the hands of their enemies, and should see their wives most cruelly harassed before their eyes, their virgins ravished and polluted, their sons torn in pieces, their little ones dashed to the ground; and lastly, everything laid waste with fire and sword, the captives banished forever from their own lands, because they had exulted over the well-beloved and most approved Son of God. And so, after their decease, when Nero had put them to death, Vespasian destroyed the name and nation of the Jews, and did all things which they had foretold as about to come to pass.

### Chap. XXII.—Arguments of Unbelievers against the Incarnation of Jesus.

I have now confirmed, as I imagine, the things which are thought false and incredible by those who are not instructed in the true knowledge of heavenly learning. But, however, that we may refute those also who are too wise, not without injury to themselves, and who detract from the credit due to divine things, let us disprove their error, that they may at length perceive that the fact ought to have been as we show that it actually was. And although with good judges either testimonies are of sufficient weight without arguments, or arguments without testimonies, we, however, are not content with the one or the other, since we are supplied with both, that we may not leave room for any one of depraved ingenuity either to misunderstand or to dispute on the opposite side. They say that it was impossible for anything to be withdrawn from an immortal nature. They say, in short, that it was unworthy of God to be willing to become man, and to burthen Himself with the infirmity of flesh; to become subject of His own accord to sufferings, to pain, and death: as though it had not been easy for Him to show Himself to men without the weakness incident to a body, and to teach them righteousness (if He so wished) with greater authority, as of one who acknowledged Himself to be God. For in that case all would have obeyed the heavenly precepts, if the influence and power of God enjoining them had been united with them. Why, then (they say), did He not come as God to teach men? Why did He render Himself so humble and weak, that it was possible for Him both to be despised by men and to be visited with punishment? Why did He suffer violence from those who are weak and mortal? Why did He not repel by strength, or avoid by His divine knowledge, the hands of men? Why did He not at least in His very death reveal His majesty? But He was led as one without strength to trial, was condemned as one who was guilty, was put to death as one who was mortal. I will carefully refute these things, nor will I permit anyone to be in error. For these things were done by a great and wonderful plan; and he who shall understand this, will not only cease to wonder that God was tortured by men, but also will easily see that it could not have been believed that he was God if those very things which he censures had not been done.

### Chap. XXIII.—Of Giving Precepts, and Acting.

If anyone gives to men precepts for living, and molds the characters of others, I ask whether he is bound himself to practice the things which he enjoins, or is not bound. If he shall not do so, his precepts are annulled. For if the things which are enjoined are good, if they place the life of men in the best condition, the instructor ought not to separate himself from the number and assemblage of men among whom he acts; and he ought himself to live in the same manner in which he teaches that men ought to live, lest, by living in another way, he himself should disparage his own precepts, and make his instruction of less value, if in reality he should relax the obligations of that which he endeavors to establish by his words. For every one, when he hears another giving precepts, is unwilling that the necessity of obeying should be imposed upon him, as though the right of liberty were taken from him. Therefore he answers his teacher in this manner: I am not able to do the things which you command, for they are impossible. For you forbid me to be angry, you forbid me to covet, you forbid me to be excited by desire, you forbid me to fear pain or death; but this is so contrary to nature, that all animals are subject to these affections. Or if you are so entirely of opinion that it is possible to resist nature, do you yourself practice the things which you enjoin, that I may know that they are possible? But since you yourself do not practice them, what arrogance is it, to wish to impose upon a free man laws which you yourself do not obey! You who teach, first learn; and before you correct the character of others, correct your own. Who could deny the justice of this answer? Nay! A teacher of this kind will fall into contempt, and will in his turn be mocked, because he also will appear to mock others.

What, therefore, will that instructor do, if these things shall be objected to him? How will he deprive the self-willed of an excuse, unless he teach them by deeds before their eyes that he teaches things which are possible? Whence it comes to pass, that no one obeys the precepts of the philosophers. For men prefer examples rather than words, because it is easy to speak, but difficult to accomplish. Would to heaven that there were as many who acted well as there are who speak well! But they who give precepts, without carrying them out into action, are distrusted; and if they shall be men, will be despised as inconsistent: if it shall be God, He will be met with the excuse of the frailty of man's nature. It remains that words should be confirmed by deeds, which the philosophers are unable to do. Therefore, since the instructors themselves are overcome by the affections which they say that it is our duty to overcome, they are able to train no one to virtue, which they falsely proclaim; and for this cause they imagine that no perfect wise man has as yet existed, that is, in whom the greatest virtue and perfect justice were in harmony with the greatest learning and knowledge. And this indeed was true. For no one since the creation of the world has been such, except Christ, who both delivered wisdom by His word, and confirmed His teaching by presenting virtue to the eyes of men.

### Chap. XXIV.—The Overthrowing of the Arguments Above Urged by Way of Objection.

Come, let us now consider whether a teacher sent from heaven can fail to be perfect. I do not as yet speak of Him whom they deny to have come from God. Let us suppose that someone were to be sent from heaven to instruct the life of men in the first principles of virtue, and to form them to righteousness. No one can doubt but that this teacher, who is sent from heaven, would be as perfect in the knowledge of all things as in virtue, lest there should be no difference between a heavenly and an earthly teacher. For in the case of a man his instruction can by no means be from within and of himself. For the mind, shut in by earthly organs, and hindered by a corrupt body, of itself can neither comprehend nor receive the truth, unless it is taught from another source. And if it had this power in the greatest degree, yet it would be unable to attain to the highest virtue, and to resist all vices, the materials of which are contained in our bodily organs. Hence it comes to pass, that an earthly teacher cannot be perfect. But a teacher from heaven, to whom His divine nature gives knowledge, and His immortality gives virtue, must of necessity in His teaching also, as in other things, be perfect and complete. But this cannot by any means happen, unless He should take to Himself a mortal body. And the reason why it cannot happen is manifest. For if He should come to men as God, not to mention that mortal eyes cannot look upon and endure the glory of His majesty in His own person, assuredly God will not be able to teach virtue; for, inasmuch as He is without a body, He will not practice the things which He will teach, and through this His teaching will not be perfect. Otherwise, if it is the greatest virtue patiently to endure pain for the sake of righteousness and duty, if it is virtue not to fear death itself when threatened, and when inflicted to undergo it with fortitude; it follows that the perfect teacher ought both to teach these things by precept, and to confirm them by practice. For he who gives precepts for the life, ought to remove every method of excuse, that he may impose upon men the necessity of obedience, not by any constraint, but by a sense of shame, and yet may leave them liberty, that a reward may be appointed for those who obey, because it was in their power not to obey if they so wished; and a punishment for those who do not obey, because it was in their power to obey if they so wished. How then can excuse be removed, unless the teacher should practice what he teaches, and as it were go before and hold out his hand to one who is about to follow? But how can one practice what he teaches, unless he is like him whom he teaches? For if he be subject to no passion, a man may thus answer him who is the teacher: It is my wish not to sin, but I am overpowered; for I am clothed with frail and weak flesh: it is this which covets, which is angry, which fears pain and death. And thus I am led on against my will; and I sin, not because it is my wish, but because I am compelled. I myself perceive that I sin; but the necessity imposed by my frailty, which I am unable to resist, impels me. What will that teacher of righteousness say in reply to these things? How will he refute and convict a man who shall allege the frailty of the flesh as an excuse for his faults, unless he himself also shall be clothed with flesh, so that he may show that even the flesh is capable of virtue? For obstinacy cannot be refuted except by example. For the things which you teach cannot have any weight unless you shall be the first to practice them; because the nature of men is inclined to faults, and wishes to sin not only with indulgence, but also with a reasonable plea. It is befitting that a master and teacher of virtue should most closely resemble man, that by overpowering sin he may teach man that sin may be overpowered by him. But if he is immortal, he can by no means propose an example to man. For there will stand forth someone persevering in his opinion, and will say: You indeed do not sin, because you are free from this body; you do not covet, because nothing is needed by an immortal; but I have need of many things for the support of this life. You do not fear death, because it can have no power against you. You despise pain, because you can suffer no violence. But I, a mortal, fear both, because they bring upon me the severest tortures, which the weakness of the flesh cannot endure. A teacher of virtue therefore ought to have taken away this excuse from men, that no one may ascribe it to necessity that he sins, rather than to his own fault. Therefore, that a teacher may be perfect, no objection ought to be brought forward by him who is to be taught, so that if he should happen to say, You enjoin impossibilities; the teacher may answer, See, I myself do them. But I am clothed with flesh, and it is the property of flesh to sin. I too bear the same flesh, and yet sin does not bear rule in me. It is difficult for me to despise riches, because otherwise I am unable to live in this body. See, I too have a body, and yet I contend against every desire. I am not able to bear pain or death for righteousness, because I am frail. See, pain and death have power over me also; and I overcome those very things which you fear, that I may make you victorious over pain and death. I go before you through those things which you allege that it is impossible to endure: if you are not able to follow me giving directions, follow me going before you. In this way all excuse is taken away, and you must confess that man is unjust through his own fault, since he does not follow a teacher of virtue, who is at the same time a guide. You see, therefore, how much more perfect is a teacher who is mortal, because he is able to be a guide to one who is mortal, than one who is immortal, for he is unable to teach patient endurance who is not subject to passions. Nor, however, does this extend so far that I prefer man to God; but to show that man cannot be a perfect teacher unless he is also God, that he may by his heavenly authority impose upon men the necessity of obedience; nor God, unless he is clothed with a mortal body, that by carrying out his precepts to their completion in actions, he may bind others by the necessity of obedience. It plainly therefore appears, that he who is a guide of life and teacher of righteousness must have a body, and that his teaching cannot otherwise be full and perfect, unless it has a root and foundation, and remains firm and fixed among men; and that he himself must undergo weakness of flesh and body, and display in himself the virtue of which he is a teacher, that he may teach it at the same time both by words and deeds. Also, he must be subject to death and all sufferings, since the duties of virtue are occupied with the enduring of suffering, and the undergoing death; all which, as I have said, a perfect teacher ought to endure, that he may teach the possibility of their being endured.

## Chap. XXV.—Of the Advent of Jesus in the Flesh and Spirit, that He Might Be Mediator between God and Man.

Let men therefore learn and understand why the Most High God, when He sent His ambassador and messenger to instruct mortals with the precepts of His righteousness, willed that He should be clothed with mortal flesh, and be afflicted with torture, and be sentenced to death. For since there was no righteousness on earth, He sent a teacher, as it were a living law, to found a new name and temple, that by His words and example He might spread throughout the earth a true and holy worship. But, however, that it might be certain that He was sent by God, it was befitting that He should not be born as man is born, composed of a mortal on both sides; but that it might appear that He was heavenly even in the form of man, He was born without the office of a father. For He had a spiritual Father, God; and as God was the Father of His spirit without a mother, so a virgin was the mother of His body without a father. He was therefore both God and man, being placed in the middle between God and man. From which the Greeks call Him Mesites, that He might be able to lead man to God—that is, to immortality: for if He had been God only (as we have before said), He would not have been able to afford to man examples of goodness; if He had been man only, He would not have been able to compel men to righteousness, unless there had been added an authority and virtue greater than that of man.

For, since man is composed of flesh and spirit, and the spirit must earn immortality by works of righteousness, the flesh, since it is earthly, and therefore mortal, draws with itself the spirit linked to it, and leads it from immortality to death. Therefore the spirit, apart from the flesh, could by no means be a guide to immortality for man, since the flesh hinders the spirit from following God. For it is frail, and liable to sin; but sin is the food and nourishment of death. For this cause, therefore, a mediator came—that is, God in the flesh—that the flesh might be able to follow Him, and that He might rescue man from death, which has dominion over the flesh. Therefore He clothed Himself with flesh, that the desires of the flesh being subdued, He might teach that to sin was not the result of necessity, but of *man's* purpose and will. For we have one great and principal struggle to maintain with the flesh, the boundless desires of which press upon the soul, nor allow it to retain dominion, but make it the slave of pleasures and sweet allurements, and visit it with everlasting death. And that we might be able to overcome these, God has opened and displayed to us the way of overcoming the flesh. And this perfect and absolutely complete virtue bestows on those who conquer, the crown and reward of immortality.

### Chap. XXVI.—Of the Cross, and Other Tortures of Jesus, and of the Figure of the Lamb under the Law.

I have spoken of humiliation, and frailty, and suffering—why God thought fit to undergo them. Now an account must be taken of the cross itself, and its meaning must be related. What the Most High Father arranged from the beginning, and how He ordained all things which were accomplished, not only the foretelling by the prophets, which preceded and was proved true in Christ, but also the manner of His suffering itself teaches. For whatever sufferings He underwent were not without meaning; but they had a figurative meaning and great significance, as had also those divine works which He performed, the strength and power of which had some weight indeed for the present, but also declared something for the future. Heavenly influence opened the eyes of the blind, and gave light to those who did not see; and by this deed He signified that it would come to pass that, turning to the nations which were ignorant of God, He might enlighten the breasts of the foolish with the light of wisdom, and open the eyes of their understanding to the contemplation of the truth. For they are truly blind who, not seeing heavenly things, and surrounded with the darkness of ignorance, worship earthly and frail things. He opened the ears of the deaf. It is plain that this divine power did not limit its exercise to this point; but He declared that it would shortly come to pass, that they who were destitute of the truth would both hear and understand the divine words of God. For you may truly call those deaf who do not hear the things which are heavenly and true, and worthy of being performed. He loosed the tongues of the dumb, so that they spoke plainly. A power worthy of admiration, even when it was in operation: but there was contained in this display of power another meaning, which showed that it would shortly come to pass that those who were lately ignorant of heavenly things, having received the instruction of wisdom, might speak respecting God and the truth. For he who is ignorant of the divine nature, he truly is speechless and dumb, although he is the most eloquent of all men. For when the tongue has begun to speak truth—that is, to set forth the excellency and majesty of the one God—then only does it discharge the office of its nature; but as long as it speaks false things it is not rightly employed: and therefore he must necessarily be speechless who cannot utter divine things. He also renewed the feet of the lame to the office of walking,—a strength of divine work worthy of praise; but the figure implied this, that

## The Writings of Lactatius

the errors of a worldly and wandering life being restrained, the path of truth was opened by which men might walk to attain the favor of God. For He is truly to be considered lame, who, being enwrapped in the gloom and darkness of folly, and ignorant in what direction to go, with feet liable to stumble and fall, walks in the way of death.

Likewise He cleansed the stains and blemishes of defiled bodies,—no slight exercise of immortal power; but this strength prefigured that by the instruction of righteousness His doctrine was about to purify those defiled by the stains of sins and the blemishes of vices. For they ought truly to be accounted as leprous and unclean, whom either boundless lusts compel to crimes, or insatiable pleasures to disgraceful deeds, and affect with an everlasting stain those who are branded with the marks of dishonorable actions. He raised the bodies of the dead as they lay prostrate; and calling them aloud by their names, He brought them back from death. What is more suitable to God, what more worthy of the wonder of all ages, than to have recalled the life which has run its course, to have added times to the completed times of men, to have revealed the secrets of death? But this unspeakable power was the image of a greater energy, which showed that His teaching was about to have such might, that the nations throughout the world, which were estranged from God and subject to death, being animated by the knowledge of the true light, might arrive at the rewards of immortality. For you may rightly deem those to be dead, who, not knowing God the giver of life, and depressing their souls from heaven to earth, run into the snares of eternal death. The actions, therefore, which He then performed for the present, were representations of future things; the things which He displayed in injured and diseased bodies were figures of spiritual things, that at present He might display to us the works of an energy which was not of earth, and for the future might show the power of His heavenly majesty.

Therefore, as His works had a signification also of greater power, so also His passion did not go before us as simple, or superfluous, or by chance. But as those things which He did signified the great efficacy and power of His teaching, so those things which He suffered announced that wisdom would be held in hatred. For the vinegar which they gave Him to drink, and the gall which they gave Him to eat, held forth hardships and severities in this life to the followers of truth. And although His passion, which was harsh and severe in itself, gave to us a sample of the future torments which virtue itself proposes to those who linger in this world, yet drink and food of this kind, coming into the mouth of our teacher, afforded us an example of pressures, and labors, and miseries. All which things must be undergone and suffered by those who follow the truth; since the truth is bitter, and detested by all who, being destitute of virtue, give up their life to deadly pleasures. For the placing of a crown of thorns upon His head, declared that it would come to pass that He would gather to Himself a holy people from those who were guilty. For people standing around in a circle are called a *corona*. But we, who before that we knew God were unjust, were thorns—that is, evil and guilty, not knowing what was good; and estranged from the conception and the works of righteousness, polluted all things with wickedness and lust. Being taken, therefore, from briars and thorns, we surround the sacred head of God; for, being called by Himself, and spread around Him, we stand beside God, who is our Master and Teacher, and crown Him King of the world, and Lord of all the living.

But with reference to the cross, it has great force and meaning, which I will now endeavor to show. For God (as I have before explained), when He had determined to set man free, sent as His ambassador to the earth a teacher of virtue, who might both by salutary precepts train men to innocence, and by works and deeds before their eyes might open the way of righteousness, by walking in which, and following his teacher, man might attain to eternal life. He therefore assumed a body, and was clothed in a garment of flesh, that He might hold out to man, for whose instruction He had come, examples of virtue and incitements to its practice. But when He had afforded an example of righteousness in all the duties of life, in order that He might teach man also the patient endurance of pain and contempt of death, by which virtue is rendered perfect and complete, He came into the hands of an impious nation, when, by the knowledge of the future which He had, He might have avoided them, and by the same power by which He did wonderful works He might have repelled them. Therefore He endured tortures, and stripes, and thorns. At last He did not refuse even to undergo death that under His guidance man might triumph over death, subdued and bound in chains with all its terrors. But the reason why the Most High Father chose that kind of death in preference to others, with which He should permit Him to be visited, is this. For someone may perchance say: Why, if He was God, and chose to die, did He not at least suffer by some honorable kind of death? Why was it by the cross especially? Why by an infamous kind of punishment, which may appear unworthy even of a man if he is free, although guilty? First of all, because He, who had come in humility that He might bring assistance to the humble and men of low degree, and might hold out to all the hope of safety, was to suffer by that kind of punishment by which the humble and low usually suffer, that there might be no one at all who might not be able to imitate Him. In the next place, it was in order that His body might be kept unmutilated, since He must rise again from the dead on the third day.

 Nor ought anyone to be ignorant of this, that He Himself, speaking before of His passion, also made it known that He had the power, when He willed it, of laying down His life and of taking it again. Therefore, because He had laid down His life while fastened to the cross, His executioners did not think it necessary to break His bones (as was their prevailing custom), but they only pierced His side. Thus His unbroken body was taken down from the cross, and carefully enclosed in a tomb. Now all these things were done lest His body, being injured and broken, should be rendered unsuitable for rising again. That also was a principal cause why God chose the cross, because it was necessary that He should be lifted up on it, and the passion of God become known to all nations. For since he who is suspended upon a cross is both conspicuous to all and higher than others, the cross was especially chosen, which might signify that He would be so conspicuous, and so raised on high, that all nations from the whole world should meet together at once to know and worship Him. Lastly, no nation is so uncivilized, no region so remote, to which either His passion or the height of His majesty would be unknown. Therefore in His suffering He stretched forth His hands and measured out the world, that even then He might show that a great multitude, collected together out of all languages and tribes, from the rising of the sun even to his setting, was about to come under His wings, and to receive on their foreheads that great and lofty sign. And the Jews even now exhibit a figure of this transaction when they mark their thresholds with the blood of a lamb. For when God was about to smite the Egyptians, to secure the Hebrews from that infliction He had enjoined them to slay a white lamb without spot, and to place on their thresholds a mark from its blood. And thus, when the first-born of the Egyptians had perished in one night, the Hebrews alone were saved by the sign of the blood: not that the blood of a sheep had such efficacy in itself as to be the safety of men, but it was an image of things to come. For Christ was the white lamb without spot; that is, He was innocent, and just, and holy, who, being slain by the same Jews, is the salvation of all who have written on their foreheads the sign of blood—that is, of the cross, on which He shed His blood. For the forehead is the top of the threshold in man, and the wood sprinkled with blood is the emblem of the cross. Lastly, the slaying of the lamb by those very persons who perform it is called the paschal feast, from the word "paschein," because it is a figure of the passion, which God, foreknowing the future, delivered by Moses to be celebrated by His people. But at that time the figure was efficacious at the present for averting the danger, that it may appear what great efficacy the truth itself is about to have for the protection of God's people in the extreme necessity of the whole world. But in what manner or in what region all will be safe who have marked on the highest part of their body this sign of the true and divine blood, I will show in the last book.

### Chap. XXVII.—Of the Wonders Effected by the Power of the Cross, and of Demons.

At present it is sufficient to show what great efficacy the power of this sign has. How great a terror this sign is to the demons, he will know who shall see how, when adjured by Christ, they flee from the bodies which they have besieged. For as He Himself, when He was living among men, put to flight all the demons by His word, and restored to their former senses the minds of men which had been excited and maddened by their dreadful attacks; so now His followers, in the name of their Master, and by the sign of His passion, banish the same polluted spirits from men. And it is not difficult to prove this. For when they sacrifice to their gods, if any one bearing a marked forehead stands by, the sacrifices are by no means favorable.

"Nor can the diviner, when consulted, give answers."

And this has often been the cause of punishment to wicked kings. For when some of their attendants who were of our religion were standing by their masters as they sacrificed, having the sign placed on their foreheads, they caused the gods of their masters to flee, that they might not be able to observe future events in the entrails of the victims. And when the soothsayers understood this, at the instigation of the same demons to whom they had sacrificed, complaining that profane men were present at the sacrifices, they drove their princes to madness, so that they attacked the temple of the god, and contaminated themselves by true sacrilege, which was expiated by the severest punishments on the part of their persecutors. Nor, however, are blind men able to understand even from this, either that this is the true religion, which contains such great power for overcoming, or that that is false, which is not able to hold its ground or to come to an engagement.

But they say that the gods do this, not through fear, but through hatred; as though it were possible for anyone to hate another, unless it be him who injures, or has the power of injuring. Yea, truly, it would be consistent with their majesty to visit those whom they hated with immediate punishment, rather than to flee from them. But since they can neither approach those in whom they shall see the heavenly mark, nor injure those whom the immortal sign as an impregnable wall protects, they harass them by men, and persecute them by the hands of others: and if they acknowledge the existence of these demons, we have overcome; for this must necessarily be the true religion, which both understands the nature of demons, and understands their subtlety, and compels them, vanquished and subdued, to yield to itself. If they deny it, they will be refuted by the testimonies of poets and philosophers. But if they do not deny the existence and malignity of demons, what remains except that they affirm that there is a difference between gods and demons? Let them therefore explain to us the difference between the two kinds, that we may know what is to be worshipped and what to be held in execration; whether they have any mutual agreement, or are really opposed to one another. If they are united by some necessity, how shall we distinguish them? Or how shall we unite the honor and worship of each kind? If, on the other hand, they are enemies, how is it that the demons do not fear the gods, or that the gods cannot put to flight the demons? Behold, someone excited by the impulse of the demon is out of his senses, raves, is mad: let us lead him into the temple of the excellent and mighty Jupiter; or since Jupiter knows not how to cure men, into the fane of Æsculapius or Apollo. Let the priest of either, in the name of his god, command the wicked spirit to come out of the man: that can in no way come to pass. What, then, is the power of the gods, if the demons are not subject to their control? But, in truth, the same demons, when adjured by the name of the true God, immediately flee. What reason is there why they should fear

Christ, but not fear Jupiter, unless that they whom the multitude esteem to be gods are also demons? Lastly, if there should be placed in the midst one who is evidently suffering from an attack of a demon, and the priest of the Delphian Apollo, they will in the same manner dread the name of God; and Apollo will as quickly depart from his priest as the spirit of the demon from the man; and his god being adjured and put to flight, the priest will be forever silent. Therefore the demons, whom they acknowledge to be objects of execration, are the same as the gods to whom they offer supplications.

If they imagine that we are unworthy of belief, let them believe Homer, who associated the supreme Jupiter with the demons; and also other poets and philosophers, who speak of the same beings at one time as demons, and at another time as gods,—of which names one is true, and the other false. For those most wicked spirits, when they are adjured, then confess that they are demons; when they are worshipped, then falsely say that they are gods; in order that they may lead men into errors, and call them away from the knowledge of the true God, by which alone eternal death can be escaped. They are the same who, for the sake of overthrowing man, have founded various systems of worship for themselves through different regions,—under false and assumed names, however, that they might deceive. For because they were unable by themselves to aspire to divinity, they took to themselves the names of powerful kings, under whose titles they might claim for themselves divine honors; which error may be dispelled, and brought to the light of truth. For if anyone desires to inquire further into the matter, let him assemble those who are skilled in calling forth spirits from the dead. Let them call forth Jupiter, Neptune, Vulcan, Mercury, Apollo, and Saturnus the father of all. All will answer from the lower regions; and being questioned they will speak, and confess respecting themselves and God. After these things let them call up Christ; He will not be present, He will not appear, for He was not more than two days in the lower regions. What proof can be brought forward more certain than this? I have no doubt that Trismegistus arrived at the truth by some proof of this kind, who spoke many things respecting God the Son which are contained in the divine secrets.

## Chap. XXVIII.—Of Hope and True Religion, and of Superstition.

And since these things are so, as we have shown, it is plain that no other hope of life is set before man, except that, laying aside vanities and wretched error, he should know God, and serve God; except he renounce this temporary life, and train himself by the principles of righteousness for the cultivation of true religion. For we are created on this condition, that we pay just and due obedience to God who created us, that we should know and follow Him alone. We are *bound* and *tied* to God by this *chain of piety*; from which religion itself received its name, not, as Cicero explained it, from carefully gathering, for in his second book respecting the nature of the gods he thus speaks: "For not only philosophers, but our ancestors also, separated superstition from religion. For they who spent whole days in prayers and sacrifices, that their children might survive them, were called superstitious. But they who handled again, and as it were carefully gathered all things which related to the worship of the gods, were called religious from carefully gathering, as some were called elegant from choosing out, and diligent from carefully selecting and intelligent from understanding. For in all these words there is the same meaning of gathering which there is in the word religious: thus it has come to pass, that in the names superstitious and religious, the one relates to a fault, the other belongs to praise." How senseless this interpretation is, we may know from the matter itself. For if both religion and superstition are engaged in the worship of the same gods, there is little or rather no difference between them. For what cause will he allege why he should think that to pray once for the health of sons is the part of a religious man, but to do the same ten times is the part of a superstitious man? For if it is an excellent thing to pray once, how much more so to do it more frequently! If it is well to do it at the first hour, then it is well to do it throughout the day. If one victim renders the deity propitious, it is plain that many victims must render him more propitious, because multiplied services oblige rather than offend. For those servants do not appear to us hateful who are assiduous and constant in their attendance, but more beloved. Why, therefore, should he be in fault, and receive a name which implies censure, who either loves his children more, or sufficiently honors the gods; and he, on the contrary, be praised, who loves them less? And this argument has weight also from the contrary. For if it is wrong to pray and sacrifice during whole days, therefore it is wrong to do so once. If it is faulty frequently to wish for the preservation of our children, therefore he also is superstitious who conceives that wish even rarely. Or why should the name of a fault be derived from that, than which nothing can be wished more honorable, nothing more just? For as to his saying, that they who diligently take in hand again the things relating to the worship of the gods are called religious from their carefully gathering; how is it, then, that they who do this often in a day lose the name of religious men, when it is plain from their very assiduity that they more diligently gather those things by which the gods are worshipped?

What, then, is it? Truly religion is the cultivation of the truth, but superstition of that which is false. And it makes the entire difference what you worship, not how you worship, or what prayer you offer. But because the worshippers of the gods imagine themselves to be religious, though they are superstitious, they are neither able to distinguish religion from superstition, nor to express the meaning of the names. We have said that the name of religion is derived from *the bond* of piety, because God has *tied* man to Himself, and *bound* him by piety; for we must serve Him as a master, and be obedient to Him as a father. And therefore Lucretius better explained this name, who says that He loosens the knots of superstitions. But they are called superstitious, not who wish their children to survive them, for we all wish this; but either those who reverence the surviving memory of the dead, or those who, surviving their parents, reverenced their images at their houses as household gods. For those who assumed to themselves new rites, that they might honor the dead as gods, whom they supposed to be taken from men and received into heaven, they called superstitious. But those who worshipped the public and ancient gods they named religious. From which Virgil says:—

"Superstition vain, and ignorant of ancient gods."

But since we find that the ancient gods also were consecrated in the same manner after their death, therefore they are superstitious who worship many and false gods. We, on the other hand, are religious, who make our supplications to the one true God.

**Chap. XXIX.—Of the Christian Religion, and of the Union of Jesus with the Father.**

Someone may perhaps ask how, when we say that we worship one God only, we nevertheless assert that there are two, God the Father and God the Son: which assertion has driven many into the greatest error. For when the things which we say seem to them probable, they consider that we fail in this one point alone, that we confess that there is another God, and that He is mortal. We have already spoken of His mortality: now let us teach concerning His unity. When we speak of God the Father and God the Son, we do not speak of them as different, nor do we separate each: because the Father cannot exist without the Son, nor can the Son be separated from the Father, since the name of Father cannot be given without the Son, nor can the Son be begotten without the Father. Since, therefore, the Father makes the Son, and the Son the Father, they both have one mind, one spirit, one substance; but the former is as it were an overflowing fountain, the latter as a stream flowing forth from it: the former as the sun, the latter as it were a ray extended from the sun. And since He is both faithful to the Most High Father, and beloved by

Him, He is not separated from Him; just as the stream is not separated from the fountain, nor the ray from the sun: for the water of the fountain is in the stream, and the light of the sun is in the ray: just as the voice cannot be separated from the mouth, nor the strength or hand from the body. When, therefore, He is also spoken of by the prophets as the hand, and strength, and word of God, there is plainly no separation; for the tongue, which is the minister of speech, and the hand, in which the strength is situated, are inseparable portions of the body.

We may use an example more closely connected with us. When anyone has a son whom he especially loves, who is still in the house, and in the power of his father, although he concede to him the name and power of a master, yet by the civil law the house is one, and one person is called master. So this world is the one house of God; and the Son and the Father, who unanimously inhabit the world, are one God, for the one is as two, and the two are as one. Nor is that wonderful, since the Son is in the Father, for the Father loves the Son, and the Father is in the Son; for He faithfully obeys the will of the Father, nor does He ever do nor has done anything except what the Father either willed or commanded. Lastly, that the Father and the Son are but one God, Isaiah showed in that passage which we have brought forward before, when he said: "They shall fall down unto Thee, and make supplication unto Thee, since God is in Thee, and there is no other God besides Thee." And he also speaks to the same purport in another place: "Thus saith God the King of Israel, and His Redeemer, the everlasting God; I am the first, and I am the last; and beside me there is no God." When he had set forth two persons, one of God the King, that is, Christ, and the other of God the Father, who after His passion raised Him from the dead, as we have said that the prophet Hosea showed, who said, "I will redeem Him from the power of the grave:" nevertheless, with reference to each person, he introduced the words, "and beside me there is no God," when he might have said "beside us;" but it was not right that a separation of so close a relationship should be made by the use of the plural number. For there is one God alone, free, most high, without any origin; for He Himself is the origin of all things, and in Him at once both the Son and all things are contained. Wherefore, since the mind and will of the one is in the other, or rather, since there is one in both, both are justly called one God; for whatever is in the Father flows on to the Son, and whatever is in the Son descends from the Father. Therefore that highest and matchless God cannot be worshipped except through the Son. He who thinks that he worships the Father only, as he does not worship the Son, so he does not worship even the Father. But he who receives the Son, and bears His name, he truly together with the Son worships the Father also, since the Son is the ambassador, and messenger, and priest of the Most High Father. He is the door of the greatest temple, He the way of light, He the guide to salvation, He the gate of life.

## Chap. XXX.—Of Avoiding Heresies and Superstitions, and what is the Only True Catholic Church.

But since many heresies have existed, and the people of God have been rent into divisions at the instigation of demons, the truth must be briefly marked out by us, and placed in its own peculiar dwelling-place, that if anyone shall desire to draw the water of life, he may not be borne to broken cisterns which hold no water, but may know the abundant fountain of God, watered by which he may enjoy perpetual light. Before all things, it is befitting that we should know both that He Himself and His ambassadors foretold that there must be numerous sects and heresies, which would break the unity of the sacred body; and that they admonished us to be on our guard with the greatest prudence, lest we should at any time fall into the snares and deceits of that adversary of ours, with whom God has willed that we should contend. Then that He gave us sure commands, which we ought always to treasure in our minds; for many, forgetting them, and abandoning the heavenly road, have made for themselves devious paths amidst windings and precipices, by which they might lead away the incautious and simple part of the people to the darkness of death: I will explain how this happened. There were some of our religion whose faith was less established, or who were less learned or less cautious, who rent the unity and divided the Church. But they whose faith was unsettled, when they pretended that they knew and worshipped God, aiming at the increase of their wealth and honor, aspired to the highest sacerdotal power; and when overcome by others more powerful, preferred to secede with their supporters, than to endure those set over them, over whom they themselves before desired to be set.

But some, not sufficiently instructed in heavenly learning, when they were unable to reply to the accusers of the truth, who objected that it was either impossible or inconsistent that God should be shut up in the womb of a woman, and that the Majesty of heaven could not be reduced to such weakness as to become an object of contempt and derision, a reproach and mockery to men; lastly, that He should even endure tortures, and be affixed to the accursed cross; and when they could defend and refute all these things neither by talent nor learning, for they did not thoroughly perceive their force and meaning, they were perverted from the right path, and corrupted the sacred writings, so that they composed for themselves a new doctrine without any root and stability. But some, enticed by the prediction of false prophets, concerning whom both the true prophets and he himself had foretold, fell away from the knowledge of God, and left the true tradition. But all of these, ensnared by frauds of demons, which they ought to have foreseen and guarded against, by their carelessness lost the name and worship of God. For when they are called Phrygians, or Novatians, or Valentinians, or Marcionites, or Anthropians, or Arians, or by any other name, they have ceased to be Christians, who have lost the name of Christ, and assumed human and external names. Therefore it is the Catholic Church alone which retains true worship.

This is the fountain of truth, this is the abode of the faith, this is the temple of God; into which if anyone shall not enter, or from which if any shall go out, he is estranged from the hope of life and eternal salvation. No one ought to flatter himself with persevering strife. For the contest is respecting life and salvation, which, unless it is carefully and diligently kept in view, will be lost and extinguished. But, however, because all the separate assemblies of heretics call themselves Christians in preference to others, and think that theirs is the Catholic Church, it must be known that the true Catholic Church is that in which there is confession and repentance, which treats in a wholesome manner the sins and wounds to which the weakness of the flesh is liable. I have related these things in the meanwhile for the sake of admonition, that no one who desires to avoid error may be entangled in a greater error, while he is ignorant of the secret of the truth. Afterwards, in a particular and separate work, we will more fully and copiously contend against all divisions of falsehoods. It follows that, since we have spoken sufficiently on the subject of true religion and wisdom, we discuss the subject of justice in the next book.

**General Notes by the American Editor.**

*I.*

(On cap. 29.)

Here we should look for something also concerning the Holy Spirit. But our author's principle is doubtless a reflection of the prevailing sentiment of the Church at this period, which was perhaps a violent exaggeration of our Lord's example (Mark iv. 33). And see something of this on p. 140, note 6, infra; also Matt. vii. 6.

*II.*

(On cap. 30.)

The simplicity with which our author gives a note of the Catholic Church, in accordance with African canons and the teaching of Cyprian, is very noteworthy. It never occurred to him that communion with any one particular See was the note. Hippolytus alone would have reminded him that the worst heretics had been in communion with both Zephyrinus and Callistus in his days (see vol. v. pp. 156 and 160; also *Ibid.*, 125,

130), and that orthodoxy had been persecuted by these bishops of Rome.

# The divine institutes
## Book V.
## Of Justice.

**Chap. I.—Of the Non-Condemnation of Accused Persons Without a Hearing of Their Cause; From What Cause Philosophers Despised the Sacred Writings; Of the First Advocates of the Christian Religion.**

I Entertain no doubt, O mighty Emperor Constantine,—since they are impatient through excessive superstition,—that if any *one* of those who are foolishly religious should take in hand this work of ours, in which that matchless Creator of all things and Ruler of this boundless world is asserted, he would even assail it with abusive language, and perhaps, having scarcely read the beginning, would dash it to the ground, cast it from him, curse it, and think himself contaminated and bound by inexpiable guilt if he should patiently read or hear these things. We demand, however, from this man, if it is possible, by the right of human nature, that he should not condemn before that he knows the whole matter. For if the right of defending themselves is given to sacrilegious persons, and to traitors and sorcerers, and if it is lawful for no one to be condemned beforehand, his cause being as yet untried, we do not appear to ask unjustly, that if there shall be anyone who shall have fallen upon this subject, if he shall read it, he read it throughout; if he shall hear it, that he put off the forming of an opinion until the end. But I know the obstinacy of men; we shall never succeed in obtaining this. For they fear lest they should be overcome by us, and be compelled at length to yield, truth itself crying out. They interrupt, therefore, and make hindrances, that they may not hear; and close their eyes, that they may not see the light which we present to them. Wherefore they themselves plainly show their distrust in their own abandoned system, since they neither venture to investigate, nor to engage with as, because they know that they are easily overpowered. And therefore, discussion being taken away,

"Wisdom is driven from among them, they have recourse to violence,"

as Ennius says; and because they eagerly endeavor to condemn as guilty those whom they plainly know to be innocent, they are unwilling to be agreed respecting innocence itself; as though, in truth, it were a greater injustice to have condemned innocence, when proved to be such, than unheard. But, as I said, they are afraid lest, if they should hear, they should be unable to condemn.

And therefore they torture, put to death, and banish the worshippers of the Most High God, that is, the righteous; nor are they, who so vehemently hate, themselves able to assign the causes of their hatred. Because they are themselves in error, they are angry with those who follow the path of truth; and when they are able to correct themselves, they greatly increase their errors by cruel deeds, they are stained with the blood of the innocent, and they tear away with violence souls dedicated to God from the lacerated bodies. Such are the men with whom we now endeavor to engage and to dispute: these are the men whom we would lead away from a foolish persuasion to the truth, men who would more readily drink blood than imbibe the words of the righteous. What then? Will our labor be in vain? By no means. For if we shall not be able to deliver these from death, to which they are hastening with the greatest speed; if we cannot recall them from that devious path to life and light, since they themselves oppose their own safety; yet we shall strengthen those who belong to us, whose opinion is not settled, and founded and fixed with solid roots. For many of them waver, and especially those who have any acquaintance with literature. For in this respect philosophers, and orators, and poets are pernicious, because they are easily able to ensnare unwary souls by the sweetness of their discourse, and of their poems flowing with delightful modulation. These are sweets which conceal poison. And on this account I wished to connect wisdom with religion, that that vain system may not at all injure the studious; so that now the knowledge of literature may not only be of no injury to religion and righteousness, but may even be of the greatest profit, if he who has learned it should be more instructed in virtues and wiser in truth.

Moreover, even though it should be profitable to no other, it certainly will be so to us: the conscience will delight itself, and the mind will rejoice that it is engaged in the light of truth, which is the food of the soul, being overspread with an incredible kind of pleasantness. But we must not despair. Perchance

"We sing not to the deaf."

For neither are affairs in so bad a condition that there are no sound minds to which the truth may be pleasing, and which may both see and follow the right course when it is pointed out to them. Only let the cup be anointed with the heavenly honey of wisdom, that the bitter remedies may be drunk by them unawares, without any annoyance, whilst the first sweetness of taste by its allurement conceals, under the cover of pleasantness, the bitterness of the harsh flavor. For this is especially the cause why, with the wise and the learned, and the princes of this world, the sacred Scriptures are without credit, because the prophets spoke in common and simple language, as though they spoke to the people. And therefore they are despised by those who are willing to hear or read nothing except that which is polished and eloquent; nor is anything able to remain fixed in their minds, except that which charms their ears by a more soothing sound. But those things which appear humble are considered anile, foolish, and common. So entirely do they regard nothing as true, except that which is pleasant to the ear; nothing as credible, except that which can excite pleasure: no one estimates a subject by its truth, but by its embellishment. Therefore they do not believe the sacred writings, because they are without any pretense; but they do not even believe those who explain them, because they also are either altogether ignorant, or at any rate possessed of little learning. For it very rarely happens that they are wholly eloquent; and the cause of this is evident. For eloquence is subservient to the world, it desires to display itself to the people, and to please in things which are evil; since it often endeavors to overpower the truth, that it may show its power; it seeks wealth, desires honors; in short, it demands the highest degree of dignity. Therefore it despises these subjects as low; it avoids secret things as contrary to itself, inasmuch as it rejoices in publicity, and longs for the multitude and celebrity. Hence it comes to pass that wisdom and truth need suitable heralds. And if by chance any of the learned have betaken themselves to it, they have not been sufficient for its defense.

Of those who are known to me, Minucius Felix was of no ignoble rank among pleaders. His book, which bears the title of *Octavius*, declares how suitable a maintainer of the truth he might have been, if he had given himself altogether to that pursuit. Septimius Tertullianus also was skilled in literature of every kind; but in eloquence he had little readiness, and was not sufficiently polished, and very obscure. Not even therefore did he find sufficient renown. Cyprianus, therefore, was above all others distinguished and renowned, since he had sought great glory to himself from the profession of the art of oratory, and he wrote very many things worthy of admiration in their particular class. For he was of a turn of mind which was ready, copious, agreeable, and (that which is the greatest excellence of style) plain and open; so that you cannot determine whether he was more embellished in speech, or more ready in explanation, or more powerful in persuasion. And yet he is unable to please those who are ignorant of the mystery except by his words; inasmuch as the things which he spoke are mystical, and prepared with this object, that they may be heard by the faithful only: in short, he is accustomed to be derided by the learned men of this age, to whom his writings have happened to be known. I have heard of a certain man who was skillful indeed, who by the change of a single letter called him Coprianus, as though he were one who had applied to old women's fables a mind which was elegant and fitted for better things. But if this happened to him whose eloquence is not unpleasant, what then must we suppose happens to those whose discourse is meagre and displeasing, who could have had neither the power of persuasion, nor subtlety in arguing, nor any severity at all for refuting?

### Chap. II.—To What an Extent the Christian Truth Has Been Assailed by Rash Men.

Therefore, because there have been wanting among us suitable and skillful teachers, who might vigorously and sharply refute public errors, and who might defend the whole cause of truth with elegance and copiousness, this very want incited some to venture to write against the truth, which was unknown to them. I pass by those who in former times in vain assailed it. When I was teaching rhetorical learning in Bithynia, having been called thither, and it had happened that at the same time the temple of God was overthrown, there were living at the same place two men who insulted the truth as it lay prostrate and overthrown, I know not whether with greater arrogance or harshness: the one of whom professed himself the high priest of philosophy; but he was so addicted to vice, that, though a teacher of abstinence, he was not less inflamed with avarice than with lusts; so extravagant in his manner of living, that though in his school he was the maintainer of virtue, the praiser of parsimony and poverty, he dined less sumptuously in a palace than at his own house. Nevertheless he sheltered his vices by his hair and his cloak, and (that which is the greatest screen) by his riches; and that he might increase these, he used to penetrate with wonderful effort to the friendships of the judges; and he suddenly attached them to himself by the authority of a fictitious name, not only that he might make a traffic of their decisions, but also that he might by this influence hinder his neighbors, whom he was driving from their homes and lands, from the recovery of their property. This man, in truth, who overthrew his own arguments by his character, or censured his own character by his arguments, a weighty censor and most keen accuser against himself, at the very same time in which a righteous people were impiously assailed, vomited forth three books against the Christian religion and name; professing, above all things, that it was the office of a philosopher to remedy the errors of men, and to recall them to the true way, that is, to the worship of the gods, by whose power and majesty, as he said, the world is governed; and not to permit that inexperienced men should be enticed by the frauds of any, lest their simplicity should be a prey and sustenance to crafty men.

Therefore he said that he had undertaken this office, worthy of philosophy, that he might hold out to those who do not see the light of wisdom, not only that they may return to a healthy state of mind, having undertaken the worship of the gods, but also that, having laid aside their pertinacious obstinacy, they may avoid tortures of the body, nor wish in vain to endure cruel lacerations of their limbs. But that it might be evident on what account he had laboriously worked out that task, he broke out profusely into praises of the princes, whose piety and foresight, as he himself indeed said, had been distinguished both in other matters, and especially in defending the religious rites of the gods; that he had, in short, consulted the interests of men, in order that, impious and foolish superstition having been restrained, all men might have leisure for lawful sacred rites, and might experience the gods propitious to them. But when he wished to weaken the grounds of that religion against which he was pleading, he appeared senseless, vain, and ridiculous; because that weighty adviser of the advantage of others was ignorant not only what to oppose, but even what to speak. For if any of our religion were present, although they were silent on account of the time, nevertheless in their mind they derided him; since they saw a man professing that he would enlighten others, when he himself was blind; that he would recall others from error, when he himself was ignorant where to plant his feet; that he would instruct others to the truth, of which he himself had never seen even a spark at any time; inasmuch as he who was a professor of wisdom, endeavored to overthrow wisdom. All, however, censured this, that he undertook this work at that time in particular, in which odious cruelty raged. O philosopher, a flatterer, and a time-server! But this man was despised, as his vanity deserved; for he did not gain the popularity which he hoped for, and the glory which he eagerly sought for was changed into censure and blame.

Another wrote the same subject with more bitterness, who was then of the number of the judges, and who was especially the adviser of enacting persecution; and not contented with this crime, he also pursued with writings those whom he had persecuted. For he composed two books, not *against* the Christians, lest he might appear to assail them in a hostile manner but *to* the Christians, that he might be thought to consult for them with humanity and kindness. And in these writings he endeavored so to prove the falsehood of sacred Scripture, as though it were altogether contradictory to itself; for he expounded some chapters which seemed to be at variance with themselves, enumerating so many and such secret things, that he sometimes appears to have been one of the same sect. But if this was so, what Demosthenes will be able to defend from the charge of impiety him who became the betrayer of the religion to which he had given his assent, and of the faith the name of which he had assumed, and of the mystery which he had received, unless it happened by chance that the sacred writings fell into his hands? What rashness was it, therefore, to dare to destroy that which no one explained to him! It was well that he either learned nothing or understood nothing. For contradiction is as far removed from the sacred writings as he was removed from faith and truth. He chiefly, however, assailed Paul and Peter, and the other disciples, as disseminators of deceit, whom at the same time he testified to have been unskilled and unlearned. For he says that some of them made gain by the craft of fishermen, as though he took it ill that some Aristophanes or Aristarchus did not devise that subject.

**Chap. III.—Of the Truth of the Christian Doctrine, and the Vanity of Its Adversaries; And that Christ Was Not a Magician.**

The desire of inventing, therefore, and craftiness were absent from these men, since they were unskillful. Or what unlearned man could invent things adapted to one another, and coherent, when the most learned of the philosophers, Plato and Aristotle, and Epicurus and Zeno, themselves spoke things at variance with one another, and contrary? For this is the nature of falsehoods, that they cannot be coherent. But their teaching, because it is true, everywhere agrees, and is altogether consistent with itself; and on this account it effects persuasion, because it is based on a consistent plan. They did not therefore devise that religion for the sake of gain and advantage, inasmuch as both by their precepts and in reality they followed that course of life which is without pleasures, and despised all things which are reckoned among good things, and since they not only endured death for their faith, but also both knew and foretold that they were about to die, and afterwards that all who followed their system would suffer cruel and impious things. But he affirmed that Christ Himself was put to flight by the Jews, and having collected a band of nine hundred men, committed robberies. Who would venture to oppose so great an authority? We must certainly believe this, for perchance some Apollo announced it to him in his slumbers. So many robbers have at all times perished, and do perish daily, and you yourself have certainly condemned many: which of them after his crucifixion was called, I will not say a God, but a man? But you perchance believed it from the circumstance of your having consecrated the homicide Mars as a god, though you would not have done this if the Areopagites had crucified him.

The same man, when he endeavored to overthrow his wonderful deeds, and did not however deny them, wished to show that Apollonius performed equal or even greater deeds. It is strange that he omitted to mention Apuleius, of whom many and wonderful things are accustomed to be related. Why therefore, O senseless one, does no one worship Apollonius in the place of God? Unless by chance you alone do so, who are worthy forsooth of that god, with whom the true God will punish you everlastingly. If Christ is a magician because He performed wonderful deeds, it is plain that Apollonius, who, according to your description, when Domitian wished to punish him, suddenly disappeared on his trial, was more skillful than He who was both arrested and crucified. But perhaps he wished from this very thing to prove the arrogance of Christ, in that He made Himself God, that the other may appear to have been more modest, who, though he performed greater actions, as this one thinks, nevertheless did not claim that for himself. I omit at present to compare the works themselves, because in the second and preceding book I have spoken respecting the fraud and tricks of the magic art. I say that there is no one who would not wish that that should especially befall him after death which even the greatest kings desire. For why do men prepare for themselves magnificent sepulchers why statues and images? Why by some illustrious deeds, or even by death undergone in behalf of their countrymen, do they endeavor to deserve the good opinions of men? Why, in short, have you yourself wished to raise a monument of your talent, built with this detestable folly, as if with mud, except that you hope for immortality from the remembrance of your name? It is foolish, therefore, to imagine that Apollonius did not desire that which he would plainly wish for if he were able to attain to it; because there is no one who refuses immortality, and especially when you say that he was both adored by some as a god, and that his image was set up under the name of Hercules, the averter of evil, and is even now honored by the Ephesians.

  He could not therefore after death be believed to be a god, because it was evident that he was both a man and a magician; and for this reason he affected divinity under the title of a name belonging to another, for in his own name he was unable to attain it, nor did he venture to make the attempt. But he of whom we speak could both be believed to be a god, because he was not a magician, and was believed to be such because he was so in truth. I do not say this, he says, that Apollonius was not accounted a god, because he did not wish it, but that it may be evident that we, who did not at once connect a belief in his divinity with wonderful deeds, are wiser than you, who on account of slight wonders believed that he was a god. It is not wonderful if you, who are far removed from the wisdom of God, understand nothing at all of those things which you have read, since the Jews, who from the beginning had frequently read the prophets, and to whom the mystery of God had been assigned, were nevertheless ignorant of what they read. Learn, therefore, if you have any sense, that Christ was not believed by us to be God on this account, because He did wonderful things, but because we saw that all things were done in His case which were announced to us by the prediction of the prophets. He performed wonderful deeds: we might have supposed Him to be a magician, as you now suppose Him to be, and the Jews then supposed Him, if all the prophets did not with one accord proclaim that Christ would do those very things. Therefore we believe Him to be God, not more from His wonderful deeds and works, than from that very cross which you as dogs lick, since that also was predicted at the same time. It was not therefore on His own testimony (for who can be believed when he speaks concerning himself?), but on the testimony of the prophets who long before foretold all things which He did and suffered, that He gained a belief in His divinity, which could have happened neither to Apollonius, nor to Apuleius, nor to any of the magicians; nor can it happen at any time. When, therefore, he had poured forth such absurd ravings of his ignorance, when he had eagerly endeavored utterly to destroy the truth, he dared to give to his books which were impious and the enemies of God the title of "truth-loving." O blind breast! O mind more black than Cimmerian darkness, as they say! He may perhaps have been a disciple of Anaxagoras, to whom snows were as black as ink. But it is the same blindness, to give the name of falsehood to truth, and of truth to falsehood. Doubtless the crafty man wished to conceal the wolf under the skin of a sheep, that he might ensnare the reader by a deceitful title. Let it be true; grant that you did this from ignorance, not from malice: what truth, however, have you brought to us, except that, being a defender of the gods, you had at last betrayed those very gods? For, having set forth the praises of the Supreme God, whom you confessed to be king, most mighty, the maker of all things, the fountain of honors, the parent of all, the creator and preserver of all living creatures, you took away the kingdom from your own Jupiter; and when you had driven him from the supreme power, you reduced him to the rank of servants. Thus your own conclusion convicts you of folly, vanity, and error. For you affirm that the gods exist, and yet you subject and enslave them to that God whose religion you attempt to overturn.

**Chap. IV.—Why This Work Was Published, and Again of Tertullian and Cyprian.**

Since, therefore, they of whom I have spoken had set forth their sacrilegious writings in my presence, and to my grief, being incited both by the arrogant impiety of these, and by the consciousness of truth itself, and (as I think) by God, I have undertaken this office, that with all the strength of my mind I might refute the accusers of righteousness; not that I should write against these, who might be crushed with a few words, but that I might once for all by one attack overthrow all who everywhere effect, or have effected, the same work. For I do not doubt that very many others, and in many places, and that not only in Greek, but also in Latin writings, have raised a monument of their own unrighteousness. And since I was not able to reply to these separately, I thought that this cause was to be so pleaded by me that I might overthrow former writers, together with all their writings, and cut off from future writers the whole power of writing and of replying. Only let them attend, and I will assuredly effect that whosoever shall know these things, must either embrace that which he before condemned, or, which is next to it, cease at length to deride it. Although Tertullian fully pleaded the same cause in that treatise which is entitled the *Apology*, yet, inasmuch as it is one thing to answer accusers, which consists in defense or denial only, and another thing to instruct, which we do, in which the substance of the whole system must be contained, I have not shrunk from this labor, that I might complete the subject, which Cyprian did not fully carry out in that discourse in which he endeavors to refute Demetrianus (as he himself says) railing at and clamoring against the truth. Which subject he did not handle as he ought to have done; for he ought to have been refuted not by the testimonies of Scripture, which he plainly considered vain, fictitious, and false, but by arguments and reason. For, since he was contending against a man who was ignorant of the truth, he ought for a while to have laid aside divine readings, and to have formed from the beginning this man as one who was altogether ignorant, and to have shown to him by degrees the beginnings of light, that he might not be dazzled, the whole of its brightness being presented to him.

For as an infant is unable, on account of the tenderness of its stomach, to receive the nourishment of solid and strong food, but is supported by liquid and soft milk, until, its strength being confirmed, it can feed on stronger nourishment; so also it was befitting that this man, because he was not yet capable of receiving divine things, should be presented with human testimonies—that is, of philosophers and historians—in order that he might especially be refuted by his own authorities. And since he did not do this, being carried away by his distinguished knowledge of the sacred writings, so that he was content with those things alone in which faith consists, I have undertaken, with the favor of God, to do this, and at the same time to prepare the way for the imitation of others. And if, through my exhortation, learned and eloquent men shall begin to betake themselves to this subject, and shall choose to display their talents and power of speaking in this field of truth, no one can doubt that false religions will quickly disappear, and philosophy altogether fall, if all shall be persuaded that this alone is religion and the only true wisdom. But I have wandered from the subject further than I wished.

## Chap. V.—There Was True Justice Under Saturnus, But It Was Banished by Jupiter.

Now the promised disputation concerning justice must be given; which is either by itself the greatest virtue, or by itself the fountain of virtue, which not only philosophers sought, but poets also, who were much earlier, and were esteemed as wise before the origin of the name of philosophy. These clearly understood that this justice was absent from the affairs of men; and they feigned that it, being offended with the vices of men, departed from the earth, and withdrew to heaven; and that they may teach what it is to live justly (for they are accustomed to give precepts by circumlocutions), they repeat examples of justice from the times of Saturnus, which they call the golden times, and they relate in what condition human life was while it delayed on the earth. And this is not to be regarded as a poetic fiction, but as the truth. For, while Saturnus reigned, the religious worship of the gods not having yet been instituted, nor any race being as yet set apart in the belief of its divinity, God was manifestly worshipped. And therefore there were neither dissensions, nor enmities, nor wars.

"Not yet had rage unsheathed maddened swords,"

as Germanicus Cæsar speaks in his poem translated from Aratus,

"Nor had discord been known among relatives."

No, nor even among strangers: but there were no swords at all to be unsheathed. For who, when justice was present and in vigor, would think respecting his own protection, since no one plotted against him; or respecting the destruction of another, since no one desired anything?

"They preferred to live content with a simple mode of life,"

as Cicero relates in his poem; and this is peculiar to our religion. "It was not even allowed to mark out or to divide the plain with a boundary: men sought all things in common;" since God had given the earth in common to all, that they might pass their life in common, not that mad and raging avarice might claim all things for itself, and that that which was produced for all might not be wanting to any. And this saying of the poet ought so to be taken, not as suggesting the idea that individuals at that time had no private property, but it must be regarded as a poetical figure; that we may understand that men were so liberal, that they did not shut up the fruits of the earth produced for them, nor did they in solitude brood over the things stored up, but admitted the poor to share the fruits of their labor:—

"Now streams of milk, now streams of nectar flowed."

And no wonder, since the storehouses of the good liberally lay open to all. Nor did avarice intercept the divine bounty, and thus cause hunger and thirst in common; but all alike had abundance, since they who had possessions gave liberally and bountifully to those who had not. But after that Saturnus had been banished from heaven, and had arrived in Latium,—

"Exiled from his throne
By Jove, his mightier heir,"—

since the people either through fear of the new king, or of their own accord, had become corrupted and ceased to worship God, and had begun to esteem the king in the place of God, since he himself, almost a parricide, was an example to others to the injury of piety,—

"The most just Virgin in haste deserted the lands;"

but not as Cicero says,

"And settled, in the kingdom of Jupiter, and in a part of the heaven."

For how could she settle or tarry in the kingdom of him who expelled his father from his kingdom, harassed him with war, and drove him as an exile over the whole world?

"He gave to the black serpents their noxious poison, And ordered wolves to prowl;"

that is, he introduced among men hatred, and envy, and stratagem; so that they were poisonous as serpents, and rapacious as wolves. And they truly do this who persecute those who are righteous and faithful towards God, and give to judges the power of using violence against the innocent. Perhaps Jupiter may have done something of this kind for the overthrow and removal of righteousness; and on this account he is related to have made serpents fierce, and to have whetted the spirit of wolves.

"Then war's indomitable rage,
And greedy lust of gain;"

and not without reason. For the worship of God being taken away, men lost the knowledge of good and evil. Thus the common intercourse of life perished from among then, and the bond of human society was destroyed. Then they began to contend with one another, and to plot, and to acquire for themselves glory from the shedding of human blood.

**Chap. VI.—After the Banishment of Justice, Lust, Unjust Laws, Daring, Avarice, Ambition, Pride, Impiety, and Other Vices Reigned.**

And the source of all these evils was lust; which, indeed, burst forth from the contempt of true majesty. For not only did they who had a superfluity fail to bestow a share upon others, but they even seized the property of others, drawing everything to their private gain; and the things which formerly even individuals labored to obtain for the common use of men, were now conveyed to the houses of a few. For, that they might subdue others by slavery, they began especially to withdraw and collect together the necessaries of life, and to keep them firmly shut up, that they might make the bounties of heaven their own; not on account of kindness, a feeling which had no existence in them, but that they might sweep together all the instruments of lust and avarice. They also, under the name of justice, passed most unequal and unjust laws, by which they might defend their plunder and avarice against the force of the multitude. They prevailed, therefore, as much by authority as by strength, or resources, or malice. And since there was in them no trace of justice, the offices of which are humanity, equity, pity, they now began to rejoice in a proud and swollen inequality, and made themselves higher than other men, by a retinue of attendants, and by the sword, and by the brilliancy of their garments. For this reason they invented for themselves honors, and purple robes, and fasces, that, being supported by the terror produced by axes and swords, they might, as it were by the right of masters, rule them, stricken with fear, and alarmed. Such was the condition in which the life of man was placed by that king who, having defeated and put to flight a parent, did not seize his kingdom, but set up an impious tyranny by violence and armed men, and took away that golden age of justice, and compelled men to become wicked and impious, even from this very circumstance, that he turned them away from God to the worship of himself; and the terror of his excessive power had extorted this.

For who would not fear him who was girded about with arms, whom the unwonted gleam of steel and swords surrounded? Or what stranger would he spare who had not even spared his own father? Whom, in truth, should he fear, who had conquered in war, and destroyed by massacre the race of the Titans, which was strong and excelling in might? What wonder if the whole multitude, pressed by unusual fear, had given themselves up to the adulation of a single man? Him they venerated, to him they paid the greatest honor. And since it is judged to be a kind of obsequiousness to imitate the customs and vices of a king, all men laid aside piety, lest, if they should live piously, they might seem to upbraid the wickedness of the king. Thus, being corrupted by continual imitation, they abandoned divine right, and the practice of living wickedly by degrees became a habit. And now nothing remained of the pious and excellent condition of the preceding age; but justice being banished, and drawing with her the truth, left to men error, ignorance, and blindness. The poets therefore were ignorant, who sung that she fled to heaven, to the kingdom of Jupiter. For if justice was on the earth in the age which they call "golden," it is plain that she was driven away by Jupiter, who changed the golden age. But the change of the age and the expulsion of justice is to be deemed nothing else, as I have said, than the laying aside of divine religion, which alone effects that man should esteem man dear, and should know that he is bound to him by the tie of brotherhood, since God is alike a Father to all, so as to share the bounties of the common God and Father with those who do not possess them; to injure no one, to oppress no one, not to close his door against a stranger, nor his ear against a suppliant, but to be bountiful, beneficent, and liberal, which Tullius thought to be praises suitable to a king. This truly is justice, and this is the golden age, which was first corrupted when Jupiter reigned, and shortly afterwards, when he himself and all his offspring were consecrated as gods, and the worship of many deities undertaken, had been altogether taken away.

**Chap. VII.—Of the Coming of Jesus, and Its Fruit; And of the Virtues and Vices of that Age.**

But God, as a most indulgent parent, when the last time approached, sent a messenger to bring back that old age, and justice which had been put to flight, that the human race might not be agitated by very great and perpetual errors. Therefore the appearance of that golden time returned, and justice was restored to the earth, but was assigned to a few; and this justice is nothing else than the pious and religious worship of the one God. But perhaps some may be inclined to ask, why, if this be justice, it is not given to all mankind, and the whole multitude does not agree to it. This is a matter of great disputation, why a difference was retained by God when He gave justice to the earth; and this I have shown in another place, and whenever a favorable opportunity shall occur it shall be explained. Now it is sufficient very briefly to signify it: that virtue can neither be discerned, unless it has vices opposed to it; nor be perfect, unless it is exercised by adversity. For God designed that there should be this distinction between good and evil things, that we may know from that which is evil the quality of the good, and also the quality of the evil from the good; nor can the nature of the one be understood if the other is taken away. God therefore did not exclude evil, that the nature of virtue might be evident. For how could patient endurance retain its meaning and name if there were nothing which we were compelled to endure? How could faith devoted to its God deserve praise, unless there were some one who wished to turn us away from God? For on this account He permitted the unjust to be more powerful, that they might be able to compel to evil; and on this account to be more numerous, that virtue might be precious, because it is rare. And this very point is admirably and briefly shown by Quintilian in "the muffled head." "For what virtue," he says, "would there be in innocence, had not its rarity furnished it with praises? But because it is provided by nature that hatred, desire, and anger drive men blindly to that object to which they have applied themselves, to be free from fault appears to be beyond the power of man. Otherwise, if nature had given to all men equal affections, piety would be nothing."

How true this is, the necessity of the case itself teaches. For if it is virtue to resist with fortitude evils and vices, it is evident that, without evil and vice, there is no *perfected* virtue; and that God might render this complete and perfect, He retained that which was contrary to it, with which it might contend. For, being agitated by evils which harass it, it gains stability; and in proportion to the frequency with which it is urged onward, is the firmness with which it is strengthened. This is evidently the cause which effects that, although justice is sent to men, yet it cannot be said that a golden age exists; because God has not taken away evil, that He might retain that diversity which alone preserves the mystery of a divine religion.

**Chap. VIII.—Of Justice Known to All, But Not Embraced; Of the True Temple of God, and of His Worship, that All Vices May Be Subdued.**

They, therefore, who think that no one is just, have justice before their eyes, but are unwilling to discern it. For what reason is there why they should describe it either in poems or in all their discourse, complaining of its absence, when it is very easy for them to be good if they wish? Why do you depict to yourselves justice as worthless, and wish that she may fall from heaven, as it were, represented in some image? Behold, she is in your sight; receive her, if you are able, and place her in the abode of your breast; and do not imagine that this is difficult, or unsuited to the times. Be just and good, and the justice which you seek will follow you of her own accord. Lay aside every evil thought from your hearts, and that golden age will at once return to you, which you cannot attain to by any other means than by beginning to worship the true God. But you long for justice on the earth, while the worship of false gods continues, which cannot possibly come to pass. But it was not possible even at that time when you imagine, because those deities whom you impiously worship were not yet produced, and the worship of the one God must have prevailed throughout the earth; of that God, I say, who hates wickedness and requires goodness; whose temple is not stones or clay, but man himself, who bears the image of God. And this temple is adorned not with corruptible gifts of gold and jewels, but with the lasting offices of virtues. Learn, therefore, if any intelligence is left to you, that men are wicked and unjust because gods are worshipped; and that all evils daily increase to the affairs of men on this account, because God the Maker and Governor of this world has been neglected; because, contrary to that which is right, impious superstitions have been taken up; and lastly, because you do not permit God to be worshipped even by a few.

But if God only were worshipped, there would not be dissensions and wars, since men would know that they are the sons of one God; and, therefore, among those who were connected by the sacred and inviolable bond of divine relationship, there would be no plotting, inasmuch as they would know what kind of punishments God prepared for the destroyers of souls, who sees through secret crimes, and even the very thoughts themselves. There would be no frauds or plundering if they had learned, through the instruction of God, to be content with that which was their own, though little, so that they might prefer solid and eternal things to those which are frail and perishable. There would be no adulteries, and debaucheries, and prostitution of women, if it were known to all, that whatever is sought beyond the desire of procreation is condemned by God. Nor would necessity compel a woman to dishonor her modesty, to seek for herself a most disgraceful mode of sustenance; since the males also would restrain their lust, and the pious and religious contributions of the rich would succor the destitute. There would not, therefore, as I have said, be these evils on the earth, if there were by common consent a general observance of the law of God, if those things were done by all which our people alone perform. How happy and how golden would be the condition of human affairs, if throughout the world gentleness, and piety, and peace, and innocence, and equity, and temperance, and faith, took up their abode! In short, there would be no need of so many and varying laws to rule men, since the law of God alone would be sufficient for perfect innocence; nor would there be any need of prisons, or the swords of rulers, or the terror of punishments, since the wholesomeness of the divine precepts infused into the breasts of men would of itself instruct them to works of justice. But now men are wicked through ignorance of what is right and good. And this, indeed, Cicero saw; for, discoursing on the subject of the laws, he says: "As the world, with all its parts agreeing with one another, coheres and depends upon one and the same nature, so all men, being naturally confused among themselves, disagree through depravity; nor do they understand that they are related by blood, and that they are all subject to one and the same guardianship: for if this were kept in mind, assuredly men would live the life of gods." Therefore the unjust and impious worship of the gods has introduced all the evils by which mankind in turn destroy one another. For they could not retain their piety, who, as prodigal and rebellious children, had renounced the authority of God, the common parent of all.

## Chap. IX.—Of the Crimes of the Wicked, and the Torture Inflicted on the Christians.

At times, however, they perceive that they are wicked, and praise the condition of the former ages, and conjecture that justice is absent because of their characters and deserts; for, though she presents herself to their eyes, they not only fail to receive or recognize her, but they even violently hate, and persecute, and endeavor to banish her. Let us suppose, in the meantime, that she whom we follow is not justice: how will they receive her whom they imagine to be the true justice, if she shall have come, when they torture and kill those whom they themselves confess to be imitators of the just, because they perform good and just actions; whereas, if they should put to death the wicked only, they would deserve to be unvisited by justice, who had no other reason for leaving the earth than the shedding of human blood? How much more so when they slay the righteous, and account the followers of justice themselves as enemies, yea, as more than enemies; who, though they eagerly seek their lives, and property, and children by sword and fire, yet are spared when conquered; and there is a place for clemency even amidst arms; or if they have determined to carry their cruelty to the utmost, nothing more is done towards them, except that they are put to death or led away to slavery! But this is unutterable which is done towards those who are ignorant of crime, and none are regarded as more guilty than those who are of all men innocent. Therefore most wicked men venture to make mention of justice, men who surpass wild beasts in ferocity, who lay waste the most gentle flock of God,—

> "Like gaunt wolves rushing from their den,
> Whom lawless hunger's sullen growl
> Drives forth into the night to prowl."

But these have been maddened not by the fury of hunger, but of the heart; nor do they prowl in a black mist, but by open plundering; nor does the consciousness of their crimes ever recall them from profaning the sacred and holy name of justice with that mouth which, like the jaws of beasts, is wet with the blood of the innocent. What must we say is especially the cause of this excessive and persevering hatred?

"Does truth produce hatred,"

as the poet says, as though inspired by the Divine Spirit, or are they ashamed to be bad in the presence of the just and good? Or is it rather from both causes? For the truth is always hateful on this account, because he who sins wishes to have free scope for sinning, and thinks that he cannot in any other way more securely enjoy the pleasure of his evil doings, than if there is no one whom his faults may displease. Therefore they endeavor entirely to exterminate and take them away as witnesses of their crimes and wickedness, and think them burthensome to themselves, as though their life were reproved. For why should any be unseasonably good, who, when the public morals are corrupted, should censure them by living well? Why should not all be equally wicked, rapacious, unchaste, adulterers, perjured, covetous, and fraudulent? Why should they not rather be taken out of the way, in whose presence they are ashamed to lead an evil life, who, though not by words, for they are silent, but by their very course of life, so unlike their own, assail and strike the forehead of sinners? For whoever disagrees with them appears to reprove them.

Nor is it greatly to be wondered at if these things are done towards men, since for the same cause the people who were placed in hope, and not ignorant of God, rose up against God Himself; and the same necessity follows the righteous which attacked the Author of righteousness Himself. Therefore they harass and torment them with studied kinds of punishments, and think it little to kill those whom they hate, unless cruelty also mocks their bodies. But if any through fear of pain or death, or by their own perfidy, have deserted the heavenly oath, and have consented to deadly sacrifices, these they praise and load with honors, that by their example they may allure others. But upon those who have highly esteemed their faith, and have not denied that they are worshippers of God, they fall with all the strength of their butchery, as though they thirsted for blood; and they call them desperate, because they by no means spare their body; as though anything could be more desperate, than to torture and tear in pieces him whom you know to be innocent. Thus no sense of shame remains among those from whom all kind feeling is absent, and they retort upon just men reproaches which are befitting to themselves. For they call them impious, being themselves forsooth pious, and shrinking from the shedding of human blood; whereas, if they would consider their own acts, and the acts of those whom they condemn as impious, they would now understand how false they are, and more deserving of all those things which they either say or do against the good. For they are not of our number, but of theirs who besiege the roads in arms, practice piracy by sea; or if it has not been in their power openly to assail, secretly mix poisons; who kill their wives that they may gain their dowries, or their husbands that they may marry adulterers; who either strangle the sons born from themselves, or if they are too pious, expose them; who restrain their incestuous passions neither from a daughter, nor sister, nor mother, nor priestess; who conspire against their own citizens and country; who do not fear the sack; who, in fine, commit sacrilege, and despoil the temples of the gods whom they worship; and, to speak of things which are light and usually practiced by them, who hunt for inheritances, forge wills, either remove or exclude the just heirs; who prostitute their own persons to lust; who, in short, unmindful of what they were born, contend with women in passivity; who, in violation of all propriety, pollute and dishonor the most sacred part of their body; who mutilate themselves, and that which is more impious, in order that they may be priests of religion; who do not even spare their own life, but sell their lives to be taken away in public; who, if they sit as judges, corrupted by a bribe, either destroy the innocent or set free the guilty without punishment; who grasp at the heaven itself by sorceries, as though the earth would not contain their wickedness. These crimes, I say, and more than these, are plainly committed by those who are worshippers of the gods.

Amidst these crimes of such number and magnitude, what place is there for justice? And I have collected a few only out of many, not for the purpose of censure, but to show their nature. Let those who shall wish to know all take in hand the books of Seneca, who was at the same time a most true describer and a most vehement accuser of the public morals and vices. But Lucilius also briefly and concisely described that dark life in these verses: "But now from morn to night, on festival and ordinary day alike, the whole people and the fathers with one accord display themselves in the forum, and never depart from it. They have all given themselves to one and the same pursuit and art that they may be able cautiously to deceive, to fight treacherously, to contend in flattery, each to pretend that he is a good man, to lie in wait, as if all were enemies to all." But which of these things can be laid to the charge of our people, with whom the whole of religion consists in living without guilt and without spot? Since, therefore, they see that both they and their people do those things which we have said, but that ours practice nothing else but that which is just and good, they might, if they had any understanding, have perceived from this, both that they who do what is good are pious, and that they themselves who commit wicked actions are impious. For it is impossible that they who do not err in all the actions of their life, should err in the main point, that is, in religion, which is the chief of all things. For impiety, if taken up in that which is the most important, would follow through all the rest. And therefore it is impossible that they who err in the whole of their life should not be deceived also in religion; inasmuch as piety, if it kept its rule in the chief point, would maintain its course in others. Thus it happens, that on either side the character of the main subject may be known from the state of the actions which are carried on.

**Chap. X.—Of False Piety, and of False and True Religion.**

It is worthwhile to investigate their piety that from their merciful and pious actions it may be understood what is the character of those things which are done by them contrary to the laws of piety. And that I may not seem to attack anyone with harshness, I will take a character from the poets, and one which is the greatest example of piety. In Maro, that king

> "Than who
> The breath of being none e'er drew,
> More brave, more pious, or more true,"—

what proofs of justice did he bring forward to us?

> "There walk with hands fast bound behind

> The victim prisoners, designed
> For slaughter o'er the flames."

What can be more merciful than this piety? *What more merciful* than to immolate human victims to the dead, and to feed the fire with the blood of men as with oil? But perhaps this may not have been the fault of the hero himself, but of the poet, who polluted with distinguished wickedness "a man distinguished by his piety." Where then, O poet, is that piety which you so frequently praise? Behold the pious Æneas:—

> "Four hapless youths of Sulmo's breed,
> And four who Ufens call their sire,
> He takes alive, condemned to bleed
> To Pallas' shade on Pallas' pyre."

Why, therefore, at the very same time when he was sending the men in chains to slaughter, did he say,

> "Fain would I grant the living peace,"

when he ordered that those whom he had in his power alive should be slain in the place of cattle? But this, as I have said, was not his fault—for he perhaps had not received a liberal education—but yours; for, though you were learned, yet you were ignorant of the nature of piety, and you believed that that wicked and detestable action of his was the befitting exercise of piety. He is plainly called pious on this account only, because he loved his father. Why should I say that

> "The good Æneas owned their plea,"

and yet slew them? For, though adjured by the same father, and

> "By young Iulus' dawning day,"

he did not spare them,

"Live fury kindling every vein"

What! Can anyone imagine that there was any virtue in him who was fired with madness as stubble, and, forgetful of the shade of his father, by whom he was entreated, was unable to curb his wrath? He was therefore by no means pious who not only slew the unresisting, but even suppliants. Here someone will say: What then, or where, or of what character is piety? Truly it is among those who are ignorant of wars, who maintain concord with all, who are friendly even to their enemies, who love all men as brethren, who know how to restrain their anger, and to soothe every passion of the mind with calm government. How great a mist, therefore, how great a cloud of darkness and errors, has over-spread the breasts of men who, when they think themselves especially pious, then become especially impious? For the more religiously they honor those earthy images, so much the more wicked are they towards the name of the true divinity. And therefore they are often harassed with greater evils as the reward of their impiety; and because they know not the cause of these evils, the blame is altogether ascribed to fortune, and the philosophy of Epicurus finds a place, who thinks that nothing extends to the gods, and that they are neither influenced by favor nor moved by anger, because they often see their despisers happy, and their worshippers in misery. And this happens on this account, because when they seem to be religious and naturally good, they are believed to deserve nothing of that kind which they often suffer. However, they console themselves by accusing fortune; nor do they perceive that if she had any existence, she would never injure her worshippers. Piety of this kind is therefore deservedly followed by punishment; and the deity offended with the wickedness of men who are depraved in their religious worship, punishes them with heavy misfortune; who, although they live with holiness in the greatest faith and innocence, yet because they worship gods whose impious and profane rites are an abomination to the true God, are estranged from justice and the name of true piety. Nor is it difficult to show why the worshippers of the gods cannot be good and just. For how shall they abstain from the shedding of blood who worship bloodthirsty deities, Mars and Bellona? Or how shall they spare their parents who worship Jupiter, who drove out his father? Or how shall they spare their own infants who worship Saturnus? How shall they uphold chastity who worship a goddess who is naked, and an adulteress, and who prostitutes herself as it were among the gods? How shall they withhold themselves from plunder and frauds who are acquainted with the thefts of Mercurius, who teaches that to deceive is not the part of fraud, but of cleverness? how shall they restrain their lusts who worship Jupiter, Hercules, Liber, Apollo, and the others, whose adulteries and debaucheries with men and women are not only known to the learned, but are even set forth in the theatres, and made the subject of songs, so that they are notorious to all? Among these things is it possible for men to be just, who, although they were naturally good, would be trained to injustice by the very gods themselves? For, that you may propitiate the god whom you worship, there is need of those things with which you know that he is pleased and delighted. Thus it comes to pass that the god fashions the life of his worshippers according to the character of his own will, since the most religious worship is to imitate.

### Chap XI.—Of the Cruelty of the Heathens against the Christians.

Therefore, because justice is burthensome and unpleasant to those men who agree with the character of their gods, they exercise with violence against the righteous the same impiety which they show in other things. And not without reason are they spoken of by the prophets as beasts. Therefore it is excellently said by Marcus Tullius: "For if there is no one who would not prefer to die than to be changed into the figure of a beast, although he is about to have the mind of a man, how much more wretched is it to be of a brutalized mind in the figure of a man! To me, indeed, it seems as much worse as the mind is more excellent than the body." Therefore they view with disdain the bodies of beasts, though they are themselves crueler than these; and they pride themselves on this account, that they were born men, though they have nothing belonging to man except the features and the eminent figure. For what Caucasus, what India, what Hyrcania ever nourished beasts so savage and so bloodthirsty? For the fury of all wild beasts rages until their appetite is satisfied; and when their hunger is appeased, immediately is pacified. That is truly a beast by whose command alone

> "With rivulets of slaughter reeks
> The stern embattled field."
> "Dire agonies, wild terrors swarm,
> And Death glares grim in many a form."

No one can befittingly describe the cruelty of this beast, which reclines in one place, and yet rages with iron teeth throughout the world, and not only tears in pieces the limbs of men, but also breaks their very bones, and rages over their ashes, that there may be no place for their burial, as though they who confess God aimed at this, that their tombs should be visited, and not rather that they themselves may reach the presence of God.

What brutality is it, what fury, what madness, to deny light to the living, earth to the dead? I say, therefore, that nothing is more wretched than those men whom necessity has either found or made the ministers of another's fury, the satellites of an impious command. For that was no honor, or exaltation of dignity, but the condemnation of a man to torture, and also to the everlasting punishment of God. But it is impossible to relate what things they performed individually throughout the world. For what number of volumes will contain so infinite, so varied kinds of cruelty? For, having gained power, every one raged according to his own disposition. Some, through excessive timidity, proceeded to greater lengths than they were commanded; others thus acted through their own particular hatred against the righteous; some by a natural ferocity of mind; some through a desire to please, and that by this service they might prepare the way to higher offices: some were swift to slaughter, as an individual in Phrygia, who burnt a whole assembly of people, together with their place of meeting. But the crueler he was, so much the more merciful is he found to be. But that is the worst kind *of persecutors* whom a false appearance of clemency flatters; he is the more severe, he the crueler torturer, who determines to put no one to death. Therefore it cannot be told what great and what grievous modes of tortures judges of this kind devised, that they might arrive at the accomplishment of their purpose. But they do these things not only on this account, that they may be able to boast that they have slain none of the innocent,—for I myself have heard some boasting that their administration has been in this respect without bloodshed,—but also for the sake of envy, lest either they themselves should be overcome, or the others should obtain the glory due to their virtue. And thus, in devising modes of punishment, they think of nothing else besides victory. For they know that this is a contest and a battle. I saw in Bithynia the præfect wonderfully elated with joy, as though he had subdued some nation of barbarians, because one who had resisted for two years with great spirit appeared at length to yield. They contend, therefore, that they may conquer and inflict exquisite pains on their bodies, and avoid nothing else but that the victims may not die under the torture: as though, in truth, death alone could make them happy, and as though tortures also in proportion to their severity would not produce greater glory of virtue. But they with obstinate folly give orders that diligent care shall be given to the tortured, that their limbs may be renovated for other tortures, and fresh blood be supplied for punishment. What can be so pious, so beneficent, so humane? They would not have bestowed such anxious care on any whom they loved. This is the discipline of the gods: to these deeds they train their worshippers; these are the sacred rites which they require. Moreover, most wicked murderers have invented impious laws against the pious. For both sacrilegious ordinances and unjust disputations of jurists are read. Domitius, in his seventh book, concerning the office of the proconsul, has collected wicked rescripts of princes, that he might show by what punishments they ought to be visited who confessed themselves to be worshippers of God.

## Chap. XII.—Of True Virtue; And of the Estimation of a Good or Bad Citizen.

What would you do to those who give the name of justice to the tortures inflicted by tyrants of old, who fiercely raged against the innocent; and though they are teachers of injustice and cruelty, wish to appear just and prudent, being blind and dull, and ignorant of affairs and of truth? Is justice so hateful to you, O abandoned minds, that ye regard it as equal with the greatest crimes? Is innocence so utterly lost in your eyes that you do not think it worthy of death only, but it is esteemed as beyond all crimes to commit no crime, and to have a breast pure from all contagion of guilt? And since we are speaking generally with those who worship gods, let us have your permission to do good with you; for this is our law, this our business, this our religion. If we appear to you wise, imitate us; if foolish, despise us, or even laugh at us, if you please; for our folly is profitable to us. Why do you lacerate, why do you afflict us? We do not envy your wisdom. We prefer this folly of ours—we embrace this. We believe that this is expedient for us,—to love you, and to confer all things upon you, who hate us.

There is in the writings of Cicero a passage not inconsistent with the truth, in that disputation which is held by Furius against justice: "I ask," he says, "if there should be two men, and one of them should be an excellent man, of the highest integrity, the greatest justice, and remarkable faith, and the other distinguished by crime and audacity; and if the state should be in such error as to regard that good man as wicked, vicious, and execrable, but should think the one who is most wicked to be of the highest integrity and faith; and if, in accordance with this opinion of all the citizens, that good man should be harassed, dragged away, should be deprived of his hands, have his eyes dug out, should be condemned, be bound, be branded, be banished, be in want, and lastly, should most justly appear to all to be most wretched; but, on the other hand, if that wicked man should be praised, and honored, and loved by all,—if all honors, all commands, all wealth, and all abundance should be bestowed upon him,—in short, if he should be judged in the estimation of all an excellent man, and most worthy of all fortune,—who, I pray, will be so mad as to doubt which of the two he would prefer to be?" Assuredly he put forth this example as though he divined what evils were about to happen to us, and in what manner, on account of righteousness; for our people suffer all these things through the perverseness of those in error. Behold, the state, or rather the whole world itself, is in such error, that it persecutes, tortures, condemns, and puts to death good and righteous men, as though they were wicked and impious. For as to what he says, that no one is so infatuated as to doubt which of the two he would prefer to be, he indeed, as the one who was contending against justice, thought this, that the wise man would prefer to be bad if he had a good reputation, than to be good with a bad reputation.

But may this senselessness be absent from us, that we should prefer that which is false to the true? Or does the character of our good man depend upon the errors of the people, more than upon our own conscience and the judgment of God? Or shall any prosperity ever allure us, so that we should not rather choose true goodness, though accompanied with all evil, than false goodness together with all prosperity? Let kings retain their kingdoms, the rich their riches, as Plautus says, the wise their wisdom; let them leave to us our folly, which is evidently proved to be wisdom, from the very fact that they envy us its possession: for who would envy a fool, but he who is himself most foolish? But they are not so foolish as to envy fools; but from the fact of their following us up with such care and anxiety, they allow that we are not fools. For why should they rage with such cruelty, unless it is that they fear lest, as justice grows strong from day to day, they should be deserted together with their decaying gods? If, therefore, the worshippers of gods are wise, and we are foolish, why do they fear lest the wise shall be allured by the foolish?

**Chapter XIII.—Of the Increase and the Punishment of the Christians.**

But since our number is continually increased from the worshippers of gods, but is never lessened, not even in persecution itself,—since men may commit sin, and be defiled by sacrifice, but they cannot be turned away from God, for the truth prevails by its own power,—who is there, I pray, so foolish and so blind as not to see on which side wisdom is? But they are blinded by malice and fury, that they cannot see; and they think that those are foolish who, when they have it in their power to avoid punishments, nevertheless prefer to be tortured and to be put to death; whereas they might see from this very circumstance, that it is not folly to which so many thousands throughout the world agree with one and the same mind. For if women fall into error through the weakness of their sex (for these persons sometimes call it a womanish and anile superstition), men doubtless are wise. If boys, if youths are improvident through their age, the mature and aged doubtless have a fixed judgment. If one city is unwise, it is evident that the other innumerable cities cannot be foolish. If one province or one nation is without prudence, the rest must have understanding of that which is right. But since the divine law has been received from the rising even to the setting of the sun, and each sex, every age, and nation, and country, with one and the same mind obeys God—since there is everywhere the same patient endurance, the same contempt of death—they ought to have understood that there is some reason in that matter, that it is not without a cause that it is defended even to death, that there is some foundation and solidity, which not only frees that religion from injuries and molestation, but always increases and makes it stronger. For in this respect also the malice of those is brought to light, who think that they have utterly overthrown the religion of God if they have corrupted men, when it is permitted them to make satisfaction also to God; and there is no worshipper of God so evil who does not, when the opportunity is given him, return to appease God, and that, too, with greater devotedness. For the consciousness of sin and the fear of punishment make a man more religious, and the faith is always much stronger which is replaced through repentance. If, therefore, they themselves, when they think that the gods are angry with them, nevertheless believe that they are appeased by gifts, and sacrifices, and incense, what reason is there why they should imagine our God to be so unmerciful and implacable, that it should appear impossible for him to be a Christian, who by compulsion and against his will has poured a libation to their gods? Unless by chance they think that those who are once contaminated are about to change their mind, so that they may now begin of their own accord to do that which they have done under the influence of torture. Who would willingly undertake that duty which began with injury? Who, when he sees the scars on his own sides, would not the more hate the gods, on account of whom he bears the traces of lasting punishment, and the marks imprinted upon his flesh? Thus it comes to pass, that when peace is given from heaven, those who were estranged from us return, and a fresh crowd of others are added on account of the wonderful nature of the virtue displayed. For when the people see that men are lacerated by various kinds of tortures, and that they retain their patience unsubdued while the executioners are wearied, they think, as is really the case, that neither the agreement of so many nor the constancy of the dying is without meaning, and that patience itself could not surmount such great tortures without the aid of God. Robbers and men of robust frame are unable to endure lacerations of this kind: they utter exclamations, and send forth groans; for they are overcome by pain, because they are destitute of patience infused into them. But in our case (not to speak of men), boys and delicate women in silence overpower their torturers, and even the fire is unable to extort from them a groan. Let the Romans go and boast in their Mutius or Regulus,—the one of whom gave himself up to be slain by the enemy, because he was ashamed to live as a captive; the other being taken by the enemy, when he saw that he could not escape death, laid his hand upon the burning hearth, that he might make atonement for his crime to the enemy whom he wished to kill, and by that punishment received the pardon which he had not deserved. Behold, the weak sex and fragile age endure to be lacerated in the whole body, and to be burned: not of necessity, for it is permitted them to escape if they wished to do so; but of their own will, because they put their trust in God.

### Chap. XIV.—Of the Fortitude of the Christians.

But this is true virtue, which the vaunting philosophers also boast of, not in deed, but with empty words, saying that nothing is so befitting the gravity and constancy of a wise man as to be able to be driven away from his sentiment and purpose by no torturers, but that it is worth his while to suffer torture and death rather than betray a trust or depart from his duty, or, overcome by fear of death or severity of pain, commit any injustice. Unless by chance Flaccus appears to them to rave in his lyrics, when he says,

"Not the rage of the million commanding things evil; Not the doom frowning near in the brows of the tyrant,
    Shakes the upright and resolute man
    In his solid completeness of soul."

And nothing can be more true than this, if it is referred to those who refuse no tortures, no kind of death, that they may not turn aside from faith and justice; who do not tremble at the commands of tyrants nor the swords of rulers, so as not to maintain true and solid liberty with constancy of mind, which wisdom is to be observed in this alone. For who is so arrogant, who so lifted up, as to forbid me to raise my eyes to heaven? Who can impose upon me the necessity either of worshipping that which I am unwilling to worship, or of abstaining from the worship of that which I wish to worship? What further will now be left to us, if even this, which must be done of one's own will, shall be extorted from me by the caprice of another? No one will effect this, if we have any courage to despise death and pain. But if we possess this constancy, why are we judged foolish when we do those things which philosophers praise? Seneca, in charging men with inconsistency, rightly says the highest virtue appears to them to consist in greatness of spirit; and yet the same persons regard him who despises death as a madman, which is plainly a mark of the greatest perverseness. But those followers of vain religions urge this with the same folly with which they fail to understand the true God; and these the Erythræan Sibyl calls "deaf and senseless," since they neither hear nor perceive divine things, but fear and adore an earthen image molded by their own fingers.

**Chap. XV.—Of Folly, Wisdom, Piety, Equity, and Justice.**

But the reason on account of which they imagine those who are wise to be foolish has strong grounds of support (for they are not deceived without reason). And this must be diligently explained by us, that they may at length (if it is possible) recognize their errors. Justice by its own nature has a certain appearance of folly, and I am able to confirm this both by divine and human testimonies. But perhaps we should not succeed with them, unless we should teach them from their own authorities that no one can be just, a matter which is united with true wisdom, unless he also appears to be foolish. Carneades was a philosopher of the Academic sect; and one who knows not what power he had in discussion, what eloquence, what sagacity, will nevertheless understand the character of the man himself from the praises of Cicero or of Lucilius, in whose writings Neptune, discoursing on a subject of the greatest difficulty, shows that it cannot be explained, even if Orcus should restore Carneades himself to life. This Carneades, when he had been sent by the Athenians as ambassador to Rome, disputed copiously on the subject of justice, in the hearing of Galba and Cato, who had been censor, who were at that time the greatest of orators. But on the next day the same man overthrew his own argument by a disputation to the contrary effect, and took away the justice which he had praised on the preceding day, not indeed with the gravity of a philosopher, whose prudence ought to be firm and his opinion settled, but as it were by an oratorical kind of exercise of disputing on both sides. And he was accustomed to do this, that he might be able to refute others who asserted anything. L. Furius, in Cicero, makes mention of that discussion in which justice is overthrown. I believe, inasmuch as he was discussing the subject of the state, he did it that he might introduce the defense and praise of that without which he thought that a state could not be governed. But Carneades, that he might refute Aristotle and Plato, the advocates of justice, in that first disputation collected all the arguments which were alleged in behalf of justice, that he might be able to overthrow them, as he did. For it was very easy to shake justice, having no roots, inasmuch as there was then none on the earth, that its nature or qualities might be perceived by philosophers. And I could wish that men, so many and of such a character, had possessed knowledge also, in proportion to their eloquence and spirit, for completing the defense of this greatest virtue, which has its origin in religion, its principle in equity! But those who were ignorant of that first part could not possess the second. But I wish first to show, summarily and concisely, what it is, that it may be understood that the philosophers were ignorant of justice, and were unable to defend that with which they were unacquainted.

Although justice embraces all the virtues together, yet there are two, the chief of all, which cannot be torn asunder and separated from it—piety and equity. For fidelity, temperance, uprightness, innocence, integrity, and the other things of this kind, either naturally or through the training of parents, may exist in those men who are ignorant of justice, as they have always existed; for the ancient Romans, who were accustomed to glory in justice, used evidently to glory in those virtues which (as I have said) may proceed from justice, and be separated from the very fountain itself. But piety and equity are, as it were, its veins: for in these two fountains the whole of justice is contained; but its source and origin is in the first, all its force and method in the second. But piety is nothing else but the conception of God, as Trismegistus most truly defined it, as we have said in another place. If, therefore, it is piety to know God, and the sum of this knowledge is that you worship Him, it is plain that he is ignorant of justice who does not possess the knowledge of God. For how can he know justice itself, who is ignorant of the source from which it arises? Plato, indeed, spoke many things respecting the one God, by whom he said that the world was framed; but he spoke nothing respecting religion: for he had dreamed of God, but had not known Him. But if either he himself or any other person had wished to complete the defense of justice, he ought first of all to have overthrown the religions of the gods, because they are opposed to piety. And because Socrates indeed tried to do this, he was thrown into prison; that even then it might be seen what was about to happen to those men who had begun to defend true justice, and to serve the only God.

The other part of justice, therefore, is equity; and it is plain that I am not speaking of the equity of judging well, though this also is praiseworthy in a just man, but of making himself equal to others, which Cicero calls equability. For God, who produces and gives breath to men, willed that all should be equal that is, equally matched. He has imposed on all the same condition of living; He has produced all to wisdom; He has promised immortality to all; no one is cut off from His heavenly benefits. For as He distributes to all alike His one light, sends forth His fountains to all, supplies food, and gives the most pleasant rest of sleep; so He bestows on all equity and virtue. In His sight no one is a slave, no one a master; for if all have the same Father, by an equal right we are all children. No one is poor in the sight of God, but he who is without justice; no one is rich, but he who is full of virtues; no one, in short, is excellent, but he who has been good and innocent; no one is most renowned, but he who has abundantly performed works of mercy; no one is most perfect, but he who has filled all the steps of virtue. Therefore neither the Romans nor the Greeks could possess justice, because they had men differing from one another by many degrees, from the poor to the rich, from the humble to the powerful; in short, from private persons to the highest authorities of kings. For where all are not equally matched, there is not equity; and inequality of itself excludes justice, the whole force of which consists in this, that it makes those equal who have by an equal lot arrived at the condition of this life.

## Chap. XVI.—Of the Duties of the Just Man, and the Equity of Christians.

Therefore, since those two fountains of justice are changed, all virtue and all truth are taken away, and justice itself returns to heaven. And on this account the true good was not discovered by philosophers, because they were ignorant both of its origin and effects: which has been revealed to no others but to our people. Someone will say, Are there not among you some poor, and others rich; some servants, and others masters? Is there not some difference between individuals? There is none; nor is there any other cause why we mutually bestow upon each other the name of brethren, except that we believe ourselves to be equal. For since we measure all human things not by the body, but by the spirit, although the condition of bodies is different, yet we have no servants, but we both regard and speak of them as brothers in spirit, in religion as fellow-servants. Riches also do not render men illustrious, except that they are able to make them more conspicuous by good works. For men are rich, not because they possess riches, but because they employ them on works of justice; and they who seem to be poor, on this account are rich, because they are not in want, and desire nothing.

Though, therefore, in lowliness of mind we are on an equality, the free with slaves, and the rich with the poor, nevertheless in the sight of God we are distinguished by virtue. And every one is more elevated in proportion to his greater justice. For if it is justice for a man to put himself on a level even with those of lower rank, although he excels in this very thing, that he made himself equal to his inferiors; yet if he has conducted himself not only as an equal, but even as an inferior, he will plainly obtain a much higher rank of dignity in the judgment of God. For assuredly, since all things in this temporal life are frail and liable to decay, men both prefer themselves to others, and contend about dignity; than which nothing is more foul, nothing more arrogant, nothing more removed from the conduct of a wise man: for these earthly things are altogether opposed to heavenly things. For as the wisdom of men is the greatest foolishness with God, and foolishness is (as I have shown) the greatest wisdom; so he is low and abject in the sight of God who shall have been conspicuous and elevated on earth. For, not to mention that these present earthly goods to which great honor is paid are contrary to virtue, and enervate the vigor of the mind, what nobility, I pray, can be so firm, what resources, what power, since God is able to make kings themselves even lower than the lowest? And therefore God has consulted our interest in placing this in particular among the divine precepts: "He that exalted himself shall be abased; and he that humbled himself shall be exalted." And the wholesomeness of this precept teaches that he who shall *simply* place himself on a level with *other* men, and carry himself with humility, is esteemed excellent and illustrious in the sight of God. For the sentiment is not false which is brought forward in Euripides to this effect:—

"The things which are here considered evil are esteemed good in heaven."

**Chap. XVII.—Of the Equity, Wisdom, and Foolishness of Christians.**

I have explained the reason why philosophers were unable either to find or to defend justice. Now I return to that which I had purposed. Carneades, therefore, since the arguments of the philosophers were weak, undertook the bold task of refuting them, because he understood that they were capable of refutation. The substance of his disputation was this: "That men enacted laws for themselves, with a view to their own advantage, differing indeed according to their characters, and in the case of the same persons often changed according to the times: but that there was no natural law: that all, both men and other animals, were borne by the guidance of nature to their own advantage; therefore that there was no justice, or if any did exist, it was the greatest folly, because it injured itself by promoting the interests of others." And he brought forward these arguments: "That all nations which flourished with dominion, even the Romans themselves, who were masters of the whole world, if they wish to be just, that is, to restore the possessions of others, must return to cottages, and lie down in want and miseries." Then, leaving general topics, he came to particulars. "If a good man," he says, "has a runaway slave, or an unhealthy and infected house, and he alone knows these faults, and on this account offers it for sale, will he give out that the slave is a runaway, and the house which he offers for sale is infected, or will he conceal it from the purchaser? If he shall give it out, he is good indeed, because he will not deceive; but still he will be judged foolish, because he will either sell at a low price or not sell at all. If he shall conceal it, he will be wise indeed, because he will consult his own interest; but he will be also wicked, because he will deceive. Again, if he should find anyone who supposes that he is selling copper ore when it is gold, or lead when it is silver, will he be silent, that he may buy it at a small price; or will he give information of it, so that he may buy it at a great price? It evidently appears foolish to prefer to buy it at a great price." From which he wished it to be understood, both that he who is just and good is foolish, and that he who is wise is wicked; and yet that it may possibly happen without ruin, for men to be contented with poverty. Therefore he passed to greater things, in which no one could be just without danger of his life. For he said: "Certainly it is justice not to put a man to death, not to take the property of another. What, then, will the just man do, if he shall happen to have suffered shipwreck, and someone weaker than himself shall have seized a plank? Will he not thrust him from the plank, that he himself may get upon it, and supported by it may escape, especially since there is no witness in the middle of the sea? If he is wise, he will do so; for he must himself perish unless he shall thus act. But if he choose rather to die than to inflict violence upon another, in this case he is just, but foolish, in not sparing his own life while he spares the life of another. Thus also, if the army of his own people shall have been routed, and the enemy have begun to press upon them, and that just man shall have met with a wounded man on horseback, will he spare him so as to be slain himself, or will he throw him from his horse, that he himself may escape from the enemy? If he shall do this, he will be wise, but also wicked; if he shall not do it, he will be just, but also of necessity foolish." When, therefore, he had thus divided justice into two parts, saying that the one was civil, the other natural, he subverted both: because the civil part is wisdom, but not justice; but the natural part is justice, but not wisdom. These arguments are altogether subtle and acute, and such as Marcus Tullius was unable to refute. For when he represents Lælius as replying to Furius, and speaking in behalf of justice, he passed them by as a pitfall without refuting them; so that the same Lælius appears not to have defended natural justice, which bad fallen under the charge of folly, but that civil justice which Furius had admitted to be wisdom, but unjust.

## Chap. XVIII.—Of Justice, Wisdom, and Folly.

With reference to our present discussion, I have shown how justice bears the resemblance of folly that it may appear that those are not deceived without reason who think that men of our religion are foolish in appearing to do such things as he proposed. Now I perceive that a greater undertaking is required from me, to show why God wished to enclose justice under the appearance of folly, and to remove it from the eyes of men, when I shall have first replied to Furius, since Lælius has not sufficiently replied to him; who, although he was a wise man, as he was called, yet could not be the advocate of true justice, because he did not possess the source and fountain of justice. But this defense is easier for us, to whom by the bounty of Heaven this justice is familiar and well known, and who know it not in name, but in reality. For Plato and Aristotle desired with an honest will to defend justice, and would have effected something, if their good endeavors, their eloquence, and vigor of intellect had been aided also by a knowledge of divine things. Thus their work, being vain and useless, was neglected: nor were they able to persuade any of men to live according to their precept, because that system had no foundation from heaven. But our work must be more certain, since we are taught of God. For they represented justice in words, and pictured it when it was not in sight; nor were they able to confirm their assertions by present examples. For the hearers might have answered that it was impossible to live as they prescribed in their disputation; so that none have as yet existed who followed that course of life. But we show the truth of our statements not only by words, but also by examples derived from the truth. Therefore Carneades understood what is the nature of justice, except that he did not sufficiently perceive that it was not folly; although I seem to myself to understand with what intention he did this. For he did not really think that he who is just is foolish; but when he knew that he was not so, but did not comprehend the cause why he appeared so, he wished to show that the truth lay hidden, that he might maintain the dogma of his own sect, the chief opinion of which is, "that nothing can be fully comprehended."

Let us see, therefore, whether justice has any agreement with folly. The just man, he says, if he does not take away from the wounded man his horse, and from the shipwrecked man his plank, in order that he may preserve his own life, is foolish. First of all, I deny that it can in any way happen that a man who is truly just should be in circumstances of this kind; for the just man is neither at enmity with any human being, nor desires anything at all which is the property of another. For why should he take a voyage, or what should he seek from another land, when his own is sufficient for him? Or why should he carry on war, and mix himself with the passions of others, when his mind is engaged in perpetual peace with men? Doubtless he will be delighted with foreign merchandise or with human blood, who does not know how to seek gain, who is satisfied with his mode of living, and considers it unlawful not only himself to commit slaughter, but to be present with those who do it, and to behold it! But I omit these things, since it is possible that a man may be compelled even against his will to undergo these things. Do you then, O Furius—or rather O Carneades, for all this speech is his—think that justice is so useless, so superfluous, and so despised by God, that it has no power and no influence in itself which may avail for its own preservation? But it is evident that they who are ignorant of the mystery of man, and who therefore refer all things to this present life, cannot know how great is the force of justice. For when they discuss the subject of virtue, although they understand that it is very full of labors and miseries, nevertheless they say that it is to be sought for its own sake; for they by no means see its rewards, which are eternal and immortal. Thus, by referring all things to the present life, they altogether reduce virtue to folly, since it undergoes such great labors of this life in vain and to no purpose. But more on this subject at another opportunity.

In the meanwhile let us speak of justice, as we began, the power of which is so great, that when it has raised its eyes to heaven, it deserves all things from God. Flaccus therefore rightly said, that the power of innocence is so great, that wherever it journeys, it needs neither arms nor strength for its protection:—

"He whose life hath no flaw, pure from guile, need not borrow
    Or the bow or the darts of the Moor, O my Fuscus!
    He relies for defense on no quiver that teems with
    Poison-steept arrows.
    Though his path be along sultry African Syrtes,
    Or Caucasian ravines, where no guest finds a shelter,
    Or the banks which Hydaspes, the stream weird with fable,
    Licks languid-flowing."

It is impossible, therefore, that amidst the dangers of tempests and of wars the just man should be unprotected by the guardianship of Heaven; and that even if he should be at sea in company with parricides and guilty men, the wicked also should not be spared, that this one just and innocent soul may be freed from danger, or at any rate may be alone preserved while the rest perish. But let us grant that the case which the philosopher proposes is possible: what, then, will the just man do, if he shall have met with a wounded man on a horse, or a shipwrecked man on a plank? I am not unwilling to confess he will rather die than put another to death. Nor will justice, which is the chief good of man, on this account receive the name of folly. For what ought to be better and dearer to man than innocence? And this must be the more perfect, the more you bring it to extremity, and choose to die rather than to detract from the character of innocence. It is folly, he says, to spare the life of another in a case which involves the destruction of one's own life. Then do you think it foolish to perish even for friendship?

Why, then, are those Pythagorean friends praised by you, of whom the one gave himself to the tyrant as a surety for the life of the other, and the other at the appointed time, when his surety was now being led to execution, presented himself, and rescued him by his own interposition? Whose virtue would not be held in such glory, when one of them was willing to die for his friend, the other even for his word which had been pledged, if they were regarded as fools. In fine, on account of this very virtue the tyrant rewarded them by preserving both, and thus the disposition of a most cruel man was changed. Moreover, it is even said that he entreated them to admit him as a third party to their friendship, from which it is plain that he regarded them not as fools, but as good and wise men. Therefore I do not see why, since it is reckoned the highest glory to die for friendship and for one's word, it is not glorious to a man to die even for his innocence. They are therefore most foolish who impute it as a crime to us that we are willing to die for God, when they themselves extol to the heavens with the highest praises him who was willing to die for a man. In short, to conclude this disputation, reason itself teaches that it is impossible for a man to be at once just and foolish, wise and unjust. For he who is foolish is unacquainted with that which is just and good, and therefore always errs. For he is, as it were, led captive by his vices; nor can he in any way resist them, because he is destitute of the virtue of which he is ignorant. But the just man abstains from all fault, because he cannot do otherwise, although he has the knowledge of right and wrong.

But who is able to distinguish right from wrong except the wise man? Thus it comes to pass, that he can never be just who is foolish, nor wise who is unjust. And if this is most true, it is plain that he who has not taken away a plank from a shipwrecked man, or a horse from one who is wounded, is not foolish; because it is a sin to do these things, and the wise man abstains from sin. Nevertheless I myself also confess that it has this appearance, through the error of men, who are ignorant of the peculiar character of everything. And thus the whole of this inquiry is refuted not so much by arguments as by definition. Therefore folly is the erring in deeds and words, through ignorance of what is right and good. Therefore he is not a fool who does not even spare himself to prevent injury to another, which is an evil. And this, indeed, reason and the truth itself dictate. For we see that in all animals, because they are destitute of wisdom, nature is the provider of supplies for itself. Therefore they injure others that they may profit themselves, for they do not understand that the committing an injury is evil. But man, who has the knowledge of good and evil, abstains from committing an injury even to his own damage, which an animal without reason is unable to do; and on this account innocence is reckoned among the chief virtues of man. Now by these things it appears that he is the wisest man who prefers to perish rather than to commit an injury, that he may preserve that sense of duty by which he is distinguished from the dumb creation. For he who does not point out the error of one who is offering the gold for sale, in order that he may buy it for a small sum, or he who does not avow that he is offering for sale a runaway slave or an infected house, having an eye to his own gain or advantage, is not a wise man, as Carneades wished it to appear, but crafty and cunning. Now craftiness and cunning exist in the dumb animals also: either when they lie in wait for others, and take them by deceit, that they may devour them; or when they avoid the snares of others in various ways. But wisdom falls to man alone. For wisdom is understanding either with the purpose of doing that which is good and right, or for the abstaining from improper words and deeds. Now a wise man never gives himself to the pursuit of gain, because he despises these earthly advantages: nor does he allow anyone to be deceived, because it is the duty of a good man to correct the errors of men, and to bring them back to the right way; since the nature of man is social and beneficent, in which respect alone he bears a relation to God.

### Chap. XIX.—Of Virtue and the Tortures of Christians, and of the Right of a Father and Master.

But undoubtedly this is the cause why he appears to be foolish who prefers to be in want, or to die rather than to inflict injury or take away the property of another,—namely, because they think that man is destroyed by death. And from this persuasion all the errors both of the common people and also of the philosophers arise. For if we have no existence after death, assuredly it is the part of the most foolish man not to promote the interests of the present life, that it may be long-continued, and may abound with all advantages. But he who shall act thus must of necessity depart from the rule of justice. But if there remains to man a longer and a better life—and this we learn both from the arguments of great philosophers, and from the answers of seers, and the divine words of prophets—it is the part of the wise man to despise this present life with its advantages, since its entire loss is compensated by immortality. The same defender of justice, Lælius, says in Cicero: "Virtue altogether wishes for honor; nor is there any other reward of virtue." There is indeed another, and that most worthy of virtue, which you, O Lælius, could never have supposed; for you had no knowledge of the sacred writings. And this reward it easily receives, and does not harshly demand. You are greatly mistaken, if you think that a reward can be paid to virtue by man, since you yourself most truly said in another place: "What riches will you offer to this man? What commands? What kingdoms? He who regards these things as human, judges his own advantages to be divine." Who, therefore, can think you a wise man, O Lælius, when you contradict yourself, and after a short interval take away from virtue that which you have given to her? But it is manifest that ignorance of the truth makes your opinion uncertain and wavering.

In the next place, what do you add? "But if all the ungrateful, or the many who are envious, or powerful enemies, deprive virtue of its rewards." Oh how frail, how worthless, have you represented virtue to be, if it can be deprived of its reward! For if it judges its goods to be divine, as you said, how can there be any so ungrateful, so envious, so powerful, as to be able to deprive virtue of those goods which were conferred upon it by the gods? "Assuredly it delights itself," he says, "by many comforts, and especially supports itself by its own beauty." By what comforts? By what beauty? Since that beauty is often charged upon it as a fault, and turned into a punishment. For what if, as Furius said, a man should be dragged away, harassed, banished, should be in want, be deprived of his hands, have his eyes put out, be condemned, put into chains, be burned, be miserably tortured also? Will virtue lose its reward, or rather, will it perish itself? By no means. But it will both receive its reward from God the Judge, and it will live, and always flourish. And if you take away these things, nothing in the life of man can appear to be so useless, so foolish, as virtue, the natural goodness and honor of which may teach us that the soul is not mortal, and that a divine reward is appointed for it by God. But on this account God willed that virtue itself should be concealed under the character of folly, that the mystery of truth and of His religion might be secret; that He might show the vanity and error of these superstitions, and of that earthly wisdom which raises itself too highly, and exhibits great self-complacency, that its difficulty being at length set forth, that most narrow path might lead to the lofty reward of immortality.

I have shown, as I think, why our people are esteemed foolish by the foolish. For to choose to be tortured and slain, rather than to take incense in three fingers, and throw it upon the hearth, appears as foolish as, in a case where life is endangered, to be more careful of the life of another than of one's own. For they do not know how great an act of impiety it is to adore any other object than God, who made heaven and earth, who fashioned the human race, breathed into them the breath of life, and gave them light. But if he is accounted the most worthless of slaves who runs away and deserts his master, and if he is judged most deserving of stripes and chains, and a prison, and the cross, and of all evil; and if a son, in the same manner, is thought abandoned and impious who deserts his father, that he may not pay him obedience, and on this account is considered deserving of being disinherited, and of having his name removed forever from his family,—how much more so does he who forsakes God, in whom the two names entitled to equal reverence, of Lord and

Father, alike meet? For what benefit does he who buys a slave bestow upon him, beyond the nourishment with which he supplies him for his own advantage? And he who begets a son has it not in his power to effect that he shall be conceived, or born, or live; from which it is evident that he is not the father, but only the instrument of generation. Of what punishments, therefore, is he deserving, who forsakes Him who is both the true Master and Father, but those which God Himself has appointed? Who has prepared everlasting fire for the wicked spirits; and this He Himself threatens by His prophets to the impious and the rebellious.

**Chap. XX.—Of the Vanity and Crimes, Impious Superstitions, and of the Tortures of the Christians.**

Therefore, let those who destroy their own souls and the souls of others learn what an inexpiable crime they commit; in the first place, because they cause their own death by serving most abandoned demons, whom God has condemned to everlasting punishments; in the next place, because they do not permit God to be worshipped by others, but endeavor to turn men aside to deadly rites, and strive with the greatest diligence that no life may be without injury on earth, which looks to heaven with its condition secured. What else shall I call them but miserable men, who obey the instigations of their own plunderers, whom they think to be gods? Of whom they neither know the condition, nor origin, nor names, nor nature; but, clinging to the persuasion of the people, they willingly err, and favor their own folly. And if you should ask them the grounds of their persuasion, they can assign none, but have recourse to the judgment of their ancestors, saying that they were wise, that they approved them, that they knew what was best; and thus they deprive themselves of all power of perception: they bid adieu to reason, while they place confidence in the errors of others. Thus, involved in ignorance of all things, they neither know themselves nor their gods. And would to heaven that they had been willing to err by themselves, and to be unwise by themselves! But they hurry away others also to be companions of their evil, as though they were about to derive comfort from the destruction of many. But this very ignorance causes them to be so cruel in persecuting the wise; and they pretend that they are promoting their welfare, that they wish to recall them to a good mind.

Do they then strive to effect this by conversation, or by giving some reason? By no means; but they endeavor to effect it by force and tortures. O wonderful and blind infatuation! It is thought that there is a bad mind in those who endeavor to preserve their faith, but a good one in executioners. Is there, then, a bad mind in those who, against every law of humanity, against every principle of justice, are tortured, or rather, in those who inflict on the bodies of the innocent such things, as neither the most cruel robbers, nor the most enraged enemies, nor the most savage barbarians have ever practiced? Do they deceive themselves to such an extent, that they mutually transfer and change the names of good and evil? Why, therefore, do they not call day night—the sun darkness? Moreover, it is the same impudence to give to the good the name of evil, to the wise the name of foolish, to the just the name of impious. Besides this, if they have any confidence in philosophy or in eloquence, let them arm themselves, and refute these arguments of ours if they are able; let them meet us hand to hand, and examine every point. It is befitting that they should undertake the defense of their gods, lest, if our affairs should increase (as they do increase daily), theirs should be deserted, together with their shrines and their vain mockeries; and since they can effect nothing by violence (for the religion of God is increased the more it is oppressed), let them rather act by the use of reason and exhortations.

Let their priests come forth into the midst, whether the inferior ones or the greatest; their flamens, augurs, and also sacrificing kings, and the priests and ministers of their superstitions. Let them call us together to an assembly; let them exhort us to undertake the worship of their gods; let them persuade us that there are many beings by whose deity and providence all things are governed; let them show how the origins and beginnings of their sacred rites and gods were handed down to mortals; let them explain what is their source and principle; let them set forth what reward there is in their worship, and what punishment awaits neglect; why they wish to be worshipped by men; what the piety of men contributes to them, if they are blessed: and let them confirm all these things not by their own assertion (for the authority of a mortal man is of no weight), but by some divine testimonies, as we do. There is no occasion for violence and injury, for religion cannot be imposed by force; the matter must be carried on by words rather than by blows, that the will may be affected. Let them unsheathe the weapon of their intellect; if their system is true, let it be asserted. We are prepared to hear, if they teach; while they are silent, we certainly pay no credit to them, as we do not yield to them even in their rage. Let them imitate us in setting forth the system of the whole matter: for we do not entice, as they say; but we teach, we prove, we show. And thus no one is detained by us against his will, for he is unserviceable to God who is destitute of faith and devotedness; and yet no one departs from us, since the truth itself detains him. Let them teach in this manner, if they have any confidence in the truth; let them speak, let them give utterance; let them venture, I say, to discuss with us something of this nature; and then assuredly their error and folly will be ridiculed by the old women, whom they despise, and by our boys. For, since they are especially clever, they know from books the race of the gods, and their exploits, and commands, and deaths, and tombs; they may also know that the rites themselves, in which they have been initiated, had their origin either in human actions, or in casualties, or in deaths. It is the part of incredible madness to imagine that they are gods, whom they cannot deny to have been mortal; or if they should be so shameless as to deny it, their own writings, and those of their own people, will refute them; in short, the very beginnings of the sacred rites will convict them. They may know, therefore, even from this very thing, how great a difference there is between truth and falsehood; for they themselves with all their eloquence are unable to persuade, whereas the unskilled and the uneducated are able, because the matter itself and the truth speaks.

Why then do they rage, so that while they wish to lessen their folly, they increase it? Torture and piety are widely different; nor is it possible for truth to be united with violence, or justice with cruelty. But with good reason they do not venture to teach anything concerning divine things, lest they should both be derided by our people and be deserted by their own. For the common people for the most part, if they ascertain that these mysteries were instituted in memory of the dead, will condemn them, and seek for some truer object of worship.

"Hence rites of mystic awe"

were instituted by crafty men, that the people may not know what they worship. But since we are acquainted with their systems, why do they either not believe us who are acquainted with both, or envy us because we have preferred truth to falsehood? But, they say, the public rites of religion must be defended. Oh with what an honorable inclination the wretched men go astray! For they are aware that there is nothing among men more excellent than religion, and that this ought to be defended with the whole of our power; but as they are deceived in the matter of religion itself, so also are they in the manner of its defense. For religion is to be defended, not by putting to death, but by dying; not by cruelty, but by patient endurance; not by guilt, but by good faith: for the former belong to evils, but the latter to goods; and it is necessary for that which is good to have place in religion, and not that which is evil. For if you wish to defend religion by bloodshed, and by tortures, and by guilt, it will no longer be defended, but will be polluted and profaned. For nothing is so much a matter of free-will as religion; in which, if the mind of the worshipper is disinclined to it, religion is at once taken away, and ceases to exist. The right method therefore is, that you defend religion by patient endurance or by death; in which the preservation of the faith is both pleasing to God Himself, and adds authority to religion. For if he who in this earthly warfare preserves his faith to his king in some illustrious action, if he shall continue to live, because more beloved and acceptable, and if he shall fall, obtains the highest glory, because he has undergone death for his leader; how much more is faith to be kept towards God, the Ruler of all, who is able to pay the reward of virtue, not only to the living, but also to the dead! Therefore the worship of God, since it belongs to heavenly warfare, requires the greatest devotedness and fidelity. For how will God either love the worshipper, if He Himself is not loved by him, or grant to the petitioner whatever he shall ask, when he draws nigh to offer his prayer without sincerity or reverence? But these men, when they come to offer sacrifice, present to their gods nothing from within, nothing of their own—no uprightness of mind, no reverence or fear. Therefore, when the worthless sacrifices are completed, they leave their religion altogether in the temple, and with the temple, as they had found it; and neither bring with them anything of it, nor take anything back. Hence it is that religious observances of this kind are neither able to make men good, nor to be firm and unchangeable. And thus men are easily led away from them, because nothing is learned in them relating to the life, nothing relating to wisdom, nothing to faith. For what is the religion of those gods? What is its power? What its discipline? What its origin? What its principle? What its foundation? What its substance? What is its tendency? Or what does it promise, so that it may be faithfully preserved and boldly defended by man? I see nothing else in it than a rite pertaining to the fingers only. But our religion is on this account firm, and solid, and unchangeable, because it teaches justice, because it is always with us, because it has its existence altogether in the soul of the worshipper, because it has the mind itself for a sacrifice. In that religion nothing else is required but the blood of animals, and the smoke of incense, and the senseless pouring out of libations; but in this of ours, a good mind, a pure breast, an innocent life: those rites are frequented by unchaste adulteresses without any discrimination, by impudent procuresses, by filthy harlots; they are frequented by gladiators, robbers, thieves, and sorcerers, who pray for nothing else but that they may commit crimes with impunity. For what can the robber ask when he sacrifices, or the gladiator, but that they may slay? What the poisoner, but that he may escape notice? What the harlot, but that she may sin to the uttermost? What the adulteress, but either the death of her husband, or that her unchastity may be concealed? What the procuress, but that she may deprive many of their property? What the thief, but that he may commit more peculations? But in our religion there is no place even for a slight and ordinary offence; and if anyone shall come to a sacrifice without a sound conscience, he hears what threats God denounces against him: that God, I say, who sees the secret places of the heart, who is always hostile to sins, who requires justice, who demands fidelity. What place is there here for an evil mind or for an evil prayer? But those unhappy men neither understand from their own crimes how evil it is to worship, since, defiled by all crimes, they come to offer prayer; and they imagine that they offer a pious sacrifice if they wash their skin; as though any streams could wash away, or any seas purify, the lusts which are shut up within their breast. How much better it is rather to cleanse the mind, which is defiled by evil desires, and to drive away all vices by the one laver of virtue and faith! For he who shall do this, although he bears a body which is defiled and sordid, is pure enough.

## Chap. XXI.—Of the Worship of Other Gods and the True God, and of the Animals Which the Egyptians Worshipped.

But they, because they know not the object or the mode of worship, blindly and unconsciously fall into the contrary practice. Thus they adore their enemies, they appease with victims their robbers and murderers, and they place their own souls to be burned with the very incense on detestable altars. The wretched men are also angry, because others do not perish in like manner, with incredible blindness of minds. For what can they see who do not see the sun? As though, if they were gods, they would need the assistance of men against their despisers. Why, therefore, are they angry with us, if they have no power to effect anything? Unless it be that they destroy their gods, whose power they distrust, they are more irreligious than those who do not worship them at all. Cicero, in his Laws, enjoining men to approach with holiness to the sacrifices, says, "Let them put on piety, let them lay aside riches; if anyone shall act otherwise, God Himself will be the avenger." This is well spoken; for it is not right to despair about God, whom you worship on this account, because you think Him powerful. For how can He avenge the wrongs of His worshippers, if He is unable to avenge His own? I wish therefore to ask them to whom especially they think that they are doing a service in compelling them to sacrifice against their will, Is it to those whom they compel? But that is not a kindness which is done to one who refuses it. But we must consult their interests, even against their will, since they know not what is good. Why, then, do they so cruelly harass, torture, and weaken them, if they wish for their safety? Or whence is piety so impious, that they either destroy in this wretched manner, or render useless, those whose welfare they wish to promote? Or do they do service to the gods? But that is not a sacrifice which is extorted from a person against his will. For unless it is offered spontaneously, and from the soul, it is a curse; when men sacrifice, compelled by proscription, by injuries, by prison, by tortures. If they are gods who are worshipped in this manner, if for this reason only, they ought not to be worshipped, because they wish to be worshipped in this manner: they are doubtless worthy of the detestation of men, since libations are made to them with tears, with groaning, and with blood flowing from all the limbs.

But we, on the contrary, do not require that anyone should be compelled, whether he is willing or unwilling, to worship our God, who is the God of all men; nor are we angry if any one does not worship Him. For we trust in the majesty of Him who has power to avenge contempt shown towards Himself, as also He has power to avenge the calamities and injuries inflicted on His servants. And therefore, when we suffer such impious things, we do not resist even in word; but we remit vengeance to God, not as they act who would have it appear that they are defenders of their gods, and rage without restraint against those who do not worship them. From which it may be understood how it is not good to worship their gods, since men ought to have been led to that which is good by good, and not by evil; but because this is evil, even its office is destitute of good. But they who destroy religious systems must be punished. Have we destroyed them in a worse manner than the nation of the Egyptians, who worship the most disgraceful figures of beasts and cattle, and adore as gods some things which it is even shameful to speak of? Have we done worse than those same who, when they say that they worship the gods, yet publicly and shamefully deride them?—for they even allow pantomimic representations of them to be acted with laughter and pleasure. What kind of a religion is this, or how great must that majesty be considered, which is adored in temples and mocked in theatres? And they who have done these things do not suffer the vengeance of the injured deity, but even go away honored and praised. Do we destroy them in a worse manner than certain philosophers, who say that there are no gods at all, but that all things are spontaneously produced, and that all things which are done happen by chance? Do we destroy them in a worse manner than the Epicureans, who admit the existence of gods, but deny that they regard anything, and say that they are neither angry nor are influenced by favor? By which words they plainly persuade men that they are not to be worshipped at all, inasmuch as they neither regard their worshippers, nor are angry with those who do not worship them. Moreover, when they argue against fears, they endeavor to effect nothing else than that no one should fear the gods. And yet these things are willingly heard by men, and discussed with impunity.

## Chap. XXII.—Of the Rage of the Demons against Christians, and the Error of Unbelievers.

They do not therefore rage against us on this account, because their gods are not worshipped by us, but because the truth is on our side, which (as it has been said most truly) produces hatred. What, then, shall we think, but that they are ignorant of what they suffer? For they act with a blind and unreasonable fury, which we see, but of which they are ignorant. For it is not the men themselves who persecute, for they have no cause of anger against the innocent; but those contaminated and abandoned spirits by whom the truth is both known and hated insinuate themselves into their minds, and goad them in their ignorance to fury. For these, as long as there is peace among the people of God, flee from the righteous, and fear them; and when they seize upon the bodies of men, and harass their souls, they are adjured by them, and at the name of the true God are put to flight. For when they hear this name they tremble, cry out, and assert that they are branded and beaten; and being asked who they are, whence they are come, and how they have insinuated themselves into a man, confess it. Thus, being tortured and excruciated by the power of the divine name, they come out of the man. On account of these blows and threats, they always hate holy and just men; and because they are unable of themselves to injure them, they pursue with public hatred those whom they perceive to be grievous to them, and they exercise cruelty, with all the violence which they can employ, that they may either weaken their faith by pain, or, if they are unable to effect that, may take them away altogether from the earth, that there may be none to restrain their wickedness. It does not escape my notice what reply can be made on the other side. Why, then, does that God of surpassing power, that mighty One, whom you confess to preside over all things, and to be Lord of all, permit these things to be done, and neither avenge nor defend His worshippers? Why, in short, are they who do not worship Him rich, and powerful, and happy? And why do they enjoy honors and kingly state, and have these very persons subject to their power and sway?

We must also give a reason for this, that no error may remain. For this is especially the cause why it is thought that religion has not the power of God, because men are influenced by the appearance of earthly and present goods, which in no way have reference to the care of the mind; and because they see that the righteous are without these goods, and that the unrighteous abound in them, they both judge that the worship of God is worthless, in which they do not see these things contained, and they imagine that the rites of other gods are true, since their worshippers enjoy riches and honors and kingdoms. But they who are of this opinion do not attentively consider the power and method of man, which consists altogether in the mind, and not in the body. For they see nothing more than is seen, namely the body; and because this is to be seen and handled, it is weak, frail, and mortal; and to this belong all those goods which are their desire and admiration, wealth, honors, and governments, since they bring pleasures to the body, and therefore are as liable to decay as the body itself. But the soul, in which alone man consists since it is not exposed to the sight of the eyes, and its goods cannot be seen, for they are placed in virtue only, must therefore be as firm, and constant, and lasting as virtue itself, in which the good of the soul consists.

### Chap. XXIII.—Of the Justice and Patience of the Christians.

It would be a lengthened task to draw forth all the appearances of virtue, to show respecting each how necessary it is for a wise and just man to be far removed from those goods, the enjoyment of which by the unjust causes the worship of their gods to be regarded as true and efficacious. As our present inquiry is concerned, it will be sufficient to prove our point from the case of a single virtue. For instance, patience is a great and leading virtue, which the public voices of the people and philosophers and orators alike extol with the highest praises. But if it cannot be denied that this is a virtue of the highest kind, it is necessary that the just and wise man should be in the power of the unjust, for obtaining patience; for patience is the bearing with equanimity of the evils which are either inflicted or happen to fall upon us. Therefore the just and wise man, because he exercises virtue, has patience in himself; but he will be altogether free from this if he shall suffer no adversity. On the other hand, the man who lives in prosperity is impatient, and is without the greatest virtue. I call him impatient, because he suffers nothing. He is also unable to preserve innocence, which virtue is peculiar to the just and wise man. But he often acts unjustly also, and desires the property of others, and seizes upon that which he has desired by injustice, because he is without virtue, and is subject to vice and sin; and forgetful of his frailty, he is puffed up with a mind elated with insolence.

From this cause the unjust, and those who are ignorant of God, abound with riches, and power, and honors. For all these things are the rewards of injustice, because they cannot be perpetual, and they are sought through lust and violence. But the just and wise man, because he deems all these things as human, as it has been said by Lælius, and his own goods as divine, neither desires anything which belongs to another, lest he should injure anyone at all in violation of the law of humanity; nor does he long for any power or honor, that he may not do an injury to anyone. For he knows that all are produced by the same God, and in the same condition, and are joined together by the right of brotherhood. But being contented with his own, and *that* a little, because he is mindful of his frailty, he does not seek for anything beyond that which may support his life; and even from that which he has he bestows a share on the destitute, because he is pious; but piety is a very great virtue. To this is added, that he despises frail and vicious pleasures, for the sake of which riches are desired; since he is temperate, and master of his passions. He also, having no pride or insolence, does not raise himself too highly, nor lift up his head with arrogance; but he is calm and peaceful, lowly and courteous, because he knows his own condition. Since, therefore, he does injury to none, nor desires the property of others, and does not even defend his own if it is taken from him by violence, since he knows how even to bear with moderation an injury inflicted upon him, because he is endued with virtue; it is necessary that the just man should be subject to the unjust, and that the wise should be insulted by the foolish, that the one may sin because he is unjust, and the other may have virtue in himself because he is just.

But if anyone shall wish to know more fully why God permits the wicked and the unjust to become powerful, happy, and rich, and, on the other hand, suffers the pious to be humble, wretched, and poor, let him take the book of Seneca which has the title, "Why many evils happen to good men, though there is a providence;" in which book he has said many things, not assuredly with the ignorance of this world, but wisely, and almost with divine inspiration. "God," he says, "regards men as His children, but He permits the corrupt and vicious to live in luxury and delicacy, because He does not think them worthy of His correction. But He often chastises the good whom He loves, and by continual labors exercises them to the practice of virtue: nor does He permit them to be corrupted and depraved by frail and perishable goods." From which it ought to appear strange to no one if we are often chastised by God for our faults. Yea, rather, when we are harassed and pressed, then we especially give thanks to our most indulgent Father, because He does not permit our corruption to proceed to greater lengths, but corrects it with stripes and blows. From which we understand that we are an object of regard to God, since He is angry when we sin. For when He might have bestowed upon His people both riches and kingdoms, as He had before given them to the Jews, whose successors and posterity we are; on this account He would have them live under the power and government of others, lest, being corrupted by the happiness of prosperity, they should glide into luxury and despise the precepts of God; as those ancestors of ours, who, oft times enervated by these earthly and frail goods, departed from discipline and burst the bonds of the law. Therefore He foresaw how far He would afford rest to His worshippers if they should keep His commandments, and yet correct them if they did not obey His precepts. Therefore, lest they should be as much corrupted by ease as their fathers had been by indulgence, it was His will that they should be oppressed by those in whose power He placed them, that He may both confirm them when wavering, and renew them to fortitude when corrupted, and try and prove them when faithful. For how can a general prove the valor of his soldiers, unless he shall have an enemy? And yet there arises an adversary to him against his will, because he is mortal, and is able to be conquered; but because God cannot be opposed, He Himself stirs up adversaries to His name, not to fight against God Himself, but against His soldiers, that He may either prove the devotedness and fidelity of His servants, or may strengthen them, until He corrects their wasting discipline by the stripes of affliction.

There is also another cause why He permits persecutions to be carried on against us, that the people of God may be increased. Nor is it difficult to show why or how this happens. First of all, great numbers are driven from the worship of the false gods by their hatred of cruelty. For who would not shrink from such sacrifices? In the next place, some are pleased with virtue and faith itself. Some suspect that it is not without reason that the worship of the gods is considered evil by so many men, so that they would rather die than do that which others do that they may preserve their life. Someone desires to know what that good is which is defended even to death, which is preferred to all things which are pleasant and beloved in this life, from which neither the loss of goods, nor of the light, nor bodily pain, nor tortures of the vitals deter them. These things have great effect; but these causes have always especially increased the number of our followers. The people who stand around hear them saying in the midst of these very torments that they do not sacrifice to stones wrought by the hand of man, but to the living God, who is in heaven: many understand that this is true, and admit it into their breast. In the next place, as it is accustomed to happen in matters of uncertainty while they make inquiry of one another, what is the cause of this perseverance, many things which relate to religion, being spread abroad and carefully observed by rumor among one another, are learned; and because these are good they cannot fail to please. Moreover, the revenge which follows, as always happens, greatly impels men to believe. Nor, indeed, is it a slight cause that the unclean spirits of demons, having received permission, throw themselves into the bodies of many; and when these have afterwards been driven out, they who have been healed cling to the religion, the power of which they have experienced. These numerous causes being collected together, wonderfully gain over a great multitude to God.

### Chap. XXIV.—Of the Divine Vengeance Inflicted on the Torturers of the Christians.

Whatever, therefore, wicked princes plan against us, God Himself permits to be done. And yet most unjust persecutors, to whom the name of God was a subject of reproach and mockery, must not think that they will escape with impunity, because they have been, as it were, the ministers of His indignation against us. For they will be punished with the judgment of God, who, having received power, have abused it to an inhuman degree, and have even insulted God in their arrogance, and placed His eternal name beneath their feet, to be impiously and wickedly trampled upon. On this account He promises that He will quickly take vengeance upon them, and exterminate the evil monsters from the earth. But He also, although He is accustomed to avenge the persecutions of His people even in the present world, commands us, however, to await patiently that day of heavenly judgment, in which He Himself will honor or punish every man according to his deserts. Therefore let not the souls of the sacrilegious expect that those whom they thus trample upon will be despised and unavenged. Those ravenous and voracious wolves who have tormented just and innocent souls, without the commission of any crimes, will surely meet with their reward. Only let us labor, that nothing else in us may be punished by men but righteousness alone: let us strive with all our power that we may at once deserve at the hands of God the avenging of our suffering and a reward.

# The divine institutes
# Book VI.
# Of True Worship.

## Chap. I.—Of the Worship of the True God, and of Innocence, and of the Worship of False Gods.

We have completed that which was the object of our undertaking, through the teaching of the Divine Spirit, and the aid of the truth itself; the cause of asserting and explaining which was imposed upon me both by conscience and faith, and by our Lord Himself, without whom nothing can be known or clearly set forth. I come now to that which is the chief and greatest part of this work—to teach in what manner or by what sacrifice God must be worshipped. For that is the duty of man, and in that one object the sum of all things and the whole course of a happy life consists, since we were fashioned and received the breath of life from Him on this account, not that we might behold the heaven and the sun, as Anaxagoras supposed, but that we might with pure and uncorrupted mind worship Him who made the sun and the heaven. But although in the preceding books, as far as my moderate talent permitted, I defended the truth, yet it may especially be elucidated by the mode of worship itself. For that sacred and surpassing majesty requires from man nothing more than innocence alone; and if anyone has presented this to God, he has sacrificed with sufficient piety and religion. But men, neglecting justice, though they are polluted by crimes and outrages of all kinds, think themselves religious if they have stained the temples and altars with the blood of victims, if they have moistened the hearths with a profusion of fragrant and old wine. Moreover, they also prepare sacred feasts and choice banquets, as though they offered to those who would taste something from them. Whatever is rarely to be viewed, whatever is precious in workmanship or in fragrance, that they judge to be pleasing to their gods, not by any reference to their divinity, of which they are ignorant, but from their own desires; nor do they understand that God is in no want of earthly resources.

For they have no knowledge of anything except the earth, and they estimate good and evil things by the perception and pleasure of the body alone. And as they judge of religion according to its pleasure, so also they arrange the acts of their whole life. And since they have turned away once for all from the contemplation of the heaven, and have made that heavenly faculty the slave of the body, they give the reins to their lusts, as though they were about to bear away pleasure with themselves, which they hasten to enjoy at every moment; whereas the soul ought to employ the service of the body, and not the body to make use of the service of the soul. The same men judge riches to be the greatest good. And if they cannot obtain them by good practices, they endeavor to obtain them by evil practices; they deceive, they carry off by violence, they plunder, they lie in wait, they deny on oath; in short, they have no consideration or regard for anything, if only they can glitter with gold, and shine conspicuous with plate, with jewels, and with garments, can spend riches upon their greedy appetite, and always walk attended with crowds of slaves through the people compelled to give way. Thus devoting themselves to the service of pleasures, they extinguish the force and vigor of the mind; and when they especially think that they are alive, they are hastening with the greatest precipitation to death. For, as we showed in the second book, the soul is concerned with heaven, the body with the earth. They who neglect the goods of the soul, and seek those of the body, are engaged with darkness and death, which belong to the earth and to the body, because life and light are from heaven; and they who are without this, by serving the body, are far removed from the understanding of divine things. The same blindness everywhere oppresses the wretched men; for as they know not who is the true God, so they know not what constitutes true worship.

## Chap. II.—Of the Worship of False Gods and the True God.

Therefore they sacrifice fine and fat victims to God, as though He were hungry; they pour forth wine to Him, as though He were thirsty; they kindle lights to Him, as though He were in darkness. But if they were able to conjecture or to conceive in their mind what those heavenly goods are, the greatness of which we cannot imagine, while we are still encompassed with an earthly body, they would at once know that they are most foolish with their empty offices. Or if they would contemplate that heavenly light which we call the sun, they will at once perceive how God has no need of their candles, who has Himself given so clear and bright a light for the use of man. And when, in so small a circle, which on account of its distance appears to have a measure no greater than that of a human head, there is still so much brilliancy that mortal eye cannot behold it, and if you should direct your eye to it for a short time mist and darkness would overspread your dimmed eyes, what light, I pray, what brightness, must we suppose that there is in God, with whom there is no night? For He has so attempered this very light, that it might neither injure living creatures by excessive brightness or vehement heat, and has given it so much of these properties as mortal bodies might endure or the ripening of the crops require. Is that man, therefore, to be thought in his senses, who presents the light of candles and torches as an offering to Him who is the Author and Giver of light? The light which He requires from us is of another kind, and that indeed not accompanied with smoke, but (as the poet says) clear and bright; I mean the light of the mind, on account of which we are called by the poets photes, which light no one can exhibit unless he has known God. But their gods, because they are of the earth, stand in need of lights, that they may not be in darkness; and their worshippers, because they have no taste for anything heavenly, are recalled to the earth even by the religious rites to which they are devoted. For on the earth there is need of a light, because its system and nature are dark. Therefore they do not attribute to the gods a heavenly perception, but rather a human one. And on this account they believe that the same things are necessary and pleasing to them as to us, who, when hungry, have need of food; or, when thirsty, of drink; or, when we are cold, require a garment; or, when the sun has withdrawn himself, require a light that we may be able to see.

From nothing, therefore, can it be so plainly proved and understood that those gods, since they once lived, are dead, as from their worship itself, which is altogether of the earth. For what heavenly influence can there be in the shedding of the blood of beasts, with which they stain their altars? Unless by chance they imagine that the gods feed upon that which men shrink from touching. And whoever shall have offered to them this food, although he be an assassin, an adulterer, a sorcerer, or a parricide, he will be happy and prosperous. Him they love, him they defend, and to him they afford all things which he shall wish for. Persius therefore deservedly ridicules superstitions of this kind in his own style: "With what bribe," he says, "dost thou win the ears of gods? Is it with lungs and rich intestines?" He plainly perceived that there is no need of flesh for appeasing the majesty of heaven, but of a pure mind and a just spirit, and a breast, as he himself says, which is generous with a natural love of honor. This is the religion of heaven—not that which consists of corrupt things, but of the virtues of the soul, which has its origin from heaven; this is true worship, in which the mind of the worshipper presents itself as an undefiled offering to God. But how this is to be obtained, how it is to be afforded, the discussion of this book will show; for nothing can be so illustrious and so suited to man as to train men to righteousness.

In Cicero, Catulus in the *Hortensius*, while he prefers philosophy to all things, says that he would rather have one short treatise respecting duty, than a long speech in behalf of a seditious man Cornelius. And this is plainly to be regarded not as the opinion of Catulus, who perhaps did not utter this saying, but as that of Cicero, who wrote it. I believe that he wrote it for the purpose of recommending these books which he was about to write on Offices, in which very books he testifies that nothing in the whole range of philosophy is better and more profitable than to give precepts for living. But if this is done by those who do not know the truth, how much more ought we to do it, who are able to give true precepts, being taught and enlightened by God? Nor, however, shall we so teach as though we were delivering the first elements of virtue, which would be an endless task, but as though we had undertaken the instruction of him who, with them, appears to be already perfect. For while their precepts remain, which they are accustomed to give correctly, with a view to uprightness, we will add to them things which were unknown to them, for the completion and consummation of righteousness, which they do not possess. But I will omit those things which are common to us with them, that I may not appear to borrow from those whose errors I have determined to convict and bring to light.

### Chap. III.—Of the Ways, and of Vices and Virtues; and of the Rewards of Heaven and the Punishments of Hell.

There are two ways, O Emperor Constantine, by which human life must proceed—the one which leads to heaven, the other which sinks to hell; and these *ways* poets have introduced in their poems, and philosophers in their disputations. And indeed philosophers have represented the one as belonging to virtues, the other to vices; and they have represented that which belongs to virtues as steep and rugged at the first entrance, in which if anyone, having overcome the difficulty, has climbed to the summit, they say that he afterwards has a level path, a bright and pleasant plain, and that he enjoys abundant and delightful fruits of his labors; but that those whom the difficulty of the first approach has deterred, glide and turn aside into the way of vices, which at its first entrance appears to be pleasant and much more beaten, but afterwards, when they have advanced in it a little further, that the appearance of its pleasantness is withdrawn, and that there arises a steep way, now rough with stones, now overspread with thorns, now interrupted by deep waters or violent with torrents, so that they must be in difficulty, hesitate, slip about, and fall. And all these things are brought forward that it may appear that there are very great labors in undertaking virtues, but that when they are gained there are the greatest advantages, and firm and incorruptible pleasures; but that vices ensnare the minds of men with certain natural blandishments, and lead them captivated by the appearance of empty pleasures to bitter griefs and miseries,—an altogether wise discussion, if they knew the forms and limits of the virtues themselves. For they had not learned either what they are, or what reward awaits them from God: but this we will show in these two books.

But these men, because they were ignorant or in doubt that the souls of men are immortal, estimated both virtues and vices by earthly honors or punishments. Therefore all this discussion respecting the two ways has reference to frugality and luxury. For they say that the course of human life resembles the letter Y, because every one of men, when he has reached the threshold of early youth, and has arrived at the place "where the way divides itself into two parts," is in doubt, and hesitates, and does not know to which side he should rather turn himself. If he shall meet with a guide who may direct him wavering to better things—that is, if he shall learn philosophy or eloquence, or some honorable arts by which he may turn to good conduct, which cannot take place without great labor—they say that he will lead a life of honor and abundance; but if he shall not meet with a teacher of temperance, that he falls into the way on the left hand, which assumes the appearance of the better,—that is, he gives himself up to idleness, sloth, and luxury, which seem pleasant for a time to one who is ignorant of true goods, but that afterwards, having lost all his dignity and property, he will live in all wretchedness and ignominy. Therefore they referred the end of those ways to the body, and to this life which we lead on earth. The poets perhaps did better, who would have it that this twofold way was in the lower regions; but they are deceived in this, that they proposed these ways to the dead. Both therefore spoke with truth, but yet both incorrectly; for the ways themselves ought to have been referred to life, their ends to death. We therefore speak better and more truly, who say that the two ways belong to heaven and hell, because immortality is promised to the righteous, and everlasting punishment is threatened to the unrighteous.

But I will explain how these ways either exalt to heaven or thrust down to hell, and I will set forth what these virtues are of which the philosophers were ignorant; then I will show what are their rewards, and also what are vices, and what their punishments. For perhaps someone may expect that I shall speak separately of vices and virtues; whereas, when we discuss the subject of good or evil, that which is contrary may also be understood. For, whether you introduce virtues, vices will spontaneously depart; or if you take away vices, virtues will of their own accord succeed. The nature of good and evil things is so fixed, that they always oppose and drive out one another: and thus it comes to pass that vices cannot be removed without virtues, nor can virtues be introduced without the removal of vices. Therefore we bring forward these ways in a very different manner from that in which the philosophers are accustomed to present them: first of all, because we say that a guide is proposed to each, and in each case an immortal: but that the one is honored who presides over virtues and good qualities, the other condemned who presides over vices and evils. But they place a guide only on the right side, and that not one only, nor a lasting one; inasmuch as they introduce any teacher of a good art, who may recall men from sloth, and teach them to be temperate. But they do not represent any as entering upon that way except boys and young men; for this reason, that the arts are learned at these ages. We, on the other hand, lead those of each sex, every age and race, into this heavenly path, because God, who is the guide of that way, denies immortality to no human being. The shape also of the ways themselves is not as they supposed. For what need is there of the letter Y in matters which are different and opposed to one another? But the one which is better is turned towards the rising of the sun, the other which is worse towards its setting: since he who follows truth and righteousness, having received the reward of immortality, will enjoy perpetual light; but he who, enticed by that evil guide, shall prefer vices to virtues, falsehood to truth, must be borne to the setting of the sun, and to darkness. I will therefore describe each, and will point out their properties and habits.

**Chap. IV.—Of the Ways of Life, of Pleasures, Also of the Hardships of Christians.**

There is one way, therefore, of virtue and the good, which leads, not, as the poets say, to the Elysian plains, but to the very citadel of the world:—

"The left gives sinners up to pain,
And leads to Tartarus' guilty reign."

For it belongs to that accuser who, having invented false religions, turns men away from the heavenly path, and leads them into the way of perdition. And the appearance and shape of this way is so composed to the sight, that it appears to be level and open, and delightful with all kinds of flowers and fruits. For there are placed in it all things which are esteemed on earth as good things—I mean wealth, honor, repose, pleasure, all kinds of enticements; but together with these also injustice, cruelty, pride, perfidy, lust, avarice, discord, ignorance, falsehood, folly, and other vices. But the end of this way is as follows: When they have reached the point from which there is now no return, it is so suddenly removed, together with all its beauty that no one is able to foresee the fraud before that he falls headlong into a deep abyss. For whoever is captivated by the appearance of present goods, and occupied with the pursuit and enjoyment of these, shall not have foreseen the things which are about to follow after death, and shall have turned aside from God; he truly will be cast down to hell, and be condemned to eternal punishment.

But that heavenly way is set forth as difficult and hilly, or rough with dreadful thorns, or entangled with stones jutting out; so that everyone must walk with the greatest labor and wearing of the feet, and with great precautions against falling. In this he has placed justice, temperance, patience, faith, chastity, self-restraint, concord, knowledge, truth, wisdom, and the other virtues; but together with these, poverty, ignominy, labor, pain, and all kinds of hardship. For whoever has extended his hope beyond the present, and chosen better things, will be without these earthly goods, that, being lightly equipped and without impediment, he may overcome the difficulty of the way. For it is impossible for him who has surrounded himself with royal pomp, or loaded himself with riches, either to enter upon or to persevere in these difficulties. And from this it is understood that it is easier for the wicked and the unrighteous to succeed in their desires, because their road is downward and on the decline; but that it is difficult for the good to attain to their wishes, because they walk along a difficult and steep path. Therefore the righteous man, since he has entered upon a hard and rugged way, must be an object of contempt, derision, and hatred. For all whom desire or pleasure drags headlong, envy him who has been able to attain to virtue, and take it ill that anyone possesses that which they themselves do not possess. Therefore he will be poor, humble, ignoble, subject to injury, and yet enduring all things which are grievous; and if he shall continue his patience unceasingly to that last step and end, the crown of virtue will be given to him, and he will be rewarded by God with immortality for the labors which he has endured in life for the sake of righteousness. These are the ways which God has assigned to human life, in each of which he has shown both good and evil things, but in a changed and inverted order. In the one he has pointed out in the first place temporal evils followed by eternal goods, which is the better order; in the other, first temporal goods followed by eternal evils, which is the worse order: so that, whosoever has chosen present evils together with righteousness, he will obtain greater and more certain goods than those were which he despised; but whoever has preferred present goods to righteousness, will fall into greater and more lasting evils than those were which he avoided. For as this bodily life is short, therefore its goods and evils must also be short; but since that spiritual life, which is contrary to this earthly life, is everlasting, therefore its goods and evils are also everlasting. Thus it comes to pass, that goods of short duration are succeeded by eternal evils, and evils of short duration by eternal goods.

Since, therefore, good and evil things are set before man at the same time, it is befitting that everyone should consider with himself how much better it is to compensate evils of short duration by perpetual goods, than to endure perpetual evils for short and perishable goods. For as, in this life, when a contest with an enemy is set before you, you must first labor that you may afterwards enjoy repose, you must suffer hunger and thirst, you must endure heat and cold, you must rest on the ground, must watch and undergo dangers, that your children, and house, and property being preserved, you may be able to enjoy all the blessings of peace and victory; but if you should choose present ease in preference to labor, you must do yourself the greatest injury: for the enemy will surprise you offering no resistance, your lands will be laid waste, your house plundered, your wife and children become a prey, you yourself will be slain or taken prisoner; to prevent the occurrence of these things, present advantage must be put aside, that a greater and more lasting advantage may be gained;—so in the whole of this life, because God has provided an adversary for us, that we might be able to acquire virtue, present gratification must be laid aside, lest the enemy should overpower us. We must be on the watch, must post guards, must undertake military expeditions, must shed our blood to the uttermost; in short, we must patiently submit to all things which are unpleasant and grievous, and the more readily because God our commander has appointed for us eternal rewards for our labors. And since in this earthly warfare men expend so much labor to acquire for themselves those things which may perish in the same manner as that in which they were acquired, assuredly no labor ought to be refused by us, by whom that is gained which can in no way be lost.

For God, who created men to this warfare, desired that they should stand prepared in battle array, and with minds keenly intent should watch against the stratagems or open attacks of our single enemy, who, as is the practice of skillful and experienced generals, endeavors to ensnare us by various arts, directing his rage according to the nature and disposition of each. For he infuses into some insatiable avarice, that, being chained by their riches as by fetters, he may drive them from the way of truth. He inflames others with the excitement of anger, that while they are rather intent upon inflicting injury, he may turn them aside from the contemplation of God. He plunges others into immoderate lusts, that, giving themselves to pleasure of the body, they may be unable to look towards virtue. He inspires others with envy, that, being occupied with their own torments, they may think of nothing but the happiness of those whom they hate. He causes others to swell with ambitious desires. These are they who direct the whole occupation and care of their life to the holding of magistracies, that they may set a mark upon the annals, and give a name to the years. The desire of others mounts higher, not that they may rule provinces with the temporal sword, but with boundless and perpetual power may wish to be called lords of the whole human race. Moreover, those whom he has seen to be pious he involves in various superstitions, that he may make them impious. But to those who seek for wisdom, he dashes philosophy before their eyes, that he may blind them with the appearance of light, lest anyone should grasp and hold fast the truth. Thus he has blocked up all the approaches against men, and has occupied the way, rejoicing in public errors; but that we might be able to dispel these errors, and to overcome the author of evils himself, God has enlightened us, and has armed us with true and heavenly virtue, respecting which I must now speak.

### Chap. V.—Of False and True Virtue; And of Knowledge.

But before I begin to set forth the separate virtues, I must mark out the character of virtue itself, which the philosophers have not rightly defined, as to its nature, or in what things it consisted; and I must describe its operation and office. For they only retained the name, but lost its power, and nature, and effect. But whatever they are accustomed to say in their definition of virtue, Lucilius puts together and expresses in a few verses, which I prefer to introduce, lest, while I refute the opinions of many, I should be longer than is necessary:—

"It is virtue, O Albinus, to pay the proper price,
To attend to the matters in which we are engaged, and in which we live.
It is virtue for a man to know the nature of everything.
It is virtue for a man to know what is right and useful and honorable,
What things are good, and what are evil.
What is useless, base, and dishonorable.
It is virtue to know the end of an object to be sought and the means *of procuring it*

It is virtue to be able to assign their value to riches.
It is virtue to give that which is really due to honor;
To be the enemy and the foe of bad men and manners, but, on the other hand, the defender of good men and manners;
To esteem these highly, to wish them well, to live in friendship with them,
Moreover, to consider the interest of one's country first;
Then those of parents, to put our own interests in the third and last place."

From these definitions, which the poet briefly puts together, Marcus Tullius derived the offices of living, following Panætius the Stoic, and included them in three books.

But we shall presently see how false these things are, that it may appear how much the divine condescension has bestowed on us in opening to us the truth. He says that it is virtue to know what is good and evil, what is base, what is honorable, what is useful, what is useless. He might have shortened his treatise if he had only spoken of that which is good and evil; for nothing can be useful or honorable which is not also good, and nothing useless and base which is not also evil. And this also appears to be thus to philosophers, and Cicero shows it likewise in the third book of the above-mentioned treatise. But knowledge cannot be virtue, because it is not within us, but it comes to us from without. But that which is able to pass from one to the other is not virtue, because virtue is the property of each individual. Knowledge therefore consists in a benefit derived from another; for it depends upon hearing. Virtue is altogether our own; for it depends upon the will of doing that which is good. As, therefore, in undertaking a journey, it is of no profit to know the way, unless we also have the effort and strength for walking, so truly knowledge is of no avail if our virtue fails. For, in general, even they who sin perceive what is good and evil, though not perfectly; and as often as they act improperly, they know that they sin, and therefore endeavor to conceal their actions. But though the nature of good and evil does not escape their notice, they are overpowered by an evil desire to sin, because they are wanting in virtue, that is, the desire of doing right and honorable things. Therefore that the knowledge of good and evil is one thing, and virtue another, appears from this, because knowledge can exist without virtue, as it has been in the case of many of the philosophers; in which, since not to have done what you knew to be right is justly censurable, a depraved will and a vicious mind, which ignorance cannot excuse, will be justly punished. Therefore, as the knowledge of good and evil is not virtue, so the doing that which is good and the abstaining from evil is virtue. And yet knowledge is so united with virtue, that knowledge precedes virtue, and virtue follows knowledge; because knowledge is of no avail unless it is followed up by action.

Horace therefore speaks somewhat better: "Virtue is the fleeing from vice, and the first wisdom is to be free from folly." But he speaks improperly, because he defined virtue by its contrary, as though he should say, That is good which is not evil. For when I know not what virtue is, I do not know what vice is. Each therefore requires definition, because the nature of the case is such that each must be understood or not understood.

But let us do that which he ought to have done. It is a virtue to restrain anger, to control desire, to curb lust; for this is to flee from vice. For almost all things which are done unjustly and dishonestly arise from these affections. For if the force of this emotion which is called anger be blunted, all the evil contentions of men will be lulled to rest; no one will plot, no one will rush forth to injure another. Also, if desire be restrained, no one will use violence by land or by sea, no one will lead an army to carry off and lay waste the property of others. Also, if the ardor of lusts be repressed, every age and sex will retain its sanctity; no one will suffer, or do anything disgraceful. Therefore all crimes and disgraceful actions will be taken away from the life and character of men, if these emotions are appeased and calmed by virtue. And this calming of the emotions and affections has this meaning, that we do all things which are right. The whole duty of virtue then is, not to sin. And assuredly he cannot discharge this who is ignorant of God, since ignorance of Him from whom good things proceed must thrust a man unawares into vices. Therefore, that I may more briefly and significantly fix the offices of each subject, knowledge is to know God, virtue is to worship Him: the former implies wisdom, the latter righteousness.

### Chap. VI.—Of the Chief Good and Virtue, and or Knowledge and Righteousness.

I have said that which was the first thing, that the knowledge of good is not virtue; and secondly, I have shown what virtue is, and in what it consists. It follows that I should show this also, that the philosophers were ignorant of what is good and evil; and this briefly, because it has been almost made plain in the third book, when I was discussing the subject of the chief good. And because they did not know what the chief good was, they necessarily erred in the case of the other goods and evils which are not the chief; for no one can weigh these with a true judgment who does not possess the fountain itself from which they are derived. Now the source of good things is God; but of evils, he who is always the enemy of the divine name, of whom we have often spoken. From these two sources good and evil things have their origin. Those which proceed from God have this object, to procure immortality, which is the greatest good; but those which arise from the other have this office, to call man away from heavenly things and sink him in earthly things, and thus to consign him to the punishment of everlasting death, which is the greatest evil. Is it therefore doubtful but that all those were ignorant of what was good and evil, who neither knew God nor the adversary of God? Therefore they referred the end of good things to the body, and to this short life, which must be dissolved and perish: they did not advance further. But all their precepts, and all the things which they introduce as goods, adhere to the earth, and lie on the ground, since they die with the body, which is earth; for they do not tend to procure life for man, but either to the acquisition or increase of riches, honor, glory, and power, which are altogether mortal things, as much so indeed as he who has labored to obtain them. Hence is that saying, "It is virtue to know the end of an object to be sought, and the means of procuring it;" for they enjoin by what means and by what practices property is to be sought, for they see that it is often sought unjustly. But virtue of this kind is not proposed to the wise man; for it is not virtue to seek riches, of which neither the finding nor the possession is in our power: therefore they are more easy to be gained and to be retained by the bad than by the good. Virtue, then, cannot consist in the seeking of those things in the despising of which the force and purport of virtue appears; nor will it have recourse to those very things which, with its great and lofty mind, it desires to trample upon and bruise under foot; nor is it lawful for a soul which is earnestly fixed on heavenly goods to be called away from its immortal pursuits, that it may acquire for itself these frail things. But the course of virtue especially consists in the acquisition of those things which neither any man, nor death itself, can take away from us. Since these things are so, that which follows is true: "It is virtue to be able to assign their value to riches:" which verse is nearly of the same meaning as the first two. But neither he nor any of the philosophers was able to know the price itself, either of what nature or what it is; for the poet, and all those whom he followed, thought that it meant to make a right use of riches,—that is, to be moderate in living, not to make costly entertainments, not to squander carelessly, not to expend property on superfluous or disgraceful objects.

Someone will perhaps say, What do you say? Do you deny that this is virtue? I do not deny it indeed; for if I should deny it, I should appear to prove the opposite. But I deny that it is true virtue; because it is not that heavenly principle, but is altogether of the earth, since it produces no effect but that which remains on the earth. But what it is to make a right use of wealth, and what advantage is to be sought from riches, I will declare more openly when I shall begin to speak of the duty of piety. Now the other things which follow are by no means true; for to proclaim enmity against the wicked, or to undertake the defense of the good, may be common to it with the evil. For some, by a pretense of goodness, prepare the way for themselves to power, and do many things which the good are accustomed to do, and that the more readily because they do them for the sake of deceiving; and I wish that it were as easy to carry out goodness in action as it is to pretend to it. But when they have begun to attain to their purpose and their wish in reaching the highest step of power, then, truly laying aside pretense, these men discover their character; they seize upon everything, and offer violence, and lay waste; and they press upon the good themselves, whose cause they had undertaken; and they cut away the steps by which they mounted, that no one may be able to imitate them against themselves. But, however, let us suppose that this duty of defending the good belongs only to the good man. Yet to undertake it is easy, to fulfil it is difficult; because when you have committed yourself to a contest and an encounter, the victory is placed at the disposal of God, not in your own power. And for the most part the wicked are more powerful both in number and in combination than the good, so that it is not so much virtue which is necessary to overcome them as good fortune. Is anyone ignorant how often the better and the juster side has been overcome? From this cause harsh tyrannies have always broken out against the citizens. All history is full of examples, but we will be content with one. Cnoeus Pompeius wished to be the defender of the good, since he took up arms in defense of the commonwealth, in defense of the senate, and in defense of liberty; and yet the same man, being conquered, perished together with liberty itself, and being mutilated by Egyptian eunuchs, was cast forth unburied.

It is not virtue, therefore, either to be the enemy of the bad or the defender of the good, because virtue cannot be subject to uncertain chances.

"Moreover, to reckon the interests of our country as in the first place."

When the agreement of men is taken away, virtue has no existence at all; for what are the interests of our country, but the inconveniences of another state or nation?—that is, to extend the boundaries which are violently taken from others, to increase the power of the state, to improve the revenues,—all which things are not virtues, but the overthrowing of virtues: for, in the first place, the union of human society is taken away, innocence is taken away, the abstaining from the property of another is taken away; lastly, justice itself is taken away, which is unable to bear the tearing asunder of the human race, and wherever arms have glittered, must be banished and exterminated from thence. This saying of Cicero is true: "But they who say that regard is to be had to citizens, but that it is not to be had to foreigners, these destroy the common society of the human race; and when this is removed, beneficence, liberality, kindness, and justice are entirely taken away." For how can a man be just who injures, who hates, who despoils, who puts to death? And they who strive to be serviceable to their country do all these things: for they are ignorant of what this being serviceable is, who think nothing useful, nothing advantageous, but that which can be held by the hand; and this alone cannot be held, because it may be snatched away.

Whoever, then, has gained for his country these goods—as they themselves call them—that is, who by the overthrow of cities and the destruction of nations has filled the treasury with money, has taken lands and enriched his country-men—he is extolled with praises to the heaven: in him there is said to be the greatest and perfect virtue. And this is the error not only of the people and the ignorant, but also of philosophers, who even give precepts for injustice, lest folly and wickedness should be wanting in discipline and authority. Therefore, when they are speaking of the duties relating to warfare, all that discourse is accommodated neither to justice nor to true virtue, but to this life and to civil institutions; and that this is not justice the matter itself declares, and Cicero has testified. "But we," he says, "are not in possession of the real and life-like figure of true law and genuine justice, we have nothing but delineations and sketches; and I wish that we followed even these, for they are taken from the excellent copies made by nature and truth." It is then a delineation and a sketch which they thought to be justice. But what of wisdom? Does not the same man confess that it has no existence in philosophers? "Nor," he says, "when Fabricius or Aristides is called just, is an example of justice sought from these as from a wise man; for none of these is wise in the sense in which we wish the truly wise to be understood. Nor were they who are esteemed and called wise, Marcus Cato and Caius Lælius, actually wise, nor those well-known seven; but from their constant practice of the 'middle duties,' they bore a certain likeness and appearance of wise men." If therefore wisdom is taken away from the philosophers by their own confession, and justice is taken away from those who are regarded as just, it follows that all those descriptions of virtue must be false, because no one can know what true virtue is but he who is just and wise. But no one is just and wise but he whom God has instructed with heavenly precepts.

**Chap. VII.—Of the Way of Error and of Truth: that It is Single, Narrow, and Steep, and Has God for Its Guide.**

For all those who, by the confessed folly of others, are thought wise, being clothed with the appearance of virtue, grasp at shadows and outlines, but at nothing true. Which happens on this account, because that deceitful road which inclines to the west has many paths, on account of the variety of pursuits and systems which are dissimilar and varied in the life of men. For as that way of wisdom contains something which resembles folly, as we showed in the preceding book, so this way, which belongs altogether to folly, contains something which resembles wisdom, and they who perceive the folly of men in general seize upon this; and as it has its vices manifest, so it has something which appears to resemble virtue: as it has its wickedness open, so it has a likeness and appearance of justice. For how could the forerunner of that way, whose strength and power are altogether in deceit, lead men altogether into fraud, unless he showed them some things which resembled the truth? For, that His immortal secret might be hidden, God placed in his way things which men might despise as evil and disgraceful, that, turning away from wisdom and truth, which they were searching for without any guide, they might fall upon that very thing which they desired to avoid and flee from. Therefore he points out that way of destruction and death which has many windings, either because there are many kinds of life, or because there are many gods who are worshipped.

The deceitful and treacherous guide of this way, that there may appear to be some distinction between truth and falsehood, good and evil, leads the luxurious in one direction, and those who are called temperate in another; the ignorant in one direction, the learned in another; the sluggish in one direction, the active in another; the foolish in one direction, the philosophers in another, and even these not in one path. For those who do not shun pleasures or riches, he withdraws a little from this public and frequented road; but those who either wish to follow virtue, or profess a contempt for things, he drags over certain rugged precipices. But nevertheless all those paths which display an appearance of honors are not different roads, but turnings off and bypaths, which appear indeed to be separated from that common one, and to branch off to the right, but yet return to the same, and all lead at the very end to one issue. For that guide unites them all, where it was necessary that the good should be separated from the bad, the strong from the inactive, the wise from the foolish; namely, in the worship of the gods, in which he slays them all with one sword, because they were all foolish without any distinction, and plunges them into death. But this way—which is that of truth, and wisdom, and virtue, and justice, of all which there is but one fountain, one source of strength, one abode—is both simple, because with like minds, and with the utmost agreement, we follow and worship one God; and it is narrow, because virtue is given to the smaller number; and steep, because goodness, which is very high and lofty, cannot be attained to without the greatest difficulty and labor.

**Chap. VIII.—Of the Errors of Philosophers, and the Variableness of Law.**

This is the way which philosophers seek, but do not find on this account, because they prefer to seek it on the earth, where it cannot appear. Therefore they wander, as it were, on the great sea, and do not understand whither they are borne, because they neither discern the way nor follow any guide. For this way of life ought to be sought in the same manner in which their course is sought by ships over the deep: for unless they observe some light of heaven, they wander with uncertain courses. But whoever strives to hold the right course of life ought not to look to the earth, but to the heaven: and, to speak more plainly, he ought not to follow man, but God; not to serve these earthly images, but the heavenly God; not to measure all things by their reference to the body, but by their reference to the soul; not to attend to this life, but the eternal life. Therefore, if you always direct your eyes towards heaven, and observe the sun, where it rises, and take this as the guide of your life, as in the case of a voyage, your feet will spontaneously be directed into the way; and that heavenly light, which is a much brighter sun to sound minds than this which we behold in mortal flesh, will so rule and govern you as to lead you without any error to the most excellent harbor of wisdom and virtue.

Therefore the law of God must be undertaken, which may direct us to this path; that sacred, that heavenly law, which Marcus Tullius, in his third book respecting the Republic, has described almost with a divine voice; whose words have subjoined, that I might not speak at greater length: "There is indeed a true law, right reason, agreeing with nature, diffused among all, unchanging, everlasting, which calls to duty by commanding, deters from wrong by forbidding; which, however, neither commands nor forbids the good in vain, nor affects the wicked by commanding or forbidding. It is not allowable to alter the provisions of this law, nor is it permitted us to modify it, nor can it be entirely abrogated. Nor, truly, can we be released from this law, either by the senate or by the people; nor is another person to be sought to explain or interpret it. Nor will there be one law at Rome and another at Athens; one law at the present time, and another hereafter: but the same law, everlasting and unchangeable, will bind all nations at all times; and there will be one common Master and Ruler of all, even God, the framer, arbitrator, and proposer of this law; and he who shall not obey this will flee from himself, and, despising the nature of man, will suffer the greatest punishments through this very thing, even though he shall have escaped the other punishments which are supposed to exist." Who that is acquainted with the mystery of God could so significantly relate the law of God, as a man far removed from the knowledge of the truth has set forth that law? But I consider that they who speak true things unconsciously are to be so regarded as though they prophesied under the influence of some spirit. But if he had known or explained this also, in what precepts the law itself consisted, as he clearly saw the force and purport of the divine law, he would not have discharged the office of a philosopher, but of a prophet. And because he was unable to do this, it must be done by us, to whom the law itself has been delivered by the one great Master and Ruler of all, God.

## Chap. IX.—Of the Law and Precept of God; Of Mercy, and the Error of the Philosophers.

The first head of this law is, to know God Himself, to obey Him alone, to worship Him alone. For he cannot maintain the character of a man who is ignorant of God, the parent of his soul: which is the greatest impiety. For this ignorance causes him to serve other gods, and no greater crime than this can be committed. Hence there is now so easy a step to wickedness through ignorance of the truth and of the chief good; since God, from the knowledge of whom he shrinks, is Himself the fountain of goodness. Or if he shall wish to follow the justice of God, yet, being ignorant of the divine law, he embraces the laws of his own country as true justice, though they were clearly devised not by justice, but by utility. For why is it that there are different and various laws amongst all people, but that each nation has enacted for itself that which it deemed useful for its own affairs? But how greatly utility differs from justice the Roman people themselves teach, who, by proclaiming war through the Fecials, and by inflicting injuries according to legal forms, by always desiring and carrying off the property of other, have gained for themselves the possession of the whole world. But these persons think themselves just if they do nothing against their own laws; which may be even ascribed to fear, if they abstain from crimes through dread of present punishment. But let us grant that they do that naturally, or, as the philosopher says, of their own accord, which they are compelled to do by the laws. Will they therefore be just, because they obey the institutions of men, who may themselves have erred, or have been unjust?—as it was with the framers of the twelve tables, who certainly promoted the public advantage according to the condition of the times. Civil law is one thing, which varies everywhere according to customs; but justice is another thing, which God has set forth to all as uniform and simple: and he who is ignorant of God must also be ignorant of justice.

But let us suppose it possible that anyone, by natural and innate goodness, should gain true virtues, such a man as we have heard that Cimon was at Athens, who both gave alms to the needy, and entertained the poor, and clothed the naked; yet, when that one thing which is of the greatest importance is wanting—the acknowledgment of God—then all those good things are superfluous and empty, so that in pursuing them he has labored in vain. For all his justice will resemble a human body which has no head, in which, although all the limbs are in their proper position, and figure, and proportion, yet, since that is wanting which is the chief thing of all, it is destitute both of life and of all sensation. Therefore those limbs have only the shape of limbs, but admit of no use, as much so as a head without a body; and he resembles this who is not without the knowledge of God, but yet lives unjustly. For he has that only which is of the greatest importance; but he has it to no purpose, since he is destitute of the virtues, as it were, of limbs.

Therefore, that the body may be alive, and capable of sensation, both the knowledge of God is necessary, as it were the head, and all the virtues, as it were the body. Thus there will exist a perfect and living man; but, however, the whole substance is in the head; and although this cannot exist in the absence of all, it may exist in the absence of some. And it will be an imperfect and faulty animal, but yet it will be alive, as he who knows God and yet sins in some respect. For God pardons sins. And thus it is possible to live without some of the limbs, but it is by no means possible to live without a head. This is the reason why the philosophers, though they may be naturally good, yet have no knowledge and no intelligence. All their learning and virtue is without a head, because they are ignorant of God, who is the Head of virtue and knowledge; and he who is ignorant of Him, though he may see, is blind; though he may hear, is deaf; though he may speak, is dumb. But when he shall know the Creator and Parent of all things, then he will both see, and hear, and speak. For he begins to have a head, in which all the senses are placed, that is, the eyes, and ears, and tongue. For assuredly he sees who has beheld with the eyes of his mind the truth in which God is, or God in whom the truth is; he hears, who imprints on his heart the divine words and life-giving precepts; he speaks, who, in discussing heavenly things, relates the virtue and majesty of the surpassing God. Therefore he is undoubtedly impious who does not acknowledge God; and all his virtues, which he thinks that he has or possesses, are found in that deadly road which belongs altogether to darkness. Wherefore there is no reason why anyone should congratulate himself if he has gained these empty virtues, because he is not only wretched who is destitute of present goods, but he must also be foolish, since he undertakes the greatest labors in his life without any purpose. For if the hope of immortality is taken away, which God promises to those who continue in His religion, for the sake of obtaining which virtue is to be sought, and whatever evils happen are to be endured, it will assuredly be the greatest folly to wish to comply with virtues which in vain bring calamities and labors to man. For if it is virtue to endure and undergo with fortitude, want, exile, pain, and death, which are feared by others, what goodness, I pray, has it in itself, that philosophers should say that it is to be sought for on its own account? Truly they are delighted with superfluous and useless punishments, when it is permitted them to live in tranquility.

For if our souls are mortal, if virtue is about to have no existence after the dissolution of the body, why do we avoid the goods assigned to us, as though we were ungrateful or unworthy of enjoying the divine gifts? For, that we may enjoy these blessings, we must live in wickedness and impiety, because virtue, that is, justice, is followed by poverty. Therefore he is not of sound mind, who, without having any greater hope set before him, prefers labors, and tortures, and miseries, to those goods which others enjoy in life. But if virtue is to be taken up, as is most rightly said by these, because it is evident that man is born to it, it ought to contain some greater hope, which may apply a great and illustrious solace for the ills and labors which it is the part of virtue to endure. Nor can virtue, since it is difficult in itself, be esteemed as a good in any other way than by having its hardship compensated by the greatest good. We can in no other way equally abstain from these present goods, than if there are other greater goods on account of which it is worthwhile to leave the pursuit of pleasures, and to endure all evils. But these are no other, as I have shown in the third book, than the goods of everlasting life. Now who can bestow these except God, who has proposed to us virtue itself? Therefore the sum and substance of everything is contained in the acknowledging and worship of God; all the hope and safety of man centers in this; this is the first step of wisdom, to know who is our true Father, and to worship Him alone with the piety which is due to Him, to obey Him, to yield ourselves to His service with the utmost devotedness: let our entire acting, and care, and attention, be laid out in gaining His favor.

### Chap. X.—Of Religion towards God, and Mercy towards Men; And of the Beginning of the World.

I have said what is due to God, I will now say what is to be given to man; although this very thing which you shall give to man is given to God, for man is the image of God. But, however, the first office of justice is to be united with God, the second with man. But the former is called religion; the second is named mercy or kindness; which virtue is peculiar to the just, and to the worshippers of God, because this alone comprises the principle of common life. For God, who has not given wisdom to the other animals, has made them safer from attack in danger by natural defenses. But because He made him naked and defenseless, that He might rather furnish him with wisdom, He gave him, besides other things, this feeling of kindness; so that man should protect, love, and cherish man, and both receive and afford assistance against all dangers. Therefore kindness is the greatest bond of human society; and he who has broken this is to be deemed impious, and a parricide. For if we all derive our origin from one man, whom God created, we are plainly of one blood; and therefore it must be considered the greatest wickedness to hate a man, even though guilty. On which account God has enjoined that enmities are never to be contracted by us, but that they are always to be removed, so that we soothe those who are our enemies, by reminding them of their relationship. Likewise, if we are all inspired and animated by one God, what else are we than brothers? And, indeed, the more closely united, because we are united in soul rather than in body. Accordingly Lucretius does not err when he says: "In short, we are all sprung from a heavenly seed; all have that same father." Therefore they are to be accounted as savage beasts who injure man; who, in opposition to every law and right of human nature, plunder, torture, slay, and banish.

On account of this relationship of brotherhood, God teaches us never to do evil, but always good. And He also prescribes in what this doing good consists: in affording aid to those who are oppressed and in difficulty, and in bestowing food on those who are destitute. For God, since He is kind, wished us to be a social animal. Therefore, in the case of other men, we ought to think of ourselves. We do not deserve to be set free in our own dangers, if we do not succor others; we do not deserve assistance, if we refuse to render it. There are no precepts of philosophers to this purport, inasmuch as they, being captivated by the appearance of false virtue, have taken away mercy from man, and while they wish to heal, have corrupted. And though they generally admit that the mutual participation of human society is to be retained, they entirely separate themselves from it by the harshness of their inhuman virtue. This error, therefore, is also to be refuted, of those who think that nothing is to be bestowed on any one. They have introduced not one origin only, and cause of building a city; but some relate that those men who were first born from the earth, when they passed a wandering life among the woods and plains, and were not united by any mutual bond of speech or justice, but had leaves and grass for their beds, and caves and grottos for their dwellings, were a prey to the beasts and stronger animals. Then, that those who had either escaped, having been torn, or had seen their neighbors torn, being admonished of their own danger, had recourse to other men, implored protection, and at first made their wishes known by nods; then that they tried the beginnings of conversation, and by attaching names to each object, by degrees completed the system of speech. But when they saw that numbers themselves were not safe against the beasts, they began also to build towns, either that they might make their nightly repose safe, or that they might ward off the incursions and attacks of beasts, not by fighting, but by interposing barriers.

  O minds unworthy of men, which produced these foolish trifles! O wretched and pitiable men, who committed to writing and handed down to memory the record of their own folly; who, when they saw that the plan of assembling themselves together, or of mutual intercourse, or of avoiding danger, or of guarding against evil, or of preparing for themselves sleeping places and lairs, was natural even to the dumb animals, thought, however, that men could not have been admonished and learned, except by examples, what they ought to fear, what to avoid, and what to do, or that they would never have assembled together, or have discovered the method of speech, had not the beasts devoured them! These things appeared to others senseless, as they really were; and they said that the cause of their coming together was not the tearing of wild beasts, but rather the very feeling of humanity itself; and that therefore they collected themselves together, because the nature of men avoided solitude, and was desirous of communion and society. The discrepancy between them is not great; since the causes are different, the fact is the same. Each might have been true, because there is no direct opposition. But, however, neither is by any means true, because men were not born from the ground throughout the world, as though sprung from the teeth of some dragon, as the poets relate; but one man was formed by God, and from that one man all the earth was filled with the human race, in the same way as again took place after the deluge, which they certainly cannot deny. Therefore no assembling together of this kind took place at the beginning; and that there were never men on the earth who could not speak except those who were infants, everyone who is possessed of sense will understand. Let us suppose, however, that these things are true which idle and foolish old men vainly say, that we may refute them especially by their own feelings and arguments.

If men were collected together on this account, that they might protect their weakness by mutual help, therefore we must succor man, who needs help. For, since men entered into and contracted fellowship with men for the sake of protection, either to violate or not to preserve that compact which was entered into among men from the commencement of their origin, is to be considered as the greatest impiety. For he who withdraws himself from affording assistance must also of necessity withdraw himself from receiving it; for he who refuses his aid to another thinks that he stands in need of the aid of none. But he who withdraws and separates himself from the body at large, must live not after the custom of men, but after the manner of wild beasts. But if this cannot be done, the bond of human society is by all means to be retained, because man can in no way live without man. But the preservation of society is a mutual sharing of kind offices; that is, the affording help, that we may be able to receive it. But if, as those others assert, the assembling together of men has been caused on account of humanity itself, man ought undoubtedly to recognize man. But if those ignorant and as yet uncivilized men did this, and that, when the practice of speaking was not yet established, what must we think ought to be done by men who are polished, and connected together by interchange of conversation and all business, who, being accustomed to the society of men, cannot endure solitude?

**Chap. XI.—Of the Persons upon Whom a Benefit is to Be Conferred.**

Therefore humanity is to be preserved, if we wish rightly to be called men. But what else is this preservation of humanity than the loving a man because he is a man, and the same as ourselves? Therefore discord and dissension are not in accordance with the nature of man; and that expression of Cicero is true, which says that man, while he is obedient to nature, cannot injure man. Therefore, if it is contrary to nature to injure a man, it must be in accordance with nature to benefit a man; and he who does not do this deprives himself of the title of a man, because it is the duty of humanity to succor the necessity and peril of a man. I ask, therefore, of those who do not think it the part of a wise man to be prevailed upon and to pity, If a man were seized by some beast, and were to implore the aid of an armed man, whether they think that he ought to be succored or not? They are not so shameless as to deny that that ought to be done which humanity demands and requires. Also, if anyone were surrounded by fire, crushed by the downfall of a building, plunged in the sea, or carried away by a river, would they think it the duty of a man not to assist him? They themselves are not men if they think so; for no one can fail to be liable to dangers of this kind. Yes, truly, they will say that it is the part of a human being, and of a brave man too, to preserve one who was on the point of perishing. If, therefore, in casualties of this nature which imperil the life of man, they allow that it is the part of humanity to give succor, what reason is there why they should think that succor is to be withheld if a man should suffer from hunger, thirst, or cold? But though these things are naturally on an equality with those accidental circumstances, and need one and the same humanity, yet they make a distinction between these things, because they measure all things not by the truth itself, but by present utility. For they hope that those whom they rescue from peril will make a return of the favor to them. But because they do not hope for this in the case of the needy, they think that whatever they bestow on men of this kind is thrown away. Hence that sentiment of Plautus is detestable:—

> "He deserves ill who gives food to a beggar;
> For that which he gives is thrown away, and
> It lengthens out the life of the other to his misery."

But perhaps the poet spoke for the actor.

What does Marcus Tullius say in his books respecting Offices? Does he not also advise that bounty should not be employed at all? For thus he speaks: "Bounty, which proceeds from our estate, drains the very source of our liberality; and thus liberality is destroyed by liberality: for the more numerous they are towards whom you practice it, the less you will be able to practice it towards many." And he also says shortly afterwards: "But what is more foolish than so to act that you may not be able to continue to do that which you do willingly?" This professor of wisdom plainly keeps men back from acts of kindness, and advises them carefully to guard their property, and to preserve their money-chest in safety, rather than to follow justice. And when he perceived that this was inhuman and wicked, soon afterwards, in another chapter, as though moved by repentance, he thus spoke: "Sometimes, however, we must exercise bounty in giving: nor is this kind of liberality altogether to be rejected; and we must give from our property to suitable persons when they are in need of assistance." What is the meaning of "suitable?" Assuredly those who are able to restore and give back the favor. If Cicero were now alive, I should certainly exclaim: Here, here,

Marcus Tullius, you have erred from true justice; and you have taken it away by one word, since you measured the offices of piety and humanity by utility. For we must not bestow our bounty on suitable objects, but as much as possible on unsuitable objects. For that will be done with justice, piety, and humanity, which you shall do without the hope of any return!

This is that true and genuine justice, of which you say that you have no real and life-like figure. You yourself exclaim in many places that virtue is not mercenary; and you confess in the books of your Laws that liberality is gratuitous, in these words: "Nor is it doubtful that he who is called liberal and generous is influenced by a sense of duty, and not by advantage." Why therefore do you bestow your bounty on suitable persons, unless it be that you may afterwards receive a reward? With you, therefore, as the author and teacher of justice, whosoever shall not be a suitable person will be worn out with nakedness, thirst, and hunger; nor will men who are rich and abundantly supplied, even to luxuriousness, assist his last extremity. If virtue does not exact a reward; if, as you say, it is to be sought on its own account, then estimate justice, which is the mother and chief of the virtues, at its own price, and not according to your advantage: give especially to him from whom you hope for nothing in return. Why do you select persons? Why do you look at bodily forms? He is to be esteemed by you as a man, whoever it is that implores you, because he considers you a man. Cast away those outlines and sketches of justice, and hold fast justice itself, true and fashioned to the life. Be bountiful to the blind, the feeble, the lame, and the destitute, who must die unless you bestow your bounty upon them. They are useless to men, but they are serviceable to God, who retains them in life, who endues them with breath, who vouchsafes to them the light. Cherish as far as in you lies, and support with kindness, the lives of men, that they may not be extinguished. He who is able to succor one on the point of perishing, if he fails to do so, kills him. But they, because they neither retain their nature, nor know what reward there is in this, while they fear to lose, do lose, and fall into that which they chiefly guard against; so that whatever they bestow is either lost altogether, or profits only for the briefest time. For they who refuse a small gift to the wretched, who wish to preserve humanity without any loss to themselves, squander their property, so that they either acquire for themselves frail and perishable things, or they certainly gain nothing by their own great loss.

For what must be said of those who, induced by the vanity of popular favor, expend on the exhibition of shows wealth that would be sufficient even for great cities? Must we not say that they are senseless and mad who bestow upon the people that which is both lost to themselves, and which none of those on whom it is bestowed receives? Therefore, as all pleasure is short and perishable, and especially that of the eyes and ears, men either forget and are ungrateful for the expenses incurred by another, or they are even offended if the caprice of the people is not satisfied: so that most foolish men have even acquired evil for themselves by evil; or if they have thus succeeded in pleasing, they gain nothing more than empty favor and the talk of a few days. Thus every day the estates of most trifling men are expended on superfluous matters. Do they then act more wisely who exhibit to their fellow-citizens more useful and lasting gifts? They, for instance, who by the building of public works seek a lasting memory for their name? Not even do they act rightly in burying their property in the earth; because the remembrance of them neither bestows anything upon the dead, nor are their works eternal, inasmuch as they are either thrown down and destroyed by a single earthquake, or are consumed by an accidental fire, or they are over through by some attack of an enemy, or at any rate they decay and fall to pieces by mere length of time. For there is nothing, as the orator says, made by the work of man's hand which length of time does not weaken and destroy. But this justice of which we speak, and mercy, flourish more every day. They therefore act better who bestow their bounty on their tribesmen and clients, for they bestow something on men, and profit them; but that is not true and just bounty, for there is no conferring of a benefit where there is no necessity. Therefore, whatever is given to those who are not in need, for the sake of popularity, is thrown away; or it is repaid with interest, and thus it will not be the conferring of a benefit. And although it is pleasing to those to whom it is given, still it is not just, because if it is not done, no evil follows. Therefore the only sure and true office of liberality is to support the needy and unserviceable.

### Chap. XII.—Of the Kinds of Beneficence, and Works of Mercy.

This is that perfect justice which protects human society, concerning which philosophers speak. This is the chief and truest advantage of riches; not to use wealth for the particular pleasure of an individual, but for the welfare of many; not for one's own immediate enjoyment, but for justice, which alone does not perish. We must therefore by all means keep in mind, that the hope of receiving in return must be altogether absent from the duty of showing mercy: for the reward of this work and duty must be expected from God alone; for if you should expect it from man, then that will not be kindness, but the lending of a benefit at interest; nor can he seem to have deserved well who affords that which he does, not to another, but to himself. And yet the matter comes to this, that whatever a man has bestowed upon another, hoping for no advantage from him, he really bestows upon himself, for he will receive a reward from God. God has also enjoined, that if at any time we make a feast, we should invite to the entertainment those who cannot invite us in return, and thus make us a recompense, so that no action of our life should be without the exercise of mercy. Nor, however, let anyone think that he is debarred from intercourse with his friends or kindness with his neighbors. But God has made known to us what is our true and just work: we ought thus to live with our neighbors, provided that we know that the one manner of living relates to man, the other to God.

Therefore hospitality is a principal virtue, as the philosophers also say; but they turn it aside from true justice, and forcibly apply it to advantage. Cicero says: "Hospitality was rightly praised by Theophrastus. For (as it appears to me) it is highly becoming that the houses of illustrious men should be open to illustrious guests." He has here committed the same error which he then did, when he said that we must bestow our bounty on "suitable" persons. For the house of a just and wise man ought not to be open to the illustrious, but to the lowly and abject. For those illustrious and powerful men cannot be in want of anything, since they are sufficiently protected and honored by their own opulence. But nothing is to be done by a just man except that which is a benefit. But if the benefit is returned, it is destroyed and brought to an end; for we cannot possess in its completeness that for which a price has been paid to us. Therefore the principle of justice is employed about those benefits which have remained safe and uncorrupted; but they cannot thus remain by any other means than if they are bestowed upon those men who can in no way profit us. But in receiving illustrious men, he looked to nothing else but utility; nor did the ingenious man conceal what advantage he hoped from it. For he says that he who does that will become powerful among foreigners by the favor of the leading men, whom he will have bound to himself by the right of hospitality and friendship. O by how many arguments might the inconsistency of Cicero be proved, if this were my object! Nor would he be convicted so much by my words as by his own. For he also says, that the more anyone refers all his actions to his own advantage, the less he is a good man. He also says, that it is not the part of a simple and open man to ingratiate himself in the favor of others, to pretend and allege anything, to appear to be doing one thing when he is doing another, to feign that he is bestowing upon another that which he is bestowing upon himself; but that this is rather the part of one who is designing and crafty, deceitful and treacherous. But how could he maintain that that ambitious hospitality was not evil intention? "Do you run round through all the gates, that you may invite to your house the chief men of the nations and cities as they arrive, that by their means you may acquire influence with their citizens; and wish yourself to be called just, and kind, and hospitable, though you are studying to promote your own advantage?" But did he not say this rather incautiously? For what is less suitable for Cicero? But through his ignorance of true justice he knowingly and with foresight fell into this snare. And that he might be pardoned for this, he testified that he does not give precepts with reference to true justice, which he does not hold, but with reference to a sketch and outline of justice. Therefore we must pardon this teacher who uses sketches and outlines, nor must we require the truth from him who admits that he is ignorant of it.

The ransoming of captives is a great and noble exercise of justice, of which the same Tullius also approved. "And this liberality," he says, "is serviceable even to the state, that captives should be ransomed from slavery, and that those of slender resources should be provided for. And I greatly prefer this practice of liberality to lavish expenditure on shows. This is the part of great and eminent men." Therefore it is the appropriate work of the just to support the poor and to ransom captives, since among the unjust if any do these things they are called great and eminent. For it is deserving of the greatest praise for those to confer benefit from whom no one expected such conduct. For he who does good to a relative, or neighbor, or friend, either deserves no praise, or certainly no great praise, because he is bound to do it, and he would be impious and detestable if he did not do that which both nature itself and relationship require; and if he does it, he does it not so much for the sake of obtaining glory as of avoiding censure. But he who does it to a stranger and an unknown person, he truly is worthy of praise, because he was led to do it by kindness only. Justice therefore exists there, where there is no obligation of necessity for conferring a benefit. He ought not therefore to have preferred this duty of generosity to expenditure on shows; for this is the part of one making a comparison, and of two goods choosing that which is the better. For that profusion of men throwing away their property into the sea is vain and trifling, and very far removed from all justice. Therefore they are not even to be called gifts, in which no one receives but he who does not deserve to receive.

Nor is it less a great work of justice to protect and defend orphans and widows who are destitute and stand in need of assistance; and therefore that divine law prescribes this to all, since all good judges deem that it belongs to their office to favor them with natural kindness, and to strive to benefit them. But these works are especially ours, since we have received the law, and the words of God Himself giving us instructions. For they perceive that it is naturally just to protect those who need protection, but they do not perceive why it is so. For God, to whom everlasting mercy belongs, on this account commands that widows and orphans should be defended and cherished, that no one through regard and pity for his pledges should be prevented from undergoing death in behalf of justice and faith, but should encounter it with promptitude and boldness, since he knows that he leaves his beloved ones to the care of God, and that they will never want protection. Also to undertake the care and support of the sick, who need someone to assist them, is the part of the greatest kindness, and of great beneficence; and he who shall do this will both gain a living sacrifice to God, and that which he has given to another for a time he will himself receive from God for eternity. The last and greatest office of piety is the burying of strangers and the poor; which subject those teachers of virtue and justice have not touched upon at all. For they were unable to see this, who measured all their duties by utility. For in the other things which have been mentioned above, although they did not keep the true path, yet, since they discovered some advantage in these things, retained as it were by a kind of inkling of the truth, they wandered to a less distance; but they abandoned this because they were unable to see any advantage in it.

Moreover, there have not been wanting those who esteemed burial as superfluous, and said that it was no evil to lie unburied and neglected; but their impious wisdom is rejected alike by the whole human race, and by the divine expressions which command the performance of the rite. But they do not venture to say that it ought not to be done, but that, if it happens to be omitted, no inconvenience is the result. Therefore in that matter they discharge the office, not so much of those who give precepts, as of those who suggest consolation, that if this shall by chance have occurred to a wise man, he should not deem himself wretched on this account. But we do not speak of that which ought to be endured by a wise man, but of that which he himself ought to do. Therefore we do not now inquire whether the whole system of burial is serviceable or not; but this, even though it be useless, as they imagine, must nevertheless be practiced, even on this account only, that it appears among men to be done rightly and kindly. For it is the feeling which is inquired into, and it is the purpose which is weighed. Therefore we will not suffer the image and workmanship of God to lie exposed as a prey to beasts and birds, but we will restore it to the earth, from which it had its origin; and although it be in the case of an unknown man, we will fulfil the office of relatives, into whose place, since they are wanting, let kindness succeed; and wherever there shall be need of man, there we will think that our duty is required. But in what does the nature of justice more consist than in our affording to strangers through kindness, that which we render to our own relatives through affection? And this kindness is much more sure and just when it is now afforded, not to the man who is insensible, but to God alone, to whom a just work is a most acceptable sacrifice. Someone will perhaps say: If I shall do all these things, I shall have no possessions. For what if a great number of men shall be in want, shall suffer cold, shall be taken captive, shall die, since one who acts thus must deprive himself of his property even in a single day, shall I throw away the estate acquired by my own labor or by that of my ancestors, so that after this I myself must live by the pity of others?

Why do you so pusillanimously fear poverty, which even your philosophers praise, and bear witness that nothing is safer and nothing calmer than this? That which you fear is a haven against anxieties. Do you not know to how many dangers, to how many accidents, you are exposed with these evil resources? These will treat you well if they shall pass without your bloodshed. But you walk about laden with booty, and you bear spoils which may excite the minds even of your own relatives. Why, then, do you hesitate to lay that out well which perhaps a single robbery will snatch away from you, or a proscription suddenly arising, or the plundering of an enemy? Why do you fear to make a frail and perishable good everlasting, or to entrust your treasures to God as their preserver, in which case you need not fear thief and robber, nor rust, nor tyrant? He who is rich towards God can never be poor. If you esteem justice so highly, lay aside the burthens which press you, and follow it; free yourself from fetters and chains that you may run to God without any impediment. It is the part of a great and lofty mind to despise and trample upon mortal affairs. But if you do not comprehend this virtue, that you may bestow your riches upon the altar of God, in order that you may provide for yourself firmer possessions than these frail ones, I will free you from fear. All these precepts are not given to you alone, but to all the people who are united in mind, and hold together as one man. If you are not adequate to the performance of great works alone, cultivate justice with all your power, in such a manner, however, that you may excel others in work as much as you excel them in riches. And do not think that you are advised to lessen or exhaust your property; but that which you would have expended on superfluities, turn to better uses. Devote to the ransoming of captives that from which you purchase beasts; maintain the poor with that from which you feed wild beasts; bury the innocent dead with that from which you provide men for the sword. What does it profit to enrich men of abandoned wickedness, who fight with beasts, and to equip them for crimes? Transfer things about to be miserably thrown away to the great sacrifice, that in return for these true gifts you may have an everlasting gift from God. Mercy has a great reward; for God promises it, that He will remit all sins. If you shall hear, He says, the prayers of your suppliant, I also will hear yours; if you shall pity those in distress, I also will pity you in your distress. But if you shall not regard nor assist them, I also will bear a mind like your own against you, and I will judge you by your own laws.

## Chap. XIII.—Of Repentance, of Mercy, and the Forgiveness of Sins.

As often, therefore, as you are asked for aid, believe that you are tried by God, that it may be seen whether you are worthy of being heard. Examine your own conscience, and, as far as you are able, heal your wounds. Nor, however, because offences are removed by bounty, think that a license is given you for sinning. For they are done away with, if you are bountiful to God because you have sinned; for if you sin through reliance on your bounty, they are not done away with. For God especially desires that men shall be cleansed from their sins, and therefore He commands them to repent. But to repent is nothing else than to profess and to affirm that one will sin no more. Therefore they are pardoned who unawares and incautiously glide into sin; he who sins willfully has no pardon. Nor, however, if any one shall have been purified from all stain of sin, let him think that he may abstain from the work of bounty because he has no faults to blot out. Nay, in truth, he is then more bound to exercise justice when he is become just, so that that which he had before done for the healing of his wounds he may afterwards do for the praise and glory of virtue. To this is added, that no one can be without fault as long as he is burthened with a covering of flesh, the infirmity of which is subject to the dominion of sin in a threefold manner—in deeds, in words, and thoughts.

By these steps justice advances to the greatest height. The first step of virtue is to abstain from evil works; the second, to abstain also from evil words; the third, to abstain even from the thoughts of evil things. He who ascends the first step is sufficiently just; he who ascends the second is now of perfect virtue, since he offends neither in deeds nor in conversation; he who ascends the third appears truly to have attained the likeness of God. For it is almost beyond the measure of man not even to admit to the thought that which is either bad in action or improper in speech. Therefore even just men, who can refrain from every unjust work, are sometimes, however, overcome by frailty itself, so that they either speak evil in anger, or, at the sight of delightful things, they desire them with silent thought. But if the condition of mortality does not suffer a man to be pure from every stain, the faults of the flesh ought therefore to be done away with by continual bounty. For it is the single work of a man who is wise, and just, and worthy of life, to lay out his riches on justice alone; for assuredly he who is without this, although he should surpass Croesus or Crassus in riches, is to be esteemed as poor, as naked, as a beggar. Therefore we must use our efforts that we may be clothed with the garment of justice and piety, of which no one may deprive us, which may furnish us with an everlasting ornament. For if the worshippers of gods adore senseless images, and bestow upon them whatever they have which is precious, though they can neither make use of them nor give thanks because they have received them, how much more just and true is it to reverence the living images of God, that you may gain the favor of the living God! For as these make use of what they have received, and give thanks, so God, in whose sight you shall have done that which is good, will both approve of it and reward your piety.

## Chap. XIV.—Of the Affections, and the Opinion of the Stoics Respecting Them; And of Virtue, the Vices, and Mercy.

If, therefore, mercy is a distinguished and excellent gift in man, and that is judged to be very good by the consent both of the good and the evil, it appears that philosophers were far distant from the good of man, who neither enjoined nor practiced anything of this kind, but always esteemed as a vice that virtue which almost holds the first place in man. It pleases me here to bring forward one subject of philosophy, that we may more fully refute the errors of those who call mercy, desire, and fear, diseases of the soul. They indeed attempt to distinguish virtues from vices, which is truly a very easy matter. For who cannot distinguish a liberal man from one who is prodigal (as they do), or a frugal man from one who is mean, or a calm man from one who is slothful, or a cautious man from one who is timid? Because these things which are good have their limits, and if they shall exceed these limits, fall into vices; so that constancy, unless it is undertaken for the truth, becomes shamelessness. In like manner, bravery, if it shall undergo certain danger, without the compulsion of any necessity, or not for an honorable cause, is changed into rashness. Freedom of speech also, if it attack others rather than oppose those who attack it, is obstinacy. Severity also, unless it restrain itself within the befitting punishments of the guilty, becomes savage cruelty.

Therefore they say, that those who appear evil do not sin of their own accord, or choose evils by preference, but that, erring through the appearance of good, they fall into evils, while they are ignorant of the distinction between good things and evil. These things are not indeed false, but they are all referred to the body. For to be frugal, or constant, or cautious, or calm, or grave, or severe, are virtues indeed, but virtues which relate to this short life. But we who despise this life have other virtues set before us, respecting which philosophers could not by any means even conjecture. Therefore they regarded certain virtues as vices, and certain vices as virtues. For the Stoics take away from man all the affections, by the impulse of which the soul is moved—desire, joy, fear, sorrow: the two former of which arise from good things, either future or present; the latter from evil things. In the same manner, they call these four (as I said) diseases, not so much inserted in us by nature as undertaken through a perverted opinion; and therefore they think that these can be eradicated, if the false notion of good and evil things is taken away. For if the wise man thinks nothing good or evil, he will neither be inflamed with desire, nor be transported with joy, nor be alarmed with fear, nor suffer his spirits to droop through sadness. We shall presently see whether they effect that which they wish, or what it is which they do effect: in the meantime their purpose is arrogant and almost mad, who think that they apply a remedy, and that they are able to strive in opposition to the force and system of nature.

## Chap. XV.—Of the Affections, and the Opinion of the Peripatetics Respecting Them.

For, that these things are natural and not voluntary, the nature of all living beings shows, which is moved by all these affections. Therefore the Peripatetics act better, who say that all these cannot be taken from us, because they were born with us; and they endeavor to show how providently and how necessarily God, or nature (for so they term it), armed us with these affections; which, however, because they generally become vicious if they are in excess, can be advantageously regulated by man,—a limit being applied, so that there may be left to man as much as is sufficient for nature. Not an unwise disputation, if, as I said, all things were not referred to this life. The Stoics therefore are mad who do not regulate but cut them out, and wish by some means or other to deprive man of powers implanted in him by nature. And this is equivalent to a desire of taking away timidity from stags, or poison from serpents, or rage from wild beasts, or gentleness from cattle. For those qualities which have been given separately to dumb animals, are altogether given to man at the same time. But if, as physicians affirm, the affection of joy has its seat in the spleen, that of anger in the gall, of desire in the liver, of fear in the heart, it is easier to kill the animal itself than to tear anything from the body; for this is to wish to change the nature of the living creature. But the skillful men do not understand that when they take away vices from man, they also take away virtue, for which alone they are making a place. For if it is virtue in the midst of the impetuosity of anger to restrain and check oneself, which they cannot deny, then he who is without anger is also without virtue. If it is virtue to control the lust of the body, he must be free from virtue who has no lust which he may regulate. If it is virtue to curb the desire from coveting that which belongs to another, he certainly can have no virtue who is without that, to the restraining of which the exercise of virtue is applied. Where, therefore, there are no vices, there is no place even for virtue, as there is no place for victory where there is no adversary. And so it comes to pass that there can be no good in this life without evil. An affection therefore is a kind of natural fruitfulness of the powers of the mind. For as a field which is naturally fruitful produces an abundant crop of briars, so the mind which is uncultivated is overgrown with vices flourishing of their own accord, as with thorns. But when the true cultivator has applied himself, immediately vices give way, and the fruits of virtues spring up.

Therefore God, when He first made man, with wonderful foresight first implanted in him these emotions of the mind, that he might be capable of receiving virtue, as the earth is of cultivation; and He placed the subject-matter of vices in the affections, and that of virtue in vices. For assuredly virtue will have no existence, or not be in exercise, if those things are wanting by which its power is either shown or exists. Now let us see what they have effected who altogether removes vices. With regard to those four affections which they imagine to arise from the opinion of things good and evil, by the eradication of which they think that the mind of the wise man is to be healed, since they understand that they are implanted by nature, and that without these nothing can be put in motion, nothing be done, they put certain other things into their place and room: for desire they substitute inclination, as though it were not much better to desire a good than to feel inclination for it; they in like manner substitute for joy gladness, and for fear caution. But in the case of the fourth they are at a loss for a method of exchanging the name. Therefore they have altogether taken away grief, that is, sadness and pain of mind, which cannot possibly be done. For who can fail to be grieved if pestilence has desolated his country, or an enemy overthrown it, or a tyrant crushed its liberty? Can anyone fail to be grieved if he has beheld the overthrow of liberty, and the banishment or most cruel slaughter of neighbors, friends, or good men?—unless the mind of any one should be so struck with astonishment that all sensibility should be taken from him. Wherefore they ought either to have taken away the whole, or this defective and weak discussion ought to have been completed; that is, something ought to have been substituted in the place of grief, since, the former ones having been so arranged, this naturally followed.

For as we rejoice in good things that are present, so we are vexed and grieved with evil things. If, therefore, they gave another name to joy because they thought it vicious, so it was befitting that another name should be given to grief because they thought it also vicious. From which it appears that it was not the object itself which was wanting to them, but a word, through want of which they wished, contrary to what nature allowed, to take away that affection which is the greatest. For I could have refuted those changes of names at greater length, and have shown that many names are attached to the same objects, for the sake of embellishing the style and increasing its copiousness, or at any rate that they do not greatly differ from one another. For both desire takes its beginning from the inclination, and caution arises from fear, and joy is nothing else than the expression of gladness. But let us suppose that they are different, as they themselves will have it. Accordingly they will say that desire is continued and perpetual inclination, but that joy is gladness bearing itself immoderately; and that fear is caution in excess, and passing the limits of moderation. Thus it comes to pass, that they do not take away those things which they think ought to be taken away, but regulate them, since the names only are changed, the things themselves remain. They therefore return unawares to that point at which the Peripatetics arrive by argument, that vices, since they cannot be taken away, are to be regulated with moderation. Therefore they err, because they do not succeed in effecting that which they aim at, and by a circuitous route, which is long and rough, they return to the same path.

## Chap. XVI.—Of the Affections, and the Refutation of the Opinion of the Peripatetics Concerning Them; what is the Proper Use of the Affections, and What is a Bad Use of Them.

But I think that the Peripatetics did not even approach the truth, who allow that they are vices, but regulate them with moderation. For we must be free even from moderate vices; yea, rather, it ought to have been at first effected that there should be no vices. For nothing can be born vicious; but if we make a bad use of the affections they become vices, if we use them well they become virtues. Then it must be shown that the causes of the affections, and not the affections themselves, must be moderated. We must not, they say, rejoice with excessive joy, but moderately and temperately. This is as though they should say that we must not run swiftly, but walk quietly. But it is possible that he who walks may err, and that he who runs may keep the right path. What if I show that there is a case in which it is vicious not only to rejoice moderately, but even in the smallest degree; and that there is another case, on the contrary, in which even to exult with transports of joy is by no means faulty? What then, I pray, will this mediocrity profit us? I ask whether they think that a wise man ought to rejoice if he sees any evil happening to his enemy; or whether he ought to curb his joy, if by the conquest of enemies, or the overthrow of a tyrant, liberty and safety have been acquired by his countrymen.

No one doubts but that in the former case to rejoice a little, and in the latter to rejoice too little, is a very great crime. We may say the same respecting the other affections. But, as I have said, the object of wisdom does not consist in the regulation of these, but of their causes, since they are acted upon from without; nor was it befitting that these themselves should be restrained; since they may exist in a small degree with the greatest criminality, and in the greatest degree without any criminality. But they ought to have been assigned to fixed times, and circumstances, and places, that they may not be vices, when it is permitted us to make a right use of them. For as to walk in the right course is good, but to wander from it is evil, so to be moved by the affections to that which is right is good, but to that which is corrupt is evil. For sensual desire, if it does not wander from its lawful object, although it be ardent, yet is without fault. But if it desires an unlawful object, although it be moderate, yet it is a great vice. Therefore it is not a disease to be angry, nor to desire, nor to be excited by lust; but to be passionate, to be covetous or licentious, is a disease. For he who is passionate is angry even with him with whom he ought not to be angry or at times when he ought not. He who is covetous desires even that which is unnecessary. He who is licentious pursues even that which is forbidden by the laws. The whole matter ought to have turned on this, that since the impetuosity of these things cannot be restrained, nor is it right that it should be, because it is necessarily implanted for maintaining the duties of life, it might rather be directed into the right way, where it may be possible even to run without stumbling and danger.

## Chap. XVII.—Of the Affections and Their Use; Of Patience, and the Chief Good of Christians.

But I have been carried too far in my desire of refuting them; since it is my purpose to show that those things which the philosophers thought to be vices, are so far from being vices, that they are even great virtues. Of others, I will take, for the sake of instruction, those which I think to be most closely related to the subject. They regard dread or fear as a very great vice, and think that it is a very great weakness of mind; the opposite to which is bravery: and if this exists in a man, they say that there is no place for fear. Does anyone then believe that it can possibly happen that this same fear is the highest fortitude? By no means. For nature does not appear to admit that anything should fall back to its contrary. But yet I, not by any skillful conclusion, as Socrates does in the writings of Plato, who compels those against whom he disputes to admit those things which they had denied, but in a simple manner, will show that the greatest fear is the greatest virtue. No one doubts but that it is the part of a timid and feeble mind either to fear pain, or want, or exile, or imprisonment, or death; and if any one does not dread all these, he is judged a man of the greatest fortitude. But he who fears God is free from the fear of all these things. In proof of which, there is no need of arguments: for the punishments inflicted on the worshippers of God have been witnessed at all times, and are still witnessed through the world, in the tormenting of whom new and unusual tortures have been devised. For the mind shrinks from the recollection of various kinds of death, when the butchery of savage monsters has raged even beyond death itself. But a happy and unconquered patience endured these execrable lacerations of their bodies without a groan. This virtue afforded the greatest astonishment to all people and provinces, and to the torturers themselves, when cruelty was overcome by patience. But this virtue was caused by nothing else than the fear of God. Therefore (as I said) fear is not to be uprooted, as the Stoics maintain, nor to be restrained, as the Peripatetics wish, but to be directed into the right way; and apprehensions are to be taken away, but so that this one only may be left: for since this is the only lawful and true one, it alone effects that all other things may not be feared. Desire also is reckoned among vices; but if it desires those things which are of the earth, it is a vice; on the other hand, if it desires heavenly things, it is a virtue. For he who desires to obtain justice, God, perpetual life, everlasting light, and all those things which God promises to man, will despise these riches, and honors, and commands, and kingdoms themselves.

    The Stoic will perhaps say that inclination is necessary for the attainment of these things, and not desire; but, in truth, the inclination is not sufficient. For many have the inclination; but when pain has approached the vitals, inclination gives way, but desire perseveres: and if it effects that all things which are sought by others are objects of contempt to him, it is the greatest virtue, since it is the mother of self-restraint. And therefore we ought rather to effect this, that we may rightly direct the affections, a corrupt use of which is vice. For these excitements of the mind resemble a harnessed chariot, in the right management of which the chief duty of the driver is to know the way; and if he shall keep to this, with whatever swiftness he may go, he will not strike against an obstacle. But if he shall wander from the course, although he may go calmly and gently, he will either be shaken over rough places, or will glide over precipices, or at any rate will be carried where he does not need to go. So that chariot of life which is led by the affections as though by swift horses, if it keeps the right way, will discharge its duty. Dread, therefore, and desire, if they are cast down to the earth, will become vices, but they will be virtues if they are referred to divine things. On the other hand, they esteem parsimony as a virtue; which, if it is eagerness for possessing, cannot be a virtue, because it is altogether employed in the increase or preservation of earthly goods. But we do not refer the chief good to the body, but we measure every duty by the preservation of the soul only. But if, as I have before taught, we must by no means spare our property that we may preserve kindness and justice, it is not a virtue to be frugal; which name beguiles and deceives under the appearance of virtue. For frugality is, it is true, the abstaining from pleasures; but in this respect it is a vice, because it arises from the love of possessing, whereas we ought both to abstain from pleasures, and by no means to withhold money. For to use money sparingly, that is, moderately, is a kind of weakness of mind, either of one fearing lest he should be in want, or of one despairing of being able to recover it, or of one incapable of the contempt of earthly things. But, on the other hand, they call him who is not sparing of his property prodigal. For thus they distinguish between the liberal man and the prodigal: that he is liberal who bestows on deserving objects, and on proper occasions, and in sufficient quantities; but that he is prodigal who lavishes on undeserving objects, and when there is no need, and without any regard to his property.

What then? Shall we call him prodigal who through pity gives food to the needy? But it makes a great difference, whether on account of lust you bestow your money on harlots, or on account of benevolence on the wretched; whether profligates, gamesters, and pimps squander your money, or you bestow it on piety and God; whether you expend it upon your own appetite, or lay it up in the treasury of justice. As, therefore, it is a vice to lay it out badly, so it is a virtue to lay it out well. If it is a virtue not to be sparing of riches, which can be replaced, that you may support the life of man, which cannot be replaced; then parsimony is a vice. Therefore I can call them by no other name than mad, who deprive man, a mild and sociable animal, of his name; who, having uprooted the affections, in which humanity altogether consists, wish to bring him to an immoveable insensibility of mind, while they desire to free the soul from perturbations, and, as they themselves say, to render it calm and tranquil; which is not only impossible, because its force and nature consist in motion, but it ought not even to be so. For as water which is always still and motionless is unwholesome and more muddy, so the soul which is unmoved and torpid is useless even to itself: nor will it be able to maintain life itself; for it will neither do nor think anything, since thought itself is nothing less than agitation of the mind. In fine, they who assert this immoveableness of the soul wish to deprive the soul of life; for life is full of activity, but death is quiet. They also rightly esteem some things as virtues, but they do not maintain their due proportion.

Constancy is a virtue; not that we resist those who injure us, for we must yield to these; and why this ought to be done I will show presently: but that when men command us to act in opposition to the law of God, and in opposition to justice, we should be deterred by no threats or punishments from preferring the command of God to the command of man. Likewise it is a virtue to despise death; not that we seek it, and of our own accord inflict it upon ourselves, as many and distinguished philosophers have often done, which is a wicked and impious thing; but that when compelled to desert God, and to betray our faith, we should prefer to undergo death, and should defend our liberty against the foolish and senseless violence of those who cannot govern themselves, and with fortitude of spirit we should challenge all the threats and terrors of the world. Thus with lofty and invincible mind we trample upon those things which others fear—pain and death. This is virtue; this is true constancy—to be maintained and preserved in this one thing alone, that no terror and no violence may be able to turn us away from God. Therefore that is a true sentiment of Cicero: "No one," he says, "can be just who fears death, or pain, or exile, or want." Also of Seneca, who says, in his books of moral philosophy: "This is that virtuous man, not distinguished by a diadem or purple, or the attendance of lictors, but in no respect inferior, who, when he sees death at hand, is not so disturbed as though he saw a fresh object; who, whether torments are to be suffered by his whole body, or a flame is to be seized by his mouth, or his hands are to be stretched out on the cross, does not inquire what he suffers, but how well." But he who worships God suffers these things without fear. Therefore he is just. By these things it is effected, that he cannot know or maintain at all either the virtues or the exact limits of the virtues, whoever is estranged from the religion of the one God.

### Chap. XVIII.—Of Some Commands of God, and of Patience.

But let us leave the philosophers, who either know nothing at all, and hold forth this very ignorance as the greatest knowledge; or who, inasmuch as they think they know that of which they are ignorant, are absurdly and arrogantly foolish. Let us therefore (that we may return to our purpose), to whom alone the truth has been revealed by God, and wisdom has been sent from heaven, practice those things which God who enlightens us commands: let us sustain and endure the labors of life, by mutual assistance towards each other; nor, however, if we shall have done any good work, let us aim at glory from it. For God admonishes us that the doer of justice ought not to be boastful, lest he should appear to have discharged the duties of benevolence, not so much from a desire of obeying the divine commands, as of pleasing men, and should already have the reward of glory which he has aimed at, and should not receive the recompense of that heavenly and divine reward. The other things which the worshipper of God ought to observe are easy, when these virtues are comprehended, that no one should ever speak falsely for the sake of deceiving or injuring. For it is unlawful for him who cultivates truth to be deceitful in anything, and to depart from the truth itself which he follows. In this path of justice and all the virtues there is no place for falsehood. Therefore the true and just traveler will not use the saying of Lucilius:—

"It is not for me to speak falsely to a man who is a friend and acquaintance;"

but he will think that it is not his part to speak falsely even to an enemy and a stranger; nor will he at any time so act, that his tongue, which is the interpreter of his mind, should be at variance with his feeling and thought. If he shall have lent any money, he will not receive interest, that the benefit may be unimpaired which succors necessity, and that he may entirely abstain from the property of another. For in this kind of duty he ought to be content with that which is his own; since it is his duty in other respects not to be sparing of his property, in order that he may do good; but to receive more than he has given is unjust. And he who does this lies in wait in some manner, that he may gain booty from the necessity of another.

But the just man will omit no opportunity of doing anything mercifully: nor will he pollute himself with gain of this kind; but he will so act that without any loss to himself, that which he lends may be reckoned among his good works. He must not receive a gift from a poor man; so that if he himself has afforded anything, it may be good, inasmuch as it is gratuitous. If anyone reviles, he must answer him with a blessing; he himself must never revile, that no evil word may proceed out of the mouth of a man who reverences the good Word. Moreover, he must also diligently take care, lest by any fault of his he should at any time make an enemy; and if anyone should be so shameless as to inflict injury on a good and just man, he must bear it with calmness and moderation, and not take upon himself his revenge, but reserve it for the judgment of God. He must at all times and in all places guard innocence. And this precept is not limited to this, that he should not himself inflict injury, but that he should not avenge it when inflicted on himself. For there sits on the judgment-seat a very great and impartial Judge, the observer and witness of all. Let him prefer Him to man; let him rather choose that He should pronounce judgment respecting his cause, whose sentence no one can escape, either by the advocacy of any one or by favor. Thus it comes to pass, that a just man is an object of contempt to all; and because it will be thought that he is unable to defend himself, he will be regarded as slothful and inactive; but if anyone shall have avenged himself upon his enemy, he is judged a man of spirit and activity—all honor and reverence him. And although the good man has it in his power to profit many, yet they look up to him who is able to injure, rather than to him who is able to profit. But the depravity of men will not be able to corrupt the just man, so that he will not endeavor to obey God; and he would prefer to be despised, provided that he may always discharge the duty of a good man, and never of a bad man. Cicero says in those same books respecting Offices: "But if anyone should wish to unravel this indistinct conception of his soul, let him at once teach himself that he is a good man who profits those whom he can, and injures no one unless provoked by injury."

Oh how he marred a simple and true sentiment by the addition of two words! For what need was there of adding these words, "Unless provoked by injury?" that he might append vice as a most disgraceful tail to a good man and might represent him as without patience, which is the greatest of all the virtues. He said that a good man would inflict injuries if he were provoked:

now he must necessarily lose the name of a good man from this very circumstance, if he shall inflict injury. For it is not less the part of a bad man to return an injury than to inflict it. For from what source do contests, from what source do fighting and contentions, arise among men, except that impatience opposed to injustice often excites great tempests? But if you meet injustice with patience, than which virtue nothing can be found truer, nothing more worthy of a man, it will immediately be extinguished, as though you should pour water upon a fire. But if that injustice which provokes opposition has met with impatience equal to itself, as though overspread with oil, it will excite so great a conflagration, that no stream can extinguish it, but only the shedding of blood. Great, therefore, is the advantage of patience, of which the wise man has deprived the good man. For this alone causes that no evil happens; and if it should be given to all, there will be no wickedness and no fraud in the affairs of men. What, therefore, can be so calamitous to a good man, so opposed to his character, as to let loose the reins to anger, which deprives him not only of the title of a good man, but even of a man; since to injure another, as he himself most truly says, is not in accordance with the nature of man? For if you provoke cattle or horses, they turn against you either with their hoof or their horn; and serpents and wild beasts, unless you pursue them that you may kill them, give no trouble. And to return to examples of men, even the inexperienced and the foolish, if at any time they receive an injury, are led by a blind and irrational fury, and endeavor to retaliate upon those who injure them. In what respect, then, does the wise and good man differ from the evil and foolish, except that he has invincible patience, of which the foolish are destitute; except that he knows how to govern himself, and to mitigate his anger, which those, because they are without virtue, are unable to curb? But this circumstance manifestly deceived him, because, when inquiry is made respecting virtue, he thought that it is the part of virtue to conquer in every kind of contention. Nor was he able in any way to see, that a man who gives way to grief and anger, and who indulges these affections, against which he ought rather to struggle, and who rushes wherever injustice shall have called him, does not fulfil the duty of virtue. For he who endeavors to return an injury, desires to imitate that very person by whom he has been injured. Thus he who imitates a bad man can by no means be good.

Therefore by two words he has taken away from the good and wise man two of the greatest virtues, innocence and patience. But, as Sallustius relates was said by Appius, because he himself practiced that canine eloquence, be wished man also to live after the manner of a dog, so as, when attacked, to bite in return. And to show how pernicious this repayment of insult is, and what carnage it is accustomed to produce, from what can a more befitting example be sought, than from the most melancholy disaster of the teacher himself, who, while he desired to obey these precepts of the philosophers, destroyed himself? For if, when attacked with injury, he had preserved patience—if he had learned that it is the part of a good man to dissemble and to endure insult, and his impatience, vanity, and madness had not poured forth those noble orations, inscribed with a name derived from another source, he would never, by his head affixed to them, have polluted the rostra on which he had formerly distinguished himself, nor would that proscription have utterly destroyed the state. Therefore it is not the part of a wise and good man to wish to contend, and to commit himself to danger, since to conquer is not in our power, and every contest is doubtful; but it is the part of a wise and excellent man not to wish to remove his adversary, which cannot be done without guilt and danger, but to put an end to the contest itself, which may be done with advantage and with justice. Therefore patience is to be regarded as a very great virtue; and that the just man might obtain this, God willed, as has been before said, that he should be despised as sluggish. For unless he shall have been insulted, it will not be known what fortitude he has in restraining himself. Now if, when provoked by injury, he has begun to follow up his assailant with violence, he is overcome. But if he shall have repressed that emotion by reasoning, he altogether has command over himself: he is able to rule himself. And this restraining of oneself is rightly named patience, which single virtue is opposed to all vices and affections. This recalls the disturbed and wavering mind to its tranquility; this mitigates, this restores a man to himself. Therefore, since it is impossible and useless to resist nature, so that we are not excited at all; before, however, the emotion bursts forth to the infliction of injury, as far as is possible let it be calmed in time. God has enjoined us not to let the sun go down upon our wrath, lest he should depart as a witness of our madness. Finally, Marcus Tullius, in opposition to his own precept, concerning which I have lately spoken, gave the greatest praises to the forgetting of injuries. "I entertain hopes," he says, "O Cæsar, who art accustomed to forget nothing except injuries." But if he thus acted—a man most widely removed not only from heavenly, but also from public and civil justice—how much more ought we to do this, who are, as it were, candidates for immortality?

**Chap. XIX.—Of the Affections and Their Use; And of the Three Furies.**

When the Stoics attempt to uproot the affections from man as diseases, they are opposed by the Peripatetics, who not only retain, but also defend them, and say that there is nothing in man which is not produced in him with great reason and foresight. They say this indeed rightly, if they know the true limits of each subject. Accordingly they say that this very affection of anger is the whetstone of virtue, as though no one could fight bravely against enemies unless he were excited by anger; by which they plainly show that they neither know what virtue is, nor why God gave anger to man. And if this was given to us for this purpose, that we may employ it for the slaying of men, what is to be thought more savage than man, what more resembling the wild beasts, than that animal which God formed for communion and innocence? There are, then, three affections which drive men headlong to all crimes: (1) anger, (2) desire, and

(3) lust. On which account the poets have said that there are three furies which harass the minds of men: anger longs for revenge, desire for riches, and lust for pleasures. But God has appointed fixed limits to all of these; and if they pass these limits and begin to be too great, they must necessarily pervert their nature, and be changed into diseases and vices. And it is a matter of no great labor to show what these limits are. Cupidity is given us for providing those things which are necessary for life; concupiscence, for the procreation of offspring; the affection of indignation, for restraining the faults of those who are in our power, that is, in order that tender age may be formed by a severer discipline to integrity and justice: for if this *time of life* is not restrained by fear, license will produce boldness, and this will break out into every disgraceful and daring action. Therefore, as it is both just and necessary to employ anger towards the young, so it is both pernicious and impious to use it towards those of our own age. It is impious, because humanity is injured; pernicious, because if they oppose, it is necessary either to destroy them or to perish. But that this which I have spoken of is the reason why the affection of anger has been given to man, may be understood from the precepts of God Himself, who commands that we should not be angry with those who revile and injure us, but that we should always have our hands over the young; that is, that when they err, we should correct them with continual stripes, lest by useless love and excessive indulgence they should be trained to evil and nourished to vices. But those who are inexperienced in affairs and ignorant of reason, have expelled those affections which have been given to man for good uses, and they wander more widely than reason demands. From this cause they live unjustly and impiously. They employ anger against their equals in age: hence disagreements, hence banishments, hence wars have arisen contrary to justice. They use desire for the amassing of riches: hence frauds, hence robberies, hence all kinds of crimes have originated. They use lust only for the enjoyment of pleasures: hence debaucheries, hence adulteries, hence all corruptions have proceeded. Whoever, therefore, has reduced

those affections within their proper limits, which they who are ignorant of God cannot do, he is patient, he is brave, he is just.

## Chap. XX.—Of the Senses, and Their Pleasures in the Brutes and in Man; and of Pleasures of the Eyes, and Spectacles.

It remains that I should speak against the pleasures of the five senses, and this briefly, for the measure of the book itself now demands moderation; all of which, since they are vicious and deadly, ought to be overcome and subdued by virtue, or, as I said a little before respecting the affections, be recalled to their proper office. The other animals have no pleasure, except the one only which relates to generation. Therefore they use their senses for the necessity of their nature: they see, in order that they may seek those things which are necessary for the preservation of life; they hear one another, and distinguish one another, that they may be able to assemble together; they either discover from the smell, or perceive from the taste, the things which are useful for food; they refuse and reject the things which are useless, they measure the business of eating and drinking by the fullness of their stomach. But the foresight of the most skillful Creator gave to man pleasure without limit, and liable to fall into vice, because He set before him virtue, which might always be at variance with pleasure, as with a domestic enemy. Cicero says, in the *Cato Major*: "In truth, debaucheries, and adulteries, and disgraceful actions are excited by no other enticements than those of pleasure. And since nature or some God has given to man nothing more excellent than the mind, nothing is so hostile to this divine benefit and gift as pleasure. For when lust bears sway there is no place for temperance, nor can virtue have any existence when pleasure reigns supreme." But, on the other hand, God gave virtue on this account that it might subdue and conquer pleasure, and that, when it passed the boundaries assigned to it, it might restrain it within the prescribed limits, lest it should soothe and captivate man with enjoyments, render him subject to its control, and punish him with everlasting death.

The pleasure arising from the eyes is various and manifold, which is derived from the sight of objects which are pleasant in intercourse with men, or in nature or workmanship. The philosophers rightly took this away. For they say that it is much more excellent and worthy of man to look upon the heaven rather than carved works, and to admire this most beautiful work adorned with the lights of the stars shining through, as with flowers, than to admire things painted and molded, and varied with jewels. But when they have eloquently exhorted us to despise earthly things, and have urged us to look up to the heaven, nevertheless they do not despise these public spectacles. Therefore they are both delighted with these, and are gladly present at them; though, since they are the greatest incitement to vices, and have a most powerful tendency to corrupt our minds, they ought to be taken away from us; for they not only contribute in no respect to a happy life, but even inflict the greatest injury. For he who reckons it a pleasure, that a man, though justly condemned, should be slain in his sight, pollutes his conscience as much as if he should become a spectator and a sharer of a homicide which is secretly committed. And yet they call these sports in which human blood is shed. So far has the feeling of humanity departed from the men, that when they destroy the lives of men, they think that they are amusing themselves with sport, being more guilty than all those whose blood-shedding they esteem a pleasure. I ask now whether they can be just and pious men, who, when they see men placed under the stroke of death, and entreating mercy, not only suffer them to be put to death, but also demand it, and give cruel and inhuman votes for their death, not being satiated with wounds nor contented with bloodshed. Moreover, they order them, even though wounded and prostrate, to be attacked again, and their caresses to he wasted with blows, that no one may delude them by a pretended death. They are even angry with the combatants, unless one of the two is quickly slain; and as though they thirsted for human blood, they hate delays.

They demand that other and fresh combatants should be given to them, that they may satisfy their eyes as soon as possible. Being imbued with this practice, they have lost their humanity. Therefore they do not spare even the innocent, but practice upon all that which they have learned in the slaughter of the wicked. It is not therefore befitting that those who strive to keep to the path of justice should be companions and sharers in this public homicide. For when God forbids us to kill, He not only prohibits us from open violence, which is not even allowed by the public laws, but He warns us against the commission of those things which are esteemed lawful among men. Thus it will be neither lawful for a just man to engage in warfare, since his warfare is justice itself, nor to accuse any one of a capital charge, because it makes no difference whether you put a man to death by word, or rather by the sword, since it is the act of putting to death itself which is prohibited. Therefore, with regard to this precept of God, there ought to be no exception at all; but that it is always unlawful to put to death a man, whom God willed to be a sacred animal.

Therefore let no one imagine that even this is allowed, to strangle newly-born children, which is the greatest impiety; for God breathes into their souls for life, and not for death. But men, that there may be no crime with which they may not pollute their hands, deprive souls as yet innocent and simple of the light which they themselves have not given. Can anyone, indeed, expect that they would abstain from the blood of others who do not abstain even from their own? But these are without any controversy wicked and unjust. What are they whom a false piety compels to expose their children? Can they be considered innocent who expose their own offspring as a prey to dogs, and as far as it depends upon themselves, kill them in a crueler manner than if they had strangled them? Who can doubt that he is impious who gives occasion for the pity of others? For, although that which he has wished should befall the child—namely, that it should be brought up—he has certainly consigned his own offspring either to servitude or to the brothel? But who does not understand, who is ignorant what things may happen, or are accustomed to happen, in the case of each sex, even through error? For this is shown by the example of Oedipus alone, confused with twofold guilt. It is therefore as wicked to expose as it is to kill. But truly parricides complain of the scantiness of their means, and allege that they have not enough for bringing up more children; as though, in truth, their means were in the power of those who possess them, or God did not daily make the rich poor, and the poor rich. Wherefore, if anyone on account of poverty shall be unable to bring up children, it is better to abstain from marriage than with wicked hands to mar the work of God.

If, then, it is in no way permitted to commit homicide, it is not allowed us to be present at all, lest any bloodshed should overspread the conscience, since that blood is offered for the gratification of the people. And I am inclined to think that the corrupting influence of the stage is still more contaminating. For the subject of comedies are the dishonoring of virgins, or the loves of harlots; and the more eloquent they are who have composed the accounts of these disgraceful actions, the more do they persuade by the elegance of their sentiments; and harmonious and polished verses more readily remain fixed in the memory of the hearers. In like manner, the stories of the tragedians place before the eyes the parricides and incest of wicked kings, and represent tragic crimes. And what other effect do the immodest gestures of the players produce, but both teach and excite lusts? Whose enervated bodies, rendered effeminate after the gait and dress of women, imitate unchaste women by their disgraceful gestures. Why should I speak of the actors of *mimes*, who hold forth instruction in corrupting influences, who teach adulteries while they feign them, and by pretended actions train to those which are true? What can young men or virgins do, when they see that these things are practiced without shame, and willingly beheld by all? They are plainly admonished of what they can do, and are inflamed with lust, which is especially excited by seeing; and every one according to his sex forms himself in these representations. And they approve of these things, while they laugh at them, and with vices clinging to them, they return more corrupted to their apartments; and not boys only, who ought not to be inured to vices prematurely, but also old men, whom it does not become at their age to sin.

What else does the practice of the Circensian games contain but levity, vanity, and madness? For their souls are hurried away to mad excitement with as great impetuosity as that with which the chariot races are there carried on; so that they who come for the sake of beholding the spectacle now themselves exhibit more of a spectacle, when they begin to utter exclamations, to be thrown into transports, and to leap from their seats. Therefore all spectacles ought to be avoided, not only that no vice may settle in our breasts, which ought to be tranquil and peaceful; but that the habitual indulgence of any pleasure may not soothe and captivate us, and turn us aside from God and from good works. For the celebrations of the games are festivals in honor of the gods, inasmuch as they were instituted on account of their birthdays, or the dedication of new temples. And at first the hunting, which are called shows, were in honor of Saturnus, and the scenic games in honor of Liber, but the Circensian in honor of Neptune. By degrees, however, the same honor began to be paid also to the other gods, and separate games were dedicated to their names, as Sisinnius Capito teaches in his book on the games. Therefore, if anyone is present at the spectacles to which men assemble for the sake of religion, he has departed from the worship of God, and has betaken himself to those deities whose birthdays and festivals he has celebrated.

### Chap. XXI.—Of the Pleasures of the Ears, and of Sacred Literature.

Pleasure of the ears is received from the sweetness of voices and strains, which indeed is as productive of vice as that delight of the eyes of which we have spoken. For who would not deem him luxurious and worthless who should have scenic arts at his house? But it makes no difference whether you practice luxury alone at home, or with the people in the theatre. But we have already spoken of spectacles: there remains one thing which is to be overcome by us, that we be not captivated by those things which penetrate to the innermost perception. For all those things which are unconnected with words, that is, pleasant sounds of the air and of strings, may be easily disregarded, because they do not adhere to us, and cannot be written. But a well-composed poem, and a speech beguiling with its sweetness, captivate the minds of men, and impel them in what direction they please. Hence, when learned men have applied themselves to the religion of God, unless they have been instructed by some skillful teacher, they do not believe. For, being accustomed to sweet and polished speeches or poems, they despise the simple and common language of the sacred writings as mean. For they seek that which may soothe the senses. But whatever is pleasant to the ear effects persuasion, and while it delights fixes itself deeply within the breast. Is God, therefore, the contriver both of the mind, and of the voice, and of the tongue, unable to speak eloquently? Yea, rather, with the greatest foresight, He wished those things which are divine to be without adornment, that all might understand the things which He Himself spoke to all.

Therefore he who is anxious for the truth, who does not wish to deceive himself, must lay aside hurtful and injurious pleasures, which would bind the mind to themselves, as pleasant food does the body: true things must be preferred to false, eternal things to those which are of short duration, useful things to those which are pleasant. Let nothing be pleasing to the sight but that which you see to be done with piety and justice; let nothing be agreeable to the hearing but that which nourishes the soul and makes you a better man. And especially this sense ought not to be distorted to vice, since it is given to us for this purpose, that we might gain the knowledge of God. Therefore, if it be a pleasure to hear melodies and songs, let it be pleasant to sing and hear the praises of God. This is true pleasure, which is the attendant and companion of virtue. This is not frail and brief, as those which they desire, who, like cattle, are slaves to the body; but lasting, and affording delight without any intermission. And if anyone shall pass its limits, and shall seek nothing else from pleasure but pleasure itself, he designs *for himself* death; for as there is perpetual life in virtue, so there is death in pleasure. For he who shall choose temporal things will be without things eternal; he who shall prefer earthly things will not have heavenly things.

## Chap. XXII.—Of the Pleasures of Taste and Smell.

But with regard to the pleasures of taste and smell, which two senses relate only to the body, there is nothing to be discussed by us; unless by chance any one requires us to say that it is disgraceful to a wise and good man if he is the slave of his appetite, if he walks along besmeared with unguents and crowned with flowers: and he who does these things is plainly foolish and senseless, and is worthless, and one whom not even a notion of virtue has reached. Perhaps someone will say, Why, then, have these things been made, except that we may enjoy them? However, it has often been said that there would have been no virtue unless it had things which it might overpower. Therefore God made all things to supply a contest between two things. Those enticements of pleasures, then, are the instruments of that whose only business it is to subdue virtue, and to shut out justice from men. With these soothing influences and enjoyments it captivates their souls; for it knows that pleasure is the contriver of death. For as God calls man to life only through virtue and labor, so the other calls us to death by delights and pleasures; and as men arrive at real good through deceitful evils, so they arrive at real evil through deceitful goods. Therefore those enjoyments are to be guarded against, as snares or nets, lest, captivated by the softness of enjoyments, we should be brought under the dominion of death with the body itself, to which we have enslaved ourselves.

## Chap. XXIII.—De Tactus Voluptate Et Libidine, Atque de Matrimonio Et Continentiâ.

Venio nunc ad eam, quæ percipitur ex tactu, voluptatem: qui sensus est quidem totius corporis. Sed ego non de ornamentis, aut vestibus, sed de solâ libidine dicendum mihi puto; quæ maxime coercenda est, quia maxime nocet. Cure excogitasset Deus duorum sexuum rationero, attribuit iis, ut se invicem appeterent, et conjunctione gauderent. Itaque ardentissimam cupiditatem cunctorum animantium corporibus admiscuit, ut in hos affectus avidissime ruerent, eaque ratione propagari et multiplicari genera possent. Quæ cupiditas et appetentia in homine vehementior et acrior invenitur; vel quia hominum multitudinem voluit esse majorem, vel quoniam virtutem soli homini dedit, ut esset laus et gloria in coercendis voluptatibus, et abstinentia sui. Seit ergo adversarius ille noster, quanta sit vis hujus cupiditatis, quam quidam necessitatem dicere maluerunt; eamque a recto et bono, ad malum et pravum transfert. Illicita enim desideria immittit, ut aliena contaminent, quibus habere propria sine delicto licet. Objicit quippe oculis irritabiles formas, suggeritque fomenta, et vitiis pabulum subministrat: tum intimis visceribus stimulos omnes conturbat et commovet, et naturalem illum incitat atque inflammat ardorem, donee irretitum hominem implicatumque decipiat. Ac ne quis esset, qui poenarum metu abstineret alieno, lupanaria quoque constituit; et pudorem infelicium mulierum publicavit, ut ludibrio haberet tam eos qui faciunt, quam quas pati necesse est.

His obscoenitatibus animas, ad sanctitatem genitas, velut in coeni gurgite demersit, pudorem extinxit, pudicitiam profligavit. Idem etiam mares maribus admiscuit; et nefandos coitus contra naturam contraque institutum Dei machinatus est: sic imbuit homines, et armavit ad nefas omne. Quid enim potest esse sanctum iis, qui ætatem imbecillam et præsidio indigentem, libidini suæ depopulandam foedandamque substraverint? Non potest hæc res pro magnitudine sceleris enarrari. Nihil amplius istos appellare possum, quam implos et parricidas, quibus non sufficit sexus a Deo datus, nisi eliare suum profane ac petulanter illudant. Hæc tamen apud illos levia, et quasi honesta sunt. Quid dicam de iis, qui abominandam non libidinem, sod insaniam potius exercent! Piget dicere: sed quid his fore credamus, quos non piget facere? et tamen dicendum est, quia fit. De istis loquor, quorum teterrima libido et execrabilis furor ne capiti quidem parcit. Quibus hoc verbis, aut qua indignatione tantum nefas prosequar? Vincit officium linguæ sceleris magnitudo. Cum igitur libido hæc edat opera, et hæc facinora designer, armandi adversus earn virtute maxima sumus. Quisquis affectus illos frænare non potest, cohibeat eos intra præ scriptum legitimi tori, ut et illud, quod avide expetat, consequatur, et tamen in peccatum non incidat. Nam quid sibi homines perditi volunt? Nempe honesta opera voluptas sequitur: si ipsam per se appetunt, justa et legitima frui licet.

Quod si aliqua necessitas prohibebit tum vero maxima adhibenda virtus erit, ut cupiditati continentia reluctetur. Nec tanturn alienis, quæ attingere non licet, veriun etiam publicis vulgatisque corporibus abstinendum, Deus præcepit; docetque nos, cum duo inter se corpora fuerint copulata, unum corpus efficere. Ita qui se coeno immerserit, coeno sit oblitus necesse est; et corpus quidem cito ablui potest: mens autem contagione impudici corporis inquinata non potest, nisi et longo tempore, et multis bonis operibus, ab ea quæ inhæ serit colluvione purgari. Oportet ergo sibi quemque proponere, duorum sexuum conjunctionem generandi causa datam esse viventibus, eamque legera his affectibus positam, ut successionera parent. Sicut autem dedit nobis oculos Deus, non ut spectemus, voluptatemque capiamus, sed ut videamus propter eos actus, qui pertinent ad vitæ necessitatem, ita genitalem corporis partem, quod nomen ipsum docet, nulla alia causa nisi efficiendæ sobolis accepimus. Huic divinæ legi summa devotione parendum est. Sint omnes, qui se discipulos Dei profitebuntur, ita morati et instituti, ut imperare sibi possint. Nam qui voluptatibus indulgent, qui libidini obsequuntur, ii animam suam corpori mancipant, ad mortemque condemnant: quia se corpori addixerunt, in quod habet mors potestatem. Unusquisque igitur, quantum potest, formet se ad verecundiam, pudorem colat, castitatem conscientia et mente tueatur; nec tantum legibus publicis pareat: sed sit supra omnes leges, qui legem Dei sequitur. Quibus bonis si assueverit, jam pudebit eum ad deteriora desciscere: modo placeant recta et honesta, quæ melioribus jucundiora sunt quam prava et inhonesta pejoribus.

Nondum omnia castitatis officio exsecutus sum: quam Deus fion modo intra privatos parietes, sed etiam præ scripto lectuli terminat; ut cum quis hobeat uxorem, neque servam, neque liberam habere insuper velit, sed matrimonio fidem server. Non enim, sicut juris publici ratio est, solo mulier adultera est, quæ habet allure, maritus outem, etiam si plures habeat, a crimine adulterii solutus est. Sed divina lex ira duos in matrimonium, quod est in corpus unum, pari jure conjungit, ut adulter habeatur, quisquis compagem corporis in diversa distraxerit. Nec ob aliam cansam Deus, cam cæteras animantes suscepto foetu maribus repugnare voluisset, solam omnium mulierem patientem viri fecit; scilicet ne foeminis repugnantibus, libido cogeret viros aliud appetere, eoque facto, castitatis gloriam non tenerent. Sed neque mulier virtutem pudicitiæ caperet, si peccare non posset. Nam quis mutum animal pudicum esse dixerit, quod suscepto foe tu mari repugnat? Quod ideo facit, quia necesse est in dolorem atque in periculum veniat, si admiserit. Nulla igitur laus est, non facere quod facere non possis. Ideo autem pudicitia in homine laudatur, quia non naturalis est, sed voluntaria. Servanda igitur fides ab utroque alteri est: immo exemplo continentia: docenda uxor, ut se caste gerat. Iniquum est enim, ut id exigas, quod præ stare ipse non possis. Quæ iniquitas effecit profecto, ut essent adulteria, foe minis ægre ferentibus præ stare se fidem non exhibentibus mutuam charitatem. Denique nulla est tam perditi pudoris adultera, quæ non hanc causam vitiis suis præ tendat; injuriam se peccando non facere, sed referre. Quod optime Quintilianus expressit: Homo, inquit, neque alieni matrimonii abstinens, neque sui custos, quæ inter se natura. connexa sunt. Nam neque maritus circa corrumpendas aliorum conjuges occupatus potest vacare domesticæ sanctitati; et uxor, cum in tale incidit matrimonium, exemplo ipso concitara, out imitari se putat, out vindicari.

Cavendum igitur, ne occasionem vitiis nostra intemperantia demus: sed assuescant invicem mores duorum, et jugum paribus animis ferant. Nos ipsos in altero cogitemus. Nam fere in hoc justitiæ summa consistit, ut non facias alteri, quidquid ipse ab altero pati nolis. Hæc sunt quæ ad continentiam præ cipiuntur a Deo. Sed tamen ne quis divina præ cepta circumscribere se putet posse, adduntur ilia, ut omnis calumnia, et occasio fraudis removeatur, adulterum esse, qui a marito dimissam duxerit, et eum qui præ tercrimen adulterii uxorem dimiserit, ut alteram ducat; dissociari enim corpus et distrahi Deus noluit. Præ terea non tanturn adulterium esse vitandum, sed etiam cogitationem; ne quis aspiciat alienam, et animo concupiscat: adulteram enim fieri mentem, si vel imaginem voluptatis sibi ipsa depinxerit. Mens est enim profecto quæ peccat; quæ immoderata: libidinis fructum cogitatione complectitur; in hac crimen est, in hac omne delictum. Nam etsi corpus nulla sit lobe maculatum, non constat tamen pudicitiæ ratio, si animus incestus est; nec illibata castitas videri potest, ubi conscientiam cupiditas inquinavit. Nec verb aliquis existimet, difficile esse fræ nos imponere voluptati, eamque vagam et errantem castitatis pudicitiæ que limitibus includere, cum propositum sit hominibus etiam vincere, ac plurimi beatam atque incorruptam corporis integritatem retinuerint, multique sint, qui hoc coe lesti genere vitæ felicissime perfruantur. Quod quidem Deus non ira fieri præ cepit, tanquam astringat, quia generari homines oportet; sed tanquam sinat. Scit enim, quantam his affectibus imposuerit necessitatem. Si quis hoc, inquit, facere potuerit, habebit eximiam incomparabilemque mercedem. Quod continentiæ genus quasi fastigium est, omniumque consummatio virtutum. Ad quam si quis eniti atque eluctari potuerit, hunc servum dominus, hunc discipulum magister agnoscet; hic terrain triumphabit, hic erit consimilis Deo, qui virtutem Dei cepit. Hæc quidem difficilia videntur; sed de eo loquimur, cui calcatis omnibus terrenis, iter in coelum paratur. Nam quia virtus in Dei agnitione consistit, omnia gravia sunt, dum ignores; ubi cognoveris, facilia: per ipsas difficultates nobis exeundum est, qui ad summum bonum tendimus.

## Chap. XXIV.—Of Repentance, of Pardon, and the Commands of God.

Nor, however, let anyone be disheartened, or despair concerning himself, if, overcome by passion, or impelled by desire, or deceived by error, or compelled by force, he has turned aside to the way of unrighteousness. For it is possible for him to be brought back, and to be set free, if he repents of his actions, and, turning to better things, makes satisfaction to God. Cicero, indeed, thought that this was impossible, whose words in the third book of the Academics are: "But if, as in the case of those who have gone astray on a journey, it were permitted those who have followed a devious course to correct their error by repentance, it would be more easy to amend rashness." It is altogether permitted them. For if we think that our children are corrected when we perceive that they repent of their faults, and though we have disinherited and cast them off, we again receive, cherish, and embrace them, why should we despair that the mercy of God our Father may again be appeased by repentance? Therefore He who is at once the Lord and most indulgent Parent promises that He will remit the sins of the penitent, and that He will blot out all the iniquities of him who shall begin afresh to practice righteousness. For as the uprightness of his past life is of no avail to him who lives badly, because the subsequent wickedness has destroyed his works of righteousness, so former sins do not stand in the way of him who has amended his life, because the subsequent righteousness has effaced the stain of his former life. For he who repents of that which he has done, understands his former error; and on this account the Greeks better and more significantly speak of *metanoia*, which we may speak of in Latin as a return to a right understanding. For he returns to a right understanding, and recovers his mind as it were from madness, who is grieved for his error; and he reproves himself of madness, and confirms his mind to a better course of life: then he especially guards against this very thing, that he may not again be led into the same snares. In short, even the dumb animals, when they are ensnared by fraud, if by any means they have extricated themselves so as to escape, become more cautious for the future, and always avoid all those things in which they have perceived wiles and snares. Thus repentance makes a man cautious and diligent to avoid the faults into which he has once fallen through deceit.

For no one can be so prudent and so circumspect as not at some time to slip; and therefore God, knowing our weakness, of His compassion has opened a harbor of refuge for man, that the medicine of repentance might aid this necessity to which our frailty is liable. Therefore, if anyone has erred, let him retrace his step, and as soon as possible recover and reform himself.

> "But upward to retrace the way,
> And pass into the light of day,
> Then comes the stress of labor."

For when men have tasted sweet pleasures to their destruction, they can scarcely be separated from them: they would more easily follow right things if they had not tasted their attractions. But if they tear themselves away from this pernicious slavery, all their error will be forgiven them, if they shall have corrected their error by a better life. And let not any one imagine that he is a gainer if he shall have no witness of his fault: for all things are known to Him in whose sight we live; and if we are able to conceal anything from all men, we cannot conceal it from God, to whom nothing can be hidden, nothing secret. Seneca closed his exhortations with an admirable sentiment: "There is," he says, "some great deity, and greater than can be imagined; and for him we endeavor to live. Let us approve ourselves to him. For it is of no avail that conscience is confirmed; we lie open to the sight of God." What can be spoken with greater truth by him who knew God, than has been said by a man who is ignorant of true religion? For he both expressed the majesty of God, by saying that it is too great for the reflecting powers of the human mind to receive; and he touched upon the very fountain of truth, by perceiving that the life of men is not superfluous, as the Epicureans will have it, but that they make it their endeavor to live to God, if indeed they live with justice and piety. He might have been a true worshipper of God, if anyone had pointed out to him God; and he might assuredly have despised Zeno, and his teacher Sotion, if he had obtained a true guide of wisdom. Let us approve ourselves to him, he says. A speech truly heavenly, had it not been preceded by a confession of ignorance. It is of no avail that conscience is confined; we lie open to the sight of God. There is then no room for falsehood, none for dissimulation; for the eyes of men are removed by walls, but the divine power of God cannot be removed by the inward parts from looking through and knowing the entire man. The same writer says, in the first book of the same work: "What are you doing? What are you contriving? What are you hiding? Your guardian follows you; one is withdrawn from you by foreign travel, another by death, another by infirm health; this one adheres to you, and you can never be without him. Why do you choose a secret place, and remove the witness? Suppose that you have succeeded in escaping the notice of all, foolish man! What does it profit you not to have a witness, if you have the witness of your own conscience?

And Tully speaks in a manner no less remarkable concerning conscience and God: "Let him remember," he says, "that he has God as a witness, that is, as I judge, his own mind, than which God has given nothing more divine to man." Likewise, in speaking of the just and good man, he says: "Therefore such a man will not dare not merely to do, but even to think, anything which he would not dare to proclaim." Therefore let us cleanse our conscience, which is open to the eyes of God; and, as the same writer says, "let us always so live as to remember that we shall have to give an account;" and let us reckon that we are looked upon at every moment, not, as he said, in some theatre of the world by men, but from above by Him who is about to be both the judge and also the witness, to whom, when He demands an account of our life, it will not be permitted anyone to deny his actions. Therefore it is better either to flee from conscience, or ourselves to open our mind of our own accord, and tearing open our wounds to pour forth destruction; which wounds no one else can heal but He alone who made the lame to walk, restored sight to the blind, cleansed the polluted limbs, and raised the dead. He will quench the ardor of desires, He will root out lusts, He will remove envy, He will mitigate anger. He will give true and lasting health. This remedy should be sought by all, inasmuch as the soul is harassed by greater danger than the body, and a cure should be applied as soon as possible to secret diseases. For if anyone has his eyesight clear, all his limbs perfect, and his entire body in the most vigorous health, nevertheless I should not call him sound if he is carried away by anger, swollen and puffed up with pride, the slave of lust, and burning with desires; but I should rather call him sound who does not raise his eyes to the prosperity of another, who does not admire riches, who looks upon another's wife with chaste eye, who covets nothing at all, does not desire that which is another's, envies no one, disdains no one; who is lowly, merciful, bountiful, mild, courteous: peace perpetually dwells in his mind.

That man is sound, he is just, he is perfect. Whoever, therefore, has obeyed all these heavenly precepts, he is a worshipper of the true God, whose sacrifices are gentleness of spirit, and an innocent life, and good actions. And he who exhibits all these qualities offers a sacrifice as often as he performs any good and pious action. For God does not desire the sacrifice of a dumb animal, nor of death and blood, but of man and life. And to this sacrifice there is neither need of sacred boughs, nor of purifications, nor of sods of turf, which things are plainly most vain, but of those things which are put forth from the innermost breast. Therefore, upon the altar of God, which is truly very great, and which is placed in the heart of man, and cannot be defiled with blood, there is placed righteousness, patience, faith, innocence, chastity, and abstinence. This is the truest ceremony, this is that law of God, as it is called by Cicero, illustrious and divine, which always commands things which are right and honorable, and forbids things which are wrong and disgraceful; and he who obeys this most holy and certain law cannot fail to live justly and lawfully. And I have laid down a few chief points of this law, since I promised that I would speak only of those things which completed the character of virtue and righteousness. If anyone shall wish to comprise all the other parts, let him seek them from the fountain itself, from which that stream flowed to us.

## Chap. XXV.—Of Sacrifice, and of an Offering worthy of God, and of the Form of Praising God.

Now let us speak briefly concerning sacrifice itself. "Ivory," says Plato, "is not a pure offering to God." What then? Are embroidered and costly textures? Nay, rather nothing is a pure offering to God which can be corrupted or taken away secretly. But as he saw this, that nothing which was taken from a dead body ought to be offered to a living being, why did he not see that a corporeal offering ought not to be presented to an incorporeal being? How much better and more truly does Seneca speak: "Will you think of God as great and placid, and a friend to be reverenced with gentle majesty, and always at hand? not to be worshipped with the immolation of victims and with much blood—for what pleasure arises from the slaughter of innocent animals?—but with a pure mind and with a good and honorable purpose. Temples are not to be built to Him with stones piled up on high; He is to be consecrated by each man in his own breast." Therefore, if anyone thinks that garments, and jewels, and other things which are esteemed precious, are valued by God, he is altogether ignorant of what God is, since he thinks that those things are pleasing to Him which even a man would be justly praised for despising. What, then, is pure, what is worthy of God, but that which He Himself has demanded in that divine law of His?

There are two things which ought to be offered, the gift and the sacrifice; the gift as a perpetual offering, the sacrifice for a time. But with those who by no means understand the nature of the Divine Being, a gift is anything which is wrought of gold or silver; likewise anything which is woven of purple and silk: a sacrifice is a victim, and as many things as are burnt upon the altar. But God does not make use either of the one or the other, because He is free from corruption, and that is altogether corruptible. Therefore, in each case, that which is incorporeal must be offered to God, for He accepts this. His offering is innocence of soul; His sacrifice praise and a hymn. For if God is not seen, He ought therefore to be worshipped with things which are not seen. Therefore no other religion is true but that which consists of virtue and justice. But in what manner God deals with the justice of man is easily understood. For if man shall be just, having received immortality, he will serve God forever.

But that men are not born except for justice, both the ancient philosophers and even Cicero suspects. For, discussing the Laws, he says: "But of all things which are discussed by learned men, nothing assuredly is of greater importance than that it should be entirely understood that we are born to justice." We ought therefore to hold forth and offer to God that alone for the receiving of which He Himself produced us. But how true this twofold kind of sacrifice is, Trismegistus Hermes is a befitting witness, who agrees with us, that is, with the prophets, whom we follow, as much in fact as in words. He thus spoke concerning justice: "Adore and worship this word, O son." But the worship of God consists of one thing, not to be wicked. Also in that perfect discourse, when he heard Asclepius inquiring from his son whether it pleased him that incense and other odors for divine sacrifice were offered to his father, exclaimed: "Speak words of good omen, O Asclepius. For it is the greatest impiety to entertain any such thought concerning that being of pre-eminent goodness. For these things, and things resembling these, are not adapted to Him. For He is full of all things, as many as exist, and He has need of nothing at all. But let us give Him thanks, and adore Him. For His sacrifice consists only of blessing." And he spoke rightly.

For we ought to sacrifice to God in word; inasmuch as God is the Word, as He Himself confessed. Therefore the chief ceremonial in the worship of God is praise from the mouth of a just man directed towards God. That this, however, may be accepted by God, there is need of humility, and fear, and devotion in the greatest degree, lest anyone should chance to place confidence in his integrity and innocence, and thus incur the charge of pride and arrogance, and by this deed lose the recompense of his virtue. But that he may obtain the favor of God, and be free from every stain, let him always implore the mercy of God, and pray for nothing else but pardon for his sins, even though he has none. If he desires anything else, there is no need of expressing it in word to one who knows what we wish; if anything good shall happen to him, let him give thanks; if any evil, let him make amends, and let him confess that the evil has happened to him on account of his faults; and even in evils let him nothing less give thanks, and make amends in good things, that he may be the same at all times, and be firm, and unchangeable, and unshaken. And let him not suppose that this is to be done by him only in the temple, but at home, and even in his very bed. In short, let him always have God with himself, consecrated in his heart, inasmuch as he himself is a temple of God. But if he has served God, his Father and Lord, with this assiduity, obedience, and devotion, justice is complete and perfect; and he who shall keep this, as we before testified, has obeyed God, and has satisfied the obligations of religion and his own duty.

# The Divine Institutes.
## Book VII.
## Of a Happy Life.

### Chap. I.—Of the World, and Those Who are About to Believe, and Those who are Not; And in This the Censure of the Faithless.

It is well: the foundations are laid, as the illustrious orator says. But we have not only laid the foundations, which might be firm and suitable for the support of the work; but we have raised the entire edifice, with great and strong buildings, almost to the summit. There remains, a matter which is much easier, either to cover or adorn it; without which, however, the former works are both useless and displeasing. For of what avail is it, either to be freed from false religions or to understand the true one? Of what avail, either to see the vanity of false wisdom, or to know what is true? Of what avail is it, I say, to defend that heavenly justice? Of what avail to hold the worship of God with great difficulties, which is the greatest virtue, unless the divine reward of everlasting blessedness attends it? Of which subject we must speak in this book, lest all that is gone before should appear vain and unprofitable: if we should leave this, on account of which they were undertaken, in uncertainty, lest anyone should by chance think that such great labors are undertaken in vain; while he distrusts their heavenly reward, which God has appointed for him who shall have despised the present sweet enjoyments of earth in comparison of solitary and unrewarded virtue. Let us satisfy this part of our subject also, both by the testimonies of the sacred writings and also by probable arguments, that it may be equally manifest that future things are to be preferred to those which are present; heavenly things to earthly; and eternal things to those which are temporal: since the rewards of vices are temporal, those of virtues are eternal.

I will therefore set forth the system of the world, that it may easily be understood both when and how it was made by God; which Plato, who discoursed about the making of the world, could neither know nor explain, inasmuch as he was ignorant of the heavenly mystery, which is not learned except by the teaching of prophets and God; and therefore he said that it was created for eternity. Whereas the case is far different, since whatever is of a solid and heavy body, as it received a beginning at some time, so it must needs have an end. For Aristotle, when he did not see how so great a magnitude of things could perish, and wished to escape this objection, said that the world always had existed, and always would exist. He did not at all see, that whatever *material thing* exists must at some time have had a beginning, and that nothing can exist at all unless it had a beginning. For when we see that earth, and water, and fire perish, are consumed, and extinguished, which are clearly parts of the world, it is understood that *that* is altogether mortal the members of which are mortal. Thus it comes to pass, that whatever is liable to destruction must have been produced. But everything which comes within the sight of the eyes must of necessity be material, and capable of dissolution. Therefore Epicurus alone, following the authority of Democritus, spoke truly in this matter, who said that it had a beginning at some time, and that it would at some time perish. Nor, however, was he able to assign any reason, either through what causes or at what time this work of such magnitude should be destroyed. But since God has revealed this to us, and we do not arrive at it by conjectures, but by instruction from heaven, we will carefully teach it, that it may at length be evident to those who are desirous of the truth, that the philosophers did not see nor comprehend the truth; but that they had so slight a knowledge of it, that they by no means perceived from what source that fragrance of wisdom, which was so pleasant and agreeable, breathed upon them.

In the meantime, I think it necessary to admonish those who are about to read this, that depraved and vicious minds, since the acuteness of their mind is blunted by earthly passions, which weigh down all the perceptions and render them weak, will either altogether fail to understand these things which we relate, or, even if they shall understand them, they will dissemble and be unwilling for them to be true: because they are drawn away by vices, and they knowingly favor their own evils, by the pleasantness of which they are captivated, and they desert the way of virtue, by the bitterness of which they are offended. For they who are inflamed with avarice and a certain insatiable thirst for riches—because, when they have sold or squandered the things in which they delight, they are unable to live in a simple style—undoubtedly prefer that by which they are compelled to renounce their eager desires. Also, they who, urged on by the incitements of lusts, as the poet says,

"Rush into madness and fire,"

say that we bring forward things plainly incredible; because the precepts about self-restraint wound their ears, which restrain them from their pleasures, to which they have given up their soul, together with their body. But those who, swollen with ambition or inflamed with the love of power, have bestowed all their efforts on the acquisition of honors, will not, even if we should bear the sun himself in our hands, believe that teaching which commands them to despise all power and honor, and to live in humility, and in such humility that they may be able to receive an injury, and if they have received one, be unwilling to return it. These are the men who cry out in any way against the truth with closed eyes. But they who are or shall be of sound mind, that is, not so immersed in vices as to be incurable, will both believe these things, and will readily approach them; and whatever things we say, they will appear to them open, and plain, and simple, and that which is chiefly necessary, true and unassailable.

No one favors virtue but he who is able to follow it; but it is not easy for all to follow it: they can do so whom poverty and want have exercised, and made capable of virtue. For if the endurance of evils is virtue, it follows that they are not capable of virtue who have always lived in the enjoyment of good things; because they have never experienced evils, nor can they endure them, through their long-continued use and desire of good things, which alone they know. Thus it comes to pass that the poor and humble, who are unencumbered, more readily believe God than the rich, who are entangled with many hindrances; yea, rather, in chains and fetters they are enslaved to the nod of desire, their mistress, which has ensnared them with inextricable bonds; nor are they able to look up to heaven, since their mind is bent down to the earth, and fixed on the ground. But the way of virtue does not admit those carrying great burthens. The path is very narrow by which justice leads man to heaven; no one can keep this unless he is unencumbered and lightly equipped. For those wealthy men, who are loaded with many and great burthens, proceed along the way of death, which is very broad, since destruction rules with extended sway. The precepts which God gives for justice, and the things which we bring forward under the teaching of God respecting virtue and the truth, are bitter and as poisons to these. And if they shall dare to oppose these things, they must own themselves to be enemies of virtue and justice. I will now come to the remaining part of the subject, that an end may be put to the work. But this remains, that we should treat of the judgment of God, which will then be established when our Lord shall return to the earth to render to everyone either a reward or punishment, according to his desert. Therefore, as we spoke in the fourth book concerning His first advent, so in this book we will relate His second advent, which the Jews also both confess and hope for; but in vain, since He must return to the confusion of those for whose call He had before come. For they who impiously treated Him with violence in His humiliation, will experience Him in His power as a conqueror; and, God requiting them, they will suffer all those things which they read and do not understand; inasmuch as, being polluted with all sins, and moreover sprinkled with the blood of the Holy One, they were devoted to eternal punishment by that very One on whom they laid wicked hands. But we shall have a separate subject against the Jews, in which we shall convict them of error and guilt.

## Chap. II.—Of the Error of the Philosophers, and of the Divine Wisdom, and of the Golden Age.

Now let us instruct those who are ignorant of the truth. It has been so determined by the arrangement of the Most High God, that this unrighteous age, having run the course of its appointed times, should come to an end; and all wickedness being immediately extinguished, and the souls of the righteous being recalled to a happy life, a quiet, tranquil, peaceful, in short, golden age, as the poets call it, should flourish, under the rule of God Himself. This was especially the cause of all the errors of the philosophers, that they did not comprehend the system of the world, which comprises the whole of wisdom. But it cannot be comprehended by our own perception and innate intelligence, which they wished to do by themselves without a teacher. Therefore they fell into various and oft times contradictory opinions, out of which they had no way of escape,

And they remained fixed in the same mire,

as the comic writer says, since their conclusion does not correspond with their assumptions; inasmuch as they had assumed things to be true which could not be affirmed, and proved without the knowledge of the truth and of heavenly things. And this knowledge, as I have often said already, cannot exist in a man unless it is derived from the teaching of God. For if a man is able to understand divine things, he will be able also to perform them; for to understand is, as it were, to follow in their track. But he is not able to do the things which God does, because he is clothed with a mortal body; therefore he cannot even understand those things which God does. And whether this is possible is easy for everyone to measure, from the immensity of the divine actions and works. For if you will contemplate the world, with all the things which it contains, you will assuredly understand how much the work of God surpasses the works of men. Thus, as great as is the difference between divine and human works, so great must be the distance between the wisdom of God and man. For because God is incorruptible and immortal, and therefore perfect because He is everlasting, His wisdom also is perfect, as He Himself is; nor can anything oppose it, because God Himself is subject to nothing.

But because man is subject to passion, his wisdom also is subject to error; and as many things hinder the life of man, so that it cannot be perpetual, so also his wisdom must be hindered by many things: so that it is not perfect in entirely perceiving the truth. Therefore there is no human wisdom, if it strives by itself to attain to the conception and knowledge of the truth; inasmuch as the mind of man, being bound up with a frail body, and enclosed in a dark abode, is neither able to wander at large, nor clearly to perceive the truth, the knowledge of which belongs to the divine nature. For His works are known to God alone. But man cannot attain this knowledge by reflection or disputation, but by learning and hearing from Him who alone is able to know and to teach. Therefore Marcus Tullius, borrowing from Plato the sentiment of Socrates, who said that the time had come for himself to depart from life, but that they before whom he was pleading his cause were still alive, says: Which is better is known to the immortal gods; but I think that no man knows. Wherefore all the sects of philosophers must be far removed from the truth, because they who established them were men; nor can those things have any foundation or firmness which are unsupported by any utterances of divine voices.

### Chap. III.—Of Nature, and of the World; And a Censure of the Stoics and Epicureans.

And since we are speaking of the errors of philosophers, the Stoics divide nature into two parts—the one which effects, the other which affords itself tractable for action. They say that in the former is contained all the power of perception, in the latter the material, and that the one cannot act without the other. How can that which handles and that which is handled be one and the same thing? If anyone should say that the potter is the same as the clay, or that the clay is the same as the potter, would he not plainly appear to be mad? But these men comprehend under the one name of nature two things which are most widely different, God and the world, the Maker and the work; and say that the one can do nothing without the other, as though God were mixed up in nature with the world. For sometimes they so mix them together, that God Himself is the mind of the world, and that the world is the body of God; as though the world and God began to exist at the same time, and God did not Himself make the world. And they themselves also confess this at other times, when they say that it was made for the sake of men, and that God could, if He willed it, exist without the world, inasmuch as God is the divine and eternal mind, separate and free from a body. And since they were unable to understand His power and majesty, they mixed Him with the world, that is, with His own work. Whence is that saying of Virgil:—

> "A spirit whose celestial flame
> Glows in each member of the frame,
> And stirs the mighty whole."

What, then, becomes of their own saying, that the world was both made and is governed by the divine providence? For if He made the world, it follows that He existed without the world; if He governs it, it is plain that it is not as the mind governs the body, but as a master rules the house, as a pilot the ship, as a charioteer the chariot. Nor, however, are they mixed with those things which they govern. For if all these things which we see are members of God, then God is rendered insensible by them, since the members are without sensibility, and mortal, since we see that the members are mortal.

I can enumerate how often lands shaken by sudden motions have either opened or sunk down precipitously; how often cities and islands have been overwhelmed by waves, and gone into the deep; marshes have inundated fruitful plains, rivers and pools have been dried up; mountains also have either fallen precipitously, or have been levelled with plains. Many districts, and the foundations of many mountains, are laid waste by latent and internal fire. And this is not enough, if God does not spare His own members, unless it is permitted man also to have some power over the body of God. Seas are built up, mountains are cut down, and the innermost bowels of the earth are dug out to draw forth riches. Why, should I say that we cannot even plough without lacerating the divine body? So that we are at once wicked and impious in doing violence to the members of God. Does God, then, suffer His body to be harassed, and endure to weaken Himself, or permit this to be done by man? Unless by chance that divine intelligence which is mixed with the world, and with all parts of the world, abandoned the first outer aspect of the earth, and plunged itself into the lowest depths, that it might be sensible of no pain from continual laceration. But if this is trifling and absurd, then they themselves were as devoid of intelligence as those are who have not perceived that the divine spirit is everywhere diffused, and that all things are held together by it, not however in such a manner that God, who is incorruptible, should Himself be mixed with heavy and corruptible elements. Therefore that is more correct which they derived from Plato that the world was made by God, and is also governed by His providence. It was therefore befitting that Plato, and those who held the same opinion, should teach and explain what was the cause, what the reason, for the contriving of so great a work; why or for the sake of whom He made it.

But the Stoics also say the world was made for the sake of men. I hear. But Epicurus is ignorant on what account or who made men themselves. For Lucretius, when he said that the world was not made by the gods, thus spoke:

"To say, again, that for the sake of men they have willed to set in order the glorious nature of the world"—

then he introduced:—

"Is sheer folly. For what advantage can our gratitude bestow on immortal and blessed beings, that for our, sake they should take in hand to administer aught?"

And with good reason. For they brought forward no reason why the human race was created or established by God. It is our business to set forth the mystery of the world and man, of which they, being destitute, were able neither to reach nor see the shrine of truth. Therefore, as I said a little before, when they had assumed that which was true, that is, that the world was made by God, and was made for the sake of men, yet, since their argument failed them in the consequences, they were unable to defend that which they had assumed. In fine, Plato, that he might not make the work of God weak and subject to ruin, said that it would remain forever. If it was made for the sake of men, and so made as to be eternal, why then are not they on whose account it was made eternal? If they are mortal on account of whom it was made, it must also itself be mortal and subject to dissolution, for it is not of more value than those for whose sake it was made. But if his argument were consistent, he would understand that it must perish because it was made, and that nothing can remain forever except that which cannot be touched.

But he who says that it was not made for the sake of men has no argument. For if he says that the Creator contrived these works of such magnitude on His own account, why then were we produced? Why do we enjoy the world itself? What means the creation of the human race, and of the other living creatures? Why do we intercept the advantages of others? Why, in short, do we grow, decrease, and perish? What reason is implied in our production itself? What in our perpetual succession? Doubtless God wished us to be seen, and to frame, as it were, impressions with various representations of Himself, with which He might delight Himself. Nevertheless, if it were so, He would esteem living creatures as His care, and especially man, to whose command He made all things subject. But with regard to those who say that the world always existed: I omit that point, that itself cannot exist without some beginning, from which they are unable to extricate themselves; but I say this, if the world always existed, it can have no systematic arrangement. For what could arrangement have effected in that which never had a beginning? For before anything is done or arranged, there is need of counsel that it may be determined how it should be done; nor can anything be done without the foresight of a settled plan. Therefore the plan precedes every work. Therefore that which has not been made has no plan. But the world has a plan by which it both exists and is governed; therefore also it was made: if it was made, it will also be destroyed. Let them therefore assign a reason, if they can, why it was either made in the beginning or will hereafter be destroyed.

And because Epicurus or Democritus was unable to teach this, he said that it was produced of its own accord, the seeds coming together in all directions; and that when these are again resolved, discord and destruction will follow. Therefore he perverted that which he had correctly seen, and by his ignorance of system entirely overthrew the whole system, and reduced the world, and all things which are done in it, to the likeness of a most trifling dream, if no plan exists in human affairs. But since the world and all its parts, as we see, are governed by a wonderful plan; since the framing of the heaven, and the course of the stars and of the heavenly bodies, which is harmonious even in variety itself, the constant and wonderful arrangement of the seasons, the varied fruitfulness of the lands, the level plains, the defenses and heaping up of mountains, the verdure and productiveness of the woods, the most salubrious bursting forth of fountains, the seasonable overflowing of rivers, the rich and abundant flowing in of the sea, the opposite and useful breathing of the winds, and all things, are fixed with the greatest regularity: who is so blind as to think that they were made without a cause, in which a wonderful disposition of most provident arrangement shines forth? If, therefore, nothing at all exists nor is done without a cause; if the providence of the Supreme God is manifest from the disposition of things, His excellency from their greatness, and His power from their government: therefore they are dull and mad who have said that there is no providence. I should not disapprove if they denied the existence of gods with this object, that they might affirm the existence of one; but when they did it with this intent, that they might say that there is none, he who does not think that they were senseless is himself senseless.

**Chap. IV.—That All Things Were Created for Some Use, Even Those Things Which Appear Evil; On What Account Man Enjoys Reason in So Frail a Body.**

But we have spoken sufficiently on the subject of providence in the first book. For if it has any existence, as appears from the wonderful nature of its works, it must be that the same providence created man and the other animals. Let us therefore see what reason there was for the creation of the human race, since it is evident, as the Stoics say, that the world was made for the sake of men, although they make no slight error in this very matter, in saying it was not made for the sake of man, but of men. For the naming of one individual comprehends the whole human race. But this arises from the fact that they are ignorant that one man only was made by God, and they think that men were produced in all lands and fields like mushrooms. But Hermes was not ignorant that man was both made by God and after the likeness of God. But I return to my subject. There is nothing, as I imagine, which was made on its own account; but whatever is made at all must necessarily be made for some purpose. For who is there either so senseless or so unconcerned as to attempt to do anything at random, from which he expects no utility, no advantage? He who builds a house does not build it merely for this purpose that it may be a house, but that it may be inhabited. He who builds a ship does not bestow his labor on this account, only that the ship may be visible, but that men may sail in it. Likewise he who designs and forms any vessel does not do it on this account, that he may only appear to have done it, but that the vessel when made may contain something necessary for use. In like manner, other things, whatever are made, are plainly not made superfluously, but for some useful purposes.

It is plain, therefore, that the world was made by God, not on account of the world itself; for since it is without sensibility, it neither needs the warmth of the sun, or light, or the breath of the winds, or the moisture of showers, or the nourishment of fruits. But it cannot even be said that God made the world for His own sake, since He can exist without the world, as He did before it was made; and God Himself does not make use of all those things which are contained in it, and which are produced. It is evident, therefore, that the world was constructed for the sake of living beings, since living beings enjoy those things of which it consists; and that these may live and exist, all things necessary for them are supplied at fixed times. Again, that the other living beings were made for the sake of man, is plain from this, that they are subservient to man, and were given for his protection and service; since, whether they are of the earth or of the water, they do not perceive the system of the world as man does. We must here reply to the philosophers, and especially to Cicero, who says: "Why should God, when He made all things on our account, make so large a quantity of snakes and vipers? Why should He scatter so many pernicious things by land and by sea?" A very wide subject for discussion, but it must be briefly touched upon, as in passing. Since man is formed of different and opposing elements, soul and body, that is, heaven and earth, that which is slight and that which is perceptible to the senses, that which is eternal and that which is temporal, that which has sensibility and that which is senseless, that which is endued with light and that which is dark, reason itself and necessity require that both good and evil things should be set before man—good things which he may use, and evil things which he may guard against and avoid.

For wisdom has been given to him on this account, that, knowing the nature of good and evil things, he may exercise the force of his reason in seeking the good and avoiding the evil. For because wisdom was not given to the other animals, they were both defended with natural clothing and were armed; but in the place of all these He gave to man that which was most excellent, reason only. Therefore He formed him naked and unarmed, that wisdom might be both his defense and covering. He placed his defense and ornament not without, but within not in the body, but in the heart. Unless, therefore, there were evils which he might guard against, and which he might distinguish from good and useful things, wisdom was not necessary for him. Therefore let Marcus Tullius know that reason was either given to man that he might take fishes on account of his own use, and avoid snakes and vipers for the sake of his own safety; or that good and evil things were set before him on this account, because he had received wisdom, the whole force of which is occupied in distinguishing things good and evil. Great, therefore, and right, and admirable is the force, and reason, and power of man, for whose sake God made the world itself and all things, as many as exist, and gave him so much honor that He set him over all things, since he alone could admire the works of God. Most excellently, therefore, does our Asclepiades, in discussing the providence of the Supreme God in that book which he wrote to me, say: "And on this account any one may with good reason think that the divine providence gave the place nearest to itself to him who was able to understand its arrangement. For that is the sun: who so beholds it as to understand why it is the sun, and what amount of influence it has upon the other parts of the system? This is the heaven, who looks up to it? This is the earth, who inhabits it? This is the sea, who sails upon it? This is fire, who makes use of it?" Therefore the Supreme God did not arrange these things on account of Himself, because He stands in need of nothing, but on account of man, who might fitly make use of them.

## Chap. V.—Of the Creation of Man, and of the Arrangement of the World, and of the Chief Good.

Let us now assign the reason why He made man himself. For if the philosophers had known this, they would either have maintained those things which they had found to be true, or would not have fallen into the greatest errors. For this is the chief thing; this is the point on which everything turns. And if any one does not possess this, the truth altogether glides away from him. It is this, in short, which causes them to be inconsistent with reason; for if this had shone upon them, if they had known all the mystery of man, the Academy would never have been in entire opposition to their disputations, and to all philosophy. As, therefore, God did not make the world for His own sake, because He does not stand in need of its advantages, but for the sake of man, who has the use of it, so also He made man himself for His own sake. What advantage is there to God in man, says Epicurus that He should make him for His own sake? Truly, that there might be one who might understand His works; who might be able both to admire with his understanding, and to express with his voice, the foresight displayed in their arrangement, the order of their creation, the power exerted in their completion. And the sum of all these things is, that he should worship God. For he who understands these things worships Him; he follows Him with due veneration as the Maker of all things, He as his true Father, who measures the excellence of His majesty according to the invention, the commencement, and completion of His works. What more evident argument can be brought forward that God both made the world for the sake of man, and man for His own sake, than that he alone of all living creatures has been so formed that his eyes are directed towards heaven, his face looking towards God, his countenance is in fellowship with his Parent, so that God appears, as it were, with outstretched hand to have raised man from the ground, and to have elevated him to the contemplation of Himself. "What, then," he says, "does the worship paid by man confer on God, who is blessed, and in want of nothing? Or if He gave such honor to man as to create the world for his sake, to furnish him with wisdom, to make him lord of all things living, and to love him as a son, why did He make him subject to death and decay? Why did He expose the object of His love to all evils? When it was befitting that man should be happy, as though closely connected with God, and everlasting as He is, to the worship and contemplation of whom he was formed."

Although we have taught these things for the most part in a scattered manner in the former books, nevertheless, since the subject now specially requires it, because we have undertaken to discuss the subject of a happy life, these things are to be explained by us more carefully and fully, that the arrangement made by God, and His work and will, may be known. Though He was always able by His own immortal Spirit to produce innumerable souls, as He produced the angels, to whom there exists immortality without any danger and fear of evils, yet He devised an unspeakable work, in what manner He might create an infinite multitude of souls, which being at first united with frail and feeble bodies, He might place in the midst between good and evil, that He might set virtue before them composed as they were of both natures; that they might not attain to immortality by a delicate and easy course of life, but might arrive at that unspeakable reward of eternal life with the utmost difficulty and great labors. Therefore, that He might clothe them with limbs which were heavy and liable to injury, since they were unable to exist in the middle void, the weight and gravity of the body sinking downwards, He determined that an abode and dwelling-place should first be built for them. And thus with unspeakable energy and power He contrived the surpassing works of the world; and having suspended the light elements on high, and depressed the heavy ones to the depths below, He strengthened the heavenly things, and established the earthly. It is not necessary at present to follow out each point separately, since we discussed them all together in the second book.

Therefore He placed in the heaven lights, whose regularity, and brightness, and motion, were most suitably proportioned to the advantage of living beings. Moreover, He gave to the earth, which He designed as their dwelling-place, fruitfulness for bringing forth and producing various things, that by the abundance of fruits and green herbs it might supply nourishment according to the nature and requirements of each kind. Then, when He had completed all things which belonged to the condition of the world, He formed man from the earth itself, which He prepared for him from the beginning as a habitation; that is, He clothed and covered his spirit with an earthly body, that, being compacted of different and opposing materials, he might be susceptible of good and evil; and as the earth itself is fruitful for the bringing forth of grain, so the body of man, which was taken from the earth, received the power of producing offspring, that, inasmuch as he was formed of a fragile substance, and could not exist for ever, when the space of his temporal life was past, he might depart, and by a perpetual succession renew that which he bore, which was frail and feeble. Why, then, did He make him frail and mortal, when He had built the world for his sake? First of all, that an infinite number of living beings might be produced, and that He might fill all the earth with a multitude; in the next place, that He might set before man virtue, that is, endurance of evils and labors, by which he might be able to gain the reward of immortality. For since man consists of two parts, body and soul, of which the one is earthly, the other heavenly, two lives have been assigned to man: the one temporal, which is appointed for the body; the other everlasting, which belongs to the soul. We received the former at our birth we attain to the latter by striving, that immortality might not exist to man without any difficulty. That earthly one is as the body, and therefore has an end; but this heavenly one is as the soul, and therefore has no limit. We received the first when we were ignorant of it, this second knowingly; for it is given to virtue, not to nature, because God wished that we should procure life for ourselves in life.

For this reason He has given us this present life, that we may either lose that true and eternal life by our vices, or win it by virtue. The chief good is not contained in this bodily life, since, as it was given to us by divine necessity, so it will again be destroyed by divine necessity. Thus that which has an end does not contain the chief good. But the chief good is contained in that spiritual life which we acquire by ourselves, because it cannot contain evil, or have an end; to which subject nature and the system of the body afford an argument. For other animals incline towards the ground, because they are earthly, and are incapable of immortality, which is from heaven; but man is upright and looks towards heaven, because immortality is proposed to him; which, however, does not come, unless it is given to man by God. For *otherwise* there would be no difference between the just and the unjust, since every man who is born would become immortal. Immortality, then, is not the consequence of nature, but the reward and recompense of virtue. Lastly, man does not immediately upon his birth walk upright, but at first on all fours, because the nature of his body and of this present life is common to us with the dumb animals; afterwards, when his strength is confirmed, he raises himself, and his tongue is loosened so that he speaks plainly, and he ceases to be a dumb animal. And this argument teaches that man is born mortal; but that he afterwards becomes immortal, when he begins to live in conformity with the will of God, that is, to follow righteousness, which is comprised in the worship of God, since God raised man to a view of the heaven and of Himself. And this takes place when man, purified in the heavenly laver, lays aside his infancy together with all the pollution of his past life, and having received an increase of divine vigor, becomes a perfect and complete man.

Therefore, because God has set forth virtue before man, although the soul and the body are connected together, yet they are contrary, and oppose one another. The things which are good for the soul are evil to the body, that is, the avoiding of riches, the prohibiting of pleasures, the contempt of pain and death. In like manner, the things which are good for the body are evil to the soul, that is, desire and lust, by which riches are desired, and the enjoyments of various pleasures, by which the soul is weakened and destroyed. Therefore it is necessary, that the just and wise man should be engaged in all evils, since fortitude is victorious over evils; but the unjust in riches, in honors, in power. For these goods relate to the body, and are earthly; and these men also lead an earthly life, nor are they able to attain to immortality, because they have given themselves up to pleasures which are the enemies of virtue. Therefore this temporal life ought to be subject to that eternal life, as the body is to the soul. Whoever, then, prefers the life of the soul must despise the life of the body; nor will he in any other way be able to strive after that which is highest, unless he shall have despised the things which are lowest. But he who shall have embraced the life of the body, and shall have turned his desires downwards to the earth, is unable to attain to that higher life. But he who prefers to live well for eternity, will live badly for a time, and will be subjected to all troubles and labors as long as he shall be on earth, that he may have divine and heavenly consolation. And he who shall prefer to live well for a time, will live ill to eternity; for he will be condemned by the sentence of God to eternal punishment, because he has preferred earthly to heavenly goods. On this account, therefore, God seeks to be worshipped, and to be honored by man as a Father, that he may have virtue and wisdom, which alone produce immortality. For because no other but Himself is able to confer that immortality, since He alone possesses it, He will grant to the piety of the man, with which he has honored God, this reward, to be blessed to all eternity, and to be forever in the presence of God and in the society of God.

N.B.—The following paragraphs to the end of the chapter are wanting many mss., and it is very doubtful whether they were written by Lactantius.

Nor can anyone shelter himself under the pretext that the fault belongs to Him who made both good and evil. For why did

He will that evil should exist if He hated it? Why did He not make good only, that no one might sin, no one commit evil? Although I have explained this in almost all the former books, and have touched upon it, though slightly, above, yet it must be mentioned repeatedly, because the whole matter turns on this point. For there could be no virtue unless He had made contrary things; nor can the power of good be at all manifest, except from a comparison with evil. Thus evil is nothing else but the explanation of good. Therefore if evil is taken away, good must also be taken away. If you shall cut off your left hand or foot, your body will not be entire, nor will life itself remain the same. Thus, for the due adjustment of the framework of the body, the left members are most suitably joined with the right. In like manner, if you make chessmen all alike, no one will play. If you shall give one color only to the circus, no one will think it worthwhile to be a spectator, all the pleasure of the Circensian games being taken away. For he who first instituted the games was a favorer of one color; but he introduced another as a rival, that there might be a contest, and some partisanship in the spectacle. Thus God, when He was fixing that which was good, and giving virtue, appointed also their contraries, with which they might contend. If an enemy and a fight be wanting, there is no victory. Take away a contest, and even virtue is nothing. How many are the mutual contests of men, and with what various arts are they carried on! No one, however, would be regarded as surpassing in bravery, swiftness, or excellence, if he had no adversary with whom he might contend. And where victory is wanting, there also glory and the reward of victory must be absent together with it. Therefore, that he might strengthen virtue itself by continual exercise, and might make it perfect from its conflict with evils, He gave both together, because each of the two without the other is unable to retain its force. Therefore there is diversity, on which the whole system of truth depends.

It does not escape my notice what may here be urged in opposition by more skillful persons. If good cannot exist without evil, how do you say that, before he had offended God, the first man lived in the exercise of good only, or that he will hereafter live in the exercise of good only? This question is to be examined by us, for in the former books I omitted it, that I might here fill up the subject. We have said above that the nature of man is made up of opposing elements; for the body, because it is earth, is capable of being grasped, of temporary duration, senseless, and dark. But the soul, because it is from heaven, is unsubstantial, everlasting, endued with sensibility, and full of luster; and because these qualities are opposed to one another, it follows of necessity that man is subject to good and evil. Good is ascribed to the soul, because it is incapable of dissolution; evil to the body, because it is frail. Since, therefore, the body and the soul are connected and united together, the good and the evil must necessarily hold together; nor can they be separated from one another, unless when they (the body and soul) are separated. Finally, the knowledge of good and of evil was given at the same time to the first man; and when he understood this, he was immediately driven from the holy place in which there is no evil; for when he was conversant with that which was good only, he was ignorant that this itself was good. But after that he had received the knowledge of good and evil, it was now unlawful for him to remain in that place of happiness, and he was banished to this common world, that he might at once experience both of those things with the nature of which he had at once become acquainted. It is plain, therefore, that wisdom has been given to man that he may distinguish good from evil—that he may discriminate between things advantageous and things disadvantageous, between things useful and things useless—that he may have judgment and consideration as to what he ought to guard against, what to desire, what to avoid, and what to follow. Wisdom therefore cannot exist without evil; and that first author of the human race, as long as he was conversant with good only, lived as an infant, ignorant of good and evil. But, indeed, hereafter man must be both wise and happy without any evil; but this cannot take place as long as the soul is clothed with the abode of the body.

But when a separation shall have been made between the body and the soul, then evil will be disunited from good; and as the body perishes and the soul remains, so evil will perish and good be permanent. Then man, having received the garment of immortality, will be wise and free from evil, as God is. He, therefore, who wishes that we should be conversant with good only, especially desires this, that we should live without the body, in which evil is. But if evil is taken away, either wisdom, as I have said, or the body, will be taken from man; wisdom, that he may be ignorant of evil; the body, that he may not be sensible of it. But now, since man is furnished with wisdom to know, and a body to perceive, God willed that both should exist alike in this life, that virtue and wisdom may be in agreement. Therefore He placed man in the midst, between both, that he might have liberty to follow either good or evil. But He mingled with evil some things which appear good, that is, various and delightful enjoyments, that by the enticements of these He might lead men to the concealed evil. And He likewise mingled with good some things which appear evil—that is, hardships, and miseries, and labors—by the harshness and unpleasantness of which the soul, being offended, might shrink back from the concealed good. But here the office of wisdom is needed, that we may see more with the mind than with the body, which very few are able to do; because while virtue is difficult and rarely to be found, pleasure is common and public. Thus it necessarily happens that the wise man is accounted as a fool, who, while he seeks good things which are not seen, permits those which are seen to slip from his hands; and while he avoids evils which are not seen, runs into evils which are before the eyes; which happens to us when we refuse neither torture nor death in behalf of the faith, since we are driven to the greatest wickedness, so as to betray the faith and deny the true God, and to sacrifice to dead and death-bearing gods. This is the cause why God made man mortal, and made him subject to evils, although he had framed the world for his sake, namely, that he might be capable of virtue, and that his virtue might reward him with immortality. Now virtue, as we have shown, is the worship of the true God.

**Chap. VI.—Why the World and Man Were Created. How Unprofitable is the Worship of False Gods.**

Now let us mark the whole argument by a brief definition. The world has been created for this purpose, that we may be born; we are born for this end, that we may acknowledge the Maker of the world and of ourselves—God; we acknowledge Him for this end, that we may worship Him; we worship Him for this end, that we may receive immortality as the reward of our labors, since the worship of God consists of the greatest labors; for this end we are rewarded with immortality, that being made like to the angels, we may serve the Supreme Father and Lord forever, and may be to all eternity a kingdom to God. This is the sum of all things, this the secret of God, this the mystery of the world, from which they are estranged, who, following present gratification, have devoted themselves to the pursuit of earthly and frail goods, and by means of deadly enjoyments have sunk as it were in mire and mud their souls, which were born for heavenly pursuits.

Let us now, in the next place, inquire whether there is anything reasonable in the worship of these gods; for if they are many, if they are worshipped only on this account by men, that they may afford them riches, victories, honors, and all things, which are of no avail except for the present; if we are produced without cause—if no providence is employed in the production of men—if we are brought forth by chance for ourselves, and for the sake of our own pleasure—if we are nothing after death,—what can be so superfluous, so empty, so vain, as the affairs of man, and the world itself? Which, though it is of incredible magnitude, and constructed with such wonderful arrangement, is nevertheless occupied with trifling subjects. For why should the breathings of the winds put the clouds in motion? Why should lightnings shine forth, thunders roar, or showers fall, that the earth may bring forth its increase, and nourish its various productions? Why, in short, should all nature labor that nothing may be wanting of those things by which the life of man is sustained, if it is vain, if we utterly perish, if there is in us nothing of greater advantage to God? But if it is unlawful to be spoken, and is not to be thought possible, that that which you see to be most in accordance with reason was not established on account of some reason of importance, what reason can there be in these errors of depraved religions, and in this persuasion of philosophers, by which they imagine that souls perish? Assuredly there is none; for what have they to say why the gods so regularly supply to men everything in its season? Is it that we may present to them corn and wine, and the odor of incense, and the blood of cattle? Which things cannot be acceptable to the immortals, because they are perishable; nor can they be of use to beings destitute of bodies, because these things have been given for the use of those possessed of bodies; and yet if they required these things, they could bestow them upon themselves when they wished. Whether, therefore, souls perish or exist forever, what principle is involved in the worship of the gods, or by whom was the world established? Why, or when, or how long, or how far were men produced, or on what account? Why do they arise, die, succeed one another, are renewed? What do the gods obtain from the worship of those who after death are about to have no existence? What do they perform, what do they promise, what do they threaten, which is worthy of men or of gods? Or if souls remain after death, what do they do or are they about to do respecting them? What need is there to them of a treasure-house of souls? From what source do they themselves arise? How, or why, or whence are they so many? Thus it comes to pass, that if you depart from that sum of things which we comprised above, all system is destroyed, and all things return to nothing.

## Chap. VII.—Of the Variety of Philosophers, and Their Truth.

And because the philosophers did not comprehend this main point, they were neither able to comprehend truth, although they for the most part both saw and explained those things of which the main point itself consists. But different persons brought forward all these things, and in different ways, not connecting the causes of things, nor the consequences, nor the reasons, so that they might join together and complete that main point which comprises the whole. But it is easy to show that almost the whole truth has been divided by philosophers and sects. For we do not overthrow philosophy, as the Academics are accustomed to do, whose plan was to reply to everything, which is rather to calumniate and mock; but we show that no sect was so much out of the way, and no philosopher so vain, as not to see something of the truth. But while they are mad with the desire of contradicting, while they defend their own arguments even though false, and overthrow those of others even though true, not only has the truth escaped from them, which they pretended that they were seeking, but they themselves lost it chiefly through their own fault. But if there had been any one to collect together the truth which was dispersed amongst individuals and scattered amongst sects, and to reduce it to a body, he assuredly would not disagree with us. But no one is able to do this, unless he has experience and knowledge of the truth. But to know the truth belongs to him only who has been taught by God. For he cannot in any other way reject the things which are false, or choose and approve of those which are true; but if even by chance he should effect this, he would most surely act the part of the philosopher; and though he could not defend those things by divine testimonies, yet the truth would explain itself by its own light. Wherefore the error of those is incredible, who, when they have approved of any sect, and have devoted themselves to it, condemn all others as false and vain, and arm themselves for battle, neither knowing what they ought to defend nor what to refute; and make attacks everywhere, without distinction, upon all things which are brought forward by those who disagree with them.

On account of these most obstinate contentions of theirs, no philosophy existed which made a nearer approach to the truth, for the whole truth has been comprised by these in separate portions. Plato said that the world was made by God: the prophets speak the same; and the same is apparent from the verses of the Sibyl. They therefore are in error, who have said either that all things were produced of their own accord or from an assemblage of atoms; since so great a world, so adorned and of such magnitude, could neither have been made nor arranged and set in order without some most skillful author, and that very arrangement by which all things are perceived to be kept together and to be governed bespeaks an artificer with a most skillful mind. The Stoics say that the world, and all things which are in it, were made for the sake of men: the sacred writings teach us the same thing. Therefore Democritus was in error, who thought that they were poured forth from the earth like worms, without any author or plan. For the reason of man's creation belongs to a divine mystery; and because he was unable to know this, he drew down man's life to nothing. Aristo asserted that men were born to the exercise of virtue; we are also reminded of and learn the same from the prophets. Therefore Aristippus is deceived, who made man subject to pleasure, that is, to evil, as though he were a beast. Pherecydes and Plato contended that souls were immortal; but this is a peculiar doctrine in our religion. Therefore Dicæarchus was mistaken, together with Democritus, who argued that souls perished with the body and were dissolved, Zeno the Stoic taught that there were infernal regions, and that the abodes of the good were separated from the wicked; and that the former enjoyed peaceful and delightful regions, but that the latter suffered punishment in dark places, and in dreadful abysses of mire: the prophets show the same thing. Therefore Epicurus was mistaken, who thought that that was an invention of the poets, and explained those punishments of the infernal regions, which are spoken of, as happening in this life. Therefore the philosophers touched upon the whole truth, and every secret of our holy religion; but when others denied it, they were unable to defend that which they had found, because the system did not agree with the particulars; nor were they able to reduce to a summary those things which they had perceived to be true, as we have done above.

### Chap. VIII.—Of the Immortality of the Soul.

The one chief good, therefore, is immortality, for the reception of which we were originally formed and born. To this we direct our course; human nature regards this; to this virtue exalts us. And because we have discovered this good, it remains that we should also speak of immortality itself. The arguments of Plato, although they contribute much to the subject, have little strength to prove and fill up the truth, since he had neither summed up and collected into one the plan of the whole of this great mystery, nor had he comprehended the chief good. For although he perceived the truth respecting the immortality of the soul, yet he did not speak respecting it as though it were the chief good. We, therefore, are able to elicit the truth by more certain signs; for we have not collected it by doubtful surmise, but have known it by divine instruction. Now Plato thus reasoned, that whatever has perception by itself, and always moves, is immortal; for that that which has no beginning of motion is not about to have an end, because it cannot be deserted by itself. But this argument would give eternal existence even to dumb animals, unless he had made a distinction by the addition of wisdom. He added, therefore, that he might escape this common linking together, that the soul of man could not be otherwise than immortal, since its wonderful skill in invention, its quickness in reflection, and its readiness in perceiving and learning, its memory of the past, and its foresight of the future, and its knowledge of innumerable arts and subjects, which other living creatures do not possess, appear divine and heavenly; because of the soul, which conceives such great things, and contains such great things, no origin can be found on earth, since it has nothing of earthly admixture united with it. But that which is ponderous in man, and liable to dissolution, must be resolved into earth; whereas that which is slight and subtle is incapable of division, and when freed from the abode of the body, as from prison, it flies to the heaven, and to its own nature. This is a brief summary of the tenets of Plato, which are widely and copiously explained in his own writings.

Pythagoras also was previously of the same sentiments, and his teacher Pherecydes, whom Cicero reported to have been the first who discoursed respecting the immortality of the soul. And although all these excelled in eloquence, nevertheless in this contest at least, those who argued against this opinion had no less authority; Dicæarchus first, then Democritus, and lastly Epicurus: so that the matter itself, respecting which they were contending, was called into doubt. Finally, Tullius also having set forth the opinions of all these respecting immortality and death, declared that he did not know what was the truth. "Which of these opinions is true," he said, "some God may see." And again he says in another place: "Since each of these opinions had most learned defenders, it cannot be divined what is certainty." But we have no need of divination, since the divinity itself has laid open to us the truth.

### Chap. IX.—Of the Immortality of the Soul, and of Virtue.

By these arguments, therefore, which neither Plato nor any other invented, the immorality of souls can be proved and perceived: which arguments we will briefly collect, since my discourse hastens on to relate the great judgment of God, which will be celebrated on the earth at the approaching end of the world. Before all things, since God cannot be seen by man, lest anyone should imagine from this circumstance that God does not exist, because He was not seen by mortal eyes, among other wonderful arrangements. He also made many things the power of which is manifest, but the substance is not seen, as the voice, smell, the wind, that by the token and example of these things we might perceive God from His power and operation and works, although He did not fall under the notice of our eyes. What is clearer than the voice, or stronger than the wind, or more forcible than smell? Yet these, when they are borne through the air and come to our senses, and impel them by their efficacy, are not distinguished by the eyesight, but are perceived by other parts of the body. In like manner, God is not to be perceived by us through the sight or other frail sense; but He is to be beheld by the eyes of the mind, since we see His illustrious and wonderful works. For as to those who have altogether denied the existence of God, I should not only refuse to call them philosophers, but even deny them the name of men, who, with a close resemblance to dumb animals, consisted of body only, discerning nothing with their mind, and referring all things to the bodily senses, who thought that nothing existed but that which they beheld with their eyes. And because they saw that adversity befell the wicked, or prosperity happened to the good, they believed that all things were carried on by fortune, and that the world was established by nature, and not by providence.

Hence they at once fell into the absurdities which necessarily followed such a sentiment. But if there is a God who is incorporeal, invisible, and eternal, therefore it is credible that the soul, since it is not seen, does not perish after its departure from the body; for it is manifest that something exists which perceives and is vigorous, and yet does not come into sight. But, it is said, it is difficult to comprehend with the mind how the soul can retain its perception without those parts of the body in which the office of perception is contained. What about God? Is it easy to comprehend how He is vigorous without a body? But if they believe in the existence of gods who, if they exist, are plainly destitute of bodies, it must be that human souls exist in the same way, since it is perceived from reason itself, and discernment, that there is a certain resemblance in man and God. Finally, that proof which even Marcus Tullius saw is of sufficient strength: that the immortality of the soul may be discerned from the fact that there is no other animal which has any knowledge of God; and religion is almost the only thing which distinguishes man from the dumb creation. And since this falls to man alone, it assuredly testifies that we may aim at, desire, and cultivate that which is about to be familiar and very near.

Can anyone, when he has considered the nature of other animals, which the providence of the Supreme God has made abject, with bodies bending down and prostrated to the earth, so that it may be understood from this that they have no intercourse with heaven, fail to understand that man alone of all animals is heavenly and divine, whose body raised from the ground, elevated countenance, and upright position, goes in quest of its origin, and despising, as it were, the lowliness of the earth, reaches forth to that which is on high, because he perceives that the highest good is to be sought by him in the highest place, and mindful of his condition in which God made him illustrious, looks towards his Maker? And Trismegistus most rightly called this looking a contemplation of God, which has no existence in the dumb animals. Since therefore wisdom, which is given to man alone, is nothing else but the knowledge of God, it is evident that the soul does not perish, nor undergo dissolution, but that it remains forever, because it seeks after and loves God, who is everlasting, by the impulse of its very nature perceiving either from what source it has sprung, or to what it is about to return. Moreover, it is no slight proof of immortality that man alone makes use of the heavenly element. For, since the nature of the world consists of two elements which are opposed to one another—fire and water—of which the one is assigned to the heaven, the other to the earth, the other living creatures, because they are of the earth and mortal, make use of the element which is earthly and heavy: man alone makes use of fire, which is an element light, rising upward, and heavenly. But those things which are weighty depress to death, and those which are light elevate to life; because life is on high, and death below. And as there cannot be light without fire, so there cannot be life without light. Therefore fire is the element of light and life; from which it is evident that man who uses it is a partaker of an immortal condition, because that which causes life is familiar to him.

The gift of virtue also to man alone is a great proof that souls are immortal. For this will not be in accordance with nature if the soul is extinguished; for it is injurious to this present life. For that earthly life, which we lead in common with dumb animals, both seeks pleasure, by the varied and agreeable fruits of which it is delighted, and avoids pain, the harshness of which, by its unpleasant sensations, injures the nature of living beings, and endeavors to lead them to death, which dissolves the living being. If, therefore, virtue both prohibits man from those goods which are naturally desired, and impels him to endure evils which are naturally avoided, it follows that virtue is an evil, and opposed to nature; and he must necessarily be judged foolish who pursues it, since he injures himself both by avoiding present goods, and by seeking equally evils, without hope of greater advantage. For when it is permitted us to enjoy the sweetest pleasures, should we not appear to be without sense if we should not prefer to live in lowliness, in want, in contempt and ignominy, or not to live at all, but to be tormented with pain, and to die, when from these evils we should gain nothing to compensate us for the pleasure which we have given up? But if virtue is not an evil, and acts honorably, inasmuch as it despises vicious and shameful pleasures, and bravely, inasmuch as it neither fears pain nor death, that it may discharge its duty, therefore it must obtain some greater good than those things are which it despises. But when death has been undergone, what further good can be hoped for except immortality?

**Chap. X.—Of Vices and Virtues, and of Life and Death.**

Let us now in turn pass on to those things which are opposed to virtue, that from these also the immortality of the soul may be inferred. All vices are for a time; for they are excited for the present. The impetuosity of anger is appeased when vengeance has been taken; the pleasure of the body puts an end to lust; desire is destroyed either by the full enjoyment of the objects which it seeks, or by the excitement of other affections; ambition, when it has gained the honors which it wished for, loses its strength; likewise the other vices are unable to stand their ground and remain, but they are ended by the very enjoyment which they desire. Therefore they withdraw and return. But virtue is perpetual, without any intermission; nor can he who has once taken it up depart from it. For if it should have any interruption, if we can at any time do without it, vices, which always oppose virtue, will return. Therefore it has not been grasped, if it deserts its post, if at any time it withdraws itself. But when it has established for itself a firm abode, it must necessarily be engaged in every act; nor can it faithfully drive away and put to flight vices, unless it shall fortify with a perpetual guard the breast which it inhabits. Therefore the uninterrupted duration of virtue itself shows that the soul of man, if it has received virtue, remains permanent, because virtue is perpetual, and it is the human mind alone which receives virtue. Since, therefore, vices are contrary to virtue, the whole systems must of necessity differ from and be contrary to each other. Because vices are commotions and perturbations of the soul; virtue, on the contrary, is mildness and tranquility of mind. Because vices are temporary, and of short duration; virtue is perpetual and constant, and always consistent with itself. Because the fruits of vices, that is, pleasures, equally with themselves, are short and temporary, therefore the fruit and reward of virtue are everlasting. Because the advantage of vices is immediate, therefore that of virtue is future.

Thus it happens that in this life there is no reward of virtue, because virtue itself still exists. For as, when vices are completed in their performance, pleasure and their rewards follow; so, when virtue has been ended, its reward follows. But virtue is never ended except by death, since its highest office is in the undergoing of death: therefore the reward of virtue is after death. In fine, Cicero, in his *Tusculan Disputations*, perceived, though with doubt, that the chief good does not happen to man except after death. "A man will go," he says, "with confident spirit, if circumstances shall so happen, to death, in which we have ascertained that there is either the chief good or no evil." Death, therefore, does not extinguish man, but admits him to the reward of virtue. But he who has contaminated himself, as the same writer says, with vices and crimes, and has been the slave of pleasure, he truly, being condemned, shall suffer eternal punishment, which the sacred writings call the second death, which is both eternal and full of the severest torments. For as two lives are proposed to man, of which the one belongs to the soul, the other to the body; so also two deaths are proposed,—one relating to the body, which all must undergo according to nature, the other relating to the soul, which is acquired by wickedness and avoided by virtue. As this life is temporary and has fixed limits, because it belongs to the body; so also death is in like manner temporary and has a fixed end, because it affects the body.

**Chap. XI.—Of the Last Times, and of the Soul and Body.**

Therefore, when the times which God has appointed for death shall be completed, death itself shall be ended. And because temporal death follows temporal life, it follows that souls rise again to everlasting life, because temporal death has received an end. Again, as the life of the soul is everlasting, in which it receives the divine and unspeakable fruits of its immortality; also its death must be eternal, in which it suffers perpetual punishments and infinite torments for its faults. Therefore things are in this position, that they who are happy in this life, pertaining to the body and the earth, are about to be miserable forever, because they have already enjoyed the good things which they preferred, which happens to those who adore false gods and neglect the true God. In the next place, they who, following righteousness, have been miserable, and despised, and poor in this life, and have often been harassed with insults and injuries on account of righteousness itself, because virtue cannot otherwise be attained, are about to be always happy, that since they have already endured evils, they may also enjoy goods. Which plainly happens to those who, having despised gods of the earth and frail goods, follow the heavenly religion of God, whose goods are everlasting, as He Himself who gave them. What shall I say of the works of the body and soul? Do not they show that the soul is not subject to death? For, as to the body, since it is itself frail and mortal, whatever works it contrives are equally perishable. For Tullius says that there is nothing which is wrought by the hands of man which is not at some time reduced to destruction, either through injury caused by men, or through length of time, which is the destroyer of all things.

But truly we see that the productions of the mind are immortal. For as many as, devoting themselves to the contempt of present things, have handed down to memory the monuments of their genius and great deeds, have plainly gained by these an imperishable name for their mind and virtue. Therefore, if the deeds of the body are mortal for this reason, because the body itself is mortal, it follows that the soul is shown to be immortal from this, because we see that its productions are not mortal. In the same manner also, the desires of the body and of the soul declare that the one is mortal, the other everlasting. For the body desires nothing except what is temporal, that is, food, drink, clothing, rest, and pleasure; and it cannot desire or attain to these very things without the assent and assistance of the soul. But the soul of itself desires many things which do not extend to the duty or enjoyment of the body; and those are not frail, but eternal, as the fame of virtue, as the remembrance of the name. For the soul even in opposition to the body desires the worship of God, which consists in abstinence from desires and lusts, in the enduring of pain, in the contempt of death. From which it is credible that the soul does not perish, but is separated from the body, because the body can do nothing without the soul, but the soul can do many and great things without the body. Why should I mention that those things which are visible to the eyes, and capable of being touched by the hand, cannot be eternal, because they admit of external violence; but those things which neither come under the touch nor under the sight, but are apparent *only* in their force and method and effect, are eternal because they suffer no violence from without? But if the body is mortal on this account, because it is equally open to the sight and to the touch, therefore the soul is immortal for this reason, because it can be neither touched nor seen.

## Chap. XII.—Of the Soul and the Body, and of Their Union and Separation and Return.

Now let us refute the arguments of those who maintain the opposite opinions, which Lucretius has related in his third book. Since, he says, the soul is born together with the body, it must necessarily die with the body. But the two cases are not similar. For the body is solid, and capable of being grasped both by the eyes and the hand; but the soul is slight, and eluding the touch and sight. The body is formed from the earth, and made firm; the soul has in it nothing concrete, nothing of earthly weight, as Plato maintained. For it could not have such great force, such great skill, such great rapidity, unless it derived its origin from heaven. The body, therefore, since it is made up of a ponderous and corruptible element, and is tangible and visible, is corrupted and dies; nor is it able to repel violence, because it comes under the sight and under the touch; but the soul, which by its slightness avoids all touch, can be dissolved by no attack. Therefore, although they are joined and connected together from birth, and the one which is formed of earthly material is, as it were, the vessel of the other, which is drawn out from heavenly fineness, when any violence has separated the two, which separation is called death, then each returns into its own nature; that which was of earth is resolved into earth; that which is of heavenly breath remains fixed, and flourishes always, since the divine spirit is everlasting. In fine, the same Lucretius, forgetting what he asserted, and what dogma he defended, wrote these verses:—

"That also which before was from the earth passes back into the earth, and that which was sent from the borders of ether is carried again by the quarters of heaven."

But this language was not for him to employ, who contended that souls perished with the bodies; but he was overcome by the truth, and the true system stole upon him unawares. Moreover, that very inference which he draws, that the soul suffers dissolution, that is, that it perishes together with the body, since they are produced together, is both false, and is capable of being turned to the opposite direction. For the body does not perish together with the soul; but when the soul departs it remains entire for many days, and frequently by medical preparations it remains entire for a very long time. For if they both perished together, as they are produced together, the soul would not hastily depart and desert the body, but both would be dispersed alike at one point of time; and the body also, while the breath still remained in it, would dissolve and perish as quickly as the soul departs: yes, truly, the body, being dissolved, the soul would vanish, as moisture poured forth from a broken vessel. For if the earthly and frail body after the departure of the soul does not immediately flow away and waste into earth, from which it has its origin, therefore the soul, which is not frail, endures to eternity, since its origin is eternal. He says, since the understanding increases in boys, and is vigorous in young men, and is lessened in the aged, it is evident that it is mortal. First, the soul is not the same thing as the mind; for it is one thing that we live, another that we reflect. For it is the mind of those who are asleep which is at rest, not the soul; and in those who are mad, the mind is extinguished, the soul remains; and therefore they are not said to be without a soul, but to be deprived of their mind. Therefore the mind, that is, the understanding, is either increased or lessened according to age. The soul is always in its own condition; and from the time when it receives the power of breathing, it remains the same even to the end, until, being sent forth from the confinement of the body, it flies back to its own abode. In the next place, the soul, although inspired by God, yet, because it is shut up in a dark abode of earthly flesh, does not possess knowledge, which belongs to divinity. Therefore it hears and learns all things, and receives wisdom by learning and hearing; and old age does not lessen wisdom, but increases it, if the age of youth has been passed in virtue; and if excessive old age shall have enfeebled the limbs, it is not the fault of the mind if the sight has vanished, if the tongue has become benumbed, if the hearing has grown deaf, but it is the fault of the body. But, it is said, the memory fails. What wonder, if the mind is oppressed by the ruin of the falling house, and forgets the past, not about to be divine on any other condition than if it shall have escaped the prison in which it is confined?

But the soul, he says, is also subject to pain and grief, and loses its senses through drunkenness, whence it is evidently frail and mortal. On this account, therefore, virtue and wisdom are necessary, that both grief, which is contracted by the suffering and the sight of unworthy objects, may be repelled by fortitude, and that pleasure may be overcome, not only by abstaining from drinking, but also from other things. For if it be destitute of virtue, if it be given up to pleasure, and thus rendered effeminate, it will become subject to death, since virtue, as we have shown, is the contriver of immortality, as pleasure is of death. But death, as I have set forth, does not entirely extinguish and destroy, but visits with eternal torments. For the soul cannot entirely perish, since it received its origin from the Spirit of God, which is eternal. The soul, he says, is sensible even of disease of the body, and suffers forgetfulness of itself; and as it grows ill, so also it is often healed. This is therefore the reason why virtue is especially to be used, that the mind—not the soul—may not be harassed by any pain of the body, or undergo oblivion of itself. And since this has its seat in a certain part of the body, when any violence of disease has vitiated that part, it is moved from its place; and as though shaken, it departs from its station, about to return when a cure and health shall have remodeled its abode. For, since the soul is united with the body, if it is destitute of virtue, it grows sick by the contagion of the body, and from sharing its frailty the weakness extends to the mind. But when it shall be disunited from the body it will flourish by itself; nor will it now be assailed by any condition of frailty, because it has laid aside its frail covering. As the eye, he says, when torn out and separated from the body, can see nothing, so also the soul, when separated, can perceive nothing, because it is itself also a part of the body. This is false, and dissimilar to the case supposed; for the soul is not a part of the body, but in the body. As that which is contained in a vessel is not a part of the vessel, and these things which are in a house are not said to be a part of the house; so the mind is not a part of the body, because the body is either the vessel or the receptacle of the soul.

Now, that is a much more empty argument which says that the soul appears to be mortal because it is not quickly sent forth from the body, but gradually unfolds itself from all the members, beginning from the extremity of the feet; as though, if it were eternal, it would burst forth in a single moment of time, which takes place in those who die by the sword. But they who are slain by disease are longer in breathing forth their spirit, so that as the limbs grow cold the soul is breathed forth. For, since it is contained in the material of the blood, as light is in the oil, that material being consumed by the heat of fevers, the extremities of the limbs must grow cold; since the more slender veins are extended into the extremities of the body, and the extreme and smaller streams are dried up when the fountain spring fails. It must not, however, be supposed that, because the perception of the body fails, the sensibility of the soul is extinguished and perishes. For it is not the soul that becomes senseless when the body fails, but it is the body which becomes senseless when the soul takes its departure, because it draws all sensibility with it. But since the soul by its presence gives sensibility to the body, and causes it to live, it is impossible that it should not live and perceive by itself, since it is in itself both consciousness and life. For as to that which says,

> "But if our mind were immortal, it would not when dying complain so much of its dissolution as it would rejoice in passing abroad and quitting its vesture like a snake,"

I never saw any one who complained of his dissolution in death; but he perhaps had seen some Epicurean philosophizing even in death, and with his latest breath discoursing about his dissolution.

How can it be known whether he feels that he is in a state of dissolution, or that he is being set free from the body, when his tongue grows dumb at his departure? For as long as he perceives and has the power of speech, he is not yet dissolved; when he has suffered dissolution, he is now unable either to perceive or to speak, so that either he is not yet able to complain of his dissolution, or he is no longer able. But, it is said, he understands before he undergoes dissolution, that he must undergo it. Why should I mention that we see many of the dying, not complaining that they are undergoing dissolution, but testifying that they are passing out, and setting forth on their journey and walking? And they signify this by gesture, or if they still are able, they express it also by their voice. From which it is evident that it is not a dissolution which takes place, but a separation; and this shows that the soul continues to exist. Other arguments of the Epicurean system are opposed to Pythagoras, who contends that souls migrate from bodies worn out with old age and death, and gain admission into those which are new and recently born; and that the same souls are always reproduced at one time in a man, at another time in a sheep, at another in a wild beast, at another in a bird; and that they are immortal on this account, because they often change their abodes, consisting of various and dissimilar bodies. And this opinion of a senseless man, since it is ridiculous and more worthy of a stage-player than of a school of philosophy, ought not even to have been refuted seriously; for he who does this appears to be afraid lest anyone should believe it. Therefore we must pass by those things which have been discussed in behalf of falsehood against falsehood; it is sufficient to have refuted those things which are against the truth.

**Chap. XIII.—Of the Soul, and the Testimonies Concerning Its Eternity.**

I have made it evident, as I think, that the soul is not subject to dissolution. It remains that I bring forward witnesses by whose authority my arguments may be confirmed. And I will not now allege the testimony of the prophets, whose system and divination consist in this alone, the teaching that man was created for the worship of God, and for receiving immortality from Him; but I will rather bring forward those whom they who reject the truth cannot but believe. Hermes, describing the nature of man, that he might show how he was made by God, introduced this statement: "And the same out of two natures—the immortal and the mortal—made one nature, that of man, making the same partly immortal, and partly mortal; and bringing this, he placed it in the midst, between that nature which was divine and immortal, and that which was mortal and changeable, that seeing all things, he may admire all things." But someone may perhaps reckon him in the number of the philosophers, although he has been placed among the gods, and honored by the Egyptians under the name of Mercury, and may give no more authority to him than to Plato or Pythagoras. Let us therefore seek for greater testimony. A certain Polites asked Apollo of Miletus whether the soul remains after death or goes to dissolution; and he replied in these verses:—

"As long as the soul is bound by fetters to the body, perceiving corruptible sufferings, it yields to mortal pains; but when, after the wasting of the body, it has found a very swift dissolution of mortality, it is altogether borne into the air, never growing old, and it remains always uninjured; for the first-born providence of God made this disposition."

What do the Sibylline poems say? Do they not declare that this is so, when they say that the time will come when God will judge the living and the dead?—whose authority we will hereafter bring forward. Therefore the opinion entertained by Democritus, and Epicurus, and Dicæarchus concerning the dissolution of the soul is false; and they would not venture to speak concerning the destruction of souls, in the presence of any magician, who knew that souls are called forth from the lower regions by certain incantations, and that they are at hand, and afford themselves to be seen by human eyes, and speak, and foretell future events; and if they should thus venture, they would be overpowered by the fact itself, and by proofs presented to them. But because they did not comprehend the nature of the soul, which is so subtle that it escapes the eyes of the human mind, they said that it perishes. What of Aristoxenus, who denied that there is any soul at all, even while it lives in the body? But as on the lyre harmonious sound, and the strain which musicians call harmony, is produced by the tightening of the strings, so he thought that the power of perception existed in bodies from the joining together of the vitals, and from the vigor of the limbs; than which nothing can be said more senseless. Truly he had his eyes uninjured, but his heart was blind, with which he did not see that he lived, and had the mind by which he had conceived that very thought. But this has happened to many philosophers that they did not believe in the existence of any object which is not apparent to the eyes; whereas the sight of the mind ought to be much clearer than that of the body, for perceiving those things the force and nature of which are rather felt than seen.

### Chap. XIV.—Of the First and Last Times of the World.

Since we have spoken of the immortality of the soul, it follows that we teach how and when it is given to man; that in this also they may see the errors of their perverseness and folly, who imagine that some mortals have become gods by the decrees and dogmas of mortals; either because they had invented arts, or because they had taught the use of certain productions of the earth, or because they had discovered things useful for the life of men, or because they had slain savage beasts. How far these things were from deserving immortality we have both shown in the former books, and we will now show, that it may be evident that it is righteousness alone which procures for man eternal life, and that it is God alone who bestows the reward of eternal life. For they who are said to have been immortalized by their merits, inasmuch as they possessed neither righteousness nor any true virtue, did not obtain for themselves immortality, but death by their sins and lusts; nor did they deserve the reward of heaven, but the punishment of hell, which impends over them, together with all their worshippers. And I show that the time of this judgment draws near, that the due reward may be given to the righteous, and the deserved punishment may be inflicted on the wicked.

Plato and many others of the philosophers, since they were ignorant of the origin of all things, and of that primal period at which the world was made, said that many thousands of ages had passed since this beautiful arrangement of the world was completed; and in this they perhaps followed the Chaldeans, who, as Cicero has related in his first book respecting divination, foolishly say that they possess comprised in their memorials four hundred and seventy thousand years; in which matter, because they thought that they could not be convicted, they believed that they were at liberty to speak falsely. But we, whom the Holy Scriptures instruct to the knowledge of the truth, know the beginning and the end of the world, respecting which we will now speak in the end of our work, since we have explained respecting the beginning in the second book. Therefore let the philosophers, who enumerate thousands of ages from the beginning of the world, know that the six thousandth year is not yet completed, and that when this number is completed the consummation must take place, and the condition of human affairs be remodeled for the better, the proof of which must first be related, that the matter itself may be plain. God completed the world and this admirable work of nature in the space of six days, as is contained in the secrets of Holy Scripture, and consecrated the seventh day, on which He had rested from His works. But this is the Sabbath-day, which in the language of the Hebrews received its name from the number, whence the seventh is the legitimate and complete number. For there are seven days, by the revolutions of which in order the circles of years are made up; and there are seven stars which do not set, and seven luminaries which are called planets, whose differing and unequal movements are believed to cause the varieties of circumstances and times.

Therefore, since all the works of God were completed in six days, the world must continue in its present state through six ages, that is, six thousand years. For the great day of God is limited by a circle of a thousand years, as the prophet shows, who says "In Thy sight, O Lord, a thousand years are as one day." And as God labored during those six days in creating such great works, so His religion and truth must labor during these six thousand years, while wickedness prevails and bears rule. And again, since God, having finished His works, rested the seventh day and blessed it, at the end of the six thousandth year all wickedness must be abolished from the earth, and righteousness reign for a thousand years; and there must be tranquility and rest from the labors which the world now has long endured. But how that will come to pass I will explain in its order. We have often said that lesser things and things of small importance are figures and previous shadowing forth of great things; as this day of ours, which is bounded by the rising and the setting of the sun, is a representation of that great day to which the circuit of a thousand years affixes its limits.

In the same manner also the fashioning of the earthly man held forth to the future the formation of the heavenly people. For as, when all things were completed which were contrived for the use of man, last of all, on the sixth day, He made man also, and introduced him into this world as into a home now carefully prepared; so now on the great sixth day the true man is being formed by the word of God, that is, a holy people is fashioned for righteousness by the doctrine and precepts of God. And as then a mortal and imperfect man was formed from the earth, that he might live a thousand years in this world; so now from this earthly age is formed a perfect man, that being quickened by God, he may bear rule in this same world through a thousand years. But in what manner the consummation will take place, and what end awaits the affairs of men, if any one shall examine the divine writings he will ascertain. But the voices also of prophets of the world, agreeing with the heavenly, announce the end and overthrow of all things after a short time, describing as it were the last old age of the wearied and wasting world. But the things which are said by prophets and seers to be about to happen before that last ending comes upon the world, I will subjoin, being collected and accumulated from all quarters.

### Chap. XV.—Of the Devastation of the World and Change of the Empires.

It is contained in the mysteries of the sacred writings that a prince of the Hebrews, compelled by want of corn, passed into Egypt with all his family and relatives. And when his posterity, remaining long in Egypt, had increased into a great nation, and were oppressed by the heavy and intolerable yoke of slavery, God smote Egypt with an incurable stroke, and freed His people, leading them through the midst of the sea, when, the waves being cut asunder and parted on either side, the people went over on dry ground. And the king of the Egyptians endeavoring to follow them as they fled, the sea returning to its place, he was cut off, with all his people. And this deed so illustrious and so wonderful, although for the present it displayed to men the power of God, was also a foreshadowing and figure of a greater deed, which the same God was about to perform at the last consummation of the times, for He will free His people from the oppressive bondage of the world. But since at that time the people of God were one, and in one nation only, Egypt only was smitten. But now, because the people of God are collected out of all languages, and dwell among all nations, and are oppressed by those bearing rule over them, it must come to pass that all nations, that is, the whole world, be beaten with heavenly stripes, that the righteous people, who are worshippers of God, may be set free. And as then signs were given by which the coming destruction was shown to the Egyptians, so at the last time wonderful prodigies will take place throughout all the elements of the world, by which the impending destruction may be understood by all nations.

Therefore, as the end of this world approaches, the condition of human affairs must undergo a change, and through the prevalence of wickedness become worse; so that now these times of ours, in which iniquity and impiety have increased even to the highest degree, may be judged happy and almost golden in comparison of that incurable evil. For righteousness will so decrease, and impiety, avarice, desire, and lust will so greatly increase, that if there shall then happen to be any good men, they will be a prey to the wicked, and will be harassed on all sides by the unrighteous; while the wicked alone will be in opulence, but the good will be afflicted in all calumnies and in want. All justice will be confounded, and the laws will be destroyed. No one will then have anything except that which has been gained or defended by the hand: boldness and violence will possess all things. There will be no faith among men, nor peace, nor kindness, nor shame, nor truth; and thus also there will be neither security, nor government, nor any rest from evils. For all the earth will be in a state of tumult; wars will everywhere rage; all nations will be in arms, and will oppose one another; neighboring states will carry on conflicts with each other; and first of all, Egypt will pay the penalties of her foolish superstitions, and will be covered with blood as if with a river. Then the sword will traverse the world, mowing down everything, and laying low all things as a crop. And—my mind dreads to relate it, but I will relate it, because it is about to happen— the cause of this desolation and confusion will be this; because the Roman name, by which the world is now ruled, will be taken away from the earth, and the government return to Asia; and the East will again bear rule, and the West be reduced to servitude. Nor ought it to appear wonderful to anyone, if a kingdom founded with such vastness, and so long increased by so many and such men, and in short strengthened by such great resources, shall nevertheless at some time fall. There is nothing prepared by human strength which cannot equally he destroyed by human strength, since the works of mortals are mortal. Thus also other kingdoms in former times, though they had long flourished, were nevertheless destroyed. For it is related that the Egyptians, and Persians, and Greeks, and Assyrians had the government of the world; and after the destruction of them all, the chief power came to the Romans also. And inasmuch as they excel all other kingdoms in magnitude, with so much greater an overthrow will they fall, because those buildings which are higher than others have more weight for a downfall.

Seneca therefore not unskillfully divided the times of the Roman city by ages. For he said that at first was its infancy under King Romulus, by whom Rome was brought into being, and as it were educated; then its boyhood under the other kings, by whom it was increased and fashioned with more numerous systems of instruction and institutions; but at length, in the reign of Tarquinius, when now it had begun as it were to be grown up, it did not endure slavery; and having thrown off the yoke of a haughty tyranny, it preferred to obey laws rather than kings; and when its youth was terminated by the end of the Punic war, then at length with confirmed strength it began to be manly. For when Carthage was taken away, which was long its rival in power, it stretched out its hands by land and sea over the whole world, until, having subdued all kings and nations, when the materials for war now failed, it abused its strength, by which it destroyed itself. This was its first old age, when, lacerated by civil wars and oppressed by intestine evil, it again fell back to the government of a single ruler, as it were revolving to a second infancy. For, having lost the liberty which it had defended under the guidance and authority of Brutus, it so grew old, as though it had no strength to support itself, unless it depended on the aid of its rulers. But if these things are so, what remains, except that death follow old age? And that it will so come to pass, the predictions of the prophets briefly announce under the cover of other names, so that no one can easily understand them. Nevertheless the Sibyls openly say that Rome is doomed to perish, and that indeed by the judgment of God, because it held His name in hatred; and being the enemy of righteousness, it destroyed the people who kept the truth. Hystaspes also, who was a very ancient king of the Medes, from whom also the river which is now called Hydaspes received its name, handed down to the memory of posterity a wonderful dream upon the interpretation of a boy who uttered divinations, announcing long before the founding of the Trojan nation, that the Roman empire and name would be taken away from the world.

## CHAP. XVI.—OF THE DEVASTATION of the World, and Its Prophetic Omens.

But, test anyone should think this incredible, I will show how it will come to pass. First, the kingdom will be enlarged, and the chief power, dispersed among many and divided, will be diminished. Then civil discords will perpetually be sown; nor will there be any rest from deadly wars, until ten kings arise at the same time, who will divide the world, not to govern, but to consume it. These, having increased their armies to an immense extent, and having deserted the cultivation of the fields, which is the beginning of overthrow and disaster, will lay waste and break in pieces and consume all things. Then a most powerful enemy will suddenly arise against him from the extreme boundaries of the northern region, who, having destroyed three of that number who shall then be in possession of Asia, shall be admitted into alliance by the others, and shall be constituted prince of all. He shall harass the world with an intolerable rule; shall mingle things divine and human; shall contrive things impious to relate, and detestable; shall meditate new designs in his breast, that he may establish the government for himself: he will change the laws, and appoint his own; he will contaminate, plunder, spoil, and put to death. And at length, the name being changed and the seat of government being transferred, confusion and the disturbance of mankind will follow. Then, in truth, a detestable and abominable time shall come, in which life shall be pleasant to none of men.

Cities shall be utterly overthrown, and shall perish; not only by fire and the sword, but also by continual earthquakes and overflowing of waters, and by frequent diseases and repeated famines. For the atmosphere will be tainted, and become corrupt and pestilential—at one time by unseasonable rains, at another by barren drought, now by colds, and now by excessive heats. Nor will the earth give its fruit to man: no field, or tree, or vine will produce anything; but after they have given the greatest hope in the blossom, they will fail in the fruit. Fountains also shall be dried up, together with the rivers; so that there shall not be a sufficient supply for drinking; and waters shall be changed into blood or bitterness. On account of these things, beasts shall fail on the land, and birds in the air, and fishes in the sea. Wonderful prodigies also in heaven shall confound the minds of men with the greatest terrors, and the trains of comets, and the darkness of the sun, and the color of the moon, and the gliding of the falling stars. Nor, however, will these things take place in the accustomed manner; but there will suddenly appear stars unknown and unseen by the eyes; the sun will be perpetually darkened, so that there will be scarcely any distinction between the night and the day; the moon will now fail, not for three hours only, but overspread with perpetual blood, will go through extraordinary movements, so that it will not be easy for man to ascertain the courses of the heavenly bodies or the system of the times; for there will either be summer in the winter, or winter in the summer. Then the year will be shortened, and the month diminished, and the day contracted into a short space; and stars shall fall in great numbers, so that all the heaven will appear dark without any lights. The loftiest mountains also will fall, and be levelled with the plains; the sea will be rendered unnavigable.

And that nothing may be wanting to the evils of men and the earth, the trumpet shall be heard from heaven, which the Sibyl foretells in this manner:—

"The trumpet from heaven shall utter its wailing voice."

And then all shall tremble and quake at that mournful sound. But then, through the anger of God against the men who have not known righteousness, the sword and fire, famine and disease, shall reign; and, above all things, fear always overhanging. Then they shall call upon God, but He will not hear them; death shall be desired, but it will not come; not even shall night give rest to their fear, nor shall sleep approach to their eyes, but anxiety and watchfulness shall consume the souls of men; they shall deplore and lament, and gnash their teeth; they shall congratulate the dead, and bewail the living. Through these and many other evils there shall be desolation on the earth, and the world shall be disfigured and deserted, which is thus expressed in the verses of the Sibyl:—

"The world shall be despoiled of beauty, through the destruction of men."

For the human race will be so consumed, that scarcely the tenth part of men will be left; and from whence a thousand had gone forth, scarcely a hundred will go forth. Of the worshippers of God also, two parts will perish; and the third part, which shall have been proved, will remain.

**Chap. XVII.—Of the False Prophet, and the Hardships of the Righteous, and His Destruction.**

But I will more plainly set forth the manner in which this happens. When the close of the times draws nigh, a great prophet shall be sent from God to turn men to the knowledge of God, and he shall receive the power of doing wonderful things. Wherever men shall not hear him, he will shut up the heaven, and cause it to withhold its rains; he will turn their water into blood, and torment them with thirst and hunger; and if anyone shall endeavor to injure him, fire shall come forth out of his mouth, and shall burn that man. By these prodigies and powers he shall turn many to the worship of God; and when his works shall be accomplished, another king shall arise out of Syria, born from an evil spirit, the over thrower and destroyer of the human race, who shall destroy that which is left by the former evil, together with himself. He shall fight against the prophet of God, and shall overcome, and slay him, and shall suffer him to lie unburied; but after the third day he shall come to life again; and while all look on and wonder, he shall be caught up into heaven. But that king will not only be most disgraceful in himself, but he will also be a prophet of lies; and he will constitute and call himself God, and will order himself to be worshipped as the Son of God; and power will be given him to do signs and wonders, by the sight of which he may entice men to adore him. He will command fire to come down from heaven, and the sun to stand and leave his course, and an image to speak; and these things shall be done at his word,—by which miracles many even of the wise shall be enticed by him. Then he will attempt to destroy the temple of God, and persecute the righteous people; and there will be distress and tribulation, such as there never has been from the beginning of the world.

As many as shall believe him and unite themselves to him, shall be marked by him as sheep; but they who shall refuse his mark will either flee to the mountains, or, being seized, will be slain with studied tortures. He will also enwrap righteous men with the books of the prophets, and thus burn them; and power will be given him to desolate the whole earth for forty-two months. That will be the time in which righteousness shall be cast out, and innocence be hated; in which the wicked shall prey upon the good as enemies; neither law, nor order, nor military discipline shall be preserved; no one shall reverence hoary locks, nor recognize the duty of piety, nor pity sex or infancy; all things shall be confounded and mixed together against right, and against the laws of nature. Thus the earth shall be laid waste, as though by one common robbery. When these things shall so happen, then the righteous and the followers of truth shall separate themselves from the wicked, and flee into solitudes. And when he hears of this, the impious king, inflamed with anger, will come with a great army, and bringing up all his forces, will surround all the mountain in which the righteous shall be situated, that he may seize them. But they, when they shall see themselves to be shut in on all sides and besieged, will call upon God with a loud voice, and implore the aid of heaven; and God shall hear them, and send from heaven a great king to rescue and free them, and destroy all the wicked with fire and sword.

## Chap. XVIII.—Of the Fortunes of the World at the Last Time, and of the Things Foretold by the Soothsayers.

That these things will thus take place, all the prophets have announced from the inspiration of God, and also the soothsayers at the instigation of the demons. For Hystaspes, whom I have named above, having described the iniquity of this last time, says that the pious and faithful, being separated from the wicked, will stretch forth their hands to heaven with weeping and mourning, and will implore the protection of Jupiter: that Jupiter will look to the earth, and hear the voices of men, and will destroy the wicked. All which things are true except one, that he attributed to Jupiter those things which God will do. But that also was withdrawn from the account, not without fraud on the part of the demons, viz., that the Son of God would then be sent, who, having destroyed all the wicked, would set at liberty the pious. Which, however, Hermes did not conceal. For in that book which is entitled the *Complete Treatise*, after an enumeration of the evils concerning which we have spoken, he added these things: "But when these things thus come to pass, then He who is Lord, and Father, and God, and the Creator of the first and one God, looking upon what is done, and opposing to the disorder His own will, that is, goodness, and recalling the wandering and cleansing wickedness, partly inundating it with much water, and partly burning it with most rapid fire, and sometimes pressing it with wars and pestilences, He brought His world to its ancient state and restored it." The Sibyls also show that it would not be otherwise than that the Son of God should be sent by His supreme Father, to set free the righteous from the hands of the wicked, and to destroy the unrighteous, together with their cruel tyrants. One of whom thus wrote:—

"He shall come also, wishing to destroy the city of the blest; and a king sent against him from the gods shall slay all the great kings and chief men: then judgment shall thus come from the Immortal to men."

Also another Sibyl:—

"And then God shall send a king from the sun, who shall cause all the earth to cease from disastrous war."

And again another:—

"He will take away the intolerable yoke of slavery which is placed on our neck, and he will do away with impious laws and violent chains."

## Chap. XIX.—Of the Advent of Christ to Judgment, and of the Overcoming of the False Prophet.

The world therefore being oppressed, since the resources of men shall be insufficient for the overthrow of a tyranny of immense strength, inasmuch as it will press upon the captive world with great armies of robbers, that calamity so great will stand in need of divine assistance. Therefore God, being aroused both by the doubtful danger and by the wretched lamentation of the righteous, will immediately send a deliverer. Then the middle of the heaven shall be laid open in the dead and darkness of the night, that the light of the descending God may be manifest in all the world as lightning: of which the Sibyl spoke in these words:—

"When He shall come, there will be fire and darkness in the midst of the black night."

This is the night which is celebrated by us in watchfulness on account of the coming of our King and God: of which night there is a twofold meaning; because in it He then received life when He suffered, and hereafter He is about to receive the kingdom of the world. For He is the Deliverer, and Judge, and Avenger, and King, and God, whom we call Christ, who before He descends will give this sign: There shall suddenly fall from heaven a sword, that the righteous may know that the leader of the sacred warfare is about to descend; and He shall descend with a company of angels to the middle of the earth, and there shall go before Him an unquenchable fire, and the power of the angels shall deliver into the hands of the just that multitude which has surrounded the mountain, and they shall be slain from the third hour until the evening, and blood shall flow like a torrent; and all his forces being destroyed, the wicked one shall alone escape, and his power shall perish from him.

Now this is he who is called Antichrist; but he shall falsely call himself Christ, and shall fight against the truth, and being overcome shall flee; and shall often renew the war, and often be conquered, until in the fourth battle, all the wicked being slain, subdued, and captured, he shall at length pay the penalty of his crimes. But other princes also and tyrants who have harassed the world, together with him, shall be led in chains to the king; and he shall rebuke them, and reprove them, and upbraid them with their crimes, and condemn them, and consign them to deserved tortures. Thus, wickedness being extinguished and impiety suppressed, the world will be at rest, which having been subject to error and wickedness for so many ages, endured dreadful slavery. No longer shall gods made by the hands be worshipped; but the images being thrust out from their temples and couches, shall be given to the fire, and shall be burnt, together with their wonderful gifts: which also the Sibyl, in accordance with the prophets, announced as about to take place:—

"But mortals shall break in pieces the images and all the wealth."

The Erythræan Sibyl also made the same promise:—

"And the works made by the hand of the gods shall be burnt up."

**Chap. XX.—Of the Judgment of Christ, of Christians, and of the Soul.**

After these things the lower regions shall be opened, and the dead shall rise again, on whom the same King and God shall pass judgment, to whom the supreme Father shall give the great power both of judging and of reigning. And respecting this judgment and reign, it is thus found in the Erythræan Sibyl:—

"When this shall receive its fated accomplishment, and the judgment of the immortal God shall now come to mortals, the great judgment shall come upon men, and the beginning."

Then in another:—

"And then the gaping earth shall show a Tartarean chaos; and all kings shall come to the judgment-seat of God."

And in another place in the same:—

"Rolling along the heavens, I will open the caverns of the earth; and then I will raise the dead, loosing fate and the sting of death; and afterwards I will call them into judgment, judging the life of pious and impious men."

Not all men, however, shall then be judged by God, but those only who have been exercised in the religion of God. For they who have not known God, since sentence cannot be passed upon them for their acquittal, are already judged and condemned, since the Holy Scriptures testify that the wicked shall not arise to judgment. Therefore they who have known God shall be judged, and their deeds, that is, their evil works, shall be compared and weighed against their good ones: so that if those which are good and just are more and weighty, they may be given to a life of blessedness; but if the evil exceed, they may be condemned to punishment. Here, perhaps, someone will say, If the soul is immortal, how is it represented as capable of suffering, and sensible of punishment? For if it shall be punished on account of its deserts, it is plain that it will be sensible of pain, and even of death. If it is not liable to death, not even to pain, it follows that it is not capable of suffering.

This question or argument is thus met by the Stoics: that the souls of men continue to exist, and are not annihilated by the intervention of death: that the souls, moreover, of those who have been just, being pure, and incapable of suffering, and happy, return to the heavenly abodes from which they had their origin, or are borne to some happy plains, where they may enjoy wonderful pleasures; but that the wicked, since they have defiled themselves with evil passions, have a kind of middle nature, between that of an immortal and a mortal, and have something of weakness, from the contagion of the flesh; and being enslaved to its desires and lusts, they contract an indelible stain and earthly blot; and when this has become entirely inherent through length of time, souls are given over to its nature, so that, though they cannot altogether be extinguished, inasmuch as they are from God, nevertheless they become liable to torment through the taint of the body, which being burnt in by means of sins, produces a feeling of pain. Which sentiment is thus expressed by the poet:—

> "Nay, when at last the life has fled,
> And left the body cold and dead,
> E'en then there passes not away
> The painful heritage of clay:
> Full many a long contracted stain
> Perforce must linger deep in grain.
> So penal sufferings they endure
> For ancient crime, to make them pure."

These things are near to the truth. For the soul, when separated from the body, is, as the same poet says, such as

> "No vision of the drowsy night,
> No airy current half so light,"

because it is a spirit, and by its very slightness incapable of being perceived, but only by us who are corporeal but capable of being perceived by God, since it belongs to Him to be able to do all things.

**Chap. XXI.—Of the Torments and Punishments of Souls.**

First of all, therefore, we say that the power of God is so great, that He perceives even incorporeal things, and manages them as He will. For even angels fear God, because they can be chastised by Him in some unspeakable manner; and devils dread Him, because they are tormented and punished by Him. What wonder is it, therefore, if souls, though they are immortal, are nevertheless capable of suffering at the hand of God? For since they have nothing solid and tangible in themselves, they can suffer no violence from solid and corporeal beings; but because they live in their spirits only, they are capable of being handled by God alone, whose energy and substance is spiritual. But, however, the sacred writings inform us in what manner the wicked are to undergo punishment. For because they have committed sins in their bodies, they will again be clothed with flesh, that they may make atonement in their bodies; and yet it will not be that flesh with which God clothed man, like this our earthly body, but indestructible, and abiding forever, that it may be able to hold out against tortures and everlasting fire, the nature of which is different from this fire of ours, which we use for the necessary purposes of life, and which is extinguished unless it be sustained by the fuel of some material. But that divine fire always lives by itself, and flourishes without any nourishment; nor has it any smoke mixed with it, but it is pure and liquid, and fluid, after the manner of water. For it is not urged upwards by any force, as our fire, which the taint of the earthly body, by which it is held, and smoke intermingled, compels to leap forth, and to fly upwards to the nature of heaven, with a tremulous movement.

The same divine fire, therefore, with one and the same force and power, will both burn the wicked and will form them again, and will replace as much as it shall consume of their bodies, and will supply itself with eternal nourishment: which the poets transferred to the vulture of Tityus. Thus, without any wasting of bodies, which regain their substance, it will only burn and affect them with a sense of pain. But when He shall have judged the righteous, He will also try them with fire. Then they whose sins shall exceed either in weight or in number, shall be scorched by the fire and burnt: but they whom full justice and maturity of virtue has imbued will not perceive that fire; for they have something of God in themselves which repels and rejects the violence of the flame. So great is the force of innocence, that the flame shrinks from it without doing harm; which has received from God this power, that it burns the wicked, and is under the command of the righteous. Nor, however, let anyone imagine that souls are immediately judged after death. For all are detained in one and a common place of confinement, until the arrival of the time in which the great Judge shall make an investigation of their deserts. Then they whose piety shall have been approved of will receive the reward of immortality; but they whose sins and crimes shall have been brought to light will not rise again, but will be hidden in the same darkness with the wicked, being destined to certain punishment.

## Chap. XXII.—Of the Error of the Poets, and the Return of the Soul from the Lower Regions.

Some imagine that these things are figments of the poets, not knowing whence the poets received them, and they say that these things are impossible; and it is no wonder that it so appears to them. For the matter is related by the poets in a manner which is different from the truth; for although they are much more ancient than the historians and orators, and other kinds of writers, yet because they were ignorant of the secret of the divine mystery, and mention of a future resurrection had reached them by an obscure rumor, yet they handed it down, when carelessly and lightly heard, after the manner of a feigned story. And yet they also testified that they did not follow a sure authority, but mere opinion, as Maro, who says,

"What ear has heard let tongue make known."

Although, therefore, they have partly corrupted the secrets of the truth, yet the matter itself is found to be truer, because it partly agrees with the prophets: which is sufficient for us as a proof of the matter. Yet some reason is contained in their error. For when the prophets proclaimed with continual announcements that the Son of God was about to judge the dead, and this announcement did not escape their notice; inasmuch as they supposed that there was no other ruler of heaven but Jupiter, they reported that the son of Jupiter was king in the lower regions, but not Apollo, or Liber, or Mercurius, who are supposed to be gods of heaven, but one who was both mortal and just, either Minos, or Æacus, or Rhadamanthus. Therefore with poetic license they corrupted that which they had received; or, the opinion being scattered through different mouths and various discourses, changed the truth. For inasmuch as they foretold that, when a thousand years had been passed in the lower regions, they should again be restored to life, as Maro said:—

> "All these, when centuries ten times told
> The wheel of destiny have rolled,
> The voice divine from far and wide
> Calls up to Lethe's river side,
> That earthward they may pass once more,
> Remembering not the things before,
> And with a blind propension yearn
> To fleshly bodies to return:"

this matter escaped their notice, that the dead will rise again, not after a thousand years from their death, but that, when again restored to life, they may reign with God a thousand years. For God will come, that, having cleansed the world from all defilement, He may restore the souls of the righteous to their renewed bodies, and raise them to everlasting blessedness. Therefore the other things are true, except the water of oblivion, which they feigned on this account, that no one might make this objection: why, therefore, did they not remember that they were at one time alive, or who they were, or what things they accomplished? But nevertheless it is not thought probable, and the whole matter is rejected, as though licentiously and fabulously invented. But when we affirm the doctrine of the resurrection, and teach that souls will return to another life, not forgetful of themselves, but possessed of the same perception and figure, we are met with this objection: So many ages have now passed; what individual ever arose from the dead, that through his example we may believe it to be possible? But the resurrection cannot take place while unrighteousness still prevails. For in this world men are slain by violence, by the sword, by ambush, by poisons, and are visited with injuries, with want, with imprisonment, with tortures, and with proscriptions. Add to this that righteousness is hated, that all who wish to follow God are not only held in hatred, but are harassed with all reproaches, and are tormented by manifold kinds of punishments, and are driven to the impious worship of gods made with hands, not by reason or truth, but by dreadful laceration of their bodies.

Ought men therefore to rise again to these same things, or to return to a life in which it is impossible for them to be safe? Since the righteous, then, are so lightly esteemed, and so easily taken away, what can we suppose would have happened if anyone returning from the dead had recovered life by a recovery of his former condition? He would assuredly be taken away from the eyes of men, lest, if he were seen or heard, all men with one accord should leave the gods and betake themselves to the worship and religion of the one God. Therefore it is necessary that the resurrection should take place once only when evil shall have been taken away, since it is befitting that those who have risen again should neither die any more, nor be injured in any way, that they may be able to pass a happy life whose death has been annulled. But the poets, knowing that this life abounds with all evils, introduced the river of oblivion, lest the souls, remembering their labors and evils, should refuse to return to the upper regions; whence Virgil says:—

> "O Father! And can thought conceive
> That happy souls this realm would leave,
> And seek the upper sky,
> With sluggish clay to reunite?
> This dreadful longing for the light,
> Whence comes it, say, and why?"

For they did not know how or when it must take place; and therefore they supposed that souls were born again, and that they returned afresh to the womb, and went back to infancy. Whence also Plato, while discussing the nature of the soul, says that it may be known from this that souls are immortal and divine, because in boys minds are pliant, and easy of perception, and because they so quickly comprehend the subjects which they learn, that they appear not then to be learning for the first time, but to be recalling them to mind and recollecting them: in which matter the wise man most foolishly believed the poets.

## Chap. XXIII.—Of the Resurrection of the Soul, and the Proofs of This Fact.

Therefore they will not be born again, which is impossible, but they will rise again, and be clothed by God with bodies, and will remember their former life, and all its actions; and being placed in the possession of heavenly goods, and enjoying the pleasure of innumerable resources, they will give thanks to God in His immediate presence, because He has destroyed all evil, and because He has raised them to His kingdom and to perpetual life. Respecting which resurrection the philosophers also attempted to speak as corruptly as the poets. For Pythagoras asserted that souls passed into new bodies; but foolishly, that they passed from men into cattle, and from cattle into men; and that he himself was restored from Euphorbus. Chrysippus says better, whom Cicero speaks of as supporting the portico of the Stoics, who, in the books which he wrote concerning providence, when he was speaking of the renewing of the world, introduced these words: "But since this is so, it is evident that nothing is impossible, and that we, after our death, when certain periods of time have again come round, are restored to this state in which we now are." But let us return from human to divine things. The Sibyl thus speaks:—

"For the whole race of mortals is hard to be believed; but when the judgment of the world and of mortals shall now come, which God Himself shall institute, judging the impious and the holy at the same time, then at length He shall send the wicked to darkness in fire. But as many as are holy shall live again on the earth, God giving them at the same time a spirit, and honor, and life."

But if not only prophets, but even bards, and poets, and philosophers, agree that there will be a resurrection of the dead, let no one ask of us how this is possible: for no reason can be assigned for divine works; but if from the beginning God formed man in some unspeakable manner, we may believe that the old man can be restored by Him who made the new man.

### Chap. XXIV.—Of the Renewed World.

Now I will subjoin the rest. Therefore the Son of the most high and mighty God shall come to judge the quick and the dead, as the Sibyl testifies and says:—

"For then there shall be confusion of mortals throughout the whole earth, when the Almighty Himself shall come on His judgment-seat to judge the souls of the quick and dead, and all the world."

But He, when He shall have destroyed unrighteousness, and executed His great judgment, and shall have recalled to life the righteous, who have lived from the beginning, will be engaged among men a thousand years, and will rule them with most just command. Which the Sibyl proclaims in another place, as she utters her inspired predictions:—

"Hear me, ye mortals; an everlasting King reigns."

Then they who shall be alive in their bodies shall not die, but during those thousand years shall produce an infinite multitude, and their offspring shall be holy, and beloved by God; but they who shall be raised from the dead shall preside over the living as judges. But the nations shall not be entirely extinguished, but some shall be left as a victory for God, that they may be the occasion of triumph to the righteous, and may be subjected to perpetual slavery. About the same time also the prince of the devils, who is the contriver of all evils, shall be bound with chains, and shall be imprisoned during the thousand years of the heavenly rule in which righteousness shall reign in the world, so that he may contrive no evil against the people of God. After His coming the righteous shall be collected from all the earth, and the judgment being completed, the sacred city shall be planted in the middle of the earth, in which God Himself the builder may dwell together with the righteous, bearing rule in it. And the Sibyl marks out this city when she says:—

"And the city which God made, this He made more brilliant than the stars, and sun, and moon."

Then that darkness will be taken away from the world with which the heaven will be overspread and darkened, and the moon will receive the brightness of the sun, nor will it be further diminished: but the sun will become seven times brighter than it now is; and the earth will open its fruitfulness, and bring forth most abundant fruits of its own accord; the rocky mountains shall drop with honey; streams of wine shall run down, and rivers flow with milk: in short, the world itself shall rejoice, and all nature exult, being rescued and set free from the dominion of evil and impiety, and guilt and error. Throughout this time beasts shall not be nourished by blood, nor birds by prey; but all things shall be peaceful and tranquil. Lions and calves shall stand together at the manger, the wolf shall not carry off the sheep, the hound shall not hunt for prey; hawks and eagles shall not injure; the infant shall play with serpents. In short, those things shall then come to pass which the poets spoke of as being done in the reign of Saturnus. Whose error arose from this source,—that the prophets bring forward and speak of many future events as already accomplished. For visions were brought before their eyes by the divine Spirit, and they saw these things, as it were, done and completed in their own sight. And when fame had gradually spread abroad their predictions, since those who were uninstructed in the mysteries of religion did not know why they were spoken, they thought that all those things were already fulfilled in the ancient ages, which evidently could not be accomplished and fulfilled under the reign of a man. But when, after the destruction of impious religions and the suppression of guilt, the earth shall be subject to God,—

"The sailor himself also shall renounce the sea, nor shall the naval pine
Barter merchandise; all lands shall produce all things.
The ground shall not endure the harrow, nor the vineyard the pruning hook;
The sturdy ploughman also shall loose the bulls from the yoke.
The plain shall by degrees grow yellow with soft ears of corn,
The blushing grape shall hang on the uncultivated brambles, And hard oaks shall distil the dewy honey.
Nor shall the wool learn to counterfeit various colors;
But the ram himself in the meadows shall change his fleece,
Now for a sweetly blushing purple, now for saffron dye;
Scarlet of its own accord shall cover the lambs as they feed.
The goats of themselves shall bring back home their udders distended with milk;
Nor shall the herds dread huge lions."

Which things the poet foretold according to the verses of the Cumæan Sibyl. But the Erythræan thus speaks:—

"But wolves shall not contend with lambs on the mountains, and lynxes shall eat grass with kids; boars shall feed with calves, and with all flocks; and the carnivorous lion shall eat chaff at the manger, and serpents shall sleep with infants deprived of their mothers."

And in another place, speaking of the fruitfulness of all things:—

"And then shall God give great joy to men; for the earth, and the trees, and the numberless flocks of the earth shall give to men the true fruit of the vine, and sweet honey, and white milk, and corn, which is the best of all things to mortals."
And another in the same manner:—

"The sacred land of the pious only will produce all these things, the stream of honey from the rock and from the fountain, and the milk of ambrosia will flow for all the just."

Therefore men will live a most tranquil life, abounding with resources, and will reign together with God; and the kings of the nations shall come from the ends of the earth with gifts and offerings, to adore and honor the great King, whose name shall be renowned and venerated by all the nations which shall be under heaven, and by the kings who shall rule on earth.

### Chap. XXV.—Of the Last Times, and of the City of Rome.

These are the things which are spoken of by the prophets as about to happen hereafter: but I have not considered it necessary to bring forward their testimonies and words, since it would be an endless task; nor would the limits of my book receive so great a multitude of subjects, since so many with one breath speak similar things; and at the same time, lest weariness should be occasioned to the readers if I should heap together things collected and transferred from all; moreover, that I might confirm those very things which I said, not by my own writings, but in an especial manner by the writings of others, and might show that not only among us, but even with those very persons who revile us, the truth is preserved, which they refuse to acknowledge. But he who wishes to know these things more accurately may draw from the fountain itself, and he will know more things worthy of admiration than we have comprised in these books. Perhaps someone may now ask when these things of which we have spoken are about to come to pass? I have already shown above, that when six thousand years shall be completed this change must take place, and that the last day of the extreme conclusion is now drawing near. It is permitted us to know respecting the signs, which are spoken by the prophets, for they foretold signs by which the consummation of the times is to be expected by us from day to day, and to be feared. When, however, this amount will be completed, those teach, who have written respecting the times, collecting them from the sacred writings and from various histories, how great is the number of years from the beginning of the world. And although they vary, and the amount of the number as reckoned by them differs considerably, yet all expectation does not exceed the limit of two hundred years. The subject itself declares that the fall and ruin of the world will shortly take place; except that while the city of Rome remains it appears that nothing of this kind is to be feared. But when that capital of the world shall have fallen, and shall have begun to be a street, which the Sibyls say shall come to pass, who can doubt that the end has now arrived to the affairs of men and the whole world? It is that city, that only, which still sustains all things; and the God of heaven is to be entreated by us and implored—if, indeed, His arrangements and decrees can be delayed—lest, sooner than we think for, that detestable tyrant should come who will undertake so great a deed, and dig out that eye, by the destruction of which the world itself is about to fall. Now let us return, to set forth the other things which are then about to follow.

**Chap. XXVI.—Of the Loosing of the Devil, and of the Second and Greatest Judgment.**

We have said, a little before, that it will come to pass at the commencement of the sacred reign that the prince of the devils will be bound by God. But he also, when the thousand years of the kingdom, that is, seven thousand *of the world*, shall begin to be ended, will be loosed afresh, and being sent forth from prison, will go forth and assemble all the nations, which shall then be under the dominion of the righteous, that they may make war against the holy city; and there shall be collected together from all the world an innumerable company of the nations, and shall besiege and surround the city. Then the last anger of God shall come upon the nations, and shall utterly destroy them; and first He shall shake the earth most violently, and by its motion the mountains of Syria shall be rent, and the hills shall sink down precipitously, and the walls of all cities shall fall, and God shall cause the sun to stand, so that he set not for three days, and shall set it on fire; and excessive heat and great burning shall descend upon the hostile and impious people, and showers of brimstone, and hailstones, and drops of fire; and their spirits shall melt through the heat, and their bodies shall be bruised by the hail, and they shall smite one another with the sword. The mountains shall be filled with carcasses, and the plains shall be covered with bones; but the people of God during those three days shall be concealed under caves of the earth, until the anger of God against the nations and the last judgment shall be ended.

Then the righteous shall go forth from their hiding-places, and shall find all things covered with carcasses and bones. But the whole race of the wicked shall utterly perish; and there shall no longer be any nation in this world, but the nation of God alone. Then for seven continuous years the woods shall be untouched, nor shall timber be cut from the mountains, but the arms of the nations shall be burnt; and now there shall be no war, but peace and everlasting rest. But when the thousand years shall be completed, the world shall be renewed by God, and the heavens shall be folded together, and the earth shall be changed, and God shall transform men into the similitude of angels, and they shall be white as snow; and they shall always be employed in the sight of the Almighty, and shall make offerings to their Lord, and serve Him forever. At the same time shall take place that second and public resurrection of all, in which the unrighteous shall be raised to everlasting punishments. These are they who have worshipped the works of their own hands, who have either been ignorant of, or have denied the Lord and Parent of the world. But their lord with his servants shall be seized and condemned to punishment, together with whom all the band of the wicked, in accordance with their deeds, shall be burnt forever with perpetual fire in the sight of angels and the righteous.

This is the doctrine of the holy prophets which we Christians follow; this is our wisdom, which they who worship frail objects, or maintain an empty philosophy, deride as folly and vanity, because we are not accustomed to defend and assert it in public, since God orders us in quietness and silence to hide His secret, and to keep it within our own conscience; and not to strive with obstinate contention against those who are ignorant of the truth, and who rigorously assail God and His religion not for the sake of learning, but of censuring and jeering. For a mystery ought to be most faithfully concealed and covered, especially by us, who bear the name of faith. But they accuse this silence of ours, as though it were the result of an evil conscience; whence also they invent some detestable things respecting those who are holy and blameless, and willingly believe their own inventions.

The address to Constantine is wanting in some mss. and editions, but is inserted in the text by Migne, as found in some important mss., and as in accordance with the style and spirit of Lactantius.

But all fictions have now been hushed, most holy Emperor, since the time when the great God raised thee up for the restoration of the house of justice, and for the protection of the human race; for while thou rules the Roman state, we worshippers of God are no more regarded as accursed and impious. Since the truth now comes forth from obscurity, and is brought into light, we are not censured as unrighteous who endeavor to perform the works of righteousness. No one any longer reproaches us with the name of God. None of us, who are alone of all men religious, is any more called irreligious; since despising the images of the dead, we worship the living and true God. The providence of the supreme Deity has raised thee to the imperial dignity, that thou mightest be able with true piety to rescind the injurious decrees of others, to correct faults, to provide with a father's clemency for the safety of men,—in short, to remove the wicked from the state, whom being cast down by pre-eminent piety, God has delivered into your hands, that it might be evident to all in what true majesty consists.

For they who wished to take away the worship of the heavenly and matchless God, that they might defend impious superstitions, lie in ruin. But thou, who defends and loves His name, excelling in virtue and prosperity, enjoys thy immortal glories with the greatest happiness. They suffer and have suffered the punishment of their guilt. The powerful right hand of God protects thee from all dangers; He bestows on thee a quiet and tranquil reign, with the highest congratulations of all men. And not undeservedly has the Lord and Ruler of the world chosen thee in preference to all others, by whom He might renew His holy religion, since thou alone didst exist of all, who mightest afford a surpassing example of virtue and holiness: in which thou mightest not only equal, but also, which is a very great matter, excel the glory of ancient princes, whom nevertheless fame reckons among the good. They indeed perhaps by nature only resembled the righteous. For he who is ignorant of God, the Ruler of the universe, may attain to a resemblance of righteousness, but he cannot attain to righteousness itself. But thou, both by the innate sanctity of thy character, and by thy acknowledgment of the truth and of God in every action, dost fully perform the works of righteousness. It was therefore befitting that, in arranging the condition of the human race, the Deity should make use of thy authority and service. Whom we supplicate with daily prayers, that He may especially guard thee whom He has wished to be the guardian of the world: then that He may inspire thee with a disposition by which thou mayest always continue in the love of the divine name. For this is serviceable to all, both to thee for happiness, and to others for repose.

## Chap. XXVII.—An Encouragement and Confirmation of the Pious.

Since we have completed the seven courses of the work which we undertook, and have advanced to the goal, it remains that we exhort all to undertake wisdom together with true religion, the strength and office of which depends on this, that, despising earthly things, and laying aside the errors by which we were formerly held while we served frail things, and desired frail things, we may be directed to the eternal rewards of the heavenly treasure. And that we may obtain these, the alluring pleasures of the present life must as soon as possible be laid aside, which soothe the souls of men with pernicious sweetness. How great a happiness must it be thought, to be withdrawn from these stains of the earth, and to go to that most just Judge and indulgent Father, who in the place of labors gives rest, in the place of death life, in the place of darkness brightness, and in the place of short and earthly goods, gives those which are eternal and heavenly: with which reward the hardships and miseries which we endure in this world, in accomplishing the works of righteousness, can in no way be compared and equaled. Therefore, if we wish to be wise and happy, not only must those sayings of Terence be reflected upon and proposed to us,

"That we must ever grind at the mill, we must be beaten, and put in fetters;"

but things much more dreadful than these must be endured, namely, the prison, chains, and tortures: pains must be undergone, in short, death itself must be undertaken and borne, when it is clear to our conscience that that frail pleasure will not be without punishment, nor virtue without a divine reward. All, therefore, ought to endeavor either to direct themselves to the right way as soon as possible, or, having undertaken and exercised virtues, and having patiently performed the labors of this life, to deserve to have God as their comforter. For our Father and Lord, who built and strengthened the heaven, who placed in it the sun, with the other heavenly bodies, who by His power weighed the earth and fenced it with mountains, surrounded it with the sea, and divided it with rivers, and who made and completed out of nothing whatever there is in this workmanship of the world; having observed the errors of men, sent a Guide, who might open to us the way of righteousness: let us all follow Him, let us hear Him, let us obey Him with the greatest devotedness, since He alone, as Lucretius says,

"Cleansed men's breasts with truth-telling precepts, and fixed a limit to lust and fear, and explained what was the chief good which we all strive to reach, and pointed out the road by which, along a narrow track, we might arrive at it in a straightforward course."

And not only pointed it out, but also went before us in it, that no one might dread the path of virtue on account of its difficulty. Let the way of destruction and deceit, if it is possible, be deserted, in which death is concealed, being covered by the attractions of pleasure.

And the more nearly each one, as his years incline to old age, sees to be the approach of that day in which he must depart from this life, let him reflect how he may leave it in purity, how he may come to the Judge in innocence; not as they do, to whose dark minds the light is denied, who, when the strength of their body now fails, are admonished in this of the last pressing necessity, that they should with greater eagerness and ardor apply themselves to the satisfying of their lusts. From which abyss let everyone free himself while it is permitted him, while the opportunity is present, and let him turn himself to God with his whole mind, that he may without anxiety await that day, in which God, the Ruler and Lord of the world, shall judge the deeds and thoughts of each. Whatever things are here desired, let him not only neglect, but also avoid them, and let him judge that his soul is of greater value than those deceitful goods, the possession of which is uncertain and transitory; for they take their departure every day, and they go forth much more quickly than they had entered, and if it is permitted us to enjoy them even to the last, they must still, without doubt, be left to others. We can take nothing with us, except a well and innocently spent life. That man will appear before God with abundant resources, that man will appear in opulence, to whom there shall belong self-restraint, mercy, patience, love, and faith. This is our inheritance, which can neither be taken away from any one, nor transferred to another. And who is there who would wish to provide and acquire for himself these goods?

Let those who are hungry come, that being fed with heavenly food, they may lay aside their lasting hunger; let those who are athirst come, that they may with full mouth draw forth the water of salvation from an ever-flowing fountain. By this divine food and drink the blind shall both see, and the deaf hear, and the dumb speak, and the lame walk, and the foolish shall be wise, and the sick shall be strong, and the dead shall come to life again. For whoever by his virtue has trampled upon the corruptions of the earth, the supreme and truthful arbiter will raise him to life and to perpetual light. Let no one trust in riches, no one in badges of authority, and no one even in royal power: these things do not make a man immortal. For whosoever shall cast away the conduct becoming a man, and, following present things, shall prostrate himself upon the ground, will be punished as a deserter from his Lord, his commander, and his Father. Let us therefore apply ourselves to righteousness, which will alone, as an inseparable companion, lead us to God; and "while a spirit rules these limbs," let us serve God with unwearied service, let us keep our posts and watches, let us boldly engage with the enemy whom we know, that victorious and triumphant over our conquered adversary, we may obtain from the Lord that reward of valor which He Himself has promised.

*General Note.*

For remarks on the dubious passages which bear upon that of p. 221, *supra*, see the *General Note* suffixed to the tractate on the *Workmanship of God*, p. 300, *infra*.

## The Epitome of the Divine Institutes.

Addressed to His Brother Pentadius.

### The Preface.—The Plan and Purport of the Whole Epitome, And of the Institutions.

Although the books of the *Divine Institutions* which we wrote a long time since to illustrate the truth and religion, may so prepare and mold the minds of the readers, that their length may not produce disgust, nor their copiousness be burthensome; nevertheless you desire, O brother Pentadius, that an epitome of them should be made for you, I suppose for this reason, that I may write something to you, and that your name may be rendered famous by my work, such as it is. I will comply with your desire, although it seems a difficult matter to comprise within the compass of one book those things which have been treated of in seven large volumes. For the whole matter becomes less full when so great a multitude of subjects is to be compressed within a narrow space; and it becomes less clear by its very brevity, especially since many arguments and examples, on which the elucidation of the proofs depends, must of necessity be omitted, since their copiousness is so great, that even by themselves they are enough to make up a book. And when these are removed, what can appear useful, what plain? But I will strive as much as the subject permits, both to contract that which is diffuse and to shorten that which is long; in such a manner, however, that in this work, in which truth is to be brought to light, matter may not seem to be wanting for copiousness, nor clearness for understanding it.

### Chap. I.—Of the Divine Providence.

First a question arises: Whether there is any providence which made or governs the world? That there is, no one doubts, since of almost all the philosophers, except the school of Epicurus, there is but one voice and one opinion, that the world could not have been made without a contriver, and that it cannot exist without a ruler. Therefore Epicurus is refuted not only by the most learned men, but also by the testimonies and perceptions of all mortals. For who can doubt respecting a providence, when he sees that the heavens and the earth have been so arranged and that all things have been so regulated, that they might be most befittingly adapted, not only to wonderful beauty and adornment, but also to the use of men, and the convenience of the other living creatures? That, therefore, which exists in accordance with a plan, cannot have had its beginning without a plan: thus it is certain that there is a providence.

**Chap. II.—That There is But One God, and that There Cannot Be More.**

Another question follows: Whether there be one God or more? And this indeed contains much ambiguity. For not only do individuals differ among themselves, but also peoples and nations. But he who shall follow the guidance of reason will understand that there cannot be a Lord except one, nor a Father except one. For if God, who made all things, is also Lord and Father, He must be one only, so that the same may be the head and source of all things. Nor is it possible for the world to exist unless all things be referred to one person, unless one hold the rudder, unless one guide the reins, and, as it were, one mind direct all the members of the body. If there are many kings in a swarm of bees, they will perish or be scattered abroad, while

"Discord attacks the kings with great commotion."

If there are several leaders in a herd, they will contend until one gains the mastery. If there are many commanders in an army, the soldiers cannot obey, since different commands are given; nor can unity be maintained by themselves, since each consults his own interests according to his humors. Thus, in this commonwealth of the world, unless there were one ruler, who was also its founder, either this mass would be dissolved, or it could not have been put together at all.

Moreover, the whole *authority* could not exist in many *deities*, since they separately maintain their own duties and their own prerogatives. No one, therefore, of them can be called omnipotent, which is the true title of God, since he will be able to accomplish that only which depends upon himself, and will not venture to attempt that which depends upon others. Vulcan will not claim for himself water, nor Neptune fire; nor will Ceres claim acquaintance with the arts, nor Minerva with fruits; nor will Mercury lay claim to arms, nor Mars to the lyre; Jupiter will not claim medicine, nor Æsculapius the thunderbolt: he will more easily endure it when thrown by another, than he will brandish it himself. If, therefore, individuals cannot do all things, they have less strength and less power; but he is to be regarded as God who can accomplish the whole, and not he who can only accomplish the smallest part of the whole.

**Chap. III.—The Testimonies of the Poets Concerning the One God.**

There is, then, one God, perfect, eternal, incorruptible, incapable of suffering, subject to no circumstance or power, Himself possessing all things, ruling all things, whom the human mind can neither estimate in thought nor mortal tongue describe in speech. For He is too elevated and great to be conceived by the thought, or expressed by the language of man. In short, not to speak of the prophets, the preachers of the one God, poets also, and philosophers, and inspired women, utter their testimony to the unity of God. Orpheus speaks of the surpassing God who made the heaven and the sun, with the other heavenly bodies; who made the earth and the seas. Also our own Maro calls the Supreme God at one time a spirit, at another time a mind, and says that it, as though infused into limbs, puts in motion the body of the whole world; also, that God permeates the heights of heaven, the tracts of the sea and lands, and that all living creatures derive their life from Him. Even Ovid was not ignorant that the world was prepared by God, whom he sometimes calls the framer of all things, sometimes the fabricator of the world.

### Chap. IV.—The Testimonies of the Philosophers to the Unity of God.

But let us come to the philosophers, whose authority is regarded as more certain than that of the poets. Plato asserts His monarchy, saying that there is but one God, by whom the world was prepared and completed with wonderful order. Aristotle, his disciple, admits that there is one mind which presides over the world. Antisthenes says that there is one who is God by nature, the governor of the whole system. It would be a long task to recount the statements which have been made respecting the Supreme God, either by Thales, or by Pythagoras and Anaximenes before him, or afterwards by the Stoics Cleanthes and Chrysippus and Zeno, or of our countrymen, by Seneca following the Stoics, and by Tullius himself, since all these attempted to define the being of God, and affirmed that the world is ruled by Him alone, and that He is not subject to any nature, since all nature derives its origin from Him.

Hermes, who, on account of his virtue and his knowledge of many arts, deserved the name of Trismegistus, who preceded the philosophers in the antiquity of his doctrine, and who is reverenced by the Egyptians as a god, in asserting the majesty of the one God with infinite praises, calls Him Lord and Father, and says that He is without a name because He does not stand in need of a proper name, inasmuch as He is alone, and that He has no parents, since He exists of Himself and by Himself. In writing to his son he thus begins: To understand God is difficult, to describe Him in speech is impossible, even for one to whom it is possible to understand Him; for the perfect cannot be comprehended by the imperfect, nor the invisible by the visible.

### Chap. V.—That the Prophetic Women—That Is, the Sibyls—Declare that there is But One God.

It remains to speak of the prophetic women. Varro relates that there were ten Sibyls,—the first of the Persians, the second the Libyan, the third the Delphian, the fourth the Cimmerian, the fifth the Erythræan, the sixth the Samian, the seventh the Cumæan, the eighth the
Hellespontian, the ninth the Phrygian, the tenth the Tiburtine, who has the name of Albunea. Of all these, he says that there are three books of the Cumæan alone which contain the fates of the Romans, and are accounted sacred, but that there exist, and are commonly regarded as separate, books of almost all the others, but that they are entitled, as though by one name, Sibylline books, excepting that the Erythræan, who is said to have lived in the times of the Trojan war, placed her name in her book: the writings of the others are mixed together.

All these Sibyls of whom I have spoken, except the Cumæan, whom none but the Quindecemviri are allowed to read, bear witness that there is but one God, the ruler, the maker, the parent, not begotten of any, but sprung from Himself, who was from all ages, and will be to all ages; and therefore is alone worthy of being worshipped, alone of being feared, alone of being reverenced, by all living beings;—whose testimonies I have omitted because I was unable to abridge them; but if you wish to see them, you must have recourse to the books themselves. Now let us follow up the remaining subjects.

### Chap. VI.—Since God is Eternal and Immortal, He Does Not Stand in Need of Sex and Succession.

These testimonies, therefore, so many and so great, clearly teach that there is but one government in the world, and one power, the origin of which cannot be imagined, or its force described. They are foolish, therefore, who imagine that the gods were born of marriage, since the sexes themselves, and the intercourse between them, were given to mortals by God for this reason, that every race might be preserved by a succession of offspring. But what need have the immortals either of sex or succession since neither pleasure nor death affects them? Those, therefore, who are reckoned as gods, since it is evident that they were born as men, and that they begat others, were plainly mortals: but they were believed to be gods, because, when they were great and powerful kings, on account of the benefits which they had conferred upon men, they deserved to obtain divine honors after death; and temples and statues being erected to them, their memory was retained and celebrated as that of immortals.

### Chap. VII.—Of the Wicked Life and Death of Hercules.

But though almost all nations are persuaded that they are gods, yet their actions, as related both by poets and historians, declare that they were men. Who is ignorant of the times in which Hercules lived, since he both sailed with the Argonauts on their expedition, and having stormed Troy, slew Laomedon, the father of Priam, on account of his perjury? From that time rather more than fifteen hundred years are reckoned. He is said not even to have been born honorably, but to have been sprung from Alcmena by adultery, and to have been himself addicted to the vices of his father. He never abstained from women, or males, and traversed the whole world, not so much for the sake of glory as of lust, nor so much for the slaughter of beasts as for the begetting of children. And though he was unvanquished, yet he was triumphed over by Omphale alone, to whom he gave up his club and lion's skin; and being clothed in a woman's garment, and crouching at a woman's feet, he received his task to execute. He afterwards, in a transport of frenzy, killed his little children and his wife Megara. At last, having put on a garment sent by his wife Deianyra, when he was perishing through ulcers, being unable to endure the pain, he constructed for himself a funeral pile on Mount OEta, and burnt himself alive. Thus it is effected, that although on account of his excellence he might have been believed to be a god, nevertheless on account of these things be is believed to have been a man.

### Chap. VIII.—Of Æsculapius, Apollo, Mars, Castor and Pollux, and of Mercurius and Bacchus.

Tarquitius relates that Æsculapius was born of doubtful parents, and that on this account he was exposed; and being taken up by hunters, and fed by the teats of a hound, was given to Chiron for instruction. He lived at Epidaurus, and was buried at Cynosuræ, as Cicero says, when he had been killed by lightning. But Apollo, his father, did not disdain to take charge of another's flock that he might receive a wife; and when he had unintentionally killed a boy whom he loved, he inscribed his own lamentations on a flower. Mars, a man of the greatest bravery, was not free from the charge of adultery, since he was made a spectacle, being bound with a chain together with the adulteress.

Castor and Pollux carried off the brides of others, but not with impunity, to whose death and burial Homer bears witness, not with poetical, but simple faith. Mercurius, who was the father of Androgynus by his intrigue with Venus, deserved to be a god, because he invented the lyre and the palæstra. Father Bacchus, after subduing India as a conqueror, having by chance come to Crete, saw Ariadne on the shore, whom Theseus had forced and deserted. Then, being inflamed by love, he united her in marriage to himself, and placed her crown, as the poets say, conspicuously among the stars. The mother of the gods herself, while she lived in Phrygia after the banishment and death of her husband, though a widow, and aged, was enamored of a beautiful youth; and because he was not faithful, she mutilated, and rendered him effeminate: on which account even now she delights in the Galli as her priests.

### Chap. IX.—Of the Disgraceful Deeds of the Gods.

Whence did Ceres bring forth Proserpine, except from debauchery? Whence did Latona bring forth her twins, except from crime? Venus having been subject to the lusts of gods and men, when she reigned in Cyprus, invented the practice of courtesanship, and commanded women to make traffic of themselves, that she might not alone be infamous. Were the virgins themselves, Minerva and Diana, chaste? Whence, then, did Erichthonius arise? Did Vulcan shed his seed upon the ground, and was man born from that as a fungus? Or why did Diana banish Hippolytus either to a retired place, or give him up to a woman, where he might pass his life in solitude among unknown groves, and having now changed his name, might be called Virbius? What do these things signify but impurity, which the poets do not venture to confess?

**Chap. X.—Of Jupiter, and His Licentious Life.**

But respecting the king and father of all these, Jupiter, whom they believe to possess the chief power in heaven,—what power had he, who banished his father Saturnus from his kingdom, and pursued him with arms when he fled? What self-restraint had he, who indulged every kind of lust? For he made Alcmena and Leda, the wives of great men, infamous through his adultery: he also, captivated with the beauty of a boy, carried him off with violence as he was hunting and meditating manly things, that he might treat him as a woman. Why should I mention his debaucheries of virgins? And how great a multitude of these there was, is shown by the number of his sons. In the case of Thetis alone he was more temperate. For it bad been predicted that the son whom she should bring forth would be more powerful than his father. Therefore he struggled with his love, that one might not be born greater than himself. He knew, therefore, that he was not of perfect virtue, greatness, and power, since he feared that which he himself had done to his father. Why, therefore, is he called best and greatest, since he both contaminated himself with faults, which is the part of one who is unjust and bad, and feared a greater than himself, which is the part of one who is weak and inferior?

### Chap. XI.—The Various Emblems Under Which the Poets Veiled the Turpitude of Jupiter.

But someone will say that these things are feigned by the poets. This is not the usage of the poets, to feign in such a manner that you fabricate the whole, but so that you cover the actions themselves with a figure, and, as it were, with a variegated veil. Poetic license has this limit, not that it may invent the whole, which is the part of one who is false and senseless, but that it may change something consistently with reason. They said that Jupiter changed himself into a shower of gold, that he might deceive Danae. What is a shower of gold? Plainly golden coins, by offering a great quantity of which, and pouring them into her bosom, he corrupted the frailty of her virgin soul by this bribe. Thus also they speak of a shower of iron, when they wish to signify a multitude of javelins. He carried off his catamite upon an eagle. What is the eagle? Truly a legion, since the figure of this animal is the standard of the legion. He carried Europa across the sea on a bull. What is the bull? Clearly a ship, which had its tutelary image fashioned in the shape of a bull. So assuredly the daughter of Inachus was not turned into a cow, nor as such did she swim across, but she escaped the anger of Juno in a ship which had the form of a cow. Lastly, when she had been conveyed to Egypt, she became Isis, whose voyage is celebrated on a fixed day, in memory of her flight.

### Chap. XII.—The Poets Do Not Invent All Those Things Which Relate to the Gods.

You see, then, that the poets did not invent all things, and that they prefigured some things, that, when they spoke the truth, they might add something like this of divinity to those whom they called gods; as they did also respecting their kingdoms. For when they say that Jupiter had by lot the kingdom of Coelus, they either menu Mount Olympus, on which ancient stories relate that Saturnus, and afterwards Jupiter, dwelt, or a part of the East, which is, as it were, higher, because the light arises thence; but the region of the West is lower, and therefore they say that Pluto obtained the lower regions; but that the sea was given to Neptune, because he had the maritime coast, with all the islands. Many things are thus colored by the poets; and they who are ignorant of this, censure them as false, but only in word: for in fact they believe them, since they so fashion the images of the gods, that when they make them male and female, and confess that some are married, some parents, and some children, they plainly assent to the poets; for these relations cannot exist without intercourse and the generation of children.

### Chap. XIII.—The Actions of Jupiter are related from the Historian Euhemerus.

But let us leave the poets; let us come to history, which is supported both by the credibility of the facts and by the antiquity of the times. Euhemerus was a Messenian, a very ancient writer, who gave an account of the origin of Jupiter, and his exploits, and all his posterity, gathered from the sacred inscriptions of ancient temples; he also traced out the parents of the other gods, their countries, actions, commands, and deaths, and even their sepulchers. And this history Ennius translated into Latin, whose words are these:—

"As these things are written, so is the origin and kindred of Jupiter and his brothers; after this manner it is handed clown to us in the sacred writing."

The same Euhemerus therefore relates that Jupiter, when he had five times gone round the world, and had distributed governments to his friends and relatives, and had given laws to men, and had wrought many other benefits, being endued with immortal glory and everlasting remembrance, ended his life in Crete, and departed to the gods, and that his sepulcher is in Crete, in the town of Gnossus, and that upon it is engraved in ancient Greek letters Zankronou, which is Jupiter the son of Saturnus. It is plain, therefore, from the things which I have related, that he was a man, and reigned on the earth.

### Chap. XIV.—The Actions of Saturnus and Uranus Taken from the Historians.

Let us pass on to former things, that we may discover the origin of the whole error. Saturnus is said to have been born of Coelus and Terra. This is plainly incredible; but there is a certain reason why it is thus related, and he who is ignorant of this rejects it as a fable. That Uranus was the father of Saturnus, both Hermes affirms, and sacred history teaches. When Trismegistus said that there were very few men of perfect learning, he enumerated among them his relatives, Uranus, Saturnus, and Mercurius. Euhemerus relates that the same Uranus was the first who reigned on earth, using these words: "In the beginning Coelus first had the chief power on earth: he instituted and prepared that kingdom for himself together with his brothers."

### Chap. XX.—Of the Gods Peculiar to the Romans.

I have spoken of the religious rites which are common to all nations. I will now speak of the gods which the Romans have peculiar to themselves. Who does not know that the wife of Faustulus, the nurse of Romulus and Remus, in honor of whom the Larentinalia were instituted, was a harlot? And for this reason she was called Lupa, and represented in the form of a wild beast. Faula also and Flora were harlots, of whom the one was the mistress of Hercules, as Verrius relates; the other, having acquired great wealth by her person, made the people her heir, and on this account the games called Floralia are celebrated in her honor.

Tatius consecrated the statue of a woman which had been found in the principal sewer, and called it by the name of the goddess Cloacina. The Romans, being besieged by the Gauls, made engines for throwing weapons of the hair of women; and on this account they erected an altar and temple to Venus Calva: also to Jupiter Pistor, because he had advised them in a dream to make all their corn into bread, and to throw it upon the enemy; and when this had been done, the Gauls, despairing of being able to reduce the Romans by famine, had abandoned the siege. Tullus Hostilius made Fear and Pallor gods. Mind is also worshipped; but if they had possessed it, they would never, I believe, have thought that it ought to be worshipped. Marcellus originated Honor and Virtue.

### Chap. XXI.—Of the Sacred Rites of the Roman Gods.

But the senate also instituted other false gods of this kind,—Hope, Faith, Concord, Peace, Chastity, Piety; all of which, since they ought truly to be in the minds of men, they have falsely placed within walls. But although these have no substantial existence outside of man, nevertheless I should prefer that they should be worshipped, rather than Blight or Fever, which ought not to be consecrated, but rather to be execrated; than Fornax, together with her sacred ovens; than Stercutus, who first showed men to enrich the ground with manure; than the goddess Muta, who brought forth the Lares; than Cumina, who presides over the cradles of infants; than Caca, who gave information to Hercules respecting the stealing of his cattle, that he might slay her brother. How many other monstrous and ludicrous fictions there are, respecting which it is grievous to speak! I do not, however, wish to omit notice of Terminus, since it is related that he did not give way even to Jupiter, though he was an unwrought stone. They suppose that he has the custody of the boundaries, and public prayers are offered to him, that he may keep the stone of the Capitol immoveable, and preserve and extend the boundaries of the Roman Empire.

### Chap. XXII.—Of the Sacred Rites Introduced by Faunus and Numa.

Faunas was the first in Latium who introduced these follies, who both instituted bloody sacrifices to his grandfather Saturnus, and wished that his father Picus should be worshipped as a god, and placed Fatua Fauna his wife and sister among the gods, and named her the good goddess. Then at Rome, Numa, who burthened those rude and rustic then with new superstitions, instituted priesthoods, and distributed the gods into families and nations, that he might call off the fierce spirits of the people from the pursuits of arms. Therefore Lucilius, in deriding the folly of those who are slaves to vain superstitions, introduced these verses:—

"Those bugbears the Lamiæ, which Faunus and Numa Pompilius and others instituted, at these he trembles; he places everything in this. As infant boys believe that every statue of bronze is a living man, so these imagine that all things reigned are true: they believe that statues of bronze contain a heart. It is a painter's gallery; nothing is real, everything fictitious."

Tullius also, writing of the nature of the gods, complains that false and fictitious gods have been introduced, and that from thus source have arisen false opinions, and turbulent errors, and almost old womanly superstitions, which opinion ought in comparison with others to be esteemed more weighty, because these things were spoken by one who was both a philosopher and a priest.

### Chap. XXIII.—Of the Gods and Sacred Rites of the Barbarians.

We have spoken respecting the gods: now we will speak of the rites and practices of their sacred institutions. A human victim used to be immolated to the Cyprian Jupiter, as Teucer had appointed. Thus also the Tauri used to offer strangers to Diana; the Latian Jupiter also was propitiated with human blood. Also before Saturnus, men of sixty years of age, according to the oracle of Apollo, were thrown from a bridge into the Tiber. And the Carthaginians not only offered infants to the same Saturnus; but being conquered by the Sicilians, to make an expiation, they immolated two hundred sons of nobles. And not more mild than these are those offerings which are even now made to the Great Mother and to Bellona, in which the priests make an offering, not with the blood of others, but with their own blood; when, mutilating themselves, they cease to be men, and yet do not pass over to the women; or, cutting their shoulders, they sprinkle the loathsome altars with their own blood. But these things are cruel.

Let us come to those which are mild. The sacred rites of Isis show nothing else than the manner in which she lost and found her little son, who is called Osiris. For first her priests and attendants, having shaved all their limbs, and beating their breasts, howl, lament, and search, imitating the manner in which his mother was affected; afterwards the boy is found by Cynocephalus. Thus the mournful rites are ended with gladness. The mystery of Ceres also resembles these, in which torches are lighted, and Proserpine is sought for through the night; and when she has been found, the whole rite is finished with congratulations and the throwing about of torches. The people of Lampsacus, offer an ass to Priapus as an appropriate victim. Lindus is a town of Rhodes, where sacred rites in honor of Hercules are celebrated with reviling. For when Hercules had taken away his oxen from a ploughman, and had slain them, he avenged his injury by taunts; and afterwards having been himself appointed priest, it was ordained that he himself, and other priests after him, should celebrate sacrifices with the same reviling. But the mystery of the Cretan Jupiter represents the manner in which he was withdrawn from his father, or brought up. The goat is beside him, by the teats of which Amalthea nourished the boy. The sacred rites of the mother of the gods also show the same thing. For because the Corybantes then drowned the cry of the boy by the tinkling of their helmets and the striking of their shields, a representation of this circumstance is now repeated in the sacred rites; but cymbals are beaten instead of helmets, and drums instead of shields, that Saturnus may not hear the cries of the boy.

**Chap. XXIV.—Of the Origin of Sacred Rites and Superstitions.**

These are the mysteries of the gods. Now let us inquire also into the origin of superstitions that we may search out by whom and at what times they were instituted. Didymus, in those books which are inscribed *Of the Explanation of Pindar*, relates that Melisseus was king of the Cretans, whose daughters were Amalthea and Melissa, who nourished Jupiter with goats' milk and honey; that he introduced new rites and ceremonies of sacred things, and was the first who sacrificed to gods, that is, to Vesta, who is called Tellus,—whence the poet says:—

"And the first of the gods,
Tellus,"—

and afterwards to the mother of the gods. But Euhemerus, in his sacred history, says that Jupiter himself, after that he received the government, erected temples in honor of himself in many places. For in going about the world, as he came to each place he united the chiefs of the people to himself in friendship and the right of hospitality; and that the remembrance of this might be preserved, he ordered that temples should be built to him, and annual festivals be celebrated by those connected with him in a league of hospitality. Thus he spread the worship of himself through all lands. But at what time they lived can easily be inferred. For Thallus writes in his history, that Belus, the king of the Assyrians, whom the Babylonians worship, and who was the contemporary and friend of Saturnus, was three hundred and twenty-two years before the Trojan war, and it is fourteen hundred and seventy years since the taking of Troy. From which it is evident, that it is not more than eighteen hundred years from the time when mankind fell into error by the institution of new forms of divine worship.

**Chap. XXV.—Of the Golden Age, of Images, and Prometheus, Who First Fashioned Man.**

The poets, therefore, with good reason say that the golden age, which existed in the reign of Saturnus, was changed. For at that time no gods were worshipped, but they knew of one God only. After that they subjected themselves to frail and earthly things, worshipping idols of wood, and brass, and stone, a change took place from the golden age to that of iron. For having lost the knowledge of God, and broken off that one bond of human society, they began to harass one another, to plunder and subdue. But if they would raise their eyes aloft and behold God, who raised them up to the sight of heaven and Himself, they never would bend and prostrate themselves by worshipping earthly things, whose folly Lucretius severely rebukes, saying:

"And they abase their souls with fear of the gods, and weigh and press them down to the earth."

Wherefore they tremble, and do not understand how foolish it is to fear those things which you have made, or to hope for any protection from those things which are dumb and insensible, and neither see nor hear the suppliant. What majesty, therefore, or deity can they have, which were in the power of a man, that they should not be made, or that they should be made into some other thing, and are so even now? For they are liable to injury and might be carried off by theft, were it not that they are protected by the law and the guardianship of man. Does he therefore appear to be in possession of his senses, who sacrifices to such deities the choicest victims, consecrates gifts, and offers costly garments, as if they who are without motion could use them? With reason, then, did Dionysius the tyrant of Sicily plunder and deride the gods of Greece when he had taken possession of it as conqueror; and after the sacrilegious acts which he had committed, he returned to Sicily with a prosperous voyage, and held the kingdom even to his old age: nor were the injured gods able to punish him.

How much better is it to despise vanities, and to turn to God, to maintain the condition which you have received from God, to maintain your name! For on this account he is called *anthropos*, because he looks upward. But he looks upward who looks up to the true and living God, who is in heaven; who seeks after the Maker and Parent of his soul, not only with his perception and mind, but also with his countenance and eyes raised aloft. But he who enslaves himself to earthly and humble things, plainly prefers to himself that which is below him. For since he himself is the workmanship of God, whereas an image is the workmanship of man, the human workmanship cannot be preferred to the divine; and as God is the parent of man, so is the man of the statue. Therefore he is foolish and senseless who adores that which he himself has made, of which detestable and foolish handicraft Prometheus was the author, who was born from Iapetus the uncle of Jupiter. For when first of all Jupiter, having obtained supreme dominion, wished to establish himself as a god, and to found temples, and was seeking for someone who was able to imitate the human figure, at that time Prometheus lived, who fashioned the image of a man from thick clay with such close resemblance, that the novelty and cleverness of the art was a wonder. At length the men of his own time, and afterwards the poets, handed him down as the maker of a true and living man; and we, as often as we praise wrought statues, say that they live and breathe. And he indeed was the inventor of earthenware images. But posterity, following him, both carved them out of marble, and molded them out of bronze; then in process of time ornament was added of gold and ivory, so that not only the likenesses, but also the gleam itself, might dazzle the eyes. Thus ensnared by beauty, and forgetful of true majesty, sensible beings considered that insensible objects, rational beings that irrational objects, living beings that lifeless objects, were to be worshipped and reverenced by them.

### Chap. XXVI.—Of the Worship of the Elements and Stars.

Now let us refute those also who regard the elements of the world as gods, that is, the heaven, the sun, and the moon; for being ignorant of the Maker of these things, they admire and adore the works themselves. And this error belongs not to the ignorant only, but also to philosophers; since the Stoics are of opinion that all the heavenly bodies are to be considered as among the number of the gods, since they all have fixed and regular motions, by which they most constantly preserve the vicissitudes of the times which succeed them. They do not then possess voluntary motion, since they obey prescribed laws, and plainly not by their own sense, but by the workmanship of the supreme Creator, who so ordered them that they should complete unerring courses and fixed circuits, by which they might vary the alternations of days and nights, of summer and winter. But if men admire the effects of these, if they admire their courses, their brightness, their regularity, their beauty, they ought to have understood how much more beautiful, more illustrious, and more powerful than these is the maker and contriver Himself, even God. But they estimated the Divinity by objects which fall under the sight of men; not knowing that objects which come within the sight cannot be eternal, and that those which are eternal cannot be discerned by mortal eyes.

### Chap. XXVII.—Of the Creation, Sin, and Punishment of Man; And of Angels, both Good and Bad.

One subject remains, and that the last: that, since it usually happens, as we read in histories, that the gods appear to have displayed their majesty by auguries, by dreams, by oracles, and also by the punishments of those who had committed sacrilege, I may show what cause produced this effect, so that no one even now may fall into the same snares into which those of old fell. When God, according to His excellent majesty, had framed the world out of nothing, and had decked the heaven with lights, and had filled the earth and the sea with living creatures, then He formed man out of clay, and fashioned him after the resemblance of His own likeness, and breathed into him that he might live, and placed him in a garden which He had planted with every kind of fruit-bearing tree, and commanded him not to eat of one tree in which He had placed the knowledge of good and evil, warning him that it would come to pass, that if he did so he would lose his life, but that if he observed the command of God he would remain immortal. Then the serpent, who was one of the servants of God, envying man because he was made immortal, enticed him by stratagem to transgress the command and law of God. And in this manner he did indeed receive the knowledge of good and evil, but he lost the life which God had given him to be forever.

Therefore He drove out the sinner from the sacred place, and banished him into this world, that he might seek sustenance by labor, that he might according to his deserts undergo difficulties and troubles; and He surrounded the garden itself with a fence of fire, that none of men even till the day of judgment might attempt secretly to enter into that place of perpetual blessedness. Then death came upon man according to the sentence of God; and yet his life, though it had begun to be temporary, had as its boundary a thousand years, and that was the extent of human life even to the deluge. For after the flood the life of men was gradually shortened, and was reduced to a hundred and twenty years. But that serpent, who from his deeds received the name of devil, that is, accuser or informer, did not cease to persecute the seed of man, whom he had deceived from the beginning. At length he urged him who was first born in this world, under the impulse of envy, to the murder of his brother, that of the two men who were first born he might destroy the one, and make the other a parricide. Nor did he cease upon this from infusing the venom of malice into the breasts of men through each generation, from corrupting and depraving them; in short, from overwhelming them with such crimes, that an instance of justice was now rare, but men lived after the manner of the beasts.

But when God saw this, He sent His angels to instruct the race of men, and to protect them from all evil. He gave these a command to abstain from earthly things, lest, being polluted by any taint, they should be deprived of the honor of angels. But that wily accuser, while they tarried among men, allured these also to pleasures, so that they might defile themselves with women. Then, being condemned by the sentence of God, and cast forth on account of their sins, they lost both the name and substance of angels. Thus, having become ministers of the devil, that they might have a solace of their ruin, they betook themselves to the ruining of men, for whose protection they had come.

**Chap. XXVIII.—Of the Demons, and Their Evil Practices.**

These are the demons, of whom the poets often speak in their poems, whom Hesiod calls the guardians of men. For they so persuaded men by their enticements and deceits, that they believed that the same were gods. In fine, Socrates used to give out that he had a demon as the guardian and director of his life from his first childhood, and that he could do nothing without his assent and command. They attach themselves, therefore, to individuals, and occupy houses under the name of Genii or Penates. To these temples are built, to these libations are daily offered as to the Lares, to these honor is paid as to the averters of evils. These from the beginning, that they might turn away men from the knowledge of the true God, introduced new superstitions and worship of gods. These taught that the memory of dead kings should be consecrated, temples be built, and images made, not that they might lessen the honor of God, or increase their own, which they lost by sinning, but that they might take away life from men, deprive them of the hope of true light, lest men should arrive at that heavenly reward of immortality from which they fell. They also brought to light astrology, and augury, and divination; and though these things are in themselves false, yet they themselves, the authors of evils, so govern and regulate them that they are believed to be true. They also invented the tricks of the magic art, to deceive the eyes. By their aid it comes to pass, that that which is appears not to be, and that which is not appears to be. They themselves invented necromancies, responses, and oracles, to delude the minds of men with lying divination by means of ambiguous issues. They are present in the temples and at all sacrifices; and by the exhibition of some deceitful prodigies, to the surprise of those who are present, they so deceive men, that they believe that a divine power is present in images and statues. They even enter secretly into bodies, as being slight spirits; and they excite diseases in the vitiated limbs, which when appeased with sacrifices and vows they may again remove. They send dreams either full of terror that they themselves may be invoked, or the issues of which may correspond with the truth, that they may increase the veneration paid to themselves. Sometimes also they put forth something of vengeance against the sacrilegious, that whoever sees it may become more timid and superstitious. Thus by their frauds they have drawn darkness over the human race, that truth might be oppressed, and the name of the supreme and matchless God might be forgotten.

### Chap. XXIX.—Of the Patience and Providence of God.

But someone says: Why, then, does the true God permit these things to be done? Why does He not rather remove or destroy the wicked? Why, in truth, did He from the beginning give power to the demon, so that there should be one who might corrupt and destroy all things? I will briefly say why He willed that this should be so. I ask whether virtue is a good or an evil. It cannot be denied that it is a good. If virtue is a good, vice, on the contrary, is an evil. If vice is an evil on this account, because it opposes virtue, and virtue is on this account a good, because it overthrows vice, it follows that virtue cannot exist without vice; and if you take away vice, the merits of virtue will be taken away. For there can be no victory without an enemy. Thus it comes to pass, that good cannot exist without an evil.

Chrysippus, a man of active mind, saw this when discussing the subject of providence, and charges those with folly who think that good is caused by God, but say that evil is not thus caused. Aulus Gellius has interpreted his sentiment in his books of *Attic Nights*; thus saying: "They to whom it does not appear that the world was made for the sake of God and men, and that human affairs are governed by providence, think that they use a weighty argument when they thus speak: If there were a providence, there would be no evils. For they say that nothing is less in agreement with providence, than that in this world, on account of which it is said that God made men, the power of troubles and evils should be so great. In reply to these things, Chrysippus, when he was arguing, in his fourth book respecting providence, said: Nothing can be more foolish than those who think that good things could have existed, if there were not evils in the same place. For since good things are contrary to evil, they must of necessity be opposed to each other, and must stand resting, as it were, on mutual and opposite support. Thus there is no contrary without another contrary. For how could there be any perception of justice, unless there were injuries? Or what else is justice, but the removal of injustice? In like manner, the nature of fortitude cannot be understood, except by placing beside it cowardice, or the nature of self-control except by intemperance. Likewise, in what manner would there be prudence, unless there were the contrary, imprudence? On the same principle, he says, why do the foolish men not require this also, that there should be truth and not falsehood? For there exist together good and evil things, prosperity and trouble, pleasure and pain. For the one being bound to the other at opposite poles, as Plato says, if you take away one, you take away both." You see, therefore, that which I have often said, that good and evil are so connected with one another, that the one cannot exist without the other. Therefore God acted with the greatest foresight in placing the subject-matter of virtue in evils which He made for this purpose, that He might establish for us a contest, in which He would crown the victorious with the reward of immortality.

**Chap. XXX.—Of False Wisdom.**

I have taught, as I imagine, that the honors paid to gods are not only impious, but also vain, either because they were men whose memory was consecrated after death; or because the images themselves are insensible and deaf, inasmuch as they are formed of earth, and that it is not right for man, who ought to look up to heavenly things, to subject himself to earthly things; or because the spirits who claim to themselves those acts of religious service are unholy and impure, and on this account, being condemned by the sentence of God, fell to the earth, and that it is not lawful to submit to the power of those to whom you are superior, if you wish to be a follower of the true God. It remains that, as we have spoken of false religion, we should also discuss the subject of false wisdom, which the philosophers profess,—men endued with the greatest learning and eloquence, but far removed from the truth, because they neither know God nor the wisdom of God. And although they are clever and learned, yet, because their wisdom is human, I shall not fear to contend with them, that it may be evident that falsehood can be easily overcome by truth, and earthly things by heavenly.

They thus define the nature of philosophy. Philosophy is the love or pursuit of wisdom. Therefore it is not wisdom itself;

for that which loves must be different from that which is loved. If it is the pursuit of wisdom, not even thus is philosophy *identical with* wisdom. For wisdom is the object itself which is sought, but the pursuit is that which seeks it. Therefore the very definition or meaning of the word plainly shows that philosophy is not wisdom itself. I will say that it is not even the pursuit of wisdom, in which wisdom is not comprised. For who can be said to devote himself to the pursuit of that to which he can by no means attain? He who gives himself to the pursuit of medicine, or grammar, or oratory, may be said to be studious of that art which he is learning; but when he has learned, he is now said to be a physician, a grammarian, or an orator. Thus also those who are studious of wisdom, after they had learned it, ought to have been called wise. But since they are called students of wisdom as long as they live, it is manifest that that is not the pursuit, because it is impossible to arrive at the object itself which is sought for in the pursuit, unless by chance they who pursue wisdom even to the end of life are about to be wise in another world. Now every pursuit is connected with some end. That, therefore, is not a right pursuit which has no end.

### Chap. XXXI.—Of Knowledge and Supposition.

Moreover, there are two things which appear to fall under the subject of philosophy—knowledge and supposition; and if these are taken away, philosophy altogether falls to the ground. But the chief of the philosophers themselves have taken away both from philosophy. Socrates took away knowledge, Zeno supposition. Let us see whether they were right in doing so. Wisdom is, as Cicero defined it, the knowledge of divine and human things. Now if this definition is true, wisdom does not come within the power of man. For who of mortals can assume this to himself, to profess that he knows divine and human things? I say nothing of human affairs; for although they are connected with divine, yet, since they belong to man, let us grant that it is possible for man to know them. Certainly he cannot know divine things by himself, since he is a man; whereas he who knows them must be divine, and therefore God. But man is neither divine nor God. Man, therefore, cannot thoroughly know divine things by himself. No one, therefore, is wise but God, or certainly that man whom God has taught. But they, because they are neither gods, nor taught by God, cannot be wise, that is, acquainted with divine and human things. Knowledge, therefore, is rightly taken away by Socrates and the Academics. Supposition also does not agree with the wise man. For every one supposes that of which he is ignorant. Now, to suppose that you know that of which you are ignorant, is rashness and folly. Supposition, therefore, was rightly taken away by Zeno. If, therefore, there is no knowledge in man, and there ought to be no supposition, philosophy is cut up by the roots.

**Chap. XXXII.—Of the Sects of Philosophers, and Their Disagreement.**

To this is added, that it is not uniform; but being divided into sects, and scattered into many and discordant opinions, it has no fixed state. For since they all separately attack and harass one another, and there is none of them which is not condemned of folly in the judgment of the rest, while the members are plainly at variance with one another, the whole body of philosophy is brought to destruction. Hence the Academy afterwards originated. For when the leading men of that sect saw that philosophy was altogether overthrown by philosophers mutually opposing each other, they undertook war against all, that they might destroy all the arguments of all; while they themselves assert nothing except one thing—that nothing can be known. Thus, having taken away knowledge, they overthrew the ancient philosophy. But they did not even themselves retain the name of philosophers, since they admitted their ignorance, because to be ignorant of all things is not only not the part of a philosopher, but not even of a man. Thus the philosophers, because they have no defense, must destroy one another with mutual wounds, and philosophy itself must altogether consume and put an end to itself by its own arms. But they say it is only natural philosophy which thus gives way. How is it with moral? Does that rest on any firm foundation? Let us see whether philosophers are agreed in this part at any rate, which relates to the condition of life.

### Chap. XXXIII.—What is the Chief Good to Be Sought in Life.

What is the chief good must be an object of inquiry, that our whole life and actions may be directed to it. When inquiry is made respecting the chief good of man, it ought to be settled to be of such a kind, first, that it have reference to man alone; in the next place, that it belong peculiarly to the mind; lastly, that it be sought by virtue. Let us see, therefore, whether the chief good which the philosophers mark out be such that it has reference neither to a dumb animal nor to the body, and cannot be attained without virtue.

Aristippus, the founder of the Cyrenaic sect, who thought that bodily pleasure was the chief good, ought to be removed from the number of philosophers, and from the society of men, because he compared himself to a beast. The chief good of Hieronymus is to be without pain, that of Diodorus to cease to be in pain. But the other animals avoid pain; and when they are without pain, or cease to be in pain, are glad. What distinction, then, will be given to man, if his chief good is judged to be common with the beasts? Zeno thought that the chief good was to live agreeably to nature. But this definition is a general one. For all animals live agreeably to nature, and each has its own nature.

Epicurus maintained that it was pleasure of the soul. What is pleasure of the soul but joy, in which the soul for the most part luxuriates, and unbends itself either to sport or to laughter? But this good befalls even dumb animals, which, when they are satisfied with pasture, relax themselves to joy and wantonness. Dinomachus and Callipho approved of honorable pleasure; but they either said the same that Epicurus did, that bodily pleasure is dishonorable; or if they considered bodily pleasures to be partly base and partly honorable, then that is not the chief good which is ascribed to the body. The Peripatetics make up the chief good of goods of the soul, and body, and fortune. The goods of the soul may be approved of; but if they require assistance for the completion of happiness, they are plainly weak. But the goods of the body and of fortune are not in the power of man; nor is that now the chief good which is assigned to the body, or to things placed without us, because this double good extends even to the cattle, which have need of being well, and of a due supply of food. The Stoics are believed to have entertained much better views, who said that virtue was the chief good. But virtue cannot be the chief good, since, if it is the endurance of evils and of labors, it is not happy of itself; but it ought to effect and produce the chief good, because it cannot be attained without the greatest difficulty and labor. But, in truth, Aristotle wandered far from reason, who connected honor with virtue, as though it were possible for virtue at any time to be separated from honor, or to be united with baseness.

Herillus the Pyrrhonist made knowledge the chief good. This indeed belongs to man, and to the soul only, but it may happen to him without virtue. For he is not to be considered happy who has either learnt anything by hearing, or has gained the knowledge of it by a little reading; nor is it a definition of the chief good, because there may be a knowledge either of bad things, or at any rate of things that are useless. And if it is the knowledge of good and useful things which you have acquired by labor, nevertheless it is not the chief good, because knowledge is not sought on its own account, but on account of something else. For the arts are learnt on this account, that they may be to us the means of gaining support, or a source of glory, or even of pleasure; and it is plain that these things cannot be the chief goods. Therefore the philosophers do not observe the rule even in moral philosophy, inasmuch as they are at variance with one another on the main point itself, that is, in that discussion by which the life is molded. For the precepts cannot be equal, or resembling one another, when some train men to pleasure, others to honor, others indeed to nature, others to knowledge; some to the pursuit, others to the avoiding of riches; some to entire insensibility to pain, others to the endurance of evils: in all which, as I have shown before, they turn aside from reason, because they are ignorant of God.

### Chap. XXXIV.—That Men are Born to Justice.

Let us now see what is proposed to the wise man as the chief good. That men are born to justice is not only taught by the sacred writings, but is sometimes acknowledged even by these same philosophers. Thus Cicero says: "But of all things which fall under the discussion of learned men, nothing assuredly is more excellent than that it should be clearly understood that we are born to justice." This is most true. For we are not born to wickedness, since we are a social and sociable animal. The wild beasts are produced to exercise their fierceness; for they are unable to live in any other way than by prey and bloodshed. These, however, although pressed by extreme hunger, nevertheless refrain from animals of their own kind. Birds also do the same, which must feed upon the carcasses of others. How much more is it befitting, that man, who is united with man both in the interchange of language and in communion of feeling, should spare man, and love him! For this is justice.

But since wisdom has been given to man alone, that he may understand God, and this alone makes the difference between man and the dumb animals, justice itself is bound up in two duties. He owes the one to God as to a father, the other to man as to a brother; for we are produced by the same God. Therefore it has been deservedly and rightly said, that wisdom is the knowledge of divine and human affairs. For it is right that we should know what we owe to God, and what to man; namely, to

God religion, to man affection. But the former belongs to wisdom, the latter to virtue; and justice comprises both. If, therefore, it is evident that man is born to justice, it is necessary that the just man should be subject to evils, that he may exercise the virtue with which he is endued. For virtue is the enduring of evils. He will avoid pleasures as an evil: he will despise riches, because they are frail; and if he has them, he will liberally bestow them, to preserve the wretched: he will not be desirous of honors, because they are short and transitory; he will do injury to no one; if he shall suffer, he will not retaliate; and he will not take vengeance upon one who plunders his property. For he will deem it unlawful to injure a man; and if there shall be anyone who would compel him to depart from God, he will not refuse tortures nor death. Thus it will come to pass, that he must necessarily live in poverty and lowliness, and in insults, or even tortures.

### Chap. XXXV.—That Immortality is the Chief Good.

What, then, will be the advantage of justice and virtue, if they shall have nothing but evil in life? But if virtue, which despises all earthly goods, most wisely endures all evils, and endures death itself in the discharge of duty, cannot be without a reward, what remains but that immortality alone is its reward? For if a happy life falls to the lot of man, as the philosophers will have it, and in this point alone they do not disagree, therefore also immortality falls to him. For that only is happy which is incorruptible; that only is incorruptible which is eternal. Therefore immortality is the chief good, because it belongs both to man, and to the soul, and to virtue. We are only directed to this; we are born to the attainment of this. Therefore God proposes to us virtue and justice, that we may obtain that eternal reward for our labors. But concerning that immortality itself we will speak in the proper place. There remains the philosophy of Logic, which contributes nothing to a happy life. For wisdom does not consist in the arrangement of speech, but in the heart and the feeling. But if natural philosophy is superfluous, and this of logic, and the philosophers have erred in moral philosophy, which alone is necessary, because they have been unable in any way to find out the chief good; therefore all philosophy is found to be empty and useless, which was unable to comprehend the nature of man, or to fulfil its duty and office.

## Chap. XXXVI.—Of the Philosophers,—Namely, Epicurus and Pythagoras.

Since I have spoken briefly of philosophy, now also I will speak a few things about the philosophers. This is especially the doctrine of Epicurus, that there is no providence. And at the same time he does not deny the existence of gods. In both respects he acts contrary to reason. For if there are gods, it follows that there is a providence. For otherwise we can form no intelligible idea of God, for it is His peculiar province to foresee. But Epicurus says He takes no care about anything. Therefore He disregards not only the affairs of men, but also heavenly things. How, therefore, or from what, do you affirm that He exists? For when you have taken away the divine providence and care, it would naturally follow that you should altogether deny the existence of God; whereas now you have left Him in name, but in reality you have taken Him away. Whence, then, did the world derive its origin, if God takes no care of anything? There are, he says, minute atoms, which can neither be seen nor touched, and from the fortuitous meeting of these all things arose, and are continually arising. If they are neither seen nor perceived by any part of the body, how could you know of their existence? In the next place, if they exist, with what mind do they meet together to effect anything? If they are smooth, they cannot cohere: if they are hooked and angular, then they are divisible; for hooks and angles project, and can be cut off. But these things are senseless and unprofitable. Why should I mention that he also makes souls capable of extinction? Who is refuted not only by all philosophers and general persuasion, but also by the answers of bards, by the predictions of the Sibyls, and lastly, by the divine voices of the prophets themselves; so that it is wonderful that Epicurus alone existed, who should place the condition of man on a level with the flocks and beasts.

What of Pythagoras, who was first called a philosopher, who judged that souls were indeed immortal, but that they passed into other bodies, either of cattle, or of birds, or of beasts? Would it not have been better that they should be destroyed, together with their bodies, than thus to be condemned to pass into the bodies of other animals? Would it not be better not to exist at all, than, after having had the form of a man, to live as a swine or a dog? And the foolish man, to gain credit for his saying, said that he himself had been Euphorbus in the Trojan war, and that, when he had been slain, he passed into other figures of animals, and at last became Pythagoras. O happy man! To whom alone so great a memory was given; or rather unhappy, who, when changed into a sheep, was not permitted to be ignorant of what he was! And would to Heaven that he alone had been thus senseless! He found also some to believe him, and some indeed among the learned, to whom the inheritance of folly passed.

### Chap. XXXVII.—Of Socrates and His Contradiction.

After him Socrates held the first place in philosophy, who was pronounced most wise even by the oracle, because he confessed that he knew one thing only,—namely, that he knew nothing. And on the authority of this oracle it was right that the natural philosophers should restrain themselves, lest they should either inquire into those things which they could not know, or should think that they knew things which they did not know. Let us, however, see whether Socrates was most wise, as the Pythian god proclaimed. He often made use of this proverb that that which is above us has also no reference to us. He has now passed beyond the limits of his opinion. For he who said that he knew one thing only, found another thing to speak of, as though he knew it; but that in vain. For God, who is plainly above us, is to be sought for; and religion is to be undertaken, which alone separates us from the brutes, which indeed Socrates not only rejected, but even derided, in swearing by a goose and a dog, as if in truth he could not have sworn by Æsculapius, to whom he had vowed a cock. Behold the sacrifice of a wise man! And because he was unable to offer this in his own person, since he was at the point of death, he entreated his friends to perform the vow after his death, lest forsooth he should be detained as a debtor in the lower regions. He assuredly both pronounced that he knew nothing, and made good his statement.

## Chap. XXXVIII.—Of Plato, Whose Doctrine Approaches More Nearly to the Truth.

His disciple Plato, whom Tully speaks of as the god of philosophers, alone of all so studied philosophy that he approached nearer to the truth; and yet, because he was ignorant of God, he so failed in many things, that no one fell into worse errors, especially because in his books respecting the state he wished all things to be common to all. This is endurable concerning property, though it is unjust. For it ought not to be an injury to anyone, if he possesses more than another through his own industry; or to be a profit to anyone, if through his own fault he possesses less. But, as I have said, this is capable of being endured in some way. Shall there be a community of wives also, and of children? Shall there be no distinction of blood, or certainty of race? Shall there be neither families, nor relationships, nor affinities, but all things confused and indiscriminate, as in herds of cattle? Shall there be no self-restraint in men, no chastity in women? What conjugal affection can there be in these, between whom on either side there is no sure or peculiar love? Who will he dutiful towards a father, when he knows not from whom he was born? Who will love a son, whom he will reckon as not his own? Moreover, he opened the senate house to women, and entrusted to them warfare, magistracies, and commands. But how great will be the calamity of that city, in which women shall discharge the duties of men! But of this more fully at another opportunity.

Zeno, the master of the Stoics, who praises virtue, judged that pity, which is a very great virtue, should be cut away, as though it were a disease of the mind, whereas it is at the same time dear to God and necessary for men. For who is there who, when placed in any evil, would be unwilling to be pitied, and would not desire the assistance of those who might succor them, which is not called forth so as to render aid, except by the feeling of pity? Although he calls this humanity and piety, he does not change the matter itself, only the name. This is the affection which has been given to man alone, that by mutual assistance we might alleviate our weakness; and he who removes this affection reduces us to the life of the beasts. For his assertion that all faults are equal, proceeds from that inhumanity with which also be assails pity as a disease. For he who makes no difference in faults, either thinks that light offences ought to be visited with severe punishments, which is the part of a cruel judge, or that great offences should be visited with slight punishments, which is the part of a worthless judge. In either case there is injury to the state. For if the greatest crimes are lightly punished, the boldness of the wicked will increase, and go on to deeds of greater daring; and if a punishment of too great severity is inflicted for slight offences, inasmuch as no one can be exempt from fault, many citizens will incur peril, who by correction might become better.

## Chap. XXXIX.—Of Various Philosophers, and of the Antipodes.

These things, truly, are of small importance, but they arise from the same falsehood. Xenophanes said that the orb of the moon is eighteen times larger than this earth of ours; and that within its compass is contained another earth, which is inhabited by men and animals of every kind. About the antipodes also one can neither hear nor speak without laughter. It is asserted as something serious, that we should believe that there are men who have their feet opposite to ours. The ravings of Anaxagoras are more tolerable, who said that snow was black. And not only the sayings, but the deeds, of some are ridiculous. Democritus neglected his land which was left to him by his father, and suffered it to become a public pasture. Diogenes with his company of dogs, who professes that great and perfect virtue in the contempt of all things, preferred to beg for his support, rather than to seek it by honest labor, or to have any property. Undoubtedly the life of a wise man ought to be to others an example of living. If all should imitate the wisdom of these, how will states exist? But perhaps the same Cynics were able to afford an example of modesty, who lived with their wives in public. I know not how they could defend virtue, who took away modesty.

Nor was Aristippus better than these, who, I believe, that he might please his mistress Lais, instituted the Cyrenaic system, by which he placed the end of the chief good in bodily pleasure, that authority might not be wanting to his faults, or learning to his vices. Are those men of greater fortitude to be more approved, who, that they might be said to have despised death, died by their own hands? Zeno, Empedocles, Chrysippus, Cleanthes, Democritus, and Cato, imitating these, did not know that he who put himself to death is guilty of murder, according to the divine right and law. For it was God who placed us in this abode of flesh: it was He who gave us the temporary habitation of the body, that we should inhabit it as long as He pleased. Therefore it is to be considered impious, to wish to depart from it without the command of God. Therefore violence must not be applied to nature. He knows how to destroy His own work. And if anyone shall apply impious hands to that work, and shall tear asunder the bonds of the divine workmanship, he endeavors to flee from God, whose sentence no one will be able to escape, whether alive or dead. Therefore they are accursed and impious, whom I have mentioned above, who even taught what are the befitting reasons for voluntary death; so that it was not enough of guilt that they were self-murderers, unless they instructed others also to this wickedness.

### Chap. XL.—Of the Foolishness of the Philosophers.

There are innumerable sayings and doings of the philosophers, by which their foolishness may be shown. Therefore, since we are unable to enumerate them all, a few will be sufficient. It is enough that it is understood that the philosophers were neither teachers of justice, of which they were ignorant, nor of virtue, of which they falsely boast. For what can they teach, who often confess their own ignorance? I omit to mention Socrates, whose opinion is well known. Anaxagoras proclaims that all things are over-spread with darkness. Empedocles says that the paths for finding out the truth of the senses are narrow. Democritus asserts that truth lies sunk in a deep well; and because they nowhere find it, they therefore affirm that no wise man has as yet existed. Since, therefore, human wisdom has no existence (Socrates says in the writings of Plato), let us follow that which is divine, and let us give thanks to God, who has revealed and delivered it to us; and let us congratulate ourselves, that through the divine bounty we possess the truth and wisdom, which, though sought by so many intellects through so many ages, philosophy was not able to discover.

### Chap. XLI.—Of True Religion and Wisdom.

Now, since we have refuted false religion, which is in the worship of the gods, and false wisdom, which is in the philosophers, let us come to true religion and wisdom. And, indeed, we must speak of them both conjointly, because they are closely connected. For to worship the true God, that and nothing else is wisdom. For that God who is supreme and the Maker of all things, who made man as the image of Himself, on this account conferred on him alone of all animals the gift of reason, that he might pay back honor to Him as his Father and his Lord, and by the exercise of this piety and obedience might gain the reward of immortality. This is a true and divine mystery. But among those, because they are not true, there is no agreement. Neither are sacred rites performed in philosophy, nor is philosophy treated of in sacred things; and on this account their religion is false, because it does not possess wisdom; and on this account their wisdom is false, because it does not possess religion. But where both are joined together, there the truth must necessarily be; so that if it is asked what the truth itself is, it may be rightly said to be either wise religion or religious wisdom.

**Chap. XLII.—Of Religious Wisdom: the Name of Christ Known to None, Except Himself and His Father.**

I will now say what wise religion, or religious wisdom, is. God, in the beginning, before He made the world, from the fountain of His own eternity, and from the divine and everlasting Spirit, begat for Himself a Son incorruptible, faithful, corresponding to His Father's excellence and majesty. He is virtue, He is reason, He is the word of God, He is wisdom. With this artificer, as Hermes says, and counsellor, as the Sibyl says, He contrived the excellent and wondrous fabric of this world. In fine, of all the angels, whom the same God formed from His own breath, He alone was admitted into a participation of His supreme power, He alone was called God. For all things were through Him, and nothing was without Him. In fine, Plato, not altogether as a philosopher, but as a seer, spoke concerning the first and second God, perhaps following Trismegistus in this, whose words I have translated from the Greek, and subjoined: "The Lord and Maker of all things, whom we have thought to be called God, created a second God, who is visible and sensible. But by sensible I mean, not that He Himself receives sensation, but that He causes sensation and sight. When, therefore, He had made this, the first, and one, and only one, He appeared to Him most excellent, and full of all good qualities." The Sibyl also says that God the guide of all was made by God, and another, that

"God the Son of God must be known,"

as those examples which I have brought forward in my books declare. Him the prophets, filled with the inspiration of the Divine Spirit, proclaimed; of whom especially Solomon in the book of Wisdom, and also his father, the writer of divine hymns—both most renowned kings, who preceded the times of the Trojan war by a hundred and eighty years—testify that He was born of God. His name is known to none, except to Himself and the Father, as John teaches in the Revelation. Hermes says that His name cannot be uttered by mortal mouth. Yet by men He is called by two names—Jesus, which is Savior, and Christ, which is King. He is called Savior on this account, because He is the health and safety of all who believe in God through Him. He is called Christ on this account, because He Himself will come from heaven at the end of this dispensation to judge the world, and, having raised the dead, to establish for Himself an everlasting kingdom.

### Chap. XLIII.—Of the Name of Jesus Christ, and His Twofold Nativity.

But lest by any chance there should be any doubt in your mind why we call Him Jesus Christ, who was born of God before the world, and who was born of man three hundred years ago, I will briefly explain to you the reason. The same person is the son of God and of man. For He was twice born: first of God, in the spirit, before the origin of the world; afterwards in the flesh of man, in the reign of Augustus; and in connection with this fact is an illustrious and great mystery, in which is contained both the salvation of men and the religion of the Supreme God, and all truth. For when first the accursed and impious worship of gods crept in through the treachery of the demons, then the religion of

God remained with the Hebrews alone, who, not by any law, but after the manner of their fathers, observed the worship handed down to them by successive generations, even until the time when they went forth out of Egypt under the leadership of Moses, the first of all the prophets, through whom the law was given to them from God; and they were afterwards called Jews. Therefore they served God, being bound by the chains of the law. But they also, by degrees going astray to profane rites, undertook the worship of strange gods, and, leaving the worship of their father, sacrificed to senseless images. Therefore God sent to them prophets filled with the Divine Spirit, to upbraid them with their sins and proclaim repentance, to threaten them with the vengeance which would follow, and announce that it would come to pass, if they persisted in the same faults, that He would send another as the bearer of a new law; and having removed the ungrateful people from their inheritance, He would assemble to Himself a more faithful people from foreign nations. But they not only persisted in their course, but even slew the messengers themselves. Therefore He condemned them on account of these deeds: nor did He any longer send messengers to a stubborn people; but He sent His own Son, to call all nations to the favor of God. Nor, however, did He shut them out, impious and ungrateful as they were, from the hope of salvation: but He sent Him to them before all others, that if they should by chance obey, they might not lose that which they had received; but if they should refuse to receive their God, then, the heirs being removed, the Gentiles would come into possession. Therefore the supreme Father ordered Him to descend to the earth, and to put on a human body, that, being subject to the sufferings of the flesh, He might teach virtue and patience not only by words, but also by deeds. Therefore He was born a second time as man, of a virgin, without a father, that, as in His first spiritual birth, being born of God alone, He was made a sacred spirit, so in His second and fleshly birth, being born of a mother only, He might become holy flesh, that through Him the flesh, which had become subject to sin, might be freed from destruction.

## Chap. XLIV.—The Twofold Nativity of Christ is Proved from the Prophets.

That these things should thus take place as I have set them forth, the prophets had before predicted. In the writings of Solomon it is thus written: "The womb of a virgin was strengthened, and conceived: and a virgin was impregned, and became a mother in great pity." In Isaiah it is thus written: "Behold, a virgin shall conceive, and bear a son, and ye shall call His name Immanuel;" which, being interpreted, is God with us. For He was with us on the earth, when He assumed flesh; and He was no less God in man, and man in God. That He was both God and man was declared before by the prophets. That He was God, Isaiah thus declares: "They shall fall down unto Thee, they shall make supplication unto Thee; since God is in Thee, and we knew it not, even the God of Israel. They shall be ashamed and confounded, all of them who oppose themselves to Thee, and shall go to confusion." Also Jeremiah: "This is our God, and there shall none other be compared unto Him; He hath found out all the way of knowledge, and hath given it unto Jacob His servant, and to Israel His beloved. Afterward He was seen upon earth, and dwelt among men." Likewise that He was man, the same Jeremiah says: "And He is man, and who knew Him?" Isaiah also thus speaks: "And the Lord shall send them a man who shall save them, and with judgment shall He heal them." Also Moses himself in the book of Numbers: "There shall come a star out of Jacob, and a man shall arise out of Israel." For this cause, therefore, being God, He took upon Him flesh, that, becoming a mediator between God and man, having overcome death, He might by His guidance lead man to God.

## Chap. XLV.—The Power and Works of Christ are Proved from the Scriptures.

We have spoken of His nativity; now let us speak of His power and works, which, when He wrought them among men, the Jews, seeing them to be great and wonderful, supposed that they were done by the influence of magic, not knowing that all those things which were done by Him had been foretold by the prophets. He gave strength to the sick, and to those languishing under various diseases, not by any healing remedy, but instantaneously, by the force and power of His word; He restored the weak, He made the lame to walk, He gave sight to the blind, He made the dumb to speak, the deaf to hear; He cleansed the polluted and unclean, He restored their right mind to those who were maddened with the attack of demons, He recalled to life and light those who were dead or now buried. He also fed and satisfied five thousand men with five loaves and two fishes. He also walked upon the sea. He also in a tempest commanded the wind to be still, and immediately there was a calm; all which things we find predicted both in the books of the prophets and in the verses of the Sibyls.

When a great multitude resorted to Him on account of these miracles, and, as He truly was, believed Him to be the Son of God, and sent from God, the priests and rulers of the Jews, filled with envy, and at the same time excited with anger, because He reproved their sins and injustice, conspired to put Him to death; and that this would happen, Solomon had foretold a little more than a thousand years before, in the book of Wisdom, using these words: "Let us defraud the righteous, for he is unpleasant to us, and upbraided us with our offences against the law. He makes his boast that he has the knowledge of God, and he called himself the Son of God. He is made to reprove our thoughts: it grieves us even to look upon him; for his life is not like the life of others, his ways are of another fashion. We are counted by him as triflers; he withdraweth himself from our ways, as from filthiness; he commended greatly the latter end of the just, and boasted that he has God for his father. Let us see, therefore, if his words be true; let us prove what end he shall have; let us examine him with rebukes and torments, that we may know his meekness and prove his patience; let us condemn him to a shameful death. Such things have they imagined, and have gone astray; for their own folly hath blinded them, and they do not understand the mysteries of God."

Therefore, being unmindful of these writings which they read, they incited the people as though against an impious man, so that they seized and led Him to trial, and with impious words demanded His death. But they alleged against Him as a crime this very thing, that He said that He was the Son of God, and that by healing on the Sabbath He broke the law, which He said that He did not break, but fulfilled. And when Pontius Pilate, who then as legate had authority in Syria, perceived that the cause did not belong to the office of the Roman judge, he sent Him to Herod the Tetrarch, and permitted the Jews themselves to be the judges of their own law: who, having received the power of punishing His guilt, sentenced Him to the cross, but first scourged and struck him with their hands, put on Him a crown of thorns, spat upon His face, gave Him gall and vinegar to eat and drink; and amidst these things no word was heard to fall from His lips. Then the executioners, having cast lots over His tunic and mantle, suspended Him on the cross, and affixed Him to it, though on the next day they were about to celebrate the Passover, that is, their festival. Which crime was followed by prodigies, that they might understand the impiety which they had committed; for at the same moment in which He expired, there was a great earthquake, and a withdrawing of the sun, so that the day was turned into night.

**Chap. XLVI.—It is Proved from the Prophets that the Passion and Death of Christ Had Been Foretold.**

And the prophets had predicted that all these things would thus come to pass. Isaiah thus speaks: "I am not rebellious, nor do

## The Writings of Lactatius

I oppose: I gave my back to the scourge, and my cheeks to the hand: I turned not away my face from the foulness of spitting." The same prophet says respecting His silence: "I was brought as a sheep to the slaughter, and as a lamb before its shearers is dumb, so He opened not His mouth." David also, in the xxxivth Psalm: "The abject were gathered together against me, and they knew me not: they were scattered, yet felt no remorse: they tempted me, and gnashed upon me with their teeth." The same also says respecting food and drink in the lxviiith Psalm: "They gave me also gall for my meat, and in my thirst they gave me vinegar to drink." Also respecting the cross of Christ: "And they pierced my hands and my feet, they numbered all my bones: they themselves have looked and stared upon me; they parted my garments among them, and cast lots upon my vesture." Moses also says in Deuteronomy: "And thy life shall hang in doubt before thine eyes, and thou shall fear day and night, and shall have none assurance of thy life." Also in Numbers: "God is not in doubt as a man, nor does He suffer threats as the son of man." Also Zechariah says: "And they shall look on me whom they pierced." Amos thus speaks of the obscuring of the sun: "In that day, saith the Lord, the sun shall go down at noon, and the clear day shall be dark; and I will turn your feasts into mourning, and your songs into lamentation." Jeremiah also speaks of the city of Jerusalem, in which He suffered: "Her sun is gone down while it was yet day; she hath been confounded and reviled, and the residue of them will I deliver to the sword." Nor were these things spoken in vain. For after a short time the Emperor Vespasian subdued the Jews, and laid waste their lands with the sword and fire, besieged and reduced them by famine, overthrew Jerusalem, led the captives in triumph, and prohibited the others who were left from ever returning to their native land. And these things were done by God on account of that crucifixion of Christ, as He before declared this to Solomon in their Scriptures, saying, "And Israel shall be for perdition and a reproach to the people, and this house shall be desolate; and every one that shall pass by shall be astonished, and shall say, Why hath God done these evils to this land, and to this house? And they shall say, Because they forsook the Lord their God, and persecuted their King, who was dearly beloved by God, and crucified Him with great degradation, therefore hath God brought upon them these evils." For what would they not deserve who put to death their Lord, who had come for their salvation?

## Chap. XLVII.—Of the Resurrection of Jesus Christ, the Sending of the Apostles, and the Ascension of the Savior into Heaven.

After these things they took His body down from the cross, and buried it in a tomb. But on the third day, before daybreak, there was an earthquake, and the stone with which they had closed the sepulcher was removed, and He arose. But nothing was found in the sepulcher except the clothes in which the body had been wrapped. But that He would rise again on the third day, the prophets had long ago foretold. David, in the xvth Psalm: "Thou wilt not leave my soul in hell, neither wilt Thou suffer Thine Holy One to see corruption." Likewise Hosea: This my Son is wise, therefore He shall not stay long in the anguish of His sons: and I will ransom Him from the hand of the grave. Where is thy judgment, O death, where is thy sting? "The same again says: "After two days He will revive us on the third day."

Therefore, after His resurrection He went into Galilee, and again assembled His disciples, who had fled through fear; and having given them commands which He wished to be observed, and having arranged for the preaching of the Gospel throughout the whole world, He breathed into them the Holy Spirit, and gave them the power of working miracles, that they might act for the welfare of men as well by deeds as words; and then at length, on the fortieth day, He returned to His Father, being carried up into a cloud. The prophet Daniel had long before shown this, saying, "I saw in the night vision, and, behold, one like the Son of man came with the clouds of heaven, and came to

## The Writings of Lactatius

the Ancient of days; and they who stood beside Him brought Him near before Him. And there was given Him a kingdom, and glory, and dominion, and all people, tribes, and languages shall serve Him; and His power is an everlasting one, which shall not pass away, and His kingdom that which shall not be destroyed." Also David in the Psalm: "The Lord said unto my Lord, Sit Thou at my right hand, until I make Thine enemies Thy footstool."

### Chap. XLVIII.—Of the Disinheriting of the Jews, and the Adoption of the Gentiles.

Since, therefore, He sits at the right hand of God, about to tread down His enemies, who tortured Him, when He shall come to judge the world, it is evident that no hope remains to the Jews, unless, turning themselves to repentance, and being cleansed from the blood with which they polluted themselves, they shall begin to hope in Him whom they denied. Therefore Esdras thus speaks: "This Passover is our Savior and our refuge. Consider and let it come into your heart that we have to abase Him in a figure: and after these things we have hoped in Him."

Now that the Jews were disinherited, because they rejected Christ, and that we, who are of the Gentiles, were adopted into their place, is proved by the Scriptures. Jeremiah thus speaks: "I have forsaken mine house, I have given mine heritage into the hands of her enemies. Mine heritage is become unto me as a lion in the forest; it hath given forth its voice against me: therefore have I hated it." Also Malachi: "I have no pleasure in you, saith the Lord, neither will I accept an offering at your hand. For from the rising of the sun even unto the going down thereof, my name shall be great among the Gentiles." Isaiah also thus speaks: "I come to gather all nations and tongues: and they shall come and see my glory." The same says in another place, speaking in the person of the Father to the Son: "I the Lord have called Thee in righteousness, and will hold Thine hand, and will keep Thee, and give Thee for a covenant of my people, for a light of the Gentiles; to open the eyes of the blind, to bring out the prisoners from the prison, and them that sit in darkness out of the prison-house."

**Chap. XLIX.—That God is One Only.**

If therefore the Jews have been rejected by God, as the faith due to the sacred writings shows, and the Gentiles, as we see, brought in, and freed from the darkness of this present life and from the chains of demons, it follows that no other hope is proposed to man, unless he shall follow true religion and true wisdom, which is in Christ, and he who is ignorant of Him is always estranged from the truth and from God. Nor let the Jews, or philosophers, flatter themselves respecting the Supreme God. He who has not acknowledged the Son has been unable to acknowledge the Father. This is wisdom, and this is the mystery of the Supreme God. God willed that He should be acknowledged and worshipped through Him. On this account He sent the prophets beforehand to announce His coming, that when the things which had been foretold were fulfilled in Him, then He might be believed by men to be both the Son of God and God.

Nor, however, must the opinion be entertained that there are two Gods, for the Father and the Son are one. For since the Father loves the Son, and gives all things to Him, and the Son faithfully obeys the Father, and wills nothing except that which the Father does, it is plain that so close a relationship cannot be separated, so that they should be said to be two in whom there is but one substance, and will, and faith. Therefore the Son is through the Father, and the Father through the Son. One honor is to be given to both, as to one God, and is to be so divided through the worship of the two, that the division itself may be bound by an inseparable bond of union. He will leave nothing to himself, who separates either the Father from the Son, or the Son from the Father.

**Chap. L.—Why God Assumed a Mortal Body, and Suffered Death.**

It remains to answer those also, who deem that it was unbecoming and unreasonable that God should be clothed with a mortal body; that He should be in subjection to men; that He should endure insults; that He should even suffer tortures and death. I will speak my sentiments, and I will sum up, as I shall be able, an immense subject in few words. He who teaches anything, ought, as I think, himself to practice what he teaches, that he may compel men to obey. For if he shall not practice them, he will detract from the faith due to his precepts. Therefore there is need of examples, that the precepts which are given may have firmness, and if anyone shall prove contumacious, and shall say that they cannot be carried out in practice, the instructor may refute him by actual fact. Therefore a system of teaching cannot be perfect, when it is delivered by words only; but it then becomes perfect, when it is completed by deeds.

Since therefore Christ was sent to men as a teacher of virtue, for the perfection of His teaching it was plainly befitting that He should act as well as teach. But if He had not assumed a human body, He would not have been able to practice what He taught,—that is, not to be angry, not to desire riches, not to be inflamed with lust, not to fear pain, to despise death. These things are plainly virtues, but they cannot be done without flesh. Therefore He assumed a body on this account, that, since He taught that the desires of the flesh must be overcome, He might in person first practice it, that no one might allege the frailty of the flesh as an excuse.

### Chap. LI.—Of the Death of Christ on the Cross.

I will now speak of the mystery of the cross, lest anyone should happen to say, If death must be endured by Him, it should have been not one that was manifestly infamous and dishonorable, but one which had some honor. I know, indeed, that many, while they dislike the name of the cross, shrink from the truth, though there is in it great reasonableness and power.

For since He was sent for this purpose, that He might open to the lowest men the way to salvation, He made Himself humble that He might free them. Therefore He underwent that kind of death which is usually inflicted on the humble, that an opportunity of imitation might be given to all. Moreover, since He was about to rise again, it was not allowable that His body should be in any way mutilated, or a bone broken, which happens to those who are beheaded. Therefore the cross was preferred, which reserved the body with the bones uninjured for the resurrection.

To these grounds it was also added, that having undertaken to suffer and to die, it was befitting that He should be lifted up. Thus the cross exalted Him both in fact and in emblem, so that His majesty and power became known to all, together with His passion. For in that He extended His hands on the cross, He plainly stretched out His wings towards the east and the west, under which all nations from either side of the world might assemble and repose. But of what great weight this sign is, and what power it has, is evident, since all the host of demons is expelled and put to flight by this sign. And as He Himself before His passion put to confusion demons by His word and command, so now, by the name and sign of the same passion, unclean spirits, having insinuated themselves into the bodies of men, are driven out, when racked and tormented, and confessing themselves to be demons, they yield themselves to God, who harasses them. What therefore can the Greeks expect from their superstitions and with their wisdom, when they see that their gods, whom they do not deny to be demons also, are subdued by men through the cross?

### Chap. LII.—The Hope of the Salvation of Men Consists in the Knowledge of the True God, and of the Hatred of the Heathens against the Christians.

There is therefore but one hope of life for men, one harbor of safety, one refuge of liberty, if, laying aside the errors by which they were held, they open the eyes of their mind and recognize God, in whom alone is the abode of truth; despise earthly things, and those made from the ground esteem as nothing philosophy, which is foolishness with God; and having undertaken true wisdom, that is, religion, become heirs of immortality. But indeed they are not so much opposed to the truth as to their own safety; and when they hear these things, they abominate them as some inexpiable wickedness. But they do not even endure to hear: they think that their ears are polluted with impiety if they hear; nor do they now refrain from reproaches, but assail them with the most insulting words; and also, if they have obtained the power, persecute them as public enemies, yea, even as worse than enemies; for enemies, when they have been vanquished, are punished with death or slavery; nor is there any torturing after the laying down of arms, although those deserved to suffer all things who wished so to act, that piety might have place among swords.

Cruelty, combined with innocence, is unheard of, nor is it worthy of the condition of victorious enemies. What is the so powerful cause of this fury? Doubtless, because they cannot contend on the ground of reason, they urge forward their cause by means of violence; and, with the subject not understood, they condemn those as most pernicious persons who have declined to make a stand respecting the fact of their innocence. Nor do they deem it sufficient that those whom they unreasonably hate should die by a speedy and simple death; but they lacerate them with refined tortures, that they may satisfy their hatred, which is not produced by any fault, but by the truth, which is hateful to those who live wickedly, because they take it ill that there are some whom their deeds cannot please. They desire in every way to destroy these, that they may be able to sin without restraint in the absence of any witness.

## Chap. LIII.—The Reasons of the Hatred against the Christians are Examined and Refuted.

But they say that they do these things for the defense of their gods. In the first place, if they are gods, and have any power and influence, they have no need of the defense and protection of men, but they manifestly defend themselves. Or how is man able to hope for aid from them, if they are unable to average even their own injuries? Therefore it is a vain and foolish thing to wish to be avengers of the gods, except that their distrust is more apparent from this. For he who undertakes the protection of the god whom he worships, admits the worthlessness of that god; but if he worships him on this account, because he thinks him powerful, he ought not to wish to defend him, by whom he himself ought to be defended. We therefore act rightly. For when those defenders of false gods, who are rebellious against the true God, persecute His name in us, we resist not either in deed or in word, but with meekness, and silence, and patience, we endure whatever cruelty is able to contrive against us. For we have confidence in God, from whom we expect that retribution will hereafter follow. Nor is this confidence ungrounded, since we have in some cases heard, and in other cases seen, the miserable ends of all those who have dared to commit this crime. Nor has anyone had it in his power to insult God with impunity; but he who has been unwilling to learn by word has learned by his own punishment who is the true God.

I should wish to know, when they compel men to sacrifice against their will, what reasoning they have with themselves, or to whom they make that offering. If it is made to the gods, that is not worship, nor an acceptable sacrifice, which is made by those who are displeasing to them, which is extorted by injury, which is enforced by pain. But if it is done to those whom they compel, it is plainly not a benefit, which anyone would not receive, he even prefers rather to die. If it is a good to which you call me, why do you invite me with evil? Why with blows, and not with words? Why not by argument, but by bodily tortures? Whence it is manifest that that is an evil, to which you do not allure me willing, but drag me refusing. What folly is it to wish to consult the good of any one against his will! If anyone, under the pressure of evils, attempts to have recourse to death, can you, if you either wrest the sword from his hand, or cut the halter, or drag him away from the precipice, or pour out the poison, boast yourself as the preserver of the man, when he, whom you think that you have preserved, does not thank you, and thinks that you have acted ill towards him, in averting from him the death which be desired, and in not permitting him to reach the end and rest from his labors? For a benefit ought not to be weighed according to the quality of the action, but according to the feelings of him who receives it. Why should you reckon as a benefit that which is an injury to me? Do you wish me to worship your gods, which I consider deadly to myself? If it is a good, I do not envy it. Enjoy your good by yourself. There is no reason why you should wish to succor my error, which I have undertaken by my judgment and inclination. If it is evil, why do you drag me to a participation in evil? Use your own fortune. I prefer to die in the practice of that which is good, than to live in evil.

### Chap. LIV.—Of the Freedom of Religion in the Worship of God.

These things may indeed be said with justice. But who will hear, when men of furious and unbridled spirit think that their authority is diminished if there is any freedom in the affairs of men? But it is religion alone in which freedom has placed its dwelling. For it is a matter which is voluntary above all others, nor can necessity be imposed upon any, so as to worship that which he does not wish to worship. Someone may perhaps pretend, he cannot wish it. In short, some, through fear of torments, or overcome by tortures, have assented to detestable sacrifices: they never do that voluntarily which they did from necessity; but when the opportunity is again given to them, and liberty restored, they again betake themselves to God, and appease Him with prayers and tears, repenting not of the will, which they had not, but of the necessity which they endured; and pardon is not denied to those who make satisfaction. What then does he accomplish who pollutes the body, since he cannot change the will?

But, in fact, men of weak understanding, if they have induced any man of spirit to sacrifice to their gods, with incredible alacrity insolently exult, and rejoice, as though they had sent an enemy under the yoke. But if anyone, neither frightened by threats nor by tortures, shall have chosen to prefer his faith to his life, cruelty puts forth all its ingenuity against him, plans dreadful and intolerable things; and because they know that death for the cause of God is glorious, and that this is a victory on our side, if, having overcome the torturers, we lay down our life in behalf of the faith and religion, they also themselves strive to conquer us. They do not put us to death, but they search out new and unheard-of tortures, that the frailty of the flesh may yield to pains, and if it does not yield, they put off further punishment, and apply diligent care to the wounds, that while the scars are yet fresh, a repetition of the torture may inflict more pain; and while they practice this torture upon the innocent, they evidently consider themselves pious, and just, and religious (for they are delighted with such sacrifices to their gods), but they term the others impious and desperate. What perversity is this, that he who is punished, though innocent, should be called desperate and impious, and that the torturer, on the other hand, should be called just and pious!

### Chap. LV.—The Heathens Charge Justice with Impiety in Following God.

But they say that those are rightly and deservedly punished, who dislike the public rites of religion handed down to them by their ancestors. What if those ancestors were foolish in undertaking vain religious rites, as we have shown before, shall we be prohibited from following true and better things? Why do we deprive ourselves of liberty, and become enslaved to the errors of others, as though bound to them? Let it be permitted us to be wise, let it be permitted us to inquire into the truth. But, however, if it pleases them to defend *the folly* of their ancestors, why are the Egyptians suffered to escape, who worship cattle and beasts of every kind as deities? Why are the gods themselves made the subjects of comic representations? And why is he honored who derides them most wittily? Why are philosophers attended to, who either say that there are no gods, or that, if there are any, they take no interest in, and do not regard the affairs of men, or argue that there is no providence at all, which rules the world?

But they alone of all are judged impious who follow God and the truth. And since this is at once justice, and wisdom, they lay to its charge either impiety or folly, and do not perceive what it is which deceives them, when they call evil good, and good evil. Many indeed of the philosophers, and especially Plato and Aristotle, spoke many things about justice, asserting and extolling that virtue with the greatest praise, because it gives to each its due, because it maintains equity in all things; and whereas the other virtues are as it were silent, and shut up within, that it is justice alone which is neither concerned for itself only, nor hidden, but altogether shows itself abroad, and is ready for conferring a benefit, so as to assist as many as possible: as though in truth justice ought to be in judges only, and those placed in any post of authority, and not in all men.

And yet there is no one of men, not even of the lowest and of beggars, who is not capable of justice. But because they did not know what it was, from what source it proceeded, and what was its mode of operation, they assigned to a few only that highest virtue, that is, the common good of all, and said that it aimed at no advantages peculiar to itself, but only the interests of others. And not without reason was Carneades raised up, a man of the greatest talent and penetration, to refute their speech, and overthrow the justice, which had no firm foundation; not because he thought that justice was to be blamed, but that he might show that its defenders brought forward no firm or certain argument respecting justice.

### Chap. LVI.—Of Justice, Which is the Worship of the True God.

For if justice is the worship of the true God (for what is so just with respect to equity, so pious with respect to honor, so necessary with respect to safety, as to acknowledge God as a parent, to reverence Him as Lord, and to obey His law or precepts?), it follows that the philosophers were ignorant of justice, for they neither acknowledged God Himself, nor observed His worship and law; and on this account they might have been refuted by Carneades, whose disputation was to this effect, that there is no natural justice, and therefore that all animals defended their own interests by the guidance of nature itself, and therefore that justice, if it promotes the advantages of others and neglects its own, is to be called foolishness. But if all people who are possessed of power, and the Romans themselves, who are masters of the whole world, were willing to follow justice, and to restore to everyone his property which they have seized by force and arms, they will return to cottages and a condition of want. And if they did this, they might indeed be just, but they must of necessity be considered foolish, who proceed to injure themselves for the advantage of others. Then, if anyone should find a man who was through a mistake offering for sale gold as mountain-brass, or silver as lead, and necessity should compel him to buy it, will he conceal his knowledge and buy it for a small sum, or will he rather inform the seller of its value? If he shall inform him, he will manifestly be called just; but he will also be foolish, for conferring an advantage upon another, and injuring himself. But it is easy *to judge* in a case of injury. What if he shall incur danger of his life, so that it shall be necessary for him either to kill another or to die, what will he do? It may happen that, having suffered shipwreck, he may find some feeble person clinging to a plank; or, his army having been defeated, in his flight he may find a wounded man on horseback: will he thrust the one from the plank, the other from his horse, that he himself may be able to escape? If he shall wish to be just, he will not do it; but he will also be judged foolish, who in sparing the life of another shall lose his own. If he shall do it, he will indeed appear wise, because he will provide for his own interests; but he will also be wicked, because he will commit a wrong.

## Chap. LVII.—Of Wisdom and Foolishness.

These things indeed are said with acuteness; but we are able very readily to reply to them. For the imitation of names causes it thus to appear. For justice bears a resemblance to foolishness, and yet it is not foolishness; and at the same time malice bears a resemblance to wisdom, and yet it is not wisdom. But as that malice is intelligent and shrewd in preserving its own interests, it is not wisdom, but cunning and craftiness; so likewise justice ought not to be called foolishness, but innocence, because the just man must be wise, and the foolish man unjust. For neither reason nor nature itself permits that he who is just should not be wise, since it is plain that the just man does nothing except that which is right and good, and always avoids that which is perverted and evil. But who will be able to distinguish between good and evil, depravity and rectitude, but he who shall be wise? But the fool acts badly, because he is ignorant of what is good and evil. Therefore he does wrong, because he is unable to distinguish between things which are perverted and those which are right. Therefore justice cannot be befitting to the foolish man, nor wisdom to the unjust. He is not then a foolish person who has not thrust off a shipwrecked man from a plank, nor a wounded man from his horse, because he has abstained from injury, which is a sin; and it is the part of the wise man to avoid sin.

But that he should appear foolish at first sight is caused by this, that they suppose the soul to be extinguished together with the body; and for this reason they refer all advantage to this life. For if there is no existence after death, it is plain that he acts foolishly who spares the life of another to his own loss, or who consults the gain of another more than his own. If death destroys the soul, we must use our endeavors to live for a longer time, and more to our own advantage; but if there remains after death a life of immortality and blessedness, the just and wise man will certainly despise this corporeal existence, with all earthly goods, because he will know what kind of a reward he is about to receive from God. Therefore let us maintain innocence, let us maintain justice, let us undergo the appearance of foolishness, that we may be able to maintain true wisdom. And if it appears to men senseless and foolish to prefer torture and death rather than to sacrifice to gods, and to escape without harm, let us however strive to exhibit faithfulness towards God by all virtue and by all patience. Let not death terrify us, nor pain subdue us, so as to prevent the vigor of our mind and constancy from being preserved unshaken. Let them call us foolish, whilst they themselves are most foolish, and blind and dull, and like sheep; who do not understand that it is a deadly thing to leave the living God, and prostrate themselves in the adoration of earthly objects; who do not know that eternal punishment awaits those who have worshipped senseless images; and that those who have neither refused tortures nor death for the worship and honor of the true God will obtain eternal life. This is the highest faith; this is true wisdom; this is perfect justice. It matters nothing to us what fools may judge, what trifling men may think. We ought to await the judgment of God, that we may hereafter judge those who have passed judgment on us.

### Chap. LVIII.—Of the True Worship of God, and Sacrifice.

I have spoken of justice, what was its nature. It follows that I show what is true sacrifice to God, what is the most just manner of worshipping Him, lest anyone should think that victims, or odors, or precious gifts, are desired by God, who, if He is not subject to hunger, and thirst, and cold, and desire of all earthly things, does not therefore make use of all these things which are presented in temples and to gods of earth; but as corporeal offerings are necessary for corporeal beings, so manifestly an incorporeal sacrifice is necessary for an incorporeal being. But God has no need of those things which He has given to man for his use, since all the earth is under His power: He needs not a temple, since the world is His dwelling; He needs not an image, since He is incomprehensible both to the eyes and to the mind; He needs no earthly lights, for He was able to kindle the light of the sun, with the other stars, for the use of man. What then does God require from man but worship of the mind, which is pure and holy? For those things which are made by the hands, or are outside of man, are senseless, frail, and displeasing. This is true sacrifice, which is brought forth not from the chest but from the heart; not that which is offered by the hand, but by the mind. This is the acceptable victim, which the mind sacrifices of itself. For what do victims bestow? What does incense? What do garments? What does silver? What gold? What precious stones,—if there is not a pure mind on the part of the worshipper? Therefore it is justice only which God requires. In this is sacrifice; in this the worship of God, respecting which I must now speak, and show in what works justice must necessarily be contained.

**Chap. LIX.—Of the Ways of Life, and the First Times of the World.**

That there are two ways of human life was unknown neither to philosophers nor to poets, but both introduced them in a different manner. The philosophers wished the one to be the way of industry, the other of idleness; but in this respect they were less correct in their statements, that they referred them to the advantages of this life only. The poets spoke better who said that one of them was the way of the just, the other of the unjust; but they err in this, that they say that they are not in this life, but in the shades below. We manifestly speak more correctly, who say that the one is the way of life, the other that of death. And here, however, we say that there are two ways; but the one on the right hand, in which the just walk, does not lead to Elysium, but to heaven, for they become immortal; the other on the left leads to Tartarus, for the unjust are sentenced to eternal tortures. Therefore the way of justice, which leads to life, is to be held by us. Now the first duty of justice is to acknowledge God as a parent, and to fear Him as a master, to love Him as a father. For the same Being who begat us, who animated us with vital breath, who nourishes and preserves us, has over us, not only as a father but also as a master, authority to correct us, and the power of life and death; wherefore twofold honor is due to Him from man, that is, love combined with fear. The second duty of justice is to acknowledge man as a brother. For if the same God made us, and produced all men on equal terms to justice and eternal life, it is manifest that we are united by the relationship of brotherhood; and he who does not acknowledge this is unjust. But the origin of this evil, by which the mutual society of men, by which the bond of relationship has been torn asunder, arises from ignorance of the true God. For he who is ignorant of that fountain of bounty can by no means be good. Hence it is that, from the time when a multitude of gods began to be consecrated and worshipped by men, justice, as the poets relate, being put to flight, every compact was destroyed, the fellowship of human justice was destroyed. Then everyone, consulting his own interest, reckoned might to be right, injured another, attacked by frauds, deceived by treachery, increased his own advantages by the inconvenience of others, did not spare relatives, or children, or parents, prepared poisoned cups for the destruction of men, beset the ways with the sword, infested the seas, gave the rein to his lust, wherever passion led him,—in short, esteemed nothing sacred which his dreadful desire did not violate. When these things were done, then men instituted laws for themselves to promote the public advantage, that they might meanwhile protect themselves from injuries. But the fear of laws did not suppress crimes, but it checked licentiousness. For laws were able to punish offences, they were unable to punish the conscience. Therefore the things which before were done openly began to be done secretly. Justice also was evaded by stealth, since they who themselves presided over the administration of the laws, corrupted by, gifts and rewards, made a traffic of their sentences, either to the escape of the evil or to the destruction of the good. To these things were added dissensions, and wars, and mutual depredations; and the laws being crushed, the power of acting with violence was assumed without restraint.

## Chap. LX.—Of the Duties of Justice.

When the affairs of men were in this condition, God pitied us, revealed and displayed Himself to us, that in Himself we might learn religion, faith, purity, and mercy; that having laid aside the error of our former life, together with God Himself we might know ourselves, whom impiety had disunited from Him, and we might choose the divine law, which unites human affairs with heavenly, the Lord Himself delivering it to us; by which law all the errors with which we have been ensnared, together with vain and impious superstitions, might be taken away. What we owe to man, therefore, is prescribed by that same divine law which teaches that whatever you render to man is rendered to God. But the root of justice, and the entire foundation of equity, is that you should not do that which you would be unwilling to suffer, but should measure the feelings of another by your own. If it is an unpleasant thing to bear an injury, and he who has done it appears unjust, transfer to the person of another that which you feel respecting yourself, and to your own person that which you judge respecting another, and you will understand that you act as unjustly if you injure another as another would if he should injure you. If we consider these things, we shall maintain innocence, in which the first step of justice is, as it were, contained. For the first thing is, not to injure; the next is, to be of service. And as in uncultivated lands, before you begin to sow, the fields must be cleansed by tearing up the thorns and cutting off all the roots of trunks, so vices must first be thrust out from our souls, and then at length virtues must be implanted, from which the fruits of immortality, being engendered by the word of God, may spring up.

**Chap. LXI.—Of the Passions.**

There are three passions, or, so to speak, three furies, which excite such great perturbations in the souls of men, and sometimes compel them to offend in such a manner, as to permit them to have regard neither for their reputation nor for their personal safety: these are anger, which desires vengeance; love of gain, which longs for riches; lust, which seeks for pleasures. We must above all things resist these vices: these trunks must be rooted up, that virtues may be implanted. The Stoics are of opinion that these passions must be cut off; the Peripatetics think that they must be restrained. Neither of them judge rightly, because they cannot entirely be taken away, since they are implanted by nature, and have a sure and great influence; nor can they be diminished, since, if they are evil, we ought to be without them, even though restrained and used with moderation; if they are good, we ought to use them in their completeness. But we say that they ought not to be taken away nor lessened. For they are not evil of themselves, since God has reasonably implanted them in us; but inasmuch as they are plainly good by nature,—for they are given us for the protection of life,—they become evil by their evil use. And as bravery, if you fight in defense of your country, is a good, if against your country, is an evil, so the passions, if you employ them to good purposes, will be virtues, if to evil uses, they will be called vices. Anger therefore has been given by God for the restraining of offences, that is, for controlling the discipline of subjects, that fear may suppress licentiousness and restrain audacity. But they who are ignorant of its limits are angry with their equals, or even with their superiors. Hence they rush to deeds of cruelty, hence they rise to slaughters, hence to wars. The love of gain also has been given that we may desire and seek for the necessaries of life. But they who are unacquainted with its boundaries strive insatiably to heap up riches. Hence poisoning, hence defrauding, hence false wills, hence all kinds of frauds have burst forth. Moreover, the passion of lust is implanted and innate in us for the procreation of children; but they who do not fix its limits in the mind use it for pleasure only. Thence arise unlawful loves, thence adulteries and debaucheries, thence all kinds of corruption. These passions, therefore, must be kept within their boundaries and directed into their right course, in which, even though they should be vehement, they cannot incur blame.

### Chap. LXII.—Of Restraining the Pleasures of the Senses.

Anger is to be restrained when we suffer an injury, that the evil may be suppressed which is imminent from a contest, and that we may retain two of the greatest virtues, harmlessness and patience. Let the desire of gain be broken when we have that which is enough. For what madness is it to labor in heaping up those things which must pass to others, either by robbery, or theft, or by proscription, or by death? Let lust not go beyond the marriage-bed, but be subservient to the procreation of children. For a too great eagerness for pleasure both produces danger and generates disgrace, and that which is especially to be avoided, leads to eternal death. Nothing is so hateful to God as an unchaste mind and an impure soul. Nor let anyone think that he must abstain from this pleasure only, quæ capitur ex foeminei corporis copulatione, but also from the other pleasures which arise from the rest of the senses, because they also are of themselves vicious, and it is the part of the same virtue to despise them. The pleasure of the eyes is derived from the beauty of objects, that of the ears from harmonious and pleasant sounds, that of the nostrils from pleasant odor, that of taste from sweet food,—all of which virtue ought strongly to resist, lest, ensnared by these attractions, the soul should be depressed from heavenly to earthly things, from things eternal to things temporal, from life immortal to perpetual punishment. In pleasures of the taste and smell there is this danger, that they are able to draw us to luxury. For he who shall be given up to these things, either will have no property, or, if he shall have any, he will expend it, and afterwards live a life to be abominated. But he who is carried away by hearing (to say nothing respecting songs, which often so charm the inmost senses that they even disturb with madness a settled state of the mind by certain elaborately composed speeches and harmonious poems, or skillful disputations) is easily led aside to impious worship. Hence it is that they who are either themselves eloquent, or prefer to read eloquent writings, do not readily believe the sacred writings, because they appear unpolished; they do not seek things that are true, but things that are pleasant; nay, to them those things appear to be most true which soothe the ears. Thus they reject the truth, while they are captivated by the sweetness of the discourse. But the pleasure which has reference to the sight is manifold. For that which is derived from the beauty of precious objects excites avarice, which ought to be far removed from a wise and just man; but that which is received from the appearance of woman hurries a man to another pleasure, of which we have already spoken above.

### Chap. LXIII.—That Shows are Most Powerful to Corrupt the Minds.

It remains to speak of public shows, which, since they have a more powerful influence on the corruption of the mind, ought to be avoided by the wise, and to be altogether guarded against, because it is said that they were instituted in celebration of the honors of the gods. For the exhibitions of shows are festivals of Saturnus. The stage belongs to Father Liber; but the Circensian games are supposed to be dedicated to Neptunus: so that now he who takes part in these shows appears to have left the worship of God, and to have passed over to profane rites. But I prefer to speak of the matter itself rather than of its origin. What is so dreadful, what so foul, as the slaughter of man? Therefore our life is protected by the most severe laws; therefore wars are detestable. Yet custom finds how a man may commit homicide without war, and without laws; and this is a pleasure to him, that he has avenged guilt. But if to be present at homicide implies a consciousness of guilt, and the spectator is involved in the same guilt as the perpetrator, then in these slaughters of gladiators, he who is a spectator is no less sprinkled with blood than he who sheds it; nor can he be free from the guilt of bloodshed who wished it to be poured out, or appear not to have slain, who both favored the slayer and asked a reward for him. What of the stage? Is it more holy,—on which comedy converses on the subject of debaucheries and amours, tragedy of incest and parricide? The immodest gestures also of players, with which they imitate disreputable women, teach the lusts, which they express by dancing. For the pantomime is a school of corruption, in which things which are shameful are acted by a figurative representation, that the things which are true may be done without shame. These spectacles are viewed by youths, whose dangerous age, which ought to be curbed and governed, is trained by these representations to vices and sins. The circus, in truth, is considered more innocent, but there is greater madness in this, since the minds of the spectators are transported with such great madness, that they not only break out into reviling, but often rise to strife, and battles, and contentions. Therefore all shows are to be avoided, that we may be able to maintain a tranquil state of mind. We must renounce hurtful pleasures, lest, charmed by pestilential sweetness, we fall into the snares of death.

**Chap. LXIV.—The Passions are to Be Subdued, and We Must Abstain from Forbidden Things.**

Let virtue alone please us, whose reward is immortal when it has conquered pleasure. But when the passions have been overcome and pleasures subdued labor in suppressing other things is easy to him who is a follower of God and of truth: he will never revile, who shall hope for a blessing from God; he will not commit perjury, lest he should mock God; but he will not even swear, lest at any time, either by necessity or through habit, he should fall into perjury. He will speak nothing deceitfully, nothing with dissimulation; he will not refuse that which he has promised, nor will he promise that which he is unable to perform; he will envy no one, since he is content with himself and with his own possessions; nor will he take away from, or wish ill to another, upon whom, perhaps, the benefits of God are more plenteously bestowed. He will not steal, nor will he covet anything at all belonging to another. He will not give his money to usury, for that is to seek after gain from the evils of others; nor, however, will he refuse to lend, if necessity shall compel anyone to borrow. He must not be harsh towards a son, nor towards a slave: he must remember that he himself has a Father and a Master. He will so act towards these as he will wish that others should act towards him. He will not receive excessive gifts from those who have less resources than himself; for it is not just that the estates of the wealthy should be increased by the losses of the wretched.

It is an old precept not to kill, which ought not to be taken in this light, as though we are commanded to abstain only from homicide, which is punished even by public laws. But by the intervention of this command, it will not be permitted us to apply peril of death by word, nor to put to death or expose an infant, nor to condemn one's self by a voluntary death. We are likewise commanded not to commit adultery; but by this precept we are not only prohibited from polluting the marriage of another, which is condemned even by the common law of nations, but even to abstain from those who prostitute their persons. For the law of God is above all laws; it forbids even those things which are esteemed lawful, that it may fulfil justice. It is a part of the same law not to utter false witness, and this also itself has a wider meaning. For if false witness by falsehood is injurious to him against whom it is spoken, and deceives him in whose presence it is spoken, we must therefore never speak falsely, because falsehood always deceives or injures. Therefore he is not a just man who, even without inflicting injury, speaks in idle discourse. Nor indeed is it lawful for him to flatter, for flattery is pernicious and deceitful; but he will everywhere guard the truth. And although this may for the present be unpleasant, nevertheless, when its advantage and usefulness shall appear, it will not produce hatred, as the poet says, but gratitude.

**Chap. LXV.—Precepts about Those Things Which are Commanded, and of Pity.**

I have spoken of those things which are forbidden; I will now briefly say what things are commanded. Closely connected with harmlessness is pity. For the former does not inflict injury, the latter works good; the former begins justice, the latter completes it. For since the nature of men is more feeble than that of the other animals, which God has provided with means of inflicting violence, and with defenses for repelling it, He has given to us the affection of pity, that we might place the whole protection of our life in mutual aid. For if we are created by one God, and descended from one man, and are thus connected by the law of consanguinity, we ought on this account to love every man; and therefore we are bound not only to abstain from the infliction of injury, but not even to avenge it when inflicted on us, that there may be in us complete harmlessness. And on this account God commands us to pray always even for our enemies. Therefore we ought to be an animal fitted for companionship and society, that we may mutually protect ourselves by giving and receiving assistance. For our frailty is liable to many accidents and inconveniences. Expect that that which you see has happened to another may happen to you also. Thus you will at length be excited to render aid, if you shall assume the mind of him who, being placed in evils, implores your aid. If anyone is in need of food, let us bestow it; if anyone meets us who is naked, let us clothe him; if anyone suffers injury from one who is more powerful than himself, let us rescue him. Let our house be open to strangers, or to those who are in need of shelter. Let our defense not be wanting to wards, or our protection to the defenseless. To ransom captives is a great work of pity, and also to visit and comfort the sick who are in poverty. If the helpless or strangers die, we should not permit them to lie unburied. These are the works, these the duties, of pity; and if anyone undertakes these, he will offer unto God a true and acceptable sacrifice. This victim is more adapted for an offering to God, who is not appeased with the blood of a sheep, but with the piety of man, whom God, because He is just, follows up with His own law, and with His own condition. He shows mercy to him whom He sees to be merciful; He is inexorable to him whom He sees to be harsh to those who entreat him. Therefore, that we may be able to do all these things, which are pleasing to God, money is to be despised, and to be transferred to heavenly treasures, where neither thief can break through, nor rust corrupt, nor tyrant take away, but it may be preserved for us under the guardianship of God to our eternal wealth.

### Chap. LXVI.—Of Faith in Religion, and of Fortitude.

Faith also is a great part of justice; and this ought especially to be preserved by us, who bear the name of faith, especially in religion, because God is before and to be preferred to man. And if it is a glorious thing to undergo death in behalf of friends, of parents, and of children, that is, in behalf of man, and if he who has done this obtains lasting memory and praise, how much more so in behalf of God, who is able to bestow eternal life in return for temporal death? Therefore, when a necessity of this kind happens, that we are compelled to turn aside from God, and to pass over to the rites of the heathens, no fear, no terror should turn us aside from guarding the faith delivered to us. Let God be before our eyes, in our heart, by whose inward help we may overcome the pain of our flesh, and the torments applied to our body. Then let us think of nothing else but the rewards of an immortal life. And thus, even though our limbs should be torn in pieces, or burnt, we shall easily endure all things which the madness of tyrannical cruelty shall contrive against us. Lastly, let us strive to undergo death itself, not unwillingly or timidly, but willingly and undauntedly, as those who know what glory we are about to have in the presence of God, having triumphed over the world and coming to the things promised us; with what good things and how great blessedness we shall be compensated for these brief evils of punishments, and the injuries of this life. But if the opportunity of this glory shall be wanting, faith will have its reward even in peace.

Therefore let it be observed in all the duties of life, let it be observed in marriage. For it is not sufficient if you abstain from another's bed, or from the brothel. Let him who has a wife seek nothing further, but, content with her alone, let him guard the mysteries of the marriage-bed chaste and undefiled. For he is equally an adulterer in the sight of God and impure, who, having thrown off the yoke, wantons in strange pleasure either with a free woman or a slave. But as a woman is bound by the bonds of chastity not to desire any other man, so let the husband be bound by the same law, since God has joined together the husband and the wife in the union of one body. On this account He has commanded that the wife shall not be put away unless convicted of adultery, and that the bond of the conjugal compact shall never be dissolved, unless unfaithfulness have broken it. This also is added for the completion of chastity, that there should be an absence not only of the offence, but even of the thought. For it is evident that the mind is polluted by the desire, though unaccomplished; and so that a just man ought neither to do, nor to wish to do, that which is unjust. Therefore the conscience must be cleansed; for God, who cannot be deceived, inspects it. The breast must be cleared from every stain, that it may be a temple of God, which is enlightened not by the gleam of gold or ivory, but by the brightness of faith and purity.

## Chap. LXVII.—Of Repentance, the Immortality of the Soul, and of Providence.

But it is true all these things are difficult to man, nor does the condition of his frailty permit that anyone should be without blemish. Therefore the last remedy is this, that we have recourse to repentance, which has not the least place among the virtues, because it is a correction of oneself; that when we have happened to fail either in deed or in word, we may immediately come to a better mind, and confess that we have offended, and entreat pardon from God, which according to His mercy He will not deny, except to those who persist in their error. Great is the aid, great the solace of repentance. That is the healing of wounds and offences that hope that the harbor of safety; and he who takes away this cuts off from himself the way of salvation, because no one can be so just that repentance is never necessary for him. But we, even though there is no offence of ours, yet ought to confess to God, and to entreat pardon for our faults, and to give thanks even in evils. Let us always offer this obedience to our Lord. For humility is dear and lovely in the sight of God; for since He rather receives the sinner who confesses his fault, than the just man who is haughty, how much more will He receive the just man who confesses, and exalt him in His heavenly kingdom in proportion to his humility! These are the things which the worshipper of God ought to hold forth; these are the victims, this the sacrifice, which is acceptable; this is true worship, when a man offers upon the altar of God the pledges of his own mind. That supreme Majesty rejoices in such a worshipper as this, as it takes him as a son and bestows upon him the befitting reward of immortality, concerning which I must now speak, and refute the persuasion of those who think that the soul is destroyed together with the body. For inasmuch as they neither knew God nor were able to perceive the mystery of the world, they did not even comprehend the nature of man and of the soul. For how could they see the consequences, who did not hold the main point? Therefore, in denying the existence of a providence, they plainly denied the existence of God, who is the fountain and source of all things. It followed that they should either affirm that those things which exist have always existed, or were produced of their own accord, or arose from a meeting together of minute seeds.

It cannot be said that that which exists, and is visible, always existed; for it cannot exist of itself without some beginning. But nothing can be produced of its own accord, because there is no nature without one who generates it. But how could there be original seeds, since both the seeds arise from objects, and, in their turn, objects from seeds? Therefore there is no seed which has not origin. Thus it came to pass, that when they supposed that the world was produced by no providence, they did not suppose that even man was produced by any plan. But if no plan was made use of in the creation of man, therefore the soul cannot be immortal. But others, on the other hand, thought there was but one God, and that the world was made by Him, and made for the sake of men, and that souls are immortal. But though they entertained true sentiments, nevertheless they did not perceive the causes, or reasons, or issues of this divine work and design, so as to complete the whole mystery of the truth, and to comprise it within some limit. But that which they were not able to do, because they did not hold the truth in its integrity, must be done by us, who know it on the announcement of God.

### Chap. LXVIII.—Of the World, Man, and the Providence of God.

Let us therefore consider what was the plan of making this so great and so immense a work. God made the world, as Plato thought, but he does not show why He made it. Because He is good, he says, and envying no one, He made the things which are good. But we see that there are both good and evil things in the system of nature. Some perverse person may stand forth, such as that atheist Theodorus was, and answer Plato: Nay, because He is evil, He made the things which are evil. How will he refute him? If God made the things which are good, whence have such great evils burst forth, which, for the most part, even prevail over those which are good? They were contained, he says, in the matter. If there were evil, therefore there were also good things; so that either God made nothing, or if He made only good things, the evil things which were not made are more eternal than the good things which had a beginning. Therefore the things which at one time began will have an end, and those which always existed will be permanent. Therefore evils are preferable. But if they cannot be preferable, they cannot indeed be more eternal. Therefore they either always existed, and God has been inactive, or they both flowed from one source. For it is more in accordance with reason that God made all things, than that He made nothing.

Therefore, according to the sentiments of Plato, the same God is both good, because He made good things, and evil, because He made evil things. And if this cannot be so, it is evident that the world was not made by God on this account, because He is good. For He comprised all things, both good and evil; nor did He make anything for its own sake, but on account of something else. A house is built not for this purpose only, that there may be a house, but that it may receive and shelter an inhabitant. Likewise a ship is built not for this purpose, that it may appear only to be a ship, but that men may be able to sail in it. Vessels also are made, not only that the vessels may exist, but that they may receive things which are necessary for use. Thus also God must have made the world for some use. The Stoics say that it was made for the sake of men; and rightly so. For men enjoy all these good things which the world contains in itself. But they do not explain why men themselves were made, or what advantage Providence, the Maker of all things, has in them.

Plato also affirms that souls are immortal, but why, or in what manner, or at what time, or by whose instrumentality they attain to immortality, or what is the nature of that great mystery, why those who are about to become immortal are previously born mortal, and then, having completed the course of their temporal life, and having laid aside the covering of their frail bodies, are transferred to that eternal blessedness,—of all this he has no comprehension. Finally, he did not explain the judgment of God, nor the distinction between the just and the unjust, but supposed that the souls which have plunged themselves into crimes are condemned thus far, that they may be reproduced in the lower animals, and thus atone for their offences, until they again return to the forms of men, and that this is always taking place, and that there is no end of this transmigration. In my opinion, he introduces some sport resembling a dream, in which there appears to be neither plan, nor government of God, nor any design.

**Chap. LXIX.—That the World Was Made on Account of Man, and Man on Account of God.**

I will now say what is that chief point which not even those who spoke the truth were able to connect together, bringing into one view causes and reasons. The world was made by God, that men might be born; again, men are born, that they may acknowledge God as a Father, in whom is wisdom; they acknowledge Him, that they may worship Him, in whom is justice; they worship Him, that they may receive the reward of immortality; they receive immortality, that they may serve God forever. Do you see how closely connected the first are with the middle, and the middle with the last? Let us look into them separately, and see whether they are consistent with each other. God made the world on account of man. He who does not see this, does not differ much from a beast. Who but man looks up to the heaven? Who views with admiration the sun, who the stars, who all the works of God? Who inhabits the earth? Who receives the fruit from it? Who has in his power the fishes, who the winged creatures, who the quadrupeds, except man? Therefore God made all things on account of man, because all things have turned out for the use of man.

The philosophers saw this, but they did not see the consequence, that He made man himself on His own account. For it was befitting, and pious, and necessary, that since He contrived such great works for the sake of man, when He gave him so much honor, and so much power, that he should bear rule in the world, man should both acknowledge God, the Author of such great benefits, who made the world itself on his account, and should pay Him the worship and honor due to Him. Here Plato erred; here he lost the truth which he had at first laid hold of, when he was silent concerning the worship of that God whom he confessed to be the framer and parent of all things, and did not understand that man is bound to God by the ties of piety, whence religion itself receives its name, and that this is the only thing on account of which souls become immortal. He perceived, however, that they are eternal, but he did not descend by the regular gradations to that opinion. For the middle arguments being taken away, he rather fell into the truth, as though by some abrupt precipice; nor did he advance further, since he had found the truth by accident, and not by reason. Therefore God is to be worshipped, that by means of religion, which is also justice, man may receive from God immortality, nor is there any other reward of a pious mind; and if this is invisible, it cannot be presented by the invisible God with any reward but that which is invisible.

**Chap. LXX.—The Immortality of the Soul is Confirmed.**

It may in truth be collected from many arguments that souls are eternal. Plato says that that which always moves by itself, and has no beginning of motion, also has no end; but that the soul of man always moves by itself, and because it is flexible for reflection, subtle for discovery, easy of perception, adapted to learning, and because it retains the past, comprehends the present, foresees the future, and embraces the knowledge of many subjects and arts, that it is immortal, since it contains nothing which is mixed with the contagion of earthly weight. Moreover, the eternity of the soul is understood from virtue and pleasure. Pleasure is common to all animals, virtue belongs only to man;

the former is vicious, the latter is honorable; the former is in accordance with nature, the latter is opposed to nature, unless the soul is immortal. For in defense of faith and justice, virtue neither fears want, nor is alarmed at exile, nor dreads imprisonment, nor shrinks from pain, nor refuses death; and because these things are contrary to nature, either virtue is foolishness, if it stands in the way of advantages, and is injurious to life; or if it is not foolishness, then the soul is immortal, and despises present goods, because other things are preferable which it attains after the dissolution of the body. But that is the greatest proof of immortality, that man alone has the knowledge of God. In the dumb animals there is no notion of religion, because they are earthly and bent down to the earth. Man is upright, and beholds the heaven for this purpose, that he may seek God. Therefore he cannot be other than immortal, who longs for the immortal. He cannot be liable to dissolution, who is connected with God both in countenance and mind. Finally, man alone makes use of the heavenly element, which is fire. For if light is through fire, and life through light, it is evident that he who has the use of fire is not mortal, since this is closely connected, this is intimately related to Him without whom neither light nor life can exist.

But why do we infer from arguments that souls are eternal, when we have divine testimonies? For the sacred writings and the voices of the prophets teach this. And if this appears to anyone insufficient, let him read the poems of the Sibyls, let him also weigh the answers of the Milesian Apollo, that he may understand that Democritus, and Epicurus, and Dicæarchus raved, who alone of all mortals denied that which is evident. Having proved the immortality of the soul, it remains to teach by whom, and to whom, and in what manner, and at what time, it is given. Since fixed and divinely appointed times have begun to be filled up, a destruction and consummation of all things must of necessity take place, that the world may be renewed by God. But that time is at hand, as far as may be collected from the number of years, and from the signs which are foretold by the prophets. But since the things which have been spoken concerning the end of the world and the conclusion of the times are innumerable, those very things which are spoken are to be laid down without adornment, since it would be a boundless task to bring forward the testimonies. If any one wishes for them, or does not place full confidence in us, let him approach to the very shrine of the heavenly letters, and being more fully instructed through their trustworthiness, let him perceive that the philosophers have erred, who thought either that this world was eternal, or that there would be numberless thousands of years from the time when it was prepared. For six thousand years have not yet been completed, and when this number shall be made up, then at length all evil will be taken away, that justice alone may reign. And how this will come to pass, I will explain in few words.

### Chap. LXXI.—Of the Last Times.

These things are said by the prophets, but as seers, to be about to happen. When the last end shall begin to approach to the world, wickedness will increase; all kinds of vices and frauds will become frequent; justice will perish; faith, peace, mercy, modesty, truth, will have no existence; violence and daring will abound; no one will have anything, unless it is acquired by the hand, and defended by the hand. If there shall be any good men, they will be esteemed as a prey and a laughing-stock. No one will exhibit filial affection to parents, no one will pity an infant or an old man; avarice and lust will corrupt all things. There will be slaughter and bloodshed. There will be wars, and those not only between foreign and neighboring states, but also intestine wars. States will carry on wars among themselves, every sex and age will handle arms. The dignity of government will not be preserved, nor military discipline; but after the manner of robbery, there will be depredation and devastation. Kingly power will be multiplied, and ten men will occupy, portion out, and devour the world. There will arise another by far more powerful and wicked, who, having destroyed three, will obtain Asia, and having reduced and subdued the others under his own power, will harass all the earth. He will appoint new laws, abrogate old ones; he will make the state his own, and will change the name and seat of the government.

Then there will be a dreadful and detestable time, in which no one would choose to live. In fine, such will be the condition of things, that lamentation will follow the living, and congratulation the dead. Cities and towns will be destroyed, at one time by fire and the sword, at another by repeated earthquakes; now by inundation of waters, now by pestilence and famine. The earth will produce nothing, being barren either through excessive cold or heat. All water will be partly changed into blood, partly vitiated by bitterness, so that none of it can be useful for food, or wholesome for drinking. To these evils will also be added prodigies from heaven, that nothing may be wanting to men for causing fear. Comets will frequently appear. The sun will be overshadowed with perpetual paleness. The moon will be stained with blood, nor will it repair the losses of its light taken away. All the stars will fall, nor will the seasons preserve their regularity, winter and summer being confused. Then both the year, and the month, and the day will be shortened. And Trismegistus has declared that this is the old age and decline of the world. And when this shall have come, it must be known that the time is at hand in which God will return to change the world. But in the midst of these evils there will arise an impious king, hostile not only to mankind, but also to God. He will trample upon, torment, harass and put to death those who have been spared by that former tyrant. Then there will be ever-flowing tears, perpetual wailings and lamentations, and useless prayers to God; there will be no rest from fear, no sleep for a respite. The day will always increase disaster, the night alarm. Thus the world will be reduced almost to solitude, certainly to fewness of men. Then also the impious man will persecute the just and those who are dedicated to God, and will give orders that he himself shall be worshipped as God. For he will say that he is Christ, though he will be His adversary. That he may be believed, he will receive the power of doing wonders, so that fire may descend from heaven, the sun retire from his course, and the image which he shall have set up may speak. And by these prodigies he shall entice many to worship him, and to receive his sign in their hand or forehead. And he who shall not worship him and receive his sign will die with refined tortures. Thus he will destroy nearly two parts, the third will flee into desolate solitudes. But he, frantic and raging with implacable anger, will lead an army and besiege the mountain to which the righteous shall have fled. And when they shall see themselves besieged, they will implore the aid of God with a loud voice, and God shall hear them, and shall send to them a deliverer.

## Chap. LXXII.—Of Christ Descending from Heaven to the General Judgment, and of the Millenarian Reign.

Then the heaven shall be opened in a tempest, and Christ shall descend with great power, and there shall go before Him a fiery brightness and a countless host of angels, and all that multitude of the wicked shall be destroyed, and torrents of blood shall flow, and the leader himself shall escape, and having often renewed his army, shall for the fourth time engage in battle, in which, being taken, with all the other tyrants, he shall be delivered up to be burnt. But the prince also of the demons himself, the author and contriver of evils, being bound with fiery chains, shall be imprisoned, that the world may receive peace, and the earth, harassed through so many years, may rest. Therefore peace being made, and every evil suppressed, that righteous King and Conqueror will institute a great judgment on the earth respecting the living and the dead, and will deliver all the nations into subjection to the righteous who are alive, and will raise the *righteous* dead to eternal life, and will Himself reign with them on the earth, and will build the holy city, and this kingdom of the righteous shall be for a thousand years. Throughout that time the stars shall be more brilliant, and the brightness of the sun shall be increased, and the moon shall not be subject to decrease. Then the rain of blessing shall descend from God at morning and evening, and the earth shall bring forth all her fruit without the labor of men. Honey shall drop from rocks, fountains of milk and wine shall abound. The beasts shall lay aside their ferocity and become mild, the wolf shall roam among the flocks without doing harm, the calf shall feed with the lion, the dove shall be united with the hawk, the serpent shall have no poison; no animal shall live by bloodshed. For God shall supply to all abundant and harmless food. But when the thousand years shall be fulfilled, and the prince of the demons loosed, the nations will rebel against the righteous, and an innumerable multitude will come to storm the city of the saints. Then the last judgment of God will come to pass against the nations. For He will shake the earth from its foundations, and the cities shall be overthrown, and He shall rain upon the wicked fire with brimstone and hail, and they shall be on fire, and slay each other. But the righteous shall for a little space be concealed under the earth, until the destruction of the nations is accomplished, and after the third day they shall come forth, and see the plains covered with carcasses. Then there shall be an earthquake, and the mountains shall be rent, and valleys shall sink down to a profound depth, and into this the bodies of the dead shall be heaped together, and its name shall be called Polyandrion. After these things God will renew the world, and transform the righteous into the forms of angels, that, being presented with the garment of immortality, they may serve God forever; and this will be the kingdom of God, which shall have no end. Then also the wicked shall rise again, not to life but to punishment; for God shall raise these also, when the second resurrection takes place, that, being condemned to eternal torments and delivered to eternal fires, they may suffer the punishments which they deserve for their crimes.

**Chap. LXXIII.—The Hope of Safety is in the Religion and Worship of God.**

Wherefore, since all these things are true and certain, in harmony with the predicted announcement of the prophets, since Trismegistus and Hystaspes and the Sibyls have foretold the same things, it cannot be doubted that all hope of life and salvation is placed in the religion of God alone. Therefore, unless a man shall have received Christ, whom God has sent, and is about to send for our redemption, unless he shall have known the Supreme God through Christ, unless he shall have kept His commandments and law, he will fall into those punishments of which we have spoken. Therefore frail things must be despised, that we may gain those which are substantial; earthly things must be scorned, that we may be honored with heavenly things; temporal things must be shunned, that we may reach those which are eternal. Let everyone train himself to justice, mold himself to self-restraint, prepare himself for the contest, equip himself for virtue, that if by any chance an adversary shall wage war, he may be driven from that which is upright and good by no force, no terror, and no tortures, may give himself up to no senseless fictions, but in his uprightness acknowledge the true and only God, may cast away pleasures, by the attractions of which the lofty soul is depressed to the earth, may hold fast innocence, may be of service to as many as possible, may gain for himself incorruptible treasures by good works, that he may be able, with God for his judge, to gain for the merits of his virtue either the crown of faith, or the reward of immortality.

**Elucidations.**
*I.*
(Princes and kings, p. 13.)

How memorable the histories, moreover, of Nebuchadnezzar and his decrees; of Darius and his also; but especially of Cyrus and his great monumental edict! The beautiful narratives of the Queen of Sheba and of the Persian consort of Queen Esther (probably Xerxes) are also manifestations of the ways of Providence in giving light to the heathen world through that "nation of priests" in Israel.

But Lactantius, who uses the Sibyls so freely, should not have omitted to show what Sibylline oracles God drew forth from "the princes of this world" also, by the illumination of the *pharos* which he established in Sion, "to be a light to lighten the Gentiles" until the great Epiphany should rise upon them in "the dayspring from on high."

I extract from a paradoxical but most entertaining author, whom I have often quoted, certain extracts from Philo, which I translate from his note in the *Soirées*. Thus:—

"Agrippa," says Philo, "having visited Jerusalem in Herod's time, was enchanted by the religion of the Jews, and could never cease to speak of it....Augustus ordered that every day, at his own expense, and under the legal forms, a bull and *two lambs* should be offered in holocaust to the Most High God on the altar at Jerusalem, though he knew that it contained no image, whether exposed or within the veil; for this great prince, surpassed by none in the philosophic spirit, felt the actual necessity in this world of an altar dedicated to a God invisible."

Philo also says:—

"Your great-grandmother Julia also made superb presents to the temple; and although women very reluctantly detach themselves from images, and rarely conceive of anything apart from sensation, this lady, nevertheless, greatly superior to her sex in culture and in natural endowments, arrived at that point in which she preferred to contemplate such things in the mind rather than in sensible objects, regarding these as mere shadows of the realities."

In the same discourse, wasting words on Caligula, Philo reminds him that Augustus "not only *admired*, nay, rather, he adored (εθαύμαζε καὶ προσέκυνει, κ.τ.λ.), this custom of employing *no sort of image to represent, materially, a nature invisible in itself.*" Poor De Maistre, who quotes this testimony against images from Philo with intense appreciation, will yet sophisticate himself and others into the very contrary in behalf of his one predominant idea of (προσκύνησις) canine self-abasement to the decrees of the Vatican. On this account I am forced to consider him a sophist as well as a fanatic; but I delight to render justice to his genius, for, wherever he talks and reasons *as a Christian* merely, he fascinates and instructs me. He never conceived of "Catholicity," and lived under the delusion of the Decretals, a disciple of the Jesuits.

*II.*

(Therefore they were neglected for many ages, p. 116.)

The explicit statements of Lactantius, and his profuse quotations from the *Sibyllina*, persuade me that these curious fragments deserve a degree of scientific attention which they have not yet received. The Fathers all cite them, when it must have exposed them to scorn and overwhelming refutation had their quotations not been found in the *Sibylline* books of their adversaries. The influence of the Jewish religion upon the Gentiles under the Babylonian and Medo-Persian monarchies must have been considerable, but after Alexander's time it was vastly increased. Many versions of select prophets were doubtless produced in Greek before the authorized Septuagint. These were soon embedded in the Sibyls' books; and I cannot think the interpolations of early Christians were all frauds, by any means. Their numerous marginal annotations crept into other copies; and very likely, in the time of our author, they were inextricably confused with the text in the greater part of the "editions," so to speak, then current with booksellers.

But in vol. viii. we shall have occasion to recur again to this interesting inquiry.

*III.*

(We made proclamation before him as children, p. 117.)

"Sicut pueri." This is *not* according to the Septuagint, ὡς παιδίον. It is not the Vulgate, of course; but its radical difference with that raises interesting inquiries: Is it a specimen of one of many African or old Italic versions? Does our author endeavor to translate from the Septuagint? May he not have had in hand a copy of Isaiah from among those which preceded the Septuagint?

The Septuagint reading finds its key in cap. lii. 7, and in the tenth verse, where the "Arm of the Lord" ("His Holy Arm") is introduced as the personal Logos Incarnate. The thirteenth and fourteenth verses predict the amazing sequel, and its practical and blessed results; and then begins cap. liii., "Who hath believed" our message. To whom is "the Arm of the Lord" revealed? "*Going* before Him (i.e., as heralds), we have proclaimed *Him* as a child, and, as *it were*, a root in a thirsty land; He has no form nor glory," etc. In other words, "We have prophesied of Him who is elsewhere predicted ("unto us a child is born") as one who from His childhood is as a rush without water,—prematurely withered,—a man of sorrows, and the Carpenter's Son."

It does not hint, therefore, the "obscurity" of the Messiah's birth, but rather what Irenæus insists upon, i.e., His (premature) old age; the worn and stricken appearance of senility in comparative youth. This is just what the messengers (Isa. lii. 7) had said in their proclamation (Isa. lii. 14) just before: "His visage was so marred more than any man, and His form more than the sons of men."

*IV.*

(There was darkness, etc., pp. 122, 240.)

In former instances, where thought has turned to Phlegon the Trallian, I have failed to refer to an author whose excess of candor sometimes gives away more than is called for, in questions on which adversaries have contrived to fasten undue importance, in order to elicit indiscreet defenses. But it is due to my readers that I should refer them to a most learned work, to be found in public libraries only, by my revered friend and instructor Dr. Jarvis. The sixth chapter (part ii.) of his *Chronological Introduction to Church History* is devoted to this matter, and I can do no better than give the summary of its contents as follows:—

"Who Phlegon was; his work lost; extracts from it by Julius Africanus and Eusebius; their works, containing these extracts, lost; all we know is from versions and later writers;

collation of extracts as given by the Armenian version of the *Chronicon* of Eusebius, St. Jerome's Latin version, the *Chronographia* of Syncellus, and the *Chronicon Paschale*; extract by Syncellus from Julius Africanus; remarks upon it; testimony of Origen concerning Phlegon's account; of John Philoponus (St. Maximus) Malala; summary of the whole; account of Phlegon's testimony; not noticed by the learned and voluminous writers of the fourth and fifth centuries when they speak of the darkness, etc.; Dr. Lardner's judgment adopted."

Lardner's view, it will be observed, is thus sustained by an independent and most competent critic. This decision puts honor on the early writers: he thinks they were unwilling to claim a corroboration from evidence about which they were not well assured.

V.

(Divine and ethnic oracles, p. 210, note 2; p. 112, note 9.)

The whole subject of ethnic oracles needs fresh study and illustration. Nothing would be more fascinating in theological inquiry, and Divine Inspiration might be richly illustrated by it, as anatomical science is clarified by "comparative anatomy." I commend this subject to men of faith, learning, and intellectual vigor. Notably, let it be observed: (1) That Balaam's ass is instanced by St. Peter as miraculously enabled to rebuke the madness of his master; and the same Apostle shortly before gives us the law as to divine inspiration in contrast. (2) Balaam himself, as mechanically as the beast he rode, had his own mouth opened (see Num. xxiv. 16–19). (3) The wicked Caiaphas in like manner (St. John xi. 51, 52) spoke prophetically, "not of himself." (4) St. Paul (Acts xvii. 28) quotes a heathen oracle very much as does our author. Now, in view of the boldness with which the early Christians follow the example of the Apostle in quoting the *Orphica* and *Sibyllina*, I cannot imagine that these citations were not honestly believed by them to be oracles of a certain sort, by which God permitted the heathen to be enlightened. Observe our author's moderate but most pregnant remark about such inspiration (on p. 170, *supra*, note 8), "*almost* with a divine

## The Writings of Lactatius

voice;" then (on p. 192) compare other *almost* inspired words of poor Tully (at note 2), and of Seneca also.

Finally, and to close the subject, the reader will readily forgive me for introducing the following citations from the "Warburton Lecture" of Dr. Edersheim, on *Prophecy and History in Relation to the Messiah* Discussing the *pseudepigraphic writings* (in Lecture Eleventh), he says as follows:—

"The Sibylline oracles, in Greek hexameters, consist, in their present form, of twelve books. *They are full of interpolations*, the really ancient portions forming part of the first two books and the largest part of book third (verses 97–807). These sections *are deeply imbued with the Messianic spirit.* They date from about the year 140 before our era, while another small portion of the same book is supposed to date from the year 32 b.c.

"As regards the promise of the Messiah, we turn in the first place, and with special interest, to the *Sibylline Oracles*. In the third book of these (such portions as I shall quote date from about 140 b.c.) the Messiah is described as 'the King sent from heaven, who would judge every man in blood and splendor of fire.' And the Vision of Messianic times opens with a reference to 'the King whom God will send from the Sun,' where we cannot fail to perceive a reference to the Seventy-second Psalm, especially as we remember that the Greek of the Seventy, *which must have been present to the Hellenist Sibyl*, fully adapted the Messianic application of the passage to a *premundane* Messiah. We also think of the picture drawn in the prophecies of Isaiah. According to the Sibylline books, King Messiah was not only to come, but He was to be specifically sent of God. He is *supermundane*, a King and a Judge of superhuman glory and splendor. And, indeed, that a superhuman kingdom, such as the Sibylline oracles paint, should have a superhuman king, seems only a natural and necessary inference....If, as certain modern critics contend, the book of Daniel is not authentic, but dates from Maccabean times, ...it may well be asked *to what king* the Sibylline oracles point, for they certainly date from that period;

and what is the relationship between the (supposed Maccabean) prophecies of the book of Daniel and the *certainly Messianic* anticipations of the undoubted literature of that period?"

Dr. Edersheim gives us the reference in the margin, to which I would call attention, as directing to the whole *pseudepigraphic* literature. But who can wonder, after what we thus learn, that Constantine was so profoundly impressed with Virgil's *Pollio*? In spite of all that has been said, I cannot but see Isaiah in its entire spirit.

## A Treatise on the Anger of God

*Addressed to Donatus.*

### Chap. I.—Of Divine and Human Wisdom.

I have often observed, Donatus, that many persons hold this opinion, which some philosophers also have maintained, that God is not subject to anger; since the divine nature is either altogether beneficent, and that it is inconsistent with His surpassing and excellent power to do injury to anyone; or, at any rate, He takes no notice of us at all, so that no advantage comes to us from His goodness, and no evil from His ill-will. But the error of these men, because it is very great, and tends to overthrow the condition of human life, must be refuted by us, lest you yourself also should be deceived, being incited by the authority of men who deem themselves wise. Nor, however, are we so arrogant as to boast that the truth is comprehended by our intellect; but we follow the teaching of God, who alone is able to know and to reveal secret things. But the philosophers, being destitute of this teaching, have imagined that the nature of things can be ascertained by conjecture. But this is impossible; because the mind of man, enclosed in the dark abode of the body, is far removed from the perception of truth: and in this the divine nature differs from the human, that ignorance is the property of the human, knowledge of the divine nature.

On which account we have need of some light to dispel the darkness by which the reflection of man is overspread, since, while we live in mortal flesh, we are unable to divine by our senses. But the light of the human mind is God, and he who has known and admitted Him into his breast will acknowledge the mystery of the truth with an enlightened heart; but when God and heavenly instruction are removed, all things are full of errors. And Socrates, though he was the most learned of all the philosophers, yet, that he might prove the ignorance of the others, who thought that they possessed something, rightly said that he knew nothing, except one thing—that he knew nothing. For he understood that that learning had nothing certain, nothing true in itself; nor, as some imagine, did he pretend to learning that he might refute others, but he saw the truth in some measure. And he testified even on his trial (as is related by Plato) that there was no human wisdom. He so despised, derided, and cast aside the learning in which the philosophers then boasted, that he professed that very thing as the greatest learning, that he had learnt that he knew nothing. If, therefore, there is no human wisdom, as Socrates taught, as Plato handed down, it is evident that the knowledge of the truth is divine, and belongs to no other than to God. Therefore God must be known, in whom alone is the truth. He is the Parent of the world, and the Framer of all things; who is not seen with the eyes, and is scarcely distinguished by the mind; whose religion is accustomed to be attacked in many ways by those who have neither been able to attain true wisdom, nor to comprehend the system of the great and heavenly secret.

### Chap. II.—Of the Truth and Its Steps, and of God.

For since there are many steps by which the ascent is made to the abode of truth, it is not easy for anyone to reach the summit. For when the eyes are darkened by the brightness of the truth, they who are unable to maintain a firm step fall back to the level ground. Now the first step is to understand false religions, and to throw aside the impious worship of gods which are made by the hand of man. But the second step is to perceive with the mind that there is but one Supreme God, whose power and providence made the world from the beginning, and afterwards continues to govern it. The third step is to know His Servant and Messenger, whom He sent as His ambassador to the earth, by whose teaching being freed from the error in which we were held entangled, and formed to the worship of the true God, we might learn righteousness. From all of these steps, as I have said, there is a rapid and easy gliding to a downfall, unless the feet are firmly planted with unshaken steadfastness.

We see those shaken off from the first step, who, though they understand things which are false, do not, however, discover that which is true; and though they despised earthly and frail images, do not betake themselves to the worship of God, of whom they are ignorant. But viewing with admiration the elements of the universe, they worship the heaven, the earth, the sea, the sun, the moon, and the other heavenly bodies.

But we have already reproved their ignorance in the second book of the *Divine Institutes*. But we say that those fall from the second step, who, though they understand that there is but one Supreme God, nevertheless, ensnared by the philosophers, and captivated by false arguments, entertain opinions concerning that excellent majesty far removed from the truth; who either deny that God has any figure, or think that He is moved by no affection, because every affection is a sign of weakness, which has no existence in God. But they are precipitated from the third step, who, though they know the Ambassador of God, who is also the Builder of the divine and immortal temple, either do not receive Him, or receive Him otherwise than faith demands; whom we have partly refuted in the fourth book of the above-named work. And we will hereafter refute more carefully, when we shall begin to reply to all the sects, which, while they dispute, have destroyed the truth.

But now we will argue against those who, falling from the second step, entertain wrong sentiments respecting the Supreme God. For some say that He neither does a kindness to anyone, nor becomes angry, but in security and quietness enjoys the advantages of His own immortality. Others, indeed, take away anger, but leave to God kindness; for they think that a nature excelling in the greatest virtue, while it ought not to be malevolent, ought also to be benevolent. Thus all the philosophers are agreed on the subject of anger, but are at variance respecting kindness. But, that my speech may descend in order to the proposed subject, a division of this kind must be made and followed by me, since anger and kindness are different, and opposed to one another. Either anger must be attributed to God, and kindness taken from Him; or both alike must be taken from Him; or anger must be taken away, and kindness attributed to Him; or neither must be taken away. The nature of the case admits of nothing else besides these; so that the truth, which is sought for, must necessarily be found in some one of these. Let us consider them separately, that reason and arrangement may conduct us to the hiding-place of truth.

**Chap. III.—Of the Good and Evil Things in Human Affairs, and of Their Author.**

First, no one ever said this respecting God, that He is only subject to anger, and is not influenced by kindness. For it is unsuitable to God, that He should be endowed with a power of this kind, by which He may injure and do harm, but be unable to profit and to do good. What means, therefore, what hope of safety, is proposed to men, if God is the author of evils only? For if this is so, that venerable majesty will now be drawn out, not to the power of the judge, to whom it is permitted to preserve and set at liberty, but to the office of the torturer and executioner. But whereas we see that there are not only evils in human affairs, but also goods, it is plain that if God is the author of evils, there must be another who does things contrary to God, and gives to us good things. If there is such a one, by what name must he be called? Why is he who injures us more known to us than He who benefits us? But if this can be nothing besides God, it is absurd and vain to suppose that the divine power, than which nothing is greater or better, is able to injure, but unable to benefit; and accordingly no one has ever existed who ventured to assert this, because it is neither reasonable nor in any way credible. And because this is agreed upon, let us pass on and seek after the truth elsewhere.

## Chap. IV.—Of God and His Affections, and the Censure of Epicurus.

That which follows is concerning the school of Epicurus; that as there is no anger in God, so indeed there is no kindness. For when Epicurus thought that it was inconsistent with God to injure and to inflict harm, which for the most part arises from the affection of anger, he took away from Him beneficence also, since he saw that it followed that if God has anger, He must also have kindness. Therefore, lest he should concede to Him a vice, he deprived Him also of virtue. From this, he says, He is happy and uncorrupted, because He cares about nothing, and neither takes trouble Himself nor occasions it to another. Therefore He is not God, if He is neither moved, which is peculiar to a living being, nor does anything impossible for man, which is peculiar to God, if He has no will at all, no action, in short, no administration, which is worthy of God. And what greater, what more worthy administration can be attributed to God, than the government of the world, and especially of the human race, to which all earthly things are subject?

What happiness, then, can there be in God, if He is always inactive, being at rest and unmoveable? If He is deaf to those who pray to Him, and blind to His worshippers? What is so worthy of God, and so befitting to Him, as providence? But if He cares for nothing, and foresees nothing, He has lost all His divinity. What else does he say, who takes from God all power and all substance, except that there is no God at all? In short, Marcus Tullius relates that it was said by Posidonius, that Epicurus understood that there were no gods, but that he said those things which he spoke respecting the gods for the sake of driving away odium; and so that he leaves the gods in words, but takes them away in reality, since he gives them no motion, no office. But if this is so, what can be more deceitful than him? And this ought to be foreign to the character of a wise and weighty man. But if he understood one thing and spoke another, what else is he to be called than a deceiver, double-tongued, wicked, and moreover foolish? But Epicurus was not so crafty as to say those things with the desire of deceiving, when he consigned these things also by his writings to everlasting remembrance; but he erred through ignorance of the truth. For, being led from the beginning by the probability of a single opinion, he necessarily fell into those things which followed. For the first opinion was, that anger was not consistent with the character of God. And when this appeared to him to be true and unassailable, he was unable to refuse the consequences; because one affection being removed, necessity itself compelled him to remove from God the other affections also. Thus, he who is not subject to anger is plainly uninfluenced by kindness, which is the opposite feeling to anger. Now, if there is neither anger nor kindness in Him, it is manifest that there is neither fear, nor joy, nor grief, nor pity. For all the affections have one system, one motion, which cannot be the case with God. But if there is no affection in God, because whatever is subject to affections is weak, it follows that there is in Him neither the care of anything, nor providence.

The disputation of the wise man extends thus far: he was silent as to the other things which follow; namely, that because there is in Him neither care nor providence, therefore there is no reflection nor any perception in Him, by which it is effected that He has no existence at all. Thus, when he had gradually descended, he remained on the last step, because he now saw the precipice. But what does it avail to have remained silent, and concealed the danger? Necessity compelled him even against his will to fall. For he said that which he did not mean, because he so arranged his argument that he necessarily came to that point which he wished to avoid. You see, therefore, to what point he comes, when anger is removed and taken away from God. In short, either no one believes that, or a very few, and they the guilty and the wicked, who hope for impunity for their sins. But if this also is found to be false, that there is neither anger nor kindness in God, let us come to that which is put in the third place.

### Chap. V.—The Opinion of the Stoics Concerning God; Of His Anger and Kindness.

The Stoics and some others are supposed to have entertained much better sentiments respecting the divine nature, who say that there is kindness in God, but not anger. A very pleasing and popular speech, that God is not subject to such littleness of mind as to imagine that He is injured by anyone, since it is impossible for Him to be injured; so that that serene and holy majesty is excited, disturbed, and maddened, which is the part of human frailty. For they say that anger is a commotion and perturbation of the mind, which is inconsistent with God. Since, when it falls upon the mind of any one, as a violent tempest it excites such waves that it changes the condition of the mind, the eyes gleam, the countenance trembles, the tongue stammers, the teeth chatter, the countenance is alternately stained now with redness spread over it, now with white paleness. But if anger is unbecoming to a man, provided he be of wisdom and authority, how much more is so foul a change unbecoming to God! And if man, when he has authority and power, inflicts widespread injury through anger, sheds blood, overthrows cities, destroys communities, reduces provinces to desolation, how much more is it to be believed that God, since He has power over the whole human race, and over the universe itself, would have been about to destroy all things if He were angry.

Therefore they think that so great and so pernicious an evil ought to be absent from Him. And if anger and excitement are absent from Him, because it is disfiguring and injurious, and He inflicts injury on no one, they think that nothing else remains, except that He is mild, calm, propitious, beneficent, the preserver. For thus at length He may be called the common Father of all, and the best and greatest, which His divine and heavenly nature demands. For if among men it appears praiseworthy to do good rather than to injure, to restore to life rather than to kill, to save rather than to destroy, and innocence is not undeservedly numbered among the virtues,—and he who does these things is loved, esteemed, honored, and celebrated with all blessings and vows,—in short, on account of his deserts and benefits is judged to be most like to God; how much more right is it that God Himself, who excels in divine and perfect virtues, and who is removed from all earthly taint, should conciliate the whole race of man by divine and heavenly benefits! Those things are spoken speciously and in a popular manner, and they allure many to believe them; but they who entertain these sentiments approach nearer indeed to the truth, but they partly fail, not sufficiently considering the nature of the case. For if God is not angry with the impious and the unrighteous, it is clear that He does not love the pious and the righteous. Therefore the error of those is more consistent who take away at once both anger and kindness. For in opposite matters it is necessary to be moved to both sides or to neither. Thus, he who loves the good also hates the wicked, and he who does not hate the wicked does not love the good; because the loving of the good arises from the hatred of the wicked, and the hating of the wicked has its rise from the love of the good. There is no one who loves life without a hatred of death, nor who is desirous of light, but he who avoids darkness. These things are so connected by nature, that the one cannot exist without the other.

If any master has in his household a good and a bad servant, it is evident that he does not hate them both, or confer upon both benefits and honors; for if he does this, he is both unjust and foolish. But he addresses the one who is good with friendly words, and honors him and sets him over his house and household, and all his affairs; but punishes the bad one with reproaches, with stripes, with nakedness, with hunger, with thirst, with fetters: so that the latter may be an example to others to keep them from sinning, and the former to conciliate them; so that fear may restrain some, and honor may excite others. He, therefore, who loves also hates, and he who hates also loves; for there are those who ought to be loved, and there are those who ought to be hated. And as he who loves confers good things on those whom he loves, so he who hates inflicts evils upon those whom he hates; which argument, because it is true, can in no way be refuted. Therefore the opinion of those is vain and false, who, when they attribute the one to God, take away the other, not less than the opinion of those who take away both. But the latter, as we have shown, in part do not err, but retain that which is the better of the two; whereas the former, led on by the accurate method of their reasoning, fall into the greatest error, because they have assumed premises which are altogether false. For they ought not to have reasoned thus: Because God is not liable to anger, therefore He is not moved by kindness; but in this manner: Because God is moved by kindness, therefore He is also liable to anger. For if it had been certain and undoubted that God is not liable to anger, then the other point would necessarily be arrived at. But since the question as to whether God is angry is more open to doubt, while it is almost perfectly plain that He is kind, it is absurd to wish to subvert that which is certain by means of an uncertainty, since it is easier to confirm uncertain things by means of those which are certain.

### Chap. VI.—That God is Angry.

These are the opinions entertained by the philosophers respecting God. But if we have discovered that these things which have been spoken are false, there remains that one last resource, in which alone the truth can be found, which has never been embraced by philosophers, nor at any time defended: that it follows that God is angry, since He is moved by kindness. This opinion is to be maintained and asserted by us; for this is the sum and turning-point on which the whole of piety and religion depend: and no honor can be due to God, if He affords nothing to His worshippers; and no fear, if He is not angry with him who does not worship Him.

### Chap. VII.—Of Man, and the Brute Animals, and Religion.

Though philosophers have often turned aside from reason through their ignorance of the truth, and have fallen into inextricable errors (for that is wont to happen to these which happens to a traveler ignorant of the way, and not confessing that he is ignorant,—namely, that he wanders about, while he is ashamed to inquire from those whom he meets), no philosopher, however, has ever made the assertion that there is no difference between man and the brutes. Nor has anyone at all, provided that he wished to appear wise, reduced a rational animal to the level of the mute and irrational; which some ignorant persons do, resembling the brutes themselves, who, wishing to give themselves up to the indulgence of their appetite and pleasure, say that they are born on the same principle as all living animals, which it is impious for man to say. For who is so unlearned as not to know, who is so void of understanding as not to perceive, that there is something divine in man? I do not as yet come to the excellences of the soul and of the intellect, by which there is a manifest affinity between man and God. Does not the position of the body itself, and the fashion of the countenance, declare that we are not on a level with the dumb creation? Their nature is prostrated to the ground and to their pasture, and has nothing in common with the heaven, which they do not look upon. But man, with his erect position, with his elevated countenance raised to the contemplation of the universe, compares his features with God, and reason recognizes reason.

And on this account there is no animal, as Cicero says, except man, which has any knowledge of God. For he alone is furnished with wisdom, so that he alone understands religion; and this is the chief or only difference between man and the dumb animals. For the other things which appear to be peculiar to man, even if there are not such in the dumb animals, nevertheless may appear to be similar. Speech is peculiar to man; yet even in these there is a certain resemblance to speech. For they both distinguish one another by their voices; and when they are angry, they send forth a sound resembling altercation; and when they see one another after an interval of time, they show the office of congratulation by their voice. To us, indeed, their voices appear uncouth, as ours perhaps do to them; but to themselves, who understand one another, they are words. In short, in every affection they utter distinct expressions of voice by which they may show their state of mind. Laughter also is peculiar to man; and yet we see certain indications of joy in other animals, when they use passionate gestures with a view to sports, hang down their ears, contract their mouth, smooth their forehead, relax their eyes to sportiveness. What is so peculiar to man as reason and the foreseeing of the future? But there are animals which open several outlets in different directions from their lairs, that if any danger comes upon them, an escape may be open for them shut in; but they would not do this unless they possessed intelligence and reflection. Others are provident for the future, as

"Ants, when they plunder a great heap of corn, mindful of the winter, and lay it up in their dwelling;"

Again,—

"As bees, which alone know a country and fixed abodes; and mindful of the winter which is to come, they practice labor in the summer, and lay up their gains as a common stock."

It would be a long task if I should wish to trace out the things most resembling the skill of man, which are accustomed to be done by the separate tribes of animals. But if, in the case of all these things which are wont to be ascribed to man, there is found to be some resemblance even in the dumb animals, it is evident that religion is the only thing of which no trace can be found in the dumb animals, nor any indication. For justice is peculiar to religion, and to this no other animal attains. For man alone bears rule; the other animals are subjected to him. But the worship of God is ascribed to justice; and he who does not embrace this, being far removed from the nature of man, will live the life of the brutes under the form of man. But since we differ from the other animals almost in this respect alone, that we alone of all perceive the divine might and power, while in the others there is no understanding of God, it is surely impossible that in this respect either the dumb animals should have more wisdom, or human nature should be unwise, since all living creatures, and the whole system of nature, are subject to man on account of his wisdom. Wherefore if reason, if the force of man in this respect, excels and surpasses the rest of living creatures, inasmuch as he alone is capable of the knowledge of God, it is evident that religion can in no way be overthrown.

**Chap. VIII.—Of Religion.**

But religion is overthrown if we believe Epicurus speaking thus:—

"For the nature of gods must ever in itself of necessity enjoy immortality together with supreme repose, far removed and withdrawn from our concerns; since, exempt from every pain, exempt from all dangers, strong in its own resources, not wanting aught of us, it is neither gained by favors nor moved by anger."

Now, when he says these things, does he think that any worship is to be paid to God, or does he entirely overthrow religion? For if God confers nothing good on any one, if He repays the obedience of His worshipper with no favor, what is so senseless, what so foolish, as to build temples, to offer sacrifices, to present gifts, to diminish our property, that we may obtain nothing? But (it will be said) it is right that an excellent nature should be honored. What honor can be due to a being who pays no regard to us, and is ungrateful? Can we be bound in any manner to him who has nothing in common with us? "Farewell to God," says Cicero, "if He is such as to be influenced by no favor, and by no affection of men. For why should I say 'may He be propitious?' for He can be propitious to no one." What can be spoken more contemptible with respect to God? Farewell to Him, he says, that is, let Him depart and retire, since He is able to profit no one. But if God takes no trouble, nor occasions trouble to another, why then should we not commit crimes as often as it shall be in our power to escape the notice of men and to cheat the public laws? Wherever we shall obtain a favorable opportunity of escaping notice, let us take advantage of the occasion: let us take away the property of others, either without bloodshed or even with blood, if there is nothing else besides the laws to be reverenced.

While Epicurus entertains these sentiments, he altogether destroys religion; and when this is taken away, confusion and perturbation of life will follow. But if religion cannot be taken away without destroying our hold of wisdom, by which we are separated from the brutes, and of justice, by which the public life may be more secure, how can religion itself be maintained or guarded without fear? For that which is not feared is despised, and that which is despised is plainly not reverenced. Thus it comes to pass that religion, and majesty, and honor exist together with fear; but there is no fear where no one is angry. Whether, therefore, you take away from God kindness, or anger, or both, religion must be taken away, without which the life of men is full of folly, of wickedness, and enormity. For conscience greatly curbs men, if we believe that we are living in the sight of God; if we imagine not only that the actions which we perform are seen from above, but also that our thoughts and our words are heard by God. But it is profitable to believe this, as some imagine, not for the sake of the truth, but of utility, since laws cannot punish conscience unless some terror from above hangs over to restrain offences. Therefore religion is altogether false, and there is no divinity; but all things are made up by skillful men, in order that they may live more uprightly and innocently. This is a great question, and foreign to the subject which we have proposed; but because it necessarily occurs, it ought to be handled, however briefly.

### Chap. IX.—Of the Providence of God, and of Opinions Opposed to It.

When the philosophers of former times had agreed in their opinions respecting providence, and there was no doubt but that the world was set in order by God and reason, and was governed by reason, Protagoras, in the times of Socrates, was the first of all who said that it was not clear to him whether there was any divinity or not. And this disputation of his was judged so impious, and so contrary to the truth and to religion, that the Athenians both banished him from their territories, and burnt in a public assembly those books of his in which these statements were contained. But there is no need to speak respecting his opinions, because he pronounced nothing certain. After these things Socrates and his disciple Plato, and those who flowed forth from the school of Plato like rivulets into different directions, namely, the Stoics and Peripatetics, were of the same opinion as those who went before them.

Afterwards Epicurus said that there was indeed a God, because it was necessary that there should be in the world some being of surpassing excellence, distinction, and blessedness; yet that there was no providence, and thus that the world itself was ordered by no plan, nor art, nor workmanship, but that the universe was made up of certain minute and indivisible seeds. But I do not see what can be said more repugnant to the truth. For if there is a God, as God He is manifestly provident; nor can divinity be attributed to Him in any other way than if He retains the past, and knows the present, and foresees the future. Therefore, in taking away providence, he also denied the existence of God. But when he openly acknowledged the existence of God, at the same time he also admitted His providence for the one cannot exist at all, or be understood, without the other. But in those later times in which philosophy had now lost its vigor there lived a certain Diagoras of Melos, who altogether denied the existence of God, and on account of this sentiment was called atheist; also Theodorus of Cyrene: both of whom, because they were unable to discover anything new, all things having already been said and found out, preferred even, in opposition to the truth, to deny that in which all preceding philosophers had agreed without any ambiguity. These are they who attacked providence, which had been asserted and defended through so many ages by so many intellects. What then? Shall we refute those trifling and inactive philosophers by reason, or by the authority of distinguished men, or rather by both? But we must hasten onwards, lest our speech should wander too far from our subject.

### Chap. X.—Of the Origin of the World, and the Nature of Affairs, and the Providence of God.

They who do not admit that the world was made by divine providence, either say that it is composed of first principles coming together at random, or that it suddenly came into existence by nature, but hold, as Straton does, that nature has in itself the power of production and of diminution, but that it has neither sensibility nor figure, so that we may understand that all things were produced spontaneously, without any artificer or author. Each opinion is vain and impossible. But this happens to those who are ignorant of the truth, that they devise anything, rather than perceive that which the nature of the subject requires. First of all, with respect to those minute seeds, by the meeting together of which they say that the whole world came into existence, I ask where or whence they are. Who has seen them at any time? Who has perceived them? Who has heard them? Had none but Leucippus eyes? Had he alone a mind, who assuredly alone of all men was blind and senseless, since he spoke those things which no sick man could have uttered in his ravings, or one asleep in his dreams?

The ancient philosophers argued that all things were made up of four elements. He would not admit this, lest he should appear to tread in the footsteps of others; but he held that there were other first principles of the elements themselves, which can neither be seen, nor touched, nor be perceived by any part of the body. They are so minute, he says, that there is no edge of a sword so fine that they can be cut and divided by it. From which circumstance he gave them the name of atoms. But it occurred to him, that if they all had one and the same nature, they could not make up different objects of so great a variety as we see to be present in the world. He said, therefore, that there were smooth and rough ones, and round, and angular, and hooked. How much better had it been to be silent, than to have a tongue for such miserable and empty uses! And, indeed, I fear lest he who thinks these things worthy of refutation, should appear no less to rave. Let us, however, reply as to one who says something. If they are soft and round, it is plain that they cannot lay hold of one another, so as to make some body; as, though anyone should wish to bind together millet into one combination, the very softness of the grains would not permit them to come together into a mass. If they are rough, and angular, and hooked, so that they may be able to cohere, then they are divisible, and capable of being cut; for hooks and angles must project, so that they may possibly be cut off.

Therefore that which is able to be cut off and torn away, will be able both to be seen and held. "These," he says, "flutter about with restless motions through empty space, and are carried hither and thither, just as we see little particles of dust in the sun when it has introduced its rays and light through a window. From these there arise trees and herbs, and all fruits of the earth; from these, animals, and water, and fire, and all things are produced, and are again resolved into the same elements." This can be borne as long as the inquiry is respecting small matters. Even the world itself was made up of these. He has reached to the full extent of perfect madness: it seems impossible that anything further should be said, and yet he found something to add. "Since everything," he says, "is infinite, and nothing can be empty, it follows of necessity that there are innumerable worlds." What force of atoms had been so great, that masses so incalculable should be collected from such minute elements? And first of all I ask, What is the nature or origin of those seeds? For if all things are from them, whence shall we say that they themselves are? What nature supplied such an abundance of matter for the making of innumerable worlds? But let us grant that he raved with impunity concerning worlds; let us speak respecting this in which we are, and which we see. He says that all things are made from minute bodies which are incapable of division.

If this were so, no object would ever need the seed of its own kind. Birds would be born without eggs, or eggs without bringing forth; likewise the rest of the living creatures without coition: trees and the productions of the earth would not have their own seeds, which we daily handle and sow. Why does a corn-field arise from grain, and again grain from a cornfield? In short, if the meeting together and collecting of atoms would affect all things, all things would grow together in the air, since atoms flutter about through empty space. Why cannot the herb, why cannot the tree or grain, arise or be increased without earth, without roots, without moisture, without seed? From which it is evident that nothing is made up from atoms, since everything has its own peculiar and fixed nature, its own seed, its own law given from the beginning. Finally, Lucretius, as though forgetful of atoms, which he was maintaining, in order that he might refute those who say that all things are produced from nothing, employed these arguments, which might have weighed against himself. For he thus spoke:—

"If things came from nothing, any kind might be born of anything; nothing would require seed."

Likewise afterwards:—

"We must admit, therefore, that nothing can come from nothing, since things require seed before they can severally be born, and be brought out into the buxom fields of air."

Who would imagine that he had brain when he said these things, and did not see that they were contrary to one another? For that nothing is made by means of atoms, is apparent from this, that everything has a definite seed, unless by chance we shall believe that the nature both of fire and water is derived from atoms. Why should I say, that if materials of the greatest hardness are struck together with a violent blow, fire is struck out? Are atoms concealed in the steel, or in the flint? Who shut them in? Or why do they not leap forth spontaneously? Or how could the seeds of fire remain in a material of the greatest coldness?

I leave the subject of the flint and steel. If you hold in the sun an orb of crystal filled with water, fire is kindled from the light which is reflected from the water, even in the most severe cold. Must we then believe that fire is contained in the water? And yet fire cannot be kindled from the sun even in summer. If you shall breathe upon wax, or if a light vapor shall touch anything—either the hard surface of marble or a plate of metal—water is gradually condensed by means of the most minute drops. Also from the exhalation of the earth or sea mist is formed, which either, being dispersed, moistens whatever it has covered, or being collected, is carried aloft by the wind to high mountains, and compressed into cloud, and sends down great rains. Where, then, do we say that fluids are produced? Is it in the vapor? Or in the exhalation? Or in the wind? But nothing can be formed in that which is neither touched nor seen. Why should I speak of animals, in whose bodies we see nothing formed without plan, without arrangement, without utility, without beauty, so that the most skillful and careful marking out of all the parts and members repels the idea of accident and chance? But let us suppose it possible that the limbs, and bones, and nerves, and blood should be made up of atoms. What of the senses, the reflection, the memory, the mind, the natural capacity: from what seeds can they be compacted? He says, From the most minute. There are therefore others of greater size. How, then, are they indivisible?

In the next place, if the things which are not seen are formed from invisible seeds, it follows that those which are seen are from visible seeds. Why, then, does no one see them? But whether anyone regards the invisible parts which are in man, or the parts which can be touched, and which are visible, who does not see that both parts exist in accordance with design? How, then, can bodies which meet together without design effect anything reasonable? For we see that there is nothing in the whole world which has not in itself very great and wonderful design. And since this is above the sense and capacity of man, to what can it be more rightly attributed than to the divine providence? If a statue, the resemblance of man, is made by the exercise of design and art, shall we suppose that man himself is made up of fragments which come together at random? And what resemblance to the truth is there in the thing produced, when the greatest and most surpassing skill can imitate nothing more than the mere outline and extreme lineaments of the body? Was the skill of man able to give to his production any motion or sensibility? I say nothing of the exercise of the sight, of hearing, and of smelling, and the wonderful uses of the other members, either those which are in sight or those which are hidden from view. What artificer could have fabricated either the heart of man, or the voice, or his very wisdom? Does any man of sound mind, therefore, think that that which man cannot do by reason and judgment, may be accomplished by a meeting together of atoms everywhere adhering to each other? You see into what foolish ravings they have fallen, while they are unwilling to assign to God the making and the care of all things

Let us, however, concede to them that the things which are earthly are made from atoms: are the things also which are heavenly? They say that the gods are without contamination, eternal, and blessed; and they grant to them alone an exemption, so that they do not appear to be made up of a meeting together of atoms. For if the gods also had been made up of these, they would be liable to be dispersed, the seeds at length being resolved, and returning to their own nature. Therefore, if there is something which the atoms could not produce, why may we not judge in the same way of the others? But I ask why the gods did not build for themselves a dwelling-place before those first elements produced the world? It is manifest that, unless the atoms had come together and made the heaven, the gods would still be suspended through the midst of empty space. By what counsel, then, by what plan, did the atoms from a confused mass collect themselves, so that from some the earth below was formed into a globe, and the heaven stretched out above, adorned with so great a variety of constellations that nothing can be conceived more embellished? Can he, therefore, who sees such and so great objects, imagine that they were made without any design, without any providence, without any divine intelligence, but that such great and wonderful things arose out of fine and minute atoms? Does it not resemble a prodigy, that there should be any human being who might say these things, or that there should be those who might believe them—as Democritus, who was his hearer, or Epicurus, to whom all folly flowed forth from the fountain of Leucippus? But, as others say, the world was made by Nature, which is without perception and figure. But this is much more absurd. If Nature made the world, it must have made it by judgment and intelligence; for it is he that makes something who has either the inclination to make it, or knowledge. If nature is without perception and figure, how can that be made by it which has both perception and figure, unless by chance anyone thinks that the fabric of animals, which is so delicate, could have been formed and animated by that which is without perception, or that that figure of heaven, which is prepared with such foresight for the uses of living beings, suddenly came into existence by some accident or other, without a builder, without an artificer?

"If there is anything," says Chrysippus, "which effects those things which man, though he is endowed with reason, cannot do, that assuredly is greater, and stronger, and wiser than man." But man cannot make heavenly things; therefore that which shall produce or has produced these things surpasses man in art, in design, in skill, and in power. Who, therefore, can it be but God? But Nature, which they supposed to be, as it were, the mother of all things, if it has not a mind, will effect nothing, will contrive nothing; for where there is no reflection there is neither motion nor efficacy. But if it uses counsel for the commencement of anything, reason for its arrangement, art for its accomplishment, energy for its consummation, and power to govern and control, why should it be called Nature rather than God? Or if a concourse of atoms, or Nature without mind, made those things which we see, I ask why it was able to make the heaven, but unable to make a city or a house? Why it made mountains of marble, but did not make columns and statues? But ought not atoms to have come together to effect these things, since they leave no position untried? For concerning Nature, which has no mind, it is no wonder that it forgot to do these things. What, then, is the case? It is plain that God, when He commenced this work of the world,—than which nothing can be better arranged with respect to order, nor more befitting as to utility, nor more adorned as to beauty, nor greater as to bulk,—Himself made the things which could not be made by man; and among these also man himself, to whom He gave a portion of His own wisdom, and furnished him with reason, as much as earthly frailty was capable of receiving, that he might make for himself the things which were necessary for his own uses.

But if in the commonwealth of this world, so to speak, there is no providence which rules, no God who administers, no sense at all prevails in this nature of things. From what source therefore will it be believed that the human mind, with its skill and its intelligence, had its origin? For if the body of man was made from the ground, from which circumstance man received his name; it follows that the soul, which has intelligence, and is the ruler of the body, which the limbs obey as a king and commander, which can neither be looked upon nor comprehended, could not have come to man except from a wise nature. But as mind and soul govern everybody, so also does God govern the world. For it is not probable that lesser and humble things bear rule, but that greater and highest things do not bear rule. In short, Marcus Cicero, in his *Tusculan Disputations*, and in his *Consolation*, says: "No origin of souls can be found on earth. For there is nothing, he says, mixed and compound in souls, or which may appear to be produced and made up from the earth; nothing moist or airy, or of the nature of fire. For in these natures there is nothing which has the force of memory, of mind and reflection, which both retains the past and foresees the future, and is able to comprise the present; which things alone are divine. For no source will ever be found from which they are able to come to man, unless it be from God." Since, therefore, with the exception of two or three vain calumniators, it is agreed upon that the world is governed by providence, as also it was made, and there is no one who ventures to prefer the opinion of Diagoras and Theodorus, or the empty fiction of Leucippus, or the levity of Democritus and Epicurus, either to the authority of those seven ancient men who were called wise, or to that of Pythagoras or of Socrates or Plato, and the other philosophers who judged that there is a providence; therefore that opinion also is false, by which they think that religion was instituted by wise men for the sake of terror and fear, in order that ignorant men might abstain from sins.

But if this is true, it follows that we are derided by the wise men of old. But if they invented religion for the sake of deceiving us, and moreover of deceiving the whole human race, therefore they were not wise, because falsehood is not consistent with the character of the wise man. But grant that they were wise; what great success in falsehood was it, that they were able to deceive not only the unlearned, but Plato also, and Socrates, and so easily to delude Pythagoras, Zeno, and Aristotle, the chiefs of the greatest sects? There is therefore a divine providence, as those men whom I have named perceived, by the energy and power of which all things which we see were both made and are governed. For so vast a system of things such arrangement and such regularity in preserving the settled orders and times, could neither at first have arisen without a provident artificer, or have existed so many ages without a powerful inhabitant, or have been perpetually governed without a skillful and intelligent ruler; and reason itself declares this. For whatever exists which has reason, must have arisen from reason. Now reason is the part of an intelligent and wise nature; but a wise and intelligent nature can be nothing else than God. Now the world, since it has reason, by which it is both governed and kept together, was therefore made by God. But if God is the maker and ruler of the world, then religion is rightly and truly established; for honor and worship are due to the author and common parent of all things.

### Chap. XI.—Of God, and that the One God, and by Whose Providence the World is Governed and Exists.

Since it is agreed upon concerning providence, it follows that we show whether it is to be believed that it belongs to many, or rather to one only. We have sufficiently taught, as I think, in our *Institutions*, that there cannot be many gods; because, if the divine energy and power be distributed among several, it must necessarily be diminished. But that which is lessened is plainly mortal; but if He is not mortal, He can neither be lessened nor divided. Therefore there is but one God, in whom complete energy and power can neither be lessened nor increased. But if there are many, while they separately have something of power and authority, the sum itself decreases; nor will they separately be able to have the whole, which they have in common with others: so much will be wanting to each as the others shall possess. There cannot therefore be many rulers in this world, nor many masters in one house, nor many pilots in one ship, nor many leaders in one herd or flock, nor many queens in one swarm. But there could not have been many suns in heaven, as there are not several souls in one body; so entirely does the whole of nature agree in unity. But if the world

> "Is nourished by a soul,
> A spirit whose celestial flame
> Glows in each member of the frame,
> And stirs the mighty whole,"

it is evident from the testimony of the poet, that there is one God who inhabits the world, since the whole body cannot be inhabited and governed except by one mind. Therefore all divine power must be in one person, by whose will and command all things are ruled; and therefore He is so great, that He cannot be described in words by man, or estimated by the senses. From what source, therefore, did the opinion or persuasion respecting many gods come to men? Without doubt, all those who are worshipped as gods were men, and were also the earliest and greatest kings; but who is ignorant that they were invested with divine honors after death, either on account of the virtue by which they had profited the race of men, or that they obtained immortal memory on account of the benefits and inventions by which they had adorned human life? And not only men, but women also. And this, both the most ancient writers of Greece, whom they call *theologi*; and also Roman writers following and imitating the Greeks, teach; of whom especially Euhemerus and our Ennius, who point out the birthdays, marriages, offspring, governments, exploits, deaths, and tombs of all of them. And Tullius, following them, in his third book, *On the Nature of the Gods*, destroyed the public religions; but neither he himself nor any other person was able to introduce the true one, of which he was ignorant. And thus he himself testified that that which was false was evident; that the truth, however, lay concealed. "Would to heaven," he says, "that I could as easily discover true things as refute those that are false!" And this he proclaimed not with dissimulation as an Academic, but truly and in accordance with the feeling of his mind, because the truth cannot be uprooted from human perceptions: that which the foresight of man was able to attain to, he attained to, that he might expose false things. For whatever is fictitious and false, because it is supported by no reason, is easily destroyed. There is therefore one God, the source and origin of all things, as Plato both felt and taught in the *Timoeus*, whose majesty he declares to be so great, that it can neither be comprehended by the mind nor be expressed by the tongue.

Hermes bears the same testimony, whom Cicero asserts to be reckoned by the Egyptians among the number of the gods. I speak of him who, on account of his excellence and knowledge of many arts, was called Trismegistus; and he was far more ancient not only than Plato, but than Pythagoras, and those seven wise men. In Xenophon, Socrates, as he discourses, says that "the form of God ought not to be inquired about: "and Plato, in his *Book of Laws*, says: "What God is, ought not to be the subject of inquiry, because it can neither be found out nor related." Pythagoras also admits that there is but one God, saying that there is an incorporeal mind, which, being diffused and stretched through all nature, gives vital perception to all living creatures; but Antisthenes, in his *Physics*, said that there was but one natural God, although the nations and cities have gods of their own people. Aristotle, with his followers the Peripatetics, and Zeno with his followers the Stoics, say nearly the same things. Truly it would be a long task to follow up the opinions of all separately, who, although they used different names, nevertheless agreed in one power which governed the world. But, however, though philosophers and poets, and those, in short, who worship the gods, often acknowledge the Supreme God, yet no one ever inquired into, no one discussed, the subject of His worship and honors; with that persuasion, in truth, with which, always believing Him to be bounteous and incorruptible, they think that He is neither angry with anyone, nor stands in need of any worship. Thus there can be no religion where there is no fear.

**Chap. XII.—Of Religion and the Fear of God.**

Now, since we have replied to the impious and detestable wisdom, or rather senselessness of some, let us return to our proposed subject. We have said that, if religion is taken away, neither wisdom nor justice can be retained: wisdom, because the understanding of the divine nature, in which we differ from the brutes, is found in man alone; justice, because unless God, who cannot be deceived, shall restrain our desires, we shall live wickedly and impiously. Therefore, that our actions should be viewed by God, pertains not only to the usefulness of common life, but even to the truth; because, if religion and justice are taken away, having lost our reason, we either descend to the senselessness of the herds; or to the savageness of the beasts, yea, even more so, since the beasts spare animals of their own kind. What will be more savage, what more unmerciful, than man, if, the fear of a superior being taken away, he shall be able either to escape the notice of or to despise the might of the laws? It is therefore the fear of God alone which guards the mutual society of men, by which life itself is sustained, protected, and governed. But that fear is taken away if man is persuaded that God is without anger; for that He is moved and indignant when unjust actions are done, not only the common advantage, but even reason itself, and truth, persuade us. We must again return to the former subjects, that, as we have taught that the world was made by God, we may teach why it was made.

## Chap. XIII.—Of the Advantage and Use of the World and of the Seasons.

If any one considers the whole government of the world, he will certainly understand how true is the opinion of the Stoics, who say that the world was made on our account. For all the things of which the world is composed, and which it produces from itself, are adapted to the use of man. Man, accordingly, uses fire for the purpose of warmth and light, and of softening his food, and for the working of iron; he uses springs for drinking, and for baths; he uses rivers for irrigating the fields, and assigning boundaries to countries; he uses the earth for receiving a variety of fruits, the hills for planting vineyards, the mountains for the use of trees and firewood, the plains for crops of grain; he uses the sea not only for commerce, and for receiving supplies from distant countries, but also for abundance of every kind of fish. But if he makes use of these elements to which he is nearest, there is no doubt that he uses the heaven also, since the offices even of heavenly things are regulated for the fertility of the earth from which we live. The sun, with its ceaseless courses and unequal intervals, completes its annual circles, and either at his rising draws forth the day for labor, or at his setting brings on the night for repose; and at one time by his departure farther towards the south, at another time by his approach nearer towards the north, he causes the vicissitudes of winter and summer, so that both by the moistures and frosts of winter the earth becomes enriched for fruitfulness, and by the heats of summer either the produce of grass is hardened by maturity, or that which is in moist places, being seethed and heated, becomes ripened. The moon also, which governs the time of night, regulates her monthly courses by the alternate loss and recovery of light, and by the brightness of her shining illumines the nights obscure with gloomy darkness, so that journeys in the summer heat, and expeditions, and works, may be performed without labor and inconvenience; since

> "By night the light stubble, by night
> The dry meadows are better mown."

The other heavenly bodies also, either at their rising or setting, supply favorable times by their fixed positions. Moreover, they also afford guidance to ships, that they may not wander through the boundless deep with uncertain course, since the pilot duly observing them arrives at the harbor of the shore at which he aims. Clouds are attracted by the breath of the winds, that the fields of sown grain may be watered with showers, that the vines may abound with produce, and the trees with fruits. And these things are exhibited by a succession of changes throughout the year, that nothing may at any time be wanting by which the life of men is sustained. But (it is said) the same earth nourishes the other living creatures, and by the produce of the same even the dumb animals are fed. Has not God labored also for the sake of the dumb animals? By no means; because they are void of reason. On the contrary, we understand that even these themselves in the same manner were made by God for the use of man, partly for food, partly for clothing, partly to assist him in his work; so that it is manifest that the divine providence wished to furnish and adorn the life of men with an abundance of objects and resources, and on this account He both filled the air with birds, and the sea with fishes, and the earth with quadrupeds. But the Academics, arguing against the Stoics, are accustomed to ask why, if God made all things for the sake of men, many things are found even opposed, and hostile, and injurious to us, as well in the sea as on the land. And the Stoics, without any regard to the truth, most foolishly repelled this. For they say that there are many things among natural productions, and reckoned among animals, the utility of which hitherto escapes notice, but that this is discovered in process of the times, as necessity and use have already discovered many things which were unknown in former ages. What utility, then, can be discovered in mice, in beetles, in serpents, which are troublesome and pernicious to man? Is it that some medicine lies concealed in them? If there is any, it will at some time be found out, namely, as a remedy against evils, whereas they complain that it is altogether evil. They say that the viper, when burnt and reduced to ashes, is a remedy for the bite of the same beast. How much better had it been that it should not exist at all, than that a remedy should be required against it drawn from itself?

They might then have answered with more conciseness and truth after this manner. When God had formed man as it were His own image, that which was the completion of His workmanship, He breathed wisdom into him alone, so that he might bring all things into subjection to his own authority and government, and make use of all the advantages of the world. And yet He set before him both good and evil things, inasmuch as He gave to him wisdom, the whole nature of which is employed in discerning things evil and good: for no one can choose better things, and know what is good, unless he at the same time knows to reject and avoid the things which are evil. They are both mutually connected with each other, so that, the one being taken away, the other must also be taken away. Therefore, good and evil things being set before it, then at length wisdom discharges its office, and desires the good for usefulness, but rejects the evil for safety. Therefore, as innumerable good things have been given which it might enjoy, so also have evils, against which it might guard. For if there is no evil, no danger—nothing, in short, which can injure man—all the material of wisdom is taken away, and will be unnecessary for man. For if only good things are placed in sight, what need is there of reflection, of understanding, of knowledge, of reason? since, wherever he shall extend his hand, that is befitting and adapted to nature; so that if anyone should wish to place a most exquisite dinner before infants, who as yet have no taste, it is plain that each will desire that to which either impulse, or hunger, or even accident, shall attract them; and whatever they shall take, it will be useful and salutary to them. What injury will it therefore be for them always to remain as they are, and always to be infants and unacquainted with affairs? But if you add a mixture either of bitter things, or things useless, or even poisonous, they are plainly deceived through their ignorance of good and evil, unless wisdom is added to them, by which they may have the rejection of evil things and the choice of good things.

You see, therefore, that we have greater need of wisdom on account of evils; and unless these things had been proposed to us, we should not be a rational animal. But if this account is true, which the Stoics were in no manner able to see, that argument also of Epicurus is done away. God, he says, either wishes to take away evils, and is unable; or He is able, and is unwilling; or He is neither willing nor able, or He is both willing and able. If He is willing and is unable, He is feeble, which is not in accordance with the character of God; if He is able and unwilling, He is envious, which is equally at variance with God; if He is neither willing nor able, He is both envious and feeble, and therefore not God; if He is both willing and able, which alone is suitable to God, from what source then are evils? Or why does He not remove them? I know that many of the philosophers, who defend providence, are accustomed to be disturbed by this argument, and are almost driven against their will to admit that God takes no interest in anything, which Epicurus especially aims at; but having examined the matter, we easily do away with this formidable argument. For God is able to do whatever He wishes, and there is no weakness or envy in God. He is able, therefore, to take away evils; but He does not wish to do so, and yet He is not on that account envious. For on this account He does not take them away, because He at the same time gives wisdom, as I have shown; and there is more of goodness and pleasure in wisdom than of annoyance in evils. For wisdom causes us even to know God, and by that knowledge to attain to immortality, which is the chief good. Therefore, unless we first know evil, we shall be unable to know good. But Epicurus did not see this, nor did any other, that if evils are taken away, wisdom is in like manner taken away; and that no traces of virtue remain in man, the nature of which consists in enduring and overcoming the bitterness of evils. And thus, for the sake of a slight gain in the taking away of evils, we should be deprived of a good, which is very great, and true, and peculiar to us. It is plain, therefore, that all things are proposed for the sake of man, as well evils as also goods.

### Chap. XIV.—Why God Made Man.

It follows that I show for what purpose God made man himself. As He contrived the world for the sake of man, so He formed man himself on His own account, as it were a priest of a divine temple, a spectator of His works and of heavenly objects.

For he is the only being who, since he is intelligent and capable of reason, is able to understand God, to admire His works, and perceive His energy and power; for on this account he is furnished with judgment, intelligence, and prudence. On this account he alone, beyond the other living creatures, has been made with an upright body and attitude, so that he seems to have been raised up for the contemplation of his Parent. On this account he alone has received language, and a tongue the interpreter of his thought, that he may be able to declare the majesty of his Lord. Lastly, for this cause all things were placed under his control that he himself might be under the control of God, their Maker and Creator. If God, therefore, designed man to be a worshipper of Himself, and on this account gave him so much honor, that he might rule over all things; it is plainly most just that he should worship Him1726 who bestowed upon him such great gifts, and love man, who is united with us in the participation of the divine justice. For it is not right that a worshipper of God should he injured by a worshipper of God. From which it is understood that man was made for the sake of religion and justice. And of this matter Marcus Tullius is a witness in his books respecting the Laws, since he thus speaks: "But of all things concerning which learned men dispute, nothing is of greater consequence than that it should be altogether understood that we are born to justice." And if this is most true, it follows that God will have all men to be just, that is, to have God and man as objects of their affection; to honor God in truth as a Father, and to love man as a brother: for in these two things the whole of justice is comprised. But he who either fails to acknowledge God or acts injuriously to man, lives unjustly and contrary to his nature, and in this manner disturbs the divine institution and law.

### Chap. XV.—Whence Sins Extended to Man.

Here perhaps someone may ask, Whence sins extended to man, or what perversion distorted the rule of the divine institution to worse things, so that, though he was born to justice, he nevertheless performs unjust works. I have already in a former place explained, that God at the same time set before him good and evil, and that He loves the good, and hates the evil which is contrary to this; but that He permitted the evil on this account, that the good also might shine forth, since, as I have often taught, we understand that the one cannot exist without the other; in short, that the world itself is made up of two elements opposing and connected with one another, of fire and moisture, and that light could not have been made unless there has also been darkness, since there cannot be a higher place without a lower, nor a rising without a setting, nor warmth without cold, nor softness without hardness. Thus also we are composed of two substances equally opposed to one another—soul and body: the one of which is assigned to the heaven, because it is slight and not to be handled; the other to the earth, because it is capable of being laid hold of: the one is firm and eternal, the other frail and mortal. Therefore good clings to the one, and evil to the other: light, life, and justice to the one; darkness, death, and injustice to the other. Hence there arose among men the corruption of their nature, so that it was necessary that a law should be established, by which vices might be prohibited, and the duties of virtue be enjoined. Since, therefore, there are good and evil things in the affairs of men, the nature of which I have set forth, it must be that God is moved to both sides, both to favor when He sees that just things are done, and to anger when He perceives unjust things.

But Epicurus opposes us, and says: "If there is in God the affection of joy leading Him to favor, and of hatred influencing Him to anger, He must of necessity have both fear, and inclination, and desire, and the other affections which belong to human weakness." It does not follow that he who is angry must fear, or that he who feels joy must grieve; in short, they who are liable to anger are less timid, and they who are of a joyful temperament are less affected with grief. What need is there to speak of the affections of humanity, to which our nature yields? Let us weigh the divine necessity; for I am unwilling to speak of nature, since it is believed that our God was never born. The affection of fear has a subject-matter in man, but it has none in God. Man, inasmuch as he is liable to many accidents and dangers, fears lest any greater violence should arise which may strike, despoil, lacerate, dash down, and destroy him. But God, who is liable neither to want, nor injury, nor pain, nor death, can by no means fear, because there is nothing which can offer violence to Him. Also the reason and cause of desire is manifest in man. For, inasmuch as he was made frail and mortal, it was necessary that another and different sex should be made, by union with which offspring might be produced to continue the perpetuity of his race. But this desire has no place in God, because frailty and death are far removed from Him; nor is there with Him any female in whose union He is able to rejoice; nor does He stand in need of succession, since He will live forever. The same things may be said respecting envy and passion, to which, from sure and manifest causes, man is liable, but to which God is by no means liable. But, in truth, favor and anger and pity have their substance in God, and that greatest and matchless power employs them for the preservation of the world.

### Chap. XVI.—Of God, and His Anger and Affections.

Someone will ask what this substance is. First of all, when evils befall them, men in their dejected state for the most part have recourse to God: they appease and entreat Him, believing that He is able to repel injuries from them. He has therefore an occasion of exercising pity; for He is not so unmerciful and a despiser of men as to refuse aid to those who are in distress. Very many, also, who are persuaded that justice is pleasing to God, both worship Him who is Lord and Parent of all, and with continual prayers and repeated vows offer gifts and sacrifices, follow up His name with praises, striving to gain His favor by just and good works. There is therefore a reason, on account of which God may and ought to favor them. For if there is nothing so befitting God as beneficence, and nothing so unsuited to His character as to be ungrateful, it is necessary that He should make some return for the services of those who are excellent, and who lead a holy life, that He may not be liable to the charge of ingratitude which is worthy of blame even in the case of a man. But, on the contrary, others are daring and wicked, who pollute all things with their lusts, harass with slaughters, practice fraud, plunder, commit perjury, neither spare relatives nor parents, neglect the laws, and even God Himself. Anger, therefore, has a befitting occasion in God.

For it is not right that, when He sees such things, He should not be moved, and arise to take vengeance upon the wicked, and destroy the pestilent and guilty, so as to promote the interests of all good men. Thus even in anger itself there is also contained a showing of kindness. Therefore the arguments are found to be empty and false, either of those who, when they will not admit that God is angry, will have it that He shows kindness, because this, indeed, cannot take place without anger; or of those who think that there is no emotion of the mind in God. And because there are some affections to which God is not liable, as desire, fear, avarice, grief, and envy, they have said that He is entirely free from all affection. For He is not liable to these, because they are vicious affections; but as to those which belong to virtue,—that is, anger towards the wicked, regard towards the good, pity towards the afflicted,— inasmuch as they are worthy of the divine power, He has affections of His own, both just and true. And if He is not possessed of them, the life of man will be thrown into confusion, and the condition of things will come to such disturbance that the laws will be despised and overpowered, and audacity alone reign, so that no one can at length be in safety unless he who excels in strength. Thus all the earth will be laid waste, as it were, by a common robbery. But now, since the wicked expect punishment, and the good hope for favor, and the afflicted look for aid, there is place for virtues, and crimes are rarer. But it is said, oft times the wicked are more prosperous, and the good more wretched, and the just are harassed with impunity by the unjust. We will hereafter consider why these things happen. In the meantime let us explain respecting anger, whether there be any in God; whether He takes no notice at all, and is unmoved at those things which are done with impiety.

### Chap. XVII.—Of God, His Care and Anger.

God, says Epicurus, regards nothing; therefore He has no power. For he who has power must of necessity regard affairs. For if He has power, and does not use it, what so great cause is there that, I will not say our race, but even the universe itself, should be contemptible in His sight? On this account he says He is pure and happy, because He is always at rest. To whom, then, has the administration of so great affairs been entrusted, if these things which we see to be governed by the highest judgment are neglected by God? Or how can he who lives and perceives be at rest? For rest belongs either to sleep or to death. But sleep has not rest. For when we are asleep, the body indeed is at rest, but the soul is restless and agitated: it forms for itself images which it may behold, so that it exercises its natural power of motion by a variety of visions, and calls itself away from false things, until the limbs are satiated, and receive vigor from rest. Therefore eternal rest belongs to death alone. Now if death does not affect God, it follows that God is never at rest. But in what can the action of God consist, but in the administration of the world? But if God carries on the care of the world, it follows that He cares for the life of men, and takes notice of the acts of individuals, and He earnestly desires that they should be wise and good. This is the will of God, this the divine law; and he who follows and observes this is beloved by God. It is necessary that He should be moved with anger against the man who has broken or despised this eternal and divine law. If, he says, God does harm to anyone, therefore He is not good. They are deceived by no slight error who defame all censure, whether human or divine, with the name of bitterness and malice, thinking that He ought to be called injurious who visits the injurious with punishment. But if this is so, it follows that we have injurious laws, which enact punishment for offenders, and injurious judges who inflict capital punishments on those convicted of crime. But if the law is just which awards to the transgressor his due, and if the judge is called upright and good when he punishes crimes,—for he guards the safety of good men who punishes the evil,—it follows that God, when He opposes the evil, is not injurious; but he himself is injurious who either injures an innocent man, or spares an injurious person that he may injure many.

I would gladly ask from those who represent God as immoveable, if anyone had property, a house, a household of slaves, and his slaves, despising the forbearance of their master, should attack all things, and themselves take the enjoyment of his goods, if his household should honor them, while the master was despised by all, insulted, and deserted: could he be a wise man who should not avenge the insults, but permit those over whom he had power to have the enjoyment of his property? Can such forbearance be found in anyone? If, indeed, it is to be called forbearance, and not rather a kind of insensible stupor. But it is easy to endure contempt. What if those things were done which are spoken of by Cicero? "For I ask, if any head of a family, when his children had been put to death by a slave, his wife slain and his house set on fire, should not exact most severe punishment from that slave, whether he would appear to be kind and merciful, or inhuman and most cruel? "But if to pardon deeds of this kind is the part of cruelty rather than of kindness, it is not therefore the part of goodness in God not to be moved at those things which are done unjustly. For the world is, as it were, the house of God, and men, as it were, His slaves; and if His name is a mockery to them, what kind or amount of forbearance is it to give up His own honors, to see wicked and unjust things done, and not to be indignant, which is peculiar and natural to Him who is displeased with sins! To be angry, therefore, is the part of reason: for thus faults are removed, and licentiousness is curbed; and this is plainly in accordance with justice and wisdom.

But the Stoics did not see that there is a distinction between right and wrong, that there is a just and also an unjust anger; and because they did not find a remedy for the matter, they wished altogether to remove it. But the Peripatetics said that it was not to be cut out, but moderated; to whom we have made a sufficient reply in the sixth book of the *Institutions*. Now, that the philosophers were ignorant of the nature of anger, is plain from their definitions, which Seneca enumerated in the books which he composed on the subject of anger. "Anger is," he says, "the desire of avenging an injury." Others, as Posidonius says, describe it as the desire of punishing him by whom you think that you have been unfairly injured. Some have thus defined it: "Anger is an incitement of the mind to injure him who either has committed an injury, or who has wished to do so." The definition of Aristotle does not differ greatly from ours; for he says that "anger is the desire of requiting pain." This is the unjust anger, concerning which we spoke before, which is contained even in the dumb animals; but it is to be restrained in man, lest he should rush to some very great evil through rage. This cannot exist in God, because He cannot be injured; but it is found in man, inasmuch as he is frail. For the inflicting of injury inflames anguish, and anguish produces a desire of revenge. Where, then, is that just anger against offenders? For this is evidently not the desire of revenge, inasmuch as no injury precedes. I do not speak of those who sin against the laws; for although a judge may be angry with these without incurring blame, let us, however, suppose that he ought to be of a sedate mind when he sentences the guilty to punishment, because he is the executor of the laws, not of his own spirit or power; for so they wish it who endeavor to extirpate anger. But I speak of those in particular who are in our own power, as slaves, children, wives, and pupils; for when we see these offend, we are incited to restrain them.

For it cannot fail to be, that he who is just and good is displeased with things which are bad, and that he who is displeased with evil is moved when he sees it practiced. Therefore we arise to take vengeance, not because we have been injured, but that discipline may be preserved, morals may be corrected, and licentiousness be suppressed. This is just anger; and as it is necessary in man for the correction of wickedness, so manifestly is it necessary in God, from whom an example comes to man. For as we ought to restrain those who are subject to our power, so also ought God to restrain the offences of all. And in order that He may do this, He must be angry; because it is natural for one who is good to be moved and incited at the fault of another. Therefore they ought to have given this definition: Anger is an emotion of the mind arousing itself for the restraining of faults. For the definition given by Cicero, "Anger is the desire of taking vengeance," does not differ much from those already mentioned. But that anger which we may call either fury or rage ought not to exist even in man, because it is altogether vicious; but the anger which relates to the correction of vices ought not to be taken away from man; nor can it be taken away from God, because it is both serviceable for the affairs of men, and necessary.

**Chap. XVIII.—Of the Punishment of Faults, that It Cannot Take Place without Anger.**

What need is there, they say, of anger, since faults can be corrected without this affection? But there is no one who can calmly see any one committing an offence. This may perhaps be possible in him who presides over the laws, because the deed is not committed before his eyes, but it is brought before him as a doubtful matter from another quarter. Nor can any wickedness be so manifest, that there is no place for a defense; and therefore it is possible that a judge may not be moved against him who may possibly be found to be innocent; and when the detected crime shall have come to light, he now no longer uses his own opinion, but that of the laws. It may be granted that he does that which he does without anger; for he has that which he may follow. We, undoubtedly, when an offence is committed by our household at home, whether we see or perceive it, must be indignant; for the very sight of a sin is unbecoming. For he who is altogether unmoved either approves of faults, which is more disgraceful and unjust, or avoids the trouble of reproving them, which a tranquil spirit and a quiet mind despises and refuses, unless anger shall have aroused and incited it. But when any one is moved, and yet through unseasonable leniency grants pardon more frequently than is necessary, or at all times, he evidently both destroys the life of those whose audacity he is fostering for greater crimes, and furnishes himself with a perpetual source of annoyances. Therefore the restraining of one's anger in the case of sins is faulty.

Archytas of Tarentum is praised, who, when he had found everything ruined on his estate, rebuking the fault of his bailiff, said, "Wretch, I would have beaten you to death if I had not been angry." They consider this to be a singular example of forbearance; but influenced by authority, they do not see how foolishly he spoke and acted. For if (as Plato says) no prudent man punishes because there is an offence, but to prevent the occurrence of an offence, it is evident how evil an example this wise man put forth. For if slaves shall perceive that their master uses violence when he is not angry, and abstains from violence when he is angry, it is evident that they will not commit slight offences, lest they should be beaten; but will commit the greatest offences, that they may arouse the anger of the perverse man, and escape with impunity. But I should praise him if, when he was enraged, he had given space to his anger, that the excitement of his mind might calm down through the interval of time, and his chastisement might be confined within moderate limits. Therefore, on account of the magnitude of the anger, punishment ought not to have been inflicted, but to have been delayed, lest it should inflict upon the offender pain greater than is just, or occasion an outburst of fury in the punisher. But how, how is it equitable or wise, that anyone should be punished on account of a slight offence, and should be unpunished on account of a very great one? But if he had learned the nature and causes of things, he never would have professed so unsuitable a forbearance, that a wicked slave should rejoice that his master has been angry with him. For as God has furnished the human body with many and various senses which are necessary for the use of life, so also He has assigned to the soul various affections by which the course of life might be regulated; and as He has given desire for the sake of producing offspring, so has He given anger for the sake of restraining faults.

But they who are ignorant of the ends of good and evil things, as they employ sensual desire for the purposes of corruption and pleasure, in the same manner make use of anger and passion for the inflicting of injury, while they are angry with those whom they regard with hatred. Therefore they are angry even with those who commit no offence, even with their equals, or even with their superiors. Hence they daily rush to monstrous1758 deeds; hence tragedies often arise. Therefore Archytas would be deserving of praise, if, when he had been enraged against any citizen or equal who injured him, he had curbed himself, and by forbearance mitigated the impetuosity of his fury. This self-restraint is glorious, by which any great evil which impends is restrained; but it is a fault not to check the faults of slaves and children; for through their escaping without punishment they will proceed to greater evil. In this case anger is not to be restrained; but even if it is in a state of inactivity, it must be aroused. But that which we say respecting man, we also say respecting God, who made man like to Himself. I omit making mention of the figure of God, because the Stoics say that God has no form, and another great subject will arise if we should wish to refute them. I only speak respecting the soul. If it belongs to God to reflect, to be wise, to understand, to foresee. to excel, and of all animals man alone has these qualities, it follows that he was made after the likeness of God; but on this account he goes on to vice, because, being mingled with frailty derived from earth, he is unable to preserve pure and uncontaminated that which he has received from God, unless he is imbued with the precepts of justice by the same God.

**Chap. XIX.—Of the Soul and Body, and of Providence.**

But since he is made up, as we have said, of two parts, soul and body, the virtues are contained in the one, and vices in the other, and they mutually oppose each other. For the good properties of the soul, which consist in restraining lusts, are contrary to the body; and the good properties of the body, which consist in every kind of pleasure, are hostile to the soul. But if the virtue of the soul shall have resisted the desires, and suppressed them, he will be truly like to God. From which it is evident that the soul of man, which is capable of divine virtue, is not mortal. But there is this distinction, that since virtue is attended with bitterness, and the attraction of pleasure is sweet, great numbers are overcome and are drawn aside to the pleasantness; but they who have given themselves up to the body and earthly things are pressed to the earth, and are unable to attain to the favor of the divine bounty, because they have polluted themselves with the defilements of vices. But they who, following God, and in obedience to Him, have despised the desires of the body, and, preferring virtue to pleasures, have preserved innocence and righteousness, these God recognizes as like to Himself.

Since, therefore, He has laid down a most holy law, and wishes all men to be innocent and beneficent, is it possible that He should not be angry when He sees that His law is despised, that virtue is rejected, and pleasure made the object of pursuit? But if He is the governor of the world, as He might to be, He surely does not despise that which is even of the greatest importance in the whole world. If He has foresight, as it is befitting that God should have, it is plain that He consults the interests of the human race, in order that our life may be more abundantly supplied, and better, and safer. If He is the Father and God of all, He is undoubtedly delighted with the virtues of men, and provoked by their vices. Therefore He loves the just, and hates the wicked. There is no need (one says) of hatred; for He once for all has fixed a reward for the good, and punishment for the wicked. But if anyone lives justly and innocently, and at the same time neither worships God nor has any regard for Him, as Aristides, and Timon, and others of the philosophers, will he escape with impunity, because, though he has obeyed the law of God, he has nevertheless despised God Himself? There is therefore something on account of which God may be angry with one rebelling against Him, as it were, in reliance upon His integrity. If He can be angry with this man on account of his pride, why not more so with the sinner, who has despised the law together with the Lawgiver? The judge cannot pardon offences, because he is subject to the will of another. But God can pardon, because He is Himself the arbitrator and judge of His own law; and when He laid down this, He did not surely deprive Himself of all power, but He has the liberty of bestowing pardon.

**Chap. XX.—Of Offences, and the Mercy of God.**

If He is able to pardon, He is therefore able also to be angry. Why, then, someone will say, does it often occur, that they who sin are prosperous, and they who live piously are wretched? Because fugitives and disinherited persons live without restraint, and they who are under the discipline of a father or master live in a more strict and frugal manner. For virtue is proved and fixed by means of ills; vices by means of pleasure. Nor, however, ought he who sins to hope for lasting impunity, because there is no lasting happiness.

"But, in truth, the last day is always to be looked for by man and no one ought to be called happy before his death and last funeral rites,"

as the not inelegant poet says. It is the end which proves happiness, and no one is able to escape the judgment of God, either when alive or after death. For He has the power both to cast down the living from on high, and to punish the dead with eternal torments. Nay, he says, if God is angry, He ought to have inflicted vengeance at once, and to have punished everyone according to his desert. But (it is replied) if He had done this, no one would survive. For there is no one who offends in no respect, and there are many things which excite to the commission of sin—age, intemperance, want, opportunity, reward. To such an extent is the frailty of the flesh with which we are clothed liable to sin, that unless God were indulgent to this necessity, perhaps too few would live. On this account He is most patient, and restrains His anger. For because there is in Him perfect virtue, it follows of necessity that His patience also is perfect, which is itself also a virtue. How many men, from having been sinners, have afterwards become righteous; from being injurious, have become good; from being wicked, have become temperate! How many who were in early life base, and condemned by the judgment of all, afterwards have turned out praiseworthy? But it is plain that this could not happen if punishment followed every offence.

The public laws condemn those who are manifestly guilty; but there are great numbers whose offences are concealed, great numbers who restrain the accuser either by entreaties or by reward, great numbers who elude justice by favor or influence. But if the divine censure should condemn all those who escape the punishment of men, there would be few or even no men on the earth. In short, even that one reason for destroying the human race might have been a just one, that men, despising the living God, pay divine honor to earthly and frail images, as though they were of heaven, adoring works made by human hands. And though God their Creator made them of elevated countenance and upright figure, and raised them to the contemplation of the heaven and the knowledge of God, they have preferred, like cattle, to bend themselves to the earth. For he is low, and curved, and bent downward, who, turning away from the sight of heaven and God his Father, worships things of the earth, which he ought to have trodden upon, that is, things made and fashioned from earth. Therefore, amidst such great impiety and such great sins of men, the forbearance of God attains this object, that men, condemning the errors of their past life, correct themselves. In short, there are many who are just and good; and these, having laid aside the worship of earthly things, acknowledge the majesty of the one and only God. But though the forbearance of God is very great and most useful; yet, although late, He punishes the guilty, and does not suffer them to proceed further, when He sees that they are incorrigible.

**Chap. XXI.—Of the Anger of God and Man.**

There remains one question, and that the last. For someone will perhaps say, that God is so far from being angry, that in His precepts He even forbids man to be angry. I might say that the anger of man ought to be curbed, because he is often angry unjustly; and he has immediate emotion, because he is only for a time. Therefore, lest those things should be done which the low, and those of moderate station, and great kings do in their anger, his rage ought to have been moderated and suppressed, lest, being out of his mind, he should commit some inexpiable crime. But God is not angry for a short time, because He is eternal and of perfect virtue, and He is never angry unless deservedly. But, however, the matter is not so; for if He should altogether prohibit anger, He Himself would have been in some measure the censurer of His own workmanship, since He from the beginning had inserted anger in the liver of man, since it is believed that the cause of this emotion is contained in the moisture of the gall. Therefore He does not altogether prohibit anger, because that affection is necessarily given, but He forbids us to persevere in anger. For the anger of mortals ought to be mortal; for if it is lasting, enmity is strengthened to lasting destruction. Then, again, when He enjoined us to be angry, and yet not to sin, it is plain that He did not tear up anger by the roots, but restrained it, that in every correction we might preserve moderation and justice. Therefore He who commands us to be angry is manifestly Himself angry; He who enjoins us to be quickly appeased is manifestly Himself easy to be appeased: for He has enjoined those things which are just and useful for the interests of society.

But because I had said that the anger of God is not for a time only, as is the case with man, who becomes inflamed with an immediate excitement, and on account of his frailty is unable easily to govern himself, we ought to understand that because God is eternal, His anger also remains to eternity; but, on the other hand, that because He is endued with the greatest excellence, He controls His anger, and is not ruled by it, but that He regulates it according to His will. And it is plain that this is not opposed to that which has just been said. For if His anger had been altogether immortal, there would be no place after a fault for satisfaction or kind feeling, though He Himself commands men to be reconciled before the setting of the sun. But the divine anger remains forever against those who ever sin. Therefore God is appeased not by incense or a victim, not by costly offerings, which things are all corruptible, but by a reformation of the morals: and he who ceases to sin renders the anger of God mortal. For this reason He does not immediately punish everyone who is guilty, that man may have the opportunity of coming to a right mind, and correcting himself.

**Chap. XXII.—Of Sins, and the Verses of the Sibyls Respecting Them Recited.**

This is what I had to say, most beloved Donatus, respecting the anger of God, that you might know how to refute those who represent God as being without emotions. It only remains that, after the practice of Cicero, I should use an epilogue by way of peroration. As he did in the *Tusculan Disputations*, when discoursing on the subject of death, so we in this work ought to bring forward divine testimonies, which may be believed, to refute the persuasion of those who, believing that God is without anger, destroy all religion, without which, as we have shown, we are either equal to the brutes in savageness, or to the cattle in foolishness; for it is in religion only—that is, in the knowledge of the Supreme God—that wisdom consists. All the prophets, being filled with the Divine Spirit, speak nothing else than of the favor of God towards the righteous, and His anger against the ungodly. And their testimony is indeed sufficient for us; but because it is not believed by those who make a display of wisdom by their hair and dress, it was necessary to refute them by reason and arguments. For they act so preposterously, that human things give authority to divine things, whereas divine things ought rather to give authority to human. But let us now leave these things, lest we should produce no effect upon them, and the subject should be indefinitely drawn out. Let us therefore seek those testimonies which they can either believe, or at any rate not oppose.

Authors of great number and weight have made mention of the Sibyls; of the Greeks, Aristo the Chian, and Apollodorus the Erythræan; of our writers, Varro and Fenestella. All these relate that the Erythræan Sibyl was distinguished and noble beyond the rest. Apollodorus, indeed, boasts of her as his own citizen and countrywoman. But Fenestella also relates that ambassadors were sent by the senate to Erythræ, that the verses of this Sibyl might be conveyed to Rome, and that the consuls Curio and Octavius might take care that they should be placed in the Capitol, which had then been restored under the care of Quintus Catulus. In her writings, verses of this kind are found respecting the Supreme God and Maker of the world:—

"The incorruptible and eternal Maker who dwells in the heaven, holding forth good to the good, a much greater reward, but stirring up anger and rage against the evil and unjust."

Again, in another place, enumerating the deeds by which God is especially moved to anger, she introduced these things:—

"Avoid unlawful services, and serve the living God. Abstain from adultery and impurity; bring up a pure generation of children; do not kill: for the Immortal will be angry with everyone who may sin."

Therefore He is angry with sinners.

## Chap. XXIII.—Of the Anger of God and the Punishment of Sins, and a Recital of the Verses of the Sibyls Respecting It; And, Moreover, a Reproof and Exhortation.

But because it is related by most learned men that there have been many Sibyls, the testimony of one may not be sufficient to confirm the truth, as we purpose to do. The volumes, indeed, of the Cumæan Sibyl, in which are written the fates of the Romans are kept secret; but the writings of all the others are, for the most part, not prohibited from being in common use. And of these another, denouncing the anger of God against all nations on account of the impiety of men, thus began:—

"Since great anger is coming upon a disobedient world, I disclose the commands of God to the last age, prophesying to all men from city to city."

Another Sibyl also said, that the deluge was caused by the indignation of God against the unrighteous in a former age that the wickedness of the human race might be extinguished:—

"From the time when, the God of heaven being enraged against the cities themselves and all men, a deluge having burst forth, the sea covered the earth."

In like manner she foretold a conflagration about to take place hereafter, in which the impiety of men should again be destroyed:—

" And at some time, God no longer soothing His anger, but increasing it, and destroying the race of men, and laying waste the whole of it by fire."

From which mention is thus made concerning Jupiter by Ovid:—

"He remembers also that it is fated that the time shall come in which the sea, the earth, and the palace of heaven, being caught by fire, shall be burnt, and the curiously wrought framework of the world be in danger."

And this must come to pass at the time when the honor and worship of the Supreme shall have perished among men. The same Sibyl, however, testifying that He was appeased by reformation of conduct and self-improvement, added these things:—

"But, ye mortals, in pity turn yourselves now, and do not lead the great God to every kind of anger."

And also a little later:—

"He will not destroy, but will again restrain His anger, if you all practice valuable piety in your minds."

Then another Sibyl declares that the Father of heavenly and earthly things ought to be loved, lest His indignation should arise, to the destruction of men:—

"Lest by chance the immortal God should be angry, and destroy the whole race of men, their life and shameless race, it is befitting that we love the wise, ever-living God the Father."

From these things it is evident that the arguments of the philosophers are vain, who imagine that God is without anger, and among His other praises reckon that which is most useless, detracting from Him that which is most salutary for human affairs, by which majesty itself exists. For this earthly kingdom and government, unless guarded by fear, is broken down. Take away anger from a king, and he will not only cease to be obeyed, but he will even be cast down headlong from his height. Yea, rather take away this affection from any person of low degree, and who will not plunder him? Who will not deride him? Who will not treat him with injury? Thus he will be able to have neither clothing, nor an abode, nor food, since others will deprive him of whatever he has; much less can we suppose that the majesty of the heavenly government can exist without anger and fear. The Milesian Apollo being consulted concerning the religion of the Jews, inserted these things in his answer:—

"God, the King and Father of all, before whom the earth trembles, and the heaven and sea, and whom the recesses of Tartarus and the demons dread."

If He is so mild, as the philosophers will have it, how is it that not only the demons and ministers of such great power, but even the heaven and earth, and the whole system of the universe, tremble at His presence? For if no one submits to the service of another except by compulsion, it follows that all government exists by fear, and fear by anger. For if anyone is not aroused against one who is unwilling to obey, it will not be possible for him to be compelled to obedience. Let anyone consult his own feelings; he will at once understand that no one can be subdued to the command of another without anger and chastisement. Therefore, where there shall be no anger, there will be no authority. But God has authority; therefore also He must have anger, in which authority consists. Therefore let no one, induced by the empty prating of the philosophers, train himself to the contempt of God, which is the greatest impiety. We all are bound both to love Him, because He is our Father; and to reverence Him, because He is our Lord: both to pay Him honor, because He is bounteous; and to fear Him, because He is severe: each character in Him is worthy of reverence. Who can preserve his piety, and yet fail to love the parent of his life? Or who can with impunity despise Him who, as ruler of all things, has true and everlasting power over all? If you consider Him in the character of Father, He supplies to us our entrance to the light which we enjoy: through Him we live, through Him we have entered into the abode of this world. If you contemplate Him as God, it is He who nourishes us with innumerable resources: it is He who sustains us, we dwell in His house, we are His household; and if we are less obedient than was befitting, and less attentive to our duty than the endless merits of our Master and Parent demanded: nevertheless it is, of great avail to our obtaining pardon, if we retain the worship and knowledge of Him; if, laying aside low and earthly affairs and goods, we meditate upon heavenly and divine things which are everlasting. And that we may be able to do this, God must be followed by us, God must be adored and loved; since there is in Him the substance of things, the principle of the virtues, and the source of all that is good.

For what is greater in power than God, or more perfect in reason, or brighter in clearness? And since He begat us to wisdom, and produced us to righteousness, it is not allowable for man to forsake God, who is the giver of intelligence and life and to serve earthly and frail things, or, intent upon seeking temporal goods, to turn aside from innocence and piety. Vicious and deadly pleasures do not render a man happy; nor does opulence, which is the inciter of lusts; nor empty ambition; nor frail honors, by which the human soul, being ensnared and enslaved to the body, is condemned to eternal death: but innocence and righteousness alone, the lawful and due reward of which is immortality, which God from the beginning appointed for holy and uncorrupted minds, which keep themselves pure and uncontaminated from vices, and from every earthly impurity. Of this heavenly and eternal reward they cannot be partakers, who have polluted their conscience by deeds of violence, frauds, rapine, and deceits; and who, by injuries inflicted upon men, by impious actions, have branded themselves with indelible stains. Accordingly it is befitting that all who wish deservedly to be called wise, who wish to be called men, should despise frail things, should trample upon earthly things, and should look down upon base things, that they may be able to be united in a most blissful relationship with God.

Let impiety and discords be removed; let turbulent and deadly dissensions be allayed, by which human societies and the divine union of the public league are broken in upon, divided, and dispersed; as far as we can, let us aim at being good and bounteous: if we have a supply of wealth and resources, let it not be devoted to the pleasure of a single person, but bestowed on the welfare of many. For pleasure is as short lived as the body to which it does service. But justice and kindness are as immortal as the mind and soul, which by good works attain to the likeness of God. Let God be consecrated by us, not in temples, but in our heart. All things which are made by the hand are destructible. Let us cleanse this temple, which is defiled not by smoke or dust, but by evil thoughts which is lighted not by blazing tapers but by the brightness and light of wisdom. And if we believe that God is always present in this temple, to whose divinity the secrets of the heart are open, we shall so live as always to have Him propitious, and never to fear His anger.

*Note by the American Editor.*

It is worthwhile to direct attention to (book vi. cap. 2) what our author has said of "*true* worship," just now, when the most violent and persistent efforts are made to sensualize Christian worship, and to explain away the testimony of the

Ante-Nicene Fathers on this important subject. The argument of our author, in its entire drift, is as applicable to our own times as to his; and, deeply as I value beauty in the public worship of God, I cannot, as a Nicene Catholic, do less than adopt the universal sentiment of the early Fathers as to the limits of decoration.

## On the Workmanship of God, or the Formation of Man

### A Treatise Addressed to His Pupil Demetrianus.

### Chap. I.—The Introduction, and Exhortation to Demetrianus.

How disturbed I am, and in the greatest necessities, you will be able to judge from this little book which I have written to you, Demetrianus, almost in unadorned words, as the mediocrity of my talent permitted, that you might know my daily pursuit, and that I might not be wanting to you, even now an instructor, but of a more honorable subject and of a better system. For if you afforded yourself a ready hearer in literature, which did nothing else than form the style, how much more teachable ought you to be in these true studies, which have reference even to the life! And I now profess to you, that I am hindered by no necessity of circumstance or time from composing something by which the philosophers of our sect which we uphold may become better instructed and more learned for the future, although they now have a bad reputation, and are commonly reproved, as living otherwise than is befitting for wise men, and as concealing their vices under the covering of a name; whereas they ought either to have remedied them, or to have altogether avoided them, that they might render the name of wisdom happy and uncorrupted, their life itself agreeing with their precepts. I, however, shrink from no labor that I may at once instruct ourselves and others. For I am not able to forget myself, and especially at that time when it is most necessary for me to remember; as also you do not forget yourself, as I hope and wish. For although the necessity of the state may turn you aside from true and just works, yet it is impossible that a mind conscious of rectitude should not from time to time look to the heaven.

I indeed rejoice that all things which are esteemed blessings turn out prosperously to you, but only on condition of their changing nothing of your state of mind. For I fear lest custom and the pleasantness of these subjects should, as usually happens, creep by degrees into your mind. Therefore I advise you,

"And repeating it, will again and again advise you,"

not to believe that you have these enjoyments of the earth as great or true blessings, since they are not only deceitful because they are doubtful, but also treacherous because they are pleasant. For you know how crafty that wrestler and adversary of ours is, and also often violent, as we now see that he is. He employs all these things which are able to entice as snares, and with such subtlety that they escape the notice of the eyes of the mind, so that they cannot be avoided by the foresight of man. Therefore it is the highest prudence to advance step by step, since he occupies the passes on both sides, and secretly places stumbling-blocks for our feet. Accordingly I advise you, either to disregard, if you are able according to your virtue, your prosperity in which you live, or not to admire it greatly. Remember your true parent, and in what city you have given your name, and of what rank you have been. You understand assuredly what I say. For I do not charge you with pride, of which there is not even a suspicion in your case; but the things which I say are to be referred to the mind, not to the body, the whole system of which has been arranged on this account, that it may be in subjection to the soul as to a master, and may be ruled by its will. For it is in a certain manner an earthen vessel in which the soul, that is, the true man himself, is contained, and that vessel indeed not made by Prometheus, as the poets say, but by that supreme Creator and Artificer of the world, God, whose divine providence and most perfect excellence it is neither possible to comprehend by the perception, nor to express in word.

I will attempt, however, since mention has been made of the body and soul, to explain the nature of each, as far as the weakness of my understanding sees through; and I think that this duty is especially to be undertaken on this account, because Marcus Tullius, a man of remarkable talent, in his fourth book on the Republic, when he had attempted to do this, concluded a subject of wide extent within narrow limits, lightly selecting the chief points. And that there might be no excuse, because he had not followed up this subject, he testified that neither inclination nor attention had been wanting to him. For in his first book concerning the Laws, when he was concisely summing up the same subject, he thus spoke: "Scipio, as it appears to me, has sufficiently expressed this subject in those books which you have read." Afterwards, however, in his second book concerning the Nature of the Gods, he endeavored to follow up the same subject more extensively. But since he did not express it sufficiently even there, I will approach this office, and will take upon myself boldly to explain that which a man of the greatest eloquence has almost left untouched. Perhaps you may blame me for attempting to discuss something in matters of obscurity, when you see that there have been men of such rashness who are commonly called philosophers, that they scrutinized those things which God willed to be abstruse and hidden, and investigated the nature of things in heaven and on earth, which are far removed from us, and cannot be examined by the eyes, nor touched by the hand, nor perceived by the senses; and yet they so dispute concerning the nature of these things, as to wish that the things which they bring forward may appear to be proved and known. What reason is there, I pray, why anyone should think it an invidious thing in us, if we wish to look into and contemplate the system of our body, which is not altogether obscure, because from the very offices of the limbs, and the uses of the several parts, it is permitted us to understand with what great power of providence each part has been made?

### Chap. II.—Of the Production of the Beasts and of Man.

For our Creator and Parent, God, has given to man perception and reason, that it might be evident from this that we are descended from Him, because He Himself is intelligence, He Himself is perception and reason. Since He did not give that power of reason to the other animals, He provided beforehand in what manner their life might be safer. For He clothed them all with their own natural hair, in order that they might more easily be able to endure the severity of frosts and colds. Moreover, He has appointed to every kind its own peculiar defense for the repelling of attacks from without; so that they may either oppose the stronger animals with natural weapons, or the feebler ones may withdraw themselves from danger by the swiftness of their flight, or those which require at once both strength and swiftness may protect themselves by craft, or guard themselves in hiding places. And so others of them either poise themselves aloft with light plumage, or are supported by hoofs, or are furnished with horns; some have arms in their mouth—namely, their teeth—or hooked talons on their feet; and none of them is destitute of a defense for its own protection.

But if any fall as a prey to the greater animals, that their race might not utterly perish, they have either been banished to that region where the greater ones cannot exist, or they have received a more abundant fruitfulness in production, that food might be supplied from them to the beasts which are nourished by blood, and yet their very multitude might survive the slaughter inflicted upon them, so as to preserve the race. But He made man—reason being granted to him, and the power of perceiving and speaking being given to him—destitute of those things which are given to the other animals, because wisdom was able to supply those things which the condition of nature had denied to him. He made him naked and defenseless, because he could be armed by his talent, and clothed by his reason. But it cannot be expressed how wonderfully the absence of those things which are given to the brutes contributes to the beauty of man. For if He had given to man the teeth of wild beasts, or horns, or claws, or hoofs, or a tail, or hairs of various color, who cannot perceive how misshapen an animal he would be, as the dumb animals, if they were made naked and defenseless? For if you take from these the natural clothing of their body, or those things by which they are armed of themselves, they can be neither beautiful nor safe, so that they appear wonderfully furnished if you think of utility, and wonderfully adorned if you think of appearance: in such a wonderful manner is utility combined with beauty.

But with reference to man, whom He formed an eternal and immortal being, He did not arm him, as the others, without, but within; nor did He place his protection in the body, but in the soul: since it would have been superfluous, when He had given him that which was of the greatest value, to cover him with bodily defenses, especially when they hindered the beauty of the human body. On which account I am accustomed to wonder at the senselessness of the philosophers who follow Epicurus, who blame the works of nature, that they may show that the world is prepared and governed by no providence; but they ascribe the origin of all things to indivisible and solid bodies, from the fortuitous meetings of which they say that all things are and were produced. I pass by the things relating to the work itself with which they find fault, in which matter they are ridiculously mad; I assume that which belongs to the subject of which we are now treating.

### Chap. III.—Of the Condition of the Beasts and Man.

They complain that man is born in a more feeble and frail condition than that in which the other animals are born: for that these, as soon as they are produced from the womb, immediately raise themselves on their feet, and express their joy by running to and fro, and are at once fit for enduring the air, inasmuch as they have come forth to the light protected by natural coverings; but man, on the contrary, being naked and defenseless, is cast forth, and driven, as it were, from a shipwreck, to the miseries of this life; who is neither able to move himself from the place where he has been born, nor to seek the nourishment of milk, nor to endure the injury of time. Therefore they say that Nature is not the mother of the human race, but a stepmother, who has dealt so liberally with the dumb creation, but has so produced man, that, without resources, and without strength, and destitute of all aid, he can do nothing else than give tokens of the state of his frailty by wailing and lamentations; "as well he may, whose destiny it is to go through in life so many ills."

And when they say these things they are believed to be very wise, because everyone without consideration is displeased with his own condition; but I contend that they are never more foolish than when they say these things. For when I consider the condition of things, I understand that nothing ought to have been otherwise than it is—not to say could have been otherwise, for God is able to do all things: but it must be, that that most provident majesty made that which was better and more right.

I should like, therefore, to ask those censurers of the divine works, what they think to be wanting in man, on account of his being born in a more feeble condition. Do they think that men are, on this account, brought up worse? Or that they advance the less to the greatest strength of age? Or that weakness is a hindrance to their growth or safety, since reason bestows the things which are wanting? But, they say, the bringing up of man costs the greatest labors: in truth, the condition of the brute creation is better, because all these, when they have brought forth their young, have no care except for their own food; from which it is effected that, their teats being spontaneously distended, the nourishment of milk is supplied to their offspring, and that they seek this nourishment by the compulsion of nature, without any trouble on the part of the mothers. How is it with birds, which have a different nature? Do they not undergo the greatest labors in bringing up their young, so that they sometimes appear to have something of human intelligence? For they either build their nests of mud, or construct them with twigs and leaves, and they sit upon the eggs without taking food; and since it has not been given to them to nourish their young from their own bodies, they convey to them food, and spend whole days in going to and fro in this manner; but by night they defend, cherish, and protect them. What more can men do? Unless it be this only, that they do not drive away their young when grown up, but retain them bound by perpetual relationship and the bond of affection. Why should I say that the offspring of birds is much more fragile than that of man? Inasmuch as they do not bring forth the animal itself from the body of the mother, but that which, being warmed by the nourishment and heat of the body of the mother, produces the animal; and this, even when animated by breath, being unfledged and tender, is not only without the power of flying, but even of walking. Would he not, therefore, be most senseless, if anyone should think that nature has dealt badly with birds, first, because they are twice born, and then because they are so weak, that they have to be nourished by food sought with labor by their parents? But they select the stronger, and pass by the more feeble animals.

I ask, therefore, from those who prefer the condition of the beasts to their own, what they would choose if God should give them the choice: would they prefer the wisdom of man together with his weakness, or the strength of the beasts together with their nature? In truth, they are not so much like the beasts as not to prefer even a much more fragile condition, provided that it be human, to that strength of theirs unattended with reason. But, in truth, prudent men neither desire the reason of man together with frailty, nor the strength of the dumb animals without reason. Therefore it is nothing so repugnant or contradictory, that either reason or the condition of nature should of necessity prepare each animal. If it is furnished with natural protection, reason is superfluous. For what will it contrive? What will it do? Or what will it plan? Or in what will it display that light of the intellect, when Nature of its own accord grants those things which are able to be the result of reason? But if it be endued with reason, what need will there be of defenses for the body, when reason once granted is able to supply the office of nature? And this has such power for the adorning and protection of man that nothing greater or better can be given by God. Finally, since man is possessed of a body which is not great, and of slight strength, and of infirm health, nevertheless, since he has received that which is of greater value, he is better equipped than the other animals, and more adorned. For though he is born frail and feeble, yet he is safe from all the dumb animals, and all those which are born with greater strength, though they are able to bear patiently the inclemency of the sky, yet are unable to be safe from man. Thus it comes to pass that reason bestows more on man than nature does on the dumb animals; since, in their case, neither greatness of strength nor firmness of body can prevent them from being oppressed by us, or from being made subject to our power.

Can anyone, then, when he sees that even elephants, with their vast bodies and strength, are subservient to man, complain respecting God, the Maker of all things, because he has received moderate strength, and a small body; and not estimate according to their deserts the divine benefits towards himself, which is the part of an ungrateful man, or (to speak more truly) of a madman? Plato, I believe, that he might refute these ungrateful men, gave thanks to nature that he was born a man. How much better and more soundly did he act, who perceived that the condition of man was better, than they did who would have preferred that they had been born beasts! For if God should happen to change them into those animals whose condition they prefer to their own, they would now immediately desire to return to their previous state, and would with great outcries eagerly demand their former condition, because strength and firmness of body are not of such consequence that you should be without the office of the tongue; or the free course of birds through the air, that you should be without the hands. For the hands are of greater service than the lightness and use of the wings; the tongue is of greater service than the strength of the whole body. What madness is it, therefore, to prefer those things which, if they were given, you would refuse to receive!

**Chap. IV.—Of the Weakness of Man.**

They also complain that man is liable to diseases, and to untimely death. They are indignant, it appears, that they are not born gods. By no means, they say; but we show from this, that man was made with no foresight, which ought to have been otherwise. What if I shall show, that this very thing was foreseen with great reason, that he might be able to be harassed by diseases, and that his life might often be cut short in the midst of its course? For, since God had known that the animal which He had made, of its own accord passed to death, that it might be capable of receiving death itself, which is the dissolution of nature, He gave to it frailty, which might find an approach for death in order to the dissolution of the animal. For if it had been of such strength that disease and sickness could not approach it, not even could death, since death is the consequence of diseases. But how could a premature death be absent from him, for whom a mature death had been appointed? Assuredly they wish that no man should die, unless when he has completed his hundredth year. How can they maintain their consistency in so great an opposition of circumstances? For, in order that no one may be capable of dying before a hundred years, something of the strength which is immortal must be given to him; and when this is granted, the condition of death must necessarily be excluded. But of what kind can that be, which can render a man firm and impregnable against diseases and attacks from without? For, inasmuch as he is composed of bones, and nerves, and flesh, and blood, which of these can be so firm as to repel frailty and death? That man, therefore, may not be liable to dissolution before that time which they think ought to have been appointed for him, of what material will they assign to him a body? All things which can be seen and touched are frail. It remains that they seek something from heaven, since there is nothing on earth which is not weak.

Since, therefore, man had to be so formed by God, that he should at some time be mortal, the matter itself required that he should be made with a frail and earthly body. It is necessary, therefore, that he should at some time receive death, since he is possessed of a body; for everybody is liable to dissolution and to death. Therefore they are most foolish who complain of premature death, since the condition of nature makes a place for it. Thus it will follow that he is subject also to diseases; for nature does not admit that infirmity can be absent from that body which is at some time to undergo dissolution. But let us suppose it to be possible, as they wish, that man is not born under those conditions by which he is subject to disease or death, unless, having completed the course of his life, he shall have arrived at the extremity of old age. They do not, therefore, see what would be the consequence if it were so arranged, that it would be plainly impossible to die at another time; but if anyone can be deprived of nourishment by another, it will be possible for him to die. Therefore the case requires that man, who cannot die before an appointed day, should have no need of the nourishment of food, because it may be taken from him; but if he shall have no need of food, he will now not be a man, but will become a god. Therefore, as I have already said, they who complain of the frailty of man, make this complaint especially, that they were not born immortal and everlasting. No one ought to die unless he is old. On this account, in truth, he ought to die, because he is not God. But mortality cannot be united with immortality: for if a man is mortal in old age, he cannot be immortal in youth; neither is the condition of death foreign to him who is at some time about to die; nor is there any immortality to which a limit is appointed. Thus it comes to pass, that the exclusion of immortality forever, and the reception of mortality for a time, place man in such a condition that he is at some time mortal.

Therefore the necessity is in all points suitable, that he ought not to have been otherwise than he is, and that it was impossible. But they do not see the order of consequences, because they have once committed an error in the main point itself. For the divine providence having been excluded from the affairs of men, it necessarily followed that all things were produced of their own accord. Hence they invented the notion of those blows and fortuitous meetings together of minute seeds, because they did not see the origin of things. And when they had thrown themselves into this difficulty, necessity now compelled them to think that souls were born together with bodies, and in like manner were extinguished together with bodies; for they had made the assumption, that nothing was made by the divine mind. And they were unable to prove this in any other way, than by showing that there were some things in which the system of providence appeared to be at fault. Therefore they blamed those things in which providence wonderfully expressed its divinity, as those things which I have related concerning diseases and premature death; whereas they ought to have considered, these things being assumed, what would be the necessary consequences (but those things which I have spoken are the consequences) if he were not liable to diseases, and did not require a dwelling, nor clothing. For why should he fear the winds, or rains, or colds, the power of which consists in this, that they bring diseases? For on this account he has received wisdom, that he may guard his frailty against things that would injure him. The necessary consequence is, that since he is liable to diseases for the sake of retaining his wisdom, he must also be liable to death; because he to whom death does not come, must of necessity be firm. But infirmity has in itself the condition of death; but where there shall be firmness, neither can old age have any place, nor death, which follows old age.

Moreover, if death were appointed for a fixed age, man would become most arrogant, and would be destitute of all humanity. For almost all the rights of humanity, by which we are united with one another, arise from fear and the consciousness of frailty. In short, all the more feeble and timid animals herd together, that, since they are unable to protect themselves by strength, they may protect themselves by their multitude; but the stronger animals seek solitudes, since they trust in their force and strength. If man also, in the same manner, had sufficient strength for the repelling of dangers, and did not stand in need of the assistance of any other, what society would there be? Or what system? What humanity? Or what would be harsher than man? What more brutal? What more savage? But since he is feeble, and not able to live by himself apart from man, he desires society, that his life, passed in intercourse with others, may become both more adorned and more safe. You see, therefore, that the whole reason of man centers most of all in this, that he is born naked and fragile, that he is attacked by diseases, that he is punished by premature death. And if these things should be taken away from man, reason also, and wisdom, must necessarily be taken away. But I am discussing too long respecting things which are manifest, since it is clear that nothing ever was made, or could have been made, without providence. And if I should now wish to discuss respecting all its works in order, the subject would be infinite. But I have purposed to speak so much concerning the body of man only, that I may show in it the power of divine providence, how great it has been in those things only which are easy of comprehension and open; for those things which relate to the soul can neither be subjected to the eyes, nor comprehended. Now we speak concerning the vessel itself of man, which we see.

### Chap. V.—Of the Figures and Limbs of Animals.

In the beginning, when God was forming the animals, He did not wish to conglobate and collect them into a round shape that they might be able easily to put themselves in motion for walking, and to turn themselves in any direction; but from the highest part of the body He lengthened out the head. He also carried out to a greater length some of the limbs, which are called feet, that, being fixed on the ground with alternate motions, they might lead forward the animal wherever his inclination had borne him, or the necessity of seeking food had called him. Moreover,

He made four limbs standing out from the very vessel of the body: two behind, which are in all animals—the feet; also two close to the head and neck, which supply various uses to animals. For in cattle and wild beasts they are feet like the hinder ones; but in man they are hands, which are produced not for walking, but for acting and controlling. There is also a third class, in which those former limbs are neither feet nor hands; but wings, which, having feathers arranged in order, supply the use of flying. Thus one formation has different forms and uses; and that He might firmly hold together the density itself of the body, by binding together greater and small bones, He compacted a kind of keel, which we call the spine; and He did not think fit to form it of one continued bone, lest the animal should not have the power of walking and bending itself. From its middle part, as it were, He has extended in a different direction transverse and flat bones, by which, being slightly curved, and almost drawn together to themselves as into a circle, the inward organs may be covered, that those parts which needed to be soft and less strong might be protected by the encircling of a solid framework. But at the end of that joining together which we have said to resemble the keel of a ship, He placed the head, in which might be the government of the whole living creature; and this name was given to it, as indeed Varro writes to Cicero, because from this the senses and the nerves take their beginning.

But those parts, which we have said to be lengthened out from the body, either for the sake of walking, or of acting, or of flying, He would have to consist of bones, neither too long, for the sake of rapidity of motion, nor too short, for the sake of firmness, but of a few, and those large. For either they are two as in man, or four as in a quadruped. And these He did not make solid, lest in walking sluggishness and weight should retard; but He made them hollow, and full of marrow within, to preserve the vigor of the body. And again, He did not make them equally extended to the end; but He conglobated their extremities with coarse knots, that they might be able more easily to be bound with sinews, and to be turned more easily, from which they are called joints. These knots He made firmly solid, and covered with a soft kind of covering, which is called cartilage; for this purpose, that they might be bent without galling or any sense of pain. He did not, however, form these after one fashion. For He made some simple and round into an orb, in those joints at least in which it was befitting that the limbs should move in all directions, as in the shoulders, since it is necessary that the hands should move and be twisted about in any direction; but others He made broad, and equal, and round towards one part, and that plainly in those places where only it was necessary for the limbs to be bent, as in the knees, and in the elbows, and in the hands themselves. For as it was at the same time pleasant to the sight, and useful, that the hands should move in every direction from that position from which they spring; so assuredly, if this same thing should happen to the elbows, a motion of that kind would be at once superfluous and unbecoming. For then the hand, having lost the dignity which it now has, through its excessive flexibility, would appear like the trunk of an elephant; and man would be altogether snake-handed,—an instance of which has been wonderfully effected in that monstrous beast. For God, who wished to display His providence and power by a wonderful variety of many things, inasmuch as He had not extended the head of that animal to such a length that he might be able to touch the earth with his mouth, which would have been horrible and hideous, and because He had so armed the mouth itself with extended tusks, that even if he touched the earth the tusks would still deprive him of the power of feeding, He lengthened out between these from the top of the forehead a soft and flexible limb, by which he might be able to grasp and lay hold of anything, lest the prominent magnitude of the tusks, or the shortness of the neck, should interfere with the arrangement for taking food.

**Chap. VI.—Of the Error of Epicurus, and of the Limbs and Their Use.**

I cannot here be prevented from again showing the folly of Epicurus. For all the ravings of Lucretius belong to him, who, in order that he might show that animals are not produced by any contrivance of the divine mind, but, as he is wont to say, by chance, said that in the beginning of the world innumerable other animals of wonderful form and magnitude were produced; but that they were unable to be permanent, because either the power of taking food, or the method of uniting and generating, had failed them. It is evident that, in order to make a place for his atoms flying about through the boundless and empty space, he wished to exclude the divine providence. But when he saw that a wonderful system of providence is contained in all things which breathe, what vanity was it (O mischievous one!) to say that there had been animals of immense size, in which the system of production ceased!

Since, therefore, all things which we see are produced with reference to a plan—for nothing but a plan can effect this very condition of being born—it is manifest that nothing could have been born without a plan. For it was previously foreseen in the formation of everything, how it should use the service of the limbs for the necessaries of life; and how the offspring, being produced from the union of bodies, might preserve all living creatures by their several species. For if a skillful architect, when he designs to construct some great building, first of all considers what will be the effect of the complete building, and previously ascertains by measurement what situation is suitable for a light weight, in what place a massive part of the structure will stand, what will be the intervals between the columns, what or where will be the descents and outlets of the falling waters and the reservoirs,—he first, I say, foresees these things, that he may begin together with the very foundations whatever things are necessary for the work when now completed,—why should anyone suppose that, in the contrivance of animals, God did not foresee what things were necessary for living, before giving life itself? For it is manifest that life could not exist, unless those things by which it exists were previously arranged.

Therefore Epicurus saw in the bodies of animals the skill of a divine plan; but that he might carry into effect that which he had before imprudently assumed, he added another absurdity agreeing with the former. For he said that the eyes were not produced for seeing, nor the ears for hearing, nor the feet for walking, since these members were produced before there was the exercise of seeing, hearing, and walking; but that all the offices of these members arose from them after their production. I fear lest the refutation of such extravagant and ridiculous stories should appear to be no less foolish; but it pleases me to be foolish, since we are dealing with a foolish man, lest he should think himself too clever. What do you say, Epicurus? Were not the eyes produced for seeing? Why, then, do they see? Their use, he says, afterwards showed itself. Therefore they were produced for the sake of seeing, since they can do nothing else but see. Likewise, in the case of the other limbs, use itself shows for what purpose they were produced. For it is plain that this use could have no existence, unless all the limbs had been made with such arrangement and foresight, that they might be able to have their use.

For what if you should say, that birds were not made to fly, nor wild beasts to rage, nor fishes to swim, nor men to be wise, when it is evident that living creatures are subject to that natural disposition and office to which each was created? But it is evident that he who has lost the main point itself of the truth must always be in error. For if all things are produced not by providence, but by a fortuitous meeting together of atoms, why does it never happen by chance, that those first principles meet together in such a way as to make an animal of such a kind, that it might rather hear with its nostrils, smell with its eyes, and see with its ears? For if the first principles leave no kind of position untried, monstrous productions of this kind ought daily to have been brought forth, in which the arrangement of the limbs might be distorted, and the use far different from that which prevails. But since all the races of animals, and all the limbs, observe their own laws and arrangements, and the uses assigned to them, it is plain that nothing is made by chance, since a perpetual arrangement of the divine plan is preserved. But we will refute Epicurus at another time. Now let us discuss the subject of providence, as we have begun.

### Chap. VII.—Of All the Parts of the Body.

God therefore connected and bound together the parts which strengthen the body, which we call bones, being knotted and joined to one another by sinews, which the mind might make use of, as bands, if it should wish to hasten forward or to lag behind; and, indeed, without any labor or effort, but with a very slight inclination, it might moderate and guide the mass of the whole body. But He covered these with the inward organs, as was befitting to each place that the parts which were solid might be enclosed and concealed. Also He mixed with the inward organs, veins as streams divided through the whole body, through which the moisture and the blood, running in different directions, might bedew all the limbs with the vital juices; and He fashioned these inward organs after that manner which was befitting to each kind and situation, and covered them with skin drawn over them, which He either adorned with beauty only, or covered with thick hair, or fenced with scales, or adorned with brilliant feathers. But that is a wonderful contrivance of God, that one arrangement and one state exhibits innumerable varieties of animals. For in almost all things which breathe there is the same connection and arrangement of the limbs. For first of all is the head, and annexed to this the neck; also the breast adjoined to the neck, and the shoulders projecting from it, the belly adhering to the breast; also the organs of generation subjoined to the belly; in the last place, the thighs and feet. Nor do the limbs only keep their own course and position in all, but also the parts of the limbs. For in the head itself alone the ears occupy a fixed position, the eyes a fixed position, likewise the nostrils, the mouth also, and in the teeth and tongue. And though all these things are the same in all animals, yet there is an infinite and manifold diversity of the things formed; because those things of which I have spoken, being either more drawn out or more contracted, are comprehended by lineaments differing in various ways. What! is not that divine, that in so great a multitude of living creatures each animal is most excellent in its own class and species?—so that if any part should be taken from one to another, the necessary result would be, that nothing would be more embarrassed for use, nothing more unshapely to look upon; as if you should give a prolonged neck to an elephant, or a short neck to a camel; or if you should attach feet or hair to serpents, in which the length of the body equally stretched out required nothing else, except that being marked as to their backs with spots, and supporting themselves by their smooth scales, with winding courses they should glide into slippery tracts. But in quadrupeds the same designer lengthened out the arrangement of the spine, which is drawn out from the top of the head to a greater length on the outside of the body, and pointed it into a tail, that the parts of the body which are offensive might either be covered on account of their unsightliness, or be protected on account of their tenderness, so that by its motion certain minute and injurious animals might be driven away from the body; and if you should take away this member, the animal would be imperfect and weak. But where there is reason and the hand, that is not so necessary as a covering of hair. To such an extent are all things most befittingly arranged, each in its own class, that nothing can be conceived more unbecoming than a quadruped which is naked, or a man that is covered.

But, however, though nakedness itself on the part of man tends in a wonderful manner to beauty, yet it was not adapted to his head; for what great deformity there would be in this, is evident from baldness. Therefore He clothed the head with hair; and because it was about to be on the top, He added it as an ornament, as it were, to the highest summit of the building. And this ornament is not collected into a circle, or rounded into the figure of a cap, lest it should be unsightly by leaving some parts bare; but it is freely poured forth in some places, and withdrawn in others, according to the comeliness of each place. Therefore, the forehead entrenched by a circumference, and the hair put forth from the temples before the ears, and the uppermost parts of these being surrounded after the manner of a crown, and all the back part of the head covered, display an appearance of wonderful comeliness. Then the nature of the beard contributes in an incredible degree to distinguish the maturity of bodies, or to the distinction of sex, or to the beauty of manliness and strength; so that it appears that the system of the whole work would not have been in agreement, if anything had been made otherwise than it is.

### Chap. VIII.—Of the Parts of Man: the Eyes and Ears.

Now I will show the plan of the whole man, and will explain the uses and habits of the several members which are exposed to view in the body, or concealed. When, therefore, God had determined of all the animals to make man alone heavenly, and all the rest earthly, He raised him erect to the contemplation of the heaven, and made him a biped, doubtless that he might look to the same quarter from which he derives his origin; but He depressed the others to the earth, that, inasmuch as they have no expectation of immortality, being cast down with their whole body to the ground, they might be subservient to their appetite and food. And thus the right reason and elevated position of man alone, and his countenance, shared with and closely resembling God his Father, bespeak his origin and Maker. His mind, nearly divine, because it has obtained the rule not only over the animals which are on the earth, but even over his own body, being situated in the highest part, the head, as in a lofty citadel, looks out upon and observes all things. He formed this its palace, not drawn out and extended, as in the case of the dumb animals, but like an orb and a globe, because all roundness belongs to a perfect plan and figure. Therefore the mind and that divine fire is covered with it, as with a vault; and when He had covered its highest top with a natural garment, He alike furnished and adorned the front part which is called the face, with the necessary services of the members.

And first, He closed the orbs of the eyes with concave apertures, from which boring Varro thought that the forehead derived its name; and He would have these to be neither less nor more than two, because no number is more perfect as to appearance than that of two: as also He made the ears two, the doubleness of which bears with it an incredible degree of beauty, both because each part is adorned with a resemblance, and that voices coming from both sides may more easily be collected. For the form itself is fashioned after a wonderful manner: because He would not have their apertures to be naked and uncovered, which would have been less becoming and less useful; since the voice might fly beyond the narrow space of simple caverns, and be scattered, did not the apertures themselves confine it, received through hollow windings and kept back from reverberation, like those small vessels, by the application of which narrow-mouthed vessels are accustomed to be filled.

These ears, then, which have their name from the drinking in of voices, from which Virgil says,

"And with these ears I drank in his voice;"

or because the Greeks call the voice itself αὐδήν, from hearing,—the ears (aures) were named as though audes by the change of a letter,—God would not form of soft skins, which, hanging down and flaccid, might take away beauty; nor of hard and solid bones, lest, being stiff and immoveable, they should be inconvenient for use. But He designed that which might be between these, that a softer cartilage might bind them, and that they might have at once a befitting and flexible firmness. In these the office of bearing only is placed, as that of seeing is in the eyes, the acuteness of which is especially inexplicable and wonderful; for He covered their orbs, presenting the similitude of gems in that part with which they had to see, with transparent membranes, that the images of objects placed opposite them, being refracted as in a mirror, might penetrate to the innermost perception. Through these membranes, therefore, that faculty which is called the mind sees those things which are without; lest you should happen to think that we see either by the striking of the images, as the philosophers discuss, since the office of seeing ought to be in that which sees, not in that which is seen; or in the tension of the air together with the eyesight; or in the outpouring of the rays: since, if it were so, we should see the ray towards which we turn with our eyes, until the air, being extended together with the eyesight, or the rays being poured out, should arrive at the object which was to be seen.

But since we see at the same moment of time, and for the most part, while engaged on other business, we nevertheless behold all things which are placed opposite to us, it is more true and evident that it is the mind which, through the eyes, sees those things which are placed opposite to it, as though through windows covered with pellucid crystal or transparent stone; and therefore the mind and inclination are often known from the eyes. For the refutation of which Lucretius employed a very senseless argument. For if the mind, he says, sees through the eye, it would see better if the eyes were torn out and dug up, inasmuch as doors being torn up together with the door-posts let in more light than if they were covered. Truly his eyes, or rather those of Epicurus who taught him, ought to have been dug out, that they might not see, that the torn-out orbs, and the burst fibers of the eyes, and the blood flowing through the veins, and the flesh increasing from wounds, and the scars drawn over at last can admit no light; unless by chance he would have it that eyes are produced resembling ears, so that we should see not so much with eyes as with apertures, than which there can be nothing more unsightly or more useless. For how little should we be able to see, if from the innermost recesses of the head the mind should pay attention through slight fissures of caverns; as, if anyone should wish to look through a stalk of hemlock, he would see no more than the capability of the stalk itself admitted! For sight, therefore, it was rather needful that the members should be collected together into an orb, that the sight might be spread in breadth and the parts which adjoined them in the front of the face, that they might freely behold all things. Therefore the unspeakable power of the divine providence made two orbs most resembling each other, and so bound them together that they might be able not only to be altogether turned, but to be moved and directed with moderation. And He willed that the orbs themselves should be full of a pure and clear moisture, in the middle part of which sparks of lights might be kept shut up, which we call the pupils, in which, being pure and delicate, are contained the faculty and method of seeing. The mind therefore directs itself through these orbs that it may see, and the sight of both the eyes is mingled and joined together in a wonderful manner.

### Chap. IX.—Of the Senses and Their Power.

It pleases me in this place to censure the folly of those who, while they wish to show that the senses are false, collect many instances in which the eyes are deceived; and among them this also, that all things appear double to the mad and intoxicated, as though the cause of that error were obscure. For it happens on this account, because there are two eyes. But hear how it happens. The sight of the eyes consists in the exertion of the soul. Therefore, since the mind, as has been above said, uses the eyes as windows, this happens not only to those who are intoxicated or mad, but even to those who are of sound mind, and sober. For if you place any object too near, it will appear double, for there is a certain interval and space in which the sight of the eyes meets together. Likewise, if you call the soul back as if to reflection, and relax the exertion of the mind, then the sight of each eye is drawn asunder, and they each begin to see separately.

If you, again, exert the mind and direct the eyesight, whatever appeared double unites into one. What wonder, therefore, if the mind, impaired by poison and the powerful influence of wine, cannot direct itself to seeing, as the feet cannot to walking when they are weak through the numbness of the sinews, or if the force of madness raging against the brain disunites the agreement of the eyes? Which is so true, that in the case of one-eyed men, if they become either mad or intoxicated, it can by no means happen that they see any object double. Wherefore, if the reason is evident why the eyes are deceived, it is clear that the senses are not false: for they either are not deceived if they are pure and sound; or if they are deceived, yet the mind is not deceived which recognizes their error.

## Chap. X.—Of the Outer Limbs of Man, and Their Use.

But let us return to the works of God. That the eyes, therefore, might be better protected from injury, He concealed them with the coverings of the eyelashes, from which Varro thinks that the eyes derived their name. For even the eyelids themselves, in which there is the power of rapid motion, and to which throbbing gives their name, being protected by hairs standing in order, afford a most becoming fence to the eyes; the continual motion of which, meeting with incomprehensible rapidity, does not impede the course of the sight, and relieves the eyes. For the pupil—that is, the transparent membrane—which ought not to be drained and to become dry, unless it is cleansed by continual moisture so that it shines clearly, loses its power. Why should I speak of the summits of the eyebrows themselves, furnished with short hair? Do they not, as it were by mounds, both afford protection to the eyes, so that nothing may fall into them from above, and at the same time ornament? And the nose, arising from the confines of these, and stretched out, as it were, with an equal ridge, at once serves to separate and to protect the two eyes. Below also, a not unbecoming swelling of the cheeks, gently rising after the similitude of hills, makes the eyes safer on every side; and it has been provided by the great Artificer, that if there shall happen to be a more violent blow, it may be repelled by the projecting parts. But the upper part of the nose as far as the middle has been made solid; but the lower part has been made with a softened cartilage annexed to it, that it may be pliant to the use of the fingers. Moreover, in this, though a single member, three offices are placed: one, that of drawing the breath; the second, that of smelling; the third, that the secretions of the brain may escape through its caverns. And in how wonderful, how divine a manner did God contrive these also, so that the very cavity of the nose should not deform the beauty of the face: which would certainly have been the case if one single aperture only were open. But He enclosed and divided that, as though by a wall drawn through the middle, and made it most beautiful by the very circumstance of its being double. From which we understand of how much weight the twofold number, made firm by one simple connection, is to the perfection of things.

For though the body is one, yet the whole could not be made up of single members, unless it were that there should be parts on the right hand or on the left. Therefore, as the two feet and also hands not only avail to some utility and practice either of walking or of doing something, but also bestow an admirable character and comeliness; so in the head, which is, as it were, the crown of the divine work, the hearing has been divided by the great Artificer into two ears, and the sight into two eyes, and the smelling into two nostrils, because the brain, in which is contained the system of the sensation, although it is one, yet is divided into two parts by the intervening membrane. But the heart also, which appears to be the abode of wisdom, although it is one, yet has two recesses within, in which are contained the living fountains of blood, divided by an intervening barrier: that as in the world itself the chief control, being twofold from simple matter, or simple from a twofold matter, governs and keeps together the whole; so in the body, all the parts, being constructed of two, might present an inseparable unity. Also how useful and how becoming is the appearance and the opening of the mouth transversely cannot be expressed; the use of which consists in two offices, that of taking food and speaking.

The tongue enclosed within, which by its motions divides the voice into words, and is the interpreter of the mind, cannot, however, by itself alone fulfil the office of speaking, unless it strikes its edge against the palate, unless aided by striking against the teeth or by the compression of the lips. The teeth, however, contribute more to speaking: for infants do not begin to speak before they have teeth; and old men, when they have lost their teeth, so lisp that they appear to have returned afresh to infancy. But these things relate to man alone, or to birds, in which the tongue, being pointed and vibrating with fixed motions, expresses innumerable inflexions of songs and various kinds of sounds. It has, moreover, another office also, which it exercises in all, and this alone in the dumb animals that it collects the food when bruised and ground by the teeth, and by its force presses it down when collected into balls, and transmits it to the belly. Accordingly, Varro thinks that the name of tongue was given to it from binding the food. It also assists the beasts in drinking: for with the tongue stretched out and hollowed they draw water; and when they have taken it in the hollow of the tongue, lest by slowness and delay it should flow away, they dash it against the palate with swift rapidity. This, therefore, is covered by the concave part of the palate as by a shell, and God has surrounded it with the enclosure of the teeth as with a wall.

But He has adorned the teeth themselves, which are arranged in order in a wonderful manner, lest, being bare and exposed, they should be a terror rather than an ornament, with soft gums, which are so named from producing teeth, and then with the coverings of the lips; and the hardness of the teeth, as in a millstone, is greater and rougher than in the other bones, that they might be sufficient for bruising the food and pasture. But how befittingly has He divided the lips themselves, which as it were before were united! The upper of which, under the very middle of the nostrils, He has marked with a kind of slight cavity, as with a valley: He has gracefully spread out the lower for the sake of beauty. For, as far as relates to the receiving of flavor, he is deceived, whoever he is, who thinks that this sense resides in the palate; for it is the tongue by which flavors are perceived, and not the whole of it: for the parts of it which are more tender on either side, draw in the flavor with the most delicate perceptions. And though nothing is diminished from that which is eaten or drunk, yet the flavor in an indescribable manner penetrates to the sense, in the same way in which the taking of the smell detracts nothing from any material.

And how beautiful the other parts are can scarcely be expressed. The chin, gently drawn down from the cheeks, and the lower part of it so closed that the lightly imprinted division appears to mark its extreme point: the neck stiff and well rounded: the shoulders let down as though by gentle ridges from the neck: the fore-arms powerful, and braced by sinews for firmness: the great strength of the upper-arms standing out with remarkable muscles: the useful and becoming bending of the elbows. What shall I say of the hands, the ministers of reason and wisdom? Which the most skillful Creator made with a flat and moderately concave bend, that if anything was to be held, it might conveniently rest upon them, and terminated them in the fingers; in which it is difficult to explain whether the appearance or the usefulness is greater. For the perfection and completeness of their number, and the comeliness of their order and gradation, and the flexible bending of the equal joints, and the round form of the nails, comprising and strengthening the tips of the fingers with concave coverings, lest the softness of the flesh should yield in holding any object, afford great adornment. But this is convenient for use, in wonderful ways, that one separated from the rest rises together with the hand itself, and is enlarged in a different direction, which, offering itself as though to meet the others, possesses all the power of holding and doing either alone, or in a special manner, as the guide and director of them all; from which also it received the name of thumb, because it prevails among the others by force and power. It has two joints standing out, not as the others, three; but one is annexed by flesh to the hand for the sake of beauty: for if it had been with three joints, and itself separate, the foul and unbecoming appearance would have deprived the hand of all grace.

Again, the breadth of the breast, being elevated, and exposed to the eyes, displays a wonderful dignity of its condition; of which this is the cause, that God appears to have made man only, as it were, reclining with his face upward: for scarcely any other animal is able to lie upon its back. But He appears to have formed the dumb animals as though lying on one side, and to have pressed them to the earth. For this reason He gave them a narrow breast, and removed from sight, and prostrate towards the earth. But He made that of man open and erect, because, being full of reason given from heaven, it was not befitting that it should be humble or unbecoming. The nipples also gently rising, and crowned with darker and small orbs, add something of beauty; being given to females for the nourishment of their young, to males for grace only, that the breast might not appear misshapen, and, as it were, mutilated. Below this is placed the fiat surface of the belly, about the middle of which the navel distinguishes by a not unbecoming mark, being made for this purpose, that through it the young, while it is in the womb, may be nourished.

### Chap. XI.—Of the Intestines in Man, and Their Use.

It necessarily follows that I should begin to speak of the inward parts also, to which has been assigned not beauty, because they are concealed from view, but incredible utility, since it was necessary that this earthly body should be nourished with some moisture from food and drink, as the earth itself is by showers and frosts. The most provident Artificer placed in the middle of it a receptacle for articles of food, by means of which, when digested and liquefied, it might distribute the vital juices to all the members. But since man is composed of body and soul, that receptacle of which I have spoken above affords nourishment only to the body; to the soul, in truth, He has given another abode. For He has made a kind of intestines soft and thin, which we call the lungs, into which the breath might pass by an alternate interchange; and He did not form this after the fashion of the uterus, lest the breath should all at once be poured forth, or at once inflate it. And on this account He did not make it a full intestine, but capable of being inflated, and admitting the air, so that it might gradually receive the breath; while the vital air is spread through that thinness, and might again gradually give it back, while it spreads itself forth from it: for the very alternation of blowing and breathing, and the process of respiration, support life in the body.

Since, therefore, there are in man two receptacles,—one of the air which nourishes the soul, the other of the food which nourishes the body,—there must be two tubes through the neck for food, and for breath, the upper of which leads from the mouth to the belly, the lower from the nostrils to the lungs. And the plan and nature of these are different: for the passage which is from the mouth has been made soft, and which when closed always adheres to itself, as the month itself; since drink and food, being corporeal, make for themselves a space for passage, by moving aside and opening the gullet. The breath, on the other hand, which is incorporeal and thin, because it was unable to make for itself a space, has received an open way, which is called the windpipe. This is composed of flexible and soft bones, as though of rings fitted together after the manner of a hemlock stalk, and adhering together; and this passage is always open. For the breath can have no cessation in passing; because it, which is always passing to and fro, is checked as by a kind of obstacle through means of a portion of a member usefully sent down from the brain, and which is called the uvula, lest, drawn by pestilential air, it should come with impetuosity and spoil the slightness of its abode, or bring the whole violence of the injury upon the inner receptacles. And on this account also the nostrils are slightly open, which are therefore so named, because either smell or breath does not cease to flow through these, which are, as it were, the doors of this tube. Yet this breathing-tube lies open not only to the nostrils, but also to the mouth in the extreme regions of the palate, where the risings of the jaws, looking towards the uvula, begin to raise themselves into a swelling. And the reason of this arrangement is not obscure: for we should not have the power of speaking if the windpipe were open to the nostrils only, as the path of the gullet is to the mouth only; nor could the breath proceeding from it cause the voice, without the service of the tongue.

Therefore the divine skill opened a way for the voice from that breathing-tube, so that the tongue might be able to discharge its office, and by its strokes divide into words the even course of the voice itself. And this passage, if by any means it is intercepted, must necessarily cause dumbness. For he is assuredly mistaken, whoever thinks that there is any other cause why men are dumb. For they are not tongue-tied, as is commonly believed; but they pour forth that vocal breath through the nostrils, as though bellowing, because there is either no passage at all for the voice to the mouth, or it is not so open as to be able to send forth the full voice. And this generally comes to pass by nature; sometimes also it happens by accident that this entrance is blocked up and does not transmit the voice to the tongue, and thus makes those who can speak dumb. And when this happens, the hearing also must necessarily be blocked up; so that because it cannot emit the voice, it is also incapable of admitting it. Therefore this passage has been opened for the purpose of speaking. It also affords this advantage, that in frequenting the bath, because the nostrils are not able to endure the heat, the hot air is taken in by the mouth; also, if phlegm contracted by cold shall have happened to stop up the breathing pores of the nostrils, we may be able to draw the air through the mouth, lest, if the passage should be obstructed, the breath should be stifled. But the food being received into the stomach, and mixed with the moisture of the drink, when it has now been digested by the heat, its juice, being in an indescribable manner diffused through the limbs, bedews and invigorates the whole body.

The manifold coils also of the intestines, and their length rolled together on themselves, and yet fastened with one band, are a wonderful work of God. For when the stomach has sent forth from itself the food softened, it is gradually thrust forth through those windings of the intestines, so that whatever of the moisture by which the body is nourished is in them, is divided to all the members. And yet, lest in any place it should happen to adhere and remain fixed, which might have taken place on account of the turnings of the coils, which often turn back to themselves, and which could not have happened without injury, He has spread over these from within a thicker juice, that the secretions of the belly might more easily work their way through the slippery substance to their outlets. It is also a most skillful arrangement, that the bladder, which birds do not use, though it is separated from the intestines, and has no tube by which it may draw the urine from them, is nevertheless filled and distended with moisture. And it is not difficult to see how this comes to pass. For the parts of the intestines which receive the food and drink from the belly are more open than the other coils, and much more delicate. These entwine themselves around and encompass the bladder; and when the meat and the drink have arrived at these parts in a mixed state, the excrement becomes more solid, and passes through, but all the moisture is strained through those tender parts, and the bladder, the membrane of which is equally fine and delicate, absorbs and collects it, so as to send it forth where nature has opened an outlet.

### Chap. XII.—De Utero, Et Conceptione Atque Sexibus.

De utero quoque et conceptione, quoniam de internis loquimur, dici necesse est, ne quid præ terisse videamur; quæ quamquam in operto latent, sensum tamen atque intelligentiam latere non possunt. Vena in maribus, quæ seminium continet, duplex est, paulo interior, quam illud humoris obscoeni receptaculum. Sicut enim renes duo sunt, itemque testes, ita et venæ seminales duæ, in una tamen compage cohæ rentes; quod videmus in corporibus animalium, cum interfecta patefiunt. Sed illa dexterior masculinum continet semen, sinisterior foemininum; et omnino in toto corpore pars dextra masculine est, sinistra veto foeminina. Ipsum semen quidam putant ex medullis tantum, quidam ex omni corpore ad venam genitalem confluere, ibique concrescere. Sed hoc, humana mens, quomodo fiat, non potest comprehendere. Item in foeminis uterus in duas se dividit partes, quæ in diversum diffussæ ac reflexæ, circumplicantur, sicut arietis cornua. Quæ pars in dextram retorquetur, masculina est; quæ in sinistram, foeminina.

Conceptum igitur Varro et Aristoteles sic fieri arbitrantur. Aiunt non tantum maribus inesse semen, verum etiam foeminis, et inde plerumque matribus similes procreari; sed earum semensanguinem esse purgatum, quod si recte cum virili mixture sit, utraque concreta et simul co-agulata informari: et primum quidem cor hominis effingi, quod in eo sit et vita omnis et sapientia; denique totum opus quadragesimo die consummari. Ex abortionibus hæ c fortasse collecta sunt. In avium tamen foetibus primurn oculos fingi dubium non est, quod in ovis sæ pe deprehendimus. Unde fieri non posse arbitror quin fictio a capite sumat exordium.

Similitudines autem in corporibus filiorum sic fieri putant. Cum semina inter se permixta coalescunt, si virile superaverit, patri similem provenire, seu marem, seu foeminam; si muliebre præ valuerit, progeniem cujusque sexus ad imaginem respondere maternam. Id autem præ valet e duobus, quod fuerit uberius; alterum enim quodammodo amplectitur et includit: hinc plerumque fled, ut unius tantum lineamenta præ tendat. Si vero æqua fuerit ex pari semente permixtio, figuras quoque misceri, ut soboles illa communis aut neutrum referre videatur, quia totum ex altero non habet; aut utrumque, quia partem de singulis mutuata est. Nam in cor-poribus animalium videmus aut confundi parentum colores, ac fieri tertium neutri generantium simile; aut utriusque sic exprimi, ut discoloribus membris per omne corpus concors mixtura varietur. Dispares quoque naturæ hoc modo fieri putantur. Cum forte in læ vam uteri partem masculinæ stirpis semen inciderit, marem quidem gigni opinatio est; sed quia sit in foeminina parte conceptus, aliquid in se habere foemineum, supra quam decus virile patiatur; vel formam insignem, vel nimium candorem, vel corporis levitatem, vel artus delicatos, vel staturam brevem, vel vocem gracilem, vel animum imbecillum, vel ex his plura. Item, si partem in dextram semen foeminini sexus influxerit, foeminam quidem procreari; sed quoniam in masculina parte concepta sit, habere in se aliquid virilita-tis, ultra quam sexus; ratio permittat; aut valida membra, aut immoderatam Iongitudinem, aut fuscum colorem, aut hispidam faciem, aut vulture indecorum, aut vocem robustam, aut animum audacem, aut ex his plura.

Si vero masculinum in dexteram, foemininum in sinistram pervenerit, utrosque foetus recte provenire; ut et foeminis per omnia naturæ suæ decus constet, et maribus tam mente, quam corpore robur virile servetur. Istud vero ipsum quam mirabile institutum Dei, quod ad conservationem generum singulorum, duos sexus maris ac foeminæ machinatus est; quibus inter se per voluptatis illecebras copulatis, successiva soboles pareretur, ne omne genus viventium conditio mortalitatis extingueret. Sed plus roboris maribus attributum est, quo facilius ad patientiam jugi maritalis foeminæ cogerentur. Vir itaque nominatus est, quod major in eo vis est, quire in foemina; et hinc virtus nomen accepit. Item mulier (ut Varro interpretatur) a mollitie, immutata et detracta littera, velut mollier; cui suscepto foetu, cum partus appropinquare jam coepit, turgescentes mammæ dulcibus succis distenduntur, et ad nutrimenta nascentis fontibus lacteis foecundum pectus exuberat. Nec enim decebat aliud quam ut sapiens animal a corde alimoniam duceret. Idque ipsum solertissime comparatum est, ut candens ac pinguis humor teneritudinem novi corporis irrigaret, donec ad capiendos fortiores cibos, et dentibus instruatur, et viribus roboretur. Sed redeamus ad propositum, ut cæ tera, quæ supersunt, breviter explicemus.

### Chap. XIII.—Of the Lower Members.

Poteram nunc ego ipsorum quoque genitalium membrorum mirificam rationem tibi exponere, nisi me pudor ab hujusmodi sermone revocaret: itaque a nobis indumento verecundiæ, quæ sunt pudenda velentur. Quod ad hanc rem attinet, queri satis est, homines impios ac profanos summum nefas admittere, qui divinum et admirabile Dei opus, ad propagandam successionem inexcogitabili ratione provisum et effectum, vel ad turpissimos quæ stus, vel ad obscoenæ libidinis pudenda opera convertunt, ut jam nihil aliud ex re sanctissima petant, quam inanem et sterilem voluptatem.

How is it with respect to the other parts of the body? Are they without order and beauty? The flesh rounded off into the *nates*, how adapted to the office of sitting! And this also more firm than in the other limbs, lest by the pressure of the bulk of the body it should give way to the bones. Also the length of the thighs drawn out, and strengthened by broader muscles, in order that it might more easily sustain the weight of the body; and as this is gradually contracted, it is bounded by the knees, the comely joints of which supply a bend which is most adapted for walking and sitting. Also the legs not drawn out in an equal manner, lest an unbecoming figure should deform the feet; but they are at once strengthened and adorned by well-turned calves gently standing out and gradually diminishing.

But in the soles of the feet there is the same plan as in the hands, but yet very different: for since these are, as it were, the foundations of the whole body, the admirable Artificer has not made them of a round appearance, lest man should be unable to stand, or should need other feet for standing, as is the case with quadrupeds; but He has formed them of a longer and more extended shape, that they might make the body firm by their flatness, from which circumstance their name was given to them. The toes are of the same number with the fingers, for the sake of appearance rather than utility; and on this account they are both joined together, and short, and put together by gradations; and that which is the greatest of these, since it was not befitting that it should be separated from the others, as in the hand, has been so arranged in order, that it appears to differ from the others in magnitude and the small space which intervenes. This beautiful union of them strengthens the pressure of the feet with no slight aid; for we cannot be excited to running, unless, our toes being pressed against the ground, and resting upon the soil, we take an impetus and a spring. I appear to have explained all things of which the plan is capable of being understood. I now come to those things which are either doubtful or obscure.

### Chap. XIV.—Of the Unknown Purpose of Some of the Intestines.

It is evident that there are many things in the body, the force and purpose of which no one can perceive but He who made them. Can anyone suppose that he is able to relate what is the advantage, and what the effect, of that slight transparent membrane by which the stomach is netted over and covered? What the twofold resemblance of the kidneys? Which Varro says are so named because streams of foul moisture arise from these; which is far from being the case, because, rising on either side of the spine, they are united, and are separated from the intestines. What is the use of the spleen? What of the liver? Organs which appear as it were to be made up of disordered blood. What of the very bitter moisture of the gall? What of the heart? Unless we shall happen to think that they ought to be believed, who think that the affection of anger is placed in the gall, that of fear in the heart, of joy in the spleen. But they will have it that the office of the liver is, by its embrace and heat, to digest the food in the stomach; some think that the desires of the amorous passions are contained in the liver.

First of all, the acuteness of the human sense is unable to perceive these things, because their offices lie concealed; nor, when laid open, do they show their uses. For, if it were so, perhaps the more gentle animals would either have no gall at all, or less than the wild beasts; the more timid ones would have more heart, the more lustful would have more liver, the more playful more spleen. As, therefore, we perceive that we hear with our ears, that we see with our eyes, that we smell with our nostrils; so assuredly we should perceive that we are angry with the gall, that we desire with the liver, that we rejoice with the spleen. Since, therefore, we do not at all perceive from what part those affections come, it is possible that they may come from another source, and that those organs may have a different effect to that which we suppose. We cannot prove, however, that they who discuss these things speak falsely. But I think that all things which relate to the motions of the mind and soul, are of so obscure and profound a nature that it is beyond the power of man to see through them clearly. This, however, ought to be sure and undoubted, that so many objects and so many organs have one and the same office—to retain the soul in the body. But what office is particularly assigned to each, who can know, except the Designer, to whom alone His own work is known?

### Chap. XV.—Of the Voice.

But what account can we give of the voice? Grammarians, indeed, and philosophers, define the voice to be air struck by the breath; from which words derive their name: which is plainly false. For the voice is not produced outside of the mouth, but within, and therefore that opinion is more probable, that the breath, being compressed, when it has struck against the obstacle presented by the throat, forces out the sound of the voice: as when we send down the breath into an open hemlock stalk, having applied it to the lips, and the breath, reverberating from the hollow of the stalk, and rolled back from the bottom, while it returns to that descending through meeting with itself, striving for an outlet, produces a sound; and the wind, rebounding by itself, is animated into vocal breath. Now, whether this is true, God, who is the designer, may see. For the voice appears to arise not from the mouth, but from the innermost breast. In fine, even when the mouth is closed, a sound such as is possible is emitted from the nostrils. Moreover, also, the voice is not affected by that greatest breath with which we gasp, but with a light and not compressed breath, as often as we wish. It has not therefore been comprehended in what manner it takes place, or what it is altogether. And do not imagine that I am now falling into the opinion of the Academy, for all things are not incomprehensible. For as it must be confessed that many things are unknown, since God has willed that they should exceed the understanding of man; so, however, it must be acknowledged that there are many which may both be perceived by the senses and comprehended by the reason. But we shall devote an entire treatise to the refutation of the philosophers. Let us therefore finish the course over which we are now running.

### Chap. XVI.—Of the Mind and Its Seat.

That the nature of the mind is also incomprehensible, who can be ignorant, but he who is altogether destitute of mind, since it is not known in what place the mind is situated, or of what nature it is? Therefore various things have been discussed by philosophers concerning its nature and place. But I will not conceal what my own sentiments are: not that I should affirm that it is so—for in a doubtful matter it is the part of a foolish person to do this; but that when I have set forth the difficulty of the matter, you may understand how great is the magnitude off the divine works. Some would have it, that the seat of the mind is in the breast. But if this is so, how wonderful is it, that a faculty which is situated in an obscure and dark habitation should be employed in so great a light of reason and intelligence; then that the senses from every part of the body come together to it, so that it appears to be present in any quarter of the limbs! Others have said that its seat is in the brain and, indeed, they have used probable arguments, saying that it was doubtless befitting that that which had the government of the whole body should especially have its abode in the highest place, as though in the citadel of the body; and that nothing should be in a more elevated position than that which governs the whole by reason, just as the Lord Himself, and Ruler of the universe, is in the highest place. Then they say, that the organs which are the ministers of each sense, that is, of hearing, and seeing, and smelling, are situated in the head, and that the channels of all these lead not to the breast, but to the brain: otherwise we must be more slow in the exercise of our senses, until the power of sensation by a long course should descend through the neck even to the breast. These, in truth, do not greatly err, or perchance not at all. For the mind, which exercises control over the body, appears to be placed in the highest part, the head, as God is in heaven; but when it is engaged in any reflection, it appears to pass to the breast, and, as it were, to withdraw to some secret recess, that it may elicit and draw forth counsel, as it were, from a hidden treasury. And therefore, when we are intent upon reflection, and when the mind, being occupied, has withdrawn itself to the inner depth, we are accustomed neither to hear the things which sound about us, nor to see the things which stand in our way. But whether this is the case, it is assuredly a matter of admiration how this takes place, since there is no passage from the brain to the breast. But if it is not so, nevertheless it is no less a matter of admiration that, by some divine plan or other, it is caused that it appears to be so. Can any fail to admire that that living and heavenly faculty which is called the mind or the soul, is of such volubility that it does not rest even then when it is asleep; of such rapidity, that it surveys the whole heaven at one moment of time; and, if it wills, flies overseas, traverses lands and cities,—in short, places in its own sight all things which it pleases, however far and widely they are removed?

And does anyone wonder if the divine mind of God, being extended through all parts of the universe, runs to and fro, and rules all things, governs all things, being everywhere present, everywhere diffused; when the strength and power of the human mind, though enclosed within a mortal body, is so great, that it can in no way be restrained even by the barriers of this heavy and slothful body, to which it is bound, from bestowing upon itself, in its impatience of rest, the power of wandering without restraint? Whether, therefore, the mind has its dwelling in the head or in the breast, can anyone comprehend what power of reason effects, that that incomprehensible faculty either remains fixed in the marrow of the brain, or in that blood divided into two parts which is enclosed in the heart; and not infer from this very circumstance how great is the power of God, because the soul does not see itself, or of what nature or where it is; and if it did see, yet it would not be able to perceive in what manner an incorporeal substance is united with one which is corporeal? Or if the mind has no fixed locality, but runs here and there scattered through the whole body,—which is possible, and was asserted by Xenocrates, the disciple of Plato,—then, inasmuch as intelligence is present in every part of the body, it cannot be understood what that mind is, or what its qualities are, since its nature is so subtle and refined, that, though infused into solid organs by a living and, as it were, ardent perception, it is mingled with all the members.

But take care that you never think it probable, as Aristoxenus said, that the mind has no existence, but that the power of perception exists from the constitution of the body and the construction of the organs, as harmony does in the case of the lyre. For musicians call the stretching and sounding of the strings to entire strains, without any striking of notes in agreement with them, harmony. They will have it, therefore, that the soul in man exists in a manner like that by which harmonious modulation exists on the lyre; namely, that the firm uniting of the separate parts of the body and the vigor of all the limbs agreeing together, makes that perceptible motion, and adjusts the mind, as well-stretched things produce harmonious sound. And as, in the lyre, when anything has been interrupted or relaxed, the whole method of the strain is disturbed and destroyed; so in the body, when any part of the limbs receives an injury, the whole are weakened, and all being corrupted and thrown into confusion, the power of perception is destroyed: and this is called death. But he, if he had possessed any mind, would never have transferred harmony from the lyre to man. For the lyre cannot of its own accord send forth a sound, so that there can be in this any comparison and resemblance to a living person; but the soul both reflects and is moved of its own accord. But if there were in us anything resembling harmony, it would be moved by a blow from without, as the strings of the lyre are by the hands; whereas without the handling of the artificer, and the stroke of the fingers, they lie mute and motionless. But doubtless he ought to have beaten by the hand that he might at length observe; for his mind, badly compacted from his members, was in a state of torpor.

### Chap. XVII.—Of the Soul, and the Opinion of Philosophers Concerning It.

It remains to speak of the soul, although its system and nature cannot be perceived. Nor, therefore, do we fail to understand that the soul is immortal, since whatever is vigorous and is in motion by itself at all times, and cannot be seen or touched, must he eternal. But what the soul is, is not yet agreed upon by philosophers, and perhaps will never be agreed upon. For some have said that it is blood, others that it is fire, others wind, from which it has received its name of anima, or animus, because in Greek the wind is called anemos and yet none of these appears to have spoken anything. For if the soul appears to be extinguished when the blood is poured forth through a wound, or is exhausted by the heat of fevers, it does not therefore follow that the system of the soul is to be placed in the material of the blood; as though a question should arise as to the nature of the light which we make use of, and the answer should be given that it is oil, for when that is consumed the light is extinguished: since they are plainly different, but the one is the nourishment of the other. Therefore the soul appears to be like light, since it is not itself blood, but is nourished by the moisture of the blood, as light is by oil.

But they who have supposed it to be fire made use of this argument, that when the soul is present the body is warm, but on its departure the body grows cold. But fire is both without perception and is seen, and burns when touched. But the soul is both endowed with perception and cannot be seen, and does not burn. From which it is evident that the soul is something like God. But they who suppose that it is wind are deceived by this, because we appear to live by drawing breath from the air. Varro gives this definition: "The soul is air conceived in the mouth, warmed in the lungs, heated in the heart, diffused into the body." These things are most plainly false. For I say that the nature of things of this kind is not so obscure, that we do not even understand what cannot be true. If anyone should say to me that the heaven is of brass, or crystal, or, as Empedocles says, that it is frozen air, must I at once assent because I do not know of what material the heaven is? For as I know not this, I know that. Therefore the soul is not air conceived in the mouth, because the soul is produced much before air can be conceived in the mouth. For it is not introduced into the body after birth, as it appears to some philosophers, but immediately after conception, when the divine necessity has formed the offspring in the womb; for it so lives within the bowels of its mother, that it is increased in growth, and delights to bound with repeated beatings. In short, there must be a miscarriage if the living young within shall die. The other parts of the definition have reference to this, that during those nine months in which we were in the womb we appear to have been dead. None, therefore, of these three opinions is true. We cannot, however, say that they who held these sentiments were false to such an extent that they said nothing at all; for we live at once by the blood, and heat, and breath. But since the soul exists in the body by the union of all these, they did not express what it was in its own proper sense; for as it cannot be seen, so it cannot be expressed.

**Chap. XVIII.—Of the Soul and the Mind, and Their Affections.**

There follows another, and in itself an inexplicable inquiry: Whether the soul and the mind are the same, or there be one faculty by which we live, and another by which we perceive and have discernment. There are not wanting arguments on either side. For they who say that they are one faculty make use of this argument, that we cannot live without perception, nor perceive without life, and therefore that that which is incapable of separation cannot be different; but that whatever it is, it has the office of living and the method of perception. On which account two Epicurean poets speak of the mind and the soul indifferently. But they who say that they are different argue in this way: That the mind is one thing, and the soul another, may be understood from this, that the mind may be extinguished while the soul is uninjured, which is accustomed to happen in the case of the insane; also, that the soul is put to rest by death, the mind by sleep, and indeed in such a manner that it is not only ignorant of what is taking place, or where it is, but it is even deceived by the contemplation of false objects. And how this takes place cannot accurately be perceived; why it takes place can be perceived. For we can by no means rest unless the mind is kept occupied by the similitudes of visions. But the mind lies hid, oppressed with sleep, as fire buried by ashes drawn over it; but if you stir it a little it again blazes, and, as it were, wakes up. Therefore it is called away by images, until the limbs, bedewed with sleep, are invigorated; for the body while the perception is awake, although it lies motionless, yet is not at rest, because the perception burns in it, and vibrates as a flame, and keeps all the limbs bound to itself.

But when the mind is transferred from its application to the contemplation of images, then at length the whole body is resolved into rest. But the mind is transferred from dark thought, when, under the influence of darkness, it has begun to be alone with itself. While it is intent upon those things concerning which it is reflecting, sleep suddenly creeps on, and the thought itself imperceptibly turns aside to the nearest appearances: thus it begins also to see those things which it had placed before its eyes. Then it proceeds further, and finds diversions for itself, that it may not interrupt the healthiest repose of the body. For as the mind is diverted in the day by true sights, so that it does not sleep; so is it diverted in the night by false sights, so that it is not aroused. For if it perceives no images, it will follow of necessity either that it is awake, or that it is asleep in perpetual death. Therefore the system of dreaming has been given by God for the sake of sleeping; and, indeed, it has been given to all animals in common; but this especially to man, that when God gave this system on account of rest, He left to Himself the power of teaching man future events by means of the dream. For narratives often testify that there have been dreams which have had an immediate and a remarkable accomplishment,1931 and the answers of our prophets have been after the character of a dream.1932 On which account they are not always true, nor always false, as Virgil testified, who supposed that there were two gates for the passage of dreams. But those which are false are seen for the sake of sleeping; those which are true are sent by God, that by this revelation we may learn impending goods or evils.

## Chap. XIX.—Of the Soul, and It Given by God.

A question also may arise respecting this, whether the soul is produced from the father, or rather from the mother, or indeed from both. But I think that this judgment is to be formed as though in a doubtful matter. For nothing is true of these three opinions, because souls are produced neither from both nor from either. For a body may be produced from a body, since something is contributed from both; but a soul cannot be produced from souls, because nothing can depart from a slight and incomprehensible subject. Therefore the manner of the production of souls belongs entirely to God alone.

"In fine, we are all sprung from a heavenly seed, all have that same Father."

as Lucretius says. For nothing but what is mortal can be generated from mortals. Nor ought he to be deemed a father who in no way perceives that he has transmitted or breathed a soul from his own; nor, if he perceives it, comprehends in his mind when or in what manner that effect is produced.

From this it is evident that souls are not given by parents, but by one and the same God and Father of all, who alone has the law and method of their birth, since He alone produces them. For the part of the earthly parent is nothing more than with a sense of pleasure to emit the moisture of the body, in which is the material of birth, or to receive it; and to this work man's power is limited, nor has he any further power. Therefore men wish for the birth of sons, because they do not themselves bring it about. Everything beyond this is the work of God,—namely, the conception itself, and the molding of the body, and the breathing in of life, and the bringing forth in safety, and whatever afterwards contributes to the preservation of man: it is His gift that we breathe, that we live, and are vigorous. For, besides that we owe it to His bounty that we are safe in body, and that He supplies us with nourishment from various sources, He also gives to man wisdom, which no earthly father can by any means give; and therefore it often happens that foolish sons are born from wise parents, and wise sons from foolish parents, which some persons attribute to fate and the stars. But this is not now the time to discuss the subject of fate. It is sufficient to say this, that even if the stars hold together the efficacy of all things, it is nevertheless certain that all things are done by God, who both made and set in order the stars themselves. They are therefore senseless who detract this power from God, and assign it to His work.

He would have it, therefore, to be in our own power, whether we use or do not use this divine and excellent gift of God. For, having granted this, He bound man himself by the mystery of virtue, by which he might be able to gain life. For great is the power, great the reason, great the mysterious purpose of man; and if anyone shall not abandon this, nor betray his fidelity and devotedness, he must be happy: he, in short, to sum up the matter in few words, must of necessity resemble God. For he is in error whosoever judges of man by his flesh. For this worthless body with which we are clothed is the receptacle of man. For man himself, can neither be touched, nor looked upon, nor grasped, because he lies hidden within this body, which is seen. And if he shall be more luxurious and delicate in this life than its nature demands, if he shall despise virtue, and give himself to the pursuit of fleshly lusts, he will fall and be pressed down to the earth; but if (as his duty is) he shall readily and constantly maintain his position, which is right for him, and he has rightly obtained,—if he shall not be enslaved to the earth, which he ought to trample upon and overcome, he will gain eternal life.

### Chap. XX.—Of Himself and the Truth.

These things I have written to you, Demetrianus, for the present in few words, and perhaps with more obscurity than was befitting, in accordance with the necessity of circumstances and the time, with which you ought to be content, since you are about to receive more and better things if God shall favor us. Then, accordingly, I will exhort you with greater clearness and truth to the learning of true philosophy. For I have determined to commit to writing as many things as I shall be able, which have reference to the condition of a happy life; and that indeed against the philosophers, since they are pernicious and weighty for the disturbing of the truth. For the force of their eloquence is incredible, and their subtlety in argument and disputation may easily deceive any one; and these we will refute partly by our own weapons, but partly by weapons borrowed from their mutual wrangling, so that it may be evident that they rather introduced error than removed it.

Perhaps you may wonder that I venture to undertake so great a deed. Shall we then suffer the truth to be extinguished or crushed? I, in truth, would more willingly fail even under this burthen. For if Marcus Tullius, the unparalleled example of eloquence itself, was often vanquished by men void of learning and eloquence,—who, however, were striving for that which was true,—why should we despair that the truth itself will by its own peculiar force and clearness avail against deceitful and captious eloquence? They indeed are wont to profess themselves advocates of the truth; but who can defend that which he has not learned, or make clear to others that which he himself does not know? I seem to promise a great thing; but there is need of the favor of Heaven, that ability and time may be given us for following our purpose. But if life is to be wished for by a wise man, assuredly I should wish to live for no other reason than that I may affect something which may be worthy of life, and which may be useful to my readers, if not for eloquence, because there is in me but a slight stream of eloquence, at any rate for living, which is especially needful. And when I have accomplished this, I shall think that I have lived enough, and that I have discharged the duty of a man, if my labor shall have freed some men from errors, and have directed them to the path which leads to heaven.

## General Note by the American Editor.

Just here I economize a little spare room to note the cynical Gibbon's ideas about Lactantius and his works. He quotes him freely, and recognizes his Ciceronian Latinity, and even the elegance of his rhetoric, and the spirit and eloquence with which he can garnish the "dismal tale" of coming judgments, based on the Apocalypse. But then, again he speaks of him as an "obscure rhetorician," and affects a doubt as to his sources of information, notably in doubting the conversation between Galerius and Diocletian which forced the latter to abdicate. This is before he decides to attribute the work on the *Deaths of Persecutors* to somebody else, or, rather, to quote its author ambiguously as Cæcilius. And here we may insert what he says on this subject, as follows:—

"It is certain that this...was composed and published while Licinius, sovereign of the East, still preserved the friendship of Constantine and of the Christians. Every reader of taste must perceive that the style is of a very different and inferior character to that of Lactantius; and such, indeed, is the judgment of Le Clerc and Lardner. Three arguments (from the title of the book and from the names of Donatus and Cæcilius) are produced by the advocates of Lactantius. Each of these proofs is, singly, weak and defective; *but their concurrence has great weight*. I have often fluctuated, and shall *tamely* follow the Colbert ms. in calling the author, whoever he was, *Cæcilius*."

After this the critic adheres to this ambiguity. I have no wish to argue otherwise. Quite as important are his notes on the *Institutes*. He states the probable conjecture of *two* original editions,—the one under Diocletian, and the other under Licinius. Then he says:—

"I am *almost* convinced that Lactantius dedicated his *Institutions* to the sovereign of Gaul at a time when Galerius, Maximin, and even Licinius, persecuted the Christians; that is, between the years a.d. 306 and a.d. 311."

On the dubious passages he remarks:—

"The first and most important of these is, indeed, wanting in twenty-eight mss., but is found in nineteen. If we weigh the comparative value of those mss., one, ... in the King of France's library, may be alleged in its favor. But the passage is omitted in the correct ms. of Bologna, which the Père de Montfaucon ascribes to the sixth or seventh century. The taste of most of the editors has *felt* the genuine style of Lactantius."

Do not many indications point to the natural suggestion of a *third* original edition, issued after the conversion of Constantine? Or the questionable passages may be the interpolations of Lactantius himself.

## Of the Manner in Which the Persecutors Died.

*ADDRESSED TO DONATUS.*

### Chap. I.

The Lord has heard those supplications which you, my best beloved Donatus, pour forth in His presence all the day long, and the supplications of the rest of our brethren, who by a glorious confession have obtained an everlasting crown, the reward of their faith. Behold, all the adversaries are destroyed, and tranquility having been re-established throughout the Roman Empire, the late oppressed Church arises again, and the temple of God, overthrown by the hands of the wicked, is built with more glory than before. For God has raised up princes to rescind the impious and sanguinary edicts of the tyrants and provide for the welfare of mankind; so that now the cloud of past times is dispelled, and peace and serenity gladden all hearts. And after the furious whirlwind and black tempest, the heavens are now become calm, and the wished-for light has shone forth; and now God, the hearer of prayer, by His divine aid has lifted His prostrate and afflicted servants from the ground, has brought to an end the united devices of the wicked, and wiped off the tears from the faces of those who mourned. They who insulted over the Divinity, lie low; they who cast down the holy temple, are fallen with more tremendous ruin; and the tormentors of just men have poured out their guilty souls amidst plagues inflicted by Heaven, and amidst deserved tortures. For God delayed to punish them, that, by great and marvelous examples, He might teach posterity that He alone is God, and that with fit vengeance He executes judgment on the proud, the impious, and the persecutors.

Of the end of those men I have thought good to publish a narrative, that all who are afar off, and all who shall arise hereafter, may learn how the Almighty manifested His power and sovereign greatness in rooting out and utterly destroying the enemies of His name. And this will become evident, when I relate *who* were the persecutors of the Church from the time of its first constitution, and *what* were the punishments by which the divine Judge, in His severity, took vengeance on them.

**Chap. II.**

In the latter days of the Emperor Tiberius, in the consulship of Ruberius Geminus and Fufius Geminus, and on the tenth of the kalends of April, as I find it written, Jesus Christ was crucified by the Jews. After He had risen again on the third day, He gathered together His apostles, whom fear, at the time of His being laid hold on, had put to flight; and while He sojourned with them forty days, He opened their hearts, interpreted to them the Scripture, which hitherto had been wrapped up in obscurity, ordained and fitted them for the preaching of His word and doctrine, and regulated all things concerning the institutions of the New Testament; and this having been accomplished, a cloud and whirlwind enveloped Him, and caught Him up from the sight of men unto heaven.

His apostles were at that time eleven in number, to whom were added Matthias, in the room of the traitor Judas, and afterwards Paul. Then were they dispersed throughout all the earth to preach the Gospel, as the Lord their Master had commanded them; and during twenty-five years, and until the beginning of the reign of the Emperor Nero, they occupied themselves in laying the foundations of the Church in every province and city. And while Nero reigned, the Apostle Peter came to Rome, and, through the power of God committed unto him, wrought certain miracles, and, by turning many to the true religion, built up a faithful and steadfast temple unto the Lord. When Nero heard of those things, and observed that not only in Rome, but in every other place, a great multitude revolted daily from the worship of idols, and, condemning their old ways, went over to the new religion, he, an execrable and pernicious tyrant, sprung forward to raze the heavenly temple and destroy the true faith. He it was who first persecuted the servants of God; he crucified Peter, and slew Paul: nor did he escape with impunity; for God looked on the affliction of His people; and therefore the tyrant, bereaved of authority, and precipitated from the height of empire, suddenly disappeared, and even the burial-place of that noxious wild beast was nowhere to be seen. This has led some persons of extravagant imagination to suppose that, having been conveyed to a distant region, he is still reserved alive; and to him they apply the Sibylline verses concerning

"The fugitive, who slew his own mother, being to come from the uttermost boundaries of the earth;"

as if he who was the first should also be the last persecutor, and thus prove the forerunner of Antichrist! But we ought not to believe those who, affirming that the two prophets Enoch and Elias have been translated into some remote place that they might attend our Lord when He shall come to judgment, also fancy that Nero is to appear hereafter as the forerunner of the devil, when he shall come to lay waste the earth and overthrow mankind.

## Chap. III.

After an interval of some years from the death of Nero, there arose another tyrant no less wicked (Domitian), who, although his government was exceedingly odious, for a very long time oppressed his subjects, and reigned in security, until at length he stretched forth his impious hands against the Lord. Having been instigated by evil demons to persecute the righteous people, he was then delivered into the power of his enemies, and suffered due punishment. To be murdered in his own palace was not vengeance ample enough: the very memory of his name was erased. For although he had erected many admirable edifices, and rebuilt the Capitol, and left other distinguished marks of his magnificence, yet the senate did so persecute his name, as to leave no remains of his statues, or traces of the inscriptions put up in honor of him; and by most solemn and severe decrees it branded him, even after death, with perpetual infamy. Thus, the commands of the tyrant having been rescinded, the Church was not only restored to her former state, but she shone forth with additional splendor, and became more and more flourishing. And in the times that followed, while many well-deserving princes guided the helm of the Roman empire, the Church suffered no violent assaults from her enemies, and she extended her hands unto the east and unto the west, insomuch that now there was not any the most remote corner of the earth to which the divine religion had not penetrated, or any nation of manners so barbarous that did not, by being converted to the worship of God, become mild and gentle.

**Chap. IV.**

This long peace, however, was afterwards interrupted. Decius appeared in the world, an accursed wild beast, to afflict the Church,—and *who* but a bad man would persecute religion? It seems as if he had been raised to sovereign eminence, at once to rage against God, and at once to fall; for, having undertaken an expedition against the Carpi, who had then possessed themselves of Dacia and Moefia, he was suddenly surrounded by the barbarians, and slain, together with great part of his army; nor could he be honored with the rites of sepulture, but, stripped and naked, he lay to be devoured by wild beasts and birds,—a fit end for the enemy of God.

**Chap. V.**

And presently Valerian also, in a mood alike frantic, lifted up his impious hands to assault God, and, although his time was short, shed much righteous blood. But God punished him in a new and extraordinary manner, that it might be a lesson to future ages that the adversaries of Heaven always receive the just recompense of their iniquities. He, having been made prisoner by the Persians, lost not only that power which he had exercised without moderation, but also the liberty of which he had deprived others; and he wasted the remainder of his days in the vilest condition of slavery: for Sapores, the king of the Persians, who had made him prisoner, whenever he chose to get into his carriage or to mount on horseback, commanded the Roman to stoop and present his back; then, setting his foot on the shoulders of Valerian, he said, with a smile of reproach, "*This* is true, and not what the Romans delineate on board or plaster." Valerian lived for a considerable time under the well-merited insults of his conqueror; so that the Roman name remained long the scoff and derision of the barbarians: and this also was added to the severity of his punishment, that although he had an emperor for his son, he found no one to revenge his captivity and most abject and servile state; neither indeed was he ever demanded back. Afterward, when he had finished this shameful life under so great dishonor, he was flayed, and his skin, stripped from the flesh, was dyed with vermilion, and placed in the temple of the gods of the barbarians, that the remembrance of a triumph so signal might be perpetuated, and that this spectacle might always be exhibited to our ambassadors, as an admonition to the Romans, that, beholding the spoils of their captived emperor in a Persian temple, they should not place too great confidence in their own strength.

Now since God so punished the sacrilegious, is it not strange that anyone should afterward have dared to do, or even to devise, aught against the majesty of the one God, who governs and supports all things?

**Chap. VI.**

Aurelian might have recollected the fate of the captived emperor, yet, being of a nature outrageous and headstrong, he forgot both *his* sin and its punishment, and by deeds of cruelty irritated the divine wrath. He was not, however, permitted to accomplish what he had devised; for just as he began to give a loose to his rage, he was slain. His bloody edicts had not yet reached the more distant provinces, when he himself lay all bloody on the earth at Cænophrurium in Thrace, assassinated by his familiar friends, who had taken up groundless suspicions against him.

Examples of such a nature, and so numerous, ought to have deterred succeeding tyrants; nevertheless they were not only not dismayed, but, in their misdeeds against God, became more bold and presumptuous.

**Chap. VII.**

While Diocletian, that author of ill, and deviser of misery, was ruining all things, he could not withhold his insults, not even against God. This man, by avarice partly, and partly by timid counsels, overturned the Roman empire. For he made choice of three persons to share the government with him; and thus, the empire having been quartered, armies were multiplied, and each of the four princes strove to maintain a much more considerable military force than any sole emperor had done in times past. There began to be fewer men who paid taxes than there were who received wages; so that the means of the husbandmen being exhausted by enormous impositions, the farms were abandoned, cultivated grounds became woodland, and universal dismay prevailed. Besides, the provinces were divided into minute portions, and many presidents and a multitude of inferior officers lay heavy on each territory, and almost on each city. There were also many stewards of different degrees, and deputies of presidents. Very few civil causes came before them: but there were condemnations daily, and forfeitures frequently inflicted; taxes on numberless commodities, and those not only often repeated, but perpetual, and, in exacting them, intolerable wrongs.

Whatever was laid on for the maintenance of the soldiery might have been endured; but Diocletian, through his insatiable avarice, would never allow the sums of money in his treasury to be diminished: he was constantly heaping together extraordinary aids and free gifts, that his original hoards might remain untouched and inviolable. He also, when by various extortions he had made all things exceedingly dear, attempted by an ordinance to limit their prices. Then much blood was shed for the veriest trifles; men were afraid to expose aught to sale, and the scarcity became more excessive and grievous than ever, until, in the end, the ordinance, after having proved destructive to multitudes, was from mere necessity abrogated. To this there were added a certain endless passion for building, and on that account, endless exactions from the provinces for furnishing wages to laborers and artificers, and supplying carriages and whatever else was requisite to the works which he projected. *Here* public halls, *there* a circus, *here* a mint, and *there* a workhouse for making implements of war; in one place a habitation for his empress, and in another for his daughter. Presently great part of the city was quitted, and all men removed with their wives and children, as from a town taken by enemies; and when those buildings were completed, to the destruction of whole provinces, he said, "They are not right, let them be done on another plan." Then they were to be pulled down, or altered, to undergo perhaps a future demolition. By such folly was he continually endeavoring to equal Nicomedia with the city Rome in magnificence.

I omit mentioning how many perished on account of their possessions or wealth; for such evils were exceedingly frequent, and through their frequency appeared almost lawful. But this was peculiar to him, that whenever he saw a field remarkably well cultivated, or a house of uncommon elegance, a false accusation and a capital punishment were straightway prepared against the proprietor; so that it seemed as if Diocletian could not be guilty of rapine without also shedding blood.

### Chap. VIII.

What was the character of his brother in empire, Maximian, called *Herculius*? Not unlike to that of Diocletian; and, indeed, to render their friendship so close and faithful as it was, there must have been in them a sameness of inclinations and purposes, a corresponding will and unanimity in judgment. Herein alone they were different, that Diocletian was more avaricious and less resolute, and that Maximian, with less avarice, had a bolder spirit, prone not to good, but to evil. For while he possessed Italy, itself the chief seat of empire, and while other very opulent provinces, such as Africa and Spain, were near at hand, he took little care to preserve those treasures which he had such fair opportunities of amassing. Whenever he stood in need of more, the richest senators were presently charged, by suborned evidences, as guilty of aspiring to the empire; so that the chief luminaries of the senate were daily extinguished.

And thus the treasury, delighting in blood, overflowed with ill-gotten wealth. Add to all this the incontinency of that pestilent wretch, not only in debauching males, which is hateful and abominable, but also in the violation of the daughters of the principal men of the state; for wherever he journeyed, virgins were suddenly torn from the presence of their parents. In such enormities he placed his supreme delight, and to indulge to the utmost his lust and flagitious desires was in his judgment the felicity of his reign. I pass over Constantius, a prince unlike the others, and worthy to have had the sole government of the empire.

## Chap. IX.

But the other Maximian (Galerius), chosen by Diocletian for his son-in-law, was worse, not only than those two princes whom our own times have experienced, but worse than all the bad princes of former days. In this wild beast there dwelt a native barbarity and a savageness foreign to Roman blood; and no wonder, for his mother was born beyond the Danube, and it was an inroad of the Carpi that obliged her to cross over and take refuge in New Dacia. The form of Galerius corresponded with his manners. Of stature tall, full of flesh, and swollen to a horrible bulk of corpulence; by his speech, gestures, and looks, he made himself a terror to all that came near him. His father-in-law, too, dreaded him excessively. The cause was this. Narseus, king of the Persians, emulating the example set him by his grandfather Sapores, assembled a great army, and aimed at becoming master of the eastern provinces of the Roman Empire. Diocletian, apt to be low-spirited and timorous in every commotion, and fearing a fate like that of Valerian, would not in person encounter Narseus; but he sent Galerius by the way of Armenia, while he himself halted in the eastern provinces, and anxiously watched the event. It is a custom amongst the barbarians to take everything that belongs to them into the field. Galerius laid an ambush for them, and easily overthrew men embarrassed with the multitude of their followers and with their baggage. Having put Narseus to flight, and returned with much spoil, his own pride and Diocletian's fears were greatly increased. For after this victory he rose to such a pitch of haughtiness as to reject the appellation of Cæsar; and when he heard that appellation in letters addressed to him, he cried out, with a stern look and terrible voice, "How long am I to be *Cæsar*? "Then he began to act extravagantly, insomuch that, as if he had been a second Romulus, he wished to pass for and to be called the offspring of Mars; and that he might appear the issue of a divinity, he was willing that his mother Romula should be dishonored with the name of adulteress. But, not to confound the chronological order of events, I delay the recital of his actions; for indeed afterwards, when Galerius got the title of emperor, his father-in-law having been divested of the imperial purple, he became altogether outrageous, and of unbounded arrogance.

While by such a conduct, and with such associates, Diocles—for *that* was the name of Diocletian before he attained sovereignty—occupied himself in subverting the commonweal, there was no evil which his crimes did not deserve: nevertheless he reigned most prosperously, as long as he forbore to defile his hands with the blood of the just; and what cause he had for persecuting them, I come now to explain.

### Chap. X.

Diocletian, as being of a timorous disposition, was a searcher into futurity, and during his abode in the East he began to slay victims, that from their livers he might obtain a prognostic of events; and while he sacrificed, some attendants of his, who were Christians, stood by, and they put the *immortal sign* on their foreheads. At this the demons were chased away, and the holy rites interrupted. The soothsayers trembled, unable to investigate the wonted marks on the entrails of the victims. They frequently repeated the sacrifices, as if the former had been unpropitious; but the victims, slain from time to time, afforded no tokens for divination. At length Tages, the chief of the soothsayers, either from guess or from his own observation, said, "There are profane persons here, who obstruct the rites." Then Diocletian, in furious passion, ordered not only all who were assisting at the holy ceremonies, but also all who resided within the palace, to sacrifice, and, in case of their refusal, to be scourged. And further, by letters to the commanding officers, he enjoined that all soldiers should be forced to the like impiety, under pain of being dismissed the service. Thus far his rage proceeded; but at that season he did nothing more against the law and religion of God. After an interval of some time he went to winter in Bithynia; and presently Galerius Cæsar came thither, inflamed with furious resentment, and purposing to excite the inconsiderate old man to carry on that persecution which he had begun against the Christians. I have learned that the cause of his fury was as follows.

**Chap. XI.**

The mother of Galerius, a woman exceedingly superstitious, was a votary of the gods of the mountains. Being of such a character, she made sacrifices almost every day, and she feasted her servants on the meat offered to idols: but the Christians of her family would not partake of those entertainments; and while she feasted with the Gentiles, they continued in fasting and prayer. On this account she conceived ill-will against the Christians, and by woman-like complaints instigated her son, no less superstitious than herself, to destroy them. So, during the whole winter, Diocletian and Galerius held councils together, at which no one else assisted; and it was the universal opinion that their conferences respected the most momentous affairs of the empire. The old man long opposed the fury of Galerius, and showed how pernicious it would be to raise disturbances throughout the world and to shed so much blood; that the Christians were wont with eagerness to meet death; and that it would be enough for him to exclude persons of that religion from the court and the army. Yet he could not restrain the madness of that obstinate man. He resolved, therefore, to take the opinion of his friends. Now this was a circumstance in the bad disposition of Diocletian, that whenever he determined to do good, he did it without advice, that the praise might be all his own; but whenever he determined to do ill, which he was sensible would be blamed, he called in many advisers, that his own fault might be imputed to other men: and therefore a few civil magistrates, and a few military commanders, were admitted to give their counsel; and the question was put to them according to priority of rank. Some, through personal ill-will towards the Christians, were of opinion that they ought to be cut off, as enemies of the gods and adversaries of the established religious ceremonies. Others thought differently, but, having understood the will of Galerius, they, either from dread of displeasing or from a desire of gratifying him, concurred in the opinion given against the Christians. Yet not even then could the emperor be prevailed upon to yield his assent. He determined above all to consult his gods; and to that end he dispatched a soothsayer to inquire of Apollo at Miletus, whose answer was such as might be expected from an enemy of the divine religion. So Diocletian was drawn over from his purpose. But although he could struggle no longer against his friends, and against Cæsar and Apollo, yet still he attempted to observe such moderation as to command the business to be carried through without bloodshed; whereas Galerius would have had all persons burnt alive who refused to sacrifice.

**Chap. XII.**

A fit and auspicious day was sought out for the accomplishment of this undertaking; and the festival of the god Terminus, celebrated on the sevens of the kalends of March, was chosen, in preference to all others, to terminate, as it were, the Christian religion.

"That day, the harbinger of death, arose,
First cause of ill, and long enduring woes;"

of woes which befell not only the Christians, but the whole earth. When that day dawned, in the eighth consulship of Diocletian and seventh of Maximian, suddenly, while it was yet hardly light, the prefect, together with chief commanders, tribunes, and officers of the treasury, came to the church in Nicomedia, and the gates having been forced open, they searched everywhere for an image of the Divinity. The books of the Holy Scriptures were found, and they were committed to the flames; the utensils and furniture of the church were abandoned to pillage: all was rapine, confusion, tumult. That church, situated on rising ground, was within view of the palace; and Diocletian and Galerius stood, as if on a watchtower, disputing long whether it ought to be set on fire. The sentiment of Diocletian prevailed, who dreaded lest, so great a fire being once kindled, some part of the city might he burnt; for there were many and large buildings that surrounded the church. Then the Pretorian Guards came in battle array, with axes and other iron instruments, and having been let loose everywhere, they in a few hours levelled that very lofty edifice with the ground.

**Chap. XIII.**

Next day an edict was published, depriving the Christians of all honors and dignities; ordaining also that, without any distinction of rank or degree, they should be subjected to tortures, and that every suit at law should be received against them; while, on the other hand, they were debarred from being plaintiffs in questions of wrong, adultery, or theft; and, finally, that they should neither be capable of freedom, nor have right of suffrage. A certain person tore down this edict, and cut it in pieces, improperly indeed, but with high spirit, saying in scorn, "These are the triumphs of Goths and Sarmatians." Having been instantly seized and brought to judgment, he was not only tortured, but burnt alive, in the forms of law; and having displayed admirable patience under sufferings, he was consumed to ashes.

### Chap. XIV.

But Galerius, not satisfied with the tenor of the edict, sought in another way to gain on the emperor. That he might urge him to excess of cruelty in persecution, he employed private emissaries to set the palace on fire; and some part of it having been burnt, the blame was laid on the Christians as public enemies; and the very appellation of *Christian* grew odious on account of that fire. It was said that the Christians, in concert with the eunuchs, had plotted to destroy the princes; and that both of the princes had well-nigh been burnt alive in their own palace. Diocletian, shrewd and intelligent as he always chose to appear, suspected nothing of the contrivance, but, inflamed with anger, immediately commanded that all his own domestics should be tortured to force a confession of the plot. He sat on his tribunal, and saw innocent men tormented by fire to make discovery. All magistrates, and all who had superintendence in the imperial palace, obtained special commissions to administer the torture; and they strove with each other *who* should be first in bringing to light the conspiracy. No circumstances, however, of the fact were detected anywhere; for no one applied the torture to any domestics of Galerius. He himself was ever with Diocletian, constantly urging him, and never allowing the passions of the inconsiderate old man to cool. Then, after an interval of fifteen days, he attempted a second fire; but that was perceived quickly, and extinguished. Still, however, its author remained unknown. On that very day, Galerius, who in the middle of winter had prepared for his departure, suddenly hurried out of the city, protesting that he fled to escape being burnt alive.

**Chap. XV.**

And now Diocletian raged, not only against his own domestics, but indiscriminately against all; and he began by forcing his daughter Valeria and his wife Prisca to be polluted by sacrificing. Eunuchs, once the most powerful, and who had chief authority at court and with the emperor, were slain. Presbyters and other officers of the Church were seized, without evidence by witnesses or confession, condemned, and together with their families led to execution. In burning alive, no distinction of sex or age was regarded; and because of their great multitude, they were not burnt one after another, but a herd of them were encircled with the same fire; and servants, having millstones tied about their necks, were cast into the sea. Nor was the persecution less grievous on the rest of the people of God; for the judges, dispersed through all the temples, sought to compel everyone to sacrifice. The prisons were crowded; tortures, hitherto unheard of, were invented; and lest justice should be inadvertently administered to a Christian, altars were placed in the courts of justice, hard by the tribunal, that every litigant might offer incense before his cause could be heard. Thus judges were no otherwise approached than divinities. Mandates also had gone to Maximian Herculius and Constantius, requiring their concurrence in the execution of the edicts; for in matters even of such mighty importance their opinion was never once asked. Herculius, a person of no merciful temper, yielded ready obedience, and enforced the edicts throughout his dominions of Italy. Constantius, on the other hand, lest he should have seemed to dissent from the injunctions of his superiors, permitted the demolition of churches,—mere walls, and capable of being built up again,—but he preserved entire that true temple of God, which is the human body.

## Chap. XVI.

Thus was all the earth afflicted; and from east to west, except in the territories of Gaul, three ravenous wild beasts continued to rage.

"Had I a hundred mouths, a hundred tongues,
A voice of brass, and adamantine lungs,
Not half the dreadful scene could I disclose,"

Or recount the punishments inflicted by the rulers in every province on religious and innocent men.

But what need of a particular recital of those things, especially to you, my best beloved Donatus, who above all others was exposed to the storm of that violent persecution? For when you had fallen into the hands of the prefect Flaccinian, no puny murderer, and afterwards of Hierocles, who from a deputy became president of Bithynia, the author and adviser of the persecution, and last of all into the hands of his successor Priscillian, you displayed to mankind a pattern of invincible magnanimity. Having been nine times exposed to racks and diversified torments, nine times by a glorious profession of your faith you foiled the adversary; in nine combats you subdued the devil and his chosen soldiers; and by nine victories you triumphed over this world and its terrors. How pleasing the spectacle to God, when He beheld you a conqueror, yoking in your chariot not white horses, nor enormous elephants, but those very men who had led captive the nations! After this sort to lord it over the lords of the earth is triumph indeed! Now, by your valor were they conquered, when you set at defiance their flagitious edicts, and, through steadfast faith and the fortitude of your soul, you routed all the vain terrors of tyrannical authority. Against you neither scourges, nor iron claws, nor fire, nor sword, nor various kinds of torture, availed aught; and no violence could bereave you of your fidelity and persevering resolution. This it is to be a disciple of God, and this it is to be a soldier of Christ; a soldier whom no enemy can dislodge, or wolf snatch, from the heavenly camp; no artifice ensnare, or pain of body subdue, or torments overthrow. At length, after those nine glorious combats, in which the devil was vanquished by you, he dared not to enter the lists again with one whom, by repeated trials, he had found unconquerable; and he abstained from challenging you any more, lest you should have laid hold on the garland of victory already stretched out to you; an unfading garland, which, although you have not at present received it, is laid up in the kingdom of the Lord for your virtue and deserts. But let us now return to the course of our narrative.

## Chap. XVII.

The wicked plan having been carried into execution, Diocletian, whom prosperity had now abandoned, set out instantly for Rome, *there* to celebrate the commencement of the twentieth year of his reign. That solemnity was performed on the twelfth of the kalends of December; and suddenly the emperor, unable to bear the Roman freedom of speech, peevishly and impatiently burst away from the city. The kalends of January approached, at which day the consulship, for the ninth time, was to be offered to him; yet, rather than continue thirteen days longer in Rome, he chose that his first appearance as consul should be at Ravenna. Having, however, begun his journey in winter, amidst intense cold and incessant rains, he contracted a slight but lingering disease: it harassed him without intermission, so that he was obliged for the most part to be carried in a litter. Then, at the close of summer, he made a circuit along the banks of the Danube, and so came to Nicomedia. His disease had now become more grievous and oppressing; yet he caused himself to be brought out, in order to dedicate that circus which, at the conclusion of the twentieth year of his reign, he had erected. Immediately he grew so languid and feeble, that prayers for his life were put up to all the gods. Then suddenly, on the ides of

December, there was heard in the palace sorrow, and weeping, and lamentation, and the courtiers ran to and fro; there was silence throughout the city, and a report went of the death, and even of the burial, of Diocletian: but early on the morrow it was suddenly rumored that he still lived. At this the countenance of his domestics and courtiers changed from melancholy to gay. Nevertheless there were who suspected his death to be kept secret until the arrival of Galerius Cæsar, lest in the meanwhile the soldiery should attempt some change in the government; and this suspicion grew so universal, that no one would believe the emperor alive, until, on the kalends of March, he appeared in public, but so wan, his illness having lasted almost a year, as hardly to be known again. The fit of stupor, resembling death, happened on the ides of December; and although he in some measure recovered, yet he never attained to perfect health again, for he became disordered in his judgment, being at certain times insane and at others of sound mind.

## Chap. XVIII.

Within a few days Galerius Cæsar arrived, not to congratulate his father-in-law on the re-establishment of his health, but to force him to resign the empire. Already he had urged Maximian Herculius to the like purpose, and by the alarm of civil wars terrified the old man into compliance; and he now assailed Diocletian. At first, in gentle and friendly terms, he said that age and growing infirmities disabled Diocletian for the charge of the commonweal, and that he had need to give himself some repose after his labors. Galerius, in confirmation of his argument, produced the example of Nerva, who laid the weight of empire on Trajan.

But Diocletian made answer, that it was unfit for one who had held a rank, eminent above all others and conspicuous, to sink into the obscurity of a low station; neither indeed was it safe, because in the course of so long a reign he must unavoidably have made many enemies. That the case of Nerva was very different: he, after having reigned a single year, felt himself, either from age or from inexperience in business, unequal to affairs so momentous, and therefore threw aside the helm of government, and returned to that private life in which he had already grown old. But Diocletian added, that if Galerius wished for the title of emperor, there was nothing to hinder its being conferred on him and Constantius, as well as on Maximian Herculius.

Galerius, whose imagination already grasped at the whole empire, saw that little but an unsubstantial name would accrue to him from this proposal, and therefore replied that the settlement made by Diocletian himself ought to be inviolable; a settlement which provided that there should be two of higher rank vested with supreme power, and two others of inferior, to assist them. Easily might concord be preserved between *two* equals, never amongst *four*; that he, if Diocletian would not resign, must consult his own interests, so as to remain no longer in an inferior rank, and the last of that rank; that for fifteen years past he had been confined, as an exile, to Illyricum and the banks of the Danube, perpetually struggling against barbarous nations, while others, at their ease, governed dominions more extensive than his, and better civilized.

Diocletian already knew, by letters from Maximian Herculius, all that Galerius had spoken at their conference, and also that he was augmenting his army; and now, on hearing his discourse, the spiritless old man burst into tears, and said, "Be it as you will."

It remained to choose *Cæsars* by common consent. "But," said Galerius, "Why ask the advice of Maximian and Constantius, since they must needs acquiesce in whatever we do?"—"Certainly they will," replied Diocletian, "for we must elect their sons."

Now Maximian Herculius had a son, Maxentius, married to the daughter of Galerius, a man of bad and mischievous dispositions, and so proud and stubborn withal, that he would

## The Writings of Lactatius

never pay the wonted obeisance either to his father or father-in-law, and on that account he was hated by them both. Constantius also had a son, Constantine, a young man of very great worth, and well meriting the high station of *Cæsar*. The distinguished comeliness of his figure, his strict attention to all military duties, his virtuous demeanor and singular affability, had endeared him to the troops, and made him the choice of every individual. He was then at court, having long before been created by Diocletian a tribune of the first order.

"What is to be done?" said Galerius, "for *that* Maxentius deserves not the office. He who, while yet a private man, has treated me with contumely, how will he act when once he obtains power?"—"But Constantine is amiable, and will so rule as hereafter, in the opinion of mankind, to surpass the mild virtues of his father."—"Be it so, if my inclinations and judgment are to be disregarded. Men ought to be appointed who are at my disposal, who will dread me, and never do anything unless by my orders."—"Whom then shall we appoint?"—"Severus."—"How! That dancer, that habitual drunkard, who turns night into day, and day into night?"—"He deserves the office, for he has approved himself a faithful paymaster and purveyor of the army; and, indeed, I have already dispatched him to receive the purple from the hands of Maximian."—"Well, I consent; but whom else do you suggest?"—"Him," said Galerius, pointing out Daia, a young man, half-barbarian. Now Galerius had lately bestowed part of his own name on that youth, and called him *Maximin*, in like manner as Diocletian formerly bestowed on Galerius the name of Maximian, for the omen's sake, because Maximian Herculius had served him with unshaken fidelity.—"Who is that you present?"—"A kinsman of mine."—"Alas!" said Diocletian, heaving a deep sigh, "you do not propose men fit for the charge of public affairs!"—"I have tried them."—"Then do *you* look to it, who are about to assume the administration of the empire: as for *me*, while I continued emperor, long and diligent have been my labors in providing for the security of the commonweal; and now, should anything disastrous ensue, the blame will not be mine."

**Chap. XIX.**

Matters having been thus concerted, Diocletian and Galerius went in procession to publish the nomination of *Cæsars*. Everyone looked at Constantine; for there was no doubt that the choice would fall on him. The troops present, as well as the chief soldiers of the other legions, who had been summoned to the solemnity, fixed their eyes on Constantine, exulted in the hope of his approaching election, and occupied themselves in prayers for his prosperity. Near three miles from Nicomedia there is an eminence, on the summit of which Galerius formerly received the purple; and *there* a pillar, with the statue of Jupiter, was placed. Thither the procession went. An assembly of the soldiers was called. Diocletian, with tears, harangued them, and said that he was become infirm, that he needed repose after his fatigues, and that he would resign the empire into hands more vigorous and able, and at the same time appoint new *Cæsars*. The spectators, with the utmost earnestness, waited for the nomination. Suddenly he declared that the *Cæsars* were Severus and Maximin. The amazement was universal. Constantine stood near in public view, and men began to question amongst themselves whether his name too had not been changed into *Maximin*; when, in the sight of all, Galerius, stretching back his hand, put Constantine aside, and drew Daia forward, and, having divested him of the garb of a private person, set him in the most conspicuous place. All men wondered who he could be, and from whence he came; but none ventured to interpose or move objections, so confounded were their minds at the strange and unlooked-for event. Diocletian took off his purple robe, put it on Daia, and resumed his own original name of Diocles. He descended from the tribunal, and passed through Nicomedia in a chariot; and then this old emperor, like a veteran soldier freed from military service, was dismissed into his own country; while Daia, lately taken from the tending of cattle in forests to serve as a common soldier, immediately made one of the life-guard, presently a tribune, and next day *Cæsar*, obtained authority to trample under foot and oppress the empire of the East; a person ignorant alike of war and of civil affairs, and from a herdsman become a leader of armies.

## Chap. XX.

Galerius having effected the expulsion of the two old men, began to consider himself alone as the sovereign of the Roman Empire. Necessity had required the appointment of Constantius to the first rank; but Galerius made small account of one who was of an easy temper, and of health declining and precarious. He looked for the speedy death of Constantius. And although that prince should recover, it seemed not difficult to force him to put off the imperial purple; for what else could he do, if pressed by his three colleagues to abdicate? Galerius had Licinius ever about his person, his old and intimate acquaintance, and his earliest companion in arms, whose counsels he used in the management of all affairs; yet he would not nominate Licinius to the dignity of *Cæsar*, with the title of *son*, for he purposed to nominate him, in the room of Constantius, to the dignity of *emperor*, with the title of *brother*, while he himself might hold sovereign authority, and rule over the whole globe with unbounded license. After that, he meant to have solemnized the *vicennial* festival; to have conferred on his son Candidianus, then a boy of nine years of age, the office of *Cæsar*; and, in conclusion, to have resigned, as Diocletian had done. And thus, Licinius and Severus being emperors, and Maximin and Candidianus in the next station of *Cæsars*, he fancied that, environed as it were by an impregnable wall, he should lead an old age of security and peace. Such were his projects; but God, whom he had made his adversary, frustrated all those imaginations.

## Chap. XXI.

Having thus attained to the highest power, he bent his mind to afflict that empire into which he had opened his way. It is the manner and practice of the Persians for the people to yield themselves slaves to their kings, and for the kings to treat their people as slaves. This flagitious man, from the time of his victories over the Persians, was not ashamed incessantly to extol such an institution, and he resolved to establish it in the Roman dominions; and because he could not do this by an express law, he so acted, in imitation of the Persian kings, as to bereave men of their liberties. He first of all degraded those whom he meant to punish; and then not only were inferior magistrates put to the torture by him, but also the chief men in cities, and persons of the most eminent rank, and this too in matters of little moment, and in civil questions. Crucifixion was the punishment ready prepared in capital cases; and for lesser crimes, fetters. Matrons of honorable station were dragged into workhouses; and when any man was to be scourged, there were four posts fixed in the ground, and to them he was tied, after a manner unknown in the chastisement of slaves. What shall I say of his apartment for sport, and of his favourite diversions? He kept bears, most resembling himself in fierceness and bulk, whom he had collected together during the course of his reign. As often as he chose to indulge his humor, he ordered some particular bear to be brought in, and men were thrown to that savage animal, rather to be swallowed up than devoured; and when their limbs were torn asunder, he laughed with excessive complacency: nor did he ever sup without being spectator of the effusion of human blood. Men of private station were condemned to be burnt alive; and he began this mode of execution by edicts against the Christians, commanding that, after torture and condemnation, they should be burnt at a slow fire. They were fixed to a stake, and first a moderate flame was applied to the soles of their feet, until the muscles, contracted by burning, were torn from the bones; then torches, lighted and put out again, were directed to all the members of their bodies, so that no part had any exemption.

Meanwhile cold water was continually poured on their faces, and their mouths moistened, lest, by reason of their jaws being parched, they should expire. At length they did expire, when, after many hours, the violent heat had consumed their skin and penetrated into their intestines. The dead carcasses were laid on a funeral pile, and wholly burnt; their bones were gathered, ground to powder, and thrown into the river, or into the sea.

### Chap. XXII.

And now *that* cruelty, which he had learned in torturing the Christians, became habitual, and he exercised it against all men indiscriminately. He was not wont to inflict the slighter sorts of punishment, as to banish, to imprison, or to send criminals to work in the mines; but to burn, to crucify, to expose to wild beasts, were things done daily, and without hesitation. For smaller offences, those of his own household and his stewards were chastised with lances, instead of rods; and, in great offences, to be beheaded was an indulgence shown to very few; and it seemed as a favor, on account of old services, when one was permitted to die in the easiest manner. But these were slight evils in the government of Galerius, when compared with what follows. For eloquence was extinguished, pleaders cut off, and the learned in the laws either exiled or slain. Useful letters came to be viewed in the same light as magical and forbidden arts; and all who possessed them were trampled upon and execrated, as if they had been hostile to government, and public enemies. Law was dissolved, and unbounded license permitted to judges,—to judges chosen from amongst the soldiery, rude and illiterate men, and let loose upon the provinces, without assessors to guide or control them.

### Chap. XXIII.

But that which gave rise to public and universal calamity, was the tax imposed at once on each province and city. Surveyors having been spread abroad, and occupied in a general and severe scrutiny, horrible scenes were exhibited, like the outrages of victorious enemies, and the wretched state of captives. Each spot of ground was measured, vines and fruit-trees numbered, lists taken of animals of every kind, and a capitation-roll made up. In cities, the common people, whether residing within or without the walls, were assembled, the marketplaces filled with crowds of families, all attended with their children and slaves, the noise of torture and scourges resounded, sons were hung on the rack to force discovery of the effects of their fathers, the most trusty slaves compelled by pain to bear witness against their masters, and wives to bear witness against their husbands, In default of all other evidence, men were tortured to speak against themselves; and no sooner did agony oblige them to acknowledge what they had not, but those imaginary effects were noted down in the lists. Neither youth, nor old age, nor sickness, afforded any exemption. The diseased and the infirm were carried in; the age of each was estimated; and, that the capitation-tax might be enlarged, years were added to the young and struck off from the old. General lamentation and sorrow prevailed. Whatever, by the laws of war, conquerors had done to the conquered, the like did this man presume to perpetrate against Romans and the subjects of Rome, because his forefathers had been made liable to a like tax imposed by the victorious Trajan, as a penalty on the Dacians for their frequent rebellions. After this, money was levied for each head, as if a price had been paid for liberty to exist; yet full trust was not reposed on the same set of surveyors, but others and others still were sent round to make further discoveries; and thus the tributes were redoubled, not because the new surveyors made any fresh discoveries, but because they added at pleasure to the former rates, lest they should seem to have been employed to no purpose. Meanwhile the number of animals decreased, and men died; nevertheless taxes were paid even for the dead, so that no one could either live or cease to live without being subject to impositions. There remained mendicants alone, from whom nothing could be exacted, and whom their misery and wretchedness secured from ill-treatment. But this pious man had compassion on them, and determining that they should remain no longer in indigence, he caused them all to be assembled, put on board vessels, and sunk in the sea. So merciful was he in making provision that under his administration no man should want! And thus, while he took effectual measures that none, under the reigned pretext of poverty, should elude the tax, he put to death a multitude of real wretches, in violation of every law of humanity.

## Chap. XXIV.

Already the judgment of God approached him, and that season ensued in which his fortunes began to droop and to waste away. While occupied in the manner that I have described above, he did not set himself to subvert or expel Constantius, but waited for his death, not imagining, however, that it was so nigh. Constantius, having become exceedingly ill, wrote to Galerius, and requested that his son Constantine might be sent to see him. He had made a like request long before, but in vain; for Galerius meant nothing less than to grant it. On the contrary, he laid repeated snares for the life of that young man, because he durst not use open violence, lest he should stir up civil wars against himself, and incur that which he most dreaded, the hate and resentment of the army. Under pretense of manly exercise and recreation, he made him combat with wild beasts: but this device was frustrated; for the power of God protected Constantine, and in the very moment of jeopardy rescued him from the hands of Galerius. At length, Galerius, when he could no longer avoid complying with the request of Constantius, one evening gave Constantine a warrant to depart, and commanded him to set out next morning with the imperial dispatches. Galerius meant either to find some pretext for detaining Constantine, or to forward orders to Severus for arresting him on the road. Constantine discerned his purpose; and therefore, after supper, when the emperor was gone to rest, he hasted away, carried off from the principal stages all the horses maintained at the public expense, and escaped. Next day the emperor, having purposely remained in his bed-chamber until noon, ordered Constantine to be called into his presence; but he learnt that Constantine had set out immediately after supper. Outrageous with passion, he ordered horses to be made ready, that Constantine might be pursued and dragged back; and hearing that all the horses had been carried off from the great road, he could hardly refrain from tears. Meanwhile Constantine, journeying with incredible rapidity, reached his father, who was already about to expire. Constantius recommended his son to the soldiers, delivered the sovereign authority into his hands, and then died, as his wish had long been, in peace and quiet.

Constantine Augustus, having assumed the government, made it his first care to restore the Christians to the exercise of their worship and to their God; and so began his administration by reinstating the holy religion.

### Chap. XXV.

Some few days after, the portrait of Constantine, adorned with laurels, was brought to the pernicious wild beast, that, by receiving that symbol, he might acknowledge Constantine in the quality of *emperor*. He hesitated long whether to receive it or not, and he was about to commit both the portrait and its bearer to the flames, but his confidants dissuaded him from a resolution so frantic. They admonished him of the danger, and they represented that, if Constantine came with an armed force, all the soldiers, against whose inclination obscure or unknown *Cæsars* had been created, would acknowledge him, and crowd eagerly to his standard. So Galerius, although with the utmost unwillingness, accepted the portrait, and sent the imperial purple to Constantine, that he might seem of his own accord to have received that prince into partnership of power with him. And now his plans were deranged, and he could not, as he intended formerly, admit Licinius, without exceeding the limited number of emperors. But *this* he devised, that Severus, who was more advanced in life, should be named *emperor*, and that Constantine, instead of the title of *emperor*, to which he had been named, should receive that of *Cæsar* in common with Maximin Daia, and so be degraded from the second place to the fourth.

### Chap. XXVI.

Things seemed to be arranged in some measure to the satisfaction of Galerius, when another alarm was brought, that his son-in-law Maxentius had been declared *emperor* at Rome. The cause was this: Galerius having resolved by permanent taxes to devour the empire, soared to such extravagance in folly, as not to allow an exemption from that thraldom even to the Roman people. Tax-gatherers therefore were appointed to go to Rome, and make out lists of the citizens. Much about the same time Galerius had reduced the Pretorian Guards. There remained at Rome a few soldiers of that body, who, profiting of the opportunity, put some magistrates to death, and, with the acquiescence of the tumultuary populace, clothed Maxentius in the imperial purple. Galerius, on receiving this news, was disturbed at the strangeness of the event, but not much dismayed. He hated Maxentius, and he could not bestow on him the dignity of *Cæsar* already enjoyed by two (Daia and Constantine); besides, he thought it enough for him to have once bestowed that dignity against his inclination. So he sent for Severus, exhorted him to regain his dominion and sovereignty, and he put under his command that army which Maximian Herculius had formerly commanded, that he might attack Maxentius at Rome. *There* the soldiers of Maximian had been oftentimes received with every sort of luxurious accommodation, so that they were not only interested to preserve the city, but they also longed to fix their residence in it.

Maxentius well knew the enormity of his own offences; and although he had as it were an hereditary claim to the services of his father's army, and might have hoped to draw it over to himself, yet he reflected that this consideration might occur to

Galerius also, and induce him to leave Severus in Illyricum, and march in person with his own army against Rome. Under such apprehensions, Maxentius sought to protect himself from the danger that hung over him. To his father, who since his abdication resided in Campania, he sent the purple, and saluted him again *Augustus*. Maximian, given to change, eagerly resumed that purple of which he had unwillingly divested himself. Meanwhile Severus marched on, and with his troops approached the walls of the city. Presently the soldiers raised up their ensigns, abandoned Severus, and yielded themselves to Maxentius, against whom they had come. What remained but flight for Severus, thus deserted? He was encountered by Maximian, who had resumed the imperial dignity. On this he took refuge in Ravenna, and shut himself up *there* with a few soldiers. But perceiving that he was about to be delivered up, he voluntarily surrendered himself, and restored the purple to him from whom he had received it; and after this he obtained no other grace but that of an easy death, for he was compelled to open his veins, and in that gentle manner expired.

**Chap. XXVII.**

But Maximian, who knew the outrageous temper of Galerius, began to consider that, fired with rage on hearing of the death of Severus, he would march into Italy, and that possibly he might be joined by Daia, and so bring into the field forces too powerful to be resisted. Having therefore fortified Rome, and made diligent provision for a defensive war, Maximian went into Gaul that he might give his younger daughter Fausta in marriage to Constantine, and thus win over that prince to his interest. Meantime Galerius assembled his troops, invaded Italy, and advanced towards Rome, resolving to extinguish the senate and put the whole people to the sword. But he found everything shut and fortified against him. There was no hope of carrying the place by storm, and to besiege it was an arduous undertaking; for Galerius had not brought with him an army sufficient to invest the walls. Probably, having never seen Rome, he imagined it to be little superior in size to those cities with which he was acquainted. But some of his legions, detesting the wicked enterprise of a father against his son-in-law, and of Romans against Rome, renounced his authority, and carried over their ensigns to the enemy. Already had his remaining soldiers begun to waver, when Galerius, dreading a fate like that of Severus, and having his haughty spirit broken and humiliated, threw himself at the feet of his soldiers, and continued to beseech them that he might not be delivered to the foe, until, by the promise of mighty largesses, he prevailed on them. Then he retreated from Rome, and fled in great disorder. Easily might he have been cut off in his flight, had any one pursued him even with a small body of troops. He was aware of his danger, and allowed his soldiers to disperse themselves, and to plunder and destroy far and wide, that, if there were any pursuers, they might be deprived of all means of subsistence in a ruined country. So the parts of Italy through which that pestilent band took its course were wasted, all things pillaged, matrons forced, virgins violated, parents and husbands compelled by torture to disclose where they had concealed their goods, and their wives and daughters; flocks and herds of cattle were driven off like spoils taken from barbarians. And thus did he, once a Roman emperor, but now the ravager of Italy, retire into his own territories, after having afflicted all men indiscriminately with the calamities of war. Long ago, indeed, and at the very time of his obtaining sovereign power, he had avowed himself the enemy of the Roman name; and he proposed that the empire should be called, not the *Roman*, but the *Dacian* empire.

### Chap. XXVIII.

After the flight of Galerius, Maximian, having returned from Gaul, held authority in common with his son; but more obedience was yielded to the young man than to the old: for Maxentius had most power, and had been longest in possession of it; and it was to him that Maximian owed on this occasion the imperial dignity. The old man was impatient at being denied the exercise of uncontrolled sovereignty, and envied his son with a childish spirit of rivalry; and therefore he began to consider how he might expel Maxentius and resume his ancient dominion. This appeared easy, because the soldiers who deserted Severus had originally served in his own army. He called an assembly of the people of Rome, and of the soldiers, as if he had been to make a harangue on the calamitous situation of public affairs. After having spoken much on that subject, he stretched his hands towards his son, charged him as author of all ills and prime cause of the calamities of the state, and then tore the purple from his shoulders. Maxentius, thus stripped, leaped headlong from the tribunal, and was received into the arms of the soldiers. Their rage and clamor confounded the unnatural old man, and, like another Tarquin the Proud, he was driven from Rome.

## Chap. XXIX.

Then Maximian returned into Gaul; and after having made some stay in those quarters, he went to Galerius, the enemy of his son, that they might confer together, as he pretended, about the settlement of the commonweal; but his true purpose was, under color of reconciliation, to find an opportunity of murdering Galerius, and of seizing his share of the empire, instead of his own, from which he had been everywhere excluded.

Diocles was at the court of Galerius when Maximian arrived; for Galerius, meaning now to invest Licinius with the ensigns of supreme power in the room of Severus, had lately sent for Diocles to be present at the solemnity. So it was performed in presence both of him and of Maximian; and thus there were six who ruled the empire at one and the same time.

Now the designs of Maximian having been frustrated, he took flight, as he had done twice before, and returned into Gaul, with a heart full of wickedness, and intending by treacherous devices to overreach Constantine, who was not only his own son-in-law, but also the child of his son-in-law; and that he might the more successfully deceive, he laid aside the imperial purple. The Franks had taken up arms. Maximian advised the unsuspecting Constantine not to lead all his troops against them, and he said that a few soldiers would suffice to subdue those barbarians. He gave this advice that an army might be left for him to win over to himself, and that Constantine, by reason of his scanty forces, might be overpowered. The young prince believed the advice to be judicious, because given by an aged and experienced commander; and he followed it, because given by a father-in-law. He marched, leaving the most considerable part of his forces behind. Maximian waited a few days; and as soon as, by his calculation, Constantine had entered the territory of the barbarians, he suddenly resumed the imperial purple, seized the public treasures, after his wont made ample donatives to the soldiery, and feigned that such disasters had befallen Constantine as soon after befell himself. Constantine was presently informed of those events, and, by marches astonishingly rapid, he flew back with his army. Maximian, not yet prepared to oppose him, was overpowered at unawares, and the soldiers returned to their duty. Maximian had possessed himself of Marseilles (he fled thither), and shut the gates. Constantine drew nigh, and seeing Maximian on the walls, addressed him in no harsh or hostile language, and demanded what he meant, and what it was that he wanted, and why he had acted in a way so peculiarly unbecoming him. But Maximian from the walls incessantly uttered abuse and curses against Constantine. Then, of a sudden, the gates on the opposite side having been unbarred, the besiegers were admitted into the city. The rebel emperor, and unnatural parent and a perfidious father-in-law, was dragged into the presence of Constantine, heard a recital made of his crimes, was divested of his imperial robe, and, after this reprimand, obtained his life.

## Chap. XXX.

Maximian, having thus forfeited the respect due to an emperor and a father-in-law, grew impatient at his abased condition, and, emboldened by impunity, formed new plots against Constantine. He addressed himself to his daughter Fausta, and, as well by entreaties as by the soothing of flattery, solicited her to betray her husband. He promised to obtain for her a more honorable alliance than that with Constantine; and he requested her to allow the bed-chamber of the emperor to be left open, and to be slightly guarded. Fausta undertook to do whatever he asked, and instantly revealed the whole to her husband. A plan was laid for detecting Maximian in the very execution of his crime. They placed a base eunuch to be murdered instead of the emperor. At the dead of night Maximian arose, and perceived all things to be favorable for his insidious purpose. There were few soldiers on guard, and these too at some distance from the bed-chamber. However, to prevent suspicion, he accosted them, and said that he had had a dream which he wished to communicate to his son-in-law. He went in armed, slew the eunuch, sprung forth exultingly, and avowed the murder. At that moment Constantine showed himself on the opposite side with a band of soldiers; the dead body was brought out of the bed-chamber; the murderer, taken in the fact, all aghast,

"Stood like a stone, silent and motionless;"

while Constantine upbraided him for his impiety and enormous guilt. At last Maximian obtained leave that the manner of his death should be at his own choice, and he strangled himself.

Thus that mightiest sovereign of Rome—who ruled so long with exceeding glory, and who celebrated his twentieth anniversary—thus that most haughty man had his neck broken, and ended his detestable life by a death base and ignominious.

## Chap. XXXI.

From Maximian, God, the avenger of religion and of His people, turned his eyes to Galerius, the author of the accursed persecution, that in his punishment also He might manifest the power of His majesty. Galerius, too, was purposing to celebrate his twentieth anniversary; and as, under that pretext, he had, by new taxes payable in gold and silver, oppressed the provinces, so now, that he might recompense them by celebrating the promised festival, he used the like pretext for repeating his oppressions. Who can relate in fit terms the methods used to harass mankind in levying the tax, and especially with regard to corn and the other fruits of the earth? The officers, or rather the executioners, of all the different magistrates, seized on each individual, and would never let go their hold. No man knew to whom he ought to make payment first. There was no dispensation given to those who had nothing; and they were required, under pain of being variously tortured, instantly to pay, notwithstanding their inability. Many guards were set round, no breathing time was granted, or, at any season of the year, the least respite from exactions. Different magistrates, or the officers of different magistrates, frequently contended for the right of levying the tax from the same persons. No threshing-floor without a tax-gatherer, no vintage without a watch, and naught left for the sustenance of the husbandman! That food should be snatched from the mouths of those who had earned it by toil, was grievous: the hope, however, of being afterwards relieved, might have made that grievance supportable; but it was necessary for everyone who appeared at the anniversary festival to provide robes of various kinds, and gold and silver besides. And one might have said, "How shall I furnish myself with those things, O tyrant void of understanding, if you carry off the whole fruits of my ground, and violently seize its expected produce?" Thus, throughout the dominions of Galerius, men were spoiled of their goods, and all was raked together into the imperial treasury, that the emperor might be enabled to perform his vow of celebrating a festival which he was doomed never to celebrate.

**Chap. XXXII.**

Maximin Daia was incensed at the nomination of Licinius to the dignity of *emperor*, and he would no longer be called *Cæsar*, or allow himself to be ranked as third in authority. Galerius, by repeated messages, besought Daia to yield, and to acquiesce in *his* arrangement, to give place to age, and to reverence the grey hairs of Licinius. But Daia became more and more insolent. He urged that, as it was he who first assumed the purple, so, by possession, he had right to priority in rank; and he set at naught the entreaties and the injunctions of Galerius. That brute animal was stung to the quick, and bellowed when the mean creature whom he had made *Cæsar*, in expectation of his thorough obsequiousness, forgot the great favor conferred on him, and impiously withstood the requests and will of his benefactor. Galerius at length, overcome by the obstinacy of Daia, abolished the subordinate title of *Cæsar*, gave to himself and Licinius that of *the Augusti*, and to Daia and Constantine that of *sons of the Augusti*. Daia, sometime after, in a letter to Galerius, took occasion to observe, that at the last general muster he had been saluted by his army under the title of *Augustus*. Galerius, vexed and grieved at this, commanded that all the four should have the appellation of *emperor*.

**Chap. XXXIII.**

And now, when Galerius was in the eighteenth year of his reign, God struck him with an incurable plague. A malignant ulcer formed itself low down in his secret parts, and spread by degrees. The physicians attempted to eradicate it, and healed up the place affected. But the sore, after having been skinned over, broke out again; a vein burst, and the blood flowed in such quantity as to endanger his life. The blood, however, was stopped, although with difficulty. The physicians had to undertake their operations anew, and at length they cicatrized the wound. In consequence of some slight motion of his body, Galerius received a hurt, and the blood streamed more abundantly than before. He grew emaciated, pallid, and feeble, and the bleeding then stanched. The ulcer began to be insensible to the remedies applied, and a gangrene seized all the neighboring parts. It diffused itself the wider the more the corrupted flesh was cut away, and everything employed as the means of cure served but to aggravate the disease.

"The masters of the healing art withdrew."

Then famous physicians were brought in from all quarters; but no human means had any success. Apollo and Æsculapius were besought importunately for remedies: Apollo did prescribe, and the distemper augmented. Already approaching to its deadly crisis, it had occupied the lower regions of his body: his bowels came out, and his whole seat putrefied. The luckless physicians, although without hope of overcoming the malady, ceased not to apply fomentations and administer medicines. The humors having been repelled, the distemper attacked his intestines, and worms were generated in his body. The stench was so foul as to pervade not only the palace, but even the whole city; and no wonder, for by that time the passages from his bladder and bowels, having been devoured by the worms, became indiscriminate, and his body, with intolerable anguish, was dissolved into one mass of corruption.

"Stung to the soul, he bellowed with the pain,
So roars the wounded bull."—Pitt

They applied warm flesh of animals to the chief seat of the disease, that the warmth might draw out those minute worms; and accordingly, when the dressings were removed, there issued forth an innumerable swarm: nevertheless the prolific disease had hatched swarms much more abundant to prey upon and consume his intestines. Already, through a complication of distempers, the different parts of his body had lost their natural form: the superior part was dry, meagre, and haggard, and his ghastly-looking skin had settled itself deep amongst his bones while the inferior, distended like bladders, retained no appearance of joints. These things happened in the course of a complete year; and at length, overcome by calamities, he was obliged to acknowledge God, and he cried aloud, in the intervals of raging pain, that he would re-edify the Church which he had demolished, and make atonement for his misdeeds; and when he was near his end, he published an edict of the tenor following:—

**Chap. XXXIV.**

"Amongst our other regulations for the permanent advantage of the commonweal, we have hitherto studied to reduce all things to a conformity with the ancient laws and public discipline of the Romans.

"It has been our aim in an especial manner, that the Christians also, who had abandoned the religion of their forefathers, should return to right opinions. For such willfulness and folly had, we know not how, taken possession of them, that instead of observing those ancient institutions, which possibly their own forefathers had established, they, through caprice, made laws to themselves, and drew together into different societies many men of widely different persuasions.

"After the publication of our edict, ordaining the Christians to betake themselves to the observance of the ancient institutions, many of them were subdued through the fear of danger, and moreover many of them were exposed to jeopardy; nevertheless, because great numbers still persist in their opinions, and because we have perceived that at present they neither pay reverence and due adoration to the gods, nor yet worship their own God, therefore we, from our wonted clemency in bestowing pardon on all, have judged it fit to extend our indulgence to those men, and to permit them again to be Christians, and to establish the places of their religious assemblies; yet so as that they offend not against good order.

"By another mandate we purpose to signify unto magistrates how they ought herein to demean themselves.

"Wherefore it will be the duty of the Christians, in consequence of this our toleration, to pray to their God for our welfare, and for that of the public, and for their own; that the commonweal may continue safe in every quarter, and that they themselves may live securely in their habitations."

## Chap. XXXV.

This edict was promulgated at Nicomedia on the day preceding the kalends of May, in the eighth consulship of Galerius, and the second of Maximin Daia. Then the prison gates having been thrown open, you, my best beloved Donatus, together with the other confessors for the faith, were set at liberty from a jail, which had been your residence for six years. Galerius, however, did not, by publication of this edict, obtain the divine forgiveness. In a few days after he was consumed by the horrible disease that had brought on a universal putrefaction. Dying, he recommended his wife and son to Licinius, and delivered them over into his hands. This event was known at Nicomedia before the end of the month. His vicennial anniversary was to have been celebrated on the ensuing kalends of March.

## Chap. XXXVI.

Daia, on receiving this news, hasted with relays of horses from the East, to seize the dominions of Galerius, and, while Licinius lingered in Europe, to arrogate to himself all the country as far as the narrow seas of Chalcedon. On his entry into Bithynia, he, with the view of acquiring immediate popularity, abolished Galerius' tax, to the great joy of all. Dissension arose between the two emperors, and almost an open war. They stood on the opposite shores with their armies. Peace, however, and amity were established under certain conditions. Licinius and Daia met on the narrow sees, concluded a treaty, and in token of friendship joined hands. Then Daia, believing all things to be in security, returned (to Nicomedia), and was in his new dominions what he had been in Syria and Egypt. First of all, he took away the toleration and general protection granted by Galerius to the Christians, and, for this end, he secretly procured addresses from different cities, requesting that no Christian church might be built within their walls; and thus he meant to make that which was his own choice appear as if extorted from him by importunity. In compliance with those addresses, he introduced a new mode of government in things respecting religion, and for each city he created a high priest, chosen from among the persons of most distinction. The office of those men was to make daily sacrifices to all their gods, and, with the aid of the former priests, to prevent the Christians from erecting churches, or from worshipping God either publicly or in private; and he authorized them to compel the Christians to sacrifice to idols, and, on their refusal, to bring them before the civil magistrate; and, as if this had not been enough, in every province he established a superintendent priest, one of chief eminence in the state; and he commanded that all those priests newly instituted should appear in white habits, that being the most honorable distinction of dress. And as to the Christians, he purposed to follow the course that he had followed in the East, and, affecting the show of clemency, he forbade the slaying of God's servants, but he gave command that they should be mutilated. So the confessors for the faith had their ears and nostrils slit, their hands and feet lopped off, and their eyes dug out of the sockets.

### Chap. XXXVII.

While occupied in this plan, he received letters from Constantine which deterred him from proceeding in its execution, so for a time he dissembled his purpose; nevertheless any Christian that fell within his power was privily thrown into the sea. Neither did he cease from his custom of sacrificing every day in the palace. It was also an invention of his to cause all animals used for food to be slaughtered, not by cooks, but by priests at the altars; so that nothing was ever served up, unless foretasted, consecrated, and sprinkled with wine, according to the rites of paganism; and whoever was invited to an entertainment must needs have returned from it impure and defiled. In all things else he resembled his preceptor Galerius. For if aught chanced to have been left untouched by Diocles and Maximian, *that* did Daia greedily and shamelessly carry off. And now the granaries of each individual were shut, and all warehouses sealed up, and taxes, not yet due, were levied by anticipation. Hence famine, from neglect of cultivation, and the prices of all things enhanced beyond measure. Herds and flocks were driven from their pasture for the daily sacrifice. By gorging his soldiers with the flesh of sacrifices, he so corrupted them, that they disdained their wonted pittance in corn, and wantonly threw it away. Meanwhile Daia recompensed his bodyguards, who were very numerous, with costly raiment and gold medals, made donatives in silver to the common soldiers and recruits, and bestowed every sort of largess on the barbarians who served in his army. As to grants of the property of living persons, which he made to his favorites whenever they chose to ask what belonged to another, I know not whether the same thanks might not be due to him that are given to merciful robbers, who spoil without murdering.

### Chap. XXXVIII.

But *that* which distinguished his character, and in which he transcended all former emperors, was his desire of debauching women. What else can I call it but a blind and headstrong passion? Yet such epithets feebly express my indignation in reciting his enormities. The magnitude of the guilt overpowers my tongue, and makes it unequal to its office. Eunuchs and panders made search everywhere, and no sooner was any comely face discovered, than husbands and parents were obliged to withdraw. Matrons of quality and virgins were stripped of their robes, and all their limbs were inspected, lest any part should be unworthy of the bed of the emperor. Whenever a woman resisted, death by drowning was inflicted on her; as if, under the reign of this adulterer, chastity had been treason. Some men there were, who, beholding the violation of wives whom for virtue and fidelity they affectionately loved, could not endure their anguish of mind, and so killed themselves. While this monster ruled, it was singular deformity alone which could shield the honor of any female from his savage desires. At length he introduced a custom prohibiting marriage unless with the imperial permission; and he made this an instrument to serve the purposes of his lewdness. After having debauched freeborn maidens, he gave them for wives to his slaves. His conflicts also imitated the example of the emperor, and violated with impunity the beds of their dependents. For who was there to punish such offences? As for the daughters of men of middle rank, any who were inclined took them by force. Ladies of quality, who could not be taken by force, were petitioned for, and obtained from the emperor by way of free gift. Nor could a father oppose this; for the imperial warrant having been once signed, he had no alternative but to die, or to receive some barbarian as his son-in-law. For hardly was there any person in the lifeguard except of those people, who, having been driven from their habitations by the Goths in the twentieth year of Diocletian, yielded themselves to Galerius and entered into his service. It was ill for humankind, that men who had fled from the bondage of barbarians should thus come to lord it over the Romans. Environed by such guards, Daia oppressed and insulted the Eastern Empire.

**Chap. XXXIX.**

Now Daia, in gratifying his libidinous desires, made his own will the standard of right; and therefore he would not refrain from soliciting the widow of Galerius, the Empress Valeria, to whom he had lately given the appellation of mother. After the death of her husband, she had repaired to Daia, because she imagined that she might live with more security in his dominions than elsewhere, especially as he was a married man; but the flagitious creature became instantly inflamed with a passion for her. Valeria was still in weeds, the time of her mourning not being yet expired. He sent a message to her proposing marriage, and offering, on her compliance, to put away his wife. She frankly returned an answer such as she alone could dare to do: first, that she would not treat of marriage while she was in weeds, and while the ashes of Galerius, *her* husband, and, by adoption, the father of Daia, were yet warm; next, that he acted impiously, in proposing to divorce a faithful wife to make room for another, whom in her turn he would also cast off; and, lastly, that it was indecent, unexampled, and unlawful for a woman of her title and dignity to engage a second time in wedlock. This bold answer having been reported to Daia, presently his desires changed into rage and furious resentment. He pronounced sentence of forfeiture against the princess, seized her goods, removed her attendants, tortured her eunuchs to death, and banished her and her mother Prisca: but he appointed no particular place for her residence while in banishment; and hence he insultingly expelled her from every abode that she took in the course of her wanderings; and, to complete all, he condemned the ladies who enjoyed most of her friendship and confidence to die on a false accusation of adultery.

## Chap. XL.

There was a certain matron of high rank who already had grandchildren by more than one son. Her Valeria loved like a second mother, and Daia suspected that her advice had produced that refusal which Valeria gave to his matrimonial offers; and therefore he charged the president Eratineus to have her put to death in a way that might injure her fame. To her two others, equally noble, were added. One of them, who had a daughter a Vestal virgin at Rome, maintained an intercourse by stealth with the banished Valeria. The other, married to a senator, was intimately connected with the empress. Excellent beauty and virtue proved the cause of their death. They were dragged to the tribunal, not of an upright judge, but of a robber. Neither indeed was there any accuser, until a certain Jew, one charged with other offences, was induced, through hope of pardon, to give false evidence against the innocent. The equitable and vigilant magistrate conducted him out of the city under a guard, lest the populace should have stoned him. This tragedy was acted at Nicæa. The Jew was ordered to the torture till he should speak as he had been instructed, while the torturers by blows prevented the women from speaking in their own defense. The innocent were condemned to die. Then there arose wailing and lamentation, not only of the senator, who attended on his well-deserving consort, but amongst the spectators also, whom this proceeding, scandalous and unheard of, had brought together; and, to prevent the multitude from violently rescuing the condemned persons out of the hands of the executioners, military commanders followed with light infantry and archers. And thus, under a guard of armed soldiers, they were led to punishment. Their domestics having been forced to flee, they would have remained without burial, had not the compassion of friends interred them by stealth. Nor was the promise of pardon made good to the feigned adulterer, for he was fixed to a gibbet, and then he disclosed the whole secret contrivance; and with his last breath he protested to all the beholders that the women died innocent.

**Chap. XLI.**

But the empress, an exile in some desert region of Syria, secretly informed her father Diocletian of the calamity that had befallen her. He dispatched messengers to Daia, requesting that his daughter might be sent to him. He could not prevail. Again and again he entreated; yet she was not sent. At length he employed a relation of his, a military man high in power and authority, to implore Daia by the remembrance of past favors. This messenger, equally unsuccessful in his negotiation as the others, reported to Diocletian that his prayers were vain.

### Chap. XLII.

At this time, by command of Constantine, the statues of Maximian Herculius were thrown down, and his portraits removed; and, as the two old emperors were generally delineated in one piece, the portraits of both were removed at the same time. Thus Diocletian lived to see a disgrace which no former emperor had ever seen, and, under the double load of vexation of spirit and bodily maladies, he resolved to die. Tossing to and fro, with his soul agitated by grief, he could neither eat nor take rest. He sighed, groaned, and wept often, and incessantly threw himself into various postures, now on his couch, and now on the ground. So he, who for twenty years was the most prosperous of emperors, having been cast down into the obscurity of a private station, treated in the most contumelious manner, and compelled to abhor life, became incapable of receiving nourishment, and, worn out with anguish of mind, expired.

### Chap. XLIII.

Of the adversaries of God there still remained one, whose overthrow and end I am now to relate.

Daia had entertained jealousy and ill-will against Licinius from the time that the preference was given to him by Galerius; and those sentiments still subsisted, notwithstanding the treaty of peace lately concluded between them. When Daia heard that the sister of Constantine was betrothed to Licinius, he apprehended that the two emperors, by contracting this affinity, meant to league against him; so he privily sent ambassadors to Rome, desiring a friendly alliance with Maxentius: he also wrote to him in terms of cordiality. The ambassadors were received courteously, friendship established, and in token of it the effigies of Maxentius and Daia were placed together in public view. Maxentius willingly embraced this, as if it had been an aid from heaven; for he had already declared war against Constantine, as if to revenge the death of his father Maximian. From this appearance of filial piety a suspicion arose, that the detestable old man had but feigned a quarrel with his son that he might have an opportunity to destroy his rivals in power, and so make way for himself and his son to possess the whole empire. This conjecture, however, had no foundation; for his true purpose was to have destroyed his son and the others, and then to have reinstated himself and Diocletian in sovereign authority.

**Chap. XLIV.**

And now a civil war broke out between Constantine and Maxentius. Although Maxentius kept himself within Rome, because the soothsayers had foretold that if he went out of it he should perish, yet he conducted the military operations by able generals. In forces he exceeded his adversary; for he had not only his father's army, which deserted from Severus, but also his own, which he had lately drawn together out of Mauritania and Italy. They fought, and the troops of Maxentius prevailed. At length Constantine, with steady courage and a mind prepared for every event, led his whole forces to the neighborhood of Rome, and encamped them opposite to the Milvian Bridge. The anniversary of the reign of Maxentius approached, that is, the sixth of the kalends of November, and the fifth year of his reign was drawing to an end.

Constantine was directed in a dream to cause *the heavenly sign* to be delineated on the shields of his soldiers, and so to proceed to battle. He did as he had been commanded, and he marked on their shields the letter X, with a perpendicular line drawn through it and turned round thus at the top, being the cipher of Christ. Having this sign (XP ), his troops stood to arms.

The enemies advanced, but without their emperor, and they crossed the bridge. The armies met, and fought with the utmost exertions of valor, and firmly maintained their ground. In the meantime a sedition arose at Rome, and Maxentius was reviled as one who had abandoned all concern for the safety of the commonweal; and suddenly, while he exhibited the Circensian games on the anniversary of his reign, the people cried with one voice, "Constantine cannot be overcome!" Dismayed at this, Maxentius burst from the assembly, and having called some senators together, ordered the Sibylline books to be searched. In them it was found that:—

"On the same day the enemy of the Romans should perish."

Led by this response to the hopes of victory, he went to the field. The bridge in his rear was broken down. At sight of that the battle grew hotter. The hand of the Lord prevailed, and the forces of Maxentius were routed. He fled towards the broken bridge; but the multitude pressing on him, he was driven headlong into the Tiber.

This destructive war being ended, Constantine was acknowledged as emperor, with great rejoicings, by the senate and people of Rome. And now he came to know the perfidy of Daia; for he found the letters written to Maxentius, and saw the statues and portraits of the two associates which had been set up together. The senate, in reward of the valor of Constantine, decreed to him the title of *Maximus* (the Greatest), a title which Daia had always arrogated to himself. Daia, when he heard that Constantine was victorious and Rome freed, expressed as much sorrow as if he himself had been vanquished; but afterwards, when he heard of the decree of the senate, he grew outrageous, avowed enmity towards Constantine, and made his title of *the Greatest* a theme of abuse and raillery.

**Chap. XLV.**

Constantine having settled all things at Rome, went to Milan about the beginning of winter. Thither also Licinius came to receive his wife Constantia. When Daia understood that they were busied in solemnizing the nuptials, he moved out of Syria in the depth of a severe winter, and by forced marches he came into Bithynia with an army much impaired; for he lost all his beasts of burden, of whatever kind, in consequence of excessive rains and snow, miry ways, cold and fatigue. Their carcasses, scattered about the roads, seemed an emblem of the calamities of the impending war, and the presage of a like destruction that awaited the soldiers. Daia did not halt in his own territories; but immediately crossed the Thracian Bosphorus, and in a hostile manner approached the gates of Byzantium. There was a garrison in the city, established by Licinius to check any invasion that Daia might make. At first Daia attempted to entice the soldiers by the promise of donatives, and then to intimidate them by assault and storm. Yet neither promises nor force availed aught. After eleven days had elapsed, within which time Licinius might have learned the state of the garrison, the soldiers surrendered, not through treachery, but because they were too weak to make a longer resistance. Then Daia moved on to Heraclea (otherwise called Perinthus), and by delays of the like nature before that place lost some days. And now Licinius by expeditious marches had reached Adrianople, but with forces not numerous. Then Daia, having taken Perinthus by capitulation, and remained there for a short space, moved forwards eighteen miles to the first station. Here his progress was stopped; for Licinius had already occupied the second station, at the distance also of eighteen miles. Licinius, having assembled what forces he could from the neighboring quarters, advanced towards Daia rather indeed to retard his operations than with any purpose of fighting, or hope of victory: for Daia had an army of seventy thousand men, while he himself had scarce thirty thousand; for his soldiers being dispersed in various regions, there was not time, on that sudden emergency, to collect all of them together.

## Chap. XLVI.

The armies thus approaching each other, seemed on the eve of a battle. Then Daia made this vow to Jupiter, that if he obtained victory he would extinguish and utterly efface the name of the Christians. And on the following night an angel of the Lord seemed to stand before Licinius while he was asleep, admonishing him to arise immediately, and with his whole army to put up a prayer to the Supreme God, and assuring him that by so doing he should obtain victory. Licinius fancied that, hearing this, he arose, and that his monitor, who was nigh him, directed how we should pray, and in what words. Awaking from sleep, he sent for one of his secretaries, and dictated these words exactly as he had heard them:—

"Supreme God, we beseech Thee; Holy God, we beseech Thee; unto Thee we commend all right; unto Thee we commend our safety; unto Thee we commend our empire. By Thee we live, by Thee we are victorious and happy. Supreme Holy God, hear our prayers; to Thee we stretch forth our arms. Hear, Holy Supreme God."

Many copies were made of these words, and distributed amongst the principal commanders, who were to teach them to the soldiers under their charge. At this all men took fresh courage, in the confidence that victory bad been announced to them from heaven. Licinius resolved to give battle on the kalends of May; for precisely eight years before Daia had received the dignity of *Cæsar*, and Licinius chose that day in hopes that Daia might be vanquished on the anniversary of *his* reign, as Maxentius had been on *his*. Daia, however, purposed to give battle earlier, to fight on the day before those kalends, and to triumph on the anniversary of his reign. Accounts came that Daia was in motion; the soldiers of Licinius armed themselves; and advanced. A barren and open plain, called Campus Serenus, lay between the two armies. They were now in sight of one another.

The soldiers of Licinius placed their shields on the ground, took off their helmets, and, following the example of their leaders, stretched forth their hands towards heaven. Then the emperor uttered the prayer, and they all repeated it after him. The host, doomed to speedy destruction, heard the murmur of the prayers of their adversaries. And now, the ceremony having been thrice performed, the soldiers of Licinius became full of courage, buckled on their helmets again, and resumed their shields. The two emperors advanced to a conference: but Daia could not be brought to peace; for he held Licinius in contempt, and imagined that the soldiers would presently abandon an emperor parsimonious in his donatives, and enter into the service of one liberal even to profusion. And indeed it was on this notion that he began the war. He looked for the voluntary surrender of the armies of Licinius; and, thus reinforced, he meant forthwith to have attacked Constantine.

### Chap. XLVII.

So the two armies drew nigh; the trumpets gave the signal; the military ensigns advanced; the troops of Licinius charged. But the enemies, panic-struck, could neither draw their swords nor yet throw their javelins. Daia went about, and, alternately by entreaties and promises, attempted to seduce the soldiers of Licinius. But he was not hearkened to in any quarter, and they drove him back. Then were the troops of Daia slaughtered, none making resistance; and such numerous legions, and forces so mighty, were mowed down by an inferior enemy. No one called to mind his reputation, or former valor, or the honorable rewards which had been conferred on him. The Supreme God did so place their necks under the sword of their foes that they seemed to have entered the field, not as combatants, but as men devoted to death. After great numbers had fallen, Daia perceived that everything went contrary to his hopes; and therefore he threw aside the purple, and having put on the habit of a slave, hasted across the Thracian Bosphorus. One half of his army perished in battle, and the rest either surrendered to the victor or fled; for now that the emperor himself had deserted, there seemed to be no shame in desertion. Before the expiration of the kalends of May, Daia arrived at Nicomedia, although distant one hundred and sixty miles from the field of battle. So in the space of one day and two nights he performed that journey. Having hurried away with his children and wife, and a few officers of his court, he went towards Syria; but having been joined by some troops from those quarters, and having collected together a part of his fugitive forces, he halted in Cappadocia, and then he resumed the imperial garb.

**Chap. XLVIII.**

Not many days after the victory, Licinius, having received part of the soldiers of Daia into his service, and properly distributed them, transported his army into Bithynia, and having made his entry into Nicomedia, he returned thanks to God, through whose aid he had overcome; and on the ides of June, while he and Constantine were consuls for the third time, he commanded the following edict for the restoration of the Church, directed to the president of the province, to be promulgated:—

"When we, Constantine and Licinius, emperors, had an interview at Milan, and conferred together with respect to the good and security of the commonweal, it seemed to us that, amongst those things that are profitable to mankind in general, the reverence paid to the Divinity merited our first and chief attention, and that it was proper that the Christians and all others should have liberty to follow that mode of religion which to each of them appeared best; so that that God, who is seated in heaven, might be benign and propitious to us, and to everyone under our government. And therefore we judged it a salutary measure, and one highly consonant to right reason, that no man should be denied leave of attaching himself to the rites of the Christians, or to whatever other religion his mind directed him, that thus the supreme Divinity, to whose worship we freely devote ourselves, might continue to vouchsafe His favor and beneficence to us. And accordingly we give you to know that, without regard to any provisos in our former orders to you concerning the Christians, all who choose that religion are to be permitted, freely and absolutely, to remain in it, and not to be disturbed any ways, or molested. And we thought fit to be thus special in the things committed to your charge, that you might understand that the indulgence which we have granted in matters of religion to the Christians is ample and unconditional; and perceive at the same time that the open and free exercise of their respective religions is granted to all others, as well as to the Christians. For it befits the well-ordered state and the tranquility of our times that each individual be allowed, according to his own choice, to worship the Divinity; and we mean not to derogate aught from the honor due to any religion or its votaries. Moreover, with respect to the Christians, we formerly gave certain orders concerning the places appropriated for their religious assemblies; but now we will that all persons who have purchased such places, either from our exchequer or from anyone else, do restore them to the Christians, without money demanded or price claimed, and that this be performed peremptorily and unambiguously; and we will also, that they who have obtained any right to such places by form of gift do forthwith restore them to the Christians: reserving always to such persons, who have either purchased for a price, or gratuitously acquired them, to make application to the judge of the district, if they look on themselves as entitled to any equivalent from our beneficence.

"All those places are, by your intervention, to be immediately restored to the Christians. And because it appears that, besides the places appropriated to religious worship, the Christians did possess other places, which belonged not to individuals, but to their society in general, that is, to their churches, we comprehend all such within the regulation aforesaid, and we will that you cause them all to be restored to the society or churches, and *that* without hesitation or controversy: Provided always, that the persons making restitution without a price paid shall be at liberty to seek indemnification from our bounty. In furthering all which things for the behoove of the Christians, you are to use your utmost diligence, to the end that our orders be speedily obeyed, and our gracious purpose in securing the public tranquility promoted. So shall that divine favor which, in affairs of the mightiest importance, we have already experienced, continue to give success to us, and in our successes make the commonweal happy. And that the tenor of this our gracious ordinance may be made known unto all, we will that you cause it by your authority to be published everywhere."

Licinius having issued this ordinance, made a harangue, in which he exhorted the Christians to rebuild their religious edifices.

And thus, from the overthrow of the Church until its restoration, there was a space of ten years and about four months.

## Chap. XLIX.

While Licinius pursued with his army, the fugitive tyrant retreated, and again occupied the passes of mount Taurus; and there, by erecting parapets and towers, attempted to stop the march of Licinius. But the victorious troops, by an attack made on the right, broke through all obstacles, and Daia at length fled to Tarsus. *There*, being hard pressed both by sea and land, he despaired of finding any place for refuge; and in the anguish and dismay of his mind, he sought death as the only remedy of those calamities that God had heaped on him. But first he gorged himself with food, and large draughts of wine, as those are wont who believe that they eat and drink for the last time; and so he swallowed poison. However, the force of the poison, repelled by his full stomach, could not immediately operate, but it produced a grievous disease, resembling the pestilence; and his life was prolonged only that his sufferings might be more severe. And now the poison began to rage, and to burn up everything within him, so that he was driven to distraction with the intolerable pain; and during a fit of frenzy, which lasted four days, he gathered handfuls of earth, and greedily devoured it. Having undergone various and excruciating torments, he dashed his forehead against the wall, and his eyes started out of their sockets. And now, become blind, he imagined that he saw God, with His servants arrayed in white robes, sitting in judgment on him. He roared out as men on the rack are wont, and exclaimed that not he, but others, were guilty. In the end, as if he had been racked into confession, he acknowledged his own guilt, and lamentably implored Christ to have mercy upon him. Then, amidst groans, like those of one burnt alive, did he breathe out his guilty soul in the most horrible kind of death.

## Chap. L.

Thus did God subdue all those who persecuted His name, so that neither root nor branch of them remained; for Licinius, as soon as he was established in sovereign authority, commanded that Valeria should be put to death. Daia, although exasperated against her, never ventured to do this, not even after his discomfiture and flight, and when he knew that his end approached. Licinius commanded that Candidianus also should be put to death. He was the son of Galerius by a concubine, and Valeria, having no children, had adopted him. On the news of the death of Daia, she came in disguise to the court of Licinius, anxious to observe what might befall Candidianus. The youth, presenting himself at Nicomedia, had an outward show of honor paid to him, and, while he suspected no harm, was killed. Hearing of this catastrophe, Valeria immediately fled. The Emperor Severus left a son, Severianus, arrived at man's estate, who accompanied Daia in his flight from the field of battle. Licinius caused him to be condemned and executed, under the pretense that, on the death of Daia, he had intentions of assuming the imperial purple. Long before this time, Candidianus and Severianus, apprehending evil from Licinius, had chosen to remain with Daia; while Valeria favored Licinius, and was willing to bestow on him that which she had denied to Daia, all rights accruing to her as the widow of Galerius. Licinius also put to death Maximus, the son of Daia, a boy eight years old, and a daughter of Daia, who was seven years old, and had been betrothed to Candidianus. But before their death, their mother had been thrown into the Orontes, in which river she herself had frequently commanded chaste women to be drowned. So, by the unerring and just judgment of God, all the impious received according to the deeds that they had done.

**Chap. LI.**

Valeria, too, who for fifteen months had wandered under a mean garb from province to province, was at length discovered in Thessalonica, was apprehended, together with her mother Prisca, and suffered capital punishment. Both the ladies were conducted to execution; a fall from grandeur which moved the pity of the multitude of beholders that the strange sight had gathered together. They were beheaded, and their bodies cast into the sea. Thus the chaste demeanor of Valeria, and the high rank of her and her mother, proved fatal to both of them.

**Chap. LII.**

I relate all those things on the authority of well-informed persons; and I thought it proper to commit them to writing exactly as they happened, lest the memory of events so important should perish, and lest any future historian of the persecutors should corrupt the truth, either by suppressing their offences against God, or the judgment of God against them. To His everlasting mercy ought we to render thanks, that, having at length looked on the earth, He deigned to collect again and to restore His flock, partly laid waste by ravenous wolves, and partly scattered abroad, and to extirpate those noxious wild beasts who had trod down its pastures, and destroyed its resting-places. Where now are the surnames of the *Jovii* and the *Herculii*, once so glorious and renowned amongst the nations; surnames insolently assumed at first by Diocles and Maximian, and afterwards transferred to their successors? The Lord has blotted them out and erased them from the earth. Let us therefore with exultation celebrate the triumphs of God, and oftentimes with praises make mention of His victory; let us in our prayers, by night and by day, beseech Him to confirm forever that peace which, after a warfare of ten years, He has bestowed on His own: and do you, above all others, my best beloved Donatus, who so well deserve to be heard, implore the Lord that it would please Him propitiously and mercifully to continue His pity towards His servants, to protect His people from the machinations and assaults of the devil, and to guard the now flourishing churches in perpetual felicity.

**Elucidation**

(On the tenth of the kalends of April)

Serious difficulties are encountered by the learned in reconciling Lactantius with himself, if, indeed, the fault be not one of his copyists rather than his own. In the fourth book of the *Institutes* his language is thus given by Baluzius:—

"Extremis temporibus Tiberii Cæsaris, ut scriptum legimus, Dominus noster Jesus Christus, a Judæis cruciatus est post diem decimum kalendarum Aprilis, duobus Geminis consulibus."

Lactantius was writing in Nicomedia, and may have quoted from memory what he had read, perhaps in the report of Pilate himself. The expression post diem decimum kalendarum Aprilis is ambiguous: and Jarvis says, "My impression is, that it means 'after the tenth day before the kalends of April;' that is, after the 23d of March."

But here our author says, according to the accurate edition of Walchius (a.d. 1715),—

"Exinde tetrarchas habuerunt usque ad Herodem, qui fuit sub imperio Tiberii Cæsaris: cujus anno quinto decimo, id est duobus Geminis consulibus, ante diem septimam Calendarum Aprilium, Judæi Christum cruci affixerunt."

But here, on the authority of forty manuscripts, Du Fresnoy reads, "ante diem decimam," which he labors to reconcile with "post diem decimum," as above. Jarvis adheres to the reading *septimam*, supported by more than fifty manuscripts, and decides for the 23d of March.

He cites Augustine to the same effect in the noted passage:—

"Ille autem mense conceptum et passum esse Christum, et Paschæ observatio et dies ecclesiis notissimus Nativitatis ejus ostendit. Qui enim mense nono natus est octavo kalendas Janvarias profecto mense primo conceptus est circa octavum kalendas Aprilis, quod tempus passionis ejus fuit."

This, Augustine considers to be "seething a kid in mother's milk," after a mystical sense; cruelly making the cross to coincide with the maternity of the Virgin, who beheld her Son an innocent victim on the anniversary of her salutation by the angel.

## Fragments of Lactantius

I. Fear, love, joy, sadness, lust, eager desire, anger, pity, emulation, admiration,—these motions or affections of the mind exist from the beginning of man's creation by the Lord; and they were usefully and advantageously introduced into human nature, that by governing himself by these with method, and in accordance with reason, man may be able, by acting manfully, to exercise those good qualities, by means of which he would justly have deserved to receive from the Lord eternal life. For these affections of the mind being restrained within their proper limits, that is, being rightly employed, produce at present good qualities, and in the future eternal rewards. But when they advance beyond their boundaries, that is, when they turn aside to an evil course, then vices and iniquities come forth, and produce everlasting punishments.

II. Within our memory, also, Lactantius speaks of meters,—the pentameter (he says) and the tetrameter.

III. Firmianus, writing to Probus on the meters of comedies, thus speaks: "For as to the question which you proposed concerning the meters of comedies, I also know that many are of opinion that the plays of Terence in particular have not the meter of Greek comedy,— that is, of Menander, Philemon, and Diphilus, which consist of trimeter verses; for our ancient writers of comedies, in the modulation of their plays, preferred to follow Eupolis, Cratinus, and Aristophanes, as has been before said." That there is a measure—that is, meter—in the plays of Terence and Plautus, and of the other comic and tragic writers, let these declare: Cicero, Scaurus, and Firmianus.

IV. We will bring forward the sentiments of our Lactantius, which he expressed in words in his third volume to Probus on this subject. The Gauls, he says, were from ancient times called Galatians, from the whiteness of their body; and thus the Sibyl terms them. And this is what the poet intended to signify when he said,—

"Gold collars deck their milk-white necks,"

when he might have used the word *white*. It is plain that from this the province was called Galatia, in which, on their arrival in it, the Gauls united themselves with Greeks, from which circumstance that region was called Gallogræcia, and afterwards Galatia. And it is no wonder if he said this concerning the Galatians, and related that a people of the West, having passed over so great a distance in the middle of the earth, settled in a region of the East.

## The Phoenix

*By an Uncertain Author. Attributed to Lactantius*

There is a happy spot, retired in the first East, where the great gate of the eternal pole lies open. It is not, however, situated near to his rising in summer or in winter, but where the sun pours the day from his vernal chariot. There a plain spreads its open tracts; nor does any mound rise, nor hollow valley open itself. But through twice six ells that place rises above the mountains, whose tops are thought to be lofty among us. Here is the grove of the sun; a wood stands planted with many a tree, blooming with the honor of perpetual foliage. When the pole had blazed with the fires of Phaethon, that place was uninjured by the flames; and when the deluge had immersed the world in waves, it rose above the waters of Deucalion. No enfeebling diseases, no sickly old age, nor cruel death, nor harsh fear, approaches hither, nor dreadful crime, nor mad desire of riches, nor Mars, nor fury, burning with the love of slaughter. Bitter grief is absent, and want clothed in rags, and sleepless cares, and violent hunger. No tempest rages there, nor dreadful violence of the wind; nor does the hoar-frost cover the earth with cold dew. No cloud extends its fleecy covering above the plains, nor does the turbid moisture of water fall from on high; but there is a fountain in the middle, which they call by the name of "living;" it is clear, gentle, and abounding with sweet waters, which, bursting forth once during the space of each month, twelve times irrigates all the grove with waters. Here a species of tree, rising with lofty stem, bears mellow fruits not about to fall on the ground. This grove, these woods, a single bird, the phoenix, inhabits,—single, but it lives reproduced by its own death. It obeys and submits to Phoebus, a remarkable attendant. Its parent nature has given it to possess this office. When at its first rising the saffron morn grows red, when it puts to flight the stars with its rosy light, thrice and four times she plunges her body into the sacred waves, thrice and four times she sips water from the living stream. She is raised aloft, and takes her seat on the highest top of the lofty tree, which alone looks down upon the whole grove; and turning herself to the fresh risings of the nascent Phoebus, she awaits his rays and rising beam. And when the sun has thrown back the threshold of the shining gate, and the light gleam of the first light has shone forth, she begins to pour strains of sacred song, and to hail the new light with wondrous voice, which neither the notes of the nightingale nor the flute of the Muses can equal with Cyrrhæan strains. But neither is it thought that the dying swan can imitate it, nor the tuneful strings of the lyre of Mercury. After that Phoebus has brought back his horses to the open heaven, and continually advancing, has displayed his whole orb; she applauds with thrice-repeated flapping of her wings, and having thrice adored the fire-bearing head, is silent. And she also distinguishes the swift hours by sounds not liable to error by day and night: an overseer of the groves, a venerable priestess of the wood, and alone admitted to thy secrets, O Phoebus. And when she has now accomplished the thousand years of her life, and length of days has rendered her burdensome, in order that she may renew the age which has glided by, the fates pressing her, she flees from the beloved couch of the accustomed grove. And when she has left the sacred places, through a desire of being born again, then she seeks this world, where death reigns. Full of years, she directs her swift flight into Syria, to which Venus herself has given the name of Phoenice; and through trackless deserts she seeks the retired groves in the place, where a remote wood lies concealed through the glens. Then she chooses a lofty palm, with top reaching to the heavens, which has the pleasing name of phoenix from the bird, and where no hurtful living creature can break through, or slimy serpent, or any bird of prey. Then Æolas shuts in the winds in hanging caverns, lest they should injure the bright air with their blasts, or lest a cloud collected by the south wind through the empty sky should remove the rays of the sun, and be a hindrance to the bird. Afterwards she builds for herself either a nest or a tomb, for she perishes that she may live; yet she produces herself. Hence she collects juices and odors, which the Assyrian gathers from the rich wood, which the wealthy Arabian gathers; which either the Pygmæan nations, or India crops, or the Sabæan land produces from its soft bosom. Hence she heaps together cinnamon and the odor of the far-scented amomum, and balsams with mixed leaves. Neither the twig of the mild cassia nor of the fragrant acanthus is absent, nor the tears and rich drop of frankincense. To these she adds tender ears of flourishing spikenard, and joins the too pleasing pastures of myrrh. Immediately she places her body about to be changed on the strewed nest, and her quiet limbs on such a couch. Then with her mouth she scatters juices around and upon her limbs, about to die with her own funeral rites. Then amidst various odors she yields up her life, nor fears the faith of so great a deposit. In the meantime her body, destroyed by death, which proves the source of life, is hot, and the heat itself produces a flame; and it conceives fire afar off from the light of heaven: it blazes, and is dissolved into burnt ashes. And these ashes collected in death it fuses, as it were, into a mass, and has an effect resembling seed. From this an animal is said to arise without limbs, but the worm is said to be of a milky color. And it suddenly increases vastly with an imperfectly formed body, and collects itself into the appearance of a well-rounded egg. After this it is formed again, such as its figure was before, and the phoenix, having burst her shell, shoots forth, even as caterpillars in the fields, when they are fastened by a thread to a stone, are wont to be changed into a butterfly. No food is appointed for her in our world, nor does anyone make it his business to feed her while unfledged. She sips the delicate ambrosial dews of heavenly nectar which have fallen from the star bearing pole. She gathers these; with these the bird is nourished in the midst of odors, until she bears a natural form. But when she begins to flourish with early youth, she flies forth now about to return to her native abode. Previously, however, she encloses in an ointment of balsam, and in myrrh and dissolved frankincense, all the remains of her own body, and the bones or ashes, and relics of herself, and with pious mouth brings it into a round form, and carrying this with her feet, she goes to the rising of the sun, and tarrying at the altar, she draws it forth in the sacred temple. She shows and presents herself an object of admiration to the beholder; such great beauty is there, such great honor abounds. In the first place, her color is like the brilliancy of that which the seeds of the pomegranate when ripe take under the smooth rind; such color as is contained in the leaves which the poppy produces in the fields, when Flora spreads her garments beneath the blushing sky. Her shoulders and beautiful breasts shine with this covering; with this her head, with this her neck, and the upper parts of her back shine. And her tail is extended, varied with yellow metal, in the spots of which mingled purple blushes. Between her wings there is a bright mark above, as Tris on high is wont to paint a cloud from above. She gleams resplendent with a mingling of the green emerald, and a shining beak of pure horn opens itself. Her eyes are large; you might believe that they were two jacinths; from the middle of which a bright flame shines. An irradiated crown is fitted to the whole of her head, resembling on high the glory of the head of Phoebus. Scales cover her thighs spangled with yellow metal, but a rosy color paints her claws with honor. Her form is seen to blend the figure of the peacock with that of the painted bird of Phasis. The winged creature which is produced in the lands of the Arabians, whether it be beast or bird, can scarcely equal her magnitude. She is not, however, slow, as birds which through the greatness of their body have sluggish motions, and a very heavy weight. But she is light and swift, full of royal beauty. Such she always shows herself in the sight of men. Egypt comes hither to such a wondrous sight, and the exulting crowd salutes the rare bird. Immediately they carve her image on the consecrated marble, and mark both the occurrence and the day with a new title. Birds of every kind assemble together; none is mindful of prey, none of fear. Attended by a chorus of birds, she flies through the heaven, and a crowd accompanies her, exulting in the pious duty. But when she has arrived at the regions of pure ether, she presently returns; afterwards she is concealed in her own regions. But oh, bird of happy lot and fate, to whom the god himself granted to be born from herself! Whether it be female, or male, or neither, or both, happy she, who enters into no compacts of Venus. Death is Venus to her; her only pleasure is in death: that she may be born, she desires previously to die. She is an offspring to herself, her own father and heir, her own nurse, and always a foster-child to herself. She is herself indeed, but not the same, since she is herself, and not herself, having gained eternal life by the blessing of death.

## A Poem on the Passion of the Lord

*Formerly Ascribed to Lactantius*

Whoever you are who approach, and are entering the precincts of the middle of the temple, stop a little and look upon me, who, though innocent, suffered for your crime; lay me up in your mind, keep me in your breast. I am He who, pitying the bitter misfortunes of men, came hither as a messenger of offered peace, and as a full atonement for the fault of men. Here the brightest light from above is restored to the earth; here is the merciful image of safety; here I am a rest to you, the right way, the true redemption, the banner of God, and a memorable sign of fate. It was on account of you and your life that I entered the Virgin's womb, was made man, and suffered a dreadful death; nor did I find rest anywhere in the regions of the earth, but everywhere threats, everywhere labors. First of all a wretched dwelling in the land of Judæa was a shelter for me at my birth, and for my mother with me: here first, amidst the outstretched sluggish cattle, dry grass gave me a bed in a narrow stall. I passed my earliest years in the Pharian regions, being an exile in the reign of Herod; and after my return to Judæa I spent the rest of my years, always engaged in fasting, and the extremity of poverty itself, and the lowest circumstances; always by healthful admonitions applying the minds of men to the pursuit of genial uprightness, uniting with wholesome teaching many evident miracles: on which account impious Jerusalem, harassed by the raging cares of envy and cruel hatred, and blinded by madness, dared to seek for me, though innocent, by deadly punishment, a cruel death on the dreadful cross. And if you yourself wish to discriminate these things more fully, and if it delights you to go through all my groans, and to experience griefs with me, put together the designs and plots, and the impious price of my innocent blood, and the pretended kisses of a disciple, and the insults and strivings of the cruel multitude; and, moreover, the blows, and tongues prepared for accusations. Picture to your mind both the witnesses, and the accursed judgment of the blinded Pilate, and the immense cross pressing my shoulders and wearied back, and my painful steps to a dreadful death. Now survey me from head to foot, deserted as I am, and lifted up afar from my beloved mother. Behold and see my locks clotted with blood, and my blood-stained neck under my very hair, and my head drained with cruel thorns, and pouring down like rain from all sides a stream of blood over my divine face. Survey my compressed and sightless eyes, and my afflicted cheeks; see my parched tongue poisoned with gall, and my countenance pale with death. Behold my hands pierced with nails, and my arms drawn out, and the great wound in my side; see the blood streaming from it, and my perforated 2081 feet, and blood-stained limbs. Bend your knee, and with lamentation adore the venerable wood of the cross, and with lowly countenance stooping to the earth, which is wet with innocent blood, sprinkle it with rising tears, and at times bear me and my admonitions in your devoted heart. Follow the footsteps of my life, and while you look upon my torments and cruel death, remembering my innumerable pangs of body and soul, learn to endure hardships, and to watch over your own safety. These memorials, if at any time you find pleasure in thinking over them, if in your mind there is any confidence to bear *anything* like my *sufferings*), if the piety due, and gratitude worthy of my labors shall arise, will be incitements to true virtue, and they will be shields against the snares of an enemy, aroused by which you will be safe, and as a conqueror bear off the palm in every contest. If these memorials shall turn away your senses, which are devoted to a perishable world, from the fleeting shadow of earthly beauty, the result will be, that you will not venture, enticed by empty hope, to trust the frail enjoyments of fickle fortune, and to place your hope in the fleeting years of life. But, truly, if you thus regard this perishable world, and through your love of a better country deprive yourself of earthly riches and the enjoyment of present things, the prayers of the pious will bring you up in sacred habits, and in the hope of a happy life, amidst severe punishments, will cherish you with heavenly dew, and feed you with the sweetness of the promised good. Until the great favor of God shall recall your happy soul to the heavenly regions, your body being left after the fates of death. Then freed from all labor, then joyfully beholding the angelic choirs, and the blessed companies of saints in perpetual bliss, it shall reign with me in the happy abode of perpetual peace.

**General Note.**

There is no ms authority for ascribing the above to Lactantius. "It does not, in the least, come up to the purity and eloquence of his style," says Dupin; and the same candid author notes the "adoration of the cross" as fatal to any such claim.

Of the following poem, on Easter, Dupin says: "It is attributed to Venantius upon the testimony of some mss. in the Vatican Library." This writer became known to Gregory of Tours, who died about a.d. 595, and seems to have succeeded him as bishop, dying soon after. Bede quotes his verse on St. Alban,—

"Albanum egregium fecunda Britannia profert,"

but styles him "presbyter Fortunatus." He was the author of a poem on *St. Martin*, and another, *In Laude Virginum*. His works were edited by Brouverius, a Jesuit.

**Find this and other great works of the Early Church Fathers at lighthousechristianpublishing.com.**

Our Father who art in heaven, hallowed be thy name.
Thy kingdom come, Thy will be done, on earth as it is in heaven.
Give us this day our daily bread and forgive us our trespasses as we forgive those who trespass against us.
And lead us not into temptation, but deliver us from evil, for Thine is the kingdom, the power and the glory. Forever and ever.

Amen

Hail Mary full of grace, the Lord is with thee. Blessed art thou amongst women and blessed is the fruit of thy womb Jesus. Holy Mary mother of God, pray for us sinners, now and the hour of our death.

www.ingramcontent.com/pod-product-compliance
Lightning Source LLC
Chambersburg PA
CBHW052128070526
44585CB00017B/1744